Before *Brown*

the MODERN SOUTH

series editors
Glenn Feldman & Kari Frederickson

Before *Brown*

Civil Rights and White Backlash in the Modern South

Edited by
GLENN FELDMAN

THE UNIVERSITY OF ALABAMA PRESS
Tuscaloosa

Copyright © 2004
The University of Alabama Press
Tuscaloosa, Alabama 35487-0380
All rights reserved
Manufactured in the United States of America

Typeface: Stone Serif and Stone Sans

∞

The paper on which this book is printed meets the minimum requirements of American National Standard for Information Science–Permanence of Paper for Printed Library Materials, ANSI Z39.48–1984.

Library of Congress Cataloging-in-Publication Data

Before Brown : civil rights and white backlash in the modern South / edited by Glenn Feldman.
    p. cm. — (The modern South)
  Includes bibliographical references and index.
  ISBN 0-8173-1431-8 (cloth : alk. paper) — ISBN 0-8173-5134-5 (pbk. : alk. paper)
  1. African Americans—Civil rights—Southern States—History—20th century. 2. Civil rights movements—Southern States—History—20th century. 3. White supremacy movements—Southern States—History—20th century. 4. Southern States—Race relations. 5. Southern States—Politics and government—1865–1950. 6. Southern States—Politics and government—1951– I. Feldman, Glenn. II. Series.
  E185.61.B36 2004
  323'.0975'0904—dc22

2004002839

For Richard . . . who's always been there

Contents

Acknowledgments — ix

Foreword — xi
Patricia Sullivan

Prologue — 1
Glenn Feldman

1. "You Don't Have to Ride Jim Crow": CORE and the 1947 Journey of Reconciliation — 21
Raymond Arsenault

2. T. R. M. Howard: Pragmatism over Strict Integrationist Ideology in the Mississippi Delta, 1942–1954 — 68
David T. Beito and Linda Royster Beito

3. "Blood on Your Hands": White Southerners' Criticism of Eleanor Roosevelt during World War II — 96
Pamela Tyler

4. "City Mothers": Dorothy Tilly, Georgia Methodist Women, and Black Civil Rights — 116
Andrew M. Manis

5. Louisiana: The Civil Rights Struggle, 1940–1954 — 144
Adam Fairclough

6. Communism, Anti-Communism, and Massive Resistance: The Civil Rights Congress in Southern Perspective — 170
Sarah Hart Brown

Contents

7. E. D. Nixon and the White Supremacists: Civil Rights
   in Montgomery   198
   John White

8. "Flag-bearers for Integration and Justice": Local Civil
   Rights Groups in the South, 1940–1954   222
   John A. Salmond

9. Winning the Peace: Georgia Veterans and the Struggle to
   Define the Political Legacy of World War II   238
   Jennifer E. Brooks

   Epilogue: Ugly Roots: Race, Emotion, and the Rise of
   the Modern Republican Party in Alabama and the South   268
   Glenn Feldman

   Notes   311

   Contributors   395

   Index   399

Acknowledgments

I OWE DEBTS to many persons who made this book possible. I acknowledge an intellectual debt to Patricia Sullivan for her fine work in pushing back the beginning date of the traditional periodization of the civil rights movement. Kari Frederickson showed an interest in this project from the beginning and made an ideal partner in coediting the Modern South series at The University of Alabama Press. The press's outside readers were generous but insightful, and I am grateful for their intelligent critiques. Jonathan Lawrence did an excellent job as copy editor. It has been a pleasure to work with the staff of The University of Alabama Press. My colleagues at the Center for Labor Education and Research in the School of Business at the University of Alabama at Birmingham have been very supportive, and I owe them my thanks: Ed Brown, Tracy Chang, center director Judi King, Business School Dean Robert Holmes, and Nick Scott. Melody P. Izard was of indispensable aid in sorting through the various word-processing programs that found their way to my desk. I am pleased with the breadth and depth of the scholars who took part in the project, and their willingness to write chapters and believe in the book. On a personal note I am thankful for my family's support, especially that of my wife, Jeannie, and my daughters, Hallie and Rebecca, who are everything. I dedicate this book to my brother Richard, who *has* always been there.

Glenn Feldman
Birmingham, Alabama
December 2003

Foreword
Patricia Sullivan

IN THE SPRING of 1917, W. E. B. Du Bois reported that twelve branches of the National Association for the Advancement of Colored People had been organized in the South. The NAACP had finally, he proclaimed, "a real first line defense facing the enemy at proper range."[1] The civil rights organization had been founded eight years earlier in response to the spread of racial discrimination and violence against blacks in the North, but the South loomed as the primary arena of struggle. These small outposts of resistance multiplied during World War I and its immediate aftermath, reaching as far as the Mississippi Delta. But the burst of activism quickly faded. The racial caste system was unyielding, written into law and custom, secured by terror, and buttressed by Supreme Court rulings, bipartisan accommodation, and sympathetic northern opinion.

In recent years, a growing body of scholarship on African American life under Jim Crow has shed light on how black southerners sustained their faith in democratic ideals as they pushed up against the constraints of a society steeped in the ideology and practice of white supremacy.[2] Individual and localized acts of defiance percolated just beneath the surface of the South's tightly proscribed racial order, breaking through here and there and stoking the possibilities of change. Meanwhile, black migration out of the South steadily altered the nation's racial landscape, slowly shifting the racial balance of national politics.

With the Great Depression and the New Deal, questions concerning the role of the federal government and the meaning of national citizenship, considered settled in the aftermath of Reconstruction, were revisited. Black voters responded to the democratic rhetoric of the New Deal and the jobs and relief it brought by enlisting in the Democratic Party, which had long been a stronghold of states' rights and white rights. The crossover of the black vote in key northern states was big news, but equally notable, if little noticed by the mainstream press, was the burgeoning effort of southern blacks to claim membership in the Democratic Party, an effort further energized by heightened black militancy during World War II. By the late 1930s, established civil rights organizations such as the NAACP, local civic associations, student groups, labor unions, and progressive interracial organizations facilitated the emergence of a sustained challenge to the legal, political, and social structure of the Jim Crow system. White southern segregationists responded defiantly.

Historians have begun to cast the years surrounding the New Deal and World War II as a formative period in the modern civil rights movement. This collection is a major contribution to this enterprise, both in terms of the individual essays and the broader context they help to establish. Organized along the fault line of civil rights activism and white southern resistance, the essays explore the rapidly changing terrain of race and politics in the South at midcentury.

The loose network of civil rights forces that emerged from the 1930s stands out in sharp relief here, capturing the rich texture of political activism that grew up in the South during this period, one that linked the NAACP, elements of the Communist Party and industrial unions, radical student activists, New Deal progressives, and more homegrown groups such as T. R. M. Howard's Regional Council of Negro Leadership. The scope of the work allows for a fuller exploration of some of the major personalities, organizations, and events that shaped the contours of the emerging movement than has been offered elsewhere. Esther Cooper Jackson, Mary Price, and Lulu White are among the leading figures discussed here, further documenting the critical roles women played as leaders, organizers, and plaintiffs. Fresh insight is offered into the relationship between the NAACP and the Communist Party, particularly as it evolved in the context of local struggles. A fascinating essay on the first Freedom Ride demonstrates how growing pressure for direct-action tactics tested the national NAACP's reliance on litigation and persuasion long before the Greensboro sit-in. Several essays explore the complex yet pivotal role of the NAACP, setting it against the broader context of the activism that shaped civil rights struggles during this era.

An interesting and compelling strand that runs through several essays concerns the interracial coalitions that worked to challenge segregation and broaden political participation in the South during the 1940s and early 1950s. The ways in which white southerners supported the burgeoning challenge to Jim Crow is a further illustration of how political possibilities in the South were radically altered in the aftermath of the Depression and the New Deal and most fully realized during the 1940s. Some were church-based, others grew from the progressive wing of the New Deal, and still others found expression through the Communist Party and its affiliated organizations, particularly the Civil Rights Congress. Although white southern supporters for black civil rights were few in number, their individual circumstances and the nature of their roles is notable. The profiles offered here provide a refreshing alternative to the often flat reading of white southern racial liberals that tends to preclude a fuller analysis of how white southerners supported and participated in the movement for civil rights at mid-century.

A politics wedded to the maintenance of white supremacy, however, shaped the response of the majority of white southerners to the growing challenge to the Jim Crow system. Essays in this volume explore how the contours of southern politics developed in tandem with the rising civil rights activism of the World II era. The forces that underwrote a commitment to "southern tradition" were varied, as is demonstrated here, and reflected the fears and anxieties that accompanied postwar readjustment and the beginnings of the cold war. Yet race remained the most potent force for mobilizing southern white political sentiment, and electoral politics became a primary arena for contesting the future of the South and the role of the region in the national political arena.

Many of the key issues and challenges that shaped struggles around race and citizenship between 1940 and 1954 were resolved in the following decade. Congress outlawed legally mandated segregation, and racial barriers to voting fell, inalterably transforming the southern landscape. But of course the story does not end there. The conservative ascendancy in national politics in the years following the civil rights movement resulted in large part from the growth of the Republican Party in the South and the fracturing of the New Deal coalition along racial lines, with appeals to the fears and resentments of disaffected whites.

Race remains a critical fault line in American life and politics. This volume helps to explain why, while also underscoring the capacity of people to struggle toward a more just and equitable society, even in the face of seemingly insurmountable odds.

Before *Brown*

Prologue
Glenn Feldman

IN RECENT YEARS there has been an explosion of scholarship on the civil rights movement. Among the broad array of writings are variations in emphasis on a number of themes: the national and local stages of "the movement"; the roles of civil rights leaders versus grassroots activists; the movement as a biracial social project for "civil rights" or a black-led "freedom struggle"; concentration on laws and political-legal solutions to America's race problem versus a stress on economic approaches; and an emphasis on the traditional demarcation of 1954–65 as opposed to other attempts at periodization. These important threads and others have been explored in various historiographical assessments of the movement.[1]

The present volume examines several of the main fault lines that exist in writing about civil rights, and perhaps a few of the more hidden lines of inquiry. It is an edited collection of essays that explores civil rights and white supremacist reaction during the critically important New Deal–World War II era and the decade following. At a fundamental level, the book is informed by two themes. First and foremost, it continues the ongoing challenge to traditional periodization of the civil rights movement by highlighting the considerable ferment in race relations during the 1930s and 1940s. In recent years civil rights scholars have stressed that the movement did not suddenly begin with the 1954 *Brown v. Board of Education* decision, or even with the 1955–56 Montgomery Bus Boycott, University of Alabama riots against the admission of Arthurine Lucy, and the lynching of Emmett Till.[2] These events—

tangible, visceral, concrete, dramatic—have long provided a tempting place of demarcation for scholars trying to make sense and order of a turbulent time. The temptation to periodize—to impose order on events that in "real life" are often much messier and harder to pinpoint exactly—is, in some respects, the siren call that tempts all historians. But recent work has traced the movement back to at least the 1930s, some of it even earlier.[3] This "backing up" of the movement represents an advance in scholarship. The present book is an effort to continue this recent trend by concentrating on the critically important 1940s and early 1950s and by exploring the movement through a variety of manifestations: the activities of politicians, civil rights leaders, religious figures, associational types, returning war veterans, labor unionists, small businessmen, grassroots activists—men and women, black and white, elites and masses, radicals, liberals, moderates, and conservatives, southern and non-southern.

While it is possible to trace the movement back to the 1930s, it is likewise possible to trace white backlash to the movement, sometimes violent, back to the Great Depression and before—a second major theme in this collection. "Civil rights" in a large sense has often been understood as the drive for a more just recognition of the rights of blacks, women, and ethnic, religious, and other minorities. Actually, though, it is best understood as a two-sided coin: the drive for civil rights *and* the militant reaction against it. The bright side of this coin, the drive for the realization of civil rights for minorities, manifested itself in the movement for enhanced civil liberties, political inclusion, economic opportunity, social justice, and fairness in employment. The dark side—the white supremacist reaction, backlash, and even violence that met this drive—existed alongside the movement for human rights. Many studies of civil rights or race relations have addressed one side of the issue with little recognition or acknowledgment of its contemporaneous counterpart. It is difficult, though, to understand either side fully without reference to the other. And it is difficult to understand the evolution of opposition to bigoted groups without also considering the parallel growth of the toleration for diversity within wider society.[4]

OLD SOUTH, NEW SOUTH, AND
THE CIVIL RIGHTS MOVEMENT

It is also tempting to look at the civil rights movement as a clear break between an Old South and a new one, between an *ancien régime* predicated on the most direct and pervasive forms of caste differentiation and a New South, a lighter and more modern South that does not condone or even carry the baggage of an earlier way of life. Would that the break were so clear. It is more compelling and far more accurate to understand the movement as a direct challenge to the past, an antithesis that—although powerful—did not possess the unqualified strength to wipe away completely the stubborn ways of several centuries. Instead, what was worked out in the South was something more like a new synthesis: an improvement in many discernible ways, but also a new thesis that retains—in ways more muted, more respectable, more clever, and perhaps that much more difficult to confront—many vestiges of the old. The civil rights movement may be understood, not as a wholesale deconstruction of the Old South, but more as a challenge that led to a reconstruction, imperfect and flawed in the way its host region has eventually assimilated it: a regional reconstruction with national implications.[5] The years under study in this volume constitute the early years of significant challenge to the old order.

Much of the old racial system had been underwritten since the Civil War by the chronic appearance of what may be called a "Reconstruction Syndrome"—a set of powerful negative attitudes that did much to shape southern history and culture for more than a century. The attitudes that made up this syndrome, fortified by race, were originally born of the psychological trauma of military defeat, occupation, abolition, and the forcible imposition of a new political order. After the initial trauma, the syndrome repeatedly manifested itself in the South—rising to the surface most clearly during those times when regional mores and folkways found themselves under siege, perceived or real. As a result, for more than a hundred years after the Reconstruction trauma, the dominant white, Anglo-Saxon, Protestant South was largely distinguished and distinguishable by repeated manifestations of the syndrome's recurring component tendencies, especially in times of acute stress: very strong anti-black, anti–federal government, anti-Yankee, anti-liberal, anti-tax, and anti-outsider/foreigner beliefs that translated into little tolerance for diversity. The Second Reconstruction, with Democratic and federal sponsorship of civil rights, demanded public and legal changes to southern life, but it also cemented and personalized the syndrome's most fundamental beliefs in the hearts and minds of a new generation of white southerners and their children. To an extent that many of us are reluctant to admit, these unfortunate tendencies still persist at, or just under, the surface of the present-day South, shaping and coloring the region's approach to politics, economics, and social mores. These tenets often appear in softer, sanitized, and more euphemistic forms. Yet appear they still do, as an almost manic concern for states' rights, local autonomy, individual freedom, fierce independence, political conservatism, sectional pride, constitutional purity, traditional values, religion, and gender roles (in fact, reverence for all things traditional, including pride in the white race's leadership and achievements), and disdain for hyphenated Americanism in favor of ethnic, racial, and cultural homogeneity: in sum, for all of the things that "made this country great."[6]

Historians, particularly historians of civil rights, must continue to be aware that the concepts they study—race, class, gender, religion, civil rights—do not exist in vacuums. They must be alert, for example, to the vital and enduring relationships among race, class, and politics in southern history. Scholars of all types have spilled much ink and not a little sweat in a variety of historiographical venues, trying to talk about race and class as categorically different concepts—even competing concepts. But race and class have been so intimately bound in the region's history that to speak of them now as completely separate entities is to rip them apart with such force that one risks doing irreparable damage to both, and—in effect—speaking about what are basically artificial and incomplete constructs. As historians expand the scope of political inquiry to streets, stores, households, parlors, and train stations, they must continue to ask "Who gets what, when, and how?" and, perhaps most important, "Why?" Southern history—including the recent past and indeed the present—is largely distinguished by what may be called a "politics of emotion." The term refers to the skillful, even ingenious, manipulation of ingrained plain-white emotions, principally over race, but, increasingly since the modern civil rights movement, by a more subtle and sophisticated appeal to white supremacy augmented by a host of powerful and related "God and country" issues: abortion, school prayer, super-patriotism, gun control, gay rights, the "character" or personal morality of political candidates, exhibition of the Confederate flag, the Ten Commandments, and so forth.

It is no longer possible, even in the South, to endorse segregation from the parameters of mainstream society. Yet it would be a mistake to believe that white supremacy has died, in the South and elsewhere in the United States, as an issue with immense political potential. We must keep sight of the fact that throughout southern history some southerners—conservative, elite, white southerners—have proven more adept at using the regional preoccupation with race, Reconstruction, and other emotional issues to preserve their privileged place in a rigidly stratified and hierarchical society. Bourbons, Redeemers, planters, and industrialists—conservative Democrats all—retained power for a century largely by persuading many plain whites to ally themselves with their class "betters" by appealing to these emotional rather than substantive issues. Most recently this has been the province of the newly ascendant—even dominant—southern GOP.[7] To a large extent, the First Reconstruction created the Solid Democratic South; the Second Reconstruction has produced an increasingly Solid Republican South.

Although open race-baiting is now in bad odor and modern Republican candidates have mastered the "Southern Strategy" well enough to couch their appeals in terms of a more subtle racism—and even stiff utterances of what many disdain as "politically correct" language—the same is not the case where religion and morality are concerned. Subtle racial appeals are still common in the modern Republican South.[8] Overt race-baiting is not. Racial appeals that are too direct threaten to pry open simple slogans like "compassionate conservatism," subjecting them to fuller and more careful scrutiny than they usually receive. In fact, slippages of overt racial talk are even capable today of precipitating a national crisis in which Republicans rush to denounce racism in order to preserve the GOP's newfound respectability on race—witness Trent Lott. Religion baiting, or impugning a candidate's "moral character," has in a very real sense become the "New Racism." To a large extent in the white South, morality baiting has replaced race-baiting as the most direct and accepted form of political intolerance in our discourse. And as southern ways continue to become American ways, the effect is increasingly apparent on a national scale. While religious and values baiting is considered respectable—even admirable—by present-day social standards, the tactic shares the same fundamental propensity to appeal to the darker angels of human nature that race-baiting once did. In the Deep South, calling someone a "baby killer" possesses the power to destroy reputations, careers, and whole programs of policy in much the same way that the epithet "nigger lover" once did.[9] Even more troubling, the "New Racism" seems to have filled a gaping void in the psyches of many white southerners who have, since the success of the civil rights movement—and, more to the point, the viability of an enfranchised black electorate—been deprived of the psychological gratification of feeling better about oneself by feeling worse about others.

RACE AND THE POLITICS OF EMOTION

Race and racism, unlike other issues, qualify as both a part of this newer "politics of emotion" and a contrasting "politics of reason." While race was for so long perhaps the most powerful emotional issue for white folk, it was also a substantive issue in many respects. Because it is impossible to separate race absolutely from class concerns (despite the best efforts and desires of some historians), race is an issue that may be found in both camps—unlike more purely emotional issues such as gun control, abortion, school prayer, patriotism, and the moral character of candidates. Although it was the most emotional of all issues in the South, race was not solely an emotional issue. White supremacy had a definite rational—if repellent—logic to its maintenance. For poor whites, middle-class whites, and the privileged, concrete economic rewards accompanied white supremacy and institutionalized racism.[10] As the primary economic competitors of blacks, poor whites stood to gain much by the preservation of white supremacy—not just in the social and psychological terms of Jim Crow but also in legal disfranchisement and in the economic rewards associated with employment discrimination and institutionalized racism. As members of a select caste, no matter how humble, plain whites enjoyed access to better parks, playgrounds, schools, libraries, jobs, restaurants, entertainments, public amenities, health care, housing, neighborhoods, and credit. Planters and industrialists profited from the preservation of white supremacy as well, both in emotional terms and in concrete economic ways, such as the perpetual supply of a cheap source of labor and a strong wedge with which to divide potential biracial class insurgency. These economic trappings of white supremacy were every bit as important and powerful as the social and psychological benefits whites gained from the legal and institutionalized caste system.[11] It is little wonder, then, that so many whites from all walks of life clung to segregation and white supremacy with such tenacity—indeed, desperation—in the face of the changes that came in the middle of the twentieth century. It is this crucial yet still relatively neglected decade and a half before *Brown* that is the focus of this book.

Whites clung so tenaciously to white supremacy not only for emotional and psychological reasons but also for rational class reasons, both for the perpetuation of their own privilege and for the future privilege of their sons and daughters. While poor whites certainly did not reach the political potential that a sustained and far-reaching biracial alliance promised, they did benefit tangibly from the status quo as the primary economic competitors of blacks. Segregation and white supremacy on the job and at the union hall benefited working-class whites, who received better pay, promotions, work assignments, and job classifications than blacks, in addition to the psychological benefits of white supremacy. They also got to attend superior public schools that were open to even the poor-white public, schools that may not have been as good as exclusive private schools but were markedly better than black schools in terms of facilities, teachers, money spent, and virtually every other measure—a subject taken up by Adam Fairclough in his probing essay on Louisiana in this volume. This ensured the children of poor whites a leg up and advantage in life, educationally and economically.

Privileged white planters and industrialists benefited more than any other group from white supremacy and did more than any other group to foster its survival—through convict-lease and the fomenting of racial tensions within labor unions, one of the few institutions that attempted some form of biracial class action—a theme explored in the essay by David and Linda Royster Beito on Dr. T. R. M. Howard of the Mississippi Delta. In states such as Alabama, the Big Mule/Black Belt coalition of wealthy planters and industrialists fought unions tooth and nail to preserve and add to their profits and to undermine a biracial coalition that possessed the potential to challenge them. Race was the most potent weapon in their arsenal for dividing a black and white workforce in coal, steel, iron, rubber, and textiles and on the docks.[12] Privileged whites also benefited from their advocacy of vocational or trade school education for blacks. As paternalists, they assumed the moral high ground as opposed to the poor-white mobs they blamed for violence against African Americans (even though "better whites" in many communities actually aided, abetted, organized, and later guaranteed clemency for these mobs).[13] But vocational education was largely geared to provide a steady supply of cheap, docile, anti-union black labor to their New South fields and factories. Finally, privileged whites used the race issue to defuse biracial political challenges, such as those of the Populists of the 1890s and the independent Greenbackers and Knights of Labor during the 1880s.[14]

A small black middle class both benefited from white supremacy and was also hurt by it. Some members of the black bourgeoisie profited from white supremacy by cooperating with the white middle class to the detriment of poor and working-class blacks; that is, they opposed unions and advocated corporate paternalism and company welfare because they profited, in a class sense, from the continued repression of poorer members of their race.[15] In this way, too, class was tied to race. Members of the black middle class also suffered from white supremacy because they saw their status, along with that of poor blacks, limited solely due to their skin color, another subject that emerges in the Beitos' essay on T. R. M. Howard. Try as they might to distinguish themselves as a "talented tenth" superior to working-class blacks, and to exist in a color-blind society in which they were judged by their relatively superior education and wealth, these members of the black middle class often saw themselves condemned, by Jim Crow and disfranchisement especially, to the same undiscriminating cell of racism as the poorer blacks whom they considered beneath them. Thus, try as they might, they could not divorce economic from race issues. Poor and working-class blacks lost all the way around and had no appreciable stake—material or psychological—in the preservation of white supremacy and Jim Crow.[16]

ADDITIONAL THEMES AND CONTROVERSIES

The southern status quo would not change in a meaningful way until the twin tumults of the Great Depression and World War II. The monumental racial changes associated with these events and the various reactions to them are the primary focus of this collection. And, while there is little question now that war and the Depression shook things up so that they never quite settled again in the same way, we should be careful, Adam Fairclough instructs us, in drawing a straight line of continuity from the 1940s to the 1960s. White backlash existed right along with the civil rights activities of the late New Deal and World War II—and only became exacerbated by the onset of the cold war in the early 1950s. John A. Salmond's essay makes clear that the activities of the Fellowship of Concerned Women and the Fellowship of Southern Churchmen, both religious-based civil rights groups, were impeded, at times very effectively, by hate mail, death threats, social opprobrium, Klan abuse, and mob violence. At times the backlash came from the hands of returning white war veterans, a topic taken up by Jennifer E. Brooks in her essay on Georgia. The sometimes fatal effects of white backlash also become obvious in weighing the career of T. R. M. Howard, who, as long as he remained within the Mississippi Delta confines of middle-class black respectability, even in his racial activism, was safe. The minute he began to directly push against the walls of Jim Crow, though, the death threats came, despite his wealth and status, eventually forcing him to flee the state for what he thought would be the kinder preserves of Chicago. And we all know the fate of Howard's young protégé, Medgar Evers.

The issue of white backlash necessarily engages one of the largest controversies among historians of the era: the "white backlash" thesis of University of Virginia law and history professor Michael J. Klarman. Klarman precipitated a historiographical firestorm by arguing that the 1954 *Brown v. Board of Education* decision actually encouraged white backlash against civil rights because it frustrated the gradual gains in race relations that had been accruing and stimulated white racial resistance because it singled out one of the most sensitive and symbolic areas of racial interaction for whites—public schooling. In effect, the landmark decision, far from ushering in an era of racial progress, actually produced negative results.[17]

The essays in this collection, while not providing the final answer to this question, do furnish fascinating and relevant evidence that directly bears on this important debate. To put it simply, to accept the Klarman thesis one must also accept the premise that nothing much of consequence had happened in the way of white resistance to civil rights prior to 1954. And that—as the essays in this collection make clear—is a dubious place from which to begin. The Klarman position also overestimates the amount and quality of what passed for racial "peace" prior to *Brown*. Various essays in this volume shed light on just how much unrest did exist prior to 1954, how much was being done to reconstitute race relations in the South, and how uneasy and imperfect the character of the allegedly pacific racial status quo was prior to 1954.

Indeed, the short-run failures of groups such as the Fellowship of Reconciliation and the Congress of Racial Equality—in their 1947 Journey of Reconciliation—at times actually laid the long-term seeds of racial change more fully realized during the 1960s. This is a point made clear in a number of the essays, particularly Raymond Arsenault's study of the first "freedom ride" through the Upper South states of Virginia, Kentucky, Tennessee, and North Carolina.

Although the cold war exposed American racism as an embarrassment on the international scene, it also increasingly allowed white supremacists to tar civil rights activists with the broad brush of un-Americanism, disloyalty, and even Communism—tactics that, unfortunately, have retained strong echoes in present-day American politics. The effects of the cold war and McCarthyism emerge in several of the essays here—those of Fairclough and the Beitos on Louisiana and T. R. M. Howard, but also in John White's essay on E. D. Nixon, John Salmond's intriguing essay on various types of grassroots activism around the South, and Raymond Arsenault's essay on the Journey of Reconciliation. In her exposition on the southwide activities of the Civil Rights Congress (CRC), Sarah Hart Brown weighs two sides of this issue. Echoes with a post-9/11 world and a Bush administration Justice Department led by John Ashcroft are loud as we read of a Birmingham activist complaining during the early 1950s that "What we have here is a wave of hysteria, rushing headlong into Fascism because we are afraid of Communism." But Brown also implicitly questions the CRC for marginalizing itself by its extremism and actual Communist connections—attributes, she argues, that made it easy for foes of civil rights to cripple the group by labeling it subversive, unpatriotic, and un-American. This point is especially driven home when we learn the identity of some of the CRC's adversaries—Eleanor Roosevelt, the impeccable racial liberal Aubrey Williams, and the NAACP's Walter White. Driven to distraction by the CRC, Williams once ordered the group to stop "send[ing] me any more of your materials—you people do far more harm than good. The best thing you can do . . . is to go out of existence."

The power of white backlash makes clear a central point that emerges over and over again in different ways throughout this volume: white native southern involvement and sympathy with the civil rights cause during the 1940s and 1950s was a distinctly minority enterprise. Currents of white activism, where they may be found, were brave, noble, praiseworthy, and even necessary for what would eventually happen during the 1960s. Yet the representativeness of such sentiment and behavior should not be overstated. It would still take grassroots black activists, "outside agitators" from the North, and considerable federal involvement to effect meaningful reform in the area of southern race relations. The gradual amelioration of southern race relations, retarded by a post-*Brown* backlash according to Michael Klarman, is in some evidence within these pages, but at nothing close to what may be called "prevailing." Far more common is what may be termed instances and evidence of white backlash, whenever and wherever deemed necessary. Even for many of the "homegrown" black activists, a strong outside influence was at work: notably for T. R. M. Howard, who had spent considerable time in California, Missouri, and the Upper South states of Kentucky and Tennessee before coming to Deep South Mississippi; and for E. D. Nixon, who, as a sleeping car porter, took regular railroad runs to Chicago, St. Louis, Miami, and Los Angeles from his home in Montgomery. Perhaps nowhere is the near-unanimity of white southern opposition to the notion of black civil rights more clearly enunciated than in the essays by Ray Arsenault on the first "freedom ride," by Adam Fairclough on Louisiana, and by Pamela Tyler on white southern reaction to Eleanor Roosevelt.

The First Lady is a ubiquitous figure in these pages, gracing the essays of Tyler, Andrew M. Manis, John White, and John Salmond, among others. Taken together, her activism in this volume is prodigious in the realm of black civil rights, as is the scorn, enmity, and outright hatred she engendered from the white South. The Eleanor Roosevelt who emerges in this collection was assertive and aggressive in her words and deeds, calling the nation to live up to its highest ideals and, in the process, exposing herself to the most hateful rumors, lies, and fantasies imaginable. Contemporary echoes with Hillary Clinton—another First Lady who evidently did not seem to "know her place," a Democratic president who could not "keep his wife" in that place, activism on behalf of liberal causes, and an almost apoplectic reaction from the white South—are strong.

Yet the activities of Mrs. Roosevelt imply more. They are, perhaps, the most visible of the contributions to black civil rights made during this period by women, but the importance and extent of the work of women activists during these years is striking. Andrew Manis writes of the considerable activities of respectable, middle-class Georgia Methodist women led by Dorothy Tilly, as does John Salmond. While appreciative of Tilly's work, Salmond casts her activism in a much more conservative light than does Manis, and in contrast to the other women he studies: the Southern Conference for Human Welfare's Virginia Durr in Alabama, Margaret Fisher in Georgia, Mary Price in North Carolina, and Mary McLeod Bethune, as well as the Fellowship of Southern Churchmen's Nelle Morton.

Almost as striking as the role of women is that of Jews. Although the sentiment behind the frequent segregationist complaint about "Communists and Jews" stirring up the civil rights issue may have been repugnant, it also contained more than a seedling of truth. In these pages we meet James Peck, Igal Roodenko, Sylvia Bernard, Leah Benemovsky, Bella Abzug, and other Jewish activists—and often they are on the cutting edge of pre-*Brown* civil rights.

The contribution of women and Jewish activists is notable in this volume, not only in its own right but also as part of a loose network of relationships among activists of different groups, states, and classes who cross paths in this book—relationships that were often cooperative but sometimes contentious. We learn that the middle-class respectability of T. R. M. Howard's activism was a breeding ground for Mississippi's Medgar, Myrlie, and Charles Evers and Fannie Lou Hamer. Thurgood Marshall and A. P. Tureaud figure prominently in Adam Fairclough's Louisiana. Sarah Hart Brown's window into the Civil Rights Congress in Texas and Florida details the activities of John Moreno Coe, James and Esther Cooper Jackson, Bella Abzug, and Sam Hall. E. D. Nixon's turbulent civil rights career in Alabama includes cameos by Virginia Durr, Roy Wilkins, A. Philip Randolph, Myles Horton, Walter White, Ella Baker, Rosa Parks, a young Martin Luther King, Fred Gray, Ralph Abernathy, Jo Ann Robinson, Mrs. Johnnie Carr, and Eleanor Roosevelt. John Salmond's survey of grassroots activists throughout the region, focusing heavily on Tennessee, Georgia, and the Carolinas, features not only the Durrs, Rosa Parks, Jo Ann Robinson, and others associated with Montgomery but also Lillian Smith, Jonathan Daniels, Frank Porter Graham, Clark Foreman, Osceola McKaine, Lucy Randolph Mason, and Bayard Rustin and George Houser of the Fellowship of Reconciliation and the Congress of Racial Equality. Rustin and Houser figure prominently in Raymond Arsenault's piece as well, as do A. Philip Randolph, James Farmer, Jim Peck, A. J. Muste, Ella Baker, and Paula Murray.

More problematic in these pages is the relationship between the NAACP and our various activists. Sarah Hart Brown describes a contentious relationship between the NAACP and the more extreme Civil Rights Congress, while the Beitos write of a similarly tense relationship between the wealthy, black physician who is the subject of their essay and the NAACP chapter in Howard's part of the Mississippi Delta. The story of the New Orleans NAACP in Fairclough's estimation is one of internecine struggle between a timid, middle-class old guard and a more aggressive new guard of working-class orientation. In Montgomery the story is much the same in John White's portrait of E. D. Nixon, who, characteristically, took on the staid local chapter frontally, leading to his capture, loss, and recapture of the chapter's presidency through these years. Ray Arsenault makes the critical political connection. He ties NAACP legal timidity to the largely conservative Republican makeup of the judiciary in the 1920s and 1930s and lays the increased aggressiveness of Thurgood Marshall, William Hastie, and Spottswood Robinson to the possibilities presented by the liberal, Democratic, New Deal judiciary of Franklin Roosevelt.

With or without fratricidal rivalries, the sheer breadth of activities documented here is imposing, from voter education and voter-registration drives, to lawsuits over equality in teacher pay, adequate recreational facilities, and harassment by the highway patrol, to boycotts of service stations that refused to allow black customers to use their bathrooms, to an "Oust Bilbo" campaign in Mississippi, to workplace activism and campaigns to get a black United Services Organization. Middle-class activism is prominent in several of the essays, as is tension between working-class and bourgeois notions of what constituted proper strategies and goals. Several of the contributors address the complicated role of organized labor, which was often a beacon in these years. Witness Franklin Roosevelt's Fair Employment Practices Committee and the CIO's industrial unionism and aid to the cause of civil rights. But labor was a frequent source of darkness as well, especially as regards the AFL's craft-related hostility to black employment rights and the blue-collar nature of much of the white backlash. John White's portrait of E. D. Nixon makes clear the profound debt of his subject to the tactics, outlook, and militancy of A. Philip Randolph's Brotherhood of Sleeping Car Porters, as do Ray Arsenault's and John Salmond's positive estimations of the role of unions. Jennifer Brooks, Adam Fairclough, and Sarah Hart Brown provide estimations that are more mixed.

This variance among the essays recalls another major historiographical debate, the "lost opportunities" thesis associated with the work of Robert Korstad, Nelson Lichtenstein, and Michael Honey. In an article that focused on Winston-Salem, North Carolina, and Detroit, Michigan, Korstad and Lichtenstein contended that an "employer offensive" that capitalized on the McCarthyistic climate of the early 1950s combined with a failure on the part of "the most characteristic institutions of American liberalism," including organized labor's leadership and the NAACP, to result in a tragic series of missed opportunities for civil rights. The liberal preference for a "legal-administrative if not a bureaucratic approach" to civil rights joined with employer hostility to slam shut a narrow window of opportunity for a radical, urban, working-class-based version of civil rights opened up by "Afro-American protest groups, leftist clergymen, and Communist-led unions and front organizations." As a result of this liberal failure, including the propensity of union leaders to be indifferent to civil rights, the reconstituted civil rights movement after 1954 found itself dominated by middle-class black church and protest groups. It was more timid in outlook, bureaucratic and legal in nature and goals, and almost preordained for modest, limited accomplishments.[18]

While the essays in this book do not solve the riddle of the argument that has ebbed and flowed for a decade and a half, they do provide evidence that questions the relevance and validity of such a sanguine and complete estimation. Perhaps most problematically, the "lost opportunities" thesis tends to conflate union leadership with rank-and-file membership when it is clear that deep and serious divisions—rather than indifference—existed on at least three levels: first, between national and state, and state and local, components of organized labor; second, between black workers and white workers; and third, between labor leaders and much of their membership. During the third-party campaigns of George Wallace in the 1960s, such divisions took on national electoral significance as the Alabamian's message of hate and rage resonated powerfully with working-class whites North and South but was vehemently opposed by national and state labor leaders. It is present today as discouraged Alabama labor leaders lament their inability to break through the "three G's" ("God, Guns, and Gays") in trying to convince a largely conservative white membership to vote Democratic in national elections. Or when organizing efforts in the right-to-work stronghold of North Carolina fail when a communications worker explains that he will never join the union or vote Democratic because Democrats are "baby-killing, queer-loving, gun-hating, liberals." Or in Columbia as the female president of the South Carolina AFL-CIO is booed and hooted out of a large paper worker hall (after having Scripture quoted to her) because she asks local unions to march alongside blacks, women, gays, and other groups to protest a mayor's public comments about homosexuals not being welcome in his seaside town.[19]

Evidence in the Brooks, Fairclough, and Brown essays in this volume suggest that the "lost opportunities" thesis relegates far too much power and influence to labor leadership to impose social and cultural values on their rank and file above and beyond purely "bread and butter" union issues of wages, benefits, safety, conditions, and job security. During the period under review here, local union rules (in collusion with white employers) often worked to block, rather than facilitate, black advancement in terms of wages, skills, seniority, and job classifications. It is fairly apparent that theses such as "lost opportunities" overestimate the rationality and class consciousness of the general electorate while undervaluing the divisive power of raw emotions on race, gender, religion, morality, and values or on hot-button issues such as guns, abortion, patriotism, and sexual orientation. The essays in this book make clear that prior to 1954 there was a yawning gap between the social and cultural progressivism of union leaders and a rank and file that—while perhaps amenable to an economic liberalism that served them—lagged far behind in other areas. The essays also demonstrate the enduring power of racial prejudice, the relevance of regional folkways, and the various emotions that impinge on political and economic behavior: fear, jealousy, anger, hatred, superiority, and insecurity—perceived and real.

Although the "lost opportunities" thesis tends to conflate union leadership with the rank and file in ways that are not particularly productive, the thesis actually has a more frequent tendency toward dichotomy that is likewise not very elucidating. Rather than presenting a gulf between restless and visionary radicals and timid, hamstrung liberals, the story that emerges in much of this book is far more nuanced. While radicals like James Peck, A. Philip Randolph, Bayard Rustin, and Buck Kester most certainly get their due, as they should, a number of the essays make clear that in various times and places, radicals and traditional liberals actually worked hand in hand toward greater civil rights. Although the NAACP was often slow and grudging in its support for the more radical direct-action techniques of groups like CORE, when push came to shove it was usually there with money, morale, and most important, legal assistance. In fact, what emerges from reading and comparing Ray Arsenault's and John Salmond's differing interpretations of the same event—the "First Freedom Ride"—is that not only did radicals and liberals find themselves working together in these years, but that actually it could have been no other way. The dichotomy is overrated. Without the *Irene Morgan* court decision to stand on—the fruit of NAACP legal incrementalism (what some critics might call a timid, bureaucratic approach to civil rights), radicals like Rustin, Peck, and James Farmer wouldn't have been riding anywhere. Yet the radicals were without question correct as well. The white South wasn't going to simply lie down and accept desegregation—no matter how many Supreme Court decisions the NAACP won. At some point, someone was going to have to go down there and ride. Thus the relationship that emerges in these pages between radicals and liberals is more fluid and cooperative, perhaps, than the one that "lost opportunities" has left us with. People seeking civil rights often had to adapt themselves to varying local conditions, seeping in where and how they could, forming themselves to the ruts and grooves that existed, rather than trying to impose a stiff blanket ideological approach. Thus an atheist like A. Philip Randolph might find himself using biblical persuasion in the Deep South. Like it or not—like each other or not—radicals and liberals needed each other during these years. Neither was able to operate in a vacuum.

Other dichotomies find little support in these pages. The "good" radical or "bad" liberal approach to civil rights does not come through unscathed. While radical and Communist energy and involvement was undeniably important and often useful, it could also be, as the chapters by Fairclough and Brown make clear, disruptive and even, at times, detrimental. In talking about dichotomies, it becomes clear that it is even impossible to talk about one NAACP as part of the liberal, bureaucratic side of civil rights. Several essays make clear that what was going on in places like New Orleans, Montgomery, and the Mississippi Delta during these years was a powerful struggle *within* the NAACP to determine just how aggressive it would be. Although T. R. M. Howard, Dorothy Tilly, and E. D. Nixon would not have defined themselves as radicals, at times they took what could be called radical action and often made great strides through almost sheer force of personality. Yet how to categorize them now? Howard derived his power through a masterful playing of the free enterprise game, through a conservative, business-oriented, moneyed approach to civil rights. Yet Medgar Evers and Amzie Moore were protégés. Tilly got much of her power from pure respectability and proper religion, yet she earned the same enmity as many more radical people who pushed the bounds of white supremacy. E. D. Nixon was a classic juxtaposition of the radical and the liberal. A devout disciple of A. Philip Randolph *and* himself a local NAACP leader, Nixon worked with Randolph and Myles Horton, but he also allied with Eleanor Roosevelt, Virginia Durr, and all of the major figures associated with the Montgomery Bus Boycott. At root, in almost diametric opposition to capitalist T. R. M. Howard, Nixon represented trade union organization and working-class aggressiveness. Yet Howard, Tilly, Nixon, and no doubt many others were all far too individualistic and charismatic to constrict to the antiseptic categories that scholars have sometimes worked with. And what of the Louisiana schoolteachers who energized civil rights in the Pelican State? Or the men who returned home to the South after World War II? Jenny Brooks's essay is a poignant testament to the transformative power of wartime experience, not only on black soldiers but on whites as well who found their assumptions and attitudes radically altered by what they saw and heard in the ultimate cauldron. How to pigeonhole them now: radicals? liberals? Does it matter? And while Sally Brown's essay points to McCarthyism and right-wing cold war politics as chilling weapons against civil rights, her interpretation tends more toward blaming the Red Scare for *killing* left-wing civil rights, not liberal timidity. In fact, liberal "timidity" comes across more as a survival mechanism than a character defect, given the prevailing climate of fear and intolerance.

As important is the role of religion in the struggles for civil rights and the backlash that met them in these pages. As with the labor issue, there was a clear break on this subject between church leadership and the beliefs and attitudes of southern flocks. While the role of elite endorsement of the *Brown* decision and white folk religious "massive resistance" is becoming increasingly well known—and we await the forthcoming work of Jane Dailey on religion and race—several of the essays in this collection describe the very important contributions black and white religious people made to the cause of civil rights. Andrew Manis and John Salmond relate the inspiring work of Georgia Methodist Dorothy Tilly and her Fellowship of the Concerned, while Salmond, in particular, also recounts the valuable activities of the Fellowship of Southern Churchmen (which included women) and the work of James Dombrowski, Howard "Buck" Kester, and Nelle Morton. We also learn of the positive role the Roman Catholic Church played in Louisiana race relations during the 1940s and its reversal during the early 1950s atmosphere of McCarthyism. The social justice and pacifist emphasis of Quaker, Dutch Reformed, and missionary Methodist beliefs played an important role in the activism of Bayard Rustin, James Peck, James Farmer, and George Houser—architects of the first and later "freedom rides." Perhaps most interesting is the religious work of A. Philip Randolph, an avowed atheist who appealed, John White tells us, to the endemic religiosity of the South by casting his arguments in explicit biblical terms and evangelical concepts.

The still largely unheralded civil rights battles fought during the 1940s and early 1950s were important, not merely in their own right or because they were part of the fiery struggle that gained national and international prominence during the mid-1950s. The period was important because it played a very large role in shaping the course of politics in the South and the nation into the next century. The 1940s and early 1950s were times of great ferment as long-standing patterns of race relations found themselves under siege—not just from far-sighted individuals but from larger forces beyond the South and even the nation's borders: a world war against fascism and a cold war in which national image became a powerful weapon.[20] New parameters meant new imperatives. The results of the race warfare that raged parallel to world war and cold war restructured not only how whites and blacks related to each other in a legal and formal sense but also the way politics itself—who held power and why—was changed for the next long phase in our nation's history.

More than a decade ago, August Meier called for scholarly investigation into the connection between the Second Reconstruction and the advent of modern Republicanism in the South. The successes of the modern civil rights movement, Meier felt, were connected to the subsequent "flight of many Southern whites from the Democratic to the Republican Party—revealing a bias that remains even though the legitimacy of black political activity is" now, at least publicly, "recognized."

Steven F. Lawson noted the acute irony in the increased popular appeal of the civil rights movement during the 1980s, a movement that "contrasted sharply" with the decade's prevailing "political conservatism" and "Reagan-era mentality that glorified the attainment of personal wealth and ignored community health." Julian Bond expressed his disappointment even more directly, writing in the early 1990s that "one reason for the sorry state of student activism on college campuses today is the current replacement of militant liberal Christians with conservative right-wing evangelicals, both white and black. Jerry Falwell, Oral Roberts, Pat Robertson, and the Fellowship of Christian Athletes have replaced James Lawson, William Sloane Coffin, Robert Spike, and the Berrigan brothers."[21]

Of considerable interest and importance is how and why the Republican Party in the South went from being an anemic party of political lepers associated with "Negro" equality to become the dominant political party in the American South. In short, there is enough evidence to at least suggest that the answer has much to do with the Republican Party's transformation on the race question, and that this change was, above any other, the single most important key to its journey from Dixie's political wilderness to viability, respectability, and, ultimately, dominance among white southerners—and hence the South at large. In this shift, the course the white South chose during the 1940s has, in retrospect, been of enormous consequence.

Yet time has brought with it a tendency toward historiographical hindsight that now second-guesses much of what transpired during the Second Reconstruction. Journalists and historians have put forth similar theories that Democratic Party identification with civil rights, accelerating during the 1960s, fractured the New Deal coalition along a racial fault line and led to the demise of a class-based liberalism once vibrant among southern whites—as well as the emasculation of the Democratic Party itself. Some have gone so far as to castigate an alleged "self-imposed intellectual isolation and intolerance" as symptomatic of a modern "Democratic party elite" and the imposition on much of America—including its own increasingly unhappy southern white and northern ethnic and working-class base—of a "liberal agenda" based on race with the tax burdens and costs "borne by others." The Democratic Party, Thomas Byrne Esdall and Mary D. Esdall tell us, by allowing itself to be identified with the Second Reconstruction, "unleashed" radical, "redistributive . . . forces that it could [not] . . . control," and in doing so it alienated its traditional, white, middle- and working-class base.[22]

Prologue   19

   These arguments—as well known, influential, and ostensibly irresistible in hindsight as they are—bear a certain kinship in blaming the victim (in this case the Democratic Party) for being victimized. They also rather conveniently ignore the moral and ethical implications of electoral strategy. What would these latter-day critics have had the Democratic Party do in 1964? Follow the example set by the Republican Party and wrestle with George Wallace to wave the flag of white supremacy? Would the country or Americans in general have been better off if the Democrats had chosen this "wiser" electoral course? And, if they *had* gone down that path, two questions still linger: What difference would there have *then* been between the two major parties on race? and How long do these authors suppose black voters would have remained a part of the Democratic Party? Would this really have been a more fruitful course for the Democratic Party to follow purely in terms of counting voters' heads? Like the Klarman thesis, these arguments tend to misplace responsibility for tribulation and adverse reactions. The Klarman thesis placed undue blame for causing backlash on a progressive and courageous judicial decision rather than on centuries of the sometimes-violent repression of basic civil liberties for a whole race of people. These interpretations tend to regard Republican exploitation of racial backlash (read: prejudice) as "legitimate," rational, and even wise, while badly underestimating or, worse yet, legitimizing the manipulative power of emotional appeals to warp perceptions and distract voters from reason-based issues by pressing the hot buttons of race, gender, sexuality, and religion. Ironically, most of these critiques emanate from liberal Democrats trying to provide constructive criticism to their party, yet the most prominent critiques about Democratic elitism, Democratic detachment from the country's "majoritarian values," and the Africanization/radicalization of the Democratic Party sound as if they could have been penned by George Wallace, Barry Goldwater, or, in more recent years, by Newt Gingrich or even Rush Limbaugh.[23] The adoption and parroting by liberal commentators of this once-extreme right-wing critique of the Democratic Party on race, morality, and values is powerful evidence in and of itself of the degree to which the conservative backlash against civil rights has been effective—and close to consuming—thanks to a revolution in modern media and the active entry of the Religious Right into politics. As the Klarman thesis places undue blame on a judicial decision that moved us closer as a country to our founding ideals, these interpretations critique a political party for identifying itself with the fundamentally noble cause of civil rights, for making tax policies mildly redistributive rather than settling for the hollow rhetoric of racial egalitarianism without economic reform, and in doing so, perhaps making itself the target of those who would demagogue issues based on civil rights and kindred rights.

1
"You Don't Have to Ride Jim Crow"
CORE and the 1947 Journey of Reconciliation
Raymond Arsenault

> You don't have to ride jim crow,
> You don't have to ride jim crow,
> Get on the bus, set any place,
> 'Cause Irene Morgan won her case,
> You don't have to ride jim crow.
> > Second stanza of the 1947 freedom song
> > "You Don't Have to Ride Jim Crow"[1]

WHEN IRENE MORGAN boarded a Greyhound bus in Hayes Store, Virginia, on July 16, 1944, she had no inkling of what was about to happen—no idea that her return trip to Baltimore would alter the course of American history. The twenty-six-year-old defense worker and mother of two had more mundane things on her mind. It was a sweltering morning in the Virginia Tidewater, and she was anxious to get home to her husband, a stevedore who worked on the docks of Baltimore's bustling inner harbor. Earlier in the summer, after suffering a miscarriage, she had taken her two young children for an extended visit to her mother's house in the remote countryside near Hayes Store, a crossroads hamlet in the Tidewater lowlands of Gloucester County. Now she was returning home for a doctor's appointment and perhaps a clean bill of health that would allow her to resume work at the Martin bomber plant where she helped build B-26 Marauders. The restful stay in Gloucester—where her mother's family had lived and worked since the early nineteenth century, and where she had visited many times since childhood—had restored some of her physical strength and renewed a cherished family bond. But it had also confirmed the stark realities of a rural folk culture shouldering the burdens of three centuries of plantation life. Despite Gloucester's proximity to Hampton Roads and Norfolk, the world war had brought surprisingly few changes to the area, most of which remained mired in suffocating poverty and an unremitting caste system.

As Irene Morgan knew all too well, Baltimore had its own problems related to race and class. Still, she could not help feeling fortunate to live in a community where it was relatively common for people of color to own homes and businesses, to vote on election day, to attend high school or college, and to aspire to middle-class respectability. Despite humble beginnings, Irene herself had experienced a tantalizing measure of upward mobility. The sixth of nine children, she had grown up in a working-class black family that had encountered more hardships than luxuries. Her father, an itinerant housepainter and day laborer, had done his best to provide for the family, but the difficulty of finding steady work in a depression-ravaged and racially segregated city had nearly broken him, testing his faith as a devout Seventh Day Adventist. Although a strong-willed mother managed to keep the family together, even after one of her daughters contracted tuberculosis, hard realities had forced Irene and her siblings to drop out of high school long before graduating. As a teenager, she worked long hours as a laundress, maid, and baby-sitter. Yet she never allowed her difficult economic circumstances or her circumscribed status as a black female to impinge on her sense of self-worth and dignity. Bright and self-assured, with a strong sense of right and wrong, she was determined to make her way in the world, despite the very real obstacles of prejudice and discrimination. As a young wife and mother preoccupied with her family, she had not yet found the time to join the National Association for the Advancement of Colored People (NAACP) or any other organization dedicated to racial uplift. But in many ways she exemplified the "new Negro" that the NAACP had been touting since the 1930s. Part of a swelling movement for human dignity and racial equality, she was ready and willing to stand up—or, if need be, sit down—for her rights as an American citizen.[2]

The Greyhound from Norfolk was jammed that morning, especially in the back where several black passengers had no choice but to stand in the aisle. As the bus pulled away from the curb, Morgan was still searching for an empty seat. When none materialized, she accepted the invitation of a young black woman who graciously offered her a lap to sit on. Later, when the bus arrived in Saluda, a county-seat town twenty miles north of Hayes Store, she moved to a seat relinquished by a departing passenger. Although only three rows from the back, she found herself sitting directly in front of a white couple—an arrangement that violated both custom and a 1930 Virginia statute prohibiting racially mixed seating on public conveyances. Since she was not actually sitting next to a white person, Morgan did not think the driver would ask her to move, and perhaps he would not have if a white couple had not boarded the bus a few seconds after she sat down. Suddenly, the driver turned toward Morgan and her seatmate, a young black woman holding an infant, and barked: "You'll have to get up and give your seats to these people." The young woman complied immediately, scurrying into the aisle near the back of the bus, but Morgan, perhaps forgetting where she was, suggested a compromise: she would be happy to exchange seats with a white passenger sitting behind her, she calmly explained, but she was too weak to stand for any length of time. Growing impatient, the driver repeated his order, this time with a barely controlled rage. Once again Morgan refused to give up her seat. As an uneasy murmur filled the bus, the driver shook his head in disgust before rushing down the steps to fetch the local sheriff.[3]

Irene Morgan's impulsive act—like Rosa Park's more celebrated refusal to give up a seat on a Montgomery bus eleven years later—placed her in a difficult and dangerous position. In such situations there were no mitigating circumstances, no conventions of humanity or paternalism that might shield her from the full force of the law. To the driver and to the sheriff of Middlesex County, the fact that she was a woman and in ill health mattered little. By challenging both the sanctity of segregation and the driver's authority, she had disturbed the delicate balance of etiquette, endangering a society that made white supremacy the cornerstone of social order. With this in mind, the sheriff and his deputy showed no mercy as they dragged her out of the bus. Both men later claimed that they resorted to force only after Morgan kicked the sheriff three times in the leg, but even they did not deny that she ultimately got the worse of the exchange. When she complained that they were hurting her arms, the deputy shouted, "Wait til I get you to jail, I'll beat your head with a stick." Charged with resisting arrest and violating Virginia's Jim Crow transit law, she spent the next seven hours slumped in the corner of a county jail cell. Late in the afternoon, after her mother posted a $500 bond, she was released by county authorities who were confident that they had made their point: no uppity Negro from Baltimore could flout the law in the Virginia Tidewater and get away with it.

As Morgan and her mother left the jail, Middlesex County officials had good reason to believe they had seen the last of the feisty young woman from Baltimore. In their experience, any Negro with a lick of sense would do whatever was necessary to avoid a court appearance. If she knew what was good for her, she would hurry back to Maryland and stay there, even if it meant forfeiting a $500 bond. They had seen this calculus of survival operate on countless occasions, and they didn't expect anything different from Morgan. What they failed to anticipate was her indomitable determination to achieve simple justice. As Morgan recalled many years later, she had paid her money, was minding her business, and sitting where she was supposed to sit—and was not going to take the insult. The incident in Saluda left her with daunting medical and financial problems, but it did not diminish her sense of outrage or her burning desire for vindication. As she waited for her day in court, discussions with friends and relatives, some of whom belonged to the Baltimore branch of the NAACP, brought the significance of her challenge to Jim Crow into focus. Her personal saga was part of a larger story—an ever-widening struggle for civil rights and human dignity that promised to recast the nature of American democracy. Driven, as one family member put it, by "the pent-up bitterness of years of seeing the colored people pushed around," Morgan embraced the responsibility of bearing witness, of confronting her oppressors, in a court of law.[4]

On October 18, 1944, Morgan stood before Middlesex County circuit judge J. Douglas Mitchell and pleaded her case. Although she represented herself as best she could, arguing that Virginia law did not apply to interstate passengers, the outcome was never in doubt. Convicted on both charges, she was fined $100 for resisting arrest and $10 and court costs for violating state segregation law. As expected, she promptly paid the first fine. But, to Judge Mitchell's dismay, she announced her intention to appeal the second conviction to the Virginia Supreme Court.[5]

Morgan's appeal raised more than a few eyebrows in the capital city of Richmond, where it was no secret that the NAACP had been searching for suitable test cases that could be used to challenge the constitutionality of the state's Jim Crow transit law. Segregated transit was a special concern in Virginia, which served as a racial and legal gateway for southbound bus and railway passengers. Crossing into the Old Dominion from the District of Columbia, which had no Jim Crow restrictions, or from Maryland, which, unlike Virginia, limited its segregationist mandate to local and intrastate passengers, could be a jarring and bewildering experience for travelers unfamiliar with the complexities of border-state life. This was an old problem, dating back at least a half century, but the number of violations and interracial incidents involving interstate passengers had multiplied in recent years, especially since the outbreak of World War II. With the proliferation of military personnel and with the rising militancy of the Double V campaign, which sought twin victories over enemies abroad and racial discrimination at home, Virginia became a legal and cultural battleground for black Americans willing to challenge the dictates of Jim Crow. As early as 1908, a survey of the "color line" by the journalist Ray Stannard Baker had revealed that "no other point of race contact is so much and so bitterly discussed among Negroes as the Jim Crow car." And this was still true thirty-six years later, according to Gunnar Myrdal, the author of the monumental 1944 study *An American Dilemma: The Negro Problem and American Democracy*. "It is a common observation," he noted, "that the Jim Crow car is resented more bitterly among Negroes than most other forms of segregation."[6]

NAACP attorneys, both in Virginia and in the national office, knew all of this and did what they could to chip away at the legal foundations of Jim Crow transit. But they were frustrated by their inability to attract the attention of the U.S. Supreme Court. *Plessy v. Ferguson,* the cornerstone of the "separate but equal" doctrine that had sustained segregationist law since 1896, had validated a Louisiana segregated coach law, and through the years the Court had been reluctant to revisit the issue in any fundamental way. In 1910, with former Klansman Edward White of Louisiana serving as chief justice, the Court ruled in *Chiles v. Chesapeake and Ohio Railway* that state segregation laws could be applied to interstate passengers. Four years later, in *McCabe v. Atchison, Topeka, and Santa Fe Railroad,* the Court showed some openness to the argument that black travelers had a legal right to equal accommodations, but this tantalizing decision only served to divert attention from the underlying reality of racial separation. According to Catherine Barnes, the leading historian of transit desegregation, for the next three decades "Southern blacks attempted only to equalize accommodations, not to undo segregation."[7]

During the 1920s and early 1930s, when conservative Republicans dominated the Court, few NAACP attorneys questioned this pragmatic strategy. But from the mid-1930s on, the increasingly liberal Roosevelt Court encouraged a reformulation of the organization's approach to the interrelated problems of racial discrimination and segregation. Affecting all aspects of the NAACP's legal war on Jim Crow, this rethinking was especially apparent in cases involving segregated transit. In 1941 the campaign for equal travel accommodations finally brought a measure of victory in *Mitchell v. Arkansas*—a unanimous decision that affirmed Illinois congressman Arthur Mitchell's claim to the same first-class service accorded white travelers. Thurgood Marshall, William Hastie, and other NAACP legal theorists were convinced that the practice of applying state laws to interstate passengers was especially vulnerable to legal challenge. Citing the interstate commerce clause and *Hall v. DeCuir*—a long-forgotten 1877 decision that, ironically, had invalidated a state law *prohibiting* racial segregation among interstate steamboat passengers—they felt confident that they could persuade the Roosevelt Court to restrict legally mandated segregation to intrastate passengers. This strategy, which called for a reversal of the 1910 *Chiles* decision, allowed the NAACP to move forward without risking a premature reconsideration of *Plessy*. Since pushing the Court too fast or too far would almost certainly lead to a setback for the cause of civil rights, a cautious and careful selection of test cases was essential. To counter the inertial presumptions of American law, the NAACP needed the right defendant in the right place at the right time.[8]

In 1942, the legal committee of the Virginia NAACP, led by three Howard University–trained attorneys—Spottswood Robinson, Oliver Hill, and Martin A. Martin—began the search for a case that would bring the interstate issue before the Court. Working closely with Marshall and the national legal staff, the committee considered and rejected a number of potential clients before discovering Irene Morgan in the fall of 1944. Almost immediately they sensed that this was the case and the defendant they needed. Not only was the basis of her conviction clear, but Morgan also had the makings of an exemplary client. She was young, attractive, articulate, and, judging by her poised performance in Saluda, strong enough to withstand the pressures of a high-profile legal battle.[9]

With Marshall's blessing, the Virginia NAACP filed a carefully crafted appellate brief emphasizing the interstate commerce clause and *Hall v. DeCuir*. But, as expected, the seven justices of the Virginia Supreme Court unanimously affirmed Morgan's conviction. In a rambling sixteen-page opinion issued on June 6, 1945, the court upheld the constitutionality of the 1930 Jim Crow transit law, reiterating the wisdom and legality of segregating all passengers, regardless of their origin or destination. Speaking for the court, Justice Herbert Gregory did not deny that *Hall v. DeCuir* established a legal precedent for invoking the commerce clause as a barrier to state statutes that interfered with interstate commerce, but he summarily dismissed the NAACP's claim that the 1930 law involved such interference. "Our conclusion," he declared, "is that the statute challenged is a reasonable police regulation and applies to both intrastate and interstate passengers. It is not obnoxious to the commerce clause of the Constitution."[10]

Gregory's plain and forthright words were just what the NAACP wanted to hear. With a little help from the Virginia Supreme Court, *Morgan v. Commonwealth of Virginia* had become a near-perfect test case. When the Virginia court denied the NAACP's petition for a rehearing in September, Spot Robinson could hardly wait to file an appeal to the U.S. Supreme Court. In January 1946 the Court agreed to hear the case, and two months later Robinson joined Marshall and Hastie for the oral argument in Washington. Even though he was the NAACP's leading authority on segregated transportation law, Robinson could not actually argue the case because he was not yet certified to appear before the Court. But during the argument he sat at the table with Marshall and Hastie. Although this was the first time that the NAACP had argued a segregated transit case in front of the Court, the organization's talented team of attorneys made short work of Virginia attorney general Abram Staples's tired arguments on behalf of the status quo. Focusing on the Virginia statute's broad reach, they argued that forcibly segregating interstate passengers violated the commerce clause, infringed upon congressional authority, and threatened the nation's tradition of free movement across state lines. Insisting that this misuse of state segregation laws placed an unnecessary and unconstitutional burden on individuals as well as interstate bus companies, the NAACP gave the Court a compelling rationale for overruling the Virginia court's judicial and racial conservatism. "Today, we are just emerging from a war in which all of the people of the United States were joined in a death struggle against the apostles of racism," the NAACP brief reminded the justices. Surely it was time for the Court to declare that federal law no longer sanctioned "disruptive local practices bred of racial notions alien to our national ideals, and to the solemn undertakings of the community of civilized nations as well."[11]

Since this was essentially the same Court that had struck down the Texas white primary in the *Smith v. Allwright* decision of April 1944, NAACP leaders were cautiously optimistic. But in the unsettled atmosphere of postwar America, no one could be certain how the Court would rule—or how white Americans would respond to an NAACP victory over Jim Crow transit. The year 1946 had already brought a number of surprises, both bitter and sweet, ranging from the brutal repression of black veterans in Columbia, Tennessee, to the signing of Jackie Robinson by the Brooklyn Dodgers. Although change was in the air, it was not entirely clear which way the nation was headed on matters of race. Two years earlier, in the wake of the white primary decision, Marshall urged delegates to the national NAACP convention to accelerate the pace of the movement for civil rights. "We must not be delayed by people who say, 'The time is not ripe,'" he had declared, "nor should we proceed with caution for fear of destroying the status quo. People who deny us our civil rights should be brought to justice now." It was in this spirit that he had encouraged his Virginia colleagues to file the *Morgan* appeal. But now, as he nervously awaited the Court's ruling, he could not help wondering if he had acted precipitously. Adding to his nervousness was the knowledge that Virginia's sharp-tongued attorney general had never lost a case in nine appearances before the Court.[12]

When the Supreme Court announced its decision on June 3, 1946, Marshall was both relieved and elated. With only one dissenting vote—that of Harold Burton, a former Republican senator from Ohio appointed to the Court in 1945—the justices sustained Morgan's appeal. In a carefully worded opinion delivered by Associate Justice Stanley Reed, a Kentucky Democrat who had spoken for the Court in the 1944 *Smith v. Allwright* decision, six justices (in June 1946, the recent death of Chief Justice Harlan Fiske Stone and the assignment of Associate Justice Robert Jackson to the Nuremberg Trials had reduced the Court to seven members) accepted the NAACP's argument that segregating interstate passengers violated the spirit of the interstate commerce clause. "As there is no Federal act dealing with the separation of races," Reed explained, "we must decide the validity of this Virginia statute on the challenge that it interferes with commerce, as a matter of balance between exercise of the local police power and the need for National uniformity in the regulations for interstate travel. It seems clear to us that seating arrangements for the different races in interstate motor travel require a single uniform rule to promote and protect national travel." Cast in narrow terms, the opinion said nothing about intrastate passengers, its applicability to other means of conveyance such as railroads, or how and when desegregation of interstate buses might be implemented. And it offered no clear sign that the Court was moving closer to an outright rejection of the *Plessy* doctrine of separate but equal. As a *Time* reporter put it, "This week seven nimble Justices ducked the racial question and settled everything on the basis of comfortable traveling." None of this surprised Marshall and the other NAACP attorneys, who had maintained modest expectations throughout the *Morgan* proceedings. For the time being, they were satisfied that, in their first appearance before the Court on a segregated transit issue, pragmatic reasoning had given them a solid victory. In the aftermath of the decision, their greatest concern was not with the narrowness of the ruling but rather with the prospects of enforcement by federal and state authorities. As with all legal controversies involving social mores or public behavior, the true value and meaning of the decision would depend on the reactions to it.[13]

The congratulatory telegrams and letters that poured into the NAACP's national headquarters hailed the *Morgan* decision as a legal milestone comparable to *Smith v. Allwright,* but NAACP officials knew that such praise from friends and allies, however welcome, was less important than the responses of editors, reporters, public officials, and bus company executives. On June 4 the *Morgan* decision was front-page news throughout the nation, but there was no consensus about its probable impact on segregated travel. Press coverage followed racial, regional, and political lines and offered a wide range of explanation and speculation. In the black press the headlines and stories tended to be expansive and even jubilant, suggesting that *Morgan* represented a landmark decision. In the major dailies of the Northeast, Midwest, and West, most of the coverage was favorable but restrained. In the white South, with few exceptions, editors and reporters downplayed the significance of the Court's ruling. Anyone who scanned the pages of the *Baltimore Afro-American,* the *New York Times,* and the *Birmingham Post-Herald,* for example, would have come away with more questions than answers. Had the Court issued a minor legal clarification that would affect a few border-state travelers in northern Virginia, or had it struck a major blow against Jim Crow? No one could be sure in the days and weeks following the decision.[14]

In this atmosphere of confusion and conflicting signals, most politicians, North and South, laid low. Former secretary of the interior Harold Ickes and former New York governor Herbert Lehman lauded the decision, and Representative Adam Clayton Powell Jr., a black Democrat representing Harlem, called *Morgan* "the most important step toward winning the peace at home since the conclusion of the war." But with a few notable exceptions, the rest of the political establishment, from President Truman on down, had little or nothing to say about the Court's ruling. Even in the Deep South, the political response was muted. One exception was Mississippi congressman Dan McGehee, who insisted the decision proved that "the Supreme Court judges are a bunch of mediocre lawyers with no judicial training, and limited experience in the practice of the law." In "taking away the rights of the States of this great republic to regulate the affairs within their borders," he added, "they did so unmindful of the trouble and bloodshed that may be caused in the future." Foreshadowing the post-*Brown* attacks on Chief Justice Earl Warren, McGehee called for judicial impeachment proceedings "against each and every one of those who have handed down such decisions."[15]

In the immediate aftermath of the *Morgan* decision, most of the public officials who were in a position to implement the ruling adopted a wait-and-see attitude. Though clearly worried about the days ahead, NAACP leaders initially regarded this restraint as a hopeful sign. "Despite intemperate attacks . . . by a few professional southerners," Executive Director Walter White announced on June 5, "we have indications [an] overwhelming majority of southerners will approve and abide by [the] decision." As time passed, however, it became increasingly clear that the vast majority of southern officials had no intention of facilitating the desegregation of interstate bus passengers. Stanley Winborne, North Carolina's utilities commissioner, admitted that the "regrettable" decision would require bus companies to "halt the practice of Jim Crowing" on interstate runs, but officials in other parts of the South were not so sure. Speaking for the Louisiana Public Service Commission, Clayton Coleman vowed that segregation among intrastate passengers "will continue to be enforced" and that even among interstate passengers no racial mixing would be allowed until the Interstate Commerce Commission (ICC) validated the Morgan ruling. Alabama governor Chauncey Sparks castigated the decision as "fertilizer for the Ku Klux Klan" and as an unconstitutional interference "with the rights to conduct their internal affairs." In Georgia, gubernatorial candidate Eugene Talmadge, one of Dixie's most notorious racial demagogues, claimed that regardless of the justices' intentions, the ruling could be easily nullified. Under his plan, black passengers passing south through Georgia would "have to get off 50 feet from the Florida line and buy another ticket," which he insisted "would make them intrastate passengers and outside the protection of the decision." Mississippi governor Thomas Bailey expressed his defiance in simpler terms: "Segregation will continue down here. Neither the whites nor the Negroes want it any other way."[16]

The tentative and often conflicting response of bus company executives compounded the confusion. In the wake of the decision, some companies promptly ordered the desegregation of intrastate buses, others all but ignored the decision, and still others waffled. In several cases, desegregation orders were issued but later reversed after state officials pressured executives to maintain traditional arrangements. Since there were no counterpressures from the ICC or the Justice Department, the sense of urgency and the likelihood of actual desegregation soon faded. By midsummer there were few signs of progress and a growing realization among civil rights advocates that the *Morgan* decision was a paper tiger. Strict segregation remained the norm on the vast majority of interstate buses, and the number of racial incidents related to interstate travel actually increased. Fueled by unmet expectations, complaints and misunderstandings multiplied, particularly in the Upper South. The result was bewilderment and frustration among interstate travelers, both on buses and on trains, where there was uncertainty about the ruling's applicability.[17]

All of this left the NAACP in a legal and political bind. The initial trumpeting of the decision placed Marshall and his colleagues in an "awkward position," according to legal scholar Mark Tushnet. Scaling down their expectations, "the legal staff had to urge Walter White to make it clear how limited the victory was," something White did not want to do. By late summer, NAACP attorneys had concluded that Justice Reed's opinion was far more problematic than they had realized in the heady days immediately following the decision. As Tushnet has written, "*Morgan* cast doubt on Northern antidiscrimination statutes, which the NAACP surely could not have welcomed. And, by apparently leaving decisions about passenger seating to carriers themselves, *Morgan* drew the NAACP in the direction of attempting to devise a constitutional challenge to decisions by private operators of busses rather than decisions by state legislatures." In other words, the decision lost most of its meaning when the primary defense of segregation no longer involved "state-action," the operating principle of the Fourteenth Amendment. Marshall, Robert Carter, and other NAACP legal theorists tried to devise a new strategy that would attack privately enforced segregation, but their deliberations proved unsuccessful. As Carter later confessed, they didn't "know just how to proceed in this type of situation." In the end they retreated to a political strategy of lobbying Congress for legislation outlawing private discrimination and of applying "extra-legal . . . pressures to get the carriers to abolish their private rules and regulations requiring segregation of the races." What this really meant, of course, was that the end of Jim Crow travel was nowhere in sight.[18]

Immediately following the *Morgan* decision, the NAACP's victorious legal strategy drew praise from a wide variety of civil rights activists, including Irene Morgan. Having left Baltimore for New York City, where she found work as a practical nurse, the transplanted New Yorker expressed confidence that the Court's decision would "abolish jim crow for northerners going south." "Jim-crow tension has been removed by the edict," she proclaimed, "and the insult and degradation to colored people is gone." Unfortunately, the situation looked much different two months later: segregated transit, with all its insults and degradation, remained firmly in place; Morgan herself was all but forgotten; and the leadership of the NAACP was ready to move on to new challenges. Despite their disappointment, Marshall and his colleagues were not about to let the *Morgan* case disrupt their long-term plan to dismantle the legal structure of Jim Crow. After more than a decade of careful legal maneuvering, they remained committed to a patient struggle based on the belief that American constitutional law provided the only viable means of achieving civil rights and racial equality. Confident that they were slowly but surely weakening the legal foundations of prejudice and discrimination, they were determined to press on in the courts.[19]

Within the NAACP, some local activists—especially in the youth councils—felt constrained by this narrow, legalistic approach, but their restlessness had little impact on the organization's national leaders, who maintained tight control over all NAACP activities. Alternative strategies—such as economic boycotts, protest marches, and picketing—were anathema in the national office, which saw itself as the guardian of the organization's respectability. Faced with the rising suspicions that the cold war fostered, the NAACP's leaders did not want to do anything to invite charges of radicalism or subversion. Even though the NAACP prided itself on being a militant organization, public association with direct-action tactics or with groups that might be termed "red" or even "pink" was to be avoided at all costs. In the postwar context such caution was understandable, but in a number of instances, including the *Morgan* case, it placed several limits on the NAACP's capacity to represent the interests of black Americans. Other than counseling patience, the nation's largest civil rights organization had no real answer to the white South's refusal to take the *Morgan* decision seriously.[20]

In the fall of 1946, the NAACP's disengagement from the fading, unresolved controversy over the *Morgan* decision created an opening for the radical wing of the civil rights movement. Though no one realized it at the time, this opening represented an important turning point in the history of the modern American freedom struggle. When the NAACP fell by the wayside, a small but determined group of radical activists seized the opportunity to take the desegregation struggle out of the courts and into the streets. Inspired by an international tradition of nonviolent direct action, this response to segregationist intransigence transcended the cautious legal realism of the NAACP. In the short run, as we shall see, their efforts to breathe life into the *Morgan* decision failed, but in the long run their use of direct action in the late 1940s planted the seeds of an idea that bore remarkable fruit a decade and a half later. Although called a "Journey of Reconciliation," this non-

CORE and the 1947 Journey of Reconciliation 33

violent foray into the world of Jim Crow represented the first formal "freedom ride."

To most Americans, then and now, the pioneer freedom riders were obscure figures, men and women who lived and labored outside the spotlight of celebrity and notoriety. During the immediate postwar era, the radical wing of the civil rights struggle was small, predominantly white, and fragmented among several organizations. Concentrated in New York, Chicago, and several other large northern cities, the radicals included followers of Mohandas Gandhi, Christian socialists, labor and peace activists, Quaker pacifists, Communists, and a varied assortment of left-wing intellectuals. Though ideologically diverse, they shared a commitment to militant agitation aimed at bringing about fundamental and even revolutionary change. Like Gandhi, who was in the final stages of demonstrating the power of nonviolent resistance in India, they dreamed of a world liberated from the scourges of racial prejudice, class oppression, and colonialism. Open to a variety of provocative tactics—economic boycotts, picketing, protest marches, sit-ins, and other forms of direct action—they operated on the radical fringe of American politics. With perhaps a few thousand adherents, the radical approach constituted something less than a mass movement at this point, but the social and political turmoil of the Great Depression and World War II had produced a vanguard of activists passionately committed to widening the scope and accelerating the pace of the struggle for civil and human rights.

In 1946 the most active members of this radical vanguard were affiliated with two interrelated organizations, the Congress of Racial Equality (CORE) and its parent organization, the Fellowship of Reconciliation (FOR). It was within these groups that the idea of the Freedom Ride was born. Founded in Chicago in 1942, CORE drew inspiration from the wartime stirrings of decolonization in Africa and Asia and from the recent success of nonviolent mass resistance in Gandhi's India. But it also drew upon a somewhat older tradition of nonviolent protest nurtured by FOR.[21]

Founded in 1914 at an international gathering of Christian pacifists, FOR maintained a steady course of dissent through war and peace. During the 1920s and 1930s, the American branch of FOR included some of the nation's leading social justice advocates, including radical economist Scott Nearing, Socialist leader Norman Thomas, American Civil Liberties Union founder Roger Baldwin, and eminent theologians such as Reinhold Niebuhr, Harry Emerson Fosdick, and Howard Thurman. Representing the interests of such a diverse group was never easy, but with the approach of World War II the organization found it increasingly difficult to satisfy both radical pacifists, who insisted on an absolutist commitment to nonviolence, and pragmatic pacifists, who acknowledged the necessity of waging war against totalitarian oppression. In 1940 the selection of an absolutist, A. J. Muste, as executive director drove most of the pragmatists out of the FOR, leaving the American branch with a small but dedicated core of radical activists. A former Dutch Reformed and Congregationalist minister who passed through Trotskyism and militant trade unionism before embracing radical pacifism and Gandhianism, Muste turned the American FOR into a vanguard of social change. Determined to make it more than a left-wing debating society, he urged his followers to dedicate their lives to the cause of nonviolence. Countering the evils of militarism and social injustice required moral discipline, personal courage, and a willingness to suffer for one's beliefs; nothing less than a total commitment to pacifist activism would do. Muste believed that American society needed a radical overhaul, especially in the area of race relations, and he welcomed the creation of CORE as a natural extension of FOR's reform program.

Muste's prescriptive model was not for everyone, even in faithful pacifist circles, but his impassioned calls for engagement and sacrifice drew a number of remarkable individuals into the FOR/CORE orbit. During the early 1940s, the FOR national office in New York became the nerve center of American Gandhianism. Crammed into a small building on upper Broadway, near Columbia University, the FOR staff of twelve shared ideas, plans, and soaring dreams of social justice. Young, well educated, and impoverished—most made less than twenty dollars a week—they lived and worked in the subterranean fringe of American life.[22]

Among the FOR/CORE stalwarts were three men destined to play pivotal roles in the Freedom Rider saga: Bayard Rustin, James Peck, and James Farmer. A founding member of CORE and the co-secretary of FOR's Race and Industrial Department, Rustin—along with co-secretary George Houser—organized and led the Journey of Reconciliation of 1947 and later served as an adviser to Martin Luther King Jr. during and after the Montgomery Bus Boycott of 1955–56. He played no direct role in the Freedom Rides of 1961 (he spent most of the early 1960s in Africa), yet perhaps more than anyone else, Rustin was the intellectual godfather of the Freedom Rider movement. Peck, a radical journalist who acted as CORE's chief publicist, was the only person to participate in both the Journey of Reconciliation and the 1961 Freedom Rides. Severely beaten by Klansmen in Alabama in May 1961, he later authored a revealing memoir of his experiences as a Freedom Rider. Farmer, like Rustin, was one of the founders of CORE. Although personal reasons prevented him from participating in the Journey of Reconciliation, he was the guiding spirit behind CORE's 1961 Freedom Rides. As national director of CORE from 1961 to 1966, he presided over the organization's resurgence, crafting and sustaining the legacy of the Freedom Rides. Together these three activists provided a critical link between the nonviolent civil rights initiatives of the 1940s and the full-blown movement of the 1960s. While none of them achieved national fame in the manner of King or Rosa Parks, each in his own way exerted a powerful influence on the development of nonviolence in the United States. Their personal stories reveal a great deal about the origins and context of the Freedom Rides and about the hidden history of the civil rights struggle—especially the complex connections between North and South, black and white, liberalism and radicalism, and religious and secular motivation.[23]

Rustin, the oldest of the three, was also the most exotic. Born in 1912 in West Chester, Pennsylvania, he was the child of Florence Rustin, an unwed teenager, and Archie Hopkins, an itinerant black laborer who barely acknowledged his son's existence. Adopted by Florence's parents, Julia and Janifer Rustin, young Bayard was raised by an extended family of grandparents, aunts, and uncles who collectively eked out a living by cooking and catering for the local Quaker gentry. Julia Rustin was a member of the local Quaker meeting before joining her husband's African Methodist Episcopal Church following their marriage in 1891. And she remained a Quaker "at Heart," naming her grandson for Bayard Taylor, a celebrated mid-nineteenth-century Quaker leader. A woman of substance and deep moral conviction, Julia was the most important influence in Bayard's upbringing and the primary source of the pacifist doctrines that would anchor his lifelong commitment to nonviolence. Indulged as the favorite child of the Rustin clan, he gained a reputation as a brilliant student and gifted singer and musician, first as one of a handful of black students at West Chester High School, where he also excelled as a track and football star, and later at all-black Wilberforce University in Ohio, where he studied history and literature and toured as the lead soloist of the Wilberforce Quartet. Despite these accomplishments, he eventually ran afoul of the Wilberforce administration by challenging the school's compulsory ROTC program and engaging in homosexual activity (he reportedly fell in love with the son of the university president). Expelled in December 1933, he returned to Pennsylvania and enrolled at Cheyney State Teachers College the following fall.

At Cheyney, where he remained for three years, Rustin gained a reputation as a multitalented student leader, distinguishing himself as a singer, a keen student of philosophy, and a committed peace activist. When Cheyney's president, Leslie Pinckney Hill, a devout black Quaker, invited the American Friends Service Committee (AFSC) to hold an international peace institute on the campus in the spring of 1937, Rustin was a willing and eager participant. Inspired by the dedicated pacifists who attended the institute and already primed for social action by his family and religious background, he soon accepted a position as a "peace volunteer" with the AFSC's Emergency Peace Campaign (EPC). During an EPC training session, he received further inspiration from Muriel Lester, a noted British pacifist and Gandhi protégé. After listening to Lester's eloquent plea for pacifism and nonviolent struggle, he threw himself into the peace campaign with an uncommon zeal that would later become his trademark. Along with three other volunteers—including Carl Rachlin, who would later serve as a CORE and Freedom Rider attorney—he spent the summer of 1937 in the upstate New York town of Auburn, where he honed his skills as a lecturer and organizer.

At the end of the summer he returned to West Chester and Cheyney, but not for long. In the early fall, propelled by a growing disenchantment with southeastern Pennsylvania's political and cultural scene and by a second scandalous (and interracial) homosexual incident, he moved northward to the alluring uncertainties of metropolitan Harlem, the unofficial capital of black America. Cast adrift from the relatively secure world of college life and facing the vagaries of the Great Depression, Rustin embarked on a remarkable odyssey of survival and discovery that propelled him through a labyrinth of radical politics and bohemian culture. Along the way he became a professional singer, a dedicated Communist, and an uncloseted homosexual. During the late 1930s he sang backup for Josh White and Huddie "Ledbelly" Ledbetter, worked as a recruiter for the Young Communist League (YCL), preached revolution and brotherhood on countless street corners, and even squeezed in a few classes at City College, all the while gaining a reputation as one of Harlem's most colorful characters.

In early 1941, the YCL asked Rustin to organize a campaign against segregation in the American armed forces, but later in the year, following the unexpected German attack on the Soviet Union, YCL leaders ordered him to cancel the campaign in the interest of Allied military solidarity. With this apparent shift away from agitation for racial and social justice, Rustin became deeply disillusioned with the Communist Party. "You can all go to hell," he told his New York comrades. "I see the Communist movement is only interested in what happens in Russia. You don't give a damn about Negroes." In June 1941 he left the Communist fold for good and transferred his allegiance to A. Philip Randolph, the legendary black Socialist and labor leader who was then planning a mass march on Washington, D.C., to protest the Roosevelt administration's refusal to guarantee equal employment opportunities for black and white defense workers. Randolph appointed Rustin the youth organizer for the march, but the two men soon had a serious falling out. After Roosevelt responded to Randolph's threatened march with an executive order creating a Fair Employment Practices Committee (FEPC), Randolph agreed to call off the march. But many of his young supporters, including Rustin, thought the protest march should continue as planned. Later in the war Rustin and Randolph resumed their friendship and collaboration, but their temporary break in 1941 prompted the young activist to look elsewhere for a political and spiritual home. Consequently, in the fall of 1941, he accepted a staff position with A. J. Muste's Fellowship of Reconciliation.

As FOR youth secretary, Rustin returned to the pacifist track he had followed as an EPC volunteer, immersing himself in the writings and teachings of Gandhi and pledging his loyalty to nonviolence, not just as a strategy for change but as a way of life. Muste encouraged and nurtured Rustin's determination to apply Gandhian precepts to the African American struggle for racial equality, and in the spring of 1942 the two men joined forces with other FOR activists to found the Committee (later "Congress") of Racial Equality. "Certainly the Negro possesses qualities essential for nonviolent direct action," Rustin wrote prophetically in October 1942. "He has long since learned to endure suffering. He can admit his own share of guilt and has to be pushed hard to become bitter. . . . He is creative and has learned to adjust himself to conditions easily. But above all he possesses a rich religious heritage and today finds the church the center of his life."[24]

As a CORE stalwart, Rustin participated in a number of nonviolent protests, including an impromptu refusal to move to the back of a bus during a trip from Louisville to Nashville in the early summer of 1942. This particular episode earned him a roadside beating at the hands of the Nashville police, who later hauled him off to jail. A month after the incident, Rustin offered the readers of the FOR journal *Fellowship* a somewhat whimsical description of his arrest:

> I was put into the back seat of the police car, between two policemen. Two others sat in front. During the thirteen-mile ride to town they called me every conceivable name and said anything they could think of to incite me to violence. . . . When we reached Nashville, a number of policemen were lined up on both sides of the hallway down which I had to pass on my way to the captain's office. They tossed me from one to another like a volleyball. By the time I reached the office, the lining of my best coat was torn, and I was considerably rumpled. I straightened myself as best I could and went in. They had my bag, and went through it and my papers, finding much of interest, especially in the *Christian Century* and *Fellowship*. Finally the captain said, "Come here, nigger." I walked directly to him, "What can I do for you?" I asked. "Nigger," he said menacingly, "you're supposed to be scared when you come in here!" "I am fortified by the truth, justice and Christ," I said. "There's no need for me to fear." He was flabbergasted and, for a time, completely at a loss for words. Finally he said to another officer, "I believe the nigger's crazy!"

In the end, the timely intervention of a sympathetic white bystander (who had witnessed the roadside beating) and the restraint of a coolheaded assistant district attorney (Ben West, a future Nashville mayor who would draw widespread praise for his moderate response to the Student Non-Violent Coordinating Committee–led sit-ins of 1960 and 1961) kept Rustin out of jail, reinforcing his suspicion that even the white South could be redeemed through nonviolent struggle.[25]

Soon after his narrow escape from Nashville justice, Rustin became a friend and devoted follower of Krishnaial Shridharani, a leading Gandhian scholar and the author of *War without Violence*. This discipleship deepened his commitment to nonviolent resistance and noncooperation with evil, and in 1943 he rejected the traditional Quaker compromise of alternative service in an army hospital. Convicted of draft evasion, he spent the next twenty-eight months in federal prison. For nearly two years he was imprisoned at the Ashland, Ohio, penitentiary, where he waged spirited if futile campaigns against everything from the censorship of reading materials to racial segregation. In August 1945 a final effort to desegregate the prison dining hall led to solitary confinement, but soon thereafter he and several other pacifist malcontents were transferred to a federal facility in Lewisburg, Pennsylvania.

Following his release from Lewisburg in June 1946, Rustin returned to New York to accept an appointment as co-secretary (with George Houser) of FOR's Race and Industrial Department, a position he promptly turned into a roving ambassadorship of Gandhian nonviolence. Though physically weak and emaciated, he took to the road, preaching the gospel of nonviolent direct action to anyone who would listen. As biographer Jervis Anderson has noted, during the critical postwar year of 1946 Rustin "functioned as a one-man civil disobedience movement in his travels across the United States. He occupied 'white only' railroad compartments; sat in at 'white only' hotels; and refused to budge unless he was forcibly ejected." All of this reinforced his dual reputation as a fearless activist and a Gandhian sage. He was both irrepressible and imaginative; and no one who knew him well was surprised when he, along with Houser, came up with the provocative idea of an interracial bus ride through the Jim Crow South. After the Journey of Reconciliation proposal was hatched, Rustin acted as a relentless advocate, eventually winning over or at least wearing down those who thought the plan was too dangerous. Without his involvement, the Journey—and perhaps even the Freedom Rides of 1961—would never have taken place.[26]

Jim Peck followed a somewhat different path to the Journey of Reconciliation. Three years younger than Rustin, he grew up in one of Manhattan's most prosperous households. The son of Samuel Peck, a wealthy clothing wholesaler (who died when Peck was eleven years old), he spent the early years of the Great Depression at Choate, a tony prep school in Wallingford, Connecticut. Despite his family's conversion from Judaism to Episcopalianism, Peck was a social outsider at Choate, which used a strict quota system to limit the number of religious and ethnic minorities on campus. The primary factor separating him from his fellow students was not religion or ethnicity, however. Politically precocious, he cultivated a reputation as an independent thinker who espoused idealistic political doctrines and preferred the company of bookish intellectuals. In the fall of 1933 he enrolled at Harvard, where he honed his skills as a writer while assuming the role of a campus radical. At Harvard he missed few opportunities to challenge the social and political conventions of the Ivy League elite, and he shocked his classmates by showing up at the freshman dance with a black date. This particular act of defiance was directed not only at "the soberly dressed Boston matrons on the sidelines" who "stared at us, whispered, and then stared again" but also at his own mother, who "referred to Negroes as 'coons'" and "frequently remarked that she would never hire one as a servant because 'they are dirty and they steal.'" By the end of his freshman year he was a pariah, and his alienation from his family and the American establishment was complete. Dropping out of school, he immigrated to Paris, where he lived as an avant-garde expatriate for two years. Set against a backdrop of authoritarian ascendancy, his years in Europe deepened his commitment to activism and social justice. In the late 1930s a severe case of wanderlust and a desire to identify with the working class led to a series of jobs as a merchant seaman, an experience that eventually propelled him into the turbulent world of radical unionism. His years at sea also reinforced his commitment to civil rights. "Living and working aboard ships with interracial crews," he later recalled, "strengthened my beliefs in equality."

Returning to the United States in 1938, Peck helped to organize the National Maritime Union, which made good use of his skills as a writer and publicist. During these years he also became a friend and follower of Roger Baldwin, the strong-willed founder of the American Civil Liberties Union. Baldwin encouraged him to become involved in a number of social justice organizations, including the War Resisters League (WRL), and helped him find work with a trade union news syndicate. By the end of the decade, Peck was an avowed pacifist who spent much of his time publicizing the activities of the WRL. Like Rustin, he refused to submit to the draft, and in 1942 he was imprisoned for his defiance. He spent almost three years in the federal prison in Danbury, Connecticut, where he helped to organize a work strike that led to the desegregation of the prison mess hall. After his release in 1945, he rededicated himself to pacifism and militant trade unionism, offering his services to a number of progressive organizations. For a time he devoted most of his energies to the WRL and to editing the *Workers Defense League News Bulletin,* but in late 1946 he became increasingly absorbed with the race issue, especially after discovering and joining CORE. Recent events had convinced him that the struggle for racial equality was an essential precondition for the social transformation of American society, and CORE's direct-action philosophy provided him with a means of acting upon his convictions. With the zeal of a new recruit, he embraced the idea of the Journey of Reconciliation, which would be his first venture as a CORE volunteer.[27]

Jim Farmer shared Peck's passion for direct action and nonviolent protest, but in most other respects, from style and temperament to racial and regional background, the two men represented a study in contrasts. Born in Marshall, Texas, in 1920, Farmer was a black southerner who had firsthand experience with the institutions of the Jim Crow South. Raised in a middle-class family, he was fortunate enough to avoid the degrading economic insecurities of the rural poor, but as the aspiring son of educated parents, he was forced to endure the painful psychological and social indignities of a racial caste system that warped and restricted his prospects. His mother, Pearl Houston Farmer, was a graduate of Florida's Bethune Cookman Institute and a former teacher; his father, James Leonard Farmer Sr., was a learned Methodist minister who had earned a Ph.D. in theology at Boston University. One of the few blacks in early-twentieth-century Texas to hold a doctoral degree, Farmer's father spoke seven languages and held academic positions at a number of black colleges, including Rust College in Holly Springs, Mississippi, and Samuel Houston College in Austin, Texas. A towering figure in black academic circles, he was nonetheless a cautious, deferential accommodationist in his dealings with whites. This inconsistency troubled his young son, who idealized his father's moral and intellectual stature but eventually recoiled from what he came to see as a cringing hypocrisy that perpetuated racial injustice.[28]

A brilliant student, young Jim Farmer entered school at the age of four and graduated from Wiley College at eighteen. At Wiley he came under the influence of Melvin Tolson, an English professor and debating coach who nurtured his young protégé's oratorical skills. Farmer possessed a deep, mellifluous voice that was perfectly suited to a dramatic style of oratory; by the time Tolson got through with him, Farmer's studied intonations carried the barest hint of an East Texas twang. This remarkable speaking voice became Farmer's trademark and the cornerstone of a grand manner that struck some observers as pretentious and condescending. Even as a teenager, he was a large and imposing figure with an ego to match. Ambitious and articulate, he felt constrained by the small-town, segregated culture of Marshall. His first taste of the outside world came in 1937, when he represented Wiley at a National Conference of Methodist Youth at Miami University in Oxford, Ohio. Although only a handful of black delegates were in attendance, Farmer emerged as one of the stars of the conference, persuading his fellow Methodists to approve a resolution urging Congress to pass anti-lynching legislation. "Everyone here wants to stop lynching," he informed the assembled delegates. "The only question is how long do we have to wait? How long, oh, Lord, how long? The purpose of this motion is not to damn the South and the many decent people who live there. . . . The purpose of this motion is to *stop lynching now*." The audience responded with a standing ovation and approval by acclamation, providing him with the "first taste of the heady wine of public acclaim." The conference later elected him to its governance committee, a remarkable achievement for a seventeen-year-old black boy from East Texas.[29]

The exhilarating triumph in Ohio reinforced Farmer's determination to become involved in the widening struggle for racial justice, and a few weeks later he accepted an invitation to attend a joint meeting of the National Negro Congress (NNC) and the Southern Negro Youth Conference. Held in Richmond, Virginia, the conference attracted some of the nation's most prominent black leaders, including A. Philip Randolph, Howard University president Mordecai Johnson, and Howard political scientist Ralph Bunche. Traveling the thousand miles to Richmond by car, Farmer and two companions, one of whom was a white delegate from the University of Texas, encountered the inevitable frustrations of finding food, shelter, and restroom facilities along the Jim Crow highways of the Deep South. By the time the young travelers arrived at the conference, they had seen and experienced enough to fuel a growing sense of outrage. But the conference itself was even more eye-opening. Here Farmer received his first exposure to the passionate militancy of left-wing politics. He also got more than a glimpse of the sectarian intrigue and political infighting between Communists and Socialists that threatened to tear the NNC apart. Founded in 1936 as a national clearinghouse for civil rights and labor organizations concerned about fair employment issues, the NNC had elected Randolph as its first chairman, but during the organization's first two years the black Socialist leader had grown increasingly suspicious of Communist activists who were reportedly exploiting the NNC for selfish political purposes. Randolph's anger boiled over at the Richmond conference, where his explosive resignation speech both shocked and thrilled Farmer.[30]

To his conservative father's dismay, Farmer was never quite the same after the Richmond conference. The dream of becoming a theologian and following in his father's footsteps was still alive, and in the fall of 1938 he dutifully entered the Howard University School of Theology, where his father had recently accepted a position as a professor of Greek and New Testament studies. But during his years at Howard the young divinity student continued to gravitate toward radical politics. Inspired by Howard Thurman, a charismatic professor of social ethics and dean of the chapel (Farmer later described him as a "mystic, poet, philosopher, preacher"), Farmer became intrigued with Gandhianism, pacifism, and radical versions of the Social Gospel. Under Thurman's direction, he wrote his thesis on "A Critical Analysis of the Interrelationships between Religion and Racism." Thurman also helped him secure a position as a part-time secretary in the Washington office of FOR, and by the time he graduated in 1941 he was completely captivated by FOR's philosophy of nonviolent interracial activism. Refusing ordination as a Methodist minister—a decision clinched by the news that his choice of pastorates was limited to all-black congregations—he accepted a full-time position as FOR's race relations secretary. Assigned to FOR's regional office in Chicago, he arrived in the Windy City in August 1941, ready, as he put it, to lead "an assault on the demons of violence and bigotry."[31]

For the next two years, Farmer spearheaded a series of direct-action campaigns in Chicago and also traveled throughout the Midwest spreading the FOR gospel of pacifism and nonviolent resistance to social injustice. Though barely old enough to vote, he exuded an aura of confidence and command that belied his youth. Some found him arrogant and a bit overbearing, but no one doubted his intelligence or his passionate belief in the struggle for racial justice. At the University of Chicago he organized an interracial study group on Gandhianism and encouraged students and others to engage in sit-ins and picketing campaigns at segregated coffeehouses, restaurants, roller rinks, and theaters. Working closely with both Rustin and Houser, FOR's white field secretary, he also created Fellowship House, an interracial men's cooperative designed to challenge a restrictive covenant that segregated the neighborhood surrounding the university. In the spring of 1942 these efforts led to the formation of the Chicago Committee of Racial Equality, which Farmer conceived as part of a national direct-action network known as the "Brotherhood Mobilization." By 1943 the organization had evolved into the Committee of Racial Equality, and a year later the name was changed to Congress of Racial Equality. At first, Muste resisted Farmer's insistence that CORE should be allowed to have its own identity somewhat independent of FOR, but the FOR chairman eventually relented. CORE's charter, adopted at the organization's first annual meeting, stated that "the purpose of the organization shall be to federate local interracial groups working to abolish the color line through direct non-violent action." Although still employed by FOR, Farmer became CORE's first national chairman, though not for long.[32]

Muste's acceptance of CORE's partial autonomy came at a price, one that eventually proved too costly for Farmer to bear. In June 1943 he received a "promotion" that required relocation to New York. "I knew at once what it all meant," he later wrote, "—New York, where they could watch me closely, and full-time so I would have less time to freewheel for CORE. I was being given bigger wings, but they would be clipped wings." Muste was not unsympathetic to the aims and activities of CORE, but his primary loyalty was to pacifism and FOR. And he expected the same from Farmer, whose primary job, in his view, was to organize and recruit new members for FOR. As long as FOR was paying Farmer's salary, the interests of the parent organization had to come first. Well aware of Muste's concerns, Farmer made a valiant effort to satisfy his obligations to FOR, but by the spring of 1945 it was clear to both men that the dual arrangement was not working. In May, following an awkward meeting in Muste's office, Farmer resigned from his FOR staff position—and from his cherished unpaid position as CORE's national chairman. Following Farmer's departure, CORE reorganized its leadership structure, creating an executive directorship filled by Houser. But the troubled relationship between FOR and CORE continued to plague both organizations in the postwar years.[33]

Farmer himself soon found work as a labor organizer with the Upholsterers International Union of North America (UIU), which sent him to Virginia, and later to High Point, North Carolina, to organize furniture workers. Throughout his stay in the Piedmont he was in close touch with Houser, who kept him abreast of CORE affairs, including the Journey of Reconciliation. Farmer found the idea "exciting and intriguing" and was sorely tempted to abandon the frustrations of union organizing and join the ride. But at this point, with a new wife to support, he could not afford to leave a steady-paying job. Turning down a chance to take part in the Journey of Reconciliation was a difficult decision that isolated him from the cause that still excited his deepest passions; and when the UIU transferred him to Cincinnati, he felt even farther removed from the action. Later, after learning that Rustin and several other old friends had been arrested in North Carolina, he "felt pangs of guilt for not having been there." Farmer's failure to take part in the Journey would bother him for many years, and only in 1961—when he returned to CORE as executive director and the leader of the Freedom Rides—would he begin to feel that he had atoned for his absence from CORE's first great adventure below the Mason-Dixon Line.[34]

The plan for an interracial bus ride through the Jim Crow South grew out of a series of discussions between Bayard Rustin and George Houser held during the summer of 1946. Like Rustin, Houser was a northerner with little firsthand experience in the South. Born in Cleveland, he traveled to the Philippines with his Methodist missionary parents and later lived in New York, California, China, and Colorado before entering Union Theological Seminary in 1939. At Union he became a committed pacifist and refused to register for the draft. Convicted of draft evasion, he served a year in federal prison. Following Houser's release in the fall of 1941, Muste hired him to run FOR's Chicago office. During the early days of CORE, he collaborated with Farmer but developed an even closer relationship with Rustin, whom he came to admire greatly. Later, as the newly appointed co-secretaries of FOR's Race and Industrial Department and as members of CORE's executive committee, the two young friends were eager to boost CORE's profile by demonstrating the utility of nonviolent direct action.[35]

For Rustin and Houser, the timing of the *Morgan* decision and the ensuing controversy over compliance and enforcement could not have been better. During its first four years, CORE had operated as "a loose federation of local groups which were united mostly by their aim of tackling discrimination by a particular method—nonviolent direct action." Because "this put emphasis almost completely on local issues and organization," Houser recalled many years later, "it was difficult to get a sense of a national movement or to develop a national strategy. One of the results of this really was that it was almost impossible for CORE to raise funds to establish itself as a separate entity." In addition to enhancing CORE's national stature and autonomy, a project like the Journey of Reconciliation promised to provide "an entering wedge for CORE into the South." As Houser explained, "We had no local groups in the South and it wasn't easy to organize them at this point, especially with the two words 'racial equality' in our name. Those were fighting words in the South. But with a definite project around which to rally, we felt there was a possibility of opening up an area seemingly out of reach." Rustin and Houser were confident that the issue of Jim Crow transit—which "touched virtually every black person, was demeaning in its effect and a source of frequent conflict"—represented a perfect target for CORE's first national project. Even if the project failed to desegregate interstate buses, "challenging discrimination in transportation, by striking a raw nerve, would get public attention."[36]

During the summer, as expectations of compliance with the *Morgan* ruling faded, the idea of a CORE-sponsored freedom ride became a frequent topic of conversation among CORE stalwarts in New York. In July the idea received an unexpected boost from Wilson Head, a courageous black World War II veteran who undertook his own freedom ride from Atlanta to Washington, D.C. Traveling on the Greyhound line and insisting on his right to sit in the front of the bus, he braved angry drivers, enraged passengers, and menacing police officers—one of whom threatened to shoot him during a brief detention in Chapel Hill, North Carolina. But somehow Head managed to make it to Washington without injury or formal arrest, a feat which suggested that testing compliance in the South might not be such a crazy notion after all. By the time CORE's executive committee met in Cleveland in mid-September, Rustin and Houser had developed a full-scale plan for the ride. After a lengthy discussion of the risks and dangers of a southern foray, the committee endorsed the idea and authorized Rustin and Houser to seek approval and funding from FOR. With a little coaxing, the FOR staff soon embraced the plan, although Muste insisted that the ride be a joint project of FOR and CORE.[37]

Over the next few months, FOR's Race and Industrial Department worked out the details, adding an educational component and ultimately limiting the scope of the ride to the Upper South. The revised plan called for "a racially mixed deputation of lecturers" who would speak at various points along the route, giving "some purpose to the trip outside of simple tests and experimentation with techniques." The riders would not only test compliance with the *Morgan* decision but also spread the gospel of nonviolence to at least part of the South. The original plan involved a regionwide journey from Washington, D.C., to New Orleans, Louisiana, but after several of CORE's southern contacts warned that an interracial journey through the Deep South would provoke "wholesale violence," Rustin and Houser reluctantly agreed to restrict the ride to the more moderate Upper South. "The deep South may be touched later," they explained, "depending on what comes out of this first experience." After much debate, they also agreed that all of the riders would be men, acknowledging that "mixing the races and sexes would possibly exacerbate an already volatile situation." This decision was a grave disappointment to several women—including Ella Baker and Paula Murray—who had been actively involved in planning the trip. Many of the planning meetings took place in the New York apartment of Natalie Mormon, who, like Baker and Murray, had considerable experience traveling through the South. But their plaintive protests against paternalistic condescension fell on deaf ears. Less controversially, Rustin and Houser also came up with an official name for the project—the Journey of Reconciliation. This redemptive phrase pleased Muste and lent an air of moral authority to the project.[38]

For reasons of safety and to ensure that the compliance tests would be valid, CORE leaders did not seek any advance publicity for the Journey, but within the confines of the movement they quietly spread the word that CORE was about to invade the South. The proposed ride received enthusiastic endorsements from a number of black leaders—most notably Howard Thurman, A. Philip Randolph, and Mary McLeod Bethune—and from several organizations, including the Fellowship of Southern Churchmen, an interracial group of liberal southern clergymen. The one organization that expressly refused to endorse the ride was, predictably, the NAACP. When CORE leaders first broached the subject with national NAACP officials in early October, Marshall and his colleagues were preoccupied with a recent District of Columbia Court of Appeals decision that extended the applicability of the *Morgan* decision to interstate railways. In *Matthews v. Southern Railway,* the Court ruled that there was not a meaningful difference between Jim Crow aboard buses and trains. For a time the ruling gave NAACP attorneys renewed hope that the *Morgan* decision would actually have an effect on interstate travel, but in the aftermath of the ruling only one railway—the Richmond, Fredericksburg, and Potomac Railroad—actually desegregated its interstate trains, while the vast majority of southern railways continued to segregate all passengers, interstate or not. Several railroad officials insisted that the ruling only applied to the District of Columbia, but to protect their companies from possible federal interference they also adopted the same "company rules" strategy used by some interstate bus lines. The basis for segregation, they now claimed, was not state law but company policy. Racial separation in railroad coaches was thus a private matter allegedly beyond the bounds of public policy or constitutional intrusion. Since such company rules were sanctioned by the *Chiles* decision, rendered by the U.S. Supreme Court in 1910, NAACP attorneys were seemingly stymied by this new strategy.[39]

In mid-November, Marshall and the NAACP legal brain trust held a two-day strategy meeting in New York to address the challenge of privatized segregation. No firm solution emerged from the meeting, but the attorneys did reach a consensus that CORE's proposal for an interracial ride through the South was a very bad idea. The last thing the NAACP needed at this point, or so its leaders believed, was a provocative diversion led by a bunch of impractical agitators. A week later Marshall went public with the NAACP's opposition to direct action. Speaking in New Orleans on the topic "The Next Twenty Years toward Freedom for the Negro in America," he criticized "well-meaning radical groups in New York" who were planning to use Gandhian tactics to breach the wall of racial segregation. Predicting a needless catastrophe, he insisted that a "disobedience movement on the part of Negroes and their white allies, if employed in the South, would result in wholesale slaughter with no good achieved." He did not mention FOR or CORE by name, nor did he divulge any details about the impending Journey of Reconciliation, but his words, which were reprinted in the *New York Times,* sent a clear warning to Muste, Rustin, and Houser. Since the Journey would inevitably lead to multiple arrests, everyone involved knew that at some point CORE would require the assistance and cooperation of NAACP-affiliated attorneys, so Marshall's words could not be taken lightly. The leaders of FOR and CORE were in no position to challenge the supremacy of the NAACP, but after some hesitation they realized that Marshall's pointed critique could not go unanswered.[40]

The response, written by Rustin and published in the *Louisiana Weekly* in early January 1947, was a sharp rebuke to Marshall and a rallying cry for the nonviolent movement:

> I am sure that Marshall is either ill-informed on the principles and techniques of non-violence or ignorant of the processes of social change.
>
> Unjust social laws and patterns do not change because supreme courts deliver just opinions. One need merely observe the continued practices of jim crow in interstate travel six months after the Supreme Court's decision to see the necessity of resistance. Social progress comes from struggle; all freedom demands a price.
>
> At times freedom will demand that its followers go into situations where even death is to be faced . . . direct action means picketing, striking and boycotting as well as disobedience against unjust conditions, and all of these methods have already been used with some success by Negroes and sympathetic whites. . . .
>
> I cannot believe that Thurgood Marshall thinks that such a program would lead to wholesale slaughter. . . . But if anyone at this date in history believes that the "white problem," which is one of privilege, can be settled without some violence, he is mistaken and fails to realize the ends to which man can be driven to hold on to what they consider privileges.
>
> This is why Negroes and whites who participate in direct action must pledge themselves to non-violence in word and deed. For in this way alone can the inevitable violence be reduced to a minimum. The simple truth is this: unless we find non-violent methods which can be used by the rank-and-file who more and more tend to resist, they will more and more resort to violence.

And court-room argumentation will not suffice for the activization which the Negro masses are today demanding.[41]

Rustin's provocative and prophetic manifesto failed to soften Marshall's opposition to direct action, but it did help to convince Marshall and NAACP executive director Walter White that CORE was determined to follow through with the Journey of Reconciliation, with or without their cooperation. CORE leaders had already announced that the two-week Journey would begin on April 9, and there was no turning back for activists like Rustin and Houser who believed that the time for resolute action had arrived. For them, all the signs—including Harry Truman's unexpected decision, in December 1946, to create a President's Committee on Civil Rights—suggested that the movement for racial justice had reached a crossroads. It was time to turn ideas into action, to demonstrate the power of nonviolence as Gandhi and others were already doing in India.[42]

With this in mind, Rustin and Houser left New York in mid-January on a scouting expedition through the Upper South states of Virginia, North Carolina, Tennessee, and Kentucky. During three weeks of reconnaissance they followed the route of the coming Journey, scrupulously obeying the laws and customs of Jim Crow transit so as to avoid arrest. At each stop along the route, they met with local civil rights and community leaders who helped to arrange housing, lecture and rally facilities, and possible legal representation for the riders to come. Some dismissed the interracial duo as an odd and misguided pair of outside agitators, but most did what they could to help. In several communities, Rustin and Houser encountered the "other" NAACP: the restless branch leaders and youth council volunteers (and even some black attorneys) who were eager to take the struggle beyond the courtroom. After Rustin returned to New York in late January, Houser traveled alone to Tennessee and Kentucky, where he continued to be impressed with the untapped potential of the black South. In the end the four-state scouting trip produced a briefcase full of commitments from church leaders and state and local NAACP officials, a harvest that pushed Marshall and his colleagues toward a grudging acceptance of the coming Journey's legitimacy. Soon Spot Robinson, Charles Houston, and even Marshall himself were offering "helpful suggestions" and promising to provide CORE with legal backup if and when the riders were arrested. Most national NAACP leaders still considered the Journey a foolhardy venture, but as its start drew near there was a noticeable closing of the ranks, a feeling of solidarity that provided the riders with a reassuring measure of legal and institutional protection. As Houser put it, with the promise of southern support and with the NAACP more or less on board, "we felt our group of participants would not be isolated victims as they challenged the local and state laws."[43]

Even so, the Journey remained a dangerous prospect, and finding sixteen qualified and dependable volunteers who had the time and money to spend two weeks on the road was not easy. The organizers' determination to enlist riders who had already demonstrated a commitment to nonviolent direct action narrowed the field and forced CORE to draw upon its own staff and other seasoned veterans of FOR and CORE campaigns. When it proved impossible to find a full complement of volunteers who could commit themselves to the entire Journey, Rustin and Houser reluctantly allowed the riders to come and go as personal circumstances dictated. In the end, less than half of the riders completed the entire trip.[44]

Despite these complications, the sixteen volunteers who traveled to Washington in early April to undergo two days of training and orientation represented a broad range of nonviolent activists. There were eight whites and eight blacks and an interesting mix of secular and religious backgrounds. In addition to Houser, the white volunteers included Jim Peck; Homer Jack, a Unitarian minister and founding member of CORE who headed the Chicago Council against Racial and Religious Discrimination; Worth Randle, a CORE stalwart and biologist from Cincinnati; Igal Roodenko, a peace activist from upstate New York; Joseph Felmet, a conscientious objector from Asheville, North Carolina, representing the Southern Workers Defense League; and two FOR-affiliated Methodist ministers from North Carolina, Ernest Bromley and Louis Adams. The black volunteers included Rustin; Dennis Banks, a jazz musician from Chicago; Conrad Lynn, a civil rights attorney from New York City; Eugene Stanley, an agronomy student at North Carolina and A&T College in Greensboro; William Worthy, a radical journalist affiliated with the New York Council for a Permanent FEPC; and three CORE activists from Cincinnati—law student Andrew Johnson, pacifist lecturer Wallace Nelson, and social worker Nathan Wright.[45]

Most of the volunteers were young men still in their twenties; several were barely out of their teens. Rustin, at age thirty-five, was the oldest. Nearly all, despite their youth, had some experience with direct action, but with the exception of Rustin's impromptu freedom ride in 1942, none of this experience had been gained in the Jim Crow South. No member of the group had ever been involved in a direct-action campaign quite like the Journey of Reconciliation, and only the North Carolinians had spent more than a few weeks in the South.

Faced with so many unknowns and the challenge of taking an untried corps of volunteers into the heart of darkness, Rustin and Houser fashioned an intensive orientation program. Meeting at FOR's Washington Fellowship House, nine of the riders participated in a series of seminars that "taught not only the principles but the practices of nonviolence in specific situations that would arise aboard the buses." Using techniques pioneered by FOR peace activists and CORE chapters, the seminars addressed expected problems by staging dramatic role-playing sessions. "What if the bus driver insulted you? What if you were actually assaulted? What if the police threatened you? These and many other questions were resolved through socio-drama in which participants would act the roles of bus drivers, hysterical segregationists, police—and you. Whether the roles had been acted correctly and whether you had done the right thing was then discussed. Socio-drama of other bus stations followed. In all of them, you were supposed to remain nonviolent, but stand firm," Jim Peck recalled. Two days of this regimen left the riders exhausted but better prepared for the challenges to come.[46]

Leaving little to chance, Rustin and Houser also provided each rider with a detailed list of instructions. Later reprinted in a pamphlet entitled "You Don't Have to Ride Jim Crow," the instructions made it clear that the task at hand was not, strictly speaking, civil disobedience but rather establishing "the fact that the word of the U.S. Supreme Court is law":

WHEN TRAVELING BY BUS WITH A TICKET FROM A POINT IN ONE STATE TO A POINT IN ANOTHER STATE:

1. If you are a Negro, sit in a front seat.
   If you are a white, sit in a rear seat
2. If the driver asks you to move, tell him calmly and courteously, "As an interstate passenger I have a right to sit anywhere in this bus. This is the law as laid down by the United States Supreme Court."
3. If the driver summons the police and repeats his order in their presence, tell him exactly what you told the driver when he first asked you to move.
4. If the police ask you to "come along" without putting you under arrest, tell him you will not go until you are put under arrest. Police have often used the tactic of frightening a person into get-

ting off the bus without making an arrest, keeping him until the bus has left and then just leaving him standing by the empty roadside. In such a case this person has no redress.
5. If the police put you under arrest, go with them peacefully. At the police station, phone the nearest headquarters of the National Association of the Advancement of Colored People, or one of their lawyers. They will assist you.
6. If you have money with you, you can get out on bail immediately. It will probably be either $25 or $50. if you don't have bail, anti-discrimination organizations will help raise it for you.
7. *If you happen to be arrested, the delay in your journey will only be a few hours. The value of your action in breaking down Jim Crow will be too great to be measured.*[47]

Additional instructions assigned specific functions to individuals or subgroups of riders and distinguished between designated testers and observers. "Just which individual sat where on each lap of our trip," Peck recalled, "would be planned at meetings of the group on the eve of departure. A few were to act as observers. They necessarily had to sit in a segregated manner. So did whoever was designated to handle bail in the event of arrest. The roles shifted on each lap of the Journey. It was important that all sixteen not be arrested simultaneously and the trip thus halted." Throughout the training sessions, Rustin and Houser reiterated that Jim Crow could not be vanquished by courage alone; careful organization, tight discipline, and strict adherence to nonviolence were also essential. An unorganized and undisciplined assault on segregation, they warned, would play into the hands of the segregationists, discrediting the philosophy of nonviolence and postponing the long-awaited desegregation of the South.[48]

When the nine riders gathered at the Greyhound and Trailways station in downtown Washington on the morning of April 9 for the beginning of the Journey, the predominant mood was anxious but upbeat. As the riders boarded the buses, the only members of the press on hand were Ollie Stewart of the *Baltimore Afro-American* and Lem Graves of the *Pittsburgh Courier,* two black journalists who had agreed to accompany the riders during the first week. Joking with the reporters, Rustin, as always, set a jovial tone that helped to relieve the worst tensions for the moment. But there was also a general air of confidence that belied the dangers ahead. Sitting on the bus prior to departure, Peck thought to himself that "it would not be too long until Greyhound and Trailways would 'give up segregation practices' in the South." Years later, following the Freedom Rides of 1961, he would look back on this early and unwarranted optimism with a jaundiced eye, but during the first stage of the Journey his hopes seemed justified.[49]

The ride from Washington to Richmond was uneventful for both groups of riders, and no one challenged their legal right to sit anywhere they pleased. For a few minutes, Rustin even sat in the seat directly behind the Greyhound driver. Most gratifying was the decision by several regular passengers to sit outside the section designated for their race. Everyone, including drivers, seemed to take desegregated transit in stride, confirming a CORE report that claimed the Jim Crow line had broken down in northern Virginia in recent months. "Today any trouble is unlikely until you get south of Richmond," the report concluded. "So many persons have insisted upon their rights and fought their cases successfully, that today courts in the northern Virginia area are not handing down guilty verdicts in which Jim Crow state laws are violated by interstate passengers." At the end of the first day, the CORE riders celebrated their initial success at a mass meeting held at the Leigh Avenue Baptist Church, and prior to their departure for Petersburg the following morning Wally Nelson delivered a moving speech on nonviolence during a chapel service at all-black Virginia Union College. At the church the enthusiasm for desegregation among local blacks was palpable, suggesting that at least some southern blacks were more militant than the riders had been led to believe. But the mood was decidedly different among the predominantly middle-class students at Virginia Union, who exhibited an attitude of detachment and denial. During a question-and-answer session, it became clear that many of the students were "unwilling to admit that they had suffered discrimination in transportation." As Conrad Lynn, who joined the Journey in Richmond, observed, the students simply "pretended that racial oppression did not exist for them."[50]

The prospects for white compliance and black militancy were less promising on the second leg of the Journey. But even in southern Virginia, where most judges and law enforcement officials had yet to acknowledge the *Morgan* decision, the riders encountered little resistance. During the short stint from Richmond to Petersburg there were no incidents other than a warning from a black passenger who remarked that although black protesters like Nelson and Lynn might get away with sitting in the front of the bus in Virginia, things would get tougher farther South. "Some bus drivers are crazy," he insisted, "and the farther South you go, the crazier they get." As if to prove the point, Rustin had a run-in with a segregationist Greyhound driver the following morning. Ten miles south of Petersburg, the driver ordered the black activist, who was seated next to Peck, to the back of the bus. After Rustin politely but firmly refused to move, the driver vowed to take care of the situation once the bus reached North Carolina. At Oxford the driver called the local police, but after several minutes of interrogation the officer in charge declined to make an arrest. During the wait most of the black passengers seemed sympathetic to Rustin's actions, but a black schoolteacher boarding the bus at Oxford scolded him for needlessly causing a forty-five-minute delay. "Please move. Don't do this," he pleaded. "You'll reach your destination either in front or in back. What difference does it make?" This would not be the last time the CORE riders would hear this kind of accommodationist rhetoric.[51]

While Rustin was dealing with the Greyhound driver's outrage, a more serious incident occurred on the Trailways bus. Before the bus left the Petersburg station, the driver informed Lynn that he could not remain in the front section reserved for whites. Lynn did his best to explain the implications of the *Morgan* decision, but the driver—unaccustomed to dealing with black lawyers—"countered that he was in the employ of the bus company, not the Supreme Court, and that he followed the company rules about segregation." The unflappable New Yorker's refusal to move led to his arrest on a charge of disorderly conduct, but only after the local magistrate talked with the bus company's attorney in Richmond. During a two-hour delay, several of the CORE riders conducted a spirited but largely futile campaign to drum up support among the regular passengers. A white navy man in uniform grumbled that Lynn's behavior merited a response from the Ku Klux Klan, and an incredulous black porter (who reminded Houser of a fawning Uncle Tom character in Richard Wright's *Black Boy*) challenged Lynn's sanity. "What's the matter with him? He's crazy. Where does he think he is?" the porter demanded, adding, "We know how to deal with him. We ought to drag him off." As a menacing crowd gathered around the bus, Lynn feared that he might be beaten up or even killed, especially after the porter screamed: "Let's take the nigger off! We don't want him down here!" But in the end he managed to escape the vigilantism of both races. Released on a $25 bail bond, he soon rejoined his comrades in Raleigh, where a large crowd of black students from St. Augustine's College gathered to hear Nelson and Roodenko hold forth on the promise of nonviolent struggle. Thanks to Lynn's composure, a relieved Nelson told the crowd, the Journey had experienced its first arrest without disrupting the spirit of nonviolence.[52]

New challenges awaited the riders in Durham, where three members of the Trailways group—Rustin, Peck, and Johnson—were arrested on the morning of April 12. While Rustin and Johnson were being hauled off for ignoring the station superintendent's order to move to the black section of the bus, Peck informed the police: "If you arrest them, you'll have to arrest me, too, for I'm going to sit in the rear." The arresting officers promptly obliged him and carted all three off to jail. When Joe Felmet and local NAACP attorney C. Jerry Gates showed up at the jail a half hour later to secure their release, the charges were dropped, but a conversation with the Trailways superintendent revealed that there was more trouble ahead. "We know all about this," the superintendent declared. "Greyhound is letting them ride. But we are not." Even more disturbing was the effort by a number of local black leaders to pressure Gates and the Durham NAACP to shun the riders as unwelcome outside agitators. A rally in support of the Journey drew an expectedly large crowd, and the local branch of the NAACP refused to abandon the riders, but the rift within Durham's black community reminded the riders that white segregationists were not the only obstruction to the movement for racial equality.[53]

The next stop was Chapel Hill, the home of the University of North Carolina (UNC). Here, for the first time, the CORE riders would depend on the hospitality of white southerners. Their host was Rev. Charles M. Jones, the courageous pastor of a Presbyterian congregation that included UNC president Frank Porter Graham—a member of President Truman's Committee on Civil Rights—and several other outspoken liberals. A native Tennessean, Jones was a member of the Fellowship of Southern Churchmen, a former member of FOR's national council, and a leading figure among Chapel Hill's white civil rights advocates. Despite the efforts of Jones and others, life in this small college town remained segregated, but there were signs that the local color line was beginning to fade. Earlier in the year, the black singer Dorothy Maynor had performed before a racially integrated audience on campus, and Jones's church had hosted an interracial union meeting sponsored by the Congress of Industrial Organizations (CIO). These and other breaches of segregationist orthodoxy signaled a rising tolerance in the university community, but they also stoked the fires of reaction among local defenders of Jim Crow. By the time the CORE riders arrived, the town's most militant segregationists were primed and ready for a confrontation that would serve warning that Chapel Hill, despite the influence of the university and its liberal president, was still a white man's country.[54]

The riders' first few hours in Chapel Hill seemed to confirm the town's reputation as an outpost of racial moderation. Jones and several church elders welcomed them at the station, and a Saturday-night meeting with students and faculty at the university went off without a hitch. On Sunday morning most of the riders, including several blacks, attended services at Jones's church and later met with a delegation representing the Fellowship of Southern Churchmen. At this point there was no hint of trouble, and the interracial nature of the gatherings, as Houser later recalled, seemed natural "in the liberal setting of this college town." As the riders boarded a Trailways bus for the next leg, they could only hope that things would continue to go as smoothly in Greensboro, where a Sunday-night mass meeting was scheduled. Since there was no Greyhound run from Chapel Hill to Greensboro, the riders divided into two groups and purchased two blocs of tickets on Trailways buses scheduled to leave three hours apart.[55]

Five of the riders—Johnson, Felmet, Peck, Rustin, and Roodenko—boarded the first bus just after lunch, but they never made it out of the station. As soon as Felmet and Johnson sat down in adjoining seats near the front of the bus, the driver ordered Johnson to the "colored" section in the rear. The two riders explained that they "were traveling together to meet speaking engagements in Greensboro and other points south" and "that they were inter-state passengers . . . 'covered' by the Irene Morgan decision." Unmoved, the driver walked to the nearby police station to arrange for their arrest. While he was gone, Rustin and Roodenko engaged several of the passengers in conversation, creating an "open forum" which revealed that many of the passengers supported Felmet and Johnson's protest. When the driver later passed out waiver cards that the bus company used to absolve itself from liability, one woman balked, declaring, "You don't want me to sign one of those. I am a damn Yankee, and I think this is an outrage." Shaking her hand, Roodenko exclaimed: "Well, there are two damn Yankees on the bus!" By this time, Felmet and Johnson had been carted off to the police station, and Peck had followed them to the station to arrange bail. But the driver soon discovered that he had two more protesters to deal with. Encouraged by the sympathetic reaction among the regular passengers, Rustin and Roodenko moved to the seat vacated by the arrested riders, which prompted a second round of arrests. Having already paid $50 each for Felmet and Johnson's release, Peck called Houser, who was still at Jones's parsonage, to bring down another $100 to get Rustin and Roodenko out of jail.[56]

While the four men waited for Houser and Jones to arrive with the

CORE and the 1947 Journey of Reconciliation   57

bail money. Peck shuttled back and forth from the police station, checking on his colleagues' bags and trying to keep tabs on the situation at the bus station. By this point the bus had been delayed almost two hours, and it was obvious to everyone at the scene that a group of "outside agitators" had provoked an incident. One bystander, a white cab driver, vowed, "They'll never get a bus out of here tonight," and a few minutes later Peck found himself surrounded by five angry cab drivers as he crossed the street. Snarling "Coming down here to stir up the niggers," one of the drivers punched Peck in the side of the head. When Peck refused to retaliate and simply asked, "What's the matter?" the man gave him "a perplexed look and started to walk away awkwardly." Two men, a black professor from North Carolina A&T College and a local white minister, urged the driver to leave Peck alone, but they were told to mind their own business. Thinking that the two sympathizers were part of the CORE group, the cab drivers rushed toward them menacingly, but after learning that the two men were North Carolinians who just happened to be at the station they let them go. Returning to the police station, Peck warned Jones and Houser that trouble was brewing.[57]

After surveying the situation, Jones concluded that the riders would have to travel to Greensboro by car. Once bond had been arranged for the arrested riders, the CORE group piled into Jones's car and headed to the parsonage for a brief stop before leaving town. Unfortunately, two cabs filled with irate whites sped after them. Peck recalled the harrowing scene: "We succeeded in getting to Reverend Jones' home before them. When we got inside and looked out the window, we saw two of the drivers getting out with big sticks. Others started to pick up rocks by the roadside. Then, two of the drivers, apparently scared, motioned to the others to stop. They drove away. But a few minutes later Reverend Jones, who since the CIO meeting in his church had been marked as a 'nigger lover,' received an anonymous phone call. 'Get the niggers out of town by midnight or we'll burn down your house,' threatened a quivering voice." Determined to get the riders out of Chapel Hill before nightfall, Jones rounded up three university students willing to drive the group to Greensboro and also called the police, who reluctantly agreed to provide an escort to the county line.[58]

As soon as the riders left, Jones took his wife and two children to a friend's house for protection, a precaution that was proved warranted by subsequent events. When Jones returned home Sunday evening accompanied by a friend, Hilton Seals, he found a crowd of angry white protesters in his front yard. The two men tried to ignore the crowd's taunts, but as they walked to the door Seals was struck with a rock. On Monday morning, Jones received a second anonymous call threatening him with death. Later in the day several cab drivers milling around the bus station attacked Martin Walker, a disabled white war veteran and university student, after he was seen "talking to a Negro woman," and a second university student, Ray Sylvester, "was knocked unconscious by a cab driver for 'being too liberal.'" During the next few days Jones received additional death threats by mail, and several anonymous calls threatened his church, prompting an emergency meeting of the congregation. When they learned of the threats, several UNC students volunteered to guard Jones's home and church, but this gesture proved unnecessary, thanks in part to UNC president Frank Graham's forceful consultation with the local police. By the end of the week the wave of intimidation had subsided, even though the controversy surrounding the incident at the bus station continued to simmer.[59]

Speaking to an overflow crowd at the university's Memorial Hall four days after the arrests, Jones defended the Journey of Reconciliation as the work of true Christians who had made "a thorough and exhaustive study of law as related to transportation in order that Christians and others might understand the law and practice it." But several students in the audience criticized the Journey's provocative tactics. "When you consider the general attitudes and practices in the South," one student insisted, "it is stupid to raise a point which can bring only friction, a crusade of going about and raising such questions cannot be merely trying to bring about reconciliation. It has as its end the creation of dissensions not here before. I cannot but damn all connected with bringing a group here merely to stir up dissension." Unmoved, Jones continued to speak out on behalf of CORE and the struggle for racial justice. For most of the Chapel Hill community, the restoration of an uneasy truce between "university liberals" and the local segregationist majority represented an acceptable resolution of the crisis. But for some the unsettling influence of the CORE riders persisted. In late April, after Rustin returned to Chapel Hill to deliver two lectures on nonviolence (one in the basement of a Methodist church and a second in a university lecture hall), one local liberal, William McGirt, wrote a letter to the *Daily Tarheel* praising Rustin as a "prophet" who had turned "a nonviolent example of resistance" into "a dramatic symbol upon which racial minorities can seize to find their freedoms courageously but without debasing their spirits with anger." "These Fellows of Reconciliation, many of whom have been in prison for their convictions," McGirt added, "are the genuine creators of a new age."[60]

In the wake of the Chapel Hill incident, the CORE riders were apprehensive about the remaining ten days of the Journey. But whatever doubts they may have had about the wisdom of continuing the trip disappeared during a rousing mass meeting in Greensboro on Sunday evening. At the Shiloh Baptist Church—the same church that would welcome the Freedom Riders fourteen years later—the congregation's emotional embrace reminded them of why they had come south seeking justice. "The church was crowded to capacity and an atmosphere of excitement prevailed," Peck recalled in 1962. "Word had spread about what had happened to us and why we were late. . . . After the usual invocation, hymn-singing, scripture-reading, and prayer, Rustin, who is a particularly talented speaker, told our story. He interrupted it only to get one or another of us to rise and tell about a specific incident or experience. Then he continued. When he finished, the people in the crowded church came forward to shake the hands and congratulate us. A number of women had tears in their eyes. A few shook my hand more than once."[61]

The mass meeting in Greensboro was the emotional high point of the Journey. For most of the riders, the last ten days on the road represented little more than a long anticlimax. There were, however, a few tense moments—and a few surprises—as the riders wound their way through the mountains of western North Carolina, Tennessee, Kentucky, and Virginia. No two bus drivers—and no two groups of passengers—were quite the same. On the leg from Greensboro to Winston-Salem, a white passenger from South Carolina expressed his disgust that no one had removed Lynn from a front seat. "In my state," he declared, "he would either move or be killed." The following day, during a Greyhound run from Winston-Salem to Statesville, Nelson occupied a front seat without incident. After the riders transferred to a Trailways bus in Statesville, however, the driver ordered him to the rear. The driver relented when Nelson explained that he was an interstate passenger protected by the *Morgan* decision, but this did not satisfy several white passengers, including a soldier who demanded to know why Nelson had not been moved or arrested. "If you want to do something about this," the driver responded, "don't blame this man [Nelson]; kill those bastards up in Washington." Following several stops north of Asheville, the white section of the bus became so crowded that two white women had to stand in the aisle. When they asked why Nelson had not been forced to give up his seat, the driver cited the *Morgan* decision. Although the women later moved to the Jim Crow section in the back, the atmosphere on the bus remained tense. "It was a relief to reach Asheville," Houser recalled many years later.[62]

Asheville was the hometown of Joe Felmet, the young Southern Workers Defense League organizer who had been arrested in Chapel Hill, and several of the riders spent the night at his parents' house. This did not please at least one neighbor, who shouted "How're your nigger friends this morning?" as Felmet and the other riders left for the station. After the riders boarded a Trailways bus headed for Knoxville, Tennessee, a white woman complained to the driver that Dennis Banks, a black musician from Chicago who had just joined the Journey, was sitting in the whites-only section. When Banks, who was sitting next to Peck, politely refused to comply with the driver's order to move, the police were summoned. Twenty minutes of haggling over the law ensued before Banks was finally arrested. The police also arrested Peck, but only after he moved to the Jim Crow section and insisted that he be treated the same as his black traveling companion.

Brought before Judge Sam Cathey, a blind and notoriously hard-edge Asheville politician, the two defendants created a sensation by hiring Curtiss Todd to represent them in court. Neither Cathey nor the local prosecutor had ever heard of the *Morgan* decision, and they had to borrow Todd's copy of the decision during the trial. An NAACP-affiliated attorney from Winston-Salem, Todd was the first black lawyer ever to practice in an Asheville courtroom. Despite this breach of local racial etiquette, Judge Cathey—who reminded the defendants that "We pride ourselves on our race relations here"—made sure that other shibboleths of Jim Crow justice remained in force. "In the courtroom where we were tried," Peck later declared, "I saw the most fantastic extreme of segregation in my experience—Jim Crow bibles. Along the edges of one Bible had been printed in large letters the words 'white.' Along the page edges of the other Bible was the word 'colored.' When a white person swore in he simply raised his right hand while the clerk held the Bible. When a Negro swore in, he had to raise his right hand while holding the colored Bible in his left hand. The white clerk could not touch the colored Bible."[63]

The Jim Crow ethos did not prevent the two defendants from receiving the same sentence—thirty days on the road gang, the maximum under North Carolina law. During a long night in the white section of the city jail, Peck discovered that many of his fellow inmates bore a special animus toward white agitators from the North. "Defending the niggers?" one oversized man bellowed, moving toward the rail-thin activist with his fists clenched. "They should have given you thirty years." Bracing for a blow, Peck blurted out: "I was just traveling with my friend and I happened to believe that men are equal." After an awkward silence, another inmate, playing the role of peacemaker, interjected: "Well, it's too bad that all men can't get along together, but they can't." With this puzzling statement, the mood shifted and the inmates decided to leave Peck alone. Banks had less trouble among the black inmates, some of whom regarded him as a hero. But both riders were relieved when Todd arrived with the required $800 bail bond a few hours later.[64]

While Peck and Banks were detained in Asheville, the rest of the riders went on to Knoxville, where they welcomed three new riders—Homer Jack, Nathan Wright, and Bill Worthy. A seasoned veteran of Chicago direct-action campaigns, Jack could hardly wait to join the Journey, but he found the "taut morale" of his CORE colleagues a bit unnerving. "The whites were beginning to know the terror that many Negroes have to live with all the days of their lives," he noted. "All members of the party were dead-tired, not only from the constant tenseness, but also from participating in many meetings and conferences at every stop."[65]

Jack himself soon experienced the emotional highs and lows of direct action in the Jim Crow South. After a full day of interracial meetings in Knoxville, he and Wright tested compliance on the night Greyhound run to Nashville. With Houser serving as the designated observer, they sat in adjoining seats four rows behind the driver. "Slowly heads began to turn around and within five minutes the driver asked Wright to go to the back of the bus," Jack recalled. "Wright answered, 'I prefer to sit here.' I said I and Wright were friends, that we were riding together, that we could legally do so because of the *Morgan* decision. The bus driver pleaded, 'Wouldn't you like to move?' We said we would like to stay where we were. The driver left the bus, apparently to talk to bus officials and police. After much ogling by passengers and bus employees . . . the driver finally reappeared and started the bus, without any more words to us." So far so good, Jack thought to himself, but as the bus left the outskirts of Knoxville he started to worry that "the hard part of the Journey was still ahead." Unaccustomed to the isolation of the rural South, he began to conjure up images of impending doom. "Ours was the first night test of the entire Journey," he later noted. "The southern night, to Northerners at least, is full of vigilante justice and the lynch rope from pine trees if not palms. We wondered whether . . . the bus company—or one of its more militant employees—would telephone ahead for a road block and vigilantes to greet us in one of the Tennessee mountain towns. Neither of us slept a moment that night. We just watched the road." When nothing of this sort actually happened, Jack felt more than a little foolish, concluding that the South, or at least Tennessee, was less benighted than he had been led to believe. "The reaction of the passengers on the trip was not one of evident anger," he observed, "and certainly not of violence. It was first surprise, then astonishment, and even tittering. On that bus, anyway, there was only apathy, certainly no eager leadership in preserving the ways of the Old South."

In Nashville, Jack and Wright—having arrived "early in the morning, exhausted, relieved, and with a bit of exhilaration of the adventure"— regaled several college classes with tales of nonviolent struggle. But at the end of the day, just before midnight, they resumed their journey of discovery, boarding a train for Louisville. This was "the first train test" attempted by the CORE riders, and no one knew quite what to expect. When a conductor spied Jack and Wright sitting in adjoining reserved seats in a whites-only coach, he collected their tickets without comment. But he soon returned, whispering to Jack: "He's your prisoner, isn't he?" After Jack responded "no," the incredulous conductor ordered Wright to "go back to the Jim Crow coach." Wright refused, citing *Morgan,* which prompted the conductor to mutter "that he never had had to face this situation before and that if we were riding back in Alabama he wouldn't have to face it: the passengers would throw us both out the window." Despite this bluster, the conductor did not follow through with his threat to have them arrested when the train stopped in Bowling Green, and Wright remained in the white coach all the way to Louisville.[66]

A second team of riders traveled from Knoxville to Louisville by Greyhound, and they too escaped arrest. Worthy and Roodenko shared a seat in the front of the bus, and no one commented on the arrangement until they reached the small town of Corbin, a hundred miles north of Knoxville. When the young black journalist refused to move to the back, the driver called the police and "hinted that there would be violence from the crowd if Worthy did not move." However, the driver and the local police relented after one of the white passengers, a woman from Tennessee, defended Worthy's legal right to sit where he pleased. Once again there was hard evidence that at least some white southerners were willing to accept desegregated transit.[67]

Several of the riders, including Jack and Wright, left the Journey in Louisville on April 19, but approximately half participated in the final four days of testing as three small groups of riders converged on Washington. Although most of these concluding bus and train trips were uneventful, there were two arrests in western Virginia—Nelson in Amherst and Banks in Culpepper. In both cases, the drivers and law enforcement officers involved evidenced confusion about the law and some reluctance to follow through with actual arrests, suggesting that Virginia officials were still trying to sort out the implications of *Morgan*. And, despite the arrests, the behavior of several bystanders indicated that race relations in Virginia were changing. In Culpepper, one courageous black woman who sold bus tickets at a local concession stand boarded the bus and offered to help Banks in any way she could, and two local whites spoke out on Banks's behalf. "If I had been you I would have fought them before letting them take me off the bus," one of them told Banks as the young musician calmly went off to jail.[68]

For the riders, the return to Washington on April 23 brought a sense of relief—and a measure of pride in their perseverance. But, to their dismay, there was no public event to mark the conclusion of their remarkable collective experience. "At the end of our Journey," Peck recalled in 1962, "there were no reporters flocking around us to ask whether it had been worth it or whether we would do it again—as they did after the Freedom Ride fourteen years later. If there had been, most of would have answered yes." The Journey's official balance sheet, as reported by CORE, listed twenty-six tests of compliance, twelve arrests, and only one act of violent resistance. But the project's accomplishments drew little attention from the mainstream press in the spring of 1947. Even among white reporters interested in racial matters, the Journey could not compete with the unfolding drama of Jackie Robinson's first few weeks in a Brooklyn Dodger uniform.[69]

In the black press the Journey fared much better, especially in the columns of the two black reporters who accompanied the riders during the first week of the trip. Ollie Stewart of the *Baltimore Afro-American,* who witnessed the confrontation in Chapel Hill and the mass meeting in Greensboro, hailed the Journey as a watershed event. He wrote in late April:

> For my part, I am glad to have had even a small part of the project—even that of an observer. History was definitely made. White and colored persons, when the whole thing was explained to them as they sat in their seats on several occasions, will never forget what they heard (or saw). The white couple who went to the very back seat and sat between colored passengers, the white ma-

rine who slept while a colored woman sat beside him, the white Southern girl who, when her mother wouldn't take a seat in the rear, exclaimed "I do not care, I'm tired"—all these people now have an awareness of the problem. The Journey of Reconciliation, with whites and colored traveling and sleeping and eating together, to my way of thinking, made the solution of segregation seem far more simple than it ever had before. I heard one man refer to the group as pioneers. I think he had something there. They wrote a new page in the history of America.[70]

In the weeks and months following the Journey, several riders published reports on their experiences. Rustin and Houser—in CORE's official report, *We Challenged Jim Crow*—offered both a day-by-day narrative and general commentary on what the Journey had revealed. "The one word which most universally describes the attitude of police, of passengers, and of the Negro and white bus riders is 'confusion,'" they concluded. "Persons taking part in the psychological struggle in the buses and trains either did not know of the *Morgan* decision or, if they did, possessed no clear understanding of it." And yet there were clear indications that the confusion could be alleviated. "Much was gained when someone in our group took the lead in discussion with bus drivers or train conductors and when police appeared," they reported, adding: "As the trip progressed it became evident that the police and the bus drivers were learning about the Irene Morgan decision as word of the 'test cases' was passed from city to city and from driver to driver." To Rustin and Houser, the Journey demonstrated "the need for incidents as 'teaching techniques.'" "It is our belief that without direct action on the part of groups and individuals, the Jim Crow pattern in the South cannot be broken," they insisted. "We are equally certain that such action must be nonviolent." Homer Jack, writing in the Unitarian magazine *Common Ground,* offered a similar assessment. "What, finally, did the Journey of Reconciliation accomplish?" he asked. He answered: "It showed progressive Americans that the *Morgan* decision must be implemented by constant 'testing'—in the spirit of goodwill—and by subsequent law enforcement. The Journey helped implement the decision at least by spreading knowledge of it to bus drivers and some law-enforcement officers (both policemen and judges) in the upper South. The Journey also showed whites and Negroes living in that area that the *Morgan* decision could be enforced without disastrous results, if the proper psychological and legal techniques were used. The Journey gave these techniques—and accompanying inspiration—to thousands of whites and Negroes in the South."[71]

As they wrote these reflections, Rustin, Houser, and Jack were well aware of the unfinished business in the courts. Six separate incidents during the Journey had produced twelve arrests, the legal and financial consequences of which were still looming large in late April 1947. Fortunately, local officials had already dropped the charges against the three men arrested in Durham, and in May the district attorney in Asheville did the same when Curtiss Todd appealed the convictions of Peck and Banks. The three Virginia arrests were under review by the state supreme court, which would eventually rule in favor of the riders. Thus, CORE's major concern was the fate of the four men arrested in Chapel Hill.[72]

On May 20, two of the four defendants—Rustin and Roodenko—went on trial in the Chapel Hill Recorder's Court. Judge Henry Whitfield, a hard-line segregationist, made no effort to hide his contempt for the defendants' three NAACP attorneys—C. Jerry Gates, Herman Taylor, and Edward Avant. After the local prosecuting attorney, T. J. Phipps, delivered "a lengthy argument to show that the Negroes really want jimcrow," the judge approvingly issued a guilty verdict, assessing Rustin court costs and sentencing Roodenko to thirty days on a road gang. Explaining the differential treatment, he termed Rustin "a poor misled nigra from the North" who bore less responsibility than white agitators who should know better, and later he added a dash of anti-Semitism to his admonition: "I presume you're Jewish, Mr. Rodensky," drawled the judge. "Well, it's about time you Jews from New York learned that you can't come down here bringing your nigras with you to upset the customs of the South." NAACP attorneys immediately filed an appeal with the Superior Court in nearby Hillsboro, but a month later Felmet and Johnson received even harsher sentences from Judge Whitfield. Johnson was fined $500 and court costs, while Felmet, as a native southerner and latter-day scalawag, was sentenced to six months on the road gang, six times the maximum allowed by law. When the prosecutor pointed out the error, Whitfield reluctantly reduced Felmet's sentence to thirty days, remarking, "I can't keep all these things in my little head."[73]

In March 1948, after summarily rejecting the defendants' claimed status as interstate passengers, Superior Court judge Chester Morris ruled that all four deserved uniform thirty-day sentences. NAACP attorneys quickly filed an appeal with the North Carolina Supreme Court, but ten months later, in January 1949, the state's highest court, as expected, upheld the convictions and ordered the four men to return to North Carolina to serve their sentences. Rustin and Houser welcomed this ruling as a basis for an appeal to the U.S. Supreme Court—an appeal that would clarify and extend the nearly three-year-old *Morgan* decision—but it soon became all too apparent that NAACP leaders had no interest in filing any further appeals. Financially strapped and preoccupied with school desegregation cases and other legal challenges to Jim Crow—including the high-profile case of Norvell Lee, a former Olympic boxer who had tried to desegregate a whites-only railway coach in northern Virginia—the NAACP national office informed CORE and FOR leaders that it could neither fund nor participate in an appeal of the North Carolina Supreme Court's decision. The NAACP claimed that a further appeal was useless because defense attorneys could no longer prove that the defendants were interstate travelers. "The black lawyer who had the ticket stubs, proving that you were interstate passengers, now claims he has lost the stubs," Roy Wilkins, the NAACP's assistant executive secretary, confessed to Rustin, "although we believe he was paid to destroy them." Rustin and others suspected that the NAACP's recalcitrance involved much more than lost ticket stubs, but there was nothing they could do to remedy the situation.[74]

NAACP attorneys had never been easy to work with, and earlier disagreements over funding and strategy had prompted FOR to form an internal committee to oversee the Chapel Hill case. Some members of the committee had actually welcomed the NAACP's disengagement, preferring to keep the struggle outside the courts. Thus they were relieved when the defendants' options were reduced to three choices: seeking a gubernatorial pardon, fighting extradition, or surrendering voluntarily to North Carolina authorities. After it became clear that a pardon was highly unlikely, the committee decided that the best means of demonstrating CORE's commitment to nonviolence was to accept the sentences. Although Andrew Johnson, who was then in his senior year at the University of Cincinnati, declined to return to North Carolina, confessing that he was "both mentally and physically unprepared to serve thirty days on the road gang," the other three defendants embraced the committee's decision. Having just returned from a three-month tour of Europe and India, where he lectured on nonviolence and American race relations and met with Gandhi's son, Devadas, Rustin predicted that his impending imprisonment would help to expose the hypocrisy of America's democratic pretensions. "Our conviction, unfortunately, is one more demonstration to the colored majority of the world of the failure of American democracy," he declared upon arriving in New York. "America cannot maintain its leadership in the struggle for world democracy as long as the conditions exist which caused our arrest and conviction. We don't fool anybody. People abroad know and are losing faith."[75]

On March 21, 1949, Rustin, Felmet, and Roodenko surrendered to authorities at the Orange County Courthouse in Hillsboro, North Carolina. Assigned to the state prison camp at Roxboro, they braced themselves for thirty days of harsh punishment and humiliation. The actual sentence turned out to be only twenty-two days, thanks to an early release for good behavior, and all three men survived the ordeal. But their experiences at Roxboro, especially Rustin's, soon became the stuff of legend among movement activists. Following his release in mid-April, Rustin wrote "Twenty-Two Days on a Chain Gang," a searing memoir of his incarceration that was later serialized in the *New York Post* and the *Baltimore Afro-American.* Laced with dark humor—including an account of Rustin's dealings with a prison guard who kept reminding him "You ain't in Yankeeland now. We don't like no Yankee ways"—the piece shocked many readers and eventually led to a legislative investigation of conditions in North Carolina prison camps.[76]

This unexpected benefit pleased Rustin and his CORE colleagues, but as the decade drew to a close it was all too obvious that the Journey of Reconciliation's primary objective remained unfulfilled. While the first freedom ride had demonstrated the viability of nonviolent direct action in the upper South, it had not precipitated wholesale desegregation or even protest on a mass scale. With few exceptions, company rules and social inertia still kept the races apart on interstate buses and trains; and no one, other than a few die-hard optimists, expected the situation to change anytime soon. As it had done so many times in the past, the shape-shifting monster known as Jim Crow had adapted to changing legal and political realities without sacrificing the cold heart of racial discrimination. Irene Morgan, like so many brave souls before her, would have to wait a little longer for the year of jubilee.[77]

2
T. R. M. Howard

Pragmatism over Strict Integrationist Ideology in the Mississippi Delta, 1942–1954

David T. Beito and Linda Royster Beito

FEW BLACKS IN Mississippi were more assertive and prominent in their support of the *Brown* decision than Dr. T. R. M. Howard. Howard's defining moment came on July 31, 1954, when he and a delegation of leading blacks used a special public meeting with the governor to spurn a "compromise" plan to maintain segregation in exchange for equalizing school spending. When Howard spoke out on this subject, he could not be easily ignored. Of all the blacks in the state, he was not only one of the wealthiest but also the head of a key civil rights organization.[1]

Howard almost seemed fated for a leadership role in civil rights. As early as the 1930s he had campaigned against Jim Crow and disfranchisement in California and Tennessee. During the 1940s he distinguished himself in black business, mutual aid, and medicine. Howard's modest background set him apart from most of the best-known civil rights figures of the time. He was born in 1908 in Murray, Kentucky, as Theodore Roosevelt Howard. His father, Arthur Howard, was a tobacco twister. His mother, Mary Chandler Howard, worked as a cook for Dr. Will Mason, the white owner of the local community hospital. Howard's parents were divorced when he was three, and he was raised by his mother, who soon remarried.[2]

When he was twelve, Howard caught the eye of Dr. Mason, who encouraged his ambitions to be a doctor. Mason hired him for various menial jobs in the hospital to give him experience. Later he helped to pay Howard's way through the four-year combination high school/junior college program of Oakwood College in Huntsville, Alabama, an all-black Seventh Day Adventist (SDA) institution that stressed "manual training" and religious instruction. During the late 1920s, Howard expressed his gratitude to his white mentor by changing his name to Theodore Roosevelt *Mason* Howard. Like Mason, he joined the SDA, which had a growing, though segregated, black membership.[3]

Howard was a popular student leader at Oakwood and was well liked by the predominantly white faculty and administrators. Like most students, he divided his time between class and various missionary activities for the SDA. Advancing the SDA faith was his main preoccupation, but his political and economic ideas reflected the self-help, gradualist philosophy of Booker T. Washington.[4]

Howard finished his undergraduate education as one of the few blacks at Union College in Lincoln, Nebraska, a small SDA liberal arts school. While there he had his first chance to bask in the national limelight at the national convention of the Anti-Saloon League of America in Detroit, winning first prize for best oration by a student. He was only twenty-two. Howard's impassioned defense of Prohibition so impressed the nearly all-white crowd that, according to an eyewitness account, "the entire audience rose in a great demonstration which lasted several minutes." As a result, the Anti-Saloon League hired Howard as a paid lecturer for the summer.[5]

The most important legacy of Howard's sojourn in Nebraska was a lifelong hatred of racial injustice. His letters to faculty at Oakwood College related his personal experiences with discrimination. Although Howard expressed dismay that whites in Nebraska were just as likely to draw the color line as those in the South, he tried not to make waves. In 1929 he wrote, "I never go in the dining hall and set down at a table where there are others, but I set at a table where there is no one, and others come and eat with me. If 'staying in my place' will cause me to get through Union with friends, I sure mean to do that." But gradually Howard's frustration began to boil over. In a 1931 letter he lamented that "segregation is becoming an administrative policy of the school" and that no member of the faculty had "any interest in me.... I must confess that some of these things are awful hard to drink down." Far more dramatic was Howard's visit to Maryville, Missouri, just after a lynching in January 1931. He later wrote movingly that he had clutched some of the ashes of the victim, a day after an angry mob had burned him alive.[6]

Howard left his mark as a community leader while he was a student at the College of Medical Evangelists (CME) in California (now Loma Linda University), the chief SDA medical school. The students at

CME, like those at Union College, were nearly all white. It did not take long for Howard to develop a reputation among blacks in Los Angeles as a "silver tongued" budding leader of intelligence, charm, wit, and overwhelming self-confidence. Among those who were impressed was Edward M. Boyd, a college student and son of a wealthy black pioneer family in Riverside. Boyd introduced Howard to his sister Helen, a popular young socialite. Through Helen and Edward, Howard gained acceptance into the black elite of Riverside and Los Angeles. Through them he met Charlotta A. Bass, the publisher of Los Angeles's leading black newspaper, the *California Eagle*. For the rest of his life, Howard moved almost effortlessly between the black bourgeoisie and the masses.[7]

In July 1933, Howard settled comfortably into the twin roles of journalist and civil rights leader. Bass hired him to be field manager and to write a regular opinion column, and for the next year and a half he covered such varied subjects as international power politics, civil rights, and prostitution. Also, in July 1933, Howard was elected president of the California Economic, Commercial, and Political League (CECPL), a three-year-old organization that worked closely with Bass. Helen N. Boyd was elected secretary. All the while, Howard kept up, though not without difficulty, with his studies at the CME.[8]

Howard's columns for the *California Eagle* were thoughtful, well informed, and wide ranging, especially for a young man whose college education had stressed vocational and medical subjects. His favorite topics, however, were black self-improvement and civil rights. He was a self-described "race man," or in modern parlance, a black nationalist. At the same time, he rarely indulged in the anti-white and Africacentric rhetoric of more extreme nationalists such as Marcus Garvey.[9]

Howard championed entrepreneurship and a program of teaching "thrift and economy." In this respect he was still very much a follower of Washington, whom he praised as a "towering genius." Howard recommended a credo of "talking about Negro business, singing Negro business, preaching Negro business, spending our money with Negro business, wearing clothing purchased at Negro business houses, eat[ing] food purchased at Negro stores and writing about Negro business. We have got to become Negro Business Conscious." Howard urged blacks to emulate Japanese Americans, who, despite their small numbers in California, had created a booming business sector and a range of philanthropic institutions. Like Washington and Malcolm X, he laid much of the blame for any shortcomings on blacks themselves. Black businesses were too often unsanitary or produced inferior products. Not surprisingly, the workaholic Howard stressed the "value of time." He related that he had stopped patronizing one of the "most fashionable" black-owned barbershops in Los Angeles because "my barber insisted on clipping one minute and talking five minutes. We are living in an age of speed and the Negro barber must realize this fact."[10]

Citing the practical benefits of this strategy, Howard recommended making the most of existing conditions. He cautioned that not every boy was "born to be a preacher, lawyer or doctor" and condemned the tendency to regard menial jobs as demeaning rather than as a means for incremental progress and race pride. Howard declared that as "long as the American people wear shoes, somebody is going to have to shine them. . . . [T]he Negro boy who shines shoes should shine them so well that every body in the community would want him to shine their shoes."[11]

Although Howard's economic program was reminiscent of Washington's, his political ideas were immediatist and confrontational. Too often, he warned, various "bone-headed, pussy-footing, grafting, selfish, dishonest preachers, lawyers, doctors and ratty good-for-nothing politicians and Uncle Toms" had hoodwinked blacks into voting against their own interests. It was essential for blacks to finance their own political campaigns: "Beware of these banquets, cigars and kegs of beer! These may prove to be all that you will ever get for your vote." He proposed a strategy of bloc voting under which a "clearinghouse" of black organizations would unite behind candidates who would protect equal rights.[12]

Howard may have had separatist tendencies, but he reacted angrily to subtle—and not so subtle—efforts by local politicians and officials in Los Angeles during the early 1930s to introduce segregation. He applauded black nurses who repelled an attempt to consign them to a "colored" dining room in the new county hospital. Howard and the CECPL, along with Bass, successfully pressured local politicians to prevent hospital administrators from circumventing the rule by offering cash to black nurses if they would dine separately.[13]

Under Howard's leadership, the CECPL's trademark was the grand holiday special event. Each of these was a combination political rally, carnival, band concert, barbecue, and picnic outing. The Memorial Day rally in San Bernardino featured such prominent speakers as novelist Upton Sinclair, then a Socialist candidate for governor. Howard's abilities as a showman shone through as he promoted the event in his column: "The artistic designs and the soft lights make it look very much like the New York Cotton Club. . . . The beautiful young women of San

Bernardino, Riverside and Redlands will serve the food on that day. There is a beautiful fountain shaped like a huge orange where only pure orange juice will be served." For the children there would be a large carnival with "four different rides and all the games that go with a carnival." Howard tried to schedule Duke Ellington as the dance band but ultimately settled for the less prominent Dixie Serenaders.[14]

Despite this time-consuming political activity, Howard completed his studies at the CME in 1935, four years after entering medical school. He was the only African American in his graduating class. At the same time, he finally persuaded Helen N. Boyd to accept his proposal of marriage. They remained married for more than forty years. Over time, her activities increasingly centered on black high society and club work.[15]

After his residency at City Hospital Number 2 in St. Louis, Howard took over as medical director of the Riverside Sanitarium in Nashville, which the SDA had just established to serve the medical needs of black members. On the surface, Howard was the perfect man for the job. He was well versed in the faith, talented, ambitious, and full of energy. But the ideal never lived up to the reality. From the beginning, Howard chafed under the tight central control. One nurse remembers that he rankled administrators by insisting that surgical patients be served ginger ale rather than water during recovery. It also seems likely that the lack of opportunities to earn compensation to supplement his low salary was a source of dissatisfaction. For whatever reason, Howard's tenure as medical director ended unhappily in 1938, only a few months after he had started. Yet he was able to bounce back and establish a medical practice in Nashville. Although Howard was a member of the executive committee of the city's chapter of the National Association for the Advancement of Colored People (NAACP), he concentrated on medicine rather than civil rights.[16]

In 1941, Howard's career took a dramatic turn. He accepted an offer to be chief surgeon of the Taborian Hospital. Located in Mound Bayou, Mississippi, the hospital had been built by the International Order of Knights and Daughters of Tabor, a group founded by former slaves shortly after the Civil War. Since the 1920s, Perry M. Smith of Mound Bayou had led the organization's Mississippi unit as chief grand mentor. As a fraternal society, the Knights and Daughters of Tabor was typical of many organizations during this period, both black and white, such as the Loyal Order of Moose, the Odd Fellows, the Masons, and the Polish National Alliance. Like these other societies, it had rituals and colorful drill teams and was organized around a system of lodges. Before the rise of the welfare state, fraternal organizations were leading providers of social welfare. Through a system of cooperative insurance, they provided members and their families services such as medical care, employment information, and orphanages.[17]

The statement of principles of the Knights and Daughters of Tabor was like that of thousands of other fraternal societies. It pledged to advance "Christianity, education, morality and temperance and the art of governing, self reliance and true manhood and womanhood." Sometimes historians have become so focused on dividing individuals into collective categories of race, class, and gender that they forget the common ground that individuals in all these categories share. Fraternal societies were leading examples of this common American heritage.[18]

The Taborian Hospital was located in the heart of the Delta region of Mississippi in the small all-black town of Mound Bayou. The community had a fascinating history. Founded in 1887 by a former slave of the brother of Confederate president Jefferson Davis, it was one of a handful of towns in the South where blacks could vote and hold office. Mound Bayou's black-controlled political environment, including a black mayor and police chief, offered an ideal nurturing environment for the hospital.[19]

When the Taborian Hospital opened in 1942, the final construction costs totaled over $100,000. The facilities included two major operating rooms, an X-ray room, a sterilizer, incubators, an electrocardiograph, a blood bank, and a laboratory. The hospital usually had two or three doctors on staff; all were black. In 1944, annual dues of $8.40 entitled an adult to thirty-one days of hospitalization, including major or minor surgery, and a $200 life insurance policy. The membership fee for a child was $1.20 per year for the same services and a $50 life insurance policy.[20]

Under Howard's tenure as chief surgeon, the Taborian Hospital met with an enormous response from blacks in the Delta. The Mississippi membership of the Knights and Daughters of Tabor mushroomed to nearly fifty thousand men, women, and children. Most of those who joined were sharecroppers and farm laborers. Despite the fact that they lived in one of the poorest regions of the United States, they were able to provide for their social welfare needs by pooling their resources. It is amazing that Howard found the time for his work as chief surgeon during these years. He delivered hundreds of babies, perhaps thousands, and performed as many as twelve operations per day.[21]

For Howard, both fraternal hospitals were springboards to the creation of an array of business enterprises in Mound Bayou. He established the first swimming pool for blacks in Mississippi, a sixteen-hundred-acre cotton and cattle plantation, a restaurant with a beer garden, a home construction firm, and even a small zoo. Howard was not afraid to display his wealth. He drove an air-conditioned Cadillac and purchased a large home. He indulged in such aristocratic pastimes as betting on horses and raising pheasant, quail, and hunting dogs. He purchased the Magnolia Mutual Life Insurance Company, a purely commercial venture, which sold both life and hospitalization insurance to blacks.[22]

Although fraternal and business interests dominated Howard's time and energy during the 1940s, he never lost interest in civil rights issues. In 1946, for example, he sent a personal appeal to Claude Barnett, the head of the Associated Negro Press of Chicago, the black version of the Associated Press, to publicize the case of Lever Rush. Rush had been executed at 1 A.M. in nearby Cleveland, Mississippi, after a hurried and secretive trial that blacks were not allowed to attend. Rush's true crime, according to Howard, was that he had a consensual sexual relationship with a white woman: "They attempted to make it a case of rape, but she stated that Rush did not persuade her or force her to do anything but what she had done over a 4 year period had been done because she had wanted to do it."[23]

Howard's most important political crusade during the decade was to lobby for a hospital for black veterans in Mound Bayou. World War II had created a need for facilities, and officials in the Veterans Administration considered Mississippi a logical location. By the last months of 1945, the campaign was under way. In pushing for the hospital, Howard worked closely with Taborian grand mentor Perry Smith, Mayor Benjamin A. Green, and many prominent black doctors in the South, especially those connected with the nearest black veterans' hospital, at Tuskegee.[24]

In this case, Howard chose pragmatism over strict integrationist ideology. He quietly lobbied white politicians in Mississippi to get backing. Along with Smith and Green, he visited the office of U.S. representative Will Whittington, whose district included Mound Bayou. White politicians in the state were receptive to the proposed hospital, at least initially, including Representative John E. Rankin, perhaps the most virulent racist in the U.S. House of Representatives. After receiving an appeal from Howard, Rankin aired his views in a telegram to Walter Sillers Jr. Widely regarded as the state's most powerful politician, Sillers had been speaker of the Mississippi House of Representatives since the 1920s, and he would later serve in the vanguard of the Magnolia State's powerful Dixiecrat movement. Rankin seemed reassured that all the staff and patients at the hospital would be black and asserted that it would be best to put it in "a Negro town or a Negro community in order to avoid friction." He did not bother to mention the needs and wishes of black veterans. His main motivation was fear that mounting medical demands by blacks would put too severe a strain on hospital segregation. Sillers's response to Rankin expressed cautious support for the hospital. Howard's efforts also paid off with notorious racial demagogue Theodore G. "the Man" Bilbo. The U.S. senator promised in a letter to Howard that if "I can help in any way I will be glad to do it."[25]

Before long, however, white support began to fall away. Location was the problem. Sillers, and to a lesser extent Whittington, backtracked after a white delegation from Merigold, only three miles from Mound Bayou, strenuously objected. In a letter withdrawing his endorsement, Sillers explained to Rankin that he did not "know there was any opposition to the negro hospital being located at Mound Bayou, otherwise I would not have encouraged the location in this county." Most ominous were "the consequences that might flow from the location of this hospital in this county where we have a population of about 75% colored and 25% white." Because of white constituents' complaints, Bilbo came to a similar conclusion.[26]

The proposal to build the hospital soon met with stiff opposition from another source when the national office of the NAACP objected to any additional segregated hospitals. A key critic was W. Montague Cobb, one of the best-known black doctors in the United States and a professor of anthropology at Howard University. Cobb described the prospect of "a new segregated hospital in the home state of Rankin and Bilbo" as "a long stride backward with seven league boots."[27]

To deal with these objections, Howard and his allies emphasized a practical argument. They depicted a hospital for black veterans in Mississippi as a fait accompli. Hence, they warned, it had become a matter of deciding whether to build it in the relatively friendly atmosphere of Mound Bayou or in a more racially intolerant community such as Greenwood or McComb. Both Howard and Mayor Green emphasized this point in letters to Representative William L. Dawson of Chicago, one of two blacks in the U.S. House of Representatives. Howard noted that Mound Bayou would not inflict "petty insults" such as curfews, which were the norm in Mississippi. Instead, it would offer "the greatest absolute freedom of any place in the entire South." In closing his appeal, Howard declared that black veterans had "seen enough hell, why stand by and see them pass through more. As the fight to keep it out of Mississippi has been lost, for God's Sake let us be sensible and choose the lesser of the evils."[28]

Although no record exists of Dawson's response, Howard made considerable headway in garnering black support. A key convert was Claude Barnett, who paved the way for Howard when he visited Tuskegee. Howard was overjoyed by the result. He reported that "to a man" influential blacks in the community, including Tuskegee University president F. D. Patterson, had told him that they supported putting the hospital in Mound Bayou.[29]

Leaders of Mound Bayou predicted a great future for their community when President Truman announced in March 1947 that the federal government would build the hospital in Mound Bayou. After years of struggle, the town finally seemed on the verge of restoring some of its lost luster. But the celebrating came to a crashing halt in January 1949 when Truman announced cancellation of the hospital, noting that current health demands had revealed that the federal government had overestimated the actual need for beds. The end of official segregation in Veterans Administration hospitals the following year dashed any lingering hopes by removing the rationale for the Mound Bayou location.[30]

By this time, other developments had already turned Howard's life in Mound Bayou upside down. Almost since he had arrived in the community, the young outsider had squared off against the dominant faction of the Knights and Daughters of Tabor, led by the elderly Perry Smith. In 1946 the showdown came to a head when Smith dismissed Howard as chief surgeon. But Howard was not a man to go quietly. His supporters launched a counterattack by running George Jefferson, a young Howard protégé, as a candidate against Smith at the next annual meeting of the Mississippi affiliate. The bitterness was intense on both sides. Howard's followers accused the current leadership of dictatorial methods and nepotism and of favoring Mound Bayou's elite at the expense of the "little people." The critics fired back by alleging that the former chief surgeon was power hungry and demanded too much compensation and, because of his extended activities, could no longer devote adequate attention to his work. The infighting rose to such intensity that the white county sheriff was asked to keep order and tally the vote. Howard's candidate lost, but it was fairly close.[31]

Within a year, Howard and over ten thousand followers had formed a rival fraternal organization, the United Order of Friendship of America (UOFA). The new organization had 149 lodges and five thousand members, nearly all former Taborians. R. L. Drew, a longtime leader in the Knights and Daughters of Tabor, became grand worthy master. The organization almost immediately announced plans for a hospital just across the street from the Taborian Hospital. Not surprisingly, Howard signed on as chief surgeon. The Friendship Clinic, which opened in 1948, was not as large as the Taborian Hospital, but it offered the same menu of services, including obstetrics, internal medicine, and major surgery.[32]

Although Howard continued to thrive as an entrepreneur, planter, doctor, and fraternal leader, his attention turned increasingly toward issues of racial injustice. This was entirely predictable. Howard's core ideas had not greatly changed since he had led the CECPL. By the end of the 1940s he had not only the motivation to step up his fight for civil rights but also the means. Howard's business and fraternal enterprises were finally on a firm foundation, thus giving him an unusual degree of economic independence.

He had other reasons as well to make the move to civil rights. Because of economic changes in the state, the prospects for such a strategy were brighter. Cotton was still king, but innovations such as flame cultivators and the introduction of commercially viable cotton harvesters were undermining old habits, loyalties, and constraints. As mechanization slowly spread, more blacks than ever abandoned farm work and left for northern cities. Although he had become a gentleman planter, Howard applauded this trend. He predicted that urban life would "make the Negro more resourceful" and warned that as "long as he had Mr. John to depend upon, he is going to depend on him." The decline of sharecropping spurred many blacks to contemplate the injustices they suffered and to seek a better life.[33]

Their political and legal status was still dismally low, but signs of improvement were not hard to detect. Throughout the 1940s the NAACP recorded seven lynchings in the state, less than in any decade since Emancipation. The constant threat of federal anti-lynching legislation (though never realized) emboldened those whites who argued that these killings harmed the image of the state and were bad for business.[34]

Meanwhile, blacks flexed their political muscles carefully and cautiously. Between 1940 and 1953, NAACP membership rose from 377 in 1940 to 1,600 while registered voters (never more than 6 percent of black adults) climbed from 2,000 to 20,000. Overseas service in World War II and new experiences in the North had encouraged political assertiveness. As Howard observed, blacks "who thought they were happy on the plantations of Mississippi have gone North to visit a friend or a relative.... They find them eating better, living in a better house, wearing better clothing, having more spending money, children going to schools and above all having a freedom of mind."[35]

It was the Regional Council of Negro Leadership (RCNL) that came to embody Howard's views on civil rights. He proposed the group's formation in November 1951 at the annual conference of the UOFA. Ironically, the original stated goal was to create a black version of the powerful all-white defender of the established order, the Delta Council, an "oversized chamber of commerce" that represented the upper crust of white business interests and planters.[36]

Howard did not explicitly endorse "separate but equal," yet his proposals were consistent with that framework. It was a framework, however, that he always pushed nearly to the breaking point. Even so, in announcing the formation of the RCNL, he took care to reassure whites: "All I ask is that we be consulted on matters that affect members of our race. We are not organizing to work against our white citizens . . . but to work with them." He called for more black representation in the leading economic and political agencies such as the Mississippi Farm Bureau.[37]

His rhetoric about imitating the Delta Council notwithstanding, Howard's organizational design more closely reflected the philosophy of Booker T. Washington—perhaps combined with a dose of W. E. B. Du Bois's doctrine of the "talented tenth"—than it did any white model. Instead of starting from the grassroots, he put the priority on harnessing the talents of blacks with a proven record of leadership in business, the professions, education, and the church. "Our major effort in the past," Howard stated, "has been focused on the masses of our people." By contrast, his goal was "to reach the masses through the chosen leaders of the masses." In many ways, he hoped to create a refined model of the old CECPL.[38]

The media fallout from Howard's plan for a Delta Council of Negro Leadership was overwhelmingly positive. This was especially true in the Memphis newspapers, many of which also served the Delta area. In a rare point of agreement, at least on race relations, the black *Tri-State Defender* and the white *Commercial Appeal* carried enthusiastic editorials of praise. The *Appeal* stated that Howard had "won international acclaim for his effort to improve health conditions among Negroes" and predicted that "the council's sponsors will meet the challenge and come out triumphant."[39]

Despite statements like this from whites, events at the end of December 1951 dampened hopes of an "equal partnership" with the white Delta Council. When Howard had first made his proposal, white Delta Council officials had reacted with a mixture of suspicion and cold politeness. Contention immediately arose over the suggested name, Delta Council of Negro Leadership. In a letter to Howard, white Delta Council official Maury S. Knowlton stated that lawyers had told him that the similarity might create confusion or difficulties for state chartering agencies. More seriously, it would undermine the "good will between your new organization and the membership of the Delta Council." Eager to mollify Knowlton, and probably regretting his earlier impulsiveness, Howard beat a rapid retreat. He pledged to drop the "Delta" from the proposed name and invited white Delta Council officials, as well as other leading whites, to attend the organizational meeting scheduled for late December.[40]

The first meeting of the new Regional Council of Negro Leadership revealed how much Howard had overestimated the prospects of white/black cooperation. The speech of B. F. Smith, manager of the Delta Council, was lukewarm at best, neither endorsing nor opposing the organization. He angered many of those present by stating that the "Delta Council is not sponsoring this organization and has never authorized the use of its name for that purpose. This announcement is made because of misleading statements which have appeared in the press." Little did Smith realize what he was doing. As a black member of the audience later wrote, "Dr. Howard did not conceive of our council as a civil rights group. But with the strife with the Delta Council, we emerged as an organization opposed to the established system." This was an exaggeration. From the outset the RCNL had endorsed civil rights causes such as voter registration and equal school terms.[41]

Both before and for some time after the falling out from the Delta Council, Howard was fairly consistent in outlook. Although he did not directly challenge "separate but equal," he zeroed in on the need to guarantee the "equal." Education as a means to end the second-class status of blacks was always one of the RCNL's top priorities. Howard often identified inadequate schools as the primary cause of the black exodus to the North. Instead of demanding integration, however, the RCNL called for equal school terms for both races. In Mississippi the law guaranteed whites eight months of school, while blacks had to settle for several months less. In a speech for the RCNL, Howard proposed rewriting the state educational law to say that "Each child, regardless of race, creed, or color shall be guaranteed eight months of school in each year." He belittled the existing black schools as a "mockery to the word education," pointing out that there were eight well-equipped high schools for five thousand white children in Bolivar County while ten thousand blacks had only two substandard ones. At the time Howard spoke, the state spent an average of three dollars for each white child compared to one dollar for a black child.[42]

Howard regarded unequal punishment for crime as one of the most glaring examples of "separate but in no case equal." He underlined the hypocrisy of white men who so readily resorted to mob violence to defend southern white womanhood from sexual assaults, either real or imagined, by blacks but did nothing to stop white men "who pester, bother or rape Negro girls." He urged his audience to remember "the shame, reproach and disgrace which has been forced upon Negro womanhood in our State," citing three recent examples, including the rape of twelve-year-old black baby-sitter by a white man, in which "absolutely nothing was done."[43]

Another example of unequal treatment was the failure of white courts to punish black-on-black crime. Agreeing with many conservative blacks, he declared that the "greatest danger to Negro life in Mississippi is not what white people do to Negroes but what the courts of Mississippi let Negroes of Mississippi do to each other." He found it deplorable that criminals in such cases often went unpunished and that murderers rarely got the electric chair: "If the killer lives on a big plantation and is a good worker and especially, if he is liked by white people, the chances are that he will come clear of his crime."[44]

Howard's outrage over a system that institutionalized racial supremacy coexisted with, and often complemented, deeply conservative views on the fundamentals. He was not a deep philosophical thinker, but he showed no affinity with, and often demonstrated hostility toward, utopian panaceas for society. Although he flirted with black nationalism of a certain type, he never embraced full-blown group consciousness. He invariably expressed admiration for American founding principles as well as the founders. "There is not a thing wrong with Mississippi today," he declared matter-of-factly, "that real Jeffersonian democracy and the religion of Jesus Christ cannot solve." Deep down he was confident about the potential of blacks, when given the opportunity, to overcome prejudice and thrive by practicing the Franklinesque virtues. He pointed to Jackie Robinson, whom he deeply admired, as an example of a man who "does the job so well that the world forgets that his skin is black. Young people[,] let efficiency and service be your watch word and making money will take care of itself."[45]

Given Howard's conservative belief in self-help, it is not surprising that his zeal for black entrepreneurship was unflagging. He warned that the "economic security of the race is tied up in the Negro's support of

Negro business. It is no encouragement to me that the religious songs that the Negroes like best are, 'Take all this world, but give me Jesus' and 'A tent or a cottage—why should I care, they are building a mansion for me more over there.'" He urged ministers to start emphasizing practical matters such as maintaining a proper diet and using "the fabrics of cotton, wool, nylon, rayon, velvet, furs and leather while we are preparing for our golden slippers." Most of all, they needed to realize that if blacks were to move forward "in this industrial age, thrift, industry and business efficiency must become an integral part of the Negro's religion." He lamented that blacks in Jackson, Mississippi, had not formed banks or insurance companies to the same degree as their counterparts in Memphis and elsewhere.[46]

As war raged in Korea and Senator Joseph McCarthy was in the middle of his crusade, Howard left little doubt where he stood on the issue of communism. He expressed his "wish that one bomb could be fashioned that would blow every Communist in America right back to Russia where they belong." He pointed with pride to the failure of "Russia and her agents" to exploit the civil rights grievances, stating that blacks "were not interested in any 'Ism' but Americanism." Like many other civil rights defenders during the period, he used the specter of communism as a cautionary lesson. If blacks' continued second-class citizenship was not dealt with, he predicted, victory in the cold war could be jeopardized. Although "America is a Christian nation, a nation that Almighty God has blessed . . . the cause of Democracy is shuddering throughout the world today because of the inequality of Democracy in regards to Negro rights."[47]

Although Howard did not greatly emphasize at first the final goal of the RCNL—an "all-out fight for unrestricted voting rights"—nor did he mince words. Promising that blacks had no interest in "social equality," he added that "we are terribly concerned about equality at the ballot box, equality in education, equality in the courts of the states, equality in the protection of our homes and equality in chances to make our daily bread."[48]

At the same time, Howard did not entirely discount white claims that many people lacked sufficient skills to exercise responsible self-government. In fact, he estimated that 50 percent of the black population was in that category. But then, he pointed out, at "least 20% of the white people of our area are not prepared for first class citizenship, yet they enjoy all of the privileges of the ballot box and every other privilege which this democracy offers its citizens." His recommendation was not to restrict the franchise but to deploy institutions such as the Delta

Council and the RCNL "to guide our people in their civic responsibilities regarding education, registration and voting, law enforcement, tax paying, the preservation of property, the value of saving and in all things which will make us stable, qualified conscientious citizens."[49]

He thundered about the hypocrisy and other consequences of this racial double standard: "Black soldiers from Mississippi are fighting and dying for a democracy they don't know one single thing about back home on the plantations of the Mississippi Delta." Howard had little patience with claims of whites to have special knowledge because they had a "mammy" or were raised around blacks. In the first of many quotations reprinted in *Jet* in December 1951, he offered this suggestion: "You have to be a black man in Mississippi at least 24 hours to understand what it means to be a Negro in Mississippi."[50]

By the time of the December meeting, the RCNL had already attracted many individuals of ability and prestige. Not surprisingly, the core leadership drew heavily from the United Order of Friendship of America. The list included Robert L. Drew; Aaron Henry, a druggist from Clarksdale and local NAACP activist; E. P. Burton, the assistant chief surgeon at the Friendship Clinic; Amzie Moore, a gas station owner and NAACP activist from Cleveland, Mississippi; and Adam Newsom, the grand worthy chaplain of the UOFA. For many, it was their first exposure to civil rights and a training ground. Henry, Moore, Drew, and Burton were to become prominent activists during the 1960s.[51]

The RCNL formed an interlocking directorate not only with the UOFA but also with the Magnolia Mutual Life Insurance Company. Eight of its eighty-three officials, including Henry, Moore, Burton, and Drew, served on the company's board of directors. Of the six top officers of the RCNL, four were directors of the Magnolia. Howard was particularly close to Henry, who was secretary of both the RCNL and the Magnolia Mutual Life Insurance Company. Henry's drugstore in Clarksdale often filled prescriptions for patients of the Friendship Clinic.[52]

Sixteen relatively autonomous committees, each headed by a respected black leader in business, education, the church, or the professions, formed the backbone of the RCNL. Howard's close allies chaired the key committees such as the Committee on Race Relations (Burton), the Committee on Voting and Registration (Levye Chapple), and most importantly the Committee on Separate but Equal (Henry). The goal of this last committee, according to Henry, was to "get an equal share of every dollar spent on the state and federal level. We said we would settle for nothing less than a 'dollar-for-dollar, brick-for-brick distribution of revenues' among Negro and white." The committee, in turn, reported to an executive board and board of directors headed by Howard. The RCNL's constitution stipulated that each town or city in the Delta with at least one thousand blacks was entitled to representation. To build mass support for the work of these committees, the RCNL made sure to hold its business meeting in a different location each year.[53]

Because of Howard's organizational design, the RCNL was well represented throughout the Delta. Only eight of its eighty-three officials were from Mound Bayou, while the rest came from every section of the Delta, including Clarksdale, Greenwood, Greenville, and Vicksburg. They included at least two college presidents, Arenia Mallory of Saints Junior College in Livingston and J. H. White, president of Mississippi Vocational University in Itta Bena. Prominent Taborians were conspicuous by their absence. By contrast, the heads of two key fraternal societies in the state, the Elks and the Afro-American Sons and Daughters, were on the list. The latter group operated Mississippi's largest black hospital, in Yazoo City.[54]

A striking pattern of the RCNL's leadership was the small number of clergy. This characteristic set it apart from those civil rights groups in the South that relied heavily on ministers, such as the Montgomery Improvement Association, founded four years later under the leadership of Martin Luther King Jr. Only seven of the eighty-three RCNL officials—and not one among the top six officers—had clerical titles. Undertakers, entrepreneurs, professionals (including eight doctors and druggists), and owners of small farms were far more visible. This was probably not an accident. Howard's rhetorical focus generally emphasized business and the professions, not the church, as the vanguards of future black success. Even if he had felt otherwise, his Seventh Day Adventist affiliation, which had waned by the 1940s, made it difficult to cultivate close ties with ministers from other denominations.[55]

A history of bad blood between Howard and Harrison Henry Humes, the most powerful black religious leader in the state, certainly did not further any prospects of winning clergy support. Humes had been president of the state General Missionary Baptist State Convention since the 1930s and published the widely read *Delta Leader*. The acrimony between the two men had first become public in 1947 when Humes, a close ally of Perry Smith, backed the firing of Howard as chief surgeon of the Taborian Hospital. The feud flared up again three years later when Howard campaigned for an unsuccessful challenger to Humes for the presidency of the state convention.[56]

Special conditions in the Delta also played a role. The life of a typical minister militated against involvement outside the church. The large church with a full-time minister, fairly common in urban areas, was rare in the Delta. Even many successful ministers lacked the independence, or the time, to take on outside leadership roles. Most were bivocational, earning their main income from other occupations, such as farming or undertaking, or had a hand-to-mouth existence as the pastor of several churches. Especially in rural areas, they were often dependent on the goodwill of whites for contributions and access to plantations. An undertaker, fraternal official, or medical doctor had greater contact with a broad segment of the masses than a typical Delta minister with a few dozen parishioners.[57]

The experience of the RCNL indicates that historians have not adequately appreciated the importance of businesspeople and professionals as pioneers in the early civil rights movement, especially in Mississippi. In forming and joining the RCNL, these men and women were pursuing a practical, though much belated, application of Booker T. Washington's dictum that voluntary associations, self-help, business investment, and property ownership were the best preconditions for civil rights. On this score, Charles Evers speculates that the self-employed individuals who formed the backbone of the RCNL were effective because they could draw on independent resources to withstand white pressure. He bluntly states that "we couldn't afford to work for no white folks. They'd fire us."[58]

The role played by ordinary members in the organization is more difficult to gauge. Most of the records that could address this issue are lost. Estimates on the size of the membership range from a low of five hundred to a high of four thousand. The higher figure is more plausible, at least for the later period. In 1954, for example, two thousand people were official delegates to a business meeting of the RCNL. Even so, the written and oral record shows almost no evidence of functioning chapters at the town or county level (as, for example, was the case with the UOFA). The RCNL's local work appears to have been generally loose and sporadic. The main contact with the rank and file was either through the committees or at the business and annual meetings. This structure, of course, was consistent, at least in theory, with Howard's vision of creating a top-down organization.[59]

The probable lack of dues-paying members makes it all the harder to assess where and how the RCNL obtained its funds. Certainly, it had expenses. It lavished free food and entertainment on people who flocked to its mass meetings. Given the ad hoc nature of many day-to-day activities at the local level, it seems unlikely that regular dues could have paid many of the bills. "Money was a problem at first, but then funds came from dues and public appeals and passing the hat at meetings," Aaron Henry remembered. "After the group was well established and publicized, we were able to rely on contributions from all over the country."[60]

Yet the dearth of chapters or a large dues-paying membership did not mean that the RCNL lacked impact at the local level. The best-known members promoted civil rights at the grassroots through an amalgam of organizations. Some overlapped so closely with the RCNL that they actually approximated de facto affiliates. In Clarksdale, for example, Henry (assisted by fellow RCNL stalwarts such as Robert L. Drew) had headed the Clarksdale chapter of the Progressive Voters League since 1946. Henry used this position to press—at first cautiously, then aggressively—for greater voting rights, better treatment in the courts, and improved facilities at black schools. Other RCNL members worked through various citizens associations and groups such as the Mississippi State Democratic Association. The role of the UOFA as a stimulant of local activism should not be underestimated. The dozens of UOFA lodges in the Delta provided not only meeting places but opportunities for people of like mind to speak to each other. Local lodge activities brought potential civil rights activists together, and lodge buildings often doubled as civil rights meeting places.[61]

NAACP branches often fulfilled the role of de facto RCNL affiliates. Key NAACP officials—such as W. A. Bender, the chaplain at Tougaloo; Emmett J. Stringer, a dentist in Columbus; and Dr. Clinton Battle, a physician in Indianola—were also in the RCNL. During the 1940s, many blacks had avoided identification with the NAACP out of fear of angering whites who widely, and wrongly, believed that it was a Communist front. In 1949 it had only three branches in the Delta, and just one had more than thirty people on the rolls. The advent of the RCNL in 1951, however, emboldened blacks to take the risk of open membership in the NAACP. Henry and Drew took the plunge in 1952 by forming a branch in Clarksdale. During the next three years, other RCNL members in Columbus (Emmett Stringer), Belzoni (George W. Lee and Gus Courts), and Cleveland (Amzie Moore) followed suit.[62]

The RCNL's working alliance with Percy Greene, the publisher of the state's most widely read black newspaper, the *Jackson Advocate*, was a critical factor in building momentum. Winning his support carried great weight with proponents of civil rights. Throughout the 1940s, often at considerable risk, Greene used the *Advocate* to champion voting rights and equal treatment for blacks. In 1946 the NAACP selected him for its national honor roll for his efforts to expose the intimidation of black voters during the Bilbo campaign. Shortly after the election of 1948, Greene founded the Mississippi State Democratic Association (also known as the Mississippi Negro Democrats) to register blacks and encourage participation in the state Democratic primary. He must have appreciated Howard's declaration that the "greatest blow to Communism in the last ten years would be for the State Democratic Executive Committee to accept Negroes of the State to full membership within the party."[63]

More than once, Greene, who was a board member of the RCNL himself, devoted a page of small type in the *Advocate* to reprinting an entire speech by Howard. An article in that paper stated that the roster of the RCNL "reads like 'Who's Who' in the state of Mississippi including . . . the great majority of the most widely known, active forward looking, and successful business and professional men, farmers, educators, and religious leaders of the state." In 1953 the *Advocate* was still praising Howard as "a high type Christian gentleman" who was "dynamic, forceful, courageous, and well informed." But the two men had not always seen eye to eye. As a longtime booster of the Taborians during the 1940s, Greene had taken sides against Howard after the factional split. Because the RCNL emphasized all the causes he had held dear in the 1940s—voting rights, economic self-help, and equal treatment—the formation of the group made him much more favorably disposed.[64]

The RCNL's most famous member was Medgar Evers. Fresh from graduation at Alcorn College, Evers had moved to Mound Bayou in July 1952 after accepting a job offer from Howard to sell insurance for the Magnolia Mutual Life Insurance Company. Evers's wife, Myrlie, worked for the company as a typist. Howard made quite an impression. Myrlie recalled that he had "a friendly smile, and a hearty handshake, and there was about him an aura of security so lacking among the vast majority of Negroes in the Delta that he stood out as different wherever he went. One look told you, he was a leader: kind, affluent, and intelligent, that rare Negro in Mississippi who had somehow beaten the system." But she also could see that not everyone shared her enthusiasm. At least some blacks "resented Dr. Howard's wealth but on the whole he was viewed as a brave man, a spokesman for the Delta Negroes, and it was widely believed that he had at least some influence with the white plantation owners." Soon after he arrived in Mound Bayou, Medgar Evers threw himself into the work of the RCNL, becoming its program director.[65]

One of the RCNL's earliest initiatives was a boycott of service stations that failed to provide restrooms for blacks. It distributed an estimated twenty thousand bumper stickers with the slogan "Don't Buy Gas Where You Can't Use the Rest Room." This demand, though consistent with the doctrine of separate but equal, was risky in the context of McCarthy-era Mississippi. The campaign galvanized ordinary blacks in the Delta as nothing had before. Throughout Mississippi, Henry remembered, "Negroes were driving up to service stations and asking in the same breath for gas to use the washroom. They would drive off when told there were no washrooms available for Negroes." Many took their business to the service stations owned by blacks, such as that of RCNL official Amzie Moore in Cleveland, Mississippi. In the middle of the campaign, the RCNL discovered that the slogan might violate anti-boycott laws, so it was revised to "We Don't Buy Gas Where You Can't Use the Restroom." Despite this, all available accounts, including those of Myrlie Evers and Aaron Henry, testify to the success of the boycott. Most white stations began to install restrooms for blacks, both because of the falloff in customers and pressure from national suppliers and chains.[66]

Even as the RCNL's service-station boycott was under way, the group ran an equally high-profile campaign against harassment by law enforcement. For decades, blacks had suffered repeated indignities ranging from petty insults to physical beatings. Howard's timing was excellent. Because the racial climate in the state had improved in the last decade, he could afford to take some risks. The campaign culminated with a ninety-minute conference with T. B. Birdsong, the commissioner of the state highway patrol. Several RCNL officials accompanied Howard, including Henry, Burton, and Drew. To put a human face on the problem, they brought along a minister and a woman from a prominent black family in Marks, both of whom alleged that a highway patrolman had slapped them. A news release for the RCNL praised Birdsong's promise to take action but advised that it would be impossible to cooperate with the department's public safety program "if highway patrolmen continue to use their badges of authority as emblems of tyranny."[67]

Meanwhile, the RCNL's Committee on Voting and Registration launched a sustained but less advertised effort for voter education. By conducting classes on the state constitution, it carefully taught blacks to learn enough about voting rules to pass muster with local registrars. Fortunately for the RCNL, it had many members from traditional Black-and-Tan Republican areas, such as Cleveland and Clarksdale, who had always voted and thus were knowledgeable about the rules. Until the 1954 U.S. Supreme Court decision, the results were generally promising. Black voter registration continued to slowly increase, reaching a then century high mark of twenty-two thousand. Henry recalls that initially "white opposition to our registration drives was disorganized and generally ineffectual. They did not believe white supremacy was in danger." The RCNL's most important threat to the old order was its effort to encourage blacks to vote in the previously all-white, and all-important, Democratic primary.[68]

Complementing this strategy, both in the 1952 campaign and later, Howard identified with the Mississippi State Democratic Association. His greatest coup was to persuade Representative William Dawson of Chicago to be the featured speaker at the first annual conference of the RCNL. No other black congressman had spoken in the state since the nineteenth century. While it was not a campaign appearance as such, Dawson, a member of the National Democratic Committee, probably accepted because it would contribute to his longtime goal to expand national black support for the party. To cap this achievement, Howard arranged for singer Mahalia Jackson to be the main entertainment.[69]

Even Howard's adversaries had no choice but to acknowledge his coup. Mayor Green, a classmate of Dawson's at Fisk University, accepted the invitation to ride in the lead car in a parade down Main Street (Highway 61) that kicked off the festivities. Black schools and colleges contributed three marching bands. An estimated seven thousand blacks crowded into a giant circus tent to hear the speakers. Most black high schools in the state closed and encouraged students to attend. After an introduction by Percy Greene, Congressman Dawson gave a speech that reflected his moderate and conciliatory outlook. He warned that "we have no right to expect leaders in politics to commit political suicide by defending us when we will not support them with our votes." Helen Howard served as official hostess as five thousand people ate meals on the lawn of the Friendship Clinic.[70]

It was another feather in Howard's cap. An editorial in the Memphis *Tri-State Defender* lauded him as "a modern 'Moses' in the leadership and inspiration" who had mastered the art of "translating the truth in terms acceptable to the dominant group." Still, the "dominant group" did not seem to be overly concerned. Although a prominent white lawyer, F. D. Feduccia, who had represented Howard, welcomed Dawson on "behalf of Mississippi," whites played almost no role and showed little interest. Despite the great crowds, many white newspapers in the state did not even mention the Chicago congressman's visit.[71]

The Dawson speech was the first of several annual grand events that came to be a hallmark of the RCNL, each, in the words of Myrlie Evers, "a huge all-day camp meeting: a combination of pep rally, old-time revival, and Sunday church picnic." In using this approach, Howard followed the same strategy he had pursued with such success during the 1930s with the California Economic, Commercial, and Political League. Standard features were a big-name national speaker from the North, musical performers, and liberal helpings of food and refreshment. To achieve maximum impact, the UOFA usually held its annual conclave just before the RCNL event in Mound Bayou. For many younger and future civil black leaders such as Fannie Lou Hamer, attendance was a life-transforming event. "Everyone would gather there," Charles Evers recalls, "and had something like a festival. And we had music, gospel and blues. We had all kinds of food. People from all over the state of Mississippi would come."[72]

Fortified by his new relationship with William Dawson, Howard deepened his participation in the Democratic campaign in the following months. In August, for example, he and fellow RCNL officials Emmett Stringer of Columbus and Levye Chapple of Greenville attended the Democratic National Convention as "observers on behalf of the Mississippi Negro Democrats Association and Negro voters of the state." Although they were not official delegates, they anticipated in a small way the efforts of Fannie Lou Hamer and the Mississippi Freedom Democrats at the national convention in 1964. A few weeks before the election, Howard met with Dawson at a Democratic Party meeting in Washington, D.C. Despite Howard's support for the Democrats, he showed sensitivity to the concerns of black Republicans by carefully depicting the RCNL as a nonpartisan organization.[73]

The annual rally in 1953 was also a success, though less spectacularly so. By scheduling GOP alderman Archibald Carey of Chicago as the speaker, Howard revealed that he would not be constrained by a partisan framework. Because of his well-received speech at the 1952 convention, Carey was regarded as the up-and-coming black Republican politician in the United States. Like Howard, Thurgood Marshall, and Adam Clayton Powell, he also came from a younger generation of leaders who had matured politically during the 1930s and 1940s. All four men were born in 1908.[74]

Howard's activism had not yet pushed him beyond the pale for whites. As before, he maintained civil, even cordial relationships with white businessmen and planters in the area. Howard's new prominence in the RCNL may have even helped him on this score, at least for a while. Some members of the white elite respected and admired Howard, but many also recognized the dangers of alienating him. According to Maurice L. Sisson, an associate of Howard's in both the Magnolia Mutual Insurance Company and the RCNL, "white people were afraid of Dr. Howard." Other acquaintances and friends from the period, such as Homer Wheaton and Charles Tisdale, have said the same.[75]

Many whites apparently believed that an ill word passed down from Howard would lead their workers to slack off or cause customers not to buy their products. Wheaton stated that "one of the threats that Howard made was that if certain things didn't improve that black folks would retaliate in every way that they knew how to do it and implied that they'll start in the white folks' home." It is almost impossible to assess whether such fears had merit, but there is no doubt that Howard had clout and did not hesitate to use it. One particular incident during this period stands out. A bank teller in Cleveland had failed to use a courtesy title when addressing the wife of one of the doctors of the Taborian Hospital. After hearing the news, Howard complained loudly and implied that a boycott would follow. Bank officials quickly apologized and promised to discipline the employee.[76]

As the RCNL picked up steam, officials in the national office of the pro-integrationist NAACP became worried. Many of them distrusted Howard. From the beginning, NAACP officials had been suspicious of the RCNL in general and of Howard in particular. An internal memo to national NAACP head Walter White from Gloster Current, director of branches in the national office in New York, characterized the new group's program as "midway of that of the NAACP and the Urban League. They work in the separate but allegedly equal framework." Ruby Hurley, the director of the NAACP's regional office based in Birmingham, was even more hostile. She described the RCNL as a "threat to us which I have recognized and have tried to combat" and dismissed Howard as a hopeless case, since efforts "to bring him around to our way of thinking" had failed completely. Contrary to the NAACP's official position, Howard had allegedly stated that "if the white people wanted to keep segregation they (the Council) would just make it very expensive for them." With great alarm and more than a hint of jealousy, she warned that the RCNL had attracted many members of the NAACP, including those "who by reasons of formal education or professional status are in natural positions of leadership." Among these was state NAACP president Emmett Stringer, a member of the RCNL's Committee on Voting and Registration.[77]

As outsiders, Current and Hurley misunderstood the RCNL, or at the very least they failed to appreciate the conditions under which it had to operate. In certain black-majority Delta counties, such as Tallahatchie, not a single black was registered to vote. Howard, Moore, and Evers were anything but timid, naive, or accommodationist. Inspired by the Mau-Mau rebellion in Kenya, Evers had even contemplated waging guerrilla warfare against the white power structure. Each of these men had repeatedly taken great risks in an unusually hostile racial climate. By their actions, they had often shown themselves quite ready to take on the status quo. At the same time, they were realists and had ample reason to believe that a direct—or even indirect—assault on the rigid segregation of the Delta would completely marginalize them. Instead, they tried to change the system by concentrating on its weakest points.[78]

They could point to recent events to illustrate that their campaigns against unequal treatment and disfranchisement could yield some incremental success. Blacks had made progress, at least relative to the past, in both of these areas, but Jim Crow was as entrenched as ever. Whites proudly proclaimed their dedication to fighting any breach in the walls of separation, but they were less likely to openly admit that blacks should be disfranchised solely because they were black.

A visible sign that the racial climate had improved was Mississippi governor Hugh White's unprecedented proposal in 1952 to equalize school spending. At the beginning of his term, White had positioned himself as a racial moderate. In November he proposed a 3 percent tax and a bond issue for a crash program to equalize school spending in five years but maintain separate schools. To sell the idea, White gave a speech in Mound Bayou in early 1953, the first ever by a sitting governor, on the occasion of the eleventh anniversary of the Taborian Hospital. A crowd of six thousand blacks in the audience cordially applauded White as well as Walter J. Sillers Jr., who also spoke. Though Howard was no friend of the Taborians, both the UOFA and the Magnolia Mutual Life Insurance Company published full-page ads welcoming him to Mound Bayou.[79]

In a speech during the month of White's visit, Howard coyly avoided a position on White's plan, stressing the need for "equality in education," but his comments left little doubt that he was skeptical. He praised the proposal as a step in the right direction, but he bluntly attributed it to "the drawn lash of the Supreme Court of America." He emphasized the enormous taxpayer expense of equalizing a system in which per-pupil spending was three dollars for whites compared to one dollar for blacks. According to Howard, "a poor state like Mississippi can not support a dual system of public education and maintain the high standards of education today. If rich states like New York, Pennsylvania and California can't do it then Mississippi can't. . . . You and I have fooled ourselves into thinking that there is such a thing as separate but equal."[80]

By the latter half of 1953, Howard and other RCNL officials had moved toward open hostility against segregation as evidence mounted that legislators did not have the political will to implement equalization. Even when faced with the looming threat of a Supreme Court ruling, they dragged their feet on the necessary funding or new taxes. Legislators' reluctance only increased after estimates began to appear that equalization would increase annual state school appropriations from $25 to $37 million.[81]

A revealing episode during the summer of 1953 fueled blacks' growing skepticism about equalization. Howard, Moore, and Evers visited the office of Walter Sillers to discuss improvements for black schools. During the meeting, Sillers kept his back to the group and avoided eye contact. He ended with some vague promises of more buildings, but few ever saw the light of day. According to journalist Adam Nossiter, "the deliberate humiliation of the episode left Evers and the others commenting bitterly on the treatment they had received. It was a lesson for the future."[82]

In November, Howard cast his lot against separate but equal in no uncertain terms. His speech came only two weeks after Coahoma County School Board officials rejected a protest by the Coahoma County Citizens Association, led by R. L. Drew, against omission of Cleveland's black high school from a proposed bond issue for a building program. White officials claimed that if they had included the school, voters would have been alienated because of the added expense. Days later, the annual conferences of branches of the state NAACP passed a resolution against the governor's equalization plan and called for an end to segregation. The same conference chose RCNL leader Emmett Stringer as head of the state NAACP.[83]

In a speech delivered at the annual conclave of the UOFA several days later, Howard announced that "every progressive Negro" should support the NAACP's stand. He predicted that a serious attempt to create truly separate but equal schools would "wreck the economy of the entire South." Howard held nothing back. In response to Governor White's claim that the "good Negroes" of Mississippi rejected the NAACP's resolution, he replied that he "would be very happy if the governor would give me a definition of a 'good Negro.' . . . As president of the Council of Negro Leadership and a taxpayer, I feel I should say to you that the thinking Negro in Mississippi knows our state cannot finance a segregated system of education which is equal but separate."[84]

By taking this stand, Howard locked horns with prominent blacks who continued to stand by the governor's equalization plan, dismissing them as "spineless" and, worse, as "Uncle Toms" and "Handkerchief Heads." Two of the best-known black defenders of White's plan were John Dewey Boyd, president of the Mississippi Negro Teachers Association, and Howard's old adversary, Harrison Henry Humes. Both had responded to the NAACP resolution by sending telegrams to the governor promising support for his agenda. Boyd exemplified a subset of black educators who regarded equalization as the best hope to improve the quality of black schools as well as to protect the jobs of administrators and teachers. Humes, who acted from similar motives, predicted that opponents were making a "colossal blunder" and argued that black schools would provide more "sympathetic teachers" for children. But Humes had to perform a delicate balancing act. He wanted to preserve his ties with white leaders, but he could not afford to alienate his large Baptist constituency. He repeatedly counseled his white segregationist allies on the dangers of delay. Failure to fully fund and implement the equalization plan on a fast timetable, he advised, "might lead to the replacing of the present conservative Negro leaders by more radical elements." If the situation did not change, he hinted, he would join these "radical elements."[85]

Particularly bitter was Howard's break with Percy Greene, who argued that the RCNL should forgo desegregation in favor of voting rights as a priority. When Howard chastised the editor for his stand at a RCNL board meeting, Greene "became furious, cursed the Council, and stormed out." Both Howard and the RCNL became objects of scorn in the *Jackson Advocate*. According to one of Greene's editorials, leaders like Howard had "adopted one of the worst traits brought up from slavery by the Negroes[,] that of trying to condemn and belittle everyone else in order to appear 'big' themselves."[86]

Howard's change in course signaled a new spirit of cooperation with the NAACP, now led by his ally Emmett Stringer. He took out a lifetime membership and became chair of the state NAACP membership board. In addition, the RCNL and the NAACP joined forces to support Medgar Evers's application to the law school of the all-white University of Mississippi in January 1954. Evers made his decision at a RCNL meeting after Stringer stated that the time was ripe to desegregate 'Ole Miss. Thurgood Marshall, then the special counsel of the NAACP, provided legal advice on how to proceed. Before rejecting the application on a technicality, the 'Ole Miss administration dragged its feet for nine months. During this time, Evers continued his work with the Magnolia Mutual Life Insurance Company and the RCNL, but he had caught the eye of NAACP leaders, who selected him to be the association's director of the northwest area of the state.[87]

When the RCNL held its annual rally in Mound Bayou beginning on May 7, 1954, Howard outdid himself. Six school bands and a sixty-piece band from Tennessee A&I paraded down Main Street while Howard and Marshall waved to the crowd from a convertible. Local merchants ordered ten tons of meat to feed the crowd of eight thousand. Once again, Howard used the event as an opportunity to hold up models of black business and agricultural success. He presented before the crowd three blacks who had risen from "sharecroppers within a short period to that of landowners now possessing land estimated close to a million dollars." The RCNL's Committee on Voting and Registration held sessions on registration and reported on its survey of voting restrictions throughout the Delta. Some of the most memorable testimony involved Forrest County, where registrars "tested" blacks by asking them to estimate how many bubbles appeared on a bar of soap. Charles Evers, Medgar's brother, stated that he had learned all twenty amendments to the state constitution to anticipate possible questions.[88]

An added sense of anticipation filled the air at the 1954 conference. The U.S. Supreme Court's ruling in *Brown v. Board of Education* was only three weeks away. Marshall and Howard urged the crowd to contribute $10,000 for lawsuits against school segregation. Marshall also held a roundtable with Benjamin Hooks and other black southern attorneys in attendance to formulate possible litigation strategies.[89]

For Howard, there was no turning back now. During the coming months the press increasingly identified him as Mississippi's best-known "militant" and "radical." This characterization became even more apt in 1954 when, in a public conference, he challenged the governor to support the Supreme Court ruling. In taking this stand, Howard underestimated both the resilience of Jim Crow and the power of blacks, including himself, to resist pressure. A massive white crackdown against dissent and black voting was under way by the middle of the year. In 1955, the controversy around Howard heated up as never before when he helped to find witnesses in the Emmett Till case to testify against the two white men who were accused of killing him. Amidst death threats, Howard finally decided to leave the state a few months after the trial. From 1956 until his death in 1976 he established several clinics in Chicago, though he was largely forgotten as a national leader.[90]

Throughout Howard's career, his approach was that of a race man who was both pragmatic and radical. He consistently pushed an agenda of self-help, black business, and political equality whenever opportunities arose. Howard could be fearless in waging war against inequality and disfranchisement, but he was not a man to tilt at windmills. In the Mississippi Delta before 1953, separate but equal was the only game in town. Howard was prepared to play the game, but only under his own rules. When separate but equal finally seemed vulnerable in Mississippi, he was equally ready to push the hardest to topple the system.

Howard was also a complicated figure. It is clear that he had abundant talents as an entrepreneur, speaker, and organizer, and he showed unusual bravery despite many threats on his life. At the same time, Howard could also be his own worst enemy, and more than once he let his boundless ego get the best of him. He was a leader, not a follower, and this sometimes made it difficult for him to work well with other people. These flaws were minor, however, when compared to his impressive accomplishments and abilities.

Long before the *Brown* decision, the Montgomery Bus Boycott, and "Freedom Marchers," T. R. M. Howard, along with other local black leaders in the South, fought a lonely struggle for political equality. Especially in Mississippi, this work was instrumental in paving the way for the later civil rights victories of the 1950s and 1960s. Howard and his fellow activist pioneers, in turn, built their successes on an earlier foundation of black self-help, mutual aid, and business investment. It is difficult to imagine the rise of the modern civil rights movement without organizations such as the Knights and Daughters of Tabor and businesses such as the Magnolia Mutual Life Insurance Company.

3
"Blood on Your Hands"
White Southerners' Criticism of Eleanor Roosevelt during World War II
Pamela Tyler

THE SOUTHERN CATALOG of her offenses ran long. Critics said that she "volunteered to intermeddle with things which concern her not—to libel and vilify . . . to foment . . . unappeasable hatred . . . to sow the seeds of strife and violence." She engaged in "false coloring of southern society" and "miserable misrepresentation," and worst of all, she was "the mouthpiece of a large and dangerous faction."[1] She, of course, was Harriett Beecher Stowe; this heated indictment was written in 1852. Nine decades later, the South, again embattled and defensive, had identified another female nemesis. Her name was Eleanor Roosevelt, and in the view of much of the white South she represented a latter-day version of Mrs. Stowe—like Stowe, a meddlesome interloper determined to alter the cherished southern way of life—but because of her influential position as First Lady, she was infinitely more dangerous than a genteel lady novelist.

Admittedly, many white southerners admired the controversial First Lady. This essay, however, will focus on condemnation from the element of the white South that disapproved of Eleanor Roosevelt's words and actions. Her southern detractors increased in number and volume as the Roosevelt administration went on, and in the last three years of FDR's life they raised their voices in a crescendo of outrage that resounded across the nation. One source of their discomfort concerned her challenge to the gender conventions that governed everyday life in the South, while another and altogether more unsettling concern sprang from their conviction that Eleanor Roosevelt actively incited blacks to challenge southern racial mores.

During FDR's presidency, white southern liberals, inspired by the transformational promise of the New Deal, had begun to press for social, economic, and racial justice; African Americans inside the region and beyond joined the effort. The Southern Conference on Human Welfare, inaugurated in Birmingham in 1938, represented one flowering of biracial endeavor. Stark limitations circumscribed the vision of white liberals, however. With a staunch belief that enlightened native southerners working for reform could lead the South out of its backwardness, they viewed energetic, purposeful federal intervention as a tactical blunder that would hamper racial progress. Even so, they embraced both an anti-lynching bill and an anti–poll tax measure. Throughout the 1930s, Congress repeatedly considered the bills amid stormy rhetoric and marathon filibusters, and although they did not pass, the positive national attention they attracted contributed to a growing southern sense of alarm as the decade ended. Sensing that the stakes were higher, southern representatives had employed unprecedented, vicious race-baiting to defeat these reforms. Increasingly, a multifaceted sense of unease racked white southerners, who felt suspicion over the federal government's agenda on race, fear of the growing clout of the National Association for the Advancement of Colored People (NAACP), and alarm over the "meddling" with race relations by non-southerners, whom they labeled "outside agitators."[2]

The onset of World War II intensified their panic as the growth of union membership and of membership in the NAACP transformed black consciousness and fueled further efforts to democratize the southern political and economic system. The previously complacent belief in southern racial harmony seemed to evaporate. Creation of the Fair Employment Practices Commission (FEPC) in the summer of 1941 by means of an executive order (the first since 1875) meant that the federal government stood ready to address racial bias in hiring in defense industries and would henceforth be investigating claims and holding hearings into employment policies in southern war plants. The anti–poll tax campaign appeared to be making progress with passage of the Soldier Vote Bill in 1942, which suspended the poll tax for soldiers and provided equal access to the ballot for black troops from the South, thus bringing suffrage to a mostly voteless sector of the population. Supporters saw it as the first step toward complete repeal of the poll tax in federal elections. Although southern opposition was vigorous and, for the time being, successful, black activism continued to expand.

Racial friction grew by leaps and bounds in the South as black troops stationed in the region tested the Jim Crow statutes defiantly, making incidents on public vehicles an almost daily occurrence. When troops from the North refused to honor regional racial etiquette, "verbal abuse, shovings, slappings, and stabbings" resulted. The publication of Gunnar Myrdal's *An American Dilemma* in 1944 put the South under even greater scrutiny for its racial theories and practices. The Swedish author confidently predicted "a redefinition of the Negro's status as a result of this war," although, because so few southern newspapers deigned to review the book, it is not likely that many southerners knew of Myrdal's views. Also in that year, the U.S. Supreme Court added its weight to the momentum of change when it struck down the all-white primary in *Smith v. Allwright*. As historian Pete Daniel expressed, "southern whites had never before been assaulted on so many fronts of the color line."[3]

It was perhaps unavoidable that Eleanor Roosevelt would become a lightning rod for southern abuse. Needing a personification of the amorphous evil called "outside agitation," southerners found it in the tall, homely wife of the president. Many observers had noted something undeniably schoolmarmish about the First Lady, an unbending aura of starchy disapproval as she went about her humanitarian activities. Perhaps it was only her self-acknowledged inability to relax and have fun, or "the right kind of fun," as she put it. Tolerant, patient, understanding ER could also be the rigidly principled ER of fixed notions concerning what people should be and should do. To one of her biographers she was "more earnest, less devious, less patient, less fun, more uncompromisingly moral" than FDR, while another noted that she became "tired, disgruntled, cold and withdrawn" when faced with "opposition and imperfection." The evidence is overwhelming that the South was hypersensitive to criticism of any kind and prone to ostracize its critics. When contemplating conditions in the region that her husband famously called "the nation's number one economic problem" (he was silent on racism's contributory role to the poverty he deplored), Eleanor radiated her disapproval. She cared deeply about justice for women, workers, the poor, and especially racial minorities, and her words and deeds, conveyed in ways that made southerners feel "scolded," posed a threat to the southern way of life, a way of life that rested on the twin pillars of class-ridden patriarchy and white supremacy. The reactions of white southerners reveal the resentment the First Lady inspired in Dixie.[4]

During the 1932 campaign, ER's comments about young women and alcohol had created a frisson of controversy that resonated in the South, where prohibition remained an imperative for many. Southerner Virginia Durr conceded that, in the 1920s and 1930s, "there was a fast set that drank gin" but maintained that "nice girls" emphatically did not imbibe. Yet ER had advised that young women should learn "how to handle gin and whiskey in moderation." Disapproving southern clergymen pounced on the remark and kept their versions of her comments circulating well into Roosevelt's second term. One shocked individual wrote that his minister said Mrs. Roosevelt had said, "mothers . . . learn your daughters to drink," and remonstrated her with, "now I can't think you could use sutch [sic] language," while a North Carolina Bible class worried that she was "lead[ing] the youth of our land astray."[5]

Her views on the domestic responsibilities of husbands constituted a challenge to the accepted southern marital system, in which wives traditionally catered to their spouses. Describing with approval an evening with a young couple during which the husband donned an apron after dinner and washed the dishes, Mrs. Roosevelt advised, "When a marriage works out this way, it is very successful."[6] In her peripatetic conduct as "Eleanor Everywhere," the First Lady abandoned the customary model of devoted helpmate creating a refuge in the home for her work-weary spouse. Traveling twenty thousand miles (frequently by air, when flight was still seen as risky business) in her husband's first year in office, without company of husband, son, or other male protector, she gave a display of "emancipated womanhood" that discomfited many in the South, as did her frequent statements to the press. Shortly into FDR's first term, Harold Ickes grumbled in his diary about Mrs. Roosevelt: "She is becoming altogether too active in public affairs and I think she is harmful rather than helpful. After all, the people did not elect her president."[7]

Many southerners shared these sentiments. By the 1936 presidential campaign there were stirrings of resentment against the First Lady among southern voters, reflecting uneasiness about her public role and the extent of her influence upon the president. A joke printed in the Greenville, South Carolina, press in 1936 alluded to that uneasiness. In the story, a speaker who praised Franklin Roosevelt was interrupted by a shout from the audience: "I don't like him!" The speaker patiently resumed his pro-FDR talk, only to be interrupted again by the same shout, now louder. Attempting to soothe, the speaker said, "He depends upon a higher power for guidance," to which the shouter responded, "And I don't like her, either!"[8]

While this is gentle, inoffensive humor, Eleanor Roosevelt's increasing public association on familiar terms with African Americans excited southern criticism of her that was pointed and resentful. Initially, southerners had not perceived the First Lady as a threat to the racial status quo in their region. Her early efforts at getting better facilities for African Americans did nothing to challenge the tenets of segregation and were in fact consonant with many white southerners' desire for some amelioration of the deprivation afflicting southern blacks. For example, through her initiative, the Eleanor Roosevelt Vocational School for Colored Youth was built at Warm Springs, Georgia. At the dedication ceremony, Georgia's superintendent of schools praised her warmly, calling her "the greatest woman, not of the year, nor of the decade, but of the century."[9] But during the 1930s, she also addressed a Washington conference on Negro education, spoke to the twenty-fifth-anniversary gathering of the Urban League, lunched on the White House patio with NAACP head Walter White, entertained the Hampton Institute choir at tea, and smilingly posed for frequent photographs with African Americans. Documentary evidence certified her racial egalitarianism; cameras and press reports recorded the First Lady's easy familiarity with black Americans. The countless ways in which she mingled with people of color made her casual attitude toward racial distinctions obvious. A widely circulated bit of doggerel attacked that attitude:

What That Man Said to "That Woman":
You kiss the niggers, I'll kiss the Jews,
We'll stay in office as long as we choose.[10]

By Roosevelt's 1936 campaign, observer Ralph Bunche detected a drumbeat of discontent with Eleanor pounding in the South. A newspaper in Virginia reported disapprovingly that she had used the word "equality" twelve times in a 1936 speech to black welfare workers and noted, in disgust, that a news photograph depicted her sitting beside a black woman "so near together that their bodies touched." An Atlanta-based right-wing organization, the Women's National Association for the Preservation of the White Race, published a newsletter in which photographs of ER, escorted by a military honor guard at Howard University and receiving flowers from a black child, were prominent. By the mid-1930s the public was aware of her support for federal anti-lynching legislation and poll tax repeal, measures that would drastically alter the racial status quo in the South.[11]

More murmurs arose in the wake of her much-publicized seating choice at the 1938 meeting of the pathbreaking interracial Southern Conference for Human Welfare in Birmingham, where she rejected the southern mores on segregated accommodations. The widely reported

Marian Anderson controversy in the spring of 1939 again inflamed southern feelings. When the Daughters of the American Revolution refused to allow the black contralto to perform a concert in their hall in Washington, the First Lady resigned her membership, expressing her "complete disagreement" with their segregation policy. Though she never mentioned the group by name, she alluded to the matter in her syndicated column, noting forthrightly, "They have taken an action which has been widely talked on in the press. To remain as a member implies approval of that action, therefore I am resigning."[12]

George Gallup found that nationally only 33 percent of respondents disapproved of the First Lady's resignation. However, in the South the disapproval figure was 57 percent.[13] One angry southern woman wrote to the president that Mrs. Roosevelt's resignation "in favor of a black woman" would "shock" the founding fathers and was "a slap in the face of our women."[14]

By decade's end, observers viewed Eleanor Roosevelt as champion of the African American population, a fact that produced snide criticism from some disapproving white southerners. Most southerners nonetheless expressed a complacent confidence that African Americans were "satisfied down here." In 1940, Senator Pat Harrison told an interviewer, "Right now, so far as the people of my state [Mississippi] are concerned, if the . . . agitators and reformers don't come in and try to cause trouble, there is mighty little to fear of the Negro."[15]

But even as Harrison dismissed the possibility of change, drastic change was brewing. From the crucible of World War II a changed black population began to emerge, men and women with a growing sense of entitlement and of their own efficacy. University of North Carolina sociologist Howard Odum wrote that by 1943 "it was as if some universal message had come through to the great mass of Negroes urging them to dream new dreams and to protest against the old order." In particular, the war transformed black servicemen. Seventy-seven percent of black enlisted men served overseas during World War II, where, despite their contributions, they experienced discriminatory treatment. Their experiences helped them to develop "a special moral claim to fairness and justice." Black civilians changed too; labor shortages on the home front meant that cooks, day laborers, laundresses, domestic servants, and field hands at last had some bargaining power to use with southern employers.[16]

African American economic gains during these years led to an accompanying surge in assertiveness in the black community that alarmed southern whites. Many sought the catalyst for the situation not in indigenous efforts among blacks themselves but rather in "the new abolitionists," namely, Socialists, Communists, the CIO, New Dealers, and, in particular, Eleanor Roosevelt. Rather than attribute agency to African Americans, it became easier to them to seek "outside agitators" who kept the pot boiling in Dixie. A government report about conditions in the South during the war noted keen displeasure with Eleanor Roosevelt among southern planters and farmers. "Employers of farm labor complain that . . . Negroes are becoming too independent. . . . Many employers . . . pay a higher price than they planned to pay," it stated. "Mrs. Roosevelt is mentioned often as being dangerous because . . . she fraternizes too much with Negroes, and she is making them want social equality." An Arkansas farmer wrote to the First Lady to complain: "The negros are refusing to work on the farms and in the houses. . . . We of the south believe that you are using your high position to stir up racial trouble." One influential Mississippi planter whom Arthur Raper interviewed in 1943 angrily branded ER as "the worst of all." He said he literally could not voice to Raper what he thought of her in the constraining presence of his wife and daughter.[17]

By the first year of the war, the American South was awash in rumors and fantasies, conjured up out of whites' dread of racial change and fed by a pervasive sense of instability bred by wartime. White southerners expressed alarm at the thought of the South denuded of white men through the draft, leaving white women helpless before predatory black males. They also worried about the effects of numbers of black men in military service, believing that they constituted a menace because of aggressive attitudes, sense of entitlement, and weapons training. Reports of blacks "plotting against the whites" increased; rumors of arsenals and massacres swirled as apprehensive folks in Dixie whispered to each other about a reported increase in sales of ice picks and knives.[18]

By far the most durable of the wartime rumors concerned the Eleanor Clubs. Immediately preceding World War II, 72 percent of all employed African American women in the South had worked as domestic servants, but the war brought southern black women a range of employment opportunities. The resulting shortage of domestic workers caught the white South by surprise, and the grumbling began. Rapidly, the grumbling transformed itself into a conspiratorial worldview: black women, inspired directly by Eleanor Roosevelt, had become militant and were rebelling, with her active encouragement, against the "southern way of life." Allegedly, their motto was "a white woman in every kitchen by Christmas." Rumored rules of the club included demands that maids be addressed as "Mrs." or "Miss" and a requirement that they come in the front doors of houses where they worked. Horrified whites told each other that, as part of their Eleanor Club initiation, maids were required to commit an act of interracial intimacy, such as dining with their white employers or bathing in their bathtubs.[19]

Historian Bryant Simon has noted the irony of white southerners who feared pitched public battles with ice-pick-toting insurrectionists, while "in the same breath . . . they also fretted about private rebellions . . . [in which black female servants] would rise up against their employers, not on distant streets, but right there in white bedrooms, kitchens, and dining rooms."[20] The shift in traditional labor relations posed a threat to traditional white supremacy, and certainly the near impossibility of securing cooks and maids at the usual low rates of pay came as an unpleasant shock to southern white women. Some pragmatists realized that economic opportunity explained the dearth of domestic servants. Wrote one white woman, "Of course they [black domestic servants] are taking advantage of the situation as all humans would do and do under the circumstances." But others stoutly maintained their belief in Eleanor Clubs (also known as Daughters of Eleanor, Sisters of Eleanor, or the Royal House of Eleanor) and a conviction that the First Lady was behind the labor shortage. Frank Daniels, editor of the *Raleigh News and Observer,* wrote his brother Jonathan, an aide to FDR, "I know you are in with all the pinkeys and liberals tied up with advancement for the Negro race. The situation here in Raleigh regarding the feeling of the white people . . . is really alarming. . . . People are . . . all upset about the Eleanor Clubs which, as you know, have as their aim putting every white woman in her own kitchen by Christmas. . . . [T]he white women just aren't going to stand for it." (He was notably silent, however, on just what white women might do.) A few weeks later he wrote again to suggest indignantly that Mrs. Roosevelt "ought to be kept at home and made to shut her mouth about the race question."[21]

Reported one observer: "In women's groups in the highest brackets of southern society . . . when it came to a discussion of the Negro and Mrs. Roosevelt, the most sordid rumors were repeated and laughed at with no thought of its reflecting upon [the South]." A southern journalist wrote: "I have heard from white people a hundred of these snide and merciless Eleanor stories on visits to the South during the past year and a half. . . . Honorable men and women, who in their personal lives are true to the rules of decency and character, spread slanderous jokes and lies about her with icy malice."[22]

The sordid and malicious nature of the Eleanor jokes circulating in the South shocked outside observers. The jokes' punch lines often fell at the highly charged intersection of sex and race. The nature of FDR's handicap led to speculation about his supposed impotence; the unorthodox contours of the Roosevelt marital arrangement fueled more speculation; ER's public association with African Americans, coupled with long-standing southern beliefs about the sexual appetites of black men, capped it all.

Eleanor Roosevelt was powerless to silence the snickering that emanated from southern homes and clubs, but she did address the issue of Eleanor Clubs. At a press conference in September 1942 she stated that they existed "only in the minds of the rumor-mongers," but her denial did nothing to quiet the conspiracy-minded. FBI director J. Edgar Hoover tried to confirm the ubiquitous rumor, assigning agents in all southern cities to pursue the investigation, to no avail. "Numerous complaints and reports of the existence of these groups failed to indicate any substantial basis for them," noted a 1943 FBI report. "In no instance have inquiries into the alleged existence of 'Eleanor Clubs' resulted in anything specific."[23] Ultimately the FBI failed to document the existence of even one Eleanor Club anywhere in the South. One southern white woman commented realistically, "It's hard for the housewives who lose their Negro servants to believe that the reason can be merely the higher wages offered by war industry. Surely housewives often think there must be some sinister organization making dear old faithful Annie act that way!"[24]

The FBI's failure to establish the reality of the Eleanor Clubs did not diminish white southerners' steadfast belief in their existence. "The FBI could uncover a Nazi spy more easily than they could these clubs," explained a Georgia housewife, "for among themselves Negroes are very loyal and so completely secretive as to their inner workings." An Alabama woman wrote to President Roosevelt: "In regard to the Negro problem they are getting so impudent insulting & attacking even white folk.... [They] just can't and will not stay in their place ... forming Eleanor Clubs all thru South[,] servants of 20 yrs service coming in at 9 A.M. and gloating over their activities."[25] The specter of black women out of "their place" and "gloating" about it left white defenders of the Jim Crow regime aghast and seeking a scapegoat.

Unwilling to accept that blacks had real grievances, white southerners targeted Eleanor Roosevelt. "You have ruined the niggers," one critic charged. "They weren't race conscious until you started hobnobbing with them."[26] Even well-bred southern women expressed themselves in extreme and mean-spirited language. Tom Sancton, a southern-born journalist writing for the *New Republic,* revealed his pain in hearing such comments from his mother and her friends in New Orleans in 1943:

> In conversation among prosperous white people, even on the steps of fashionable churches after the sermon is over, one hears a most callous and un-Christlike kind of talk. Much of it concerns the difficulty of finding Negro maids. "We will never be able to get good maids again until the government stops paying their husbands those ridiculous salaries." The hearts of the kindest and gentlest of southern women seem steeled against the Negro and anything affecting his wellbeing. In rare instances one will hear a still, small voice speak up like the voice of conscience. "Well, I think the Negroes ought to get more money; they certainly don't have a thing in the world now." But a chorus of resentment drowns out such a remark and someone is bound to add, like a line in a stage play, "*You* must belong to an Eleanor Club, my dear."[27]

Jessie Daniel Ames carried out a study of southern black women in domestic work in the 1930s, which confirmed the extent of their exploitation and shocked Ames in revealing the indignant and callous attitudes of white women. Ames encountered less anger and opposition among white women for her anti-lynching stance than for her advocacy of better wages for maids and cooks. "Ye Gods," she remembered, "oh, they were indignant, and they wouldn't do their own cooking. . . . The women could take all of this other, but this matter of what they paid the cooks was their own business. And I was just interfering, giving them ideas."[28]

Southerners saw that Eleanor Roosevelt was frequently photographed with African Americans and knew that she readily accepted invitations to speak to national meetings of black organizations. The whole South soon teemed with Eleanor stories that stressed her ostentatious interracial social intimacy. According to rumors, she had registered at a hotel in a small southern town and demanded accommodations for four black women traveling with her. She had spurned a dinner prepared by "the nice white people" of Tuskegee to go off to a "colored" banquet in the company of "a big black Negro." An FBI report recorded a tale that she had driven off "in an huff" when navy officials had refused to sanction a delegation from Hampton Institute to accompany her during a ship christening at Newport News. The stories, obviously calculated to reflect on Mrs. Roosevelt's discretion and good judgment, caused the president's staff headaches as they tried to refute them. When FDR's press secretary contacted ER's secretary, Malvina Thompson, about one of the tales, she replied in exasperation, "Of course the story about Mrs. Roosevelt going to *any* hotel *anywhere* and demanding accommodations for four Negro women is just plain bunk. She certainly knows this country too well and has too much sense to even think of doing anything like that."[29]

Southern white supremacists, however, did not agree that she had "too much sense" to undermine the racial order in their region; instead, they saw her as a meddling racial liberal bent on demolishing all racial distinctions. Given the opportunity to dispense a snub, some responded with a solid phalanx of ostracism. For example, when Eleanor Roosevelt accepted an invitation to travel to Salisbury, North Carolina, in 1942 to address a convention of the African Methodist Episcopal Church, her black hosts attempted to find a white home in which she could stay, but they were unable to do so because, as one observer remembered, "no 'nice' home would receive her." Thus spurned, the First Lady stayed in the town's hotel. Frank Daniels wrote to his brother, "Quite frankly, people in North Carolina did not want her to even come to the state," and added with feeling, "it makes me sick for people to push for Negro equality."[30]

In the spring of 1943, a Florida newspaperman confided to FDR's press secretary, fellow southerner Steve Early, that "Mrs. Roosevelt grows more unpopular every month. The people in this part of the country think she is too arrogant, too officious, and too busy sticking her nose in too many other people's business. And they just plain don't like it! Her pestiferous activities are hurting the President, Steve. . . . Eleanor should have her tongue tied for the duration, and ever after."[31]

In the summer of 1943, black-white tensions in Detroit transformed the city into a cauldron of racial mayhem, requiring the intervention of federal troops to restore order. Thirty-four people died in the chaos, and all but nine were black. As a stunned nation asked itself why, a Mississippi editor lost no time in providing his answer. "It is blood on your hands, Mrs. Eleanor Roosevelt," he thundered. "More than any other person you are morally responsible for those race riots in Detroit. . . . You have been personally proclaiming and practicing social equality at the White House and wherever you go."[32] A Texan confided to J. Edgar Hoover, "If you are looking for the cause of the race riots, you can find it in the White House, Mrs. *Eleanor Roosevelt.*" He pleaded, "Can't the F.B.I. *shut* her up?"[33]

In the wake of the Detroit riots, reactionary elements in the South lashed out more freely at the First Lady as a tangible symbol of all that they hated and feared. Senator Theodore Bilbo of Mississippi, who referred to her as "old lady Roosevelt" when addressing his constituents at home, repeatedly introduced his repatriation bill to send blacks to Africa, and in 1944 he sneered, on the floor of Congress, that Mrs. Roosevelt should be sent with them and made their "queen." This comment brought him predictable hate mail from correspondents of both races and sexes who detested his crude racism, but he also received floods of approbation. The majority of white women who wrote to applaud Senator Bilbo were transplanted southerners then experiencing the wartime frictions of overcrowded transportation, housing, and recreation facilities in northern and western locales. In hyperbolic terms that revealed the sexual subtext underlying so much of southern racism, they deplored the trend toward "social equality" and denounced the "mongrelization" of the white race, penning their horrors while contemplating black men as sexual predators. Because ER had conspicuously promoted greater social intimacy with African Americans and refused to acknowledge a color bar as legitimate, these letters frequently denounced her.[34]

In February 1944 the Associated Press reported Mrs. Roosevelt's presence at the opening in Washington, D.C., of a CIO–sponsored servicemen's canteen that "invites both white and Negro servicemen and has both white and Negro hostesses." News that she had joined in the singing of songs such as "Waltzing Matilda" and "Let Me Call You Sweetheart" sparked paroxysms of outrage among white southerners, who flooded the First Lady with responses. Some were angry, others stunned and incredulous that she had lent her sanction to this violation of the most basic taboo, the one against interracial intimacy. Enclosing the "heartbreaking" clipping "which hurt me very deeply," a Tennessee woman wrote to "ask . . . if this is true." Though stating that she had "defended your work among the negroes," another woman said, "your recent endorsement of the U.S.O. [*sic*] incident in Washington is going too far and is most offensive to true Southerners." Signing herself "An Outraged Woman," a correspondent demanded, "Do you realize how dangerous to racial purity is the stand you have taken?" She foresaw "intermarriage and subsequent flooding the nation with mulattoes." An angry southern girl defiantly denounced the president's wife and predicted white backlash when the troops returned from overseas:

I know you are a Negro lover. . . . I think it is mighty sorry in you to even ask us girls to dance with those negros. The blame negro's have gotten to where they think we white people should work for them. . . . I also saw your picture in the middle of negro men & women, that goes to show how sorry you are. May I be permitted to say this, when our soldier boys return home the negro's will get the daylights knocked out of them if ever they talk back to even one boy. (We can always bet on our boys.)[35]

Other correspondents, also aghast at what they read of ER's activities, directed their concerns to the president. Frequently enclosing clippings about the offensive behavior, they implored FDR to rein in his wife. "How could the first lady of the United States condone such an unsavory thing?" "I want you to check the fifth column activities of Eleanor Roosevelt." "Would you please suggest that Mrs. Roosevelt confine her duties more to the White House."[36]

Many white southerners, material beneficiaries of New Deal reforms, began to worry that the practical political consequences of ER's racial liberalism would be to deny a fourth term to a president whose popularity remained high in the South. "Folks are for Roosevelt in Alabama but not for Mrs. R. Her too friendly attitude on the rights of Negroes is not only disgusting but is an affront to Alabama folks, women especially," wrote a southern constituent to his senator. Another Alabamian attempted to warn the president of the consequences of his wife's behavior: "Now my husband & I love you & believe you have done more than *any* president for our country. . . . Some people hate you & your wife (as they express it like they would a rattlesnake) & if you are defeated, the stand you have taken & activities of your wife, her magazine articles in their [African Americans'] behalf, will be the *sole* reason the South is not with you." A worried Mississippian wrote that Republican candidate Thomas Dewey's campaign was spreading stories in his state of ER's efforts to "equalize the colored with the whites," a matter he hoped his president would address "for your benefit, and mine *as a working man.*" Others in Dixie took up the pen to announce that their political allegiance to FDR had evaporated: "I have been a Democrat all my life," one wrote, "but I am frank to say that your and Mrs. Roosevelt's 'nigger' activities . . . have set me wholeheartedly against you and your administration and any efforts you may make to secure a fourth term."[37]

An examination of Eleanor Roosevelt's exact words on race reveals a benign friendliness toward African Americans, characterized by moderation and circumspection. She certainly expressed a more overt racial liberalism than did the president, but she could hardly be called a firebrand. In 1943 she wrote a curious article for the *Negro Digest*. Counseling patience in a well-meaning but patronizing tone, she warned placidly, "If I were a Negro, I would not do too much demanding," adding, "I would try to remember that unfair and unkind treatment will not harm me if I do not let it touch my spirit." On more than one occasion she bowed to localism, stating that no one from New York had the right to come into the South and tell southerners what to do about race. Mindful of the southern assumption that any change in the status quo would lead to "social equality," she commented soothingly, "We cannot force people to accept friends for whom they have no liking." She wrote to a white southerner that she had "never advocated social equality or intermarriage."[38] Comments like these provoked emphatic agreement among nearly all white southerners.

However, it could not be denied that the First Lady flouted the deepest traditions of southern racial etiquette. She *routinely* advocated four basic rights for every citizen: "equality before the law; equality of education; equality to hold a job according to his ability; equality of participation through the ballot in the government." She *routinely* attributed to African Americans positive traits that white southerners absolutely denied. "Because the south has created a picture, a charming one of mammys, old-fashioned butlers and gardeners and day laborers, we must not believe that that is the whole picture. They have rarely shown us the picture of the intellectual or of the soldier or of the inventor ... but they do exist," she asserted. She *routinely* paid tribute to black leaders "whom I know and admire and respect," lifting them by her choice of words to a level that white southerners rejected as utterly inappropriate.[39]

Southern conservatives found most threatening of all the fact that she *routinely* rejected the elemental racial taboo against interracial contact without hierarchical protocols. She mentioned her "really close friendship" with Mary McLeod Bethune; noted that Walter White called her "Eleanor"; revealed that she "always" kissed Edith Sampson; observed that she found A. Philip Randolph "charming and nice looking"; and wrote happily of "seeing Negro guests at my table."[40] Gunnar Myrdal's research indicates that white southerners almost unanimously rated barriers against interracial marriage and interracial social relations as their paramount concerns. Myrdal posited a "white man's rank order of discrimination" in which he showed that intermarriage and interracial sexual relations offended white southerners most of all, followed closely by behaviors such as "dancing, bathing, eating, drinking together . . . handshaking, hat lifting, use of titles, house entrance to be used, social forms when meeting on streets and in work."[41] Lillian Smith remembered that she "knew by the time I was twelve that no 'well-bred' southerner would call a Negro 'mister' or invite him into the living room or sit by him in public places." Her education into southern mores also taught her that it was possible to be "a gentlewoman and an arrogant callous creature in the same moment."[42]

When Eleanor Roosevelt wrote, "We must keep moving forward steadily, removing *restrictions which have no sense,* and fighting prejudice,"[43] most Americans might have read those words as an innocuous platitude supporting progress and general reform. The white South, however, heard a clarion call to topple the southern way of life. How it shocked them to learn that, in Mrs. Roosevelt's judgment, the most important restrictions in their world had "no sense." This highly influential woman, the well-known, much-quoted wife of the president, denied the legitimacy of the entire southern racial system. Accordingly, she became notorious across the South as a proponent of racial equality, a symbol of outside interference, and a thoroughly dangerous woman.

The spectacle of an intelligent woman of high status deliberately seeking the company of African Americans and interacting with them pleasantly on terms of social equality so jarred white southerners that some reached an extreme conclusion: Eleanor Roosevelt was not entirely white herself. "I don't mean to be rude," inquired an Alabama woman, "but do you have colored blood in your family, as you seem to derive so much pleasure from associating with colored folks?" The First Lady responded that she knew of no black ancestry. But, she added, she would not attempt to deter her children from marrying African American partners.[44]

The First Lady's jolting public stance on race relations came at a juncture when African Americans really were behaving differently. Improved job opportunities meant a previously unknown degree of freedom from subservience. Many refused to perform manual labor at all, while those who did so could demand better wages for their services. More money bought better wardrobes; stylish new clothes worn with a confident carriage clashed with the old image of deferential underlings dressed in tatters and castoffs. Black servicemen stationed in the South frequently defied Jim Crow traditions and engaged in provocative behaviors such as throwing the seating screens off streetcars and buses, demanding service in public establishments, refusing to give way to whites on sidewalks, and blowing kisses to white girls. To white southerners, it must have seemed as if the world was lurching precariously off its axis.[45]

Washington abetted this tectonic shift. The president announced that FEPC nondiscriminatory clauses were mandatory for all government contracts. One house of Congress passed an anti–poll tax measure while the other staved off its passage only by a strenuous filibuster. The U.S. Supreme Court eviscerated the all-white primary in *Smith v. Allwright.* The Soldier Vote Bill enabled servicemen, including southern black men, to cast absentee ballots. Registering the seismic nature of the changes, semi-skilled, non-union white workers in the South could only look forward with apprehension to a dismal tomorrow of competing for jobs with black workers, a situation they foresaw as driving down wages for all and leading inevitably to a dark future of "used cars, secondhand appliances, and worn-down neighborhoods." Black ballots would ultimately mean black officeholders, or, as a Tennessee clerk of elections put it, "some big black son-of-a-bitch sitting up in the courthouse sending white men to jail." When the potential horrors of black economic and political empowerment placed their way of life under attack on multiple fronts, embattled white southerners adopted a siege mentality.[46]

How strongly did white southerners believe in "the southern way of life"? An almost all-white electorate elected and reelected political leaders like "Cotton Ed" Smith, Eugene Talmadge, and Theodore Bilbo, who flaunted rather than camouflaged their vitriolic racism. When a black clergyman rose to deliver the invocation at the 1936 Democratic National Convention, an incensed Smith had stormed out, raging, "By God, he's black as melted midnight!" "We in the South love the Negro in his place," Talmadge bellowed during his 1942 campaign, "but his place is at the back door!" Campaigning in Mississippi, Bilbo told an appreciative audience, "I am a real friend of the Negro—I am making arrangements to send every damn one back to Africa." "I am willing to take the negro as a Christian brother," Bilbo said, "but damned if I can take him as a son-in-law." Moderate opponents deplored the Talmadges and the Bilbos, but they too were no less committed to segregation; they merely used a less toxic rhetoric to defend the southern way of life. Said Ellis Arnall, the moderates' candidate against Talmadge in 1942, "Why if a Negro ever tried to get in a white school in the section where I live, the sun would not set on his head." Four years later, his successor as moderate standard-bearer pledged sternly, "I will never permit the mixing of the races in Georgia . . . in any . . . manner which violates our southern traditions."[47]

Average white southerners accepted these views. They frequently wrote to Franklin and Eleanor Roosevelt to try to explain the realities of race relations and of the "natural" traits of African Americans. "The race is like a mule[; it] can't stand good treatment & behave," wrote an Alabama woman. Repeatedly, correspondents fell back on a refrain which insisted that "outsiders" could never understand the race problem in their region. A Texas attorney wrote to the president, "People of the North and East cannot possibly appreciate it. The only way to know the Negro problem in the South is to live in the area." Alleging that "many of them are not two jumps ahead of an ape," he blamed the First Lady for inspiring blacks to demand rights. "The efforts of Mrs. Roosevelt to help them are being greatly misinterpreted by the Negroes and it is causing them to become belligerent and extremely bad mannered." "If you had lived among them 68 years as I have you could understand how we of the South feel & no power on earth can change us," wrote another. "Have you ever lived in the South among the Negroes?" demanded a Texas woman. "We do not mistreat the Negro down here but we know we have to keep them in their place else they will rule us."[48]

A southern racist reaction against the rising aspirations of African Americans and their allies was predictable. Perhaps more noteworthy is the response of the small coterie of southern intellectuals and writers. These elite southern liberals registered a consensus that segregation must be maintained, that "outside interference" was detrimental, and that the South alone could and should handle the problems of racial relations there. Mark Ethridge, liberal publisher of the *Louisville Courier-Journal* and chair of the FEPC, stated in June 1942 that "there is no power in the world—not even in all the mechanized armies of the earth, Allied and Axis—which could now force the southern white people to the abandonment of the principle of social segregation." John Temple Graves, Virginius Dabney, and David Cohn all published dire warnings about the gravity of the racial situation in the South, and *all* identified Eleanor Roosevelt as a major instigator of unreasonable, ill-considered, provocative demands among blacks.[49]

What *black* southerners felt about ER was the other side of the coin. Increasingly, they read the African American newspapers printed in Chicago, Pittsburgh, and other northern cities and saw her lauded warmly for her racial egalitarianism. The *Chicago Defender,* for example, printed a full-page color illustration of the First Lady, captioning her "above rebuke of partisan lip." Crediting her with creating a new spirit and reshaping civilization, the copy trumpeted: "Ecclesiastes complained, 'But a Woman I have not Found.' Not so with you and the times, FOR HERE IS ELEANOR ROOSEVELT!"[50] After a conference of black intellectuals and writers met in Durham, North Carolina, to consider postwar race relations, the University of North Carolina Press in 1944 published their ideas as *What the Negro Wants*, a book of fourteen essays. Several contributors mentioned Eleanor Roosevelt in highly positive terms. A. Philip Randolph deplored "the vile and vicious attacks upon the First Lady, by die-hard Tories," while Doxey Wilkerson praised her for her bold efforts toward "the further liberation of our people." Rayford Logan noted with approval that she refused to condemn interracial marriage; Roy Wilkins noted that southern whites "bemoaned" her inspiring southern blacks to demand change. Sterling Brown highlighted her "genuine and gracious democracy" which had made her the target for southern abuse. The courage she displayed taking sides in controversies in which race was paramount won her the anonymous affection and respect of countless black men and women all across the Jim Crow South.[51]

As tensions mounted, white southerners made dire predictions of a coming racial Armageddon of horrific proportions, a war after the war, and they routinely laid responsibility for this apocalyptic eventuality at Eleanor Roosevelt's door. An FBI report from Birmingham, Alabama, revealed that a local businessman had said that "the Negro situation in the South is on the lips of every business man in this section . . . and that if someone did not take action concerning the activities of Mrs. ROOSEVELT our union would be disrupted." Birmingham journalist John Temple Graves wrote to Senator Lister Hill, "You can't imagine the talk that's going the rounds here now on the Negro question, the prominent people who are saying we are all going to have to get our guns out again." A young woman urged the First Lady to "get among the white people here [Alabama] and listen what they are talking about." The wife of an overseas serviceman, she implored ER to cease her activities on behalf of minorities lest they provoke the returning veterans to "kill every negro in the south . . . if these negros are not put back in there [sic] places." Accusing the First Lady of being "utterly—yes woefully—ignorant of the Negro problem," a Mississippi businessman warned that "if meddling continues (and it will) we will sooner or later have a race war—and the whole thing will be solved—for all of the 'minority' will be killed." He added pointedly, "and the 'crusaders' will be out of work." Enclosing a news story of the rape of a white soldier's wife to which a black suspect had confessed, another warned her bluntly: "Believe me you are playing with fire."[52]

Apocalyptic predictions, howls of outrage, denunciations of the First Lady—all were heard in amplitude in the American South of the World War II era. By that time, the once-insecure and shy Eleanor Roosevelt was conducting herself with confidence and autonomy. Travels, lectures, newspaper columns, and radio broadcasts gave her an unprecedented degree of exposure and publicity which many southern men and women deplored as unladylike and unbecoming. In the 1940s, former president Jimmy Carter's father baited his outspoken wife, Lillian, when he felt she was behaving too independently by saying pointedly, "All right, *Eleanor.*" It was not meant to be a compliment. Lillian Carter recalled that her husband hated to see Eleanor Roosevelt's picture in the papers and usually made an unkind remark about her.[53] During the war, Frank Daniels sent a blunt request to his brother in the White House: "Tell Papa to keep Mama at home."[54] Three decades after the war, the television character Archie Bunker spoke words that expressed the feelings of many white southerners. Quarreling with his liberal feminist antagonist Maude, Archie blustered, "Let me tell you one thing about my President, Richard E. [sic] Nixon: he knows how to keep his wife, Pat, at home. Roosevelt could never do that with Eleanor, she was always on the loose, running around with the coloreds, telling them that they was getting the short end of the stick. She was the one who discovered the coloreds in this country. We never knew they was there."[55]

To anyone whose idea of order required submissive women in domestic settings, the First Lady's frequent public comings and goings were an affront, as were her seemingly endless public comments on all concerns of the day. To many, the world seemed upside down. Girls in coveralls wielded rivet guns and acetylene torches; decorous courtships of usual duration were abandoned for speeded-up wartime romances; morals and manners no longer emphasized the desirability of "sugar and spice and everything nice." Many traditionally minded southerners saw Eleanor Roosevelt as a powerful catalyst bringing unwanted change in the realm of gender expectations because, by her conduct, she demonstrated rejection of their idea of "ladylike" behavior.[56]

Much more alarming to the traditional South, the First Lady spoke out consistently and eloquently about the American dilemma of race. Time and again she rejected the white southern formula for racial harmony. As she explained patiently to a southern critic, "I am not letting my ideals, as you call them, blind me to the facts. I am afraid that many people are letting their prejudices blind them to the real facts," adding firmly, "The colored people in the South . . . have never been given their rights as citizens of the United States." Gently but insistently, she directed attention to the glaring gap between creed and deed in American race relations. In so doing, she offended and infuriated many white southerners. One of them wrote to J. Edgar Hoover that he, "like all true Southerners," resented "Mrs. Roosevelt's persistent and seemingly determined efforts to choke the Negro race down our throats."[57]

During the war, a southern-born journalist labeled Eleanor Roosevelt "the most hated symbol the middle-class white South has had since Harriett Beecher Stowe."[58] Rejecting her message, white southerners went a step further and demonized the messenger. Defensive and infuriated, the morally isolated South was stumbling through a reenactment of a drama in the mid–twentieth century that it had played out in the mid–nineteenth century as well. The "hated symbol" did not live to see the curtain rung down, but by the time she died in 1962 she surely knew how the play would end, and so did the South. Her efforts at shaping the script had earned her nothing but vitriolic reviews from agitated southern critics. Their rage against Eleanor Roosevelt, whom they saw as a "meddler" bent on destroying their way of life, metastasized to truly enormous proportions during World War II.

4
"City Mothers"
Dorothy Tilly, Georgia Methodist Women, and Black Civil Rights
Andrew M. Manis

SOMETIME IN THE 1950s, an editor of a large southern newspaper advised a group of college students, "If you do not know what social action to take, watch the Methodist women, and where they lead, follow."[1] Similar instructions were issued in 1982 when John Patrick McDowell pointed historians toward Methodist women if they wanted to see evidence of the Social Gospel in the American South.[2] Both the editor and the scholar were correct in isolating the women of the Methodist Church as the vanguard of southern white church people's efforts to sow seeds of racial change in the pre–civil rights era. More specifically, what in this essay begins as a survey of Methodist attitudes and actions related to race and civil rights will move to a more individualized argument—that the work of Atlanta laywoman Dorothy Tilly and the Methodist women she led embodied white Protestant work to foster better race relations based on racial justice. This telling focuses on Tilly's activities both within and outside the Methodist Church, highlighting her role in leading Georgia Methodist women to work for racial justice in America.

Dorothy Rogers Tilly was born in Hampton, Georgia, in 1883, the daughter of Methodist minister Richard Wade Rogers. A lifelong Methodist, Dorothy served as president of a youth missions organization when she was twelve years old. She graduated from Georgia Methodist schools, from Reinhardt (Junior) College, and in 1901 from Macon's Wesleyan College, where her mother was also an alumna. Two years later she married a University of Georgia graduate, Milton Eben Tilly, who became a successful chemical distributor in Atlanta. The couple lived there for the rest of their lives, attending Haygood Memorial Methodist Church and investing themselves in race-relations work through various Methodist organizations. By the time of her death in 1970, Dorothy had been honored with Wesleyan College's Distinguished Achievement Award and named "the outstanding Methodist woman of the first quarter century" by the Methodist Church's Women's Society for Christian Service of the Southeast Jurisdiction Church. Extending her efforts beyond her denomination, Tilly had also become a friend of Eleanor Roosevelt's, a member of President Truman's Committee on Civil Rights, and one of the most influential women in the South.[3]

Tilly's influence was built upon, but grew far beyond, her Methodist activities—to politics, to interracial dialogue, and to what she considered a religious calling to help Methodist and other Christian women monitor racial justice in local legal systems throughout Georgia and the South. This race-relations "mission" came to be expressed most vigorously in the Fellowship of the Concerned (FOC), which she founded in 1949. By her own testimony, Tilly compared this "calling" to the ministerial call that brought black Methodist missionary John Stewart into Christian service. As Stewart had received a "calling [that] gave no rest," so had the women of the FOC answered "calling voices that would not be stilled: voices calling, 'Let the people know what is happening in the courts.'" Until the FOC died in 1970, along with its diminutive leader, Methodist and other southern women, black and white, worked alongside each other and with the Southern Regional Council to help bring local southern practices "in closer accord with the ideals of Christianity and Judaism, to strengthen and broaden democracy, to build a society in which every person can be confident of security and justice."[4] As a result, Tilly and her followers supplemented the work of "city fathers" to become "city mothers" keeping a watchful eye on law and order and racial justice in communities across the South.[5]

Because of Tilly's lifelong Methodist affiliation and Methodist education, and because her involvement with Methodist women's organizations launched her into wider circles of influence, an examination of the actions and racial attitudes of the Methodist Church is warranted. From within the Methodist fellowship emerged women's organizations that became the vanguard of the Social Gospel and concern for race relations in the South. In time these women's organizations would be the first Methodist groups to move beyond calling for truly "separate but equal" facilities to advocate the complete eradication of Jim Crow.

These organizations not only nurtured Dorothy Tilly and other southern white women of social conscience but set the pace in race relations for the dominant religious institutions of the post–World War II South.

THE METHODIST CHURCH AND
SOUTHERN RACE RELATIONS

The Methodist Church's record on race can be viewed in at least three distinct periods. Two of these periods are those before and after the 1939 reunification of the Northern Methodist Episcopal Church with the Methodist Episcopal Church, South. The third is the period after the U.S. Supreme Court's landmark ruling in *Brown v. Board of Education*.

Methodist Opinion before Brown

After the political reunion of North and South in the Compromise of 1877, a more perfect reunion was effected culturally and militarily when southern and northern soldiers fought together against common enemies in the Spanish-American War and in World War I against the German kaiser. By the end of the Progressive Era, Methodists and other white southerners settled into a spectrum of three common racial views, none of which opted for equality between the races. The most virulent expression was what Joel Williamson has called the radical stance, which supported a vigorous defense of white supremacy. Radicals mounted a staunch defense of white privilege against images of blacks as inferior beings quickly descending into bestiality in the absence of the erstwhile civilizing influence of slavery. In this response could be found a level of fear and hatred that expressed itself in terror, lynchings, and the use of the epithet "nigger."[6]

The numerically dominant stance was that of a paternalism which saw African Americans as a "child race" that was inclined toward retrogression unless aided industrially, intellectually, and morally by beneficent whites. Reflecting this view, Methodist writer Elmer T. Clark articulated what virtually became the race-relations motto of the white South until deep into the civil rights movement: "The Christian white man of the South is the Negro's best friend and always has been."[7] This paternalism was, of course, committed to preserving segregation, as in 1926 when the *Alabama Christian Advocate* criticized Methodist bishops for dining with African Methodist bishops and their wives in an integrated fashion: "Now, when Negro men and their wives and white men and their wives sit down together at the same banquet table, it is what we in the South call social equality . . . [that] will lead to social equality of other sorts, and social equality ultimately leads to intermarriage."[8]

Out of this Christian paternalism, which included a dose of Social Gospel progressivism, came a strong Methodist critique of lynching and race riots. For Georgia progressives like Dorothy Tilly, the race-baiting 1906 gubernatorial contest between Hoke Smith and Clark Howell and the Atlanta race riot of the same year had a powerful effect. Two years later the disfranchisement of black Georgians similarly stimulated a third approach to race relations that can be called interracialism. Early on, this approach accepted the concept of "separate but equal" but sought to work together with blacks to push local and state governments to shore up the equality of Jim Crow arrangements. As the century wore on, however, Methodists were in the forefront of these efforts, mostly through the denomination's women's groups and the person of Will W. Alexander, the founder of the Committee on Interracial Cooperation (CIC). Founded in 1919, this organization embodied the somewhat conservative interracialist spirit. After 1944, however, when it was transformed into the Southern Regional Council, the organization gradually developed a restrained critique of segregation itself.[9]

In this social context, Tilly was converted to working in race relations with the help of her husband, Milton. Casting about for some meaningful Christian activity, Dorothy was advised to consider the plight of African Americans in her own city. One night Milton drove her through Atlanta's black slums to the service entrance of the Piedmont Hotel, where she observed black children raiding garbage cans for food. With her husband's encouragement, she determined to go to work on the problem. Soon thereafter she became involved with the CIC and its sister organization, the Association of Southern Women for the Prevention of Lynching.[10]

Leading the way in race work among Methodists was the Woman's Missionary Council (WMC). Beginning in the early twentieth century, by the 1920s the WMC appointed a Committee on Race Relations to study the needs of southern blacks. Eventually, in July 1920 Carrie Parks Johnson and Estelle Haskin from the WMC met with ten members of the National Association of Colored Women at Tuskegee Institute to discuss possibilities for working together. That meeting resulted in the Memphis Woman's Interracial Conference in October of that year.[11] Joining the women in opposition to lynching and the Ku Klux Klan were a number of Methodist newspapers in the South, among them the *Nashville Christian Advocate,* the *North Carolina Christian Advocate,* and the *Wesleyan (Macon, Ga.) Christian Advocate,* which wondered how southerners could "identify secret methods, sectionalism, partisanism, and racial hatred with American democracy." The editor admonished his readers to resist the Klan as an "Un-American and undemocratic order."[12]

In the 1920s and 1930s, despite occasional sparring over segregation between some northern Methodists and their southern counterparts, the impulse toward reunion gradually drew the two wings together until a Plan of Re-unification was approved and the two fellowships became the Methodist Church in May 1939.[13] Race, however, became the major sticking point over the place of black Methodists in the new structure. More than three hundred thousand blacks within the Methodist Church were constituted into a separate, racially determined Central Jurisdiction. Only on such a basis were the southern churches and conferences willing to agree to the plan. As a compromise, black Methodists eventually overcame their initial misgivings, becoming convinced that the arrangement would be a temporary compromise that would in the meantime give them a larger, more unified voice in church affairs.[14]

Reunification made the Methodist Church the largest Protestant denomination in the United States. Ironically, as W. Edward Orser has noted, on the eve of World War II, when segregation would be questioned in many areas of American society, the large and influential Methodist Church had achieved unification by institutionalizing segregation in its own structure. Orser further argued that this left the Methodists "virtually voiceless" on the race question.[15] The women of the denomination, however, constituted the important exception. Significantly, within the Methodist connection the WMC's Study Group became the only white group within the Methodist Episcopal Church or the Methodist Episcopal Church, South, to join black Methodists in opposing the Plan of Re-unification and its proposed Central Jurisdiction. The women wondered whether the plan's "ethical imperfections" would be permanent or be flexible enough to allow future efforts "toward a more brotherly union."[16]

Events of the war years brought race into national consciousness to an unprecedented degree. Fighting in the European theater against Hitler's patently racist ideology shed light on American racial discrimination as never before and raised the practical issues of discrimination in the armed services and in the defense industry.[17] The black press, with its powerful strain of isolationism, was initially divided on the war. "Our war," claimed the *Pittsburgh Courier,* "is not against Hitler in Europe, but against the Hitlers in America."[18] Eventually, however, while pointing out the irony of fighting Nazism while Jim Crow continued his reign over the southern United States, the black press led the Double V campaign—calling for victory against racism, first in the war and second in America itself. The war had thus become an opportunity to point out the nation's hypocrisy and shame it toward racial justice.

Events during the war shook racial conventions and long-standing practices. Franklin Roosevelt's establishment of a Fair Employment Practices Committee in response to A. Philip Randolph's threatened "March on Washington" inserted the federal government into the racial customs of hiring practices in the South. Northern and black troops bivouacked in southern towns, often disregarding the regional customs of Jim Crow and, in the process, shocking southern sensibilities. The activities of First Lady Eleanor Roosevelt and other high-profile New Dealers challenged racial traditions in ways implicit and explicit. The U.S. Supreme Court's decision in *Smith v. Allwright* helped to establish the federal judiciary as another place where southern racial customs might come under siege. And Gunnar Myrdal's *An American Dilemma,* published in the same year as the *Smith* case, exposed Jim Crow and other southern racial customs to the glaring light of global scrutiny.

The mainstream and the church press gradually followed the black press's lead, and arguments noting the similarity between segregationist and Nazi ideology slowly began appearing in white newspapers and magazines. In 1942, L. O. Hartman, editor of the northern Methodist paper *Zion's Herald,* denounced the Methodist Church's acceptance of segregation, both in church and society, which he saw symbolized in its acceptance of the Central Jurisdiction. "In these days of war, with discrimination against the Negro becoming a nation-wide scandal, we are tongue-tied." Particularly tongue-tied was Methodism's official organ, the (Chicago) *Christian Advocate,* which "indicated the unwillingness of an important segment of the church to make an issue of what already had been settled."[19]

It is important, however, not to overstate this supposed silence, as even the often-cautious College of Methodist Bishops sounded themes similar to those found among the critics of segregation. In 1944 the bishops issued a statement on race in which they asserted that "the continent of Europe is drenched with blood because of the German doctrine of a superior race. In this country a minority group of 13 million Negroes is compelled to remain a detached racial unit, is accorded a sub-Christian status, is given an uncertain standard of livelihood, and all by the artificial standards which arise from racial grouping.... Racial minorities scattered throughout the earth are demanding to know what is meant by the affirmation of democracy that all men are created equal." Some of the denominational papers argued likewise, such as a 1947 article titled "White Supremacy—Master Race": "The notion of 'white supremacy' is a belief that the white race is inherently superior to all other races and should dominate other races politically, economically, and socially. It bears a striking resemblance to the phrase 'master race,' so frequently heard on the lips of the Nazis. It cannot stand... the indictment of the Christian faith. It is an idea against which millions of Americans fought a World War, and many died."[20] Methodist women, as we shall see, were even more forthright.

Even some traditionalists on race used the same arguments, as in the case of Benjamin F. Neal, a judge in Montezuma, Georgia. In the fall of 1948, when Georgia educators met in Milledgeville for a conference that included blacks, the proceedings were interrupted by shouts of "Nigger" from the audience, and Klan insignias were drawn on the sides of buildings. In addition, the culprits attempted to intimidate the African American educators by following them out of town. Neal denounced such activities as reflecting "the spirit of Hitlerism," adding that "their ambitions and their methods are not unlike those used by Hitler to subjugate the races he claimed inferior to the Master Race."[21]

What is remarkable about these comments is that some two months earlier the *Wesleyan Christian Advocate* had printed a conservative think piece on race and civil rights by the same judge. Neal argued that segregation in black church life was self-determined, so that the "black man" could "more freely give vent to the emotionalism of his nature." He defended the disfranchisement of blacks as a means of removing political corruption. He clung to notions of black inferiority, wherein the great mass of African Americans were "utterly incompetent to intelligently exercise the right of franchise and totally unfitted for jury duty." While claiming that whites had "given a pretty good home to the Negro," he bluntly asserted that "this is a white man's economy, a white man's civilization, and we in the South are unwilling for our standards of morality, for our social status, and for the future of our children and grandchildren to have its moral standards crushed and our ideals of common decency and the social relationships of life destroyed.... If our Jim Crow laws should be abolished and all segregation eliminated, the culture of the South would be destroyed; the morals of our people would degenerate beyond description, the religious life of both races would be demoralized and many of our churches destroyed."[22] Perspectives of this kind lay in wait for greater amplification with the announcement of the *Brown* decision.

Methodist Opinion after Brown

The postwar South was of course rocked by the Supreme Court's *Brown* ruling. Knowing the difficulty of implementing the decision quickly, the Methodist bishops' initial statement supported the ruling as "in keeping with the attitudes of the Methodist Church," citing a 1952 General Conference statement on race. The bishops underscored the church's opportunity to provide leadership to the South, asserting: "We accept this responsibility, for one of the foundations stones of our faith is the belief that all men are brothers, equal in the sight of God. In that faith we declare our support of the ruling of the Supreme Court."[23] In stronger terms, the Methodist Board of Social and Economic Relations encouraged all Methodist churches "to move resolutely forward toward the goal of full participation of the people of all races in the life of the Church and the Community." Arguing that segregation clearly violated doctrines of the fatherhood of God, the brotherhood of man, and the Kingdom of God, the board asserted: "We, therefore have no choice but to denounce it [segregation] as evil. This we do without equivocation."[24] Similarly, a group of young Methodists, meeting at the Southeastern Regional Leadership Training Conference at Lake Junaluska, North Carolina, unanimously approved a strong resolution of support on June 13, 1954, asserting: "We stand wholly in support of and applaud the Supreme Court ruling." The students further called upon every level of the Methodist Church to write letters to political and religious leaders in support of the decision.[25]

Unlike the Baptists and Presbyterians, the Methodist Church was at the time of *Brown* the only truly national denomination containing a southern wing. Methodists in the South, confined mostly to the Southeastern Jurisdiction, found their defense of segregation a minority view within their church. Thus, by the 1956 General Conference, southern Methodists winced as the larger denomination received the bishops' word that "the principle of Christian brotherhood is no longer debatable" and approved a statement entitled "The Methodist Church and Race." This document was a vigorous affirmation that the "Master permits no discrimination because of race, color, or national origin," and concluded: "There must be no place in the Methodist Church for racial discrimination or enforced segregation."[26]

Understandably, the church's southern bishops, in their attempt to mediate between their segregationist members and the national denomination, expressed a cautious support of *Brown* while warning racial liberals not to push too far too fast. Bishop William T. Watkins of Louisville, Kentucky, frankly told a group of southern ministers in 1955 that "there are areas of brotherhood we are not in position to enter yet." He added: "We prefer to bring reflection on ourselves by confessing that we have not yet become fully Christian in the area of Christian brotherhood, rather than by casting an aspersion on the Christian religion by implying that it does not require us to be a full brother to the Negro." Then, in language later incorporated in a statement by the bishops of the Southeastern Jurisdiction the next year, Watkins said: "The door to new areas of racial brotherhood simply cannot be blasted open. It must be opened from within. Any violent assault will not only fail but will keep the door closed indefinitely. Our slower pace is a swifter way to arrive at the goal. Whoever doubts this simply does not know the South."[27]

Echoing the caution of the bishops, a North Georgia Conference resolution reminded church members that they were "Christian citizens in a democracy" who, according to the Methodist Discipline, were duty bound "to observe and obey the laws and commands of the governing or supreme authority in the country." Beyond this, the conference reiterated its support of the public schools and the need for white and black Christians to work to better understand each other.[28]

Public statements of even qualified support for *Brown* were hardly received without a murmur, especially in the Southeastern Jurisdiction. Before the bishops could even leave Chicago, their 1954 meeting place, a North Carolina attorney sent them a blistering telegram: "It is with righteous indignation I condemn you, as will all other self-respecting white and colored people in America condemn you, for undertaking to use the Methodist Church and its nine million communicants as an instrumentality in bringing about desegregation in American schools. . . . It is unthinkable that the Bishops . . . of the Methodist Church would allow themselves to be drawn into a political fight, which, if successful, would destroy the ethnological divisions of man created by God and give us a nation of mongrelized races."[29]

In Montgomery, Alabama, Rev. Stanley Frazer, pastor of St. James Methodist Church, mounted a spirited defense of segregation along with his criticisms of the Supreme Court and its supporters within the Methodist Church. In a lengthy article, Frazer called upon lay members of the General Conference to "stand solidly against the choice of any one as a delegate who may help to bring about a situation that will create endless dissension in our Church." He argued that God had put his children in racial families with distinctive physical and ideological characteristics, establishing "'the bounds of their habitations' [Acts 17:26] on different continents." To call segregation an "un-Christian thing" was simply "not supported by the authority of the Holy Bible." In McCarthyite fashion he indulged in guilt by association, accusing the NAACP and the Southern Conference Educational Fund of being Communist organizations. He added: "If an 'un-Christian thing' is being done, it is by those who seek to use the Church to further political ends and to force on the rank and file of the American people a condition of strife that is distasteful to the thoughtful people of both races."[30]

Frazer ended 1954 by leading a meeting of Methodists opposed to the abolition of the Central Jurisdiction and in organizing Methodists from six different conferences into an interstate group called the Association of Methodist Ministers and Laymen. Their agenda was to oppose "any legislation or movement that seeks to 'liberalize' our present policy on racial matters." He began the next calendar year complaining to Bishop Arthur J. Moore of Atlanta about "the continuing pressure of the integrationists in every department of our Church work."[31] Over the next four years, Frazer's organization attracted more than thirty-four thousand members. It also drafted and influenced the Alabama legislature to pass the Dumas Bill, which allowed any local church to go into state court to claim title to any church property if at least 65 percent of the adult membership agreed to secede from the national denomination. Designed to circumvent Methodist Church law and allow a local church to withdraw from the Methodist Church over the issue of racial segregation, the bill was eventually declared unconstitutional.[32]

Alongside the laity's specific criticisms of the *Brown* ruling stood other, more veiled complaints. In 1952 the Board of Stewards of the Lindale (Georgia) Methodist Church approved a resolution "opposing this cancerous growth of Communism in our great Church. . . . [W]e deplore the socialistic and Communistic actions and teachings of some of the contributors to the literature published by our Methodist Publishing House." The statement also called upon Bishop Moore to make every effort to "rid our Church of persons who either knowingly or through ignorance would destroy our Church and our sacred way of life." Connecting such subversion with criticism of segregation, a few months later a laywoman from Sylvester, Georgia, complained about Methodist Sunday school literature: "Have we gone so far Leftist that our commentators *must* use a writer of Lillian Smith's caliber?" The writer enclosed a copy of the lesson, which included a quotation from the liberal Methodist's *Killers of the Dream*.[33] A few weeks before *Brown* was announced, another Georgia Methodist complained about what she saw as anti-Americanism in her denomination. She would be surprised, she asserted, to see a church conference enthusiastically salute the American flag. Connecting this malady with a certain perspective on race matters, she sarcastically complained: "Our Methodist Church . . . [is] constantly belittling America. 'America is a big, rich bully' and 'poor, dear Russia is trying so hard.' Russia's millions of degraded human slaves are not mentioned but 'the *horrible* treatment accorded colored people in America' is of prime importance."[34]

These comments reveal that Georgia Methodist women were not unanimous in supporting progressive change in church and society on matters of segregation and race relations. Nonetheless, in January 1957, in the midst of the white South's "massive resistance" to desegregation, a group of prominent Methodists met in Atlanta for one of many denomination-wide Interracial Leadership Conferences. One of the conference workshops, which examined Methodist progress in race relations up to that point, credited the women and youth "for leading out in example against race prejudice and in integration of groups meetings of various kinds. They seem more liberal in this respect than the men's groups."[35] Thus there is good evidence, especially when the involvement of Dorothy Tilly and her colleagues is considered, that women did more than merely issue statements of goodwill. Indeed, they led the way in the Methodist Church and became the most progressive element in the white South.

Women had long been more identified with issues of conscience and religious upbringing than men, both in the South and in other regions. But the activism of these Methodist women also occurred during a time when gender roles were changing rapidly. Long consigned by public decree to the separate sphere of the household, during the 1940s women entered the workforce in significant numbers to replace men who had gone off to fight in World War II. As a result, women bearing blowtorches and rivet guns became bound up in the American public's conception of patriotic duty during wartime and also challenged conventional notions of separate spheres for the sexes. First Lady Eleanor Roosevelt's unprecedented travel and activism challenged racial customs but also redefined gender expectations and boundaries. This was especially important because race and sex had long been at the center of the most combustible of social issues in the South.

DOROTHY TILLY AND METHODIST WOMEN'S ORGANIZATIONS

Since antebellum times, Christian activism among white southern women found expression—at least to the extent allowed by the male heads of their households—in mission work among the slaves. The wife of Frederick Douglass's owner was certainly not unique in teaching their young slave to read, and by the time of the Civil War, Methodist women were busying themselves in similar pursuits. One Georgia woman implored her bishop, "The field, of all others, for the care and labor of Southern women is the mission to the colored people. . . . Bishop, give us work; we can do it, not at once perhaps, but let us begin."[36]

The Methodist tradition ensured that women who entered the Civil War years with the slaves as their mission field would continue to work among the freedpersons into the twentieth century. Wesleyan-Armenian theology avoided the extreme Calvinist conception of original sin and allowed for the possibility of human improvement. John Wesley's own ethical activities and preaching formed another element in the Methodist tradition that was conducive to social reform. The combination of this tradition and the practice of southern women working among African Americans created just one area of the Social Gospel activities John Patrick McDowell has described.

By the 1920s, Methodist leader Carrie Parks Johnson served as part-time chairperson of the WMC's Commission on Race Relations and as the part-time director of women's work for the Commission on Interracial Cooperation. In this dual capacity, she informed southern churchwomen about conditions among African Americans and organized women to work for better race relations in the South. She diligently recruited Methodists for CIC work and used the CIC as a resource for Methodist work. Alice G. Knotts estimates that Methodist women made up more than half of all the women involved in interracial dialogues and race-relations studies. A south Georgia Methodist women's auxiliary participated in a variety of interracial activities, including providing for blacks a public rest room, a clinic, a nurse, a playground, and day care facilities. Taking seriously the "equal" in "separate but equal," the women's groups would not move toward challenging Jim Crow until the World War II era. As Knotts argues, however, they legitimized interracial work and gradually, "knowingly or unknowingly," undermined segregation.[37] As the war and its aftermath brought issues of racial justice into clearer focus, Methodist women's organizations worked on a three-pronged race-relations agenda that included education, the continued anti-lynching crusade, and eventually civil rights and politics. Out of this context emerged southern Methodism's unlikely leader, Dorothy Tilly, and her Fellowship of the Concerned.

Educational Work

By the mid-1940s the Women's Division of the Board of Missions, particularly its department of Christian Social Relations and Local Church Activities (CSR/LCA), had increased its interest in human rights and publicly called upon church and society to ensure these inherent rights to persons of all races. Through various educational programs the CSR/LCA sought to induce Methodists to exercise moral leadership in replacing racial and religious bigotry and oppression with civil liberties and peace. In addition, from 1943 on the women's organization committed itself to interracial meetings several times a year, issuing invitations based on geographical location rather than race or jurisdiction. They also became the Methodist Church's strongest advocates for participation in World Communion Sunday and Race Relations Sunday.[38] In sharp contrast to general public opinion in the South, and to the generally cautious tones by the bishops, the Women's Division in 1944 became the first agency within Methodism to declare segregation as evil.[39]

Soon thereafter they began a large-scale campaign to change the denomination's attitudes and policies on race. In 1945 the Women's Division called a denominational commission to "advocate full participation by people of all races in all aspects of the church's life in nondiscriminatory ways, including participation in 'non-racial congregations and conferences.'" That same year the CSR/LCA recommended that its societies "work immediately for the equalization of educational opportunity in the United States for all people without regard to race, creed, or place of residence."[40] The division went even further, becoming the first Methodist organization formally to call for the abolition of the Central Jurisdiction. Their memorial asked the 1948 General Conference to "take such steps as may be necessary to abolish this pattern of segregation in the Methodist Church."[41]

In the 1950s the Women's Division adopted a "Charter on Racial Policies," which became the organization's primary tool to influence public education and federal housing policies in the South. Committing itself to creating "a fellowship and social order without racial barriers," the women asserted, "Time marches on! The ground swell of human equality under God is becoming unmistakably the ground swell of human equality under law! . . . [W]e must plant the right seeds." Specifically, planting the seeds meant Methodist women working in their churches and communities to provide general information about segregation, in particular to publicize conditions in schools for blacks, to bring parents of both races together to discuss problems, and to solicit state and federal funds for all public schools "without discrimination in any form."[42]

In the first weeks after the *Brown* ruling, while many in the Southeastern Jurisdiction were temporizing and issuing cautious public statements, the General Assembly of Methodist Women quickly went on record as the first Methodist agency to support the decision. Their statement "rejoiced" in the ruling and affirmed a new urgency in working to eliminate segregation from the nation and the denomination.[43] Similarly, the Women's Division welcomed the Court's ruling as an opportunity to press forward in integrating Methodist schools. Two years later the same organization petitioned the General Conference to request "that the institutions of the church, local churches, colleges, universities, theological schools, hospitals, and homes carefully study their policies and practices as they relate to race, making certain that these policies and practices are Christian."[44]

Reflecting this perspective, one Georgia Methodist woman refused to let Alabama pastor Stanley Frazer's treatise in defense of segregation go unanswered, taking on the minister point by point. She reminded readers of the *Wesleyan Christian Advocate* that "large conferences of Methodist youth and Methodist women all over the South have been passing resolutions" to abolish segregation within the Methodist Church for "more than a decade now." She underscored the interracial and nonpaternalistic work of Methodist women, sharply noting:

> It seems on analysis that the only group which falls into a category within the church, that has not been moving decidedly toward inter-racial co-operation is the men . . . it is they who have failed to see how strong . . . [and] deeply-rooted this feeling is among young adults, the youth, many of the women, and some of the older adults in Methodist churches in every state of the South. The same lack of sensitivity, unfortunately, has persisted among some of the men who are ministers in our Annual Conference. That they have listened politely to the resolutions presented by the women and passed over them as being "sentiment[al]" or "too hasty." That they have scorned the statements of the Methodist Youth Fellowship and groups of young adults as long the "hotheadedness of youth" and [the] "unfortunate results of agitators."

To Frazer's point that blacks preferred their own schools and churches, she raised what she considered the obvious question: "Would you really want membership in a church where you were not welcome, where your children would be shunned by some and ignored by others?" Those who want integration, "being human beings and not psychopaths, ... will wait until they get an honest welcome." On Frazer's point that the *Brown* decision was politically motivated, she replied that the Court made its decision "to reassure the rest of the world, whose population is overwhelmingly colored, that our nation means what we declare in our intentions to work with them for a peaceful world." Finally, "with all the force of conviction" she could muster, she rejected the Montgomery minister's biblical interpretation that segregation was by God's will and design, citing Peter and Paul's New Testament insights into the inclusiveness of the Christian gospel and Jesus' willingness to minister to Samaritans.[45]

Dorothy Tilly's activism emerged naturally out of this well-developed tradition of female Methodist social concern. Beyond her local church membership in Atlanta, she was active in the North Georgia Conference, serving on a number of committees concerned with children, tenancy, and race relations. She had served on the Women's Division's Committee on Rural Life since 1933. From 1940 to 1948 she was secretary of Christian Social Relations of the Woman's Society of Christian Service, through which she made contact with Methodist women of nine southern states. Three times she was elected as a delegate to the General Conference.[46] Outside Tilly's specifically Methodist involvements, her activities included serving as field secretary of the women's division of the Southern Regional Council (which she regarded as "a mission of the Methodist Church in her part of the world"), the Georgia Interracial Committee, the Georgia Council of Church Women, and the Georgia Conference of Social Work. In 1944 she was a lobbyist in Washington to save the Farm Security Administration.[47]

In the late 1930s, Tilly conducted leadership seminars at Paine College, a historically black Methodist school in Augusta, Georgia, designed to train black women for leadership in their churches.[48] She spearheaded a drive to establish a state school to train delinquent African American girls. Working with black women's clubs in the state, her efforts raised money for the project, bought a plot of land, and put a building on it with additional aid from the federal government's Works Progress Administration. When a proposal for funding failed to pass the state legislature, Tilly mobilized twenty-eight thousand angry churchwomen to lobby the legislators, who eventually passed the appropriation over the veto of Governor Eugene Talmadge. When the school opened in an interracial dedication service, a participating pastor said,

"I dedicated that which has already been consecrated by the tears of the women of both races in Georgia.... As many a preacher will tell you, when it comes to courage to do the right thing, the women are far ahead of the men."[49]

Anti-Lynching

Not all Methodist women opposed lynching or developed progressive views of African Americans. Perhaps the most widely known woman in turn-of-the-century Georgia, Rebecca Latimer Felton, represented a radical counterpart to the likes of Dorothy Tilly or Jessie Daniel Ames, president of the Association of Southern Women for the Prevention of Lynching (ASWPL). Active in the Holiness movement of Georgia Methodism, Felton also became a powerful force in Democratic politics after the death of her husband, Dr. William H. Felton, who had served as an influential member of the U.S. House of Representatives from Georgia. Along with Tom Watson, she wielded wide influence in the state and became the first woman to serve in the U.S. Senate, appointed to complete Watson's term after his death in 1920.[50]

Far from a progressive on race, Felton complained about the possible election of Teddy Roosevelt, who had drawn southern fire for inviting Booker T. Washington to eat with him in the White House. She sardonically warned: "Voter, take your choice. Shall this be a white man's government, or a mixture of black, tan, and white?" In an 1898 letter to the *Atlanta Journal* she weighed in on the lynching question: "When you take the negro into your embrace ... and make him believe he is your man and brother, ... so long will lynching prevail.... [I]f it requires lynching to protect woman's dearest possession from ... drunken human beasts, then I say lynch a thousand a week if necessary."[51]

By the time of Felton's death in 1930, women like Dorothy Tilly and Jessie Daniel Ames had moved through their involvement with the Commission on Interracial Cooperation and had branched out into the ASWPL. Although the number of lynchings had declined after the 1930s, the September 7, 1940, lynching of Austin Callaway in La Grange, Georgia, marked the first in the state in two years and brought a wave of protests from across the nation. The Methodist women of the La Grange district in annual session on September 16 issued a statement, as did the La Grange Ministerial Association.[52] Methodist women all over Georgia then renewed their efforts to bring attention to failures of racial justice in the courts, lauding leaders who upheld justice, advocating clemency in race-based cases, and pressuring public officials to sign the anti-lynching pledges. In 1941 Ames wrote to Lillian Smith indicating that out of forty-three thousand pledge signatures filed with the ASWPL, all but three thousand were identified as Methodist women.[53]

Dorothy Tilly was centrally involved with these activities. Since Rebecca Felton's justification of lynching as the protection of southern white women was echoed all across the South, Tilly and the others made a persuasive counterargument that the collective voice of white women could carry great weight when "raised in protest against violence and to prove that no so such measures were required, effective, or to be tolerated in a civilized and democratic society."[54]

In 1941 Tilly helped Methodist women mount an economic boycott of the businesses of every Klan member in the South Georgia Conference. The boycott also resulted in the first anti-lynching law passed by the state's general assembly. On another occasion she faced down a Mississippi lynch mob by standing in the doorway of a jail and quietly persuading the mob to break up and return to their homes. Five years later she investigated a race riot in Columbia, Tennessee, along with the lynching of two couples in Monroe, Georgia. Two days after the incident, Tilly quietly canvassed the town and gradually gathered the full story. One woman told her she had heard rumors and had even observed what she had thought to be a rehearsal for the lynching. When Tilly asked the woman what she did in response, the woman simply confessed she had not known what to do. Having received a similar reply from a minister in Columbia, Tennessee, Tilly wrote a leaflet for future use, one instructing concerned citizens: "Call the sheriff and tell him you expect him to do his duty. Call and tell the state patrol the same. Call the local editor, the state-wide papers, the ministers, the civic leaders, and the headquarters of the network—the Southern Regional Council in Atlanta."[55]

Politics and Civil Rights

Tilly's anti-lynching and educational activities often overlapped, as they also provided her entrée into politics. Her efforts to establish the school for African American girls had put her at cross purposes with Governor Talmadge, and she led large numbers of Methodist women to support his opponent, Ellis Arnall, in the 1942 gubernatorial election. Along the campaign trail, Arnall had made a public remark that seemed to condone lynching, and women of the CIC mounted a letter campaign to convince him that women in the state rejected lynching. Arnall's supporters arranged a meeting between the candidate and Tilly, who convinced him that he was in danger of losing the support of churchwomen throughout the state. To make amends, he agreed to issue a statement opposing "mob violence in all its insidious forms." In the midst of this crusade, a reporter asked Tilly what was happening in the South. She replied, "Nothing that wasn't happening in my girlhood. There have always been Southerners who put humanity above color."[56]

In 1934, out of her work with the Farm Security Administration, Tilly became acquainted with Eleanor Roosevelt, who shared many of her concerns related to racial justice, particularly federal anti-lynching legislation. The First Lady often spoke at women's organization meetings, and in April 1944 Tilly and several other Methodist women were invited to visit her in the White House. On that visit Tilly invited the First Lady to speak at an assembly of Methodist women at Lake Junaluska, North Carolina, in July. In introducing Mrs. Roosevelt to the group, Tilly said the seminar was focused on the condition of minority groups in America and designed to help women "think through our Christian citizenship responsibilities for these groups and establish a program of action." Roosevelt's speech dealt with race relations as one of many problems awaiting the postwar world. The war, she argued, had underscored the issue of race relations, which she called a national as well as a southern problem. "The thing that makes it important nationally," she continued, "is the way America is being watched by other countries to see if we cope with our minority problems better than they do. The whole question of our religious belief will be examined as well as our political beliefs. They expect us as the greatest and strongest Democracy to take the lead in giving the same rights to all people."[57]

Tilly and Eleanor Roosevelt continued their friendship over the years, with Tilly visiting her in her Hyde Park, New York, home in 1947. Two years later, in her memoir, Roosevelt indicated her deep regard for Tilly:

> I had great admiration for the courage of Mrs. M. E. Tilly of Atlanta, Georgia, who was the executive secretary of the Methodist women's organization. I was told that whenever a lynching occurred, she went alone or with a friend, as soon as she heard of it, to investigate the circumstances. Only a Southern woman could have done this, but even for a Southern woman it seemed to me to require great moral as well as physical courage. She is a Christian who believes in all Christ's teachings, including the concept

that all men are brothers; and though she is a white Southern woman she deeply resents the fact that white Southern women are so often used as a pretext for lynching.[58]

It was likely through a recommendation from Eleanor Roosevelt that Tilly was invited to serve on President Truman's Committee on Civil Rights.

To Secure These Rights

One day in late 1945 the phone rang at the Tilly residence in Atlanta. It was the White House calling to invite Dorothy to serve on the President's Committee on Civil Rights. Hearing the invitation, the sixty-two-year-old woman buckled with surprise and gasped, "Who me?" Her excited husband stood next to her, cheering her on and urging, "Say yes! You can do it!"[59] She quickly accepted the assignment to travel to Washington almost every week for the next several months to help the committee study racial conditions throughout the nation and make recommendations to the president and Congress. The only white woman and one of only two southerners on the committee, she and fellow southerner Frank Porter Graham, president of the University of North Carolina, fully supported the end of segregation but worked to make sure the committee saw it as a national problem rather than merely a southern one. Together they successfully softened the committee's final report so that the South would not be singularly castigated for its racial policies. She also argued strongly that federal aid to segregated schools be maintained. Throughout their deliberations, Tilly worked to keep the other members of the committee abreast of developments and the social realities in the South, along with pointing out instances where other regions provided less-than-sterling examples of race relations.[60]

Published on October 29, 1947, the 178-page report *To Secure These Rights* called for the "elimination of segregation based on race, color, creed, or national origin, from American life." The committee cited U.S. Supreme Court justice John Harlan's dissent to the *Plessy* decision, which argued that racial segregation implied an unconstitutional badge of inferiority, anticipating the eventual language of the *Brown* ruling. The report thus argued that equality within segregation was "one of the outstanding myths of American history." The report further proposed a federal anti-lynching law, the abolition of all obstacles to voting (especially the poll tax), the end of segregation in the military and in public housing and accommodations, and cutting off federal funds to all recipient bodies continuing to practice segregation. In addition, the report called for the establishment of a permanent commission on civil rights, a joint congressional committee, a Civil Rights Division of the Justice Department, and a permanent Fair Employment Practices Committee. It was one of the most important government statements on civil rights in American history. Tilly and Graham added a mild dissent indicating that while they favored the end of segregation, they opposed "its imposition by federal laws and sanctions."[61]

Methodist women were bursting with pride in their "favorite daughter," and within weeks of the report's publication they had Tilly make a comprehensive report of the committee's work to the Women's Division. The department of CSR/LCA also convinced the entire Women's Division to support the policies and to issue a statement commending President Truman and urging him "to rectify current discriminations in health, education, and employment" within the federal government. The Women's Division eagerly committed itself to helping circulate the report throughout the nation. Tilly had made a sixty-page list of women she wanted to receive a copy of *To Secure These Rights,* and she personally sent out copies to more than a hundred church leaders across the country. Following her lead, that spring the executive committee included in its budget additional funds to purchase and distribute six thousand copies of the report. One correspondent wrote Tilly that she was "glad your Committee used the word 'immediately' in regards to abolishing segregation. We too often try to excuse our inactivities, absolving ourselves from all blame by thinking and preaching that action must not take place until the next generation."[62]

Dorothy Tilly spent most of the two years after the publication of the report discussing its proposals with church congregations and lay audiences all over the United States. In 1949 she appeared in thirty states. To sometimes critical white southerners she defended her support of the committee's report: "I do not believe that there is anyone in the United States, who, had he been with us and seen the things we did, would have signed his name to any less strong a report." Large crowds attended her talks, and fan letters poured in congratulating her for participating in the study. She told reporters that she had "received only twelve letters opposing my work."[63]

She reviewed the report and was one of the main speakers at a Southern Regional Council meeting in Atlanta in February 1948. Some four hundred persons from eleven states attended the conference, which published a report called "The Condition of Our Rights." Six days later, Herman Talmadge's segregationist newspaper, *The Statesman,* devoted its entire news section to denouncing the meeting.[64] Speaking on her home turf, Tilly addressed the North Georgia Conference Wesleyan Service Guild on June 26–27, 1948, holding her audience spellbound as she called on her fellow Christian women to help battle hate in America:

> More than 20,000,000 people are denied justice in this land because of national origin, color, or the faith of their fathers. We must work harder and pray harder to make this a land of liberty. . . . It is up to Christians to heal the sore spots all over our country. The hardest part of the golden rule is to want for someone else what you want for yourself. Democracy, brotherhood, and human rights are the practical expressions of the eternal worth of every child of God.[65]

She carried the same message to venues outside the South, recognizing that the battle was national, not just regional. Speaking at the February 13, 1949, annual interracial service of the Springfield, Illinois, Council of Churches, Tilly told the audience, "Brotherhood is the basis for peace, and brotherhood must begin with the church." A reporter for the *Springfield Register* told readers that Tilly was "representative of what Southern white women are doing to abolish 'Jim Crowism,' lynching, segregated schools, and other discriminatory customs." She implored the audience to help uproot hate, "America's public enemy No. 1":

> In our nation 22 million persons are denied opportunity for employment in fields in which they have been trained; many are denied justice, medical care in hours of need, and a voice in your government. . . . Our heads have outgrown our hearts; our minds have developed faster than our morals and science has outstripped our spirits. We invented gunpowder and atomic bombs before we acquired the morality to use them wisely. We learned the secrets of chemistry before we grew enough spiritually to refuse to make poison gas. We brought in the machine age before we had the morals to manage it. . . . One hundred seventy-three years after the Declaration of Independence, which says that all persons are created equal, and 82 years after Lincoln's Gettysburg Address . . . [it] now becomes our duty to see that our communities give civil rights to our citizens, regardless of race, color, or creed. Our world is a battle between those who would exploit the hatred in it and those who would strengthen the fellowship within it. Violence may be infectious, but liberty and courage are also infectious.[66]

Ever the optimist, Tilly was sure, in the words of a later sermon by Martin Luther King Jr., that the "arm of the moral universe" was bending "toward justice." In early 1950 she told a Louisville, Kentucky, audience that civil rights reforms were catching on at the grassroots level: "I am encouraged by progress seen in Kentucky where you have admitted Negroes to your state university, and by progress in my home state of Georgia, where we have whipped the white primary and the poll tax." Always recruiting new soldiers into the struggle, she assured them, "There are no sacrifices to fighting for what's right and the compensations are many. I have had the most satisfactory, thrilling, and stirring life possible."[67]

One pragmatic result of Tilly's far-flung advocacy tour was the boost she gave to President Truman's election plans in the hotly contested 1948 presidential contest. Having watched his high-profile civil rights policies alienate large portions of the white South, Truman desperately needed the help of influential southerners like Tilly. Although she was reluctant to campaign for the president overtly, her membership on the Civil Rights Committee and her vocal support of its conclusions constituted an implied endorsement. Just after Truman's upset victory, Channing Tobias, director of New York's Phelps-Stokes Fund and a fellow member of the Civil Rights Committee, wrote Tilly with his thanks: "I deeply appreciate your message referring to the election of President Truman. . . . I am glad that Georgia, in spite of its many weaknesses, rebuffed the Dixiecrats and came up strongly in the Truman column. I know you had a lot to do with this through the exercise of your strong influence with the church women of both races throughout the state."[68] Following Tilly's lead, Methodist women sought to use their influence in the next election cycle. In the 1952 presidential election, the department of CSR/LCA issued "A Call to Methodist Women," reminding them of their citizenship responsibilities to elect persons who would "seek to enact laws and protect rights of all persons regardless of race, creed, or nationality."[69]

In the aftermath of her service to the White House, Tilly capitalized on her fame by corresponding with U.S. Attorney General Tom C. Clark as well as many governors, sheriffs, and judges throughout the South. She advocated improvements in the court system and more fairness in civil rights cases, especially those involving lynchings.[70] Out of her solicitude for these issues, particularly lynching, and in light of the demise of the ASWPL, Tilly found her inspiration to create a new organization of churchwomen to continue these efforts.

The Fellowship of the Concerned

Before and after the *Brown* decision, it was in the activities of the Fellowship of the Concerned that Dorothy Tilly and other Methodist women most clearly "mothered" their communities toward racial justice and better race relations. Like all good mothers who watch out for pain among their children and try to ease it, who guide their children in growing up to do the right thing in responsible citizenship, these "city mothers" kept vigilant watch over their communities and enabled them to experience growth in race matters.

In the summer of 1949, Tilly visited Greenville, South Carolina, to attend the trial of thirty-one whites charged with the lynching of an African American named Willie Earle. She watched as the racial jokes of the defense attorneys and the muffled laughter of the all-white jury made a mockery of the trial. Particularly angered when the jury acquitted all of the defendants, Tilly became convinced that the presence of more fair-minded local church people, the sort of women in her own circle of contacts, would bring such injustice into the light of day where it could be ameliorated. She hit upon the idea of recruiting a cadre of Methodist and other churchwomen to become a presence in their communities to observe and inform the larger population of racial unfairness in their courts, police departments, and election systems. Believing that "there's so much goodness everywhere, there's not a spot we can't reach," she determined to build a network of local watchdogs in every county seat in the South.[71]

Putting her ideas into action, Tilly brought together 165 leaders of religious women's groups on September 8–9, 1949, for a conference at Atlanta's Wesley Memorial Methodist Church. She told the conferees: "I am concerned that our constitutional freedoms are not shared by all our people. My religion convinces me that they must be and gives me courage to study, work, and lead others to the fulfillment of equal justice under the law." Many of the women drawn to the meeting had never before participated in an interracial luncheon. Reminding them that black citizens often suffered discrimination from white judges and juries, Tilly asserted that America's moral leadership in the world, placed upon the nation by its religious convictions and its world position, demanded that such failures of democracy be corrected. "The remedies," she added, "lie with us in our own communities."[72] Recognizing that her audience had come because of concerns similar to her own, she proposed a new interracial, interdenominational organization that would take up and expand the work of the now-defunct ASWPL: the Fellowship of the Concerned (FOC).

In the aftermath of the Willie Earle lynching trial, one of the first projects Tilly took on was a counterattack on a Klan-sympathizing member of the South Carolina Assembly. Alexander Miller, a regional director of the Anti-Defamation League, phoned her to report that a legislator had invited Grand Dragon Sam Green of the Georgia Klan to speak to the Palmetto State's legislature. Tilly immediately consulted her massive index file of ministers and leaders of women's groups across the South. She quickly notified key people in South Carolina, who avalanched the assemblyman with hundreds of protest letters. He eventually rescinded his invitation to Green and denounced Tilly as "this foreign woman from Georgia for poking into South Carolina's affairs." A year later South Carolina passed an anti-Klan law. Tilly was thus among the first white southerners to be pilloried as an "outside agitator." To what she considered a ludicrous charge, she gave a simple reply: "What happens to any person in this country is the business of the whole country."[73]

Early on, working closely with the Southern Regional Council, Tilly held workshops in Atlanta and elsewhere that focused on school desegregation and justice in the courts. Like many other civil rights activists and Supreme Court watchers in the period, she anticipated numbered days for segregation and believed that the women of the South could be the "shock absorbers" of social change. These early workshops were designed to train churchwomen what to look for and what questions to ask of local officials, along with tactics for nudging them toward racial justice. Developing sharp fund-raising skills, Tilly also tapped her contacts in foundations and religious organizations for donations to fund FOC conferences.[74]

FOC workshops trained members to visit local sheriffs, judges, and other officials, to publicize their visits, and particularly to report their findings to Southern Regional Council headquarters, where a file was established on each community. For the use of FOC contacts in each locality, Tilly developed a questionnaire for each area under scrutiny. For example, in the area of administration, FOC women asked officials about the organization and personnel of their police departments, their salary scales, how they attracted qualified officers, and whether they employed African American officers. As to training, they inquired into the hours of instruction given police, the subjects taught, and whether they were instructed in the laws, ordinances, and constitutional procedures relating to civil liberties. Regarding performance, their questionnaires uncovered the number of blacks arrested compared to the number of whites as well as the number of homicides of both races. They asked whether there were marked differences in the nature of the homicides, whether places of amusement were adequately patrolled, and whether police departments had any preventative activities designed to avoid racial conflict. In the area of community relations, they sought to determine African Americans' feelings about the police in their communities. Were there trouble areas in housing, recreation, or other public services?[75]

Tilly's troops informed themselves about local conditions in the courts as well, operating with a specific goal: "Know your courts as you know your schools." The FOC women made their influence felt as they encouraged better selection and training for police and worked for the hiring of black policemen. They publicly commended officials who showed courage and integrity in race relations, and they called attention to violations. Later, when their agenda expanded to overseeing election laws and practices, the women sought to make sure registration and voting procedures were fair, both in theory and in practice. They publicly opposed state registration measures that threatened the security of any voters, and they urged officials to train poll workers "in the proper performance of their duties, and volunteered to serve as local election managers and clerks." They also worked to shape public opinion by discussing problems with local newspaper editors. In particular, they commended the adoption of improved journalistic practices in the handling of "racial news"—for example, by applying the titles "Mr." or "Mrs." to African Americans as well as whites.[76]

Once trained, the women signed the FOC Pledge, part of which read: "I, as a church woman, am concerned that our constitutional freedoms are not shared by all of our people.... I am willing to sit in the courts and to visit police and other law enforcement agencies to learn how law is administered in my community. I will work with others in times of tension to see that the rights of all are protected."[77] Before long, whenever unjust practices were uncovered in a local community, word somehow got to Tilly, who in turn contacted someone on the scene, and often went there herself. On her organization's mothering success, she commented: "We may not always get justice, but we can get public opinion so stirred up that the same thing can't ever happen in that community again."[78]

Often the work of these women had to be carried out in secret. In 1956 Tilly had promised the editor of the *Methodist Woman* an article on what southern churchwomen were doing to allay tensions in the South. In the interim, however, escalating tensions forced Tilly to inform the editor that for the protection of her FOC colleagues, she would not be able to discuss their activities fully. "The women are still meeting and working," she wrote, "but are giving no publicity to what they are doing. They are very bravely trying to work, in spite of opposition so great that it might affect their husband's business—and in some instances, it has already affected their standing in the community."[79] Sometimes women told their husbands they were going shopping or visiting relatives rather than informing them that they were attending FOC workshops. Tilly reveled in their courage, saying that their slogan was "to find a conviction that will not rest, a faith that will not shrink, and courage that will not waiver."[80] In addition, some were silent members of the FOC network—the conscience-tortured wives of Klansmen, whose value to the movement, Tilly said, "lies in their keeping their eyes and ears open and their mouths shut."[81]

Naturally, the petite crusader in her flowery hats could not manage these "subversive activities" without virulent opposition and harassment. Just after the publication of *To Secure These Rights,* a newspaper editor denounced Tilly as "a parasite who while living upon funds furnished by the Methodist Church had rendered much of her service to the cause of Socialism and Communism."[82] Before Tilly even managed to leave Washington to return home, her husband received a bomb threat. Atlanta mayor William Hartsfield provided police protection, and the Justice Department dispatched FBI agents to their home. Not knowing whether the cars cruising the alley behind his home were the Klan or the police, Milton Tilly lost a night's sleep in the aftermath of the threat.[83]

Tilly also received hate mail and harassing phone calls. She received an anonymous letter with the heading, "To the Two Southern Residents of the Civil Rights (?) Committee." It read: "You are not worthy to live in the South. The Southern public knows that you are not Southerners. The damage that has already been done is irreparable.... You cheap publicity seekers and nigger lovers such as Eleanor Roosevelt, President (?) Truman, and others ... will be the direct cause of more lynchings than have ever, or would have ever occurred." As to African Americans: "Their feeble minds, and yours, cannot grasp the resulting chaos your recommendations will bring. [Y]ou are bringing about insolence, bigotry, as well as assault, rape, murder, and a number of other outrages. We admit that the murder of 4 Negroes in Georgia was a dreadful affair, but ... something had to be done. [B]y this action, possibly

4 thousand lives were saved. Leave the South to the Southerners. [W]e have handled the situation for a century and we will continue to do so."[84]

Interestingly, Methodist women more generally were getting a taste of the same medicine. During the same month that Senator Joseph McCarthy began his anti-Communist crusade, an article in the conservative *Reader's Digest* criticized "Methodism's Pink Fringe." Interracial meetings and civil rights legislation sponsored by the Women's Division provided critics with "evidence" that Methodist women were Communists.[85]

In a notorious 1958 episode, segregationist editor Bill Cleghorn dispatched photographers to an FOC meeting in Montgomery, Alabama. Reporters went along to record the license plate numbers of the attendees, and Cleghorn published the names and business connections of the women's husbands. As a result, the Montgomery FOC women received harassing phone calls for the next several weeks. A livid Tilly wrote to Cleghorn accusing him of trampling the women's basic constitutional rights. In response to such efforts at intimidation, she admonished her colleagues in Alabama: "The men in the car, the uninvited guest, and the editor are too *little* to intimidate praying women. Don't let them—defeat them. Don't give that much power over your lives."[86] To counter her own crank phone calls, Tilly often tried to evangelize her callers or played a recording of the Lord's Prayer. "It always helps me," she noted, "and it silences the one at the other end of the phone."[87]

The FOC was largely the organizational extension of Dorothy Tilly's crusading spirit and indomitable personality. She managed the work of the organization single-handedly, with no other officers and no secretarial help. There were no membership dues, and meetings were held irregularly. By early 1950, however, more than four thousand women, mostly from the Peach State, had affiliated with the FOC.[88]

Assessing the results of Tilly's work, particularly that with the FOC, is difficult, although she was perennially upbeat about the good she and her colleagues were doing. A few days after the formation of the FOC, six women visited the editors of the two Atlanta newspapers to remind them of the unfavorable publicity their stories were giving the South. They reminded them of the racial slurs implicit when they told only of black crime but not black accomplishments. They further called on the editors to discontinue the practice of segregating stories about African Americans, and urged them to use "Mr." and "Mrs." with the names of blacks. The following Sunday the *Atlanta Constitution* carried a prominent two-column story (with photographs) of the inauguration of the president of the African American Gammon Theological Seminary.[89]

Another example of FOC success was an occasion when Tilly got word of a south Georgia community where a black schoolhouse had been burned. After whites had moved out of the community, an empty school building was donated to blacks in the community, who raised $100 to repair one of the two rooms as a community center. When the center was officially opened, a white man told the blacks, "You will never hold another meeting in that schoolhouse," and the next day the building was burned to the ground. Tilly rounded up two women from the community and contacted a local minister and the sheriff. The FOC committee raised money to rebuild the structure in order to "build back race relations." Tilly told reporters she did it simply by giving the facts to "a few good people in the community, who in turn stir up the consciences of the rest." After all, she often pointed out, "There is not a spot in the South without its good, liberal-minded people who are terribly hurt when disaster and disgrace fall on the community through broken human relationships. They are eager to do something that will say to the Negroes and to the outside world, 'We have had no part in this evil thing.'"[90]

Explaining the religious and civil rights work of the Methodist and other churchwomen she led, Tilly often spoke of seeking "a way to ease the tensions of our section and make it a proving ground for democracy."[91] In this manner, the Fellowship of the Concerned sowed seeds that would later come to fruition. They shone their lights on unfairness and pushed their southern communities toward justice. Like good "city mothers," they used their powers of encouragement to help their communities reach their potential in matters of race relations. In their straight-laced, Methodist piety, they also embodied a powerful Social Gospel.

5
Louisiana
The Civil Rights Struggle, 1940–1954
Adam Fairclough

ITS ORIGINS AS A French and Spanish colony and the particular character of New Orleans—in 1940 the South's largest port and biggest city—gave Louisiana a unique cultural profile. Its large Catholic element and its diverse population of Creoles, Cajuns, and more recent immigrants sharply distinguished the Pelican State from other southern states. But these cultural differences, insofar as they influenced race relations, should not be exaggerated. New Orleans, despite its easygoing hedonism, affirmed white supremacy no less avidly than cities in Alabama or Georgia. Moreover, Protestant northern Louisiana was culturally indistinguishable from the rest of the South and seemed scarcely more hospitable to blacks than neighboring Arkansas and Mississippi.

In 1940, blacks in Louisiana—about a third of the state's total population—suffered from severe social, economic, and political disadvantages. Jim Crow laws and customs circumscribed their lives and exposed them to daily humiliations. Excluded from the democratic process—even as defined by Louisiana's corrupted version of democracy—blacks were politically invisible, figuring in political campaigns only as the objects of scorn and abuse. White employers and white workers relegated blacks to lower-tier jobs and barred them from entire sectors of the economy. State government and local school boards ensured that whites received, per capita, the lion's share of public funds earmarked for public education. The criminal justice system and the machinery of law enforcement—judges, juries, prosecutors, lawyers, sheriffs, and policemen—constituted the all-white bulwark of a political structure designed to intimidate and subordinate the black population.

To be sure, the South was not a cultural monolith, and a careful study of race relations reveals local variations and minor exceptions. By and large, the states on the periphery of the old Confederacy, which had proportionately larger white populations, treated blacks less harshly. Similarly, states such as Texas and Virginia displayed a more generous attitude toward black education. Variations and exceptions, however, confirmed the rule. A few small pockets of black voting—in boss-run Memphis, Tennessee, for example—did not alter the overall picture of black political exclusion. Nor did modest encouragement of black secondary education in the peripheral states entail a commitment on the part of whites to equality of opportunity. Moreover, whites throughout the South, in overwhelming numbers, endorsed racial segregation in principle and practice. Despite the onrush of modernization, which seemed to be eroding the social and economic basis of white supremacy, the possibility of an integrated society did not enter their minds except as a constant threat to be kept at bay.

From the perspective of the twenty-first century, historians can see that the solidity of the South's caste system in 1940 was more apparent than real. Indeed, if the classic "age of segregation" extended from 1896 to 1954—from *Plessy* to *Brown*—then the term "caste system" is a misnomer. As its relative brevity indicates, white supremacy was never secure. One of the defining features of "caste," writes sociologist Charles S. Johnson, is the stability guaranteed by "mutual acceptance of and adjustment to" the system. In other words, in a true caste system whites need not employ coercion, and blacks would passively accept their inferior status. There should be no friction or violence. Yet this was palpably not the case in the South, where, despite the apparent rigidity of segregation, race relations were ambiguous, uncertain, and charged with tension. Blacks never accepted the validity or permanency of white supremacy. Rather than view blacks as a racial caste, Johnson believed, it was more accurate to describe them as a minority group, for "the essence of minority status is self-consciousness and struggle."[1]

Johnson's research in Louisiana on the eve of U.S. entry into World War II—an "ecological survey" conducted by a team from Fisk University with the help of local blacks—reinforced his skepticism about applying caste theory to the American South. In a recent analysis of the evidence collected by Johnson's researchers, who worked mainly in Louisiana's small cities and rural parishes, historian Phillip J. Johnson detected a "pattern of black assertiveness and white flexibility" that suggested "gradual change and adjustment throughout the 1930s and into the 1940s." In a recent study focusing on rural Louisiana, Greta De Jong also draws attention to black resistance, arguing that historians have tended to overestimate the chilling effect of white repression during the early decades of the twentieth century.[2]

Context, however, is everything. There was a difference, both qualitative and quantitative, in black resistance before and after 1940. Before that date—used, of course, as a rough yardstick, not a precise dividing line—black resistance rarely expressed itself as open protest, and even organized civil rights activity attracted relatively little support. One can, it is true, trace a continuous record of civil rights activism in Louisiana back to 1914, when a group of blacks in Shreveport organized a branch of the National Association for the Advancement of Colored People (NAACP), the first in the Deep South, which was followed in 1915 by the stronger and more enduring New Orleans chapter. And it is certainly true that instances of black resistance to white authority—as when blacks forcefully and sometimes violently confronted landlords, employers, sheriffs, and bus drivers—were surprisingly common. Apparent continuities, however, are deceptive. Before 1940, for example, very few blacks joined the NAACP, which presented no real threat to white supremacy (despite the fact that many whites understood that the NAACP represented a serious *potential* threat). Moreover, individual instances of spontaneous black defiance did not add up to a serious challenge to white domination; whites easily disposed of them through legal prosecutions and, if necessary, extralegal violence. Before about 1940, then, blacks in Louisiana commanded such meager resources, and could expect so little in the way of external assistance, that open, organized challenges to white supremacy were infrequent and ineffective. The mass of the black population exhibited little confidence in their ability to break out of segregation. As Richard H. King has argued, too much emphasis upon continuities obscures what was fresh, original, and dynamic about the civil rights movement of the 1950s and 1960s.[3]

Still, the civil rights movement did not emerge fully formed in the mid-1950s. It had a period of gestation. The late 1930s and 1940s saw a transformation of black activism that laid the groundwork for the civil rights movement of the 1950s and 1960s. Yet the civil rights movement was not a straightforward continuation of 1940s developments. Whether we see the 1940s as a "pre–civil rights movement" or as the first chapter of a two-chapter story (the second being the more familiar

Montgomery-to-Memphis tale), two important discontinuities separated the black activism of the Roosevelt-Truman era from civil rights struggles of the post-*Brown* years. First, the cold war had disruptive and repressive effects upon the American Left, of which the civil rights struggle was a part. Federal anti-communism and McCarthyite inquisitions destroyed left-wing organizations, split the Congress of Industrial Organizations (CIO), weakened civil rights groups, and limited the scope of political debate.[4] Second, although the *Brown* decision represented a triumph for the NAACP—the culmination of a legal campaign that began in the mid-1930s—it also provoked a ferocious counterattack from the South's ultra-segregationists that in 1956 shattered the NAACP. This crisis compelled blacks in the South, including Louisiana, to improvise new organizations and devise new tactics.[5]

In what ways, then, did Louisiana exemplify the notion that something vital occurred during the "long 1940s"—between about 1938 and 1954? A brief list of contrasts between these two dates is instructive:

- In 1938 Louisiana boasted fewer than 1,000 black voters; sixteen years later the total surpassed 100,000, and by 1956 it would reach 161,000.
- In 1938, in a field near the north Louisiana town of Ruston, thousands of whites turned out to gawk at the dangling corpse of nineteen-year-old W. C. Williams, who had been lynched in classic southern style by a mob. Although the identities of the killers were public knowledge, a local grand jury failed to return any indictments. By 1954, eight years had passed since the occurrence of the state's last lynching, the murder of twenty-eight-year-old John C. Jones near Minden, an act perpetrated by a small group of men acting furtively. After an FBI investigation, Jones's alleged killers faced a criminal trial in a federal court in Shreveport.
- In 1938 Louisiana spent $51 on the education of each white child but only $14 on each black child. By 1952 the figures were $151 and $99.
- In 1938 racial segregation appeared to be a monolithic system that brooked no exceptions. By 1954, however, black policemen were serving in all of Louisiana's major cities; New Orleans had integrated City Park, as well as its public libraries; black graduate students were attending Louisiana State University; and black undergraduates had been, or were about to be, admitted to state colleges in Lake Charles, Lafayette, and Hammond.[6]

These contrasts are even more impressive if one considers the unpromising political context before 1945. President Franklin D. Roosevelt was notoriously reluctant to challenge southern racism: dependent upon the support of southern congressional leaders, he acquiesced in racial segregation, refused to support a federal anti-lynching law, and generally avoided the issue of racial discrimination. With some exceptions—the activities of Eleanor Roosevelt and notably the insistence of Secretary of the Interior Harold L. Ickes that blacks should receive a proportionate share of Works Progress Administration benefits—the New Deal for the most part conformed to the racial preferences of the white South.

The major exception to Roosevelt's hands-off policy with regard to racial matters was Executive Order 8802, which banned racial discrimination in defense-related industries and set up the Fair Employment Practices Committee (FEPC). But this concession to black leaders, prompted by A. Philip Randolph's threatened "March on Washington," had a marginal effect upon southern employment patterns. In New Orleans, the Delta shipyard company resisted FEPC pressure to hire black welders, employing only sixty blacks among its six-thousand-strong workforce.[7] When the first black welders appeared at a shipyard in Morgan City, they encountered such hostility from whites that a state official withdrew them "unhurt but still unemployed."[8] A training school for black welders in New Iberia evoked such white hostility that it lasted barely a week: the black leaders responsible for its establishment—the leaders of the local NAACP—were expelled from the parish on the orders of Sheriff Gilbert Ozenne and Superintendent of Schools Lloyd G. Porter. Several were beaten.[9] Worse violence occurred in other states: FEPC directives sparked riots in the dockyards of Mobile, Alabama, and Beaumont, Texas.[10] Roosevelt, well aware of the need to shore up his political support among white southerners, downgraded the FEPC. It survived his death by only a year.

The political situation in Louisiana was hardly propitious for African Americans. Despite the displacement of a conservative oligarchy by an insurgent group led by Huey P. Long, the political conflicts that gripped the state between 1928 and 1940 did little to enhance the status of Louisiana's blacks. While Long generally eschewed the race-baiting oratory of contemporaries like Theodore Bilbo (Mississippi), Tom Heflin (Alabama), and Gene Talmadge (Georgia), in other respects the "Kingfish" was a typical southern politician when it came to the race question. He defended lynching, never questioned racial segregation, indulged in racial slurs against his political opponents, and permitted widening disparities between black and white schools. Although he abolished the poll tax, at a stroke doubling the number of white voters, Long resolutely opposed black suffrage. Moreover, if he was personally indifferent to racial issues, his henchmen included Gerald L. K. Smith and Leander Perez, two of the most extreme racists in the South.[11]

Louisiana, of course, was not insulated from the broader left-wing currents of the 1930s. The CIO struggled to gain a foothold in the Pelican State, where union organizers were confronted by violence and intimidation from policemen and American Federation of Labor (AFL) goons. By 1945 several CIO unions had finally established a presence in New Orleans. The Communist Party began working in Louisiana in 1936, operating from a base in New Orleans. In addition to establishing a strong covert presence in the CIO—the unions it controlled included Local 206 of the Transport Workers Union—the party also fostered black organizations like the Southern Negro Youth Congress, supported biracial groups such as the Southern Conference for Human Welfare (SCHW), and organized the Louisiana Farmers Union in an effort to organize sharecroppers and tenant farmers. After the war the Communist Party organized the Civil Rights Congress; it boasted an active chapter in New Orleans.

What did all this radical activity amount to? Was it the "autonomous, labor-oriented civil rights movement" that, according to Korstad and Lichtenstein, kick-started the "civil rights era . . . dramatically and decisively, in the early 1940s"? Yes and no. The rise of the CIO and the energetic activities of the Communist Party gave a temporary boost to the civil rights struggle, but the strength and duration of that infusion should not be exaggerated. The collective membership of the CIO unions was a small fraction of the total workforce. The bulk of white union members remained in AFL unions, most of which were hostile to blacks and sometimes excluded them outright. Moreover, even the CIO unions organized along segregated lines, generally downplaying official antidiscrimination policies in order not to alienate white members. A few, like the Marine Cooks and Stewards and the Food, Tobacco and Agricultural Workers, took equality of opportunity more seriously, but these were usually among the smallest labor organizations. As Alan Draper has pointed out, historians who contend that the CIO was capable of challenging Jim Crow "have built their case on marginal unions." The influence of the Communist Party in Louisiana was likewise marginal. Although New Orleans was a key Communist Party base in the South, the party had less than two hundred members in the entire state. After 1940 it effectively abandoned its efforts to expand into rural areas via the Louisiana Farmers Union. Moreover, the party's inconsistent tactics hampered its antidiscrimination policies and inspired distrust among the party's non-Communist allies. Abrupt flip-flops in 1939 and 1941 clearly exposed its devotion to the Soviet Union, thereby weakening its influence and severely disrupting organizations like the SCHW.[12]

If there is little evidence that domestic politics, national or state, changed to the advantage of blacks before 1945, perhaps World War II weakened white supremacy. It is now more than thirty years since Richard Dalfiume asserted that the first half of the 1940s represented "the forgotten years of the Negro revolution."[13] Since then, however, although dozens of books and articles have examined the domestic impact of the war, no consensus has emerged regarding the overall effect of that conflict upon race relations. Although it has become something of a truism that the war heightened racial tensions, and that black soldiers returned home from Europe and the Pacific with a determined resolve to oppose segregation and discrimination, numerous studies have disputed the idea that World War II represented a decisive turning point for blacks. Harvard Sitkoff, in particular, has long articulated a skepticism about Dalfiume's thesis, insisting that black wartime militancy was more rhetorical than real and that government pressure and the riots of 1943 persuaded mainstream black leaders to shy away from radical tactics. When such leaders showed no disposition to openly challenge segregation, it was hardly surprising that blacks in the South failed to respond to Randolph's proposals for mass nonviolent direct action. Hence, while segregated public transportation was a continual focus of racial tension during the war, the countless individual flare-ups on trains, streetcars, and buses—some of which led to the arrest, beating, and even death of black passengers—never congealed into a coherent protest against segregation.[14]

What, then, accounted for the sea change in race relations exemplified by the rise of black voting, the *Brown* decision, and the Montgomery Bus Boycott? One factor of enormous—indeed decisive—significance was the growing potency of the NAACP. From a low point in the early 1930s, when the Great Depression devastated its financial base and the Communist Party threatened to steal its popular constituency, the NAACP made a strong recovery to become, in the 1940s, the cutting edge of the civil rights struggle. A campaign against racial discrimination in public education, waged through the courts under the direction of Charles Houston and Thurgood Marshall, boosted the NAACP's effectiveness. The growth of the organization's membership, an expansion that got under way in the late 1930s and accelerated spectacularly during the war, meant that for the first time in its history the NAACP acquired a broad base of popular support.

By charting the NAACP's progress in Louisiana we can see how this growth rested upon both national strategy and local organization. The litigation of Houston and Marshall, which targeted the entire South, including the border states, could not succeed, or even get under way, without local plaintiffs and locally raised defense funds. These support networks operated through local NAACP branches; however, they sometimes had to first *capture* local branches in order to orient them toward the NAACP's national strategy.

New Orleans provided a classic example of what was happening in big-city branches across the country, as an insurgent faction challenged an entrenched branch leadership. In 1939 the New Orleans chapter claimed only three hundred members in a city that boasted a black population of 156,000. Insurance company executives, undertakers, and doctors dominated the branch's executive committee, comprising an interlocking directorate that shared business, political, and family ties. Under the guidance of these men, the branch made little effort to attract new members, showed scant interest in the economic plight of the black working class, and was excessively cautious in pursuing the NAACP's civil rights agenda. When it had resorted to court action, the chapter refused to utilize the services of A. P. Tureaud, one of the few black attorneys in the state, and instead retained white lawyers who were venal, incompetent, or both. After the loss of two lawsuits—one filed against the registrar of voters, the other against the Municipal Auditorium Commission—a group of malcontents entered their own slate of candidates in the 1939 branch elections. Calling themselves "The Group," the insurgents started their own newspaper, the *New Orleans Sentinel*, and kept Thurgood Marshall, head of the NAACP Legal Defense Fund, apprised of their tactics. It took them two years of organizing and maneuvering, but in 1941 The Group finally ousted the old guard and took control of the branch.

The significance of this leadership shift was threefold. First, it marked a victory for race unity over color-caste consciousness among blacks. The NAACP's efforts in New Orleans had long been bedeviled by the division between the Creoles of color—many of whom descended from the French-speaking *gens de couleur libre* (free Negroes) of antebellum times—and the majority black population. The Creoles were often lighter in complexion and usually Roman Catholic rather than Protestant. Although they had ceased to speak French by the 1930s, they still distinguished themselves from "American Negroes," and they remained clannish and inward looking, their sense of identity reinforced by strong social networks, both formal and informal. Geography perpetuated the Creoles' separateness. Concentrated in certain trades, the Creoles clustered in the city's Seventh Ward, situated below the French Quarter, the home of Corpus Christi Church and St. Augustine High School, both of which served black Catholics. The Protestant "American Negroes," on the other hand, usually darker in complexion and the descendants of slaves, lived above Canal Street, beyond the French Quarter and the central business district. This cultural cleavage was profound: Creoles venturing into black neighborhoods "uptown" feared hostility and aggression; "American Negroes" rarely strayed into the Seventh Ward. Although the distinction between "downtown" and "uptown" persists to this day, by 1941 it no longer prevented cooperative action among Creoles and non-Creoles.

Second, the triumph of The Group testified to rising class consciousness among blacks, itself an important factor in blurring the distinction between Creoles and Americans. In the 1930s, under pressure from challenges from the Communist Party and other rivals, the NAACP began to place much more emphasis upon economic issues and the plight of the black poor. Keenly aware that the Great Depression had hit blacks with disproportionate severity, the NAACP's national leadership threw its support behind organized labor, decisively backing the CIO's efforts to recruit black workers and its campaign to organize American industry. Walter White's support for the United Auto Workers in the Ford strike of 1941 exemplified the new NAACP-CIO alliance.

The Group closely reflected the NAACP's new orientation toward organized labor. Although its members were, according to the African American class structure, middle class rather than working class, they included schoolteachers, who in New Orleans had been unionized since 1937; mailmen, who belonged to the National Alliance of Postal Employees; and a couple of CIO organizers. The Group's newspaper, the *Sentinel,* was leftish in outlook and sympathetic to labor unions.

A 1940 strike by black insurance agents dramatically exposed class divisions within the New Orleans branch: The Group supported the agents' efforts to form a CIO union, but many branch officers—men who had an ownership stake in the insurance companies—opposed the strike. Although the agents won recognition from only one of the four companies, the strike ultimately strengthened The Group. The anti-CIO bias of the branch's executive committee was clearly out of step with national NAACP policy, and an effort by one branch official to organize a company union prompted the national board of directors to publicly rebuke him. The strikers, on the other hand, not only inspired widespread popular support but also created two new leaders, Daniel Byrd and Ernest Wright, both of whom became stalwarts of the civil rights struggle. Byrd, a native of Arkansas who grew up in Indiana, was elected president of the New Orleans branch in 1941 and then, as full-time executive director, oversaw the expansion of branch membership to six thousand during the war years. After the war he worked as a field secretary for the NAACP Legal Defense Fund. Ernest Wright emerged from the insurance strike as a popular hero—he had served time in jail—and, cultivating the support of the Communist Party, built on his position as a CIO organizer to found his own organization, the People's Defense League (PDL). Although the NAACP soon came to distrust Wright—he and Byrd became bitter enemies—Wright's PDL championed the same causes and aroused popular support for the civil rights struggle.

Third, the advent of The Group had enormous significance for the NAACP's legal campaign against unequal public education. With crucial support from black teachers, expressed through the Louisiana Colored Teachers Association, a statewide organization, and Local 527 of the American Federation of Teachers, a black unit that covered New Orleans, the branch engaged A. P. Tureaud to file a lawsuit in federal court against the Orleans Parish School Board. Acting on behalf of elementary school principal Joseph McKelpin, the suit alleged that the lower salaries paid to black teachers constituted illegal racial discrimination and violated the Fourteenth Amendment.

This was a precedent-making action in several respects. The McKelpin suit marked the first occasion on which the New Orleans NAACP retained a colored attorney and also the first time the branch worked closely with Thurgood Marshall. Marshall's experience, garnered from dealing with white lawyers and officials throughout the South, made all the difference. Counseling the inexperienced Tureaud on legal tactics, Marshall stressed that "The thing we have to bear in mind is that the pressure is on the school board and not on us.... It is just like a checker game, and it is now their move." The first lawsuit of its kind in Louisiana, it resulted in a favorable decision, federal district judge Wayne G. Borah sustained the plaintiff's position, and the school board agreed to equalize salaries by September 1943. Tureaud filed similar suits in a handful of other parishes. Despite legal setbacks and the difficulty of sustaining teachers' morale in the face of economic reprisals—school boards invariably fired the plaintiffs—white officials eventually threw in the towel, and in 1948 the state legislature enacted across-the-board equalization. Although limited in scope, the salary equalization campaign was a significant victory. It put money into teachers' pockets, elevated teachers' status as professionals, and vindicated the NAACP's strategy of using the courts to attack inequalities in public education.[15]

Although this account has so far focused on New Orleans, the NAACP grew stronger throughout Louisiana between 1935 and 1945. Monroe and Baton Rouge were home to substantial chapters in the 1930s, the dormant Shreveport branch was reorganized in 1936, and new branches were chartered in Lake Providence and other small towns. The war dramatically accelerated the NAACP's expansion: in 1940 it claimed fourteen branches in Louisiana; in 1946 it boasted thirty-three branches and a total of ten thousand members. Wartime conditions not only fostered record membership levels but also strengthened the NAACP as a state organization. The Alexandria office, hitherto only fitfully active, found itself surrounded by military bases, and it received a stream of complaints from black soldiers concerning mistreatment in the army and discrimination whenever they traveled off the base. When three soldiers were accused of raping a white waitress at Camp Livingstone and were sentenced to death, the branch became the focal point of a case that gained national attention—a "little Scottsboro" that brought Thurgood Marshall to Louisiana in a successful bid to save their lives. This case spurred the formation, in 1943, of the Louisiana State Conference of Branches, which held regular meetings for the purpose of exchanging information, bolstering morale, and promoting a common program.[16]

For the first time, Louisiana's NAACP branches began to operate in a coordinated statewide fashion. One key to the organization's newfound effectiveness was an agreement between the Louisiana Education Association (LEA) and the NAACP Legal Defense Fund. In 1943 the LEA agreed to finance all the Legal Defense Fund's educational cases in Louisiana, for which they received the services of Thurgood Marshall and A. P. Tureaud. It was "a kind of package deal," Tureaud recalled: the LEA wanted Marshall, but the latter insisted on being associated with a local attorney. Tureaud was a fortunate choice; although cautious and conservative, he displayed competence and commitment. From the 1940s to the 1960s, this quintessential New Orleans Creole—family man, devout Catholic, and bon vivant—handled virtually all of the NAACP's litigation in Louisiana.[17]

The LEA's own contribution went further than the promotion of court cases. Former Ruston schoolteacher J. K. Haynes, who in 1947 became the LEA's first full-time executive secretary, worked hard to strengthen the NAACP in the northern parishes, and public school teachers often made up the backbone of local branches. By the early 1950s the LEA was also supporting voter-registration campaigns and sponsoring, with the Prince Hall Masons, leadership-training institutes at Southern University. The LEA's elastic membership criteria, which allowed bus drivers, Parent-Teacher Association leaders, and custodians to join, broadened its roots in black communities; with the emergence of a significant black vote, white politicians learned to respect its political influence. "The leadership of LEA was extremely forceful (some would say uppity), and it was extremely successful," recalled a white official of the National Education Association. "They stuck their noses in places where school people should be afraid to enter."[18]

The rise of black voting between 1940 and 1955 represented, on the surface, the most abrupt contrast with the preceding four decades. The raw figures for the number of registered black voters were impressive: 1,029 (1944); 7,561 (1946); 22,000 (1948); 65,000 (1950); 95,000 (1952); 107,000 (1952); 127,000 (1955). Black political organizations, nearly all of them locally based, sprouted across the state. Some of them were NAACP branches by another name; others mirrored the principal white political factions; still others were efforts to shake down gullible politicians by promising to "deliver" a certain number of votes in exchange for money. The NAACP-backed Louisiana Progressive Voters League tried to coordinate voter registration and political action across the state, although it had few resources and only a limited influence. Still, by 1956, when black registration had climbed to 161,000, black voters were a force to be reckoned with, accounting for a healthy 16 percent of the total electorate. It was small wonder that many white politicians now openly appealed to black voters, spoke to black audiences, and cultivated black leaders—including men like A. P. Tureaud and J. K. Haynes.

Examining the surge of black voting during these years, one cannot help being struck by the sheer energy and persistence of black registration campaigns, as well as the number and variety of groups involved in them. Political education, of course, required money, and organizations like the LEA, the Prince Hall Masons, and the Knights of Peter Claver (composed of black Catholics) could supply it. In New Orleans, the well-heeled International Longshoremen's Association sponsored registration classes and bought radio time. Although the Southern Negro Youth Congress folded in 1948, its "right-to-vote" campaign, launched at a conference in New Orleans in 1940, helped to waken blacks from their political slumber. From the pulpits of the Baptist Church—not as a whole especially prominent in the civil rights cause—some ministers preached voter registration year in and year out. In New Orleans, for example, Rev. Abraham Lincoln Davis, pastor of New Zion Baptist Church and president of the Interdenominational Ministerial Alliance, probably did more than anyone else to popularize voting among the city's black Protestants.

National developments, of course, provided a favorable context for the black political renaissance. In *Smith v. Allwright* (1944) the U.S. Supreme Court outlawed the all-white primary election, a decision of limited scope and impact that nonetheless expressed a growing intolerance on the part of that tribunal for the South's blatant racial discrimination. Sensitive to such judicial signals, as well as to the pro–civil rights stance of the Truman administration, federal district and appeals courts began to rule in favor of black plaintiffs who sued registrars for rejecting their applications. In *Hall v. Nagel* (1946), a case relating to St. John the Baptist Parish, the U.S. Court of Appeals for the Fifth Circuit decreed that disfranchised blacks could sue in federal court without having to first go through the state courts. Four years later, U.S. District judge J. Skelly Wright enjoined the registrar of Washington Parish from refusing to enroll black voters. A year later Louisiana's Democratic Party finally stopped trying to exclude blacks from voting in the primaries in defiance of the Supreme Court's 1944 ruling. And in 1952 Judge Gaston Porterie ordered the registrar of Bossier Parish to stop turning away black applicants on the grounds that they could not supply two white voters to "identify" them. In others parishes lawsuits never came to court: registrars saw that they would lose and began registering blacks.[19]

For many white politicians, as in the case of army veteran delesseps S. Morrison, first elected mayor of New Orleans in 1946, race was an issue of secondary importance. Morrison regarded blacks as inferiors and believed in racial segregation, but he was not an inflexible white supremacist. Prepared to accept a degree of change, he saw race as a matter to be managed and controlled. Contemporaries like Russell B. Long (son of the Kingfish), who was elected to the U.S. Senate in 1948, shared Morrison's pragmatic approach to race.

Louisiana's factionalized politics both encouraged blacks to seek the ballot and encouraged many white politicians to allow them to vote. The rise to power of Huey Long, who dominated state politics between 1928 and 1935, did little to empower blacks directly, but it did provide them with political inspiration and political education. Blacks appreciated Long's refusal to indulge in race-baiting campaign rhetoric, and they chuckled over his alleged remark on racial purity: "You could feed all the pure whites in Louisiana with a nickel's worth of red beans and a dime's worth of rice." They also believed that Long's appeal to the poor transcended race and that the Kingfish went out of his way to let blacks hear his message. When Long visited New Iberia, recalled Matthew Polk, a young teacher at the time, he spoke in the auditorium of a white high school. "No Negro had entered that gymnasium before, except as janitor. Long parked his car at city hall and invited us into the gym." According to Rev. J. H. Scott, a farmer, minister, and NAACP leader in East Carroll Parish, Long inspired hope in blacks, who "saw the poor whites who had not been voting begin to vote and to get recognition." A. P. Tureaud reflected that Long "awakened [blacks] to the possibility of what an aggressive leader could do" and made them aspire to "become a part of this aggressiveness and leadership."[20]

The polarization of Louisiana politics into pro-Long and anti-Long factions endured for a quarter of a century after Huey Long's assassination in 1935. This persistent bifactionalism tempted white politicians, in the wake of *Smith v. Allwright,* to allow some blacks to vote in order to gain an electoral advantage over their rivals. Most of these politicians were allies of Earl Long, and the rate of black registration rose sharply after he was first elected governor in 1948. Because they stressed economic issues rather than race, and because they tended to live outside the old plantation areas and were not faced with potential black majorities, Longite politicians found it easier to appeal to blacks and had less to fear from them.

The small city of Monroe illustrates how a complex interplay of personal, economic, and political relationships eroded, or at least modified, white supremacy in an area of northern Louisiana often considered intransigently racist. When Arnold Bernstein became mayor in 1919, Monroe boasted one of the worst records for lynchings in the nation. During his eighteen-year tenure, Bernstein, a Jewish businessman, helped to dispel Monroe's reputation for violent racism. He opposed the Ku Klux Klan and discouraged police brutality. He also paid for a black schoolteacher, Henry Carroll, to attend Southern University. Later mayors, including Harvey Beloit and John Coon, continued Bernstein's policies of racial moderation.[21]

In the late 1940s, Henry Carroll emerged as the key mediator between the white and black communities in Monroe, as well as an important black supporter of Earl Long. His career and influence depended upon the patronage of powerful whites—first Bernstein (who died in 1939), then James A. Noe. Noe was a wealthy politician with close links to the Long machine, with extensive business interests that included ownership of a radio station and, later, a television station. Through the intercession of Noe's wife, Anna, a member of the school board, Henry Carroll, was selected to be principal of Monroe Colored High School, a position he held for more than twenty years. The Noes then helped Carroll to secure a new school building, which was renamed Carroll High School. When Noe's radio station began broadcasting a weekly program, *The Voice of the South,* devoted to the black community, Carroll acted as commentator. Later, Carroll hosted a children's show on Noe's television station. When, after 1948, black voter registration became a significant factor in Monroe politics, Carroll became one of Noe's closest political allies. "His endorsement of a candidate was almost tantamount to full Negro support at the polls, and Carroll never backed a candidate not supported by his friend and backer James A. Noe."[22]

In 1956 the White Citizens Councils challenged the registration of most of Monroe's black voters, Carroll included. Carroll immediately sought Noe's help. Incensed by the voter purge—which was clearly aimed at Earl Long and his political allies—Noe dashed to the courthouse and would have come to blows with William M. Shaw, a state-appointed attorney and Citizens Council ringleader, had not Carroll physically restrained him. Later, after he regained his composure, Noe warned that if the Citizens Councils purged black voters, "they will, as well, disfranchise our Italians, our Jews, our Catholics, or even our Protestants."[23]

The correlation between Longite political control and high levels of black voter registration—and between anti-Longite control and low black voter registration—was never precise. For one thing, by 1952 over a third of the black voters resided in Shreveport, Baton Rouge, and New Orleans—cities controlled by anti-Longite politicians. In 1956, Earl Long won a landslide victory in the gubernatorial primary, losing in only thirteen of Louisiana's sixty-four parishes. In four of the thirteen anti-Long parishes, black registration was nil or negligible: in one it stood at 10 percent, in five it varied from 11 to 49 percent, and in three it surpassed 50 percent. In staunchly pro-Long Washington Parish, on the other hand, black registration stood at only 27 percent. In fact, because many politicians switched their allegiances from election to election, coherent factions were hard to identify. Nevertheless, blacks themselves had little doubt that the Long machine favored black voting more positively than its opponents. Moreover, the *strongest* opponents of black voting tended to be the most vehement and consistent opponents of Earl Long. Thompson Clarke, a convinced anti-Longite politician, served as district attorney for Tensas, East Carroll, Madison, and West Feliciana Parishes, where no blacks voted. Willie Rainach, the most conservative member of the Louisiana senate, represented Claiborne Parish, where black registration was insignificant. Leander H. Perez—once a Longite but by the 1950s one of Earl Long's most formidable enemies—ensured that the registrar of Plaquemines Parish kept blacks off the rolls.[24]

In the parishes of southern Louisiana, especially in the French-speaking region of Acadiana—"Cajun" country—the Catholic Church encouraged black registration. Indeed, the correlation between black voting and Catholicism is stronger than that between black voting and Longism. French-speaking politicians like U.S. senator Allan J. Ellender and U.S. congressman Jimmie Domengeaux had been just as outspoken in their opposition to black voting as their Anglo-Saxon counterparts in northern Louisiana. But in 1951 Bishop Jules Jeanmard of the Lafayette diocese issued a pastoral letter in which he condemned "the official who has resort to subterfuge in order to rob a citizen, otherwise qualified, of his right to register and vote, because of the color of his skin." Blacks were soon voting in large proportions throughout Cajun country. By 1956, one study showed, black registration in Louisiana's twenty-five predominantly Catholic parishes stood at 51 percent, more than twice the level in the mainly Protestant parishes.[25]

Black voting did not uproot white supremacy, nor did it abolish segregation. It nonetheless profoundly influenced race relations. St. Landry Parish provided a particularly dramatic example. In 1950 the NAACP regarded St. Landry, although a typical Cajun area, as one of the most repressive in the state. When A. P. Tureaud filed a suit to equalize school facilities, he could only induce blacks to petition the school board if they signed as representatives of organizations rather than as individuals. Even so, the plaintiffs began to withdraw their names, one by one, after suffering economic retaliation, jail beatings, and face-to-face threats from the district attorney, J. Y. Fontenot. On June 5, 1950, an organizer from the Louisiana Progressive Voters League, Alvin H. Jones, accompanied a group of blacks from the hamlet of Lebeau—where a white Catholic priest had encouraged blacks to seek the ballot—to the parish courthouse in Opelousas. Upon entering the office of the registrar of voters, they were set upon by whites. Jones suffered severe head wounds and died eighteen months later. In 1951 three blacks sued the registrar of voters: a deputy sheriff slew one of the plaintiffs outside a tavern; the other two plaintiffs fled the parish.[26]

Less than a year later, however, black lawyer Richard B. Millspaugh received a phone call from local bigwig L. Austin Fontenot Sr. (father of the district attorney) assuring him that blacks would be able to register without fear of harassment or assault. In two years the number of black voters increased from none to two thousand, and in the November 1954 elections blacks helped to end the thirteen-year tenure of Mayor T. W. Huntington. The incoming sheriff, D. J. "The Cat" Doucet, removed all restrictions on black registration, and by 1956 the number of black voters stood at thirteen thousand, more than 80 percent of the potential and 40 percent of the total electorate. Like Sheriff Tom Poppell of McIntosh County, Georgia, the hero/villain of Melissa Fay Greene's *Praying for Sheetrock,* Doucet benefited from extensive corruption—he tolerated gambling and prostitution—but enjoyed overwhelming black support. A benevolent despot, Doucet cultivated the black vote through small favors: if someone fell ill, for example, he would dispatch a police car to carry the person to the hospital. In the late 1950s he successfully defended St. Landry's liberal registration policy against racist efforts to eliminate black voters.[27]

In addition to NAACP-backed lawsuits, pressure from the federal government also helped to change white minds in St. Landry Parish. Although the federal government consistently refused to intervene on behalf of blacks in the South during this period, NAACP officials remained in close contact with the Department of Justice, which began to deploy the FBI in investigations of alleged civil rights violations. Pressed by the NAACP, the FBI investigated the fatal assault of Alvin Jones, interviewing dozens of witnesses but failing to identify the assailants. Such probes, while undertaken with palpable lack of enthusiasm by the FBI and usually, like this one, inconclusive, nevertheless warned white officials that if they subjected blacks to intimidation and violence, their actions would not pass unnoticed.[28]

Hence, for all their success in fending off the threat of federal intervention in southern race relations—best exemplified by Congress's failure to enact any part of President Truman's civil rights program—Louisiana's political leaders knew that federal pressure was growing, not merely FBI investigations but also U.S. Supreme Court decisions that affected the rulings of federal judges in Louisiana. World War II had to a large extent discredited racism as an ideology, and the cold war had made the federal government embarrassingly aware that southern segregation was a diplomatic liability. By 1948 racial integration was, in theory if not in practice, the official policy of the federal government. While die-hard segregationists insisted that white supremacy could be preserved intact by means of intensified resistance, a growing number of Louisiana's politicians concluded that racial segregation could only be preserved in substance if whites made concessions on the margins and accorded the black population a greater measure of justice and opportunity.

Concessions should not be exaggerated. For example, when white politicians permitted a degree of black voting, they carefully controlled the level of black registration. In New Orleans, for example, where the governor appointed the registrar of voters directly, black registration remained "stuck" at about twenty-five thousand, less than a quarter of the potential, despite persistent registration campaigns by black organizations. In other words, despite his racial liberalism, Earl Long did not wish to see too large a black electorate in New Orleans, whose popular mayor, "Chep" Morrison, was a political rival. Statewide, blacks made up only 15 percent of the total electorate in the mid-1950s. Even in parishes with higher levels of black voting, white control of the registration process meant that the black vote tended to be an administered and manipulated one. In Jefferson Parish, for example, Sheriff Frank "King" Clancy had the ability to deliver the black vote to any gubernatorial candidate of his choice. In rural areas, especially, blacks stood in awe of the "high sheriff"—an elected official with more power than his counterpart in many other states—and followed his political guidance. Even so, the competitive factionalism of Louisiana politics meant that in many parishes, including the cities, black voters wielded some influence.[29]

The effect of black voting on race relations should not be underestimated. The Montgomery Bus Boycott of 1955–56 is rightly regarded as a major turning point, the occasion when a civil rights struggle became a civil rights *movement* and when blacks demonstrated the effectiveness of mass nonviolent direct action as a weapon against segregation. Yet the apparent suddenness of this change—which surprised and astonished contemporary observers—disguised the fact that the incorporation of blacks into the South's political system, however partial and imperfect, made possible the kind of open confrontation that ten years earlier had been unthinkable.[30] Together with the looming prospect of federal intervention, voting not only encouraged black ambitions but also helped to eliminate much of the violence that, manifest and latent, had underpinned white supremacy before 1940. Although the civil rights movement precipitated acts of white violence and led to a number of deaths, a remarkable fact about the period from 1955 to 1965 is that white violence was relatively limited and black casualties relatively few. The ability of the civil rights movement to focus national and world attention on that limited amount of violence testified not only to the tactical skill of the movement's leaders but also to the sea change that had occurred between 1940 and 1955.

The most obvious example of that sea change was the passing of lynching from the southern scene. After falling away sharply during the 1920s and experiencing a small upsurge during the early years of the Depression, lynching declined rapidly in the 1930s—so rapidly, in fact, that in June 1940 sociologist Monroe Work of Tuskegee Institute, the most careful compiler of relevant statistics, declared that no lynchings had taken place at all during the previous twelve months. Although the NAACP disputed, with good reason, the narrowness of Work's definition of lynching, it was clear that the South's political leaders were attempting to stamp out the traditional practice whereby white civilians summarily executed blacks in cold blood. In July 1940, when the authorities in Natchitoches arrested a black organizer of the Louisiana Farmers Union, state attorney general Eugene Stanley warned the district attorney that there was to be "no lynching!" With the federal government increasingly concerned about mob violence, he explained, "We've got to be careful. The State is on the spot." Ironically, at a time when the nation was more aware of lynching than ever before—1940 was the year that Abe Meeropol wrote the Billie Holliday hit "Strange Fruit"—lynching had almost disappeared.[31]

The South still seemed an inhospitable environment for open protest. In 1943, A. Philip Randolph's call for nonviolent direct action in the South fell upon deaf ears. Four years later, Thurgood Marshall publicly disapproved of the kind of direct-action tactics being advocated by the Congress of Racial Equality—deliberately violating segregation laws on interstate buses, for example—on the grounds that they would only provoke bloodshed. The political climate of the postwar years further discouraged direct action: McCarthyism associated radical protest with communism; liberalism feared that mass action fostered authoritarianism. Between 1945 and 1955, according to historians August Meier and Elliott Rudwick, nonviolent direct action "nearly ceased to be a weapon in the black protest struggle." Louisiana seemed no exception. Even peaceful picketing evoked repression: the city of New Orleans had one policy toward labor unions, another toward civil rights groups. In 1947, for example, the NAACP formed a "Consumers League" that organized a boycott of four Canal Street department stores. The boycott collapsed, however, when the police refused to allow blacks to picket the stores.

Even local Communists felt that conditions in New Orleans made public protests impractical. When instructed by a party official in New York to picket the state supreme court, Dillard University teacher Oakley Johnson flatly refused: "picket lines here would be slightly suicidal."[32]

But appearances were deceptive. Across the South, although unnoticed as part of regional pattern, instances of direct action were multiplying. They often involved young people. In October 1946, for example, four hundred children in Lumberton, North Carolina, protested against their dilapidated school buildings by trooping out of their classrooms. Led by members of the NAACP Youth Council and supported by their elders, the young strikers paraded through town bearing placards: "How Can I Learn When I am Cold?" and "It Rains on Me." They stayed out of school for nine days. Five years later, in Farmville, Virginia, sixteen-year-old Barbara Johns led a similar student strike, a protest that generated a lawsuit against the school board—one of the *Brown* cases. In Louisiana, also in 1951, parents and children in Alexandria picketed the Rapides Parish courthouse after the school board delayed the beginning of the school term in response to a labor shortage in the cotton fields. Early in 1953, black children in Lafayette boycotted Paul Breaux High School—newly built "but still not up to the physical plant of the white schools." NAACP official Daniel Byrd estimated that more than nine-tenths of the children took part in this protest.[33]

The most significant outbreak of direct action in Louisiana—and the one that foreshadowed the Montgomery Bus Boycott most clearly—occurred in Baton Rouge, the state capital, in June 1953. The bus boycott in Baton Rouge closely resembled its more famous counterpart in several important respects: it was organized by an umbrella group, "an organization of organizations"; it was led by a young Baptist minister who was a relative newcomer to his city; it demanded a fair application of "separate but equal" rather than an end to segregation itself; it mobilized taxis and private cars to provide an alternative transportation system; and it enjoyed solid support from the black community for as long as it lasted. The principal difference, of course, is that the Baton Rouge protest lasted less than a week, the Montgomery Bus Boycott more than a year. Nevertheless, it would be wrong to claim—despite the fact that *Brown v. Board of Education* separated the two events—that the Montgomery Bus Boycott expressed, in its opening phase at least, a higher level of militancy than the boycott in Baton Rouge. It was to a large extent the willingness of white politicians and bus company officials in Baton Rouge to offer a compromise acceptable to the blacks, compared with the intransigence of their white counterparts in Montgomery, that accounted for the brevity of the one protest and the longevity of the other.[34]

The background and politics of the Baton Rouge Bus Boycott are interesting. As in other cities, World War II intensified black discontent over public transportation, both fueling resentment over racial segregation and revealing the shortcoming of transportation systems that failed to adequately service black neighborhoods, which sometimes lay outside city boundaries. In 1942 blacks organized the Union Taxi Line (UTL), which obtained cab insurance from Chicago when unable to obtain it from local insurers. Six years later, continuing dissatisfaction with the city bus company prompted the UTL to begin its own bus service, eventually running about sixty vehicles. However, white officials responded by instigating a grand jury investigation of the UTL, which resulted in the indictment of its manager for fraud. At the same time, white bus drivers went on strike in a successful effort to close down the black-operated buses. Their employer, the white-owned company, acquired a monopoly franchise from the city.[35]

The company's commitment to providing "full and fair" service—a stipulation of its franchise—did not end black discontent. In 1953 the NAACP pressed the city to relax segregation so that black passengers would not have to stand over empty seats that were reserved for whites. This demand chimed with the company's own desire to utilize its vehicles more efficiently. The result was Ordinance 222, passed by the city council in March 1953, which provided for "first-come, first-served" segregated seating—blacks filling the bus from the rear forward and whites seating themselves from the front toward the back. This was the system that had been practiced in Mobile, Alabama, since 1917. Once again, however, white bus drivers went on strike, this time in protest against the perceived arrogance of black passengers, whom the NAACP had advised not to move if ordered to do so. "That Negro outfit . . . is telling Negroes they have a right to sit anywhere they want," complained one driver. Having been reassured that they could enforce the old policy of reserving the front seats for white passengers, the drivers returned to work. At that point blacks launched their boycott.[36]

As in Montgomery, rising black voter registration encouraged blacks in Baton Rouge to feel that white politicians, including Mayor Jesse Webb Jr., would be sensitive to their concerns. Perhaps unwisely, the boycott organization, the United Defense League (UDL), called off the protest when the city council passed Ordinance 251, which reserved the two short front seats for whites and the long rear seat for blacks. The

UDL's belief that it could successfully challenge the new ordinance in the state courts betrayed naïveté: its lawsuit did not stand a chance. Although stopping far short of victory—indeed, it must be counted a defeat—the short-lived boycott revealed the potential power of mass action. The UDL's meetings drew up to eight thousand people; the boycott cost the bus company $1,600 a day in lost revenue.[37]

But the Baton Rouge Bus Boycott also underlined that working-class whites were still deeply attached to racial segregation and that much of this attachment stemmed from a determination to maintain an economic advantage over blacks. The demise of the FEPC—despised as much by white workers as by white employers—meant that the racially segmented labor market outlasted World War II by at least twenty years. In effect, racial discrimination in private employment remained the norm. White workers not only managed to reverse black employment gains in industries like shipbuilding but also succeeded in excluding blacks from the better-paid jobs expanding in sectors such as trade, financial services, and government.

In New Orleans, for example, blacks comprised a third of the population in 1950 but made up a mere 0.08 percent of the workers employed by NOPSI (the city's public utilities company), which employed no black bus drivers at all until 1961. Blacks made up only 0.054 percent of the municipal workforce: the city employed no black firemen and only a handful of black policemen. The president of the New Orleans local of the United Steelworkers (AFL) reported no black members, adding that "the present membership does not wish to have any." Five years later, a CIO official in Baton Rouge opined that "the Negro is a somewhat inferior race." Despite one or two bright spots—teachers' pay improved, and the position of blacks in the post office got better—the economic condition of blacks in Louisiana deteriorated relative to whites. In New Orleans, for example, the proportion of white workers classified as "white collar" increased from 32 percent to 55 percent between 1940 and 1960, but the proportion of blacks in this category grew at a snail's pace, from 8 percent to just 10 percent. Large numbers of blacks were being pushed off the land by the decline of small farming and the introduction of the mechanical cotton picker; however, they encountered so few attractive employment possibilities in the towns and the cities that many left the state altogether. While the white workforce increased by 83,000 in the 1940s, the number of black workers declined by 46,000. During the 1950s, interstate migration gave Louisiana a net gain of 42,000 whites and a net loss of 92,000 blacks.[38]

As political analyst Samuel Lubell noted in 1951, the combination of industrialization and racial discrimination diminished the importance of black labor to the southern economy and prolonged the life of white supremacy. Placed in this economic context, therefore, the gains that blacks were chalking up in education and voter registration looked less impressive. Even such an apparently clear-cut advance as the elimination of lynching had to be balanced against the persistence of police brutality—including many lethal shootings every year—and a criminal justice system loaded against blacks, where "legal lynchings" were still a disturbing reality. Despite U.S. Supreme Court rulings, blacks were still routinely excluded from jury duty: no blacks served on juries in Livingston Parish, for example, before 1966; in New Orleans, the blanket exclusion of "day laborers" meant that no blacks ever served on grand juries, a system of racial discrimination that Justice John Minor Wisdom described as "neutral, principled, and—foolproof."[39]

In June 1950 the NAACP Legal Defense Fund officially abandoned its tactic of seeking equal educational facilities, deciding instead to press for the admission of blacks to white public schools, colleges, and universities. Completely consistent with the NAACP's basic philosophy, this strategic decision to attack segregation head-on had received tacit but strong encouragement from the U.S. Supreme Court—its 1950 decision in *Sweatt v. Painter* breached segregation at the University of Texas—and from the Truman administration itself, which in the same year took the momentous step of integrating the armed services. Moreover, the central role of public education in sustaining the edifice of white supremacy made the NAACP's decision to attack segregation all but inevitable. *Plessy v. Ferguson* had to go. In line with the new policy, A. P. Tureaud filed a suit against Louisiana State University on behalf of Roy S. Wilson, who had been denied admission to its law school. Two years later, in September 1952, he filed suits against the school boards of Orleans Parish (New Orleans) and St. Helena Parish, seeking the admittance of black children to white schools.

Yet the NAACP's decision raised serious practical difficulties, and the possible consequences of integration remained unclear. Although it involved confronting white officials in federal courtrooms, the tactic of seeking equalization accorded with the gradualist tactics whereby blacks in the South, from the era of Booker T. Washington on, had sought to improve their schools and colleges within the framework of racial segregation. Those tactics had met with increasing success since the 1930s and had elicited a good deal of white support, but the pursuit of integration risked alienating whites and jeopardizing the educational benefits that were slowly being achieved within "separate but equal."

Black plaintiffs also exposed themselves to retaliation and reprisal. In addition, nobody really knew what shape integration would or should take: it initially involved small numbers of black children seeking admission to white schools. Would it eventually lead to wholesale racial mixing, with black and white institutions merging and losing their racial identities completely? Integration was a leap in the dark, and Tureaud warned Marshall that it might be difficult to find plaintiffs. Daniel Byrd echoed that view, advising Marshall that the shift in policy would need to be carefully explained to NAACP members in Louisiana: "This is something entirely new and the branches are uninformed."[40]

In truth, blacks in Louisiana held a variety of views about integration. Some fully endorsed the NAACP's total opposition to racial segregation. This was especially true of New Orleans Creoles like A. P. Tureaud and branch president Arthur J. Chapital—the latter quit the Catholic Church over racial segregation, refused to join the Prince Hall Masons, and vigorously opposed the establishment of a New Orleans campus of all-black Southern University. On the other hand, while hardly any blacks spoke out against the NAACP's new policy, many harbored mixed feelings about it, viewing the issue of segregation in pragmatic terms. The question of the black public colleges became an early bone of contention. In 1947 Louisiana opened a law school at Southern University. The NAACP wanted blacks to shun this second-rate facility, correctly regarding it as a blatant attempt to head off integration. Yet such were the difficulties in entering Louisiana State University, even after 1950, that the Southern University School of Law graduated most of the newly qualified black lawyers in the state. Although the merger of black and white public universities was not yet on the NAACP's agenda, it was already clear that black colleges commanded significant loyalty.

Not surprisingly, many black schoolteachers felt little enthusiasm for integration. White segregationists warned that many would lose their jobs in the event of integration, and even the NAACP accepted that there would be fewer black teachers in a fully integrated school system. Many teachers also felt a justifiable pride in their schools. Most of them had been educated by black teachers, and they resented the NAACP's contention that an education received in a black school could never be equal to that received in a white one. "I didn't think of my school as inferior," recalled Louise Metoyer Bouisse, who had attended Bayou Road School in New Orleans. "In fact I'm sure I had some very good teachers." Black teachers also appreciated the dramatic improvements that were taking place in the public schools. In New Iberia, for example, the new Jonas B. Henderson High School was on a par with the best white school. In addition to an improved physical plant, which included an air-conditioned auditorium, children enjoyed a broader curriculum. Teachers taught fewer periods, had smaller classes, and concentrated on their specialties. The school board had done a "magnificent job" of equalization, thought local teacher Edran Auguster.[41]

Other groups had similar reservations about the practical consequences of integration. In many cases blacks had banded together to protect common interests and were naturally reluctant to disband. In New Orleans, for example, many black workers had distrusted the interracial appeals of white organizers from the CIO, preferring to remain in segregated AFL locals. The most formidable group of black workers in the city, the longshoremen, stayed with the segregated International Longshoremen's Association (ILA) rather than join the leftish and interracial International Longshoremen's and Warehousemen's Union. As Bruce Nelson has argued, black longshoremen had sound reasons for this choice: despite its notoriety as corrupt and mob-connected, the ILA offered black dockworkers greater autonomy and job security. Within the postal service, the National Alliance of Postal Employees effectively represented the interests of black workers—it exists to this day. Black professional organizations were largely the product of exclusion from white organizations; many of their members nevertheless rejected the logic that integration would render them unnecessary.[42]

In 1954 the euphoria that accompanied the *Brown* ruling made it impossible to consider the question of integration in all of its complexity. Few doubted that the NAACP had won a historic victory, whatever the imponderables. Lone dissenters received short shrift, recalled NAACP lawyer Constance Baker Motley: Oliver Hill was "hooted down— especially by Thurgood" for suggesting that blacks were less concerned about segregated schools than about segregated streetcars and buses.[43]

Downplaying early warning signs that whites would oppose integration to the bitter end, the NAACP exuded optimism. In 1953 Daniel Byrd advised Marshall that the superintendent of schools in St. Helena Parish was "looking for integration within the next three years." At a regional gathering of NAACP officials in Atlanta a year later, the Louisiana representative, Dr. E. A. Johnson, confirmed that integration was an imminent possibility in both St. Helena Parish and New Orleans. "If we can succeed in building a climate of opinion favorable to immediate desegregation," the NAACP told its branches, "legal action may not be necessary." This upbeat view certainly accorded with the editorials that appeared in leading Louisiana newspapers after the *Brown* ruling. According to the *New Orleans Times-Picayune,* for example, "All the

South can do—all the states and localities can do—is shoulder the burden the court has placed upon them." The Catholic hierarchy in Louisiana appeared even more supportive: "We fully recognize and approve of the decision," stated the superintendent of Catholic schools in New Orleans. Despite the disappointing weakness of *Brown II,* the NAACP's optimism held up until the end of 1955, when the landslide election victory of Earl Long—the arch-segregationist candidate was buried—put a racial liberal back in the governor's mansion.[44]

When the ultra-segregationists, led by William N. Rainach and Leander H. Perez, unleashed their carefully planned counterattack in March 1956, the NAACP was taken completely off guard. Few had believed that Louisiana would become one of the strongholds of opposition to integration; few predicted the extent to which the Catholic Church would cave in to segregationist pressure; nobody foresaw the extremes to which the "massive resistance" movement would go. Nevertheless, the changes wrought between 1940 and 1954 proved too deeply rooted to be eradicated. The NAACP was decimated, but it survived, and other groups sprang up to take the strain. The Citizens Councils purged black voters, but many white politicians opposed the purges, and with the assistance of the federal government—the Department of Justice, the Civil Rights Commission, and federal judges such as J. Skelly Wright—blacks stopped them. The young activists of the 1960s, despite their disdain for the organization, built upon foundations laid by the NAACP.

6
Communism, Anti-Communism, and Massive Resistance
The Civil Rights Congress in Southern Perspective

Sarah Hart Brown

> You who laid old Hitler low—
> Don't be scared of old Bilbo.
> Just like Hitler's friend, Tojo,
> Bilbo, too, has got to go!
> Civil Rights Congress rhyme, 1946[1]

THE RETURN OF black soldiers who had "laid old Hitler low" clearly brought new spirit and energy to the fight against Jim Crow; confidence after the victory even encouraged some liberal white southerners to envision a coming revolution in race relations. But as the country's wartime rapprochement with the Soviet Union cooled and the Iron Curtain descended, idealistic expectations about a brave new postwar world became suspect and increasingly vulnerable. Segregationists in Congress, like the Mississippi senator referred to in the ditty above, suffered few qualms when Americans whom they considered "radicals" labeled them fascist or compared them to Hitler and Tojo.

On the other hand, when southern politicians labeled their liberal and leftist opponents "Communists" their epithets often hit easy marks. In the 1930s white supremacists vilified the Left, especially Communists, for such iconoclasm as advocacy of integrated unions for steelworkers and sharecroppers. A Communist-led legal organization, the International Labor Defense, publicized race-based southern justice during the prolonged trials of the famous "Scottsboro boys" rape cases, and although the party never enrolled large numbers of southerners, individual Communists enlisted in almost every southern campaign against racism and poverty. During the same period, Communists invented the term "popular front" to characterize alliances of the liberal center and the Left constituted to accomplish common goals.

Southern coalitions that developed in the 1930s included the Southern Conference for Human Welfare (SCHW, 1938–48), a regionwide reform movement supported by the Roosevelt administration and led by southern liberal politicians and social activists, but including a few Communists; and the Southern Negro Youth Congress (SNYC, 1937–48), an alliance of southern young people led by dedicated members of the Communist Party.[2] While the philosophical underpinnings of these two groups differed, their work on the ground had great similarities and included interests in voting rights, labor organization, and race relations. Though often very fragile unions, popular front alliances like SCHW and SNYC presented a public facade of Left-liberal harmony in the years before and during the war. But southern popular front groups were early casualties of the cold war and a rising fear of racial change; these two groups thrived until 1948, when both died in a swirl of rumor and accusation, spurned by both center liberals and conservatives. By the late 1940s the idea that left-wing reformers had ulterior motives had become accepted gospel in the South; mass-action campaigns and protests added substance and fire to the claims of southern politicians and journalists that these crusaders bred un-American ideas. Anti-communism became not only a useful political tool for southern candidates but a respectable shield against changes in "the southern way of life." For at least a decade after the end of World War II—and beyond that period, though with gradually declining effectiveness outside the South—anti-communism served white supremacists well.

The Civil Rights Congress (CRC) was established in 1946, just as the Red Scare took wing and the influence of popular front groups like SCHW and SNYC reached a brief postwar high. Beyond all other leftist challengers, the CRC measured up to southern segregationists' expectations about the subversive nature of civil rights agitation. David Caute, an early scholar of postwar anti-communism, characterized the organization as a legal defense and advocacy group whose causes "were invariably the Party's causes," and evidence suggests that the CRC's leaders maintained close personal, if not institutional, ties to the Communist Party. Created from a merger of the International Labor Defense, the National Negro Congress, and the National Federation for Constitutional Liberties, the CRC existed under pressure from the Federal Bureau of Investigation (FBI) and other federal agencies until 1956, when the Subversive Activities Control Board finally forced its dissolution. Its major legal cases involved either the defense of Communists (most famously the defense of eleven Communist Party leaders in the Foley Square Smith Act trials of 1949) or the defense of blacks indicted under questionable circumstances, especially rape cases.[3]

In *We Cry Genocide,* an extraordinary volume about lynching in America, the founders of the CRC called southern apartheid part of a "consistent, conscious policy of every branch of the [U.S.] government," the goal of which was repression of dissent and protection of profits for a capitalist elite.[4] To change the South and the nation, the CRC instituted a three-pronged program. First and continually, propaganda campaigns highlighted the indecency and injustice of the South's race-based society. In 1946, as a part of its first major southern crusade, the CRC invented the poetic indictment of Theodore G. Bilbo, the outlandish racist senator from Mississippi, recorded at the beginning of this essay. Just before it succumbed to pressure from the U.S. government and ceased operation in 1956, the organization sponsored the painstakingly documented *Genocide,* which it presented to the United Nations with great fanfare. In between, numerous, sometimes worldwide campaigns enlisted support for victims of Jim Crow justice. These efforts linked to the second part of the CRC's southern program, involvement in court cases, primarily those judged to be "legal lynchings." Sometimes the CRC provided lawyers and legal advice to defendants. When this option retreated in the face of local counsel or because attorneys of the National Association for the Advancement of Colored People (NAACP) took responsibility, the CRC participated primarily as an instrument of propaganda, shining light on proceedings and treatment of prisoners and inviting public pressure and criticism. On the ground as cases progressed, working lawyers—even those hired by the CRC—occasionally saw this as helpful but often found it an irritant or worse. Lawyers laboring within the system to free their clients, especially in the South, sometimes complained that the appearance of outside interference, especially pressure from northern or leftist agitators, damaged their chances. Dissension between the CRC and its natural allies in the NAACP and other liberal civil rights organizations often resulted from such disagreements. The third prong of CRC southern strategy is the least known. Throughout the organization's ten-year history its leaders labored to establish local CRC branches, southern groups to help generate support for its legal and publicity efforts. While three local chapters experienced short-lived success, the combination of anti-communism and white supremacy, a lethal antidote to leftist (even liberal) organizing in the postwar South, largely defeated this effort in the region. This essay considers the CRC's ten-year drive to change the South—its publicity crusades, its branches, and the cases it championed—and attempts to assess its southern legacy.

Although the SCHW and SNYC had enlisted southern leadership, with a few very notable exceptions the CRC's leaders were African Americans or Jews from the North and West (even if they lived in the South), and most of them were Communists.[5] Fund-raising efforts by well-known left-wing celebrities and gifts from institutions such as the Robert Marshall and Field Foundations sustained the CRC's southern work as well as its civil liberties and civil rights efforts outside the South. William Patterson, born in the San Francisco area in 1890 and a graduate of the Hastings Law School of the University of California, headed the CRC from the late 1940s through the mid-1950s. The son of an immigrant from St. Lucia but on his mother's side grandson of a Virginia slave and her white master, Patterson had been involved in left-wing causes since World War I and a member of the Communist Party since 1926. He had worked on the Sacco and Vanzetti case in the 1920s and the Scottsboro trials in the 1930s. In its varied and very persuasive literature, CRC leaders always maintained that a politically diverse group of supporters created and sustained the organization, that its only interest lay in protecting constitutionally guaranteed civil rights and liberties, and that it was neither led nor controlled by the Communist Party. But both the political lineage of the chairman and of several members of the national staff and the sources of the CRC's funding point to a close, if unofficial, alliance with the party.[6]

Sometimes the statements of Chairman Patterson and his staff seemed designed not only to instruct their natural constituency but to shock conservative anti-Communists and centrist liberals alike. They never ignored the propaganda potential of their cases. In 1950 CRC members led a successful national campaign for Lieutenant Leon Gilbert, a twice-wounded World War II veteran sentenced to death for refusal to obey an order in Korea. After President Truman commuted Gilbert's sentence the organization issued a celebratory press release, but the writer of the CRC document still lamented that in his court-martial "Lt Gilbert was a victim of the government's criminal policy of Jim Crow," and criticized Truman's sentence of "twenty years at hard labor" as "an act of hypocrisy only a little less infamous than previous attempts to execute this Negro officer." Later, as CRC members lobbied for the lieutenant's early release, another CRC bulletin asserted that "What is needed in every city and town . . . is the unity of the Negro people, unity of Negro and white workers, unity of Negro and progressive white Americans. . . . Jim Crow can be smashed, the thought-control Smith Act repealed, and the Bill of Rights preserved."[7] Patterson frequently asserted that black Americans should be taught to understand American racism as a systemic problem: "I think no opportunity should be missed where the Negro people could be shown the effort made by high places to freeze them in a secondary category," he wrote to John Moreno Coe, a white attorney from Pensacola, Florida. He added that he did not believe the case being litigated for the CRC by Coe (or any case involving discriminatory southern justice) to be "an ordinary criminal case" but rather a highly political matter. Those associated with such cases had an obligation to make injustices known to "Negro youth in particular," he wrote to Coe. "The courts," he believed, "are not neutral . . . the courts are agents of reaction."[8]

The CRC's "Oust Bilbo" campaign surely reflected what white supremacists called "the party line," that is, a view subversive to southern custom and segregationist law that they linked to Soviet Communism and American treason. Despite the fact that the little rhyme's target had become an embarrassment to many in his own party (including many southern Democrats), the "southern white supremacy = fascism" equation it proclaimed made the "Oust Bilbo" campaign a red flag. At a time when, as Numan Bartley has said, "the very word *liberal* had disappeared from the southern political lexicon, except as a term of opprobrium," radical sentiments like those expressed by Patterson and public campaigns against entrenched southern politicians, even Bilbo, seemed tailor made for exploitation by supporters of the antebellum status quo.[9]

Despite the confusions about policy and control as the Communist Party mutated from "party" to "association" and back again in 1945 and 1946, it remained clear to both blacks and whites that southern Communists and their allies were uniquely willing to organize and fight publicly against inequality and injustice. In addition, a review of the CRC's activities and accomplishments would indicate to most observers that its leaders illustrated genuine interest in the legal, social, and economic issues involved in the cases they undertook and real concern about the personal welfare of their oppressed and underserved constituency. In other words, the CRC's agenda was not merely or exclusively political, and few poor southerners expressed concern to the anti-Bilbo campaigners of 1946 about whether American Communists followed Moscow's line or, as was frequently charged, "used" black followers or poor workers for their own purposes. At the first meeting of the Texas CRC, Colonel Roscoe Conklin Simmons "warned against being influenced by name-calling. 'If you believe in liberty, they call you a Communist,' he said; 'Anything that will free me, that's what I am.'" Obviously Communists saw African Americans as potential revolutionary workers and racial discrimination as fodder for anti-establishment propaganda; still, they expressed concern about civil rights issues in times and places when others were silent. Economic intimidation and outright terrorism always limited the public activities of the CRC's potential allies, but their experiences also endowed black southerners with a real appreciation of the risks taken by the small band of "outside agitators" who came to labor in the South.[10]

Although few southerners enlisted openly as workers for the CRC, opposition to Bilbo had long been a popular cause among black Mississippians, and, in fact, among African Americans and white liberals North and South. First elected in 1935, the senior senator from Mississippi issued campaign harangues containing some of the most toxic racial oratory in the annals of American politics. Especially during and just after World War II, Bilbo, like some other southerners in Congress, found race-baiting very useful for the maintenance of his political position. According to biographer Chester M. Morgan, despite Bilbo's early and earnest support for the New Deal, his "infamy as the 'archangel of white supremacy' was richly deserved." As incitements to violence and intimidation, few public statements surpass his well-known assertion that "the way to keep the nigger from the polls is to see him the night before." He filibustered against the Fair Employment Practices Commission (FEPC), berated the liberal press, targeted "old lady Roosevelt, Harold Ickes and Hank Wallace, together with all the Negroes, Communists, negro lovers and advocates of social equality who poured out their slime and money in Mississippi," and wrote a tract Morgan calls a "volatile defense of white supremacy": *Take Your Choice: Separation or Mongrelization.*[11] In the year after the Allied victory against Hitler and his "friend Tojo," Bilbo's bigotry conspicuously echoed not only the designers of the "Mississippi Plan" to disfranchise and segregate blacks in the 1890s but the ideas of the recently defeated fascist foes themselves. The CRC's leaders highlighted these similarities in their campaign literature.

They found willing allies for the 1946 "Oust Bilbo" campaign among SNYC leaders who had been working as organizers in Birmingham since the late 1930s. During World War II, Esther Cooper Jackson and Louis Burnham had promoted a Double V campaign, led voter-registration drives in concert with the NAACP and other groups, monitored FEPC hearings, and continued their local work for racial justice. "Most black Communists," Robin Kelley asserts, "believed the war would inevitably alter Jim Crow in the South," but "they also understood—better than the national Party leadership—that change would not happen by itself."[12]

When Tennessean Laurent Franz, a recent University of North Carolina student and now the southern organizer for the fledgling CRC, came to call on the Birmingham activists in 1946, they had already formed a political agenda for that election year. Reflecting their youthful optimism about the future, SNYC leaders made a voter-registration campaign aimed at black veterans their first order of business after the war. The organization joined the NAACP, the Congress of Industrial Organizations (CIO) Political Action Committee, and the new state committees of the SCHW in "a loose regional confederation to promote the democratization of southern politics." When it began work in Mississippi, SNYC's drive to increase the vote joined the CRC's simultaneous campaign to defeat Senator Bilbo.[13]

In September, Franz (who, like SNYC's leaders, had become a Communist while in college) reported from Mississippi about efforts to influence the Senate against Bilbo. Although realistically he did not believe mass meetings or sending large delegations of black Mississippians to Washington would be possible, Franz hoped that by "working through the national organizations which have Negro membership in Mississippi, working through the Negro churches, and keeping up a well-planned campaign in the Negro press nationally" the CRC could produce petitions and resolutions "urging the Senate to act on the complaint already filed." He intended to print postcards to be signed by black Mississippians and forwarded to important senators. Franz's plan to reach the hearts and minds of black Americans through their own organizations and the black press and to generate a mass lobby effort with supporting publicity aimed at affecting official action would be typical of CRC advocacy organizing over the next ten years, whether the matter at hand was saving one beleaguered defendant or appealing to Congress or the United Nations.[14]

The CRC's broadly based National Committee to Oust Bilbo also sent attorney Emmanuel Block and others into Mississippi to collect depositions about Bilbo's depredations,[15] "his corruption, his warm ties with the Ku Klux Klan, and the fiendish tactics he used to prevent blacks from voting," and they "distributed 185,000 petitions in thirty-two states supporting this effort." The dissemination of such accounts and petitions among center-liberals in the United States and Europe—a method that enraged southerners in Congress and embarrassed the U.S. government—also became standard operating procedure for the CRC. Gerald Horne, author of the only comprehensive history of the CRC, says that "this stress on 'mass action'—picketing, demonstrations, petitioning—was self-consciously what distinguished the CRC from its sometimes allies" like the NAACP or the American Civil Liberties Union (ACLU). The NAACP joined the fight against Bilbo, for example, by quietly submitting to a Senate investigating committee an exhaustive report detailing violations of voting rights in the June primary campaign. In Mississippi, while the CRC collected depositions and signatures, SNYC aided the campaign to defeat Bilbo by trying to increase the numbers of eligible voters who would normally cast ballots against him; at the least, they would further document discrimination against black voters.[16]

Because the northern wing of his own party also detested Bilbo, as did most Republicans, the Mississippian simultaneously became the subject of an internal inquiry into his campaign financing and other matters by Senate colleagues who hoped to censure him or deny him his seat. When a committee of the Senate came to Mississippi to investigate financing irregularities and charges of voter intimidation in the Democratic Party primary just past, CRC and SNYC workers encouraged local participation. Almost two hundred blacks appeared before the committee to give testimony, the majority of them World War II veterans; sixty-eight persons attested to "the pervasive pattern of unlawful behavior and racial terrorism that had characterized the Senate primary." During the primary, one stated, SNYC's James Jackson had been arrested when he brought a group of veterans to the precinct polling place located, beyond all reason, on the front porch of Senator Bilbo's house. Since the U.S. Supreme Court had ended the white primary in 1944, these former soldiers presumed to vote in the Democratic primary, even if they had to go into the lion's den to do it. The Senate committee finally established that Bilbo had violated campaign spending laws and frightened away voters, but in a straight party vote it exonerated him. Eventually the full Senate resolved to deny him his seat, but the motion was tabled on account of the senator's failing health (he was suffering from advanced cancer of the mouth and throat).[17] When Bilbo died in 1947, his colleague James Eastland became Mississippi's senior senator. Bilbo's foes saw little improvement; Eastland would become the Senate champion at red-baiting the emerging civil rights movement.

U.S. senators from Mississippi did not, of course, fight alone in Washington. After Bilbo was denied his seat, Rev. Charles F. Hamilton of Aberdeen, Mississippi, wrote to Laurent Franz to congratulate the CRC on its victory. But, he said, "a contest was also filed last January against [Mississippi congressman John E.] Rankin. His unseating would be much more valuable." Rankin's district, in which Rev. Hamilton resided, presented the perfect example of an electorate shrunken by disfranchisement of blacks and poor whites: the congressman had been reelected by 10,400 votes in a district with over 200,000 adult inhabitants. Although many southern congressmen sat on the House Un-American Activities Committee (HUAC) over the years, none showed more dedication than Rankin, who recognized early on the opportunities for self-preservation offered by anti-communism. During the war Rankin had called the FEPC "the beginning of a Communistic dictatorship the likes of which America never dreamed," and he aggressively opposed the GI Bill because it proposed to help black and white veterans equally. Soon after his reelection and about the time of Bilbo's death, Rankin and other members of HUAC avenged the CRC's attempts to influence Mississippi politics with the scathing "Report on the Civil Rights Congress," which began by asserting that "having adopted a line of militant skullduggery against the United States," the Communist Party had set up the CRC to protect its own as it pursued a "campaign of Communist lawlessness." Accepted as gospel by the FBI, congressional and state anti-Communist committees, and most Americans, the report haunted the CRC for the next ten years.[18]

In the year after the 1946 campaign both SNYC and the SCHW faced disastrous red-baiting.[19] Cornered by the fearful spirit of the times and anxious to retain their own viability, former sympathizers, especially the CIO and the NAACP, withdrew financial support or ended cooperation with groups they (or their own enemies in the government) perceived to be part of the old "popular front." In 1948 SNYC held its last "All-Southern Negro Youth Conference," and the SCHW lost its labor support and collapsed. Even before that, SNYC leader Esther Cooper Jackson and her husband, James, fled the South. He became an organizer and educator for the Communist Party in the Ford plant in Detroit. She worked for the Detroit branch of the CRC and for the Progressive Party, under whose banner former vice-president Henry Wallace ran for the presidency in 1948.[20]

After the demise of SNYC and the SCHW, the CRC and a small but militantly integrationist remnant of the southern conference movement, the similarly named Southern Conference Education Fund (SCEF), were the primary representatives of left-wing, popular front liberalism still operating in the South. SCEF single-mindedly pushed to end Jim Crow and disfranchisement, retained tax-exempt status as an educational organization for most of its life, and continued to publish the monthly *Southern Patriot* through the peak years of the civil rights movement. Often accused, SCEF remained purposefully non-Communist, but like its parent, the SCHW, it did not require political tests for its staff or board members. Headquartered in New Orleans, SCEF kept an all-southern board and staff, though it conducted fund-raising drives among friends across the country. The CRC, on the other hand, worked for justice in the South and always tried to engender southern membership, but its leadership and the large majority of its members, as well as its funding support, remained among leftists, including known Communists, in the North and West. Not only "civil rights" defenders, the CRC's adherents championed anti-government litigation in prominent civil liberties cases of the Red Scare era with equal fervor. William Patterson and his CRC staff, like the International Labor Defense lawyers before them, became the prototypical "outside agitators" in the South.

Patterson and those who worked with him in the New York office wanted desperately to develop "inside" agitators, permanent southern branches with local leadership that might sustain regional cases and campaigns. Most of the CRC's civil rights cases originated in southern courts, and short-term local pressure groups that supported particular cases or prisoners were useful, but the task of building permanent local constituencies in the region proved exceptionally difficult. Information from national sources like HUAC and the FBI fed local anti-CRC rhetoric of newspapers, law enforcement agencies, and state and local anti-Communist committees and made organizing very difficult in the South. "Strong" branches, CRC national field organizer Aubrey Grossman claimed, existed "in Los Angeles, San Francisco, Oakland, Seattle, Chicago, Milwaukee, Detroit, Philadelphia and New York, and chapters with 'some promise' in Denver, Cleveland, Pittsburgh, and Honolulu," but he could find none of consequence in the southern or border states.[21]

Although his assessment is close to the truth, Grossman neglected a few southern groups—especially those in Houston, Miami, and New Orleans—that functioned for a time as legitimate CRC branches. Smaller and more ephemeral groups operated briefly in Memphis, Tennessee, Asheville, North Carolina, and Macon, Georgia, and Patterson and his field organizers spent a great deal of time encouraging individual supporters in other southern towns. But Laurent Franz's 1946 assessment that the time was not "ripe, irrespective of our work on cases here, for a CRC organization in Jackson" could still be supported by the situation in Mississippi ten years later. In Alabama and North and South Carolina only promising beginnings arose, then disappointments. Patterson and organizer Milton Wolff believed a viable Georgia group would develop around Macon newspaperman (and state Progressive

Party chairman) Larkin Marshall and one of his contacts in Columbus, but in the end, much correspondence and visiting produced negligible results. Except for the outpost in southern Louisiana, in the Deep South states there were cases and allies but not real chapters. Even the southern branches that seemed to have staying power ceased to operate several years before the national organization died in 1956, victims of harassment by conservative local civic organizations, terrorist groups, grand juries, police "red squads," state committees, HUAC and its corresponding Senate committee, and the FBI. But the histories of the three largest southern CRC branches, at least, warrant some discussion.[22]

The Houston branch began in the summer of 1946, when Sylvia Bernard (now Sylvia Bernard Hall Thompson), a young woman from an upper-middle-class San Antonio home and recent graduate of a course of study at the Communist-sponsored Jefferson School of Social Science in New York, responded to a call to help with the establishment of the Texas Civil Rights Congress. Southern organizer Laurent Franz, on leave from the anti-Bilbo campaign, joined Bernard in Houston and persuaded the local NAACP to share space in its Houston office. This unusual arrangement, especially if measured by the developing tension between the two corresponding national organizations, depended on the largess of Houston NAACP head Lulu White, a strong and charismatic leader who encouraged cooperation among all organizations working for civil rights and civil liberties. The NAACP branch also agreed to become one of the sponsors of the first Texas CRC conference in July 1946. This conference began on a Sunday morning, when most Texas preachers would be busy at church, so when the committee decided the meeting should be opened with a prayer they dispatched Bernard, granddaughter of a prominent Texas rabbi, to find a minister. Her family credentials impressed the clergyman she found, who agreed to come but asked: "Listen, will there be any Communists there?" Bernard, a party member, replied that there might be, since civil rights "was their meat, too." The rabbi told her the story of being "the only non-Communist" in "a mass action group" in his college days, and he voiced concern over the present state of the Red Scare in Texas, but in the end he gave the opening prayer.[23]

At its first conference, the Texas CRC formed a state board whose membership list reads like a popular front organization of the 1930s, with members from the NAACP, the United Negro and Allied Veterans, the National Lawyers Guild, the University of Texas faculty, and several labor unions. Thompson commented on the stirring keynote address by liberal attorney Ben Ramey, who, in his "white suit and white Panama hat, exuded a kind of country gentleman aura." The conference passed a resolution supporting another speaker, Herman Sweatt, a recent black applicant for admission to the University of Texas Law School; Ben Ramey would become a member of the NAACP legal team representing Sweatt. Soon after the conference, Ramey joined the successful firm of Houston labor lawyers Mandell and Wright; Arthur Mandell joined the CRC in 1946 and attended its national conventions in Detroit that year and in Chicago the following year. He and other CRC lawyers authored a supporting amicus brief when the NAACP appealed Sweatt's successful, precedent-setting case to the U.S. Supreme Court in 1950.[24]

Just weeks after the Texas conference, during the 1946 primary, the CRC chairman reported to the national office that the branch had sent members to speak at "practically every political meeting . . . on the general subject of voting as a basic civil right," had sent representatives to several trade union meetings, and had sponsored, in conjunction with the NAACP, "a mass meeting protesting the Georgia murders and calling for immediate federal action to stop the wave of mob violence around the South." By the end of its first year, the Texas CRC had established branches in Austin, Dallas, El Paso, and Waco.[25]

But success in Texas was short-lived. All of the chapters faced harassment from the FBI and local police within a very short time, becoming concrete examples of the deadly combination of "black" and "red" alliances in the postwar South. Defense of a Communist who refused to testify in an immigration case led the FBI to the Dallas branch, a chapter that "carried a high profile for a while." Evidence of trouble brewing in Houston can be found in Lulu White's change of heart under pressure in late 1947; J. Edgar Hoover spoke to Thurgood Marshall, who informed local leader White about the dangers of sharing office space with the suspect CRC. After the Texas CRC arranged for the defense of two Maritime Union workers arrested for selling the *Daily Worker,* an FBI agent reported that the CRC was "strictly . . . a front for the Communist Party." Chapter leader and civil liberties lawyer Morris Bogdanow defended a German couple in a highly publicized 1949 deportation case, during which leaders of the Texas Communist Party resorted to the Fifth Amendment. As the complicated trial progressed, Houston's newspapers, according to historian Don E. Carleton, "impressed on their readers a vision of a city crawling with subversives." In early 1950 the Houston CRC branch still published its monthly newsletter, but that spring Bogdanow wrote to William Patterson that "CRC mail is snatched and any meetings held will be raided by police . . . there are several unidentified spies within the organization who undoubtedly helped disrupt." He asked that mail from the New York office be discontinued until notice from Houston. Despite the growing anti-red hysteria in Houston, Bogdanow defended Communist Party members arrested (and beaten in custody) for distributing the Stockholm Peace Petition on June 26—the day after the Korean War began.[26] Houston police then arrested Bogdanow at a watermelon party at the Negro Elk's Lodge. They charged him with "violating Texas segregation laws by 'mingling with Negroes'" and wrote on the police docket that "this white man . . . has been with several persons . . . known to belong to or have something to do with the Communist party." Carleton says that "the summer of 1950 . . . marked the end of Houston's pathetically small Communist party." At the end of the year, when members of the CRC gathered for a meeting in Austin, an FBI informant reported "thirty-eight people present, half Black and half white, about four Chicanos—and the subject of the meeting was Jim Crow."[27]

In New Orleans, members of an active CRC branch held meetings, disseminated information, and supported causes at least from 1948 through 1951. During that time Oakley Johnson, a white professor of English at predominantly black Dillard College and a Communist since 1919, held forth as the group's primary leader. The Louisiana CRC worked on voter registration during the 1948 presidential campaign, publicized and protested cases of police brutality, took up the cause of several black men on Louisiana's death row, and participated fully in the national CRC campaign to defend Mississippian Willie McGee, who died in the electric chair in 1951. The group formed as an outgrowth of the "Committee for Justice in the Brooks Case," which Johnson called a "police lynching" in Gretna, a small town across the Mississippi River from New Orleans. Roy Cyril Brooks attempted to help a woman who had deposited her last nickel in the bus coin machine when she realized she was on the wrong bus; he offered to ride on her nickel and give her his. The driver refused to allow this exchange. He called a nearby policeman, who took Brooks at gunpoint to the courthouse grounds about a block away, where he shot him in the back and killed him. A newspaper photographer saw the shooting and cleverly hid one exposed plate before the police smashed his camera. Pictures of Brooks's body, sent to liberal friends of the CRC in Congress, forced the attorney general's hand, and the FBI entered the case. As a result, though he was never suspended from his job, Gretna authorities charged the policeman, Alvin Bladsacker, with manslaughter. Two years later, despite mass protests by the committee, a jury acquitted him.[28]

Four members of the original "Brooks committee" became founders of the Louisiana CRC, among them Johnson's two co-chairmen, A. A. O'Brien of the Food, Tobacco and Agricultural Workers (Brook's union) and Louis Brown, secretary of the Gretna (Jefferson Parish) NAACP, and two other local labor union leaders, Theodore Means of the Furriers Union and Andrew Nelson of the Longshoremen and Warehousemen's Union. By 1950 Louis Brown's name appeared on letterhead as "president" and Oakley Johnson's as "executive secretary." But as anti-communism gripped New Orleans and the nation, problems surfaced. Both unions and the NAACP began purging Communists, and members who also belonged to the Louisiana CRC were suspect. After the furor over the Brooks case died down, several of the early board members, including Brown, resigned and tried to energize the Gretna NAACP chapter as an alternative. Among the unionists, longshoremen remained the most loyal to the organization.[29]

The Louisiana CRC also occasionally accommodated a changing group of Communist Party workers who came to New Orleans (like James Jackson, Jack O'Dell, or Sylvia Bernard and her first husband, Sam Hall), students, local office workers, and even a few employees of the school system. At least two members of the Tulane University faculty—Robert Hodes of the medical school and Mitchell Franklin of the law school—probably associated with the group through their friendship with Johnson and others in his circle. For a time a lively group of Louisiana CRC leaders and their friends met for informal occasions in the homes of Oakley and Mary Lea Johnson or Robert and Jane Hodes, joined there by undercover FBI agents (two of them medical students) who secretly recorded their conversations. Most participants were probably non-Communist liberals, though at one time or another almost all Louisiana CRC members known to local, state, or federal law enforcement officers were called Communists in hearing rooms or in the press. Gerald Horne counts about one hundred Louisiana CRC members in 1949, "although Johnson complained that they had 'few active members,'" a problem that "increased the work load on Johnson, who was equal to the task." In 1951 Johnson wrote to Aubrey Grossman asking for two hundred CRC membership cards. "Quite a number of the rank and filers here are demanding membership cards . . . also, in line with Pat's [William Patterson's] recent suggestions for re-organizing and reviving our LCRC [Louisiana CRC], we think it would be good to build a nucleus of organized CRC members for the new organizer to start with."[30]

Johnson's time in New Orleans was coming to a close, as foes closed in on all sides. Since he had taken refuge in the First and Fifth Amendments before a federal grand jury in 1949, he had become, in the words of Adam Fairclough, "an embarrassment to Albert Dent, Dillard's president, and a serious annoyance to the university's board of trustees, which was headed by staunch anti-communist Edgar B. Stern." At the same time, the Louisiana NAACP (especially its New Orleans leadership) treated Johnson and the Louisiana CRC "as enemies, not allies," refusing to allow Johnson to speak at branch meetings and ostracizing Louisiana CRC members and other leftists. He wrote to William Patterson in May 1951 that as he had expected, his contract at Dillard had not been renewed for 1951–52. When he asked the university president "the *reason* for the failure to reappoint me, he said there was *no specific reason,* that the University merely wished to make a change [Johnson's emphasis]." Johnson asked if "pressure had been brought because I belonged to a supposed 'subversive' organization, the CRC, [and the president] said no pressure had been brought." But, the dismissed professor added, "this does not tally with what was told my department head."[31]

Less than two years later Johnson's friend Robert Hodes faced dismissal from Tulane University, ostensibly because he could not get along with other researchers in his department. At a hearing before Tulane's board of trustees, Hodes's attorney concluded that "the real reason for Dr. Hodes's termination was the displeasure of the Medical School administration with the nature of his political beliefs." When questioned about this possibility, one department member replied, "I think it is an important factor," and said Hodes had lacked good judgment about when (and to whom) he expressed his opinions; another thought the problem was simply "the department's attitude toward political thinking." Both Johnson and Hodes were active in integrationist causes, spoke out against the Korean War, and belonged to the CRC. The Louisiana CRC had recently spearheaded the defense of Roosevelt Ward, a young black man suspected of being a Communist and accused of evading service in Korea. This high-profile case reached the U.S. Supreme Court just a few weeks after Hodes's hearing. Florida attorney John Moreno Coe and Alvin Jones, a black lawyer and voting rights activist from New Orleans, litigated the Ward case for the CRC. Much to the chagrin of the draft board chairman (reportedly a local Ku Klux Klan leader), when Coe finally argued the case before the U.S. Supreme Court he convinced the justices to overturn the local board's ruling.[32]

In the early 1950s the *New Orleans States* and *Times Picayune* published articles blasting liberals, leftists, and draft dodgers, and the "Americanism Committee" of the New Orleans Young Men's Business Club conducted an anti-Communist campaign on radio and television and in the public schools. In that climate neither group of university administrators could ignore the radicalism of these professors. Unfortunately for Johnson, he found new employment at a small black college in Houston at exactly the moment the CRC in Texas faced its own troubles with red-baiting. His reputation as leader of the Louisiana CRC followed him, so he "was sacked in 1952, [again] because of FBI meddling." After Oakley Johnson left New Orleans, Lee Brown of the International Longshoremen and Warehousemen's Union tried to hold the Louisiana CRC together, but the chapter "basically disintegrated" by the end of 1951.[33]

Members of the CRC chapter formed in Miami in 1948 faced a local situation surprisingly similar to that of their colleagues in New Orleans. The common view of Miami as a fairly liberal and cosmopolitan city—in Raymond A. Mohl's words, a city "South of the South"—does not hold up for the period before 1960, if then. South Florida underwent tremendous demographic change in the first twenty years after World War II; reaction to these changes came in waves of racism and anti-Semitism that would have made John Rankin proud. The Klan posted signs welcoming visitors to the city just after the war, and a surge of violence that began in 1946 with cross and house burnings to keep blacks out of white neighborhoods peaked in 1951 with dynamite bombings of a black housing complex, churches, and synagogues and continued into the late 1950s. The Miami CRC chapter operated in what Mohl calls a "schizophrenic" atmosphere: in spite of its "tourist industry and transplanted northerners," Miami "exhibited many of the elements of the 'Deep South' on issues of race relations, labor organizing, and federal power."[34]

The national CRC office sometimes seemed to have difficulty understanding the environment in which its southernmost branch functioned. CRC field organizer Milton Wolff reprimanded the new Miami chapter in 1949, calling it "all fouled up" and "based on the white middle-classes in Miami; and what the hell, they are the accomplices, willingly or otherwise, of the oppressors of the Negro people here." Many CRC members in Miami were white, mostly Jewish New Yorkers who came South during the war years and brought Lower East Side radicalism with them, and they both felt the stings of local anti-Semitism and adamantly opposed "the oppressors of the Negro people" in their adopted city. Bobby Graff, a Communist and social justice activist who had migrated to Miami from Detroit with her husband, Emmanuel, led the CRC in 1949. Some labor unionists and a few black radicals had also joined the group, including active CIO organizers. If the branch wanted ammunition to answer Wolff's implied accusation that it shied away from public confrontation on the race issue, it might have pointed to such impediments to liberal social action as an active local grand jury, a visit of HUAC to Miami in 1948, and, as a result of those hearings, empanelment of a federal grand jury in 1949 to consider possible indictments of Dade County "subversives." It might also have noted the brutalities of the Miami Police Department, which, "through intimidation and terror, played a powerful role in maintaining white supremacy and the color line well past mid-century."[35]

Like the New Orleans chapter, the branch in Miami grew out of a particular case, though in Miami civil liberties violations, not racial violence, inspired establishment of the organization. Perhaps this provoked Wolff's concern, though the case certainly qualifies as one that would interest the defenders of the "Communist Eleven" at Foley Square; and in the Florida case, the defenders succeeded. A former garment worker named Leah Adler Benemovsky wrote notes to various people inviting them to attend a meeting with visiting Communist dignitaries in early 1948. In the aftermath of the meeting, and just before HUAC came to Miami for the first time, she was caught in a "dragnet" sponsored by a local grand jury. When questioned about party membership or participants in the meeting, Benemovsky took refuge in the Fifth Amendment. Denying her right to refuse to testify, a Dade County judge found her guilty of contempt and sentenced her to jail for ninety days without bail. Sylvia Bernard Hall and her first husband, Sam Hall, then working for the Communist Party in Alabama, traveled to Miami to help, and Sam, accompanied by the party's district organizer from Louisiana, Irving Goff, visited Benemovsky in jail. Sylvia described her incarcerated comrade as a shy person, the daughter of immigrants, "a dedicated party worker of the 'old school.'"[36]

Two years before the Roosevelt Ward (draft evasion) case with the Louisiana CRC, Pensacolian John Moreno Coe agreed to serve as Benemovsky's lawyer. Coe took the case to the Florida Supreme Court twice in the months just before the 1948 presidential election—a busy time for him, since he also headed Henry Wallace's Progressive Party in Florida. When the high court heard substantive arguments they threw out the lower court's ruling; the majority opinion classified Benemovsky as a "political" Communist, not a "criminal" one. She had a right, in other words, to refuse to answer the county solicitor who attempted to link her with "criminal communism."[37] This interesting decision came only a few months before CRC lawyers lost the case of the eleven Communist Party leaders in New York, and it encouraged Miami's Left-liberal community, many of them already active in the Progressive Party, some of them Communists, to establish a chapter of the CRC.

Leaders of the Miami CRC quickly began a correspondence with the national office about local problems. In one letter the chapter secretary asked for advice about three matters: a case in which police broke both arms of black defendant Charles Hunter during "questioning"; an interracial square dance held by "Young Progressives and the Paul Robeson Club" that was broken up by police, who "roared up in squad cars . . . and after separating them into white and Negro . . . threatened to arrest them on grounds of inciting a riot"; and the need for "a prominent speaker who could appear in Miami." In respect to the last, the chapter thought that "the Dean of Canterbury or Paul Robeson would be tremendous." The reply from the CRC's Len Goldsmith insisted that the Miami group follow up on the Hunter case, which could "well become the center of a great deal of CRC activity" because "it has all the elements of drama and human interest that make possible a broad campaign and [could] reach sections of the community that are rarely involved in ordinary CRC cases." The second matter Goldsmith considered "equally important." He agreed with the chapter's plan to hold an interracial New Year's Eve Party and suggested that every minister in town be invited, along with photographers and some attorneys ready to challenge police interference as "a violation of the First Amendment of the Constitution, the right to peaceably assemble." On the question of speakers he demurred—the Canterbury Dean, a supporter, had returned to England, and the CRC could not commit for Robeson; but they would cooperate as much as they could.[38]

The two cases that Goldsmith emphasized, and several other incidents of police brutality and harassment like them, did become important projects of the Miami CRC in its first year. Publicizing the outrageous brutality of Lake County sheriff Willis McCall in the infamous Groveland rape case in central Florida, and raising funds for the defendants in that case, involved members of the Miami CRC from 1948 until 1951. They also participated in the organization of a Right-to-Work Committee that pushed for an end to segregation in local unions and, in early 1949, as the federal grand jury began its work, did what it could to protect their members, prepare themselves for interrogation, and deal with defections. "Fight energetically any ideas that the organization is infiltrated with enemies, that it will not be able to grow, that there are not adequate forces to handle it there, that the American people are not ready to fight back, that their defeat is inevitable," instructed William Patterson.[39]

But CRC members faced mounting odds in Miami. The *Miami Daily News* published a long series of inflammatory articles that listed members of the Progressive Party and the CRC and suggested that members of both groups were Communists. When the CRC held an anti-Klan rally, the newspaper responded with a column calling the CRC a secret Communist organization. The rally had been held, the CRC answered in an open letter to the newspaper, "to rally the community for an all-out effort against the Klan," which was terrorizing blacks and progressive whites in Miami. The newspaper succeeded only in making "Klan threats and intimidations" worse. FBI agents followed Bobby Graff and other CRC leaders and tapped their telephones, and newspapermen hounded them. One gossip column noted Graff's "good connections in the Communist Party" based on a visit to Miami by Mrs. Gus Hall, "wife of one of the eleven top commies now on trial in New York," who was presently "sunning herself in Mrs. Graff's unproletarian home in the southeast section." In May 1950, Graff wrote to Patterson about the "serious problems facing the progressive forces here . . . our numbers are decreasing and very few replacements" and admitted that the CRC chapter was "practically non-existent."[40]

The story of the rise and fall of chapters in Houston, New Orleans, and Miami, while replete with evidence about lonely leftist activists, southern resistance, and local anti-communism, tells only one small part of the history of the CRC in the South. The organization became even more widely known because of a few highly publicized cases that exposed southern justice to the world. One important example is the case of Rosa Lee Ingram, a Georgia tenant farmer sentenced to life in prison in 1947, along with two of her sons, for killing a white man who sexually harassed her. The attacker threatened Ingram with his rifle, and in the ensuing struggle one of her sons picked up the gun and hit the assailant with it, killing him. This case engendered letters and petitions to Governor Herman Talmadge and Presidents Harry S Truman and Dwight D. Eisenhower from all over the world, and brought five delegations of protesting women to Georgia. (Mrs. Talmadge, it is said, invited the white women in but would not allow black women to enter the governor's mansion.) Esther Cooper Jackson, still a staff member of the Detroit CRC, gathered three thousand signatures on petitions by going door-to-door, appealing to church groups, and canvassing union members "at the Ford plant." Every May from 1947 until 1955 the CRC publicized a special "Mother's Day Appeal" for the Ingram case. The NAACP carried most of the legal burden in the case, but the CRC's huge international campaign may have been even more important in finally securing the Ingrams' release in 1955. Nevertheless, the relationship between the NAACP and the CRC was never smooth; the NAACP often disavowed CRC activities, both to shield itself from "guilt by association" and because its lawyers found the CRC's extralegal efforts distasteful.[41]

Another significant southern CRC case shared (again, with difficulty) by the CRC and the NAACP began, and ended, while the Ingrams sat in jail. The "Martinsville (Virginia) Seven" faced execution in 1951, convicted of gang-raping a white woman in 1949. As it publicized the appeal of this case, and in other such rape cases, the CRC's leaders first aimed to expose the disparity in sentences for rape between blacks and whites in the South. Second, they wanted to showcase that disparity as "legal lynching," that is, not simply as evidence of southern injustice but as part of an overall strategy for maintaining white supremacy and discouraging black advancement in the United States. NAACP lawyers shared the CRC's first goal but not the second, believing such an approach to be self-defeating and understanding that, in cold war terms, its advocates would be considered disloyal. In appealing the case, NAACP lawyers pointed to the effect of racial injustice on U.S. efforts to win the hearts and minds of the world in the cold war struggle, a view that influenced many liberal integrationists in the 1950s. The CRC organized an enormous mass-action protest movement to overturn the sentences of the Martinsville Seven, and later to have their sentences commuted, all to no avail. Eric Rise, student of the cause célèbre, says that neither the CRC nor the NAACP strategy worked because "Communism and civil rights were too closely linked in the minds of most southerners to permit any capitulation to either the NAACP or the CRC." Even the NAACP's more mainstream arguments did not work, because "the emphasis on inequitable treatment of black defendants paralleled radical attacks on the American legal system." The NAACP's consternation about CRC organizing tactics may have been justified in this case; Rise concludes that the desire of Virginia's governor not to "appear to be bowing to the radical influence" at least in part prompted his refusal to grant clemency to any of the Martinsville Seven.[42]

After the Benemovsky victory in Florida, lawyer John Moreno Coe took part in several important southern CRC matters, including the most celebrated CRC rape case, that of Mississippian Willie McGee. This case had all the elements of southern drama: allegations of rape of a southern white woman by a young black man, a hostile local populace, and, like the Ingram and Martinsville cases, interference in southern justice by "outside agitators." The national NAACP did not participate in McGee's defense, and his early defense lawyers were reluctant advocates at best. Local attorneys appointed by the court (in the beginning) or hired by the CRC after Laurent Franz and others investigated the case "were almost disbarred . . . virtually ruined economically," and one, frightened by a personal threat, "left the courtroom before summing up and before the case went to the jury." Perhaps even more than the other cases, the McGee case attracted national and international press and contributions from all parts of the United States and Europe. There were rallies and marches in Chicago, Detroit, Louisville, New Orleans, and New York, petitions to Congress and the president, and contributions from labor unions, church groups, and local chapters of the NAACP and the ACLU. When a "white women's delegation" traveled to Mississippi in 1951 under CRC sponsorship to protest McGee's inability to get a fair trial, it was jailed briefly for disturbing the peace.[43]

The state charged McGee in 1945 with rape of a white Laurel, Mississippi, housewife with whom, according to local rumors and his own wife's testimony during the appeals, he had had a long-term sexual relationship. When his mother asked him why he confessed to the crime, he answered, "I signed to be living when you got here." Black eyewitnesses placed him in another part of town at the time the woman's husband alleged the rape took place; unfortunately, no white eyewitnesses came forward. The McGee case reached the U.S. Supreme Court four times, twice being remanded to Hinds County for retrial. After the third high court hearing, a CRC press release charged state and federal courts with "collusion" in the case, a "conspiracy" to keep McGee on death row that could "go on indefinitely."[44]

John Coe and fellow CRC attorney Bella Abzug of New York worked on the final appeal of the McGee case in January 1951. They based the new appeal to the federal district court on several grounds: denial of equal protection of the law, that is, of federally guaranteed civil rights, because Mississippi executed only black men for rape; perjured trial testimony; and a confession they believed to be forced by physical violence, but null in any case because McGee faced certain lynching had he told the truth. After a denial from the district court, they presented a petition, unsuccessfully, to the U.S. Supreme Court, and then to Governor Fielding Wright, who denied clemency. The state of Mississippi placed its traveling electric chair in the yard of the Laurel courthouse, where the case began, and executed McGee in a public ceremony on May 8, 1951. People cheered when he died, a fact the CRC noted in its several postmortem announcements. The day after the execution, John

Coe, a southern lawyer often called "radical" or "Communist" by his neighbors in the conservative Florida Panhandle, wrote to Abzug in words that his friend William Patterson would have approved. He had "thought of poor Willie," he said, "a poor human being sacrificed on the altar of brutality and intransigence of the 'master race.'"[45]

Coe had litigated two very different CRC cases immediately before he entered the McGee case, each involving white clients and almost identical local ordinances that made it illegal for Communists to reside within the city limits of Jacksonville, Florida, and Birmingham, Alabama. On August 29, 1950, a front-page story in the *Jacksonville Times-Union* announced, "First Arrest Made Under Red Statute—Alexander W. Trainor, 54, Detained by Police." Trainor, the only Communist registered in Duval County, said he had changed parties since he first registered in 1947 and merely forgot to change his registration. Coe won the case in circuit court, citing the Florida Supreme Court decision in *Benemovsky v. Sullivan* as well as the First and Fourteenth Amendments as grounds for asserting the unconstitutionality of the ordinance. While complimenting Coe's "able argument," a local reporter noted how the CRC lawyer "adroitly avoided the real point at issue here," the essence of the foreign-controlled, malevolent Communist Party.[46]

Two weeks later Coe argued successfully against Birmingham in federal district court. "What we have is a wave of hysteria," he told the court, "rushing headlong into Fascism because we are afraid of Communism." Called the "Bull Connor" ordinance, the Birmingham law in question had been created by then–city commissioner (future police chief) Eugene T. Connor. Connor hated Communists, a truth well known since his early occupation as a "union-buster" for Birmingham's steel companies, and Alabama native Sam Hall, the defendant in this case, had been called "The City's Top Commie" in a local newspaper. Long watched by the brutal "Red Squad" of the Birmingham Police Department, Hall publicly acknowledged his employment as a full-time Communist Party worker and even ran newspaper advertisements defending the party's right to exist.[47]

Hall wrote articles for Communist-supported weeklies and headed the small Communist Party in Alabama in the late 1940s. Police maintained constant surveillance of Hall's house and followed both Hall and his wife, Sylvia, on everyday errands. According to Sylvia, Sam kept a loaded rifle by the bed and firecrackers on the window sills to serve as a warning in case of attack by the Klan or its allies. Their last travail in the steel city began the day after the Korean War started in 1950.

Police arrested Sam Hall as the couple sought to obtain signatures for the same Stockholm Peace Petition that had put Texas Communists at risk. Whatever means of support Hall might have, read the vagrancy indictment, was "disreputable." The Halls found a Birmingham lawyer to arrange Sam's bond and left for New York to attend meetings there. While driving through Georgia they heard on the car radio about the anti-Communist ordinance's passage and assumed that they would be arrested and jailed if they returned to Birmingham.[48]

In New York, Hall consulted William Patterson of the CRC, who contacted John Moreno Coe. The couple returned to Birmingham only after the constitutionality of the ordinance had been successfully challenged in federal court. Coe won that case and beat the "disreputable" vagrancy charge, and then the couple returned just long enough to pick up their belongings and entrust the sale of their house to friends. They went first to New Orleans, where Sam Hall finally met his lawyer at the home of Oakley Johnson, during Coe's litigation of Roosevelt Ward's draft evasion case. After New Orleans, like many others in their situation in the early 1950s, the Halls hid "underground" for the next three years, until Sam died of brain cancer in New York in 1954.[49]

Some CRC cases, like those of Trainor and Hall, received little publicity outside the local press, but the CRC's national and international mass-action crusades, especially the many involving race and rape, had propaganda value for their wider cause. Most such cases came from southern courts, but some important race discrimination cases, like that of the Trenton Six in New Jersey (which the CRC labeled "A Northern Scottsboro") and the Gilbert court-martial, originated in courts outside the South. Cases like these helped to validate CRC leaders' claim that the racial injustice perpetuated by courts and lynch mobs was a national issue and a federal responsibility.

Commenting on "To Secure These Rights," the 1947 report about southern inequality and lynching that became the basis of President Truman's civil rights proposals to Congress, an official CRC document proclaimed pessimistically: "The genocidal policies of the Government of the United States against the Negro people of the United States, against its own citizens, are so evident that the Government itself is forced to acknowledge them." This statement comes from a remarkable book presented as a petition to the United Nations in 1951: *We Cry Genocide: The Historic Petition to the United Nations for Relief from a Crime of the United States Government against the Negro People*. Part 2 of the petition cites the legal basis for the study: "Shocked by the Nazis' barbaric murders of Poles, Russians, Czechs and other nationals on the sole basis of 'race' under Hitler's law—just as Negroes are murdered on the basis of 'race' in the United States under Mississippi, Virginian, and Georgia law—the General Assembly of the United Nations adopted the Genocide Convention on December 9, 1948."[50]

Written by William Patterson with considerable help from other contributors, including Oakley Johnson and Florida writer and activist Stetson Kennedy, *We Cry Genocide* applies the principles of the United Nations Genocide Convention to race relations in the United States. It is a 238-page indictment of American justice, especially southern justice. "We shall prove," it says, that "the object of this genocide . . . is the perpetuation of political and economic power . . . [and] its end is to increase the profits and unchallenged control by a reactionary clique." Laid out like a legal brief, after introductory statements in each section it is a laborious compendium of evidence—encyclopedic, almost mind-numbing lists and descriptions of thousands of legal and illegal lynchings of the postwar years. On its cover are statements from the address of Justice Robert Jackson at the opening of the Nuremberg Trials, accusing not "little people" but "men who possess themselves of great power" of "planned and intended conduct that involved moral as well as legal wrong" in Nazi Germany. The intent is a clear indictment of American racism as perpetuated or allowed to prosper by American elites. The language is radical, strident, and as much anti-capitalist as anti-racist. In less metaphoric terms, the message remains "Just like Hitler's friend, Tojo, Bilbo, too, has got to go," with Bilbo as the stand-in for American leadership in general.[51]

Patterson led one group to Paris and presented the CRC's petition to the United Nations there; Paul Robeson led another CRC delegation to the UN's New York headquarters. In Paris, Patterson asked the UN to apply the Genocide Convention to the United States, likening contemporary African Americans to German Jews under Hitler. He castigated the American Bar Association and the American Legion, both of which had lobbied against U.S. ratification of the Genocide Convention. Upon Patterson's return, the U.S. government relieved him of his passport, and a direct, systematic effort to build the government's case against the CRC ensued. By 1956, beset by a Subversive Activities Control Board ruling that it hand over records, and with Patterson under indictment for contempt because he refused to comply, the CRC closed its doors. In its last year, it protested the lynching of Emmett Till and the subsequent verdict of acquittal in Mississippi courts. In one release the organization called for a new mass-action campaign against lynching and the poll tax and "the impeachment of Senator James O. Eastland, who calls for violation of the desegregation order of the Supreme Court, which is a violation of his oath of office."[52]

William Patterson never left the Communist Party; he became the editor of the *Daily Worker* in 1958, wrote an autobiography, *The Man Who Cried Genocide,* in 1971, and was a prolific political writer until his death in 1980. The Communist Party in the United States had all but died long before then, in the wake of Stalinism, the cold war, American anti-communism, and de-Stalinization during the Khrushchev years. Its membership shrank from a postwar high of about eighty thousand (out of a total population of about 150 million) around the time the CRC was established, to about twelve thousand when the CRC collapsed in 1956, to about three thousand after Khrushchev denounced Stalin and invaded Hungary in 1958. The years of the CRC were the years of the party's decline, and attacks on one fueled attacks on the other. Even if the CRC had not introduced *We Cry Genocide,* and Patterson not been prosecuted, it is difficult to see how the radical legal aid organization could have survived much past 1956. Cold war pressure overpowered the party and organizations connected to it, no matter how uncertain the connection. By the time Patterson died, the American party was so small as to be ineffectual, a gathering of ancient partisans, most of whom had simply looked on as the civil rights movement—and the New Left—passed them by.[53]

Still, the CRC that Patterson headed from 1946 to 1956 bequeathed a legacy of protest under fire to the southerners of the civil rights generation. The case can be made that leftist reformers, especially Communist Party members, provided the seedbed, if not the ideology, for the activism that became the postwar civil rights movement. By the late 1950s, Esther Cooper Jackson and most of her friends had joined the reformist southern movement led by Martin Luther King Jr. and others; she edited *Freedomways,* a periodical devoted to telling the story of the civil rights struggle, from 1961 until 1986. Her coeditor, Jack O'Dell, had been an organizer for the National Maritime Union active in CRC activities in New Orleans in the time of Oakley Johnson; and he worked for King's Southern Christian Leadership Conference in the early 1960s, until pressure from the FBI and the Kennedy administration forced his release. Angela Davis, Black Panther supporter and the most famous Communist of the 1970s, was the daughter of SNYC activists from Birmingham. Many of the sons and daughters of her leftist allies of the late 1930s and 1940s, Jackson says, labored in the voting rights and public accommodations drives of the civil rights movement. Robert Hodes's son moved back to New Orleans to provide legal assistance to civil rights workers. In the introduction to the collection *Freedomways Reader,* Julian Bond wrote that, while race remained the central issue, the older activists who were the periodical's editors taught activists of the 1960s that "race was immensely complicated by greed, that prejudice and poverty were necessarily linked, and that it would take organized mass action to carry the day for freedom."[54]

The notion that these early radical organizers were the forerunners of the more successful civil rights activists of the 1950s and 1960s is very appealing. Civil rights historians looking for continuity sometimes refer to the band of young progressives who created the Southern Negro Youth Congress as the "first SNCC" (Student Non-Violent Coordinating Committee, 1960–70). Although it is doubtful that many SNCC members of the 1960s knew about their supposed predecessors (and founding leadership by Communist Party members was missing in SNCC's case), the linkages of purpose and methodology are easy to discern. Based among young college-educated southerners, both organizations had ties to supportive groups in the North, declined to require political tests for membership, and worked for political and economic justice at the grassroots. And other links come naturally to mind. Depositions taken by the CRC in the "Oust Bilbo" campaign cannot fail to remind us of the depositions taken during the Mississippi Freedom Democratic Challenge, both sets aimed at reforming the Mississippi Democratic Party. CRC lawyers of the earlier period are not unlike the heroic civil rights lawyers who faced recalcitrant southern judges to protect Freedom Riders, sit-in participants, and other protestors. Both the Mississippi Freedom Democratic Party and the Voter Education Project of the 1960s involved "local people" who were part of the generation nurtured by voting rights and equal justice crusaders of SNYC and the CRC.

But the view that radical crusaders in the civil rights arena accomplished little except to "stiffen white resistance," on the one hand, or muddy the water for liberal civil rights activists, on the other, has long been widely accepted.[55] The CRC did not restrict its agenda to civil rights, or its civil rights protests to the courts, and in the process it added to the leverage of its opponents. Communism remained a national issue until well past 1954, when *Brown v. Board of Education* shook the foundations of southern law and custom, or 1956, when the CRC issued its last manifesto. Even after fervent anti-communism quieted in the rest of the country, well past the mid-1960s, white southerners listened to FBI reports about Martin Luther King Jr. and imagined links between agitation for civil rights and the goals of the Soviet

Union. And while conservatives equated civil rights with communism, many single-minded liberal civil rights advocates worried about the diverse purposes of Communists and their allies. Unlike their sometime allies on the far Left, by the mid-1950s most center liberals (black and white) saw the end of segregation and disfranchisement as the primary goals of the civil rights movement, and they seemed to be making some progress. Communism and loyalty issues endangered that progress and brought their primary goals into question.

Responding to such perceptions, the civil rights establishment circled its wagons and shunned the CRC. The NAACP's Walter White helped with the State Department's attempts to counter reaction to *We Cry Genocide*. UN delegate Ralph Bunche, a longtime acquaintance, snubbed William Patterson in Paris. Eleanor Roosevelt wondered in print "if [Patterson] has decided to transfer his citizenship to the Soviets." By 1951, Dr. Benjamin E. Mays of Morehouse College, a respected progressive and an original co-chairman of the CRC, had quit his participation. Even Aubrey Williams, chairman of the militantly integrationist SCEF for many years, struck out against the CRC. In response to a mailing about the McGee case, he wrote, "Don't send me any more of your materials—you people do far more harm than good. The best thing you can do for Willie McGee is to go out of existence." After Senator James Eastland brought the Senate's anti-Communist committee to New Orleans for hearings aimed at SCEF in 1954, Benjamin Mays quit that suspected board as well. SCEF may be a case in point. Although the group remained decidedly non-Communist and politically unaffiliated throughout its history, it never disavowed the former Communists or other leftists among its supporters; and the New Orleans NAACP refused to cooperate with SCEF or even to grant its executive director a membership card. Even the appearance of impropriety mattered a great deal, because in the delicate political climate of the 1950s it endangered accomplishment of the liberal agenda. Alliances with Communists were patently impossible.[56]

The "anti-Communist" roots of what would come to be called southern "massive resistance" reach far back into the region's history; after World War II, invigorated by the urgency of postwar activism, this distinctive kind of southern anti-radicalism gradually became a coherent political force. As historian Adam Fairclough notes in his book about civil rights in Louisiana, the impetus for this was national as well as regional, encouraged by the anti-Communist agenda of the Truman and Eisenhower administrations. "By fostering a conservative political climate that stigmatized criticism of the established order as 'un-

American,'" he writes, "the Cold War enabled southern segregationists to link integration with subversion." Sometimes it seemed that the mass-action campaigns of the left wing encouraged and enabled southern segregationists. Identifying Communists among the agitators for civil rights afforded a certain respectability to the movement to preserve the racial status quo and served to quiet its liberal or moderate opponents. Southern leaders perfected the use of anti-communism as a tool of "massive resistance" during and after the war, and it flourished between 1946 and 1956, the years of the CRC. In a land stagnated by fear of outsiders and steeped in the hypocrisy of the "Lost Cause," all progressives fended off accusations of radicalism, alienism, and anti-Americanism. CRC activists were particularly exposed, easy targets. The ideal weapon of reaction, certainly more acceptable nationwide than white supremacy, anti-communism remained a great benefit for the makers of "massive resistance" throughout the 1950s and 1960s. Southern segregationists gladly joined right-wing collaborators across the country in a public, spirited hunt for Soviet sympathizers, and their anti-radicalism included and intimidated southern liberals as well as left-wing radicals. It is no wonder that liberal activists distanced themselves from the Left. The NAACP barely lived through the Red Scare, almost by joining it; the vulnerable CRC could not. In the end the weapons of the Right were simply more powerful than the defenses of the Left. Center liberalism may have survived through adaptation, but by the mid-1950s the old left-wing progressivism of the 1930s and 1940s lay dying at the feet of anti-communism and "massive resistance."[57]

7
E. D. Nixon and the White Supremacists
Civil Rights in Montgomery
John White

IN NOVEMBER 1985, part of the fortieth-anniversary issue of *Ebony* magazine was devoted to a celebration of "Four Decades of Black Progress." A photographic essay entitled "Forty Who Made a Difference" featured short profiles of "movers and shakers" who had "helped make the world a better place for blacks." Those honored for their civil rights activities included Daisy Bates, who led the desegregation protest at Little Rock High School in 1952, and Ezell Blair, Joseph McNeil, David Richmond, and Franklin McCain, the North Carolina A&T students who sat down at a Greensboro lunch counter in 1960. Also featured were James Farmer of the Congress of Racial Equality, Roy Wilkins of the National Association for the Advancement of Colored People (NAACP), Dorothy Height of the National Council of Negro Women, Whitney Young of the National Urban League, and A. Philip Randolph, organizer of the Brotherhood of Sleeping Car Porters (BSCP) and leader of the 1963 March on Washington, D.C. Better known, perhaps, to *Ebony* readers were Martin Luther King Jr., "leader of the Montgomery Bus Boycott," and Mrs. Rosa Parks, whose "refusal to give a White man her seat on a bus in Montgomery, Alabama, became one of the most significant spark plugs in Black history."[1]

Before the month was out, John H. Johnson, publisher of *Jet* and *Ebony*, received an embittered letter from an Alabama subscriber to both magazines. Protesting his exclusion from the "listing [of] people that has made some form of contribution to civil rights" in *Ebony*'s feature, the writer set the record straight:

I organized the first Welfare League in 1935; organized the Voters League in 1939; fought for a USO Club for blacks in Montgomery in 1941; in 1944 I led 750 people around the court house to prove to white people that blacks wanted to register just like everybody else. I was the first black to run for public office in Montgomery. I got Mrs. Rosa Parks out of jail and I got her to let me use her case for a test case. It was I who called the people together to organize a Bus Boycott; it was I who selected Dr. M. L. King, Jr., as Chairman and it was I who raised over $100,000 to operate on.

He did not, the writer continued, "want people to build me up just to make me a big man," but simply to tell "children all over the country the truth." Johnson was admonished as "one of the people who ought to tell the truth through your press, because if I had gotten Mrs. Parks out of jail, paid her fine and kept my mouth shut, a lot of people would never have known Rev. King or Mrs. Parks." The civil rights movement, the writer concluded, "grew out of the Bus Boycott, and I started the whole movement." The letter was signed, "Respectfully yours, Dr. E. D Nixon."[2]

E. D. Nixon had been a notable figure in Montgomery's African American community for at least twenty years before the city's famous bus boycott, and despite his bombastic tone there was considerable substance to his claims. As an active member of two nationally based organizations—the BSCP and the NAACP—that were pledged to fight the precepts and practices of white supremacy, E. D. Nixon always placed local concerns at the top of his agenda for change.

Nixon's checkered career also exemplifies the contention that during the Jim Crow era in the South, leaders of African American communities—often divided by interracial tensions and jealousies—attempted to create "an alternative culture emphasizing collectivist values, mutuality and fellowship" in a hostile environment where "white dominated public space was vigilantly undemocratic and potentially dangerous."[3] These values, in Nixon's case, derived primarily from his identification with the BSCP and its leader, A. Philip Randolph.

Through the BSCP, Nixon learned the practical and strategic value of waging collective action. Through a series of what can be described as minor, everyday workplace battles, Nixon learned how concerted union action could, and did, challenge unjust employer activity that was both economic and racial in nature. Fighting these small battles and drawing upon group goals and group strength schooled Nixon and other black unionists of his day for later and larger civil rights struggles.

The testimonies of BSCP members support this view. Mrs. Rosina Tucker, international secretary-treasurer of the Ladies Auxiliary of the BSCP and president of the Washington, D.C., chapter, affirmed that membership in the BSCP "brought out qualities of strength and courage in the porters and their wives. They became leaders in their communities, bought homes, sent their children to college." The brotherhood, she believed, "laid the foundation for the civil rights movement. It inspired black people by proving that they could get results. The [Pullman] porter changed the image of blacks from strike breakers to strong union men."[4] As Bernard Mergen notes: "The [Pullman] porter was unique among black workers in that he came into prolonged and intimate contact with large and diverse numbers of whites. The Pullman was a kind of theater with seats on a single aisle by day, which was transformed (by the porter impresario), by night into twenty-four individual theaters. The uniform, insignia, and paraphernalia of the porter, from his iron step to his whisk broom, were prominent stage props in the scene he played."[5]

Edgar Daniel Nixon was born on King Street in Montgomery on July 23, 1899, the fifth of eight children. His father, Wesley M. Nixon, was a tenant farmer and a Primitive Baptist preacher. Edgar remembered wryly that "my daddy had two wives, and he had bad luck with all the children. He was only able to raise seventeen of us!"[6] His mother, Sue Ann Chappell, a cook and maid, hoped that her son would become a lawyer or a doctor, but she died when Edgar was ten and he was brought up in rural Autauga County (which he loathed) by a paternal aunt, Winnie Bates, a laundress and Seventh Day Adventist. His aunt would often send her young nephew to the local slaughterhouse, where "you could buy a cow head for a dime"—which she would clean and cook. Nixon's most vivid memory of his impoverished childhood in a "four-room house" was the problem of lighting: "The [gas] company would put a meter in your place, and to turn on the gas, you had to put in a quarter. When the time was running out, I'd stand there and hold on to the quarter until the lights flickered down, getting the last second out of what we'd paid for."[7]

The young Nixon received little more than a third-grade education, and at the age of fourteen he left home and became self-supporting. After several jobs, including work in a meatpacking plant, on a construction crew, and at a Birmingham store, Nixon became a baggage handler at Montgomery's Union Station. In 1923 he became a Pullman porter—"I'd been wanting one of those jobs on the Pullman car ever since I got down there and saw those porters standing up side the train with those white coats on, sharp and everything"—a position he held until his retirement in 1964, and made regular runs from Montgomery to Miami, Chicago, St. Louis, and Los Angeles.[8]

Although Pullman porters were regarded as the elite of the African American working class, Nixon resented the degrading treatment they received from the Pullman Company and white passengers. By 1924 Pullman porters earned sixty dollars a month, but they were expected to buy their meals and equipment and were not paid for the time spent in preparing the coaches for journeys. They also had to contend with disgruntled passengers. If one had mislaid his wallet, he might accuse a porter of having stolen it. "A whole lot of porters were searched and humiliated, and [then] they found the man had left it at home."[9] But Nixon's experiences on the railroad also widened his horizons and increased his self-esteem. He liked to recall that "I was over twenty years old before I knew the whole world wasn't like Montgomery. I decided not to be a coward and move up North where things were different, but to keep my home in Montgomery and start fighting for what I thought was right."[10] Moreover, his travels convinced Nixon that southern segregation laws were both unjust and immoral.

Functionally illiterate, Nixon taught himself to read while working as a Pullman porter. "If you got on a train with a newspaper or book," he recalled, "and you left it in your room and went to the dining car, by the time you come back I'd done read it almost. And I made a memorandum of words that I couldn't understand."[11] In 1928, Nixon—now married to his second wife, Arlet, and with a son by his first marriage—heard A. Philip Randolph speak at the YMCA in St. Louis, demanding a salary increase for Pullman porters to $150 a month. Nixon—who was earning only $72.50 a month—put a dollar in the collection box and immediately joined the fledgling BSCP. He asserted: "When I heard Randolph speak, it was like a light. He done more to bring me in the fight for civil rights than anybody."[12] Nixon revered Randolph as "the greatest black man we had in the last one hundred years" and as the mentor who had provided him with the skills and confidence to challenge the white supremacists: "I was able to make a contribution solely because we had the Brotherhood and I wasn't afraid."[13] The values of collective struggle instilled in members of the BSCP were central to Nixon and his subsequent career in civil rights. As he put it, the BSCP and his long association with Randolph "gave me the know-how and the courage to organize the [Montgomery] Bus Boycott, and if I had not had that training that I received under the able leadership of Mr. Randolph, the Bus Boycott would have been a failure."[14]

For Randolph, the BSCP was an organization to promote race pride as well as to improve the working conditions of its members. Echoing the motto of Marcus Garvey's Universal Negro Improvement Association, the major black nationalist movement of the 1920s, an early issue of the BSCP's newspaper, *The Black Worker,* demanded: "Up with Race Pride and Class Pride, Long Live the Spirit of the New Negro."[15] Aware also of the power of black religion, Randolph, a professed atheist, appealed to his members in biblical and evangelical terms and held meetings in black churches.

Nixon's membership in the fledgling BSCP did much to increase his confidence in dealing with intimidation and taunts from his white superiors in the Pullman Company. Returning to Montgomery after his first meeting with Randolph, Nixon recalled:

> When I got home, before I got off the train, the superintendent there told me, "I understand you attended the meeting of the Brotherhood yesterday in St. Louis." I said, "Yes I did." So he says, "I'll tell you right now, we're not going to have any of our porters attending the Brotherhood meeting[s]." I says, "Well, if somebody told you I attended the meeting there, maybe they told you also that I joined yesterday." And before he could answer me I said, "Of course, before I joined I thought about what lawyer I wanted to handle my case if you started to mess with my job. And that's what I'm going to do—I'm going to drag anybody into court that messes with my job." And I didn't even know a lawyer's name at that time. But I bluffed him out so that he didn't bother me. And from then on I was a strong supporter of A. Philip Randolph.[16]

Nixon founded the Montgomery division of the BSCP in 1938 and served as its president for twenty-five years, making it into Alabama's most notable black union. But there were problems in recruiting porters for the brotherhood because the Pullman Company would not allow discussion of union matters during work time. Nixon's solution, derived from Randolph's example, was to find porters wherever he could in Montgomery—in churches, bars, and fraternal lodges—and ask them to join the union. "If a man went to church, I would go and talk to him about the service, the minister, what the church was doing in the com-

E. D. Nixon and the White Supremacists 203

munity and such things, and then kind of lead the conversation around to the idea that if he joined the Brotherhood we would get higher pay and be able to give more to the church and do more in the community. Or if I knew a man liked to go out and have a few drinks with friends, I would find him at the Elks club, and go in there and ask him for dues for the Brotherhood."[17]

Active involvement in the BSCP increased Nixon's standing in Montgomery's African American community and stimulated his growing political awareness. On one occasion, a former white railroad employee in Montgomery who had persistently harassed black porters obtained a job at a furniture store that they patronized. Borrowing enough money from the bank to pay off the porters' debts, Nixon led his colleagues to the store and informed the startled manager that unless the individual was sacked, they would immediately close their accounts. The offending employee was promptly fired.[18]

When the brotherhood finally secured a contract with the Pullman Company in 1937, Nixon memorized every section of the personnel rules and used them to advantage. He told the story of a white passenger who frequently boarded his train at Decatur, Alabama:

> He'd drop his bag down the side of the train and tell me, "Go get that bag, boy!" It happened a dozen times or more. We finally got a clause put into our contract where if a passenger wanted to accuse us of anything, he had to have a witness to whatever you were supposed to have done or said before he could do anything about it. When we got that clause, that was the time for us! He got on the train one evening and told me, "Go get that bag, boy!" just like that. So I went on and got the bag and come back and he followed me in the car and I carried the bag to his room, and when I got there, I slammed the door and I cussed him with everything I could think of. I told him if he ever called me "boy" again, I would break his neck. He didn't have no witnesses and I took advantage of that. After that, when he got on the train, he would say, "Porter, would you please get my bag?" But I had to teach him a lesson. And it took him by surprise because he didn't expect a black man to say that to him.[19]

Issues of status and etiquette were involved in another episode that Nixon related to his friend Studs Terkel, a Chicago-based broadcaster and author:

> I was once called in. The supervisor wrote me up, said I was talkin' to "some woman." The woman was my wife. I said, "Mr. Maloney, that woman is Mrs. Nixon. And I'm gonna demand you respect her as Mrs. Nixon, just as you would expect me to respect Mrs. Maloney as Mrs. Maloney. And I want my statement in the record." It knocked him for a deck of tombstones. They found me guilty of dereliction of duty. He gave me eight days on the ground. You get no pay for that time. The Chicago office of the [Pullman] Company said eight days. The local man made it eighteen days. So I said to my wife: "They're askin' for a fight and they're gonna get it." The Brotherhood appealed to the [National Labor] Relations Board. I was found not guilty, and the Pullman Company had to pay me for all the time lost.[20]

Despite his personal courage and evident contempt for white racists, Nixon (often threatened by the Ku Klux Klan) was only too well aware of the dangers faced by African American men in their daily lives. He was, therefore, compelled to administer a stern lesson in racial etiquette to Virginia Durr—who with her husband, Clifford Durr, was one of Montgomery's most visible (and committed) white liberals. After she had known Nixon for several years, Mrs. Durr met him in the post office.

> I said, "Why hello, Ed." People called him Ed Nixon. He didn't say anything. I held out my hand and said, "Hello, Ed." And he didn't take my hand. I went on back to the office with the mail and in about fifteen minutes, he came up and sat down. "Now, Mrs. Durr, I want to get something straight with you. Don't ever call me Ed again. If I called you Virginia, I'd be lynched. Suppose in the post office you said, 'Hello Ed.' And I said, 'Hello, Virginia.' You got me in trouble right there and then. And to shake my hand in public that way, that's going to get me in trouble. Now when I can call you Virginia, you can call me Ed. And I'll shake your hand in public when it's safe. You ought to have better sense than come up to a black man in the public post office and say 'Hello, Ed.' And put out your hand."

Reflecting on the episode, Durr realized that she had inadvertently ignored the constraints that Jim Crow placed on whites as well as on blacks and had placed her friend in a potentially dangerous situation.[21]

Nixon also relished telling the story of an overweight Pullman porter named Cooley and the Pullman Company's attempt to "get rid of him." An equally obese white superintendent boarded the train at Montgomery and made himself comfortable in the drawing room. When the train reached Atlanta, the superintendent told the conductor to "write up Cooley as no good," since he had allegedly failed to close the toilet doors during the entire journey. Nixon zestfully contested the ruling on the grounds of "weight and width":

> The superintendent stated that Porter Cooley didn't lock the toilet doors from Montgomery to Atlanta. There were seventeen stops between. That means the superintendent would have to get out of that drawing room and walk to the other end of the car and back thirty-four times. He'd have to pass Cooley each time. If he weighed some 300 odd pounds and Cooley weighed close to 300, together they weighed close to 600 pounds. The aisle of a Pullman car [is] about thirty inches. It just wasn't wide enough. He couldn't pass him once, let alone thirty-four times. I pointed this out. We won the case.[22]

But the increasing use of the automobile and the decline of the railroads saw a nationwide decline in BSCP membership. By 1952, the Montgomery division was desperately short of funds and had only nine paid-up members. Nixon's repeated appeals for help from Randolph could not prevent the closures of lines and the consequent loss of porters' jobs.

Nixon's first involvement in community rights came in 1925, after two black children drowned while swimming in a city drainage ditch. He organized an unsuccessful petition to build a swimming pool for African Americans, and remembered that "after that incident I knew there would not be any recreation or any form of civil rights for black people unless they were ready and willing to fight for it."[23] During the 1930s, Nixon assisted Myles Horton of the interracial Highlander Folk School in Tennessee in an attempt to organize Alabama's cucumber pickers into a union.

In 1943 Nixon founded the Montgomery Welfare League, which helped indigent African Americans secure relief payment and jobs with the New Deal's Works Progress Administration. Realizing that the league was, in effect, an organization dependent on donations, Nixon founded the Citizens' Overall Committee, which campaigned for jobs and improved pay and began to attract local press attention for Nixon's brave stands on civic issues.[24] The committee did effect some tangible improvements in the daily lives of black Montgomerians. In 1944 Nixon complained to J. B. Hill, president of the Louisville and Nashville Railroad, about the squalid conditions in the "Ladies rest room in the Colored Waiting Room" at Montgomery's Union Station. The room was filthy and often waterlogged, while drinking water was available only "in an open end keg with the faucet in the side and the water is carried in one of the buckets used for mopping the men's rest room." Paper cups were in short supply, and on one occasion a male passenger had retrieved two beer bottles from the keg.[25] That some improvements were made as a consequence of Nixon's protest is evident in a letter to Hill, thanking him on behalf of "the Negro people of Montgomery for your consideration in the Ladies rest room and the Water Cooler in the Colored waiting room at the Union Station."[26] Nixon was also able to prevent the construction of a separate "shed" at the station where black passengers would have purchased tickets without having to pass through the waiting room, which was for whites only.[27]

Nixon was also a member of the Montgomery Negro and Civic Improvement League (MNCIL), founded in 1936 by Dr. Roman T. Adair, one of the first African American physicians to practice in Alabama and the medical director at Alabama State College.[28] The group's purpose was to support black voter-registration efforts through litigation on behalf of those who had been denied the franchise because of race. In 1938 it sent a tactfully worded petition to the Montgomery County Board of Registrars in which it protested the process employed for the registration of blacks and whites. "Literacy" tests, applied by registrars in other Alabama counties, were not used in Montgomery. Instead, questions were asked orally by registrars, who filled in the blanks for white applicants, whereas blacks had to fill out their own blanks in front of the registrar. Blacks were also required to have two white witnesses appear in person and sign for them. In practice, few whites actually appeared, and when they did they were closely questioned about their knowledge of the black applicant. Since most African Americans in the city and county had moved there from other areas, they were, in any case, unlikely to be able to produce white sponsors.

In its appeal, the MNCIL complained of these practices and described itself as representing "a large group of Negro citizens, who are embracing the principles of good citizenship, observance of law and order, and are ardent supporters of both federal and state constitutions." In July 1938, a delegation of prominent black doctors and educators, representing the MNCIL, appeared before the registration board, only to have their request that African American voters be allowed to act as witnesses for black applicants rejected. A year later, the chair of the Montgomery County Board of Registrars, interviewed by Gunnar Myrdal, frankly stated her attitude toward the political aspirations and prospects of black Alabamians:

> All niggers—uneducated and educated—have one idea in their mind—they want equality; but look on them for yourself. You don't mean that we could have them in our churches, bury them in our cemeteries, have [them] in our schools and in our homes any more than we have apes or other animals. It is necessary to keep the Negro from voting, for voting would lead to social equality. The niggers are in the majority in this county and in Alabama. They would take over the power in the state. The white people are never going to give them this power.[29]

During 1939 and 1940 fewer than one hundred African Americans were placed on Montgomery's registration rolls, and practically all of these were from the educated upper class.

With more success, the MNCIL sponsored "Good Conduct" campaigns and engaged in community drives for the Red Cross, the United Appeal, and the March of Dimes. During World War II it organized bond drives, one of which resulted in the purchase by black Montgomerians of more than $150,000 worth of bonds. In 1941 the MNCIL discussed the recreational needs of African American servicemen in Montgomery. Nixon was particularly concerned at the lack of a United Services Organization (USO) facility for black military personnel passing through or stationed in the city. He later recalled:

> When the war came, there wasn't a lounge in the railroad station for the Negro soldiers, like the whites had, where they could relax and leave their bags. And they didn't have a USO club for Negro soldiers in all Montgomery. It was out of the question to think that we could go into the USO club for whites. We had the Negro Civic Improvement League then, and a committee went to find out why we didn't have a USO club for Negroes. When this committee reported back that we couldn't have a club because we didn't have 1,000 Negro soldiers, I said to the League President, "I don't know how, but I am going out lone-handed for a USO club."

While working as a Pullman porter, Nixon encountered Loula Dunn, commissioner for the Alabama Department of Public Welfare, on his train and pressed her on the matter. He also wrote to Eleanor Roosevelt to explain the situation. The First Lady sent James Geater, special investigator for the Federal Security Agency (FSA), to Montgomery along with the athlete Jesse Owens. Geater's first remark to Nixon was: "I been with the recreation department for fourteen years, and I ain't never heard a Negro cry loud enough that would make Mrs. Roosevelt send me down here to see what it was all about."[30] Later, when Eleanor Roosevelt was a passenger on his train, Nixon requested—and received—an audience with her, marking the beginning of their lifelong friendship.

In June 1942, a USO Club—or "A Recreation Center for Colored Servicemen in the Armed Forces of the United States"—was opened at 215 Monroe Street in Montgomery. Again, as a consequence of Nixon's effective lobbying, the Citizens' Overall Committee secured the use of a small USO lounge for black military personnel at Union Station. But as with many of Nixon's subsequent activities, these episodes revealed class and status divisions within Montgomery's African American community. At the dedication of the USO Club, Nixon's contributions were not mentioned, and he was not even notified of the opening of the USO facility at Union Station. As one of his supporters observed, Nixon's innovative attacks on racial proscription and segregation deserved to "be respected by those of his own racial group for whom he has had the forwardness and initiative to intercede." They should also acknowledge his considerable achievements and offer "wholehearted co-operation in the realization of other projects upon which he is now working."[31]

Dismayed by the unwillingness of the conservative Montgomery branch of the NAACP to engage in direct-action protests, Nixon, despite white hostility, organized the Montgomery Voter's League in 1940 to register black voters. Following the U.S. Supreme Court's *Smith v. Allwright* decision of April 1944, which invalidated the discriminatory white primary in Texas, he led 750 African Americans to the board of registrars, demanding to be placed on the electoral rolls. Nixon himself had paid the thirty-six-dollar poll tax in Montgomery and had tried to register to vote for ten years. Only after filing a lawsuit and threatening another was he registered in 1945. From May to October 1944, Nixon took five months' leave from his porter's job and traveled extensively throughout Alabama in an attempt to organize black voters. Partly as a result of his efforts, the number of African American voters in the state increased from 25,000 in 1940 to 600,000 by 1948. In that year Nixon described himself as being "very busy in this fight for the right to vote for Negroes," but he acknowledged that the "crackers here have done a good job of keeping the Negro afraid and also keeping him unlearned."[32]

In 1947, Nixon, on behalf of the NAACP, protested against segregated admission to the Freedom Train, a touring exhibition—sponsored by the American Heritage Foundation—of such historic documents as the Declaration of Independence, the original manuscript of the "Star Spangled Banner," and the Japanese surrender treaty ending World War II—when it visited Montgomery.[33] The *Alabama Tribune*, under the headline "Local Freedom Train Comm[ittee] Snubs NAACP," carried a statement by Rosa Parks, secretary of the local branch, asserting that news of the visit of the Freedom Train to Montgomery, scheduled for December 27, 1947, immediately prompted "the militant Montgomery Branch NAACP President Mr. E. D. Nixon into action. He [had] sought to determine Montgomery's stand on racial discrimination in regards to the program and viewing the Freedom Train." Nixon and E. G. Jackson, manager of the *Tribune,* had met with Montgomery mayor John L. Goodwyn but received no assurance that admission to the train would be on a nonsegregated basis. Since the Montgomery branch of the NAACP was "firm in its stand against all racial discrimination," it felt "solemn anxiety" about the Freedom Train's imminent arrival.[34]

Following an NAACP directive that local branches should seek active participation in planning for visits of the Freedom Train, Nixon discovered that in Montgomery, as in Birmingham, "not a single colored person" had been included in the city's planning committee. Failing to receive any reassurances from Mayor Goodwyn that this omission would be rectified, Nixon urged NAACP executive secretary Walter White "to see to it that no discrimination against any race is used in Montgomery or any other Southern town, even if it calls for by-passing the city."[35] Nixon also informed the American Heritage Foundation of the apparent resolve of Montgomery officials to enforce segregation when the Freedom Train visited the city and requested that "you save us further embarrassment" by taking Montgomery off the train's itinerary.[36]

Rosa Parks subsequently notified Gloster Current, the NAACP's director of branches, that "President [E. D.] Nixon is militantly opposing the 'two lines for the colored and white races' plan to view the train,'" as well as the all-white composition of Montgomery's Freedom Train Committee. In conclusion, she warned, "the Montgomery branch cannot welcome the Freedom Train under a Jim Crow pattern."[37]

In the event, thanks to the uncompromising position taken by

Nixon—and possibly as a response by the Montgomery city fathers to the cancellation of the Freedom Train's scheduled visit to Birmingham—it did stop in Alabama's capital city, where segregation practices were temporarily suspended. The *Montgomery Advertiser* duly reported: "Both white people and Negroes stood side by side to read for themselves the Emancipation Proclamation. Two Negro girls were the first to be admitted when the train opened at 10:00 AM for inspection," and until closing time "the one, continuous line which extended for blocks was filled with practically equal numbers of the two races."[38] Governor James E. "Big Jim" Folsom and his two young daughters had been early visitors to the exhibit, and the United Press reported that "as the state's chief executive entered the streamlined coaches, he was trailed by two small Negro children and their parents. It was hard to tell whether the youngsters were more moved by the six-foot, eight-inch governor, or the imposing array of documents." The United Press International release also suggested that the huge turnout might have been partly due to the tenth annual North-South football game that was being held in Montgomery.[39]

As a leading member of the Progressive Democratic Association, a separate organization of black Alabamians excluded from the Democratic Party, Nixon was a co-signer of "An Open Letter" to the *Montgomery Advertiser* in 1953 that protested against a scheduled appearance in Montgomery of Davis Lee, the African American publisher of a Newark, New Jersey, newspaper. Lee had argued that the desegregation of public schools would result in the loss of many black teachers—a point that Nixon scornfully discounted. When Lee appeared at Montgomery's municipal auditorium, he addressed a meager audience of seventy-five, of whom only twenty-five were African Americans.

In May 1954, Nixon filed as a candidate in the Montgomery Democratic primary for a place on the county Democratic Executive Committee—making him the first African American to seek public office in Alabama since the Reconstruction era. He lost to the white candidate by just ninety-seven votes. He was, however, chosen as "Man of the Year" by African American readers of the *Alabama Journal* and was characterized as "very unassuming, yet militant, aggressive, yet not a radical."[40]

Nixon made headlines of a different kind the following year when he tried to purchase a ticket to the Democratic Party's Jefferson-Jackson Day Dinner in Birmingham, Alabama. Refused admission to an all-white gathering, Nixon—described by the *Montgomery Advertiser* as the "NAACP Mau Mau Chief"—protested against his exclusion. In response, the principal scheduled speaker, Governor G. Mennen Williams of Michigan, canceled his appearance.[41] The *Alabama Tribune*, an African American newspaper, editorialized that Nixon, "a certified Democrat, and also one by choice," had applied for a ticket, only to be informed that "local laws" prevented the admission of black Democrats to the dinner.[42]

Despite this setback, and with the African American vote an increasingly significant factor in Montgomery politics, Nixon successfully pressured Montgomery County commissioner Dave Birmingham in 1954 into hiring four black police officers. The Progressive Democratic Association now began to itemize black grievances—which included the humiliating treatment of African American passengers on Montgomery's buses. Always alert and sensitive to practices of racial exclusion, Nixon during the 1950s went three years without a telephone in Montgomery rather than accept one on a four-party "all-colored" line.

On September 3, 1954, following the U.S. Supreme Court's *Brown v. Board of Education* decision, Nixon attempted (unsuccessfully) to enroll twenty-three African American students at the new all-white William R. Harrison High School in Montgomery. Black pupils had previously attended Abraham's Vineyard Elementary School only a short distance from Harrison, "an outmoded structure that had been scheduled to be closed and its students bussed elsewhere until black parents petitioned the local school board not to close the neighborhood school."[43] In May 1955, the Montgomery chapter of the NAACP planned its celebration of the first anniversary of *Brown*. Nixon was quoted as saying that "we had not done very much about implementing" the Court's landmark decision and that "the NAACP and other organizations should join in letting it be known in Washington that segregation in public schools must be abolished."[44] In fact, Nixon's membership in the Montgomery branch of the NAACP was always vexed. He was frequently involved in acrimonious disputes with the local chapter and its conservative, middle-class elite grouped around Alabama State College.

A year after its formation in the summer and fall of 1918, the Montgomery branch of the NAACP had nearly six hundred members—second only to Birmingham in the state's branches. But the Montgomery chapter was afflicted by quarrels between its college and non-college members. The first secretary, William Porter, lamented the failure of Montgomery's African American working class to appreciate the importance of supporting the organization.[45] A founding member of the reorganized Montgomery branch in 1928, Nixon felt that it suffered from both corrupt and inadequate leadership. Defeated in his first bid for branch president in 1944, he was elected in 1946 and remained in office until 1950 when Robert L. Matthews, the man he had beaten in 1945, replaced him.

Immediately after his 1944 defeat, Nixon—as president of the Citizens' Overall Committee—wrote to Walter White, secretary of the NAACP, complaining that the election had been "one of the most nasty I have ever seen held in a NAACP branch." Matthews, Nixon alleged, had broken "all records in violating the constitution of the Association" and had rigged the election by appointing the nominating committee and recruiting "about 15 people who came to the meeting, paid dues and voted." Nixon also charged Matthews with incompetence, citing as evidence the fact that out of a black population of fifty thousand, the Montgomery NAACP branch had only about four hundred members. Nixon claimed that his bitterness was not over having lost the election but rather over the manner in which it had been conducted, with Matthews's supporters openly buying votes for their candidate. In a postscript, Nixon restated his 1944 platform, with its call for three thousand new members "instead of 400," a NAACP office in downtown Montgomery, a redress committee, and a voting drive.[46]

Reporting to Ella Baker, the NAACP's director of branches, after a two-day visit to Montgomery in the spring of 1945, Assistant Branch Field Director Donald Jones noted that the branch was in "a bad way due to a lack of competent leadership," judged Matthews to be "hopeless," and suggested that his election as president was "because he works for the Pilgrim Insurance Company which has had one of its personnel as President for the last several years, obviously for prestige purposes." Jones believed that Nixon was "the strongest man in the community in civic affairs, pretty influential among the rank-and-file," and he (accurately) predicted that Nixon would "win the next election and improve the situation." But Jones also added a cautionary postscript: "The big trouble with Nixon is that he fancies himself as an amateur detective. While I was there he was deeply involved in a criminal investigation and his talk was mostly of other cases in which he played the role of sleuth. Were he President, we'd have to watch the branch pretty closely to keep it from turning into a detective bureau and nothing else."[47]

In his 1945 election manifesto, Nixon called for a more aggressive NAACP branch in Montgomery and pledged to make it a popularly based organization.[48] During his 1945 campaign, Nixon confided to one of his supporters: "I do not believe in a one man administration. But I do believe in the organization having a public office where people can find the official man when one is needed. We need a more militant NAACP in Montgomery because we need a program to offer the people, because we need to return the NAACP to the people as their organization."[49]

During his first year in office, Nixon personally signed twenty-two hundred members into the Montgomery chapter, but he was concerned that members felt they had fulfilled their obligations once they had paid their annual dues. On the other hand, those who did engage in branch activities only did so when their jobs and other commitments permitted. Living up to his characterization by Donald Jones as a "sleuth," Nixon personally investigated many cases involving police brutality, rapes of African American women, lynchings, and murders. In one instance he managed to persuade Alabama governor Chauncey Sparks to commute the death sentences of three African American men found guilty of raping a white woman to terms of life imprisonment. On another occasion, in the early 1930s, Nixon had appeared before Sparks to request that a reward be posted for information leading to the arrest of those responsible for the murder of a black student, Amanda Baker. A $250 reward was subsequently posted by the governor—the first state reward offered in a crime against a black victim.[50] Openly critical of southern white liberals and their black allies who failed to act decisively on racial issues, Nixon recalled that on his way to see Governor Sparks about the Amanda Baker outrage he "passed a church where the Southern Conference for Human Welfare were having a meeting, talking about the terrible things going on."

> I went in and was sitting in the back when the chairman, [an] elderly white woman seen me and said, "I see we got a new face here this morning and I'm going to let the gentleman come up and identify himself. So I walked up and said, "Good morning— I'm E. D. Nixon, President of the NAACP, and I'm on my way to see Governor Sparks to ask for a reward for the arrest and conviction of the guilty Party who committed the crime against Amanda Baker, and all I want to ask is if there is one man or woman here, white or black, that has the courage to go with me, because if there is, I'd be glad to have you." I stood there for a few minutes, and not a word did I get out of them. Finally I said, "Madam chairman, I'm sorry I've taken up your time, and I see now that nobody here really believes in what you are talking about."[51]

In March 1947 the Montgomery branch of the NAACP celebrated the thirty-ninth anniversary of the founding of the NAACP with a rally at Holt Street Baptist Church. The program featured a short profile of the incumbent president as being "well versed in the problems confronting Negroes in Montgomery." Nixon had also "spent long hours working toward the time when the two races will have a better understanding as regards each other." He was widely respected, "and many members of our race rely upon his judgment." Among the contributors to the souvenir program was the Montgomery division of the BSCP.[52]

Mrs. Johnnie Carr, an active member of the NAACP in Montgomery in the 1940s and still a leading figure in the city's African American community, was one beneficiary of Nixon's judgment. The city was using Oak Park, near her home, as a dumping ground for manure, and the area soon became infested with flies. Despite protests from local residents, the dumping continued. When she called Nixon, he advised her to collect one hundred dollars and sue the city. He also recommended the services of two white attorneys who filed suit on behalf of the residents, and the offending dump was eventually cleared.[53]

By the mid-1950s, Nixon's connections with organized labor and the NAACP, his friendships with prominent white liberals in Montgomery, and his standing with the city's African American working-class community made him a force to be reckoned with. Jo Ann Gibson Robinson, who was to play a pivotal role in the Montgomery Bus Boycott, recalled that by 1955 Nixon was "acquainted with most of the members of the police and sheriff's departments, with judges and jailers, and with people at city hall. Also, he knew most of the lawyers in the city, black and white." Whenever violations of civil rights occurred, "the victims involved would telephone Mr. Nixon, and he would go to their rescue. He was a friend to all who were in trouble and appealed to him for help. He simply seemed to get pleasure out of helping people, especially those who could not help themselves."[54]

Fred D. Gray, the African American attorney who was also to be a key figure in the Montgomery Bus Boycott, had earlier received Nixon's help in obtaining affidavits to register as a law student and take the Alabama bar exam. He related that "if anyone ever had problems with the city police or any matter where they thought their civil rights were being denied, they would always contact E. D. Nixon."[55] Rev. Ralph D. Abernathy, Martin Luther King's successor as leader of the Southern Christian Leadership Conference (SCLC), characterized Nixon as "an aggressive and fearless fighter for the rights of Negro people in Montgomery for many years, a Pullman porter [who] does not have a formal education, but a very courageous man. Long before the bus crisis he was meeting threats and turning them back in language as picturesque as a Missouri mule skinner."[56]

In his own account of the Montgomery Bus Boycott, King called Nixon "a foe of injustice" who had always "worked fearlessly to achieve the rights of his people, to arouse the Negroes from their apathy," and "one of the chief voices in the Negro community in the arena of civil rights, a symbol of the hopes and aspirations of the long oppressed people of the State of Alabama."[57] Rosa Parks remembered that Nixon "was one of the most active African Americans in Montgomery. He was a proud, dignified man who carried himself straight as an arrow."[58]

Nixon's repeated and sometimes self-serving accounts of his role in the events immediately following Rosa Parks's arrest and the formation of the Montgomery Improvement Association (MIA) have been variously interpreted. What is certain is that his activities—as strategist, treasurer, and fund-raiser for the MIA—owed much to his (differing) experiences in the BSCP and the NAACP.

The Women's Political Council (WPC) in Montgomery, organized in 1949 to urge African American women to vote, lodged several complaints with the city commission about the mistreatment of black female passengers on the city's bus line but had achieved little success. Numerous incidents—all involving African American women—had angered the black community. The most notable case was the arrest on March 2, 1955, of Claudette Colvin, a teenager, who had refused to vacate her seat when ordered to do so by a white bus driver. After Colvin pleaded not guilty to violating Alabama's segregation laws, Nixon discovered that she was unmarried and pregnant and decided that she was not a good choice for a test case against Jim Crow transportation.

The arrest of Rosa Parks on December 1, 1955, provided Nixon—and Jo Ann Robinson, the most active member of the WPC—with their opportunity. Nixon paid Rosa Parks's bail bond and then gained her permission to use her arrest as a test case of the segregation laws. Together with the WPC, Nixon decided that the protest should take the form of a one-day boycott of the Montgomery City Lines by its black passengers. He also called Joe Azbell, a sympathetic reporter on the *Montgomery Advertiser,* alerting him to the proposed boycott and the pamphlets about to be printed by Jo Ann Robinson advising blacks to stay off the buses on the day of Rosa Parks's court appearance. This astute move provided the protesters with valuable, free publicity. Again, it was Nixon who forcefully persuaded the city's African American ministers—

meeting at Martin Luther King's prestigious Dexter Avenue Baptist Church—to lend their public support to the protest after it was decided to extend the one-day boycott indefinitely. Not least, Nixon supported King's election as president of the MIA, convinced that "the success of the boycott would depend largely on a black preacher who could communicate with, motivate and inspire the masses."[59]

Nixon was acutely aware that the MIA needed both publicity and substantial funds to sustain its operations. The warmest responses to his appeals came from southern branches of the BSCP. Members of the Birmingham, Alabama, district branch cabled their congratulations on "your untiring effort in the great struggle to obtain justice and due consideration for all citizens of Montgomery as well as the entire South." The Asheville, North Carolina, division of the BSCP informed him that its members had passed a resolution "commending you and the organizations which you head for the firm, vigorous and courageous stand in behalf of matters of great importance to all concerned."[60]

In March 1956, Nixon was the guest speaker at a BSCP-sponsored meeting of the National Committee for Rural Schools in New York City. He seized the opportunity to tell delegates of the origins and progress of the ongoing boycott and of his own role in calling Montgomery's black ministers following the arrest of Rosa Parks. He also explained the MIA's "many objectives." Although its original aim had been "to adjust the seating arrangements on the bus[es] within the existing law," Nixon told his audience that the MIA was about to file suit in a federal court to challenge the constitutionality of segregation on Montgomery's public transport system. He also described the organization of the MIA's transportation committee and the operation of the forty-seven pick-up stations and three hundred cars that were taking African Americans to work—"and providing a better job than the Montgomery bus line has done in 20 years." After the MIA achieved its new objectives, it would stay in existence to fight police brutality and other forms of racial discrimination. Nixon then told the amused delegates a story about a small boy going down the street with a basket, selling puppies. When a lady asked their price, the boy replied "twenty-five cents." She was tempted, but decided against a purchase. The next day she met the boy again and asked him if the puppies were still for sale. The boy said that they were and that they now cost fifty cents. Asked why the price had doubled overnight, the boy said: "Their eyes are open." To much laughter, Nixon supplied the moral to this story: "The Negroes' eyes are open in Montgomery and they aren't being sold for 25 cents anymore."[61]

The following day, Nixon's mentor, A. P. Randolph, informed delegates that it cost thirty-five hundred dollars a week to keep the car pool running and asked for their support. Nixon then stressed the importance of the mass meetings in Montgomery in maintaining the dynamic of the boycott, and the financial contributions that the MIA was receiving from across the country. Montgomery's African Americans were "tired of being Jim Crowed on the Montgomery City Line or any other form of transportation" and would continue their protest "until the court says they don't have to do it." He ended with an appeal for donations; delegates were urged to "put your hand in your pocket and make a contribution. Whether it's large or small, the MIA will be eternally grateful."[62]

Nixon made a great impression when he appeared in May 1956 at a civil rights rally in New York City's Madison Square Garden together with Eleanor Roosevelt, A. Philip Randolph, the Alabama-born film actress Tallulah Bankhead, Congressman Adam Clayton Powell, and Martin Luther King. The last scheduled speaker, Nixon brought the audience of sixteen thousand to its feet when he announced: "I'm E. D. Nixon from Montgomery, Alabama, a city that is known as the Cradle of the Confederacy and that has stood still for more than ninety-three years until Rosa Parks was arrested and thrown in jail like a common criminal, and 50,000 Negroes rose up and caught hold of the cradle and began to rock it and the segregated slats began to fall. I am from *that* city."[63] Roy Wilkins, head of the NAACP, was also present and recalled that with Nixon's dramatic statement "people began to shout and yell and thump one another on the back, and the Garden resonated with enough joy and hope to keep us all going for months afterward."[64]

As the boycott continued, Martin Luther King was increasingly presented in the media as both its originator and its driving force, but Nixon's activities were extensively recorded in the *Black Worker*. The December 1955 issue announced: "Bro. Nixon Steps Up the Fight for Civil Rights," and concluded, "our hats are doffed to you once again, Brother Nixon."[65] In April 1956 the Chicago division of the BSCP hosted "A Salute to A. Philip Randolph," and Nixon was the keynote speaker before six hundred guests. The *Black Worker* duly reported that Nixon had presented them with "a ringside view of the important undertaking being carried on successfully by the Negroes in Alabama."[66]

Unlike the BSCP, however, the NAACP was more critical of the unfolding drama in Montgomery. When the newly formed MIA resolved to extend the one-day bus boycott, Nixon hoped that the Montgomery branch of the NAACP would offer its support, but he was told that the

New York office would first have to be consulted. Nixon—who had already decided that a new organization was needed to coordinate the protest—was not prepared to wait. He was aware that the state of Alabama was threatening to outlaw the NAACP, and this could be fatal to the boycott if the MIA was seen to be its auxiliary. His fears were justified. On June 1, 1956, in the sixth month of the boycott, devout segregationist Judge Walter B. Jones of the Montgomery Circuit Court granted Alabama attorney general John Patterson an injunction that banned the NAACP from operating in the state. With a blithe disregard for the truth, Patterson claimed that the NAACP was "organizing, supporting, and financing an illegal boycott by the Negro residents of Montgomery."[67] When the NAACP refused to surrender its membership and contribution lists to Patterson, Jones imposed a fine of $100,000 for contempt, effectively crippling its operations in the state.

In fact, the executive leadership of the NAACP was less than enthusiastic over the initial goals and direct-action strategies of the Montgomery Bus Boycott. Since the MIA's original demands were only for greater courtesy from bus drivers, the hiring of African American drivers for black neighborhoods, and the seating of passengers on a first-come, first-served basis, Wilkins believed that the MIA merely wanted to make segregation "more polite." The NAACP was pledged to "knock it out completely" and was not prepared to go to Montgomery "simply to ask Jim Crow to have better manners."[68]

Only with the mass indictment of boycott leaders and car-pool drivers in Montgomery and the MIA's challenge (in *Browder v. Gayle*) to Alabama's segregation laws did the NAACP intervene directly in the boycott. Responding to a call from Nixon, Thurgood Marshall, chief counsel for the NAACP, promised that he would assist in the legal defense of those indicted. Wilkins then pledged his total support of the boycott to Dr. King. Reflecting on the outcome of events in Montgomery twenty years earlier, Wilkins claimed it as a victory for "all the years of fighting and organizing done by the BSCP and the NAACP." In particular, he praised the efforts and example of E. D. Nixon, "the true godfather of the boycott," a man who was "straight as a ramrod, tough as a mule, and braver than a squad of marines," who had "locked Dr. King into history."[69]

E. D. Nixon, novelist Alexander Haley believed, "helped to nationalize the Montgomery movement" through his long-standing affiliation with the BSCP and labor unions that also gave him "the foresight and organizational skills to impress and mobilize Montgomery's black community."[70] But Nixon was increasingly unhappy with the middle-class leadership of the MIA, irregular accounting methods in its handling of funds, and what he regarded (with some justification) as the patronizing attitude of Martin Luther King. In November 1957, after discussions with King and Abernathy, Nixon submitted his resignation as MIA treasurer, citing the pressure of work as a Pullman porter and dissatisfaction with his treatment by the MIA leadership as prime causes of his departure. Nixon also informed Dr. King: "Since I have only been treasurer in name and not reality, it will not be hard to find someone to do what I have been doing, even a school boy." He concluded bitterly: "I resent being treated as a newcomer to the MIA. It is my dream, hope and hard work since 1932."[71]

Never committed to King's philosophy of nonviolent direct action, Nixon was not involved in any of the Southern Christian Leadership Conference's later campaigns in Alabama or in Chicago. He also criticized the SCLC for moving into local situations that had been initiated by grassroots activists and then stealing the limelight from them.

In 1964, when Nixon retired after more than forty-one years of Pullman service, the BSCP paid him an apt and judicious tribute, summarizing his civil rights activities before and during the Montgomery Bus Boycott:

> No member of the Brotherhood has had a more colorful record in Pullman service or in the Brotherhood. Brother E. D. Nixon was "Mr. Brotherhood" for Montgomery, serving both as secretary-treasurer and its only President. [He] was the first to organize a campaign in Montgomery, Alabama to get Negroes registered to vote, and was himself a candidate for local office. Having been the courageous and able Alabama State President of the NAACP, he was an early target for the bigots. Nevertheless, none of these activities changed his course of action or discouraged him from pursuing his objectives.[72]

After his retirement, Nixon became heavily involved in community work in Montgomery—raising funds for the care of the sick and organizing annual summer camps for the city's black children, including the "E. D. Nixon Summer Olympics." He served as community service adviser to Young Forte Village, a housing project in Montgomery with fifteen thousand residents, mostly teenagers. Increasingly concerned with *human* rights, during the 1970s Nixon also worked with the Alabama Coalition against Hunger and the Red Cross, with groups supporting the welfare of the elderly, and with groups opposing capital punishment. A lifelong advocate of racial integration, he rejected the rhetoric and separatist program of the Black Power movement during the 1960s. (To the consternation of many of his former admirers, Nixon supported the "reformed" George Wallace in his gubernatorial campaigns.)

In his last years, Nixon complained bitterly that his role in the Montgomery Bus Boycott had been largely forgotten, and he frequently disparaged Martin Luther King's exaggerated reputation as the instigator and organizer of the protest. Ironically, at the end of his life the disgruntled Nixon was a recipient of many awards and honors, including a resolution by the Alabama House of Representatives in 1971 commending his outstanding services to the state.

The historic marker, erected on September 6, 1986, in front of Nixon's home on Clinton Street, Montgomery, records that

> E. D. Nixon, Sr., posted bail for segregation law violator Rosa Parks. In her defense, Nixon gathered the support of Montgomery blacks in implementing the successful 1955–56 Montgomery Bus Boycott. His commitment and active involvement as a grassroots organizer, civic leader and founder of the Montgomery NAACP chapter has paralleled local movements for the advancement of blacks. As chief strategist of the Montgomery Bus Boycott, Nixon spearheaded a local protest, which launched a massive movement of social reform and earned him recognition as "The Father of the Civil Rights Movement."

Notably absent from this tribute is any mention of Nixon's campaigns against white supremacy *before* 1955 and his lifetime association with the BSCP. Yet as he fervently believed, this union—with its empowerment of black workers—had inspired his own determination to destroy the humiliations and lunacies of racial discrimination and segregation.

Writing in 1948 about his travels in the United States, the French socialist Daniel Guerin believed that he had detected a growing empathy between the leading civil rights organizations and organized labor. African American working-class unionism—best exemplified by A. Philip Randolph and the BSCP—was beginning to forge alliances with the Congress of Industrial Organizations and the American Federation of Labor. At all levels of the workforce, Guerin noted, "a new generation of Negro cadres is developing, realistic and modern, formed in the tough school of trade unionism." He predicted that "the effects of this germination will soon be fully felt both in labor and the Negro community." In the South this change had been particularly evident in

Montgomery, Alabama, where E. D. Nixon, "a vigorous colored union militant," was "the leading spirit in his city both of the local union of Sleeping Car Porters and the local branch of the NAACP. What a difference from other branches of the Association, which are controlled by dentists, pastors and undertakers! Nixon has both feet on the ground. He is linked to the masses. He speaks their language. He has organized the work of race defense with the precision and method of a trade unionist. Men like E. D. Nixon (to name only him) incarnate the alliance which has at last been consummated between the race and labor."[73] Guerin's prediction of a meaningful alliance between labor unions and the emerging civil rights movement was too sanguine; his estimate of E. D. Nixon in the era of white supremacy can hardly be bettered.

8
"Flag-bearers for Integration and Justice"
Local Civil Rights Groups in the South, 1940–1954

John A. Salmond

LATE IN 1944, as World War II drew to a close, the Left-leaning southerner and former New Dealer Aubrey Willis Williams believed a new liberal spirit was stirring in the South. "There seems to be a bottom deep awakening," he wrote, "a breaking up of the thick shed that has for decades covered the South; a stirring, or to use a good Southern term of 50 years ago, a refreshing. An unmistakable assertion of decency, and a turning on people who live by exploiting hatred, religious bigotry by trading in people's prejudices and fears." Williams believed that this spirit could, if boldly seized, end the region's economic and racial caste systems.[1]

Williams was not the only southern liberal who thought he could feel these winds of change. His friend Clifford Durr was similarly optimistic. So, albeit briefly, was the writer Lillian Smith, and even the tough-minded journalist Jonathan Daniels knew that change was on the way, like it or not. One reason why liberals felt as they did was the seeming proliferation of grassroots agencies for social and economic change that occurred at war's end. Locally based groups, some with national linkages, that emerged to challenge the southern status quo and, in particular, to confront directly the issue of racial segregation with the aim of ending it immediately rapidly became a feature of the postwar mosaic. This essay will examine three such organizations in order to give some recognition to these largely forgotten precursors of the civil rights revolution of the 1960s and to explain why their initial promise was usually foreshortened—why, in fact, Aubrey Williams's "bottom deep awakening," his "refreshing," did not develop into a more swiftly flowing stream.[2]

The Southern Conference for Human Welfare (SCHW) was the most radical of those groups dedicated to southern change. Formed in the charged atmosphere of the late New Deal, it survived a divisive attempt by American Communists to direct its agenda and emerged in 1945 determined to extend its influence and programs. In particular, its president, Clark Foreman, was insistent that it should develop an active local presence in the South to take advantage of the liberal tide he, too, believed was cresting. In 1945, therefore, the SCHW established state committees throughout the region, aiming to shift the SCHW's focus from fund-raising and lobbying in Washington and New York to grassroots activism, particularly in the area of voting rights. Osceola McKaine, an African American veteran of World War I, once owner of a Belgian nightclub, and a long-term activist, was hired as SCHW field secretary to coordinate the expanded program and to get African Americans more involved.[3]

By this time the SCHW had established state affiliates in Georgia, Virginia, Alabama, and North Carolina and was well on the way to doing so in South Carolina, Louisiana, Texas, Arkansas, Tennessee, and Florida. Of these, the three most effective were those in Georgia, Alabama, and North Carolina. Taking advantage of the relatively liberal political climate symbolized by the election of Ellis Arnall to the governorship, the Committee for Georgia, under its energetic director, Margaret Fisher, worked enthusiastically to support Arnall's liberal perspectives, and in particular his disinclination to oppose the recent U.S. Supreme Court decision to outlaw the white primary. Initially, the committee worked effectively to promote a range of measures enlarging social and economic democracy in Georgia, to the extent that the veteran labor organizer and founding SCHW member Lucy Randolph Mason could dare to hope that "we are touching the tap roots of democracy in this state, and are going to release new forces for good and right." For a time, as the committee boldly attacked Georgia's county-unit voting system, which greatly disadvantaged urban voters, or supported quietly the New Dealish Helen Douglas Mankin's successful campaign to win the U.S. House of Representatives seat vacated midterm by majority whip Robert Ramspeck, there seemed grounds for such optimism.[4]

The Committee for Alabama, certainly the furthest to the left of those established, as historian Patricia Sullivan has written, "continued much of the work initiated during the 1930s by the Communist Party and CIO activists around civil liberties and voter registration." It, too, benefited briefly from the liberal climate that sustained James E. Folsom's successful gubernatorial campaign in 1946. Committee for Alabama members worked tirelessly for Folsom, who won in a landslide. He received more than 90 percent of the small number of black votes cast as many black voters went to the polls for the first time, registered as a result of SCHW activity.[5]

Numerically, the strongest of the state committees was that in North Carolina, which was headed by Mary Price. Based in the liberal climate of Chapel Hill and enthusiastically backed by the University of North Carolina's president, Dr. Frank Porter Graham, himself a former SCHW national president, the Committee for North Carolina had a membership that included black and white college presidents, businessmen, lawyers, journalists, and even politicians, as well as "a large college student contingent many of whom were veterans." One of Price's many projects was to have prominent black leaders tour the state, address integrated meetings to show it could be done, and then form local branches in the successful aftermath, using the students as the recruiters. They did not always proceed smoothly, but one built around Mary McLeod Bethune, the distinguished educator, New Deal administrator, and friend to First Lady Eleanor Roosevelt, was an outstanding success. She spoke in Greensboro, Durham, and Winston-Salem to enthusiastic crowds. As a consequence, membership soared in these three cities. "Great strides are being made," Price reported to her board in March 1946. "We are a going concern." With more than a thousand paid-up members, they certainly were—for a time.[6]

The Committee for North Carolina (CNC), like its counterparts elsewhere, became heavily involved in voter registration and in lobbying legislators. As Sullivan points out, Mary Price registered as a lobbyist and spent much of her time in Raleigh, working for minimum-wage legislation and for measures promoting equal expenditure on black and white education and opposing right-to-work measures. Committee members, and especially the students, spearheaded a statewide voter-education drive, making good use of Osceola McKaine's experience as they did so. By January 1946, five student chapters had been established —at the University of North Carolina at Chapel Hill, Duke University, North Carolina College for Negroes, Bennett College, and the Women's College of the University of North Carolina at Greensboro—under McKaine's direction in order to facilitate voter-registration activity.[7]

Whenever possible, Price and her members confronted segregation directly. In 1946 the CNC's annual meeting was held in the Raleigh municipal auditorium, despite the local segregation laws. John Hope Franklin, then a young historian and a member of the CNC, recalled that on another occasion they met at the Washington Duke Hotel in Durham. When the integrated group was refused service in the dining room, the white members "went out to the white places and brought food in and we all ate together. For the 1940's this was real wild stuff, but they did it. That's the kind of thing Mary Price and them were doing." In North Carolina, as in other states, the work of the CNC initially seemed to bear out Aubrey Williams's sense of possibility.[8]

If the work of the SCHW and its state committees represented the leftist end of the reform spectrum, that of Dorothy Tilly and her Fellowship of the Concerned (FOC) epitomized political respectability. Tilly herself was certainly no revolutionary, but rather the entirely conventional, deeply religious wife of an Atlanta businessman, with a fondness for wearing hats decorated with roses, who nevertheless had by 1946 acquired sufficient reputation as a battler against the evils of segregation that she was the only southern woman appointed to President Truman's Committee on Civil Rights. As director of Women's Work for the Southern Regional Council (SRC), she was sometimes referred to as "the most influential woman in the South."[9]

In 1949, with the support of the SRC, Tilly founded the FOC to give direction to one of her myriad activities, ensuring the racially based dispensation of justice in southern courts. She had been working on equal justice issues as an individual since World War I, imbued, as she once put it, by her conviction that southern churchwomen "have often been able to start a movement for social reform long before society as a whole was ready to consider such a change" and that her job was to lead by example. Thus she was often to be found in southern courtrooms, a gray-haired, middle-aged lady, on her own, there to bear silent witness against any injustice. Sometimes, according to reports, "the mere presence of a well-dressed observer in the court-room was enough to insure fair play from a bigoted jury and an indifferent judge." More often than not, however, her presence alone could not prevent injustice from occurring. In 1947 she sat alone in a courtroom in Greenville, South Carolina, during the trial of thirty-one taxi drivers charged with the lynching of a local black man, Willie Earle. It had left a "special kind of mark on her," she later reported, "to see the defendants and the jury making a brazen mockery of the trial, openly talking and cracking jokes back and forth." People needed to know about such enormity, she thought. "If they did, they would stop it." If "good people" filled the courtrooms, she believed, "just their presence" would stop injustices such as those she had recently seen, not only in Greenville but throughout rural Georgia.[10]

Thus was born the Fellowship of the Concerned, so named, Tilly explained, "because it was built on our concern" about the state of justice in southern courts. The idea was simple: groups of women would attend trials, as she herself had been doing, as observers for justice. The FOC had no constitution and collected no dues; all "members" were required to do was to sign a pledge that read, in part, "I will sit in the courts and I will . . . learn how justice operates in my community. I will work with others in times of tension to see the rights of all are protected." From her small Atlanta office, Tilly coordinated this all-woman network herself.[11]

Tilly's ambitious aim was to recruit a membership covering every county seat in the South, and though this was never realized, the FOC's achievements were nonetheless impressive. Within a year of its founding there were networks in twelve southern states—most of Georgia was covered, as were half the counties in Kentucky, fourteen in South Carolina, eight in North Carolina, and seven in Tennessee. More than three thousand women already had their names on the books, with the number rising steadily. Soon they were doing much more than observing court procedures. They watched the polls at local elections on behalf of black voters and worked for equal treatment in local school finances. In Louisville, Kentucky, FOC women ran a roster on Saturday nights at the city hospital, checking on emergency room procedures. Quickly observing that no black doctors were permitted to practice there even though the bulk of the patients were African Americans, they lobbied successfully to have that convention overturned. After the *Brown* decision was handed down, FOC women became active in many communities working for the peaceful integration of their schools. In Montgomery, Alabama, they provided quiet support to Rosa Parks, to the young Martin Luther King Jr., and to Jo Ann Robinson and those others sustaining the bus boycott that was, eventually, to be the catalyst for southern transformation. Convinced through their court experiences that the roots of much black crime could be traced to shockingly inadequate living conditions, Tilly and her band became crusaders for fairness in public housing development. She may not have blanketed the South completely, but their influence was entirely for good. As Jo Ann Robinson once said of the FOC women, they were "islands of healing in a land of hurt."[12]

Dorothy Tilly and her women, though often the recipients of obscene hate mail, even of death threats and occasional Klan excoriation, were able to continue their work into the 1960s. They were, after all, thoroughly respectable middle-class women, often, with their husbands, pillars of their communities, imbued with a spirit of Christian love and determined to bring out the goodness in all southerners. Though they may have been irritants to many, they were scarcely political revolutionaries, nor did they radically challenge traditional southern value systems. The same could not as easily be said of the Fellowship of Southern Churchmen (FSC), another agency for racial change in the postwar South, also largely lost to the civil rights story.

Historian Robert F. Martin has described the FSC as "a loosely knit interdenominational and interracial association" of Christians "troubled by their region's mores" and determined to change them. Founded in 1934, it was finally disbanded in 1963, "a little cadre of Christians," primarily a "fellowship group . . . an association of Christian men and women who gathered periodically for study, discussion and prayer about the significant issues of the day." Its importance lay in providing a sense of community among its often beleaguered members rather than its pursuit of an activist social agenda. Only in the years immediately after World War II did the FSC broaden its structure and develop and clarify its aims to the extent that it entered the ranks of those grassroots groups actively fighting against segregation. For a few years, in fact, it functioned at the battle's cutting edge.[13]

Founded in 1934 by the young Christian socialist James A. Dombrowski, who later became executive director of the SCHW, the FSC was initially directed by one of the most remarkable figures in the history of southern radicalism, Howard Anderson "Buck" Kester. Best known for his role in the formation of the Southern Tenant Farmers Union, this iconoclastic, passionate Christian socialist was involved in a myriad of social justice struggles in the 1930s and 1940s. Kester gave the FSC its initial focus as a discussion forum, a place where members could renew their sense of purpose and then return to the picket line, the factory floor, or the field to continue their work on "behalf of the disinherited and the oppressed." In 1943 Kester resigned his position as FSC director, however, and his successor, Nelle Morton, lost no time in moving its office from Kester's home in Black Mountain, North Carolina, to the university town of Chapel Hill—or in changing the direction of its activities.[14]

Nelle Morton had a distinguished background as a teacher, social worker, and Christian activist. A native of Sullivan County, Tennessee, with degrees from North Carolina's Flora McDonald College and the

Biblical Seminary in New York, she moved into full-time church work after a brief stint as a public school teacher, with a particular focus on youth work. Active for some years in the FSC, she quickly resolved to change its focus, using its location in the relatively liberal Chapel Hill and building on the postwar idealism of the student body to turn it from a group of like-minded people giving each other mutual support into an organization of committed Christians whose ideals impelled them to work actively for social change and racial justice.[15]

In Chapel Hill, Morton found strong support among the town's clergy and its liberal community, mostly attached to the university. Rev. Charles Jones, minister of the Chapel Hill Presbyterian Church, was a dedicated FSC member, and for a time the FSC office was located in the church's basement. J. C. Herrin and Warren Ashby were also staunch allies, as was Aubrey Williams Jr., son of the former New Dealer, and Allard Lowenstein, later to become a civil rights activist, a close associate of Robert F. Kennedy's, and a U.S. congressman. In partnership with supporters such as these, Morton rapidly chartered an activist social role for the FSC, fighting for racial justice. She believed the organization should work closely with other agencies, such as the SCHW, whenever possible, but that it should also develop distinct strategies and approaches and, above all, stress the religious basis for its actions.[16]

Of those strategies, none was more distinctive than the use Morton and the FSC made of student work camps. The work camp idea was not new. They had begun in Europe after World War I and were soon enthusiastically taken up by most Protestant churches. The simple philosophy behind them was to bring Christian young people together for a period of time, in a particular community, "to work with their hands without pay, on some useful project," designed to help individuals, families, and communities solve their problems. The campers, too, benefited "from the spiritual experience which comes to a group drawn together by such high purpose." Morton hoped to use such camps in the fight to break down racial segregation. By living together in an interracial situation, young Christian southerners would not only lose the lingering racial barriers they themselves possessed but also provide examples for the communities in which they worked.[17]

Fortunately, there was a community in which a prototype camp could easily be developed. Rev. Eugene Smathers, an FSC member and a Presbyterian minister in the rural community of Big Lick near Crossville, in the Cumberland plateau of eastern Tennessee, had created a cooperative community there, helping his parishioners to improve the standard and marketing of their crops, to develop recreational programs, and, most important, to create from scratch a community health center known as the House of Health. In February 1945 he invited Nelle Morton to plan a work camp for his community, and in July eight young people, including a Japanese American, a Cuban American, and an African American, went to Big Lick. This was the first FSC fellowship camp, and it proved such an enormous success in terms of "the equality of the inter-group life, the practical expression of Christian brotherhood," and the quality of the work done that plans for a similar camp in 1946 were immediately drawn up. The South, Smathers exultantly believed, was indeed changing. The camp's success was a testament to this.[18]

The experience of the campers at Big Lick the following year was not quite so pleasant, but it reflected the future more accurately. The camp began on July 1 without incident, and as before, the group, which included one young black man, planned to live in the House of Health while building a recreation hall, helping clear school grounds, teaching canning techniques to the locals, and conducting Bible schools for their children. After only a week, however, there were signs of trouble. Smathers invited the local community to a social in the church hall to meet the campers, but they refused to come "as long as that Negro was in there." Later a jeering crowd gathered at the House of Health; some threw rocks. Though shaken, Smathers tried again a week later. He held another social, but this time the crowd was even uglier, again throwing rocks, jeering, and threatening to attack the campers, especially "the black boy, Billy." Most of the local parents refused to let their children attend the Bible school because of Billy. Sadly, Smathers decided the camp should disband after only two weeks' work. He felt immensely despondent at what had happened, for which he blamed war veterans from neighboring communities rather than his parishioners. It was the FSC's first taste of the hostility its work could cause, and there would be more to come.[19]

Nevertheless, the FSC's second interracial project was a resounding success—but then it was carried out, not in the South, but on the high seas. The United Nations Relief and Rehabilitation Agency (UNRRA) was at the time organizing the transportation of livestock from the United States to Europe in order to rebuild the Continent's devastated farm stock. Thus a steady stream of "cattle boats" crossed the Atlantic throughout the year. Although crewed by regular sailors, each ship also carried a number of animal attendants, including veterinarians, who did not need to hold seamen's tickets. All types of organizations, including church groups, were allowed to recruit such people, and here

Morton saw a chance. She applied for and received permission on behalf of the FSC "to recruit an interracial crew of 30 attendants, 2 veterinarians and one supervisor" to take an UNRRA ship to Poland, the first mixed crew to be so selected. The ship would sail on June 15, 1946, for an eight-week voyage, with "a recreational and educational" program planned for the return journey, when there was little regular work to do. Given that attendants were paid $150 plus expenses, it was hardly surprising that Morton received enough applications to fill three such boats.[20]

Morton sifted through the applications carefully, having been told privately by UNRRA officials that if the experiment was successful the agency would never again segregate its crews. Deciding to choose only southerners committed to an interracial future, she had no difficulty filling her quota. The young men came from twenty-three different schools and colleges, black and white, in the South. The whole venture was an outstanding success. Stock losses were fewer than on any previous trip, while those who participated said it was worth it for the interracial aspect alone—for many their first such experience. Hibbard Thatcher, a Chapel Hill student who made the trip, recalled nearly forty years later that it was a "precious kind of experience." Its success thrust Morton's concern at the failure of the Big Lick project into the background as she and her group determined to develop their interracial witness further in 1947.[21]

Thus, in 1947 the FSC made its decision to go to Tyrell County, in North Carolina's eastern Black Belt, to work with the African American community there. Some years before, S. P. Dean, a local black farmer, had formed the Light of Tyrell Credit Union, which, according to an FSC newsletter, had "saved the homes of many sharecroppers and small farmers in the county." The FSC board was particularly anxious to become linked to Dean's work. Although a second work camp was planned for Phoebus, Virginia, where campers would build a community house while living at the nearby all-black Hampton Institute, it was toward Tyrell County that the FSC looked most eagerly to extend its southern witness.[22]

In her memoirs, Morton recalled that "everything went well" with the Tyrell camp until a few days before its closing date. Her recollection was faulty. In fact, from the time the ten campers, including a young black man, Nat Garth, arrived in the county seat of Columbia they were met with suspicion and hostility. Columbia, with a population of around eight hundred people, three hundred of them black, was a typical eastern North Carolina town. Racial attitudes there were more akin to those found in the Alabama Black Belt or the Mississippi Delta than in the more liberal college and university communities from which the campers came. The young people, who had hoped to live at the local black school, found that permission to do so had been withdrawn, forcing them to crowd into Dean's home. For a long time they were unable to get repaired a truck that was essential to carry them to the work project, a farm property that they planned to convert into a community store. Moreover, the mayor and other local whites intimidated Dean so badly that he was incapable of providing any leadership. By mid-July the project was on the verge of closing, the campers thoroughly sick of their enforced idleness and more than a little frightened by the sustained hostility of the white community.[23]

In the end they decided to stay. The truck was finally repaired, the campers moved from Dean's house to a converted fowl house at the work project, and morale started to improve as they began to work in earnest. But then came disaster, in the thoughtless shape of a visit from the Phoebus campers, including three white women. They arrived in Columbia in an open truck, all in full view, "entering the small town singing and waving banners." Their friends were delighted to greet them. There were hugs and kisses all round before the interracial group had a picnic, went for a swim in the river, and then played some volleyball, still in their swimming attire, and still in public view.[24]

The visit was the last straw for the local people, their patience already sorely tried by the group's earlier behavior. That night a mob of three hundred men, mostly armed, invaded the camp, forcing the campers to hide in ditches and cornfields. Even then, the campers were determined to stay. Only after the local sheriff, Ray Cahoon, warned them that if they did not leave immediately a mob "twice as big" would come the following night to "get them" did they pack up and go home, the project uncompleted. Most white North Carolinians supported the sheriff. The *Greensboro Daily News* reflected their views when, after having chided the young people for not being "housebroken," it stated that given they were "intruders" in the region, the residents' reaction was justified. Said Sheriff Cahoon, "I don't know of any laws preventing white folks from living with Negroes, but it is not customary for intelligent white people to do that, [and] I do know that people here don't think much of it."[25]

The retreat from Tyrell County caused anguished debate within the FSC ranks as to whether they should continue to witness to the white South through racially integrated group living and work, or whether such activity should be restricted to a property the agency had recently acquired through benefaction, in Buckeye Cove, near Swannanoa, North Carolina, seven miles east of Asheville in the heart of the southern Appalachians. To Morton that would signal retreat, the more so since some members doubted the wisdom of any further integrated activity, wherever it was held. The times were just not right. Morton had her way—in the short term. Two further work projects were scheduled for 1948, one in Crossville, Cumberland County, Tennessee, which was a success, and one in Atlanta that failed so comprehensively that it brought that phase of the FSC's activities to an end.[26]

The idea behind the Atlanta project was simple. Described as a students-in-industry camp, it involved young people living communally at the black Gannon Theological Seminary, finding jobs locally on an individual basis, and coming together each evening to talk about their day's experiences, to pray, and to reflect on their situations "in the light of the larger problems of the South." Seven young men—six white and one black—were recruited and moved into Gannon in early June.[27]

Nothing went smoothly for the young men. They had difficulty finding jobs, time hung increasingly heavily on their hands, and they started to get on each other's nerves. In an attempt to relieve this growing tension, Frank McCallister, director of the Georgia Workers Education Service, one of the project's sponsors, made a decision he would soon bitterly regret. He offered the use of his conference room for a party, with Rosalie Oakes of the Atlanta Young Women's Christian Association undertaking to "recruit some girls . . . who were adjusted to interracial groups." The campers were enthusiastic, and a date was set, July 16. They baked cookies, brought ginger ale and grape juice, the girls duly arrived, and the place soon started to swing. The group was having a great time together, playing folk games, singing folk and union songs, and dancing the Virginia Reel when a large contingent of Atlanta's police arrived, brandishing arrest warrants alleging the running of an illegal dance and of violating the city's segregation ordinances. Though these warrants were eventually not acted upon, the police charged everyone present with disorderly conduct and disturbing the peace. Then they left, and so did the demoralized campers and their female guests, the night of fun and relaxation ruined.[28]

The matter did not end there. The Atlanta newspapers made much of the incident, stressing that interracial dancing had occurred and listing the names of those present. In the hardening southern racial climate, that was enough. Some of the young women who had attended the party lost their jobs as a consequence, and all the participants were fined for disturbing the peace, having decided to plead guilty to save costs and avoid further embarrassment to their families. It was a sad end to an innocent affair—and to the FSC's interracial work camp program in the South, except those subsequently held on its Swannanoa property. For Nelle Morton it was also the end of her dream of using the camps to attack segregation by example. She left office in 1949, sadly conceding failure, though at the same time she was cheered by the success of other projects she had initiated since 1945, especially those involving the wider Chapel Hill community. As she reflected on her work, some of these projects helped to counter her deep disappointment at the collapse of the camp ideal.[29]

One such success took place in January 1947, when the FSC was able to organize an integrated concert by the black mezzo-soprano Dorothy Maynor only because Frank Graham agreed to its being held on campus. It was a huge success. An unfriendly newspaper report conceded that 1,300 people had attended, including Graham and 225 blacks, to listen to Maynor sing works by Mendelssohn, Debussy, and Dvořák as well as some favorite spirituals. The seating was completely integrated, the applause tumultuous. "On two occasions," sniffed the newspaper, "the negress, Maynor, took the white piano player, her accompanist, by the hand after the completion of a song, the applause redoubling." Although the unfriendly columnist thought the concert was "part of a movement to trample underfoot Southern traditions," FSC members believed it to be a shining example of the irrelevance of race, at the same time recognizing that there was scarcely another southern community in which it could have been held so free of incident.[30]

The Chapel Hill community figured in a further FSC-connected enterprise later the same year, one with deep significance for the future. In September 1946, Morton had received a letter from George Houser and Bayard Rustin of the New York–based Fellowship of Reconciliation telling her that it was organizing an interracial group to ride on interstate buses in the South, testing recent U.S. Supreme Court judgments outlawing segregation on such travel. They sought FSC endorsement of the plan. What Morton did not know at the time was that the Congress of Racial Equality (CORE) was behind the idea, and thus the plan provides a fascinating preview of the famous CORE-sponsored Freedom Rides of 1961—now part of the fabric of the civil rights revolution. Morton's thoughtful reply agreed in principle with the trip but stressed the need for careful advanced planning, including the importance of having lawyers briefed at each stopping point. Above all, she insisted that as many southerners as possible be included in the party, thus avoiding the appearance of the enterprise being an invasion of "outside agitators" from the North—advice that, had it been heeded, might have prevented the disaster the trip soon became.[31]

Those first Freedom Riders, all of them from the North, duly set out on April 9, 1947. In Chapel Hill they first struck real trouble; indeed, as Morton later put it, the ride "blew up" there. On April 13 four members of the team, including Rustin, boarded a bus for Greensboro. When the two blacks refused a request to move to the back of the bus, all four were arrested. Local taxi drivers, incensed because the riders had previously tried to integrate their cabs, threatened violence, but the FSC saved the day. Rev. Charles Jones, at considerable personal risk, sheltered the four in his home overnight and smuggled them out of town the next day. As George Houser later told Morton, it was his "first experience in trying to do anything in an organized fashion in the South," and he simply had not understood the degree of difficulty involved. He had now found out the hard way and was grateful to Jones and the FSC for their advice and assistance.[32]

The story did not end there, of course. The four riders were duly tried in Chapel Hill, found guilty of violating North Carolina's segregation laws, and sentenced to thirty days in jail on the ground that because they were involved in intrastate, not interstate, travel, the U.S. Supreme Court's recent judgment in *Morgan v. Virginia* did not apply. The decision was upheld on appeal, no gubernatorial pardon was forthcoming, and in March 1949 three of the four convicted men arrived in Raleigh to serve their time. They were met by an interracial delegation organized by the FSC.[33]

Nor did the FSC's involvement stop there. Knowing the treatment the men were likely to receive on the road gangs to which they were sent, Morton arranged for teams of students to visit them regularly, hoping through that means to prevent their cruel treatment. More important, she organized similar teams to "walk along with them" while they were at work, both to raise their morale and to reduce the possibility of violence. When the three men were released in April, a few days early and in good health, Rustin gratefully acknowledged the importance of the FSC's efforts to protect them. "Whenever I think of the great work we have to do," he told Morton, "I am more and more appreciative of the job which you are doing from Chapel Hill. When I think of the ease with which certain types of progress can be made in New York as compared with the more serious problems that Southern Christians and liberals face, I always feel that I should take my hat off to those of you who continue in the struggle." Morton must have appreciated his sentiments as she prepared to leave the FSC. She would have wanted to share them with the Chapel Hill community, which had provided such strong support.[34]

With Morton's departure, the FSC's days as an activist agency were over. For more than a year it languished leaderless, until in 1951 Buck Kester was prevailed upon to return to his old post of executive secretary. But he had no interest in continuing Morton's social agenda. Instead the FSC soon switched back to its original function, that of a discussion forum and a place to which like-minded people could retreat, to rest and to refresh themselves morally and spiritually before once again working in an increasingly hostile southern world. Kester himself lived on the FSC's property in Swannanoa, and people came to him and to the fellowship center there. Although the FSC members thrilled as the pace of southern change quickened, especially after the arrival of Martin Luther King Jr. on the scene, they had little influence upon the movement. In 1963, recognizing this, the few remaining FSC members voted it out of existence.[35]

The state committees of the SCHW, the FOC, and the Chapel Hill phase of the FSC all exemplify the spirit of possibility that southern interracial liberals glimpsed in the immediate postwar years. Margaret Fisher, Mary Price, Dorothy Tilly, Nelle Morton, and those with whom they worked believed for a time that their hour was at hand, that the transformations the war had occasioned would reach deep into their region and strike a fatal blow to entrenched economic privilege and the racial caste system. In the short term they were wrong. The forces arrayed against them remained too strong, and such little influence as they could bring to bear scarcely survived the unsettled first two years. By 1947, the lineaments of segregation seemed as strong as ever.

It is worth noting here the importance of women as leaders in these interracial liberal agencies. Nelle Morton, Mary Price, and Dorothy Tilly, along with women such as Virginia Durr, Lucy Randolph Mason, Charlotte Hawkins Brown, and Lillian Smith, exemplify a growing group of dedicated southern women, black and white, who were centrally involved in the struggle to bring racial decency and social justice to their region. They were not feminists; nor were they exclusively or even primarily concerned with women's issues. Yet their active involvement as leaders in these agencies of change pointed the way to the role of women as activists in the tumultuous years ahead.

By 1947 the liberals had a new enemy to fight: the hardening climate of opinion caused by the onset of the cold war, when any advocate of radical social action could easily be branded Communist and thus marginalized. This was particularly true in the case of the SCHW. From its foundation in 1938 it had been vulnerable to charges of Communist control, and these were renewed with increased vigor as it tried to expand its influence after 1945. In time these worried the SCHW's chief source of financial support, the CIO, sufficiently for the union to close off the financial spigot, and with that went much of its effectiveness. From 1946, for example, Mary Price in North Carolina constantly warned that the CNC's existence was in danger through lack of funds. "The plain and hard fact," she told James Dombrowski, "is that if the Committee for North Carolina is to survive we must have some money. I love my work," she said, "and I have faith in the progressive future of North Carolina, but I am not willing to be harassed about money as I have been for the past three months." With the snapping of the CIO lifeline, her pleas had no chance of success.[36]

The communism issue also divided the SCHW membership fatally. At the national level, staunch supporters like Lucy Randolph Mason left its ranks, while it caused similar splits in the state committees. In February 1948 the CNC's executive board brought the issue into the open when it passed a resolution requiring "each and every member" of the board to declare in writing "whether he or she is a member of the Communist Party; whether or not he or she is opposed to the antidemocratic political weapons which the Communist Party has employed" whenever it had gained power. Those who refused to sign, ran the resolution, should seriously consider resigning. Some, like the declared Communist Junius Scales, had already done so, and others now followed his example. Mary Price, who had unsuccessfully opposed the resolution's passage, decided to stay on in the interim, at the same time acknowledging that her committee's usefulness as a force for change in North Carolina was ended. In the wake of Margaret Fisher's resignation as director, the Committee for Georgia had folded the previous year, beset by financial problems, by increasing tension with the SCHW over policy direction (including the communism issue), and by general warweariness and lack of faith. As for the national SCHW, its life, too, was almost over. Following Clark Foreman's decision to devote its remaining resources to Henry Wallace's quixotic third-party campaign for the presidency in 1948—which cost him the support of those former New Dealers like Aubrey Williams who were not yet prepared to desert the Democrats—and targeted by the rising tide of red-baiters in the land, it quietly wound up its activities. The state committees had already gone, as the "bottom deep awakening" came to a lonely end.[37]

The FSC's effectiveness as a social agency was also finished by 1949, again blunted by the intransigence of the white South and the hostility displayed toward those working for change, for which they were unprepared. Of these three groups, only Dorothy Tilly's FOC survived the counterattack, perhaps because of her eminent respectability, but also because the cause of legal justice was not as potentially threatening as social integration or political involvement. The three of them, however, all deserve recollection, especially as we search these immediate postwar years for the origins of the great movement of the 1960s and the southern grassroots for local heroes and heroines. They were all, as Hibbard Thatcher said of the FSC in 1985, "the flag-bearers of work for integration and for justice and for peace."[38]

9
Winning the Peace
Georgia Veterans and the Struggle to Define the Political Legacy of World War II
Jennifer E. Brooks

IN TRAVELING AROUND the nation and throughout the European and Pacific theaters during World War II, soldiers from the South encountered cultures, economies, and political ideas beyond the realm of southern tradition. After the war, armed with new exemptions from poll taxes, Georgia soldiers injected a strong dose of uncertainty into state politics.[1] Local dynasties pondered the electoral potential that the veterans represented: Would they vote to defend southern tradition and, by extension, the right of incumbents to rule? Or had wartime service altered their attitude to the southern status quo?

In Georgia, black and white veterans confirmed both the worst fears and best hopes of political pundits across the region. They launched numerous powerful and multifaceted assaults on the provincial and undemocratic nature of southern politics, expressing an energetic sense of civic duty and entitlement derived by and large from service in the war. Above all, Georgia's veterans wanted their well-deserved share of political and economic opportunities unleashed by the war. When they returned home from the service, however, they confronted a conservative, complacent, and often reactionary leadership determined to hold on to the power and privileges that had long perpetuated Bourbon rule. For veterans weary of war and eager to take advantage of new opportunities, postwar Georgia posed a disturbing conundrum: achieving the quality of life they believed they had earned required waging another war—this time at home—against the political, economic, and racial traditions that upheld the one-party South. An account of their efforts to

Struggle to Define the Political Legacy of World War II 239

achieve these goals illustrates the difficulty in determining whether World War II was an agent of political continuity in Georgia and the South.

The activities that black and white veterans pursued were fraught with contradiction. For example, those who assaulted the citadels of southern racial tradition confronted other veterans policing the ramparts of white supremacy. These contradictions, however, make veteran activism a useful barometer by which to measure the war's political impact. Through their efforts to implement often conflicting understandings of the war's meaning, southern veterans did much to define the political legacy of the war as disruptive and contradictory for Georgia and the South. They destabilized conservative Democratic hegemony, made racial reform and economic development the key issues of the postwar era, and determined that the politics of growth would prevail over the politics of progressive racial reform. It was a complicated political legacy, one that testified to the war's role in generating considerable political and social turmoil.

African American veterans who returned to Georgia were determined to exercise their rights of citizenship.[2] They organized to protest their veterans' benefits, protested police brutality, and used voter-registration drives to increase black political influence. Through it all, Georgia's black veterans asserted a strong moral claim to citizenship, respect, and justice, which they felt should reward their service in war. Their efforts helped to elevate postwar registration and voting to unprecedented levels, boosted postwar movements for progressive reform, and eventually touched off a reactionary backlash. In the wake of the white primary's demise in Georgia in 1946, this surge in black political activism made race a key issue in postwar politics throughout the state.[3]

Service in the war both increased black soldiers' frustration with racial injustices and boosted their expectations for the future. W. W. Law, a black veteran from Savannah, Georgia, found military service to be a series of disheartening encounters with the barriers and humiliations of Jim Crow. When drafted, Law recalled, "I asked for frontline duty as an infantry soldier. But they assigned me to the quartermaster, as was typical." After he was inducted, Law ran into trouble almost immediately. Assigned to Kessler Airfield's aviation battalion in Biloxi, Mississippi, he clashed with his company commander, a white man from Mississippi. "We were being assigned chores on the base of picking up match stems and cigarette butts," Law recalled, "and I objected and was called before my commander, and we had a discussion on leadership."

A headstrong young man, Law informed the commander that "a proper leader would be a person who could inspire his people into formation, and this was not inspirational work." After this discussion, "he found a way to transfer me out because I did not go along with the proceedings."[4]

Historians of black soldiers during the war have demonstrated that experiences such as Law's were far from unusual. Despite such encounters, however, many black servicemen remained convinced that the war ultimately would improve black life in the South. "There was a tendency among Negro soldiers," army researchers found, "to expect or hope for an increase in rights and privileges, improved treatment, and better economic status after the war," with southern blacks tending to be more optimistic than those from the North. In fact, 43 percent of those soldiers surveyed expected to have "more rights and privileges" after the war, and 42 percent believed that "in the long run Negro soldiers [would] be better off . . . after they got out of the Army than they were before they went into the Army."[5] Confident in the value of their own contribution to victory, many apparently headed home expecting, or at least hoping, to find a changed environment. "A lot of guys . . . didn't expect to find the same situation that we left," explained Tuskegee war veteran Otis Pinkard, in part because many blacks believed that southern whites had a moral imperative to acknowledge and reward blacks' wartime participation by recognizing their civic, political, and economic rights.[6]

Thus, many black veterans returned to Georgia certain that their contribution to victory would give them greater opportunities than they had enjoyed before the war.[7] They soon discovered that few white southerners agreed. Horace Bohannon, a field agent for the Southern Regional Council's Veteran Services Project, noted that white citizens in Ft. Valley, Georgia, for example, nervously anticipated trouble from the "returning Negro veteran . . . dissatisfied with conditions" and expected white southerners to " 'pick on' the returning veteran to try and steer him 'back into his place.' "[8] Both predictions were accurate.

As soon as the war ended, whites in Georgia and throughout the South began a campaign of discrimination against black veterans that impeded both their utilization of wartime skills and their access to the job-training, unemployment, and educational benefits guaranteed by the GI Bill. A group consisting primarily of black teachers, principals, and school administrators attending a summer seminar in 1946 at Atlanta University reported that employment discrimination was widespread. A Bibb County, Georgia, teacher and minister declared, "I be-

Struggle to Define the Political Legacy of World War II   241

lieve that the single greatest problem confronting the returning Negro veteran is . . . obtaining employment." An Atlanta-area student agreed: "The veterans in my community are having difficulty getting suitable job placement in newly acquired skills. In most cases," he stated, "these men were in a low income bracket prior to the war, but while in service they learned how to do better jobs." Now, he noted, veterans "are unwilling to accept the old job as before." "For myself I was not able to find a job because I was not able to do the kind of work they wanted done," lamented a veteran from Hogansville, Georgia. "I can operate any kind of office equipment but I was refused a job in this line of work." He concluded that "the Negro veterans are merely being pushed around."[9] The American Council of Race Relations found in 1946 that of 246 approved on-the-job federal training programs in Georgia, black veterans participated in only half a dozen.[10] High hopes for a better job, more economic security, and a "chance to make it" came crashing down in the cruel light of the Jim Crow day, and a Warm Springs, Georgia, principal noted that "for the most part the returning soldiers seemed not to be able to readjust themselves."[11]

In the immediate postwar years, however, intransigent southern whites confronted a determined, ambitious, and experienced foe who staunchly resisted the forces of white reaction and southern tradition. Georgia's black veterans organized the Georgia Veterans League (GVL), a statewide association headquartered in Atlanta with four chapters throughout the state.[12] According to Horace Bohannon, who was a member, the GVL had two to three hundred members statewide, with sixty or so of those in the Fulton County (Atlanta) chapter.[13]

Organized to facilitate black veterans' access to GI Bill benefits, the GVL hoped, according to John B. Turner, the Fulton County commander, "to aid returning veterans in adjusting themselves to community life." Through an office established in Atlanta in early 1946, the GVL's trained black counselors assisted veterans in applying for GI benefits, because, as Bohannon recalled, black veterans often did not "feel quite at home talking to a white representative," and "if you had credential as a representative of a veterans' group . . . you got a much better ear than if you were somebody that [just] got off the train."[14]

More importantly, these veterans quickly learned that "there was no need of applying for a job as radio announcer. . . . You weren't going to get it. . . . You had to stay within these artificial barriers." In order to address this discrimination in wages and hiring, the GVL also pledged to fight for equal pay for equal work and for employment in all professions and occupations. The group also advocated equal park, recreational, public health, and hospital facilities; improved and equal schools for black children; equal justice under the law; and black policemen and firemen. Promising to cooperate with organized labor, black-owned businesses, and organizations working for community improvement, veterans of the GVL aimed to use "every intelligent and honorable means" to combat discrimination, including the "ballot, publicity, picketing, parades, and boycotts," all of which, according to Horace Bohannon, "made a difference in the black community."[15]

Indeed, participation by veterans lent a new moral legitimacy to voter-registration campaigns, some of which had begun before or during the war. As Doyle Combs, a World War II veteran and later a leader of the National Association for the Advancement of Colored People (NAACP) in northeast Georgia, explained, defending the American way of life abroad fostered a deep conviction in the determined right to political freedom at home. After leaving the army, Combs was determined to vote because "I lost a portion of my body for this country," even though "I didn't have no right to fight whatsoever [be]cause I didn't have no rights in the United States of America, as a black man." Having physically sacrificed "to protect my own rights," Combs was determined to "die for my rights" and even "kill for my rights: if necessary."[16] The sense of civic entitlement that veterans like Combs articulated underlay the practical realization that the franchise represented the only realistic avenue to increased black political power. "We demand . . . full civil and political rights and protection for every person," declared the GVL, and "the League will work for every Negro of age becoming a registered voter." Voter registration was a requirement for membership in the GVL.[17]

Thus, in communities throughout Georgia and the South, black veterans organized, joined, and led voter-registration drives that aimed to boost black participation in the first postwar Democratic Party primaries. Their commitment and enthusiasm helped increase black registration and voting to unprecedented levels and disrupted the civic complacency at the heart of Bourbon rule. Two of the most energetic and successful drives occurred in Savannah and Atlanta. Both campaigns drew large numbers of black citizens to county courthouses to register and to precincts and polls to vote.

An enthusiastic insurgent campaign launched in Savannah by the moderately reformist and business progressive Citizens Progressive League, a new civic organization consisting primarily of white veterans and citizens, attracted broad interest in the spring of 1946. If enough blacks voted to assist in ousting the mossback political machine headed

Struggle to Define the Political Legacy of World War II 243

by Chatham County attorney John Bouhan, a local Democratic Party boss, blacks surmised, then they might increase their influence with the new city administration and state legislative delegation. With this in mind, a newly organized black World War II–Veterans Association (WW2-VA) launched an enthusiastic voter-registration campaign in the early spring, fulfilling its pledge to "take a leading role in politics" in order to improve "the political and economic position of all of its colored citizens."[18]

Calling on all registered voters and every organization to lend a hand, the WW2-VA conducted a house-to-house canvass and mass meetings to encourage registration and voting. Black citizens responded in overwhelming numbers. Pastors led large numbers of their parishioners to register, and undertakers donated hearses to carry people to the courthouse. On July 5, the last day to register, black citizens—with lunchboxes and children in tow—came in "droves," jamming the courthouse and the surrounding park. They were ready to stand in line all day if necessary to enforce, as one elderly citizen told a reporter, "the will of the Lord that us colored folks vote."[19] Indeed, the voter-registration project by the WW2-VA turned out enough black voters to give the margin of victory to the Citizens Progressive League, which swept state legislative and local offices as well as the membership of the county Democratic committee.[20]

In Atlanta, veterans helped to spearhead an equally vigorous registration drive aimed at the 1946 campaigns for governor and the Fifth District congressional seat. The All Citizens Registration Committee (ACRC) registered more than twenty thousand black voters in the spring and summer of 1946, and black veterans were crucial to the drive's success.[21] Ex-GI David Watson served as director of ACRC headquarters and executive secretary of the voter drive. In canvassing black neighborhoods, veterans in the GVL drew on the following script to make a powerful moral appeal against blacks' civic apathy and fear. "I spent over two years, a part of which was overseas, in the armed services," veterans told prospective registrants, and "I had hopes that my services would provide *you* with freedom from want and fear. Above all else I wanted to maintain *your* freedom of Speech. Now that the war has been won," veterans testified, "the most difficult job ahead of us is to win the *peace* here at home. . . . If you will become a *registered voter* we may be able to win the *peace*." Political participation, veterans argued, was the key to unlocking the restrictive hold of southern racial tradition over black opportunity and freedom. "If we are to be treated fairly in this state, if we want to stop police brutality, get justice in the courts,

Negro Policemen, equal education, health, and recreational facilities," GVL leader Clarence Stephen declared, "then we must have a voice in our government. The ballot must be our weapon against the enemies of democracy at home in Georgia."[22]

Initially, the ACRC drive was successful. The campaign registered almost twenty-two thousand new black voters, who became the core of the new black political strength in Atlanta. However, the county-unit system nullified the popular majorities that black voters helped to give Helen Douglas Mankin, the gubernatorial candidate. Nonetheless, increased black registration quickly drew official attention. In Atlanta, Mayor William B. Hartsfield and the board of aldermen finally agreed to hire black police officers, while in Savannah the new Citizens Progressive League administration appointed a Negro Advisory Committee, hired nine black police officers, and began school and recreational improvements in black neighborhoods.[23] Black veterans initiated and joined similar registration drives across the state, often boosting voter registration and turnout to historic levels.[24]

As these campaigns illustrate, African American veterans who returned to Georgia and the South believed that their contribution to American victory overseas had real value. Their determination to implement the sense of civic entitlement that resulted had important political repercussions in a region that habitually circumscribed black freedom and opportunity. The organized protests and voter-registration drives in which these veterans participated had significant results. In Georgia, these efforts netted between 135,000 and 150,000 registered black voters in 1946 alone. Between 85,000 and 100,000 black citizens actually voted that year, helping provide popular majorities to both Helen Douglas Mankin and James V. Carmichael. Moreover, black voters played a key role in defeating entrenched political machines in Savannah and Augusta in 1946 and in electing a new mayor in Macon in 1947. The following year around 200,000 black citizens registered statewide for the gubernatorial race between Melvin E. Thompson and Herman E. Talmadge. By the time of the *Brown v. Board of Education* decision in 1954, over one million African Americans were registered to vote in the South. By forcefully demanding racial and democratic reform, black veterans helped to disrupt the civic complacency that sustained the Solid South.[25] Their efforts made the issue of racial change especially controversial in postwar elections throughout the state.

Black veterans were not alone in their fight to define the war's political legacy in racially progressive terms. White veterans from the South probably did not expect their military service to generate doubt and uncertainly in their regional loyalties. While many white southerners entered the service certain of the immutability of Jim Crow, some found that the war undermined that conviction.[26] Defending a discriminatory nation against a racially intolerant enemy posed a disturbing irony. War-induced disenchantment with southern racial practices and political traditions turned into outright opposition when veterans were confronted with the persistent vitality of reactionary conservatism at home. They joined black veterans in combating political inequality and injustice and ultimately mounted a spirited attack on the county-unit system, a discriminatory apportionment of the state legislative representation and electoral votes that tilted power and policy against the interests of blacks, workers, and urban dwellers. Their efforts provided an interracial component to progressive postwar movements— though they were less successful in battling racial hatred and tyranny at home than they had been overseas.

Despite an official policy of segregation in the armed forces, the exigencies of the war required interaction between black and white GIs. Black servicemen performed their duties ably despite discrimination and mistreatment. In this light, the notion that they deserved unequal treatment because of their race grew less convincing as the war progressed. "I spent four and a half years in the army, twenty months overseas," Henry C. Rivers of Griffin, Georgia, remarked, and "I have been around and fought with Negro soldiers and I have nothing to hold against them." A white sergeant from Texas agreed. He had not cared about discrimination before the war, but his wartime experiences convinced him that white southerners should not "abuse the colored people any more," because blacks as well as whites had died serving their country.[27] Few white veterans, however, recalled the liberalizing impact of their wartime service as vividly as did Georgian Harold Fleming.

Fleming had attended Harvard before the war but, as he later recalled, "was still pretty much a victim of [his] own upbringing." Though he looked with "disdain on redneck stuff on the crasser forms of prejudice [and] discrimination," Fleming was "pretty damn unenlightened" on the racial issues of the day. Upon graduating from Officer Candidate School, he took command of black troops in the Quartermaster Corps on Okinawa. The experience "was critical" in transforming him from a relatively "unenlightened" southern moderate into an outright racial liberal.[28]

Commanding black troops was "a very traumatic kind of experience," Fleming recalled, because "you were a white straw boss in a very discriminatory segregated Army, and you felt discriminated against."

As a white officer commanding black troops, "you lived where they lived [and] you were a second class citizen because your privates were black." Fleming took exception to the practice of confiscating black soldiers' ammunition and weapons while they guarded Japanese prisoners of war in remote areas subject to guerrilla attack. White GIs performing the same duty were armed, but "they blatantly . . . made us turn in every round. . . . The big fear of the brass, who were mostly Southern . . . was fraternization between the black soldiers and the POWs. They didn't trust them worth a damn." To Fleming, this experience was pivotal. "It was a good way to learn about race relations," he recalled, because "you could really see it plain if you had any sense of fairness and if you weren't just under the total mercy of your prejudices." "It was just the sheer human experience of 'good, God, how can these men stand it, why do they do it?' Here they are being called on to follow the rules, shape up, be a good soldier, work your ass off, be ready to die for your country and then they would crap all over you without apology. 'Not a single one of you black bastards is good enough to be an officer even with your own people. You don't get the Quonset huts. You stay in tents and mud. All the Quonset huts go to a white unit that landed yesterday even though you have been here six months.'" "It was that kind of stuff," Fleming concluded, "and I understood why they were bitter. The amazing thing is that they functioned at all."[29]

Service with black GIs afforded disturbing lessons in racism, and the war's destructiveness also caused soldiers to search for a meaning that justified such tremendous cost in human life and property. In this sense, the war magnified the value of the freedoms and opportunities that most white southerners took for granted. James Mackay, a Georgia veteran and postwar liberal politician, believed that his fifty-two months aboard a Coast Guard cutter during the war "taught [him] what freedom is." As a first lieutenant on a destroyer escort, Mackay saw several shipmates die: "I lost thirty-one shipmates and I had to hose down the brains of my buddies on my own ship." Mackay had been at sea with them long enough to recognize "who they were by looking at their shoes, covered with blankets." Before then, he states, "I had taken freedom for granted," but when "the executive officer said to me—'Mackay, is there anything, anything, worth the deaths of these guys. They're not going to live their lives.' And I said 'of course, there's only one thing' . . . it is clear that they died to secure the right of all of us to go behind the curtain and cast our ballot without anybody knowing how we voted or having anything to do with how we voted."[30]

Likewise, serving as a marine corps chaplain in the Pacific theater during World War II made Joseph Rabun, a Baptist preacher in Telfair County, Georgia, far "more conscious of the precious importance of life and dignity." As a marine "sky pilot," Rabun came under enemy fire on Guadalcanal, Bougainville, Saipan, and Guam, where he ministered to the dying and wounded. His beliefs about the war, which developed during his marine corps service while he was in his late thirties and informed his liberal political views afterward, included the ideas "that the war was fought against the anti-Christ, that the war was fought against forces that would shackle and ground men down instead of set him free; that the war was fought against an ideology which held that because of race one man was better than another."[31]

For Mackay and Rabun and, no doubt, others, the war's devastation seemed a pointless tragedy unless meaning could be found to vindicate the death and destruction it wreaked—and that meaning could not apply only to the fight abroad. If preserving democracy, justice, and freedom justified such a sacrifice overseas, then the same rights had to be defended at home. Many of the organizations through which veterans pursued a progressive agenda explicitly drew this connection. Military service may have educated these veterans in much more than the tactics and strategy of warfare, particularly in exposing the hypocrisy of American racial practices, but it often took the reality of postwar conditions at home to turn disenchantment into active rebellion against the political and racial status quo.[32] Harold Fleming found that the racial violence and political turmoil that plagued postwar Georgia intensified his disillusionment and demoralization, which had begun overseas. "When I came back I was sick of the whole goddamn business," Fleming later recalled. "I was mad at the Army and mad at the system." And then, much to his chagrin, "Talmadge came back in," and then a white mob in Walton County, Georgia, lynched four black citizens in the summer of 1946. These events, which "laid the base for total disgust that built up over the preceding year," made it more than he could bear to think of "settling and having a normal life in that setting when that kind of thing could take place and where you could have a guy saying the things that Talmadge said, reelected governor after all." However, after a brief return to Harvard, Fleming came back to Georgia in the summer of 1947. That fall he joined the Southern Regional Council at the urging of Ralph McGill, editor of the *Atlanta Constitution.* "I didn't know there was anybody in the South, anybody white," Fleming explained, "who had my egalitarian values or wanted to see society move away from segregation and discrimination."[33]

White veterans like Fleming returned to the South and joined organizations devoted to fighting against discrimination and intolerance and for progressive social change. Many joined the interracial progressive American Veterans Committee (AVC), which had more than twenty chapters in the southern states, including several in Georgia.[34] Through the AVC, white veterans worked alongside black veterans to obtain full GI benefits, to address problems of housing and employment, and especially to challenge discriminatory practices. The Atlanta chapter protested police brutality against black veterans and called for the integration of the city police force. In addition to raffling appliances to raise money and conducting membership drives, the Atlanta-area AVC, according to Johnny Glustrom, its president, also worked "for civil rights in close cooperation with other groups." The Atlanta chapter won the national AVC's new George W. Norris Award for "outstanding work" on behalf of American civil rights in 1950–51. In particular, the award cited the chapter's efforts to improve housing for black Atlantans, its support of litigation to "eliminate discrimination" in Atlanta schools, and its ongoing and "vigorous" fight against the Ku Klux Klan.[35]

Not content to rely on pronouncements and petitions, Georgia's progressive white veterans also campaigned for political change. In particular, they worked to elect moderate-to-liberal candidates who advocated programs and policies in keeping with their own reformist sympathies. In Atlanta they joined black citizens in rallying behind the candidacy of Helen Douglas Mankin in her bid for reelection in 1946 to the House of Representatives from Georgia's Fifth Congressional District.[36] For example, George Stoney, an army veteran and AVC member, left his job with the federal housing authority in Atlanta to head Mankin's reelection bid. He recruited volunteers from his associates in the AVC who became a core of support for Mankin throughout the myriad difficulties of her campaign. Among those AVC supporters was Calvin Kytle, who backed Mankin because of her impressive record in supporting price controls, President Truman's veto of the anti-labor Case Bill, federal aid to education, veterans' housing, and improved relations between business and labor. "Since March [of 1946]," reasoned Kytle, "Mrs. Mankin represented the one cause for cheer in Georgia's otherwise depressing political situation."[37]

White veterans in the AVC and black veterans in the ACRC helped Mankin win the majority of the popular vote in the Fifth District primary on July 17, 1946. Enthusiasm and commitment, however, could not overcome the power of Georgia's discriminatory county-unit system. Mankin's reactionary opponent, James C. Davis, won enough

Struggle to Define the Political Legacy of World War II 249

county-unit votes to nullify her popular majority. This disheartening outcome—achieved, many suspected, through manipulation and fraud—convinced progressive veterans of the futility of trying to accomplish substantive change without first achieving electoral reform. Veterans believed that freeing Georgia's electorate from the discriminatory restrictions that perpetuated a truncated vote and nullified popular democracy was a crucial first step to fulfilling what they regarded as the war's mandate for democratic reform.[38] Thus the fight against Germany, Japan, and Italy overseas ultimately generated a battle against the county-unit system at home.

Within a few days of Mankin's defeat, progressive white and black veterans formed Georgia Veterans for Majority Rule (GVMR). The GVMR sponsored two federal lawsuits aimed at overturning the county-unit system as a violation of the Fourteenth Amendment's equal protection clause.[39] The plaintiffs alleged that the unit system of voting deprived the residents of Georgia's more populous counties the right to have their votes counted on the same effective basis as the votes of residents in less populous counties. As an example, under the county-unit system 106 votes in Georgia's largest county equaled 1 vote in the smallest. Thus, the plaintiffs argued, the county-unit system constituted "a deliberate, express, and unreasonable discrimination in varying degrees against all voters residing in any but the smallest counties."[40]

Progressive veterans organized the GVMR with the assistance of the Southern Conference for Human Welfare (SCHW) in order to raise the money and support necessary to carry their case all the way to the U.S. Supreme Court.[41] White veterans in the AVC were the majority of the staff in the central office in Atlanta, and they led a structure of committees throughout the state to facilitate those efforts. The central committee included James Mackay and Calvin Kytle, while other veterans headed GVMR committees in each congressional district and on several college and university campuses.[42]

Fund-raising letters sent to prospective donors in Georgia explained how these veterans defined their civic obligations and cause in relation to the recent war. "We are a group of Georgia men and women who served in World War II," they stated, "and who are now fighting for a better state. We need your support." Through urban-rural discrimination, GVMR veterans alleged, the county-unit system "had made it possible for corrupt politicians to control votes in our rural areas." Moreover, "as servicemen we saw in other countries the poverty, corruption, and disease that were the product of minority rule," the GVMR proclaimed, and "now as citizen-veterans we mean to do everything we can to wipe out minority rule back here home in Georgia." In fact, "the question of majority rule is the fundamental issue facing the world today.... We feel strongly that as long as this system persists Georgia is in danger of the same sort of dictatorship we went to war to defeat."[43]

The veterans' impassioned pleas helped to raise funds; nevertheless, they lost the case. The U.S. Supreme Court refused to overturn a lower federal decision sustaining the constitutionality of the county-unit system. Indeed, the climate of fear and suspicion that permeated postwar Georgia made organizing for any progressive cause a difficult and even risky gamble.[44] Like many other southern reformers, progressive white veterans proceeded cautiously, straddling the fence when it came to the racial implications of their political attacks. Veterans in the GVMR, for example, sidestepped the race issue by never mentioning it directly as they pursued legal action against the county-unit system. Others vacillated between racial progressivism on the one hand and political expediency on the other. War veteran R. W. Hayes testified before a Georgia state legislative committee against a bill to restore the white primary in 1947. Condemning the bill as "thoroughly undemocratic," he pleaded with the committee to not "sink back to the period of 1865" and to "free Georgia from its Reconstruction complex." After all, he noted, "if the Negro was good enough to carry a gun in the war, and pay taxes, he should vote." He also warned that the white primary bill posed "the imminent danger of forcing the colored citizens into a colored bloc due to present antagonism."[45]

Even white veterans who dared to challenge the racial status quo expressed a progressivism that had its racial limits. Given the reactionary climate in postwar Georgia, it was the rare white southerner who had the moral conviction and courage to risk community censure, opprobrium, and personal safety for the cause of black political freedom. Nonetheless, despite their caution and sometimes equivocation, progressive white veterans did challenge the political traditions, racial discrimination, and civic complacency that they believed betrayed the war's democratic purpose. In this sense the war did serve as an agent of social change, not only by heightening the racial consciousness and activism of black soldiers but also by convincing some white veterans of the moral righteousness of racial reform. Within two years of the war's end, southern veterans of both races had helped an unprecedented number of black citizens become registered voters, mounted a broad and diverse challenge to Jim Crow, and organized to attack the state's most blatantly discriminatory political custom.

In addition to Georgia veterans who were eager to create a more progressive and democratic future for the region, there were reactionary white veterans who understood the racial implications of the war's impact in very different terms. These veterans belonged to the Ku Klux Klan and the neo-fascist Columbians, Inc., and supported Governor Eugene Talmadge and the white primary. They expressed an understanding of the war that demonstrated its capacity to produce division and reaction as much as unity and reform. Their support of reactionaries and conservatives determined to defend southern political traditions at all costs limited what progressive veterans were able to achieve and helped turn the state's first postwar elections into a popular referendum on what the racial legacy of the war would be.

Veterans who returned to Georgia in the first year after the war found plenty of reason to be disappointed. At first, economic observers, industrial developers, and the media anticipated the end of the war with nervous optimism, predicting in 1945 that the state would weather the trials of reconversion easily. Rosy predictions, however, gave way to worried ruminations on the layoffs that followed V-J Day.[46] By September 6 employment officials of the state's War Manpower Commission announced that there were 36,016 displaced war workers in Georgia, most whom were seeking jobs comparable in pay, skill, and training to what they had done during the war. It seemed to be a fruitless effort. By January 1946 Savannah reported a "sharp rise since V-J Day" in unemployment, with around three thousand jobless receiving unemployment benefits.[47]

Difficulty in adjusting to civilian life was not unique to southern white veterans. Ex-servicemen and -women throughout the United States experienced problems, at least initially, in reintegrating into postwar society.[48] However, conditions that existed in other regions had special racial implications in the Deep South. White veterans encountered economic difficulties just as campaigns for progressive reform were adding to reconversion's destabilization of the local and regional economic, political, and social environment. In this context, some white veterans in Georgia construed the problems of reintegration in specifically racial terms.

Certainly, many areas of the region and state had undergone significant change since the war began. War industries and military cantonments attracted black-white competition for scarce jobs during the period of reconversion, and a wave of black voter-registration drives, the occasional individual rebellion against Jim Crow, and ongoing campaigns by the NAACP, the SCHW, and the CIO indicated that the battlements of white supremacy were under attack. In the chaotic and competitive environment of postwar reconversion, some white veterans fell back on a long tradition of racial scapegoating to expunge their fears of social change and their frustrations with and resentment of postwar conditions.[49]

While infiltrating the Klan in Georgia in 1946, author Stetson Kennedy found that the KKK used "horror stories of social equality" to attract veterans, who made up 10 percent or more of its membership.[50] At a September meeting of Atlanta Klavern no. 1, a young veteran "declared that he was working in the Chevrolet plant in Atlanta and that he was proud that 76 fellow workers were members of the Klan." In fact, "he stated that he and his fellows planned to keep organizing until they had the majority of workmen in Chevrolet in the Klan."[51] Indeed, veterans were often active members in the Georgia Klan's Klavalier Klub, reportedly the "storm trooper arm" or "whipping squad" that carried out so-called direct-line activity.[52] Informants in Georgia's Klavalier Klubs reported that veterans made up about half of those who asked to join the Klan's inner circle. Immediately after the war, these Klubs reportedly intimidated, beat, and murdered more than one black cab driver, reported on alleged interracial transgressions, kidnapped and flogged at least one black citizen, and organized against moderate and liberal candidates for state and local offices.[53]

For those veterans who found the Klan to be too passé or tame, the Columbians, Inc., of Atlanta offered an attractive alternative.[54] Sporting khaki shirts, black ties, and armbands with an SS-like thunderbolt emblem, members of the Columbians vented racial and religious resentments in a pseudo-martial atmosphere. Several sources commented on the active participation of at least a few ex-soldiers in this organization. For example, "Ned," an informant, reported to "AF" that at one meeting, Bill Couch, reportedly an army officer on terminal leave, "appeared in full uniform wearing the Columbians lightning bolt silver emblem on his shirt pocket" and that speaker P. M. Adams "praised the 'group of veterans who have sacrificed to get this thing started.'" In addition, John Zimmerlee sported his "G.I. shirt and trousers" as Hoke GeWinner "charged . . . that the reason veterans cannot find housing is that unscrupulous real estate dealers are selling white property to Negroes, thus forcing all whites in the neighborhood to move." In fact, lamented the Atlanta chapter of the American Veterans Committee, "there are veterans in the Columbians. Men who fought as we did; men who fired guns and learned fear, as we did. Did these men, all through the long battles, think they were on the wrong side?"[55]

While the Klan worked to thwart black economic advancement and

Struggle to Define the Political Legacy of World War II   253

to enforce a traditional code of racial behavior, the Columbians specialized in policing the lines of residential segregation. During the fall of 1946, veterans who were members of the Columbians waged a brief campaign of intimidation and violence against African Americans living on the fringes of transitional white neighborhoods in Atlanta. On October 28 three Columbians blackjacked Clifford Hines in an unprovoked attack, ostensibly to protect a white family from "Negroes" moving in. A few days later, Columbian "regulators" prevented Frank Jones, a black man, from occupying his newly purchased house in the Ashby Street section. A Columbian sign demarcated Jones's house for the "White Community only," and various reports put war veterans James Akins and R. I. Whitman on a picket line in front of the house carrying signs that read "Zoned for Whites." Authorities arrested three Columbians, including Akins and Whitman, for disorderly conduct and inciting a riot.[56]

The activities of veterans in the Klan and the Columbians reflected their fear of racial reform, of black competition, and of a breakdown in the traditional code of racial behavior. Herman Talmadge, son of Eugene Talmadge (Georgia's reigning demagogue) and a veteran of the Pacific theater, declared that the real issue in 1946 was to "determine whether or not we will fight to preserve our Southern traditions and heritages as we fought on our ships at sea and as we fought on foreign soil."[57] Such determination to defend white supremacy had important political ramifications, and the racial legacy of World War II became a source of controversy at the center of many of the state's first postwar elections.

Indeed, in February 1946 Helen Douglas Mankin won the popular vote in a special election for representative from the Fifth Congressional District of Georgia, and the pivotal role of Atlanta blacks rang like a fire bell in the night to racial conservatives alarmed at the potential power of an organized and active black electorate. This fear grew as the All Citizens Registration Committee successfully boosted black registration and voting. Meanwhile, Eugene Talmadge kicked off his fourth bid for the gubernatorial seat. Campaigning largely on a platform of white supremacy, Talmadge promised to reinstate the white primary, preserve the county-unit system, and generally keep black southerners "in their place." His message attracted veterans already uncomfortable with the direction in which Georgia appeared to be headed.

Some veterans vowed allegiance to the reactionary Talmadge and hostility to the liberal Mankin in explicit terms. "I am glad I live in Georgia and not in Fulton County," proclaimed Guy Alford, a combat veteran from Emanuel County. "Helen Douglas Mankin is the biggest political freak or fraud in Georgia," he continued, and "certainly has never added or reflected any credit on the Democratic Party in Fulton County."[58] Jimmy Gaston of Atlanta announced that he had "awakened while in Guam, Iwo Jima, and Okinawa." As "a veteran of many South Pacific invasions," Gaston declared, he knew "what it means to lose buddies and friends. . . . I and all of my friends are for Mr. Talmadge."[59] Similarly, while serving in the navy at Norfolk, Virginia, J. D. Dickens "watched the recent gubernatorial race with considerable interest," regarding Talmadge as "the only man in the race that could qualify in a real Southern Democratic primary." After five and a half years in the navy, Dickens added, he looked forward to a Georgia where "Old Gene will be around for the next four years."[60] William Tyson of Nashville, Georgia, took issue with the *Atlanta Journal*'s claim that veterans of the recent war would disapprove of Talmadge. "These boys died so we could be free to go to the polls and vote for the man we think most worthy of holding office," Tyson angrily proclaimed. After losing "many friends while serving in the Army, and [with] two brothers wounded in ETO," he planned, along with his brothers, to "go to the polls and vote for Eugene Talmadge." Moreover, he promised, "we will also talk to our many good friends and pull every vote for Mr. Talmadge possible." After all, "we feel it is our duty because we believe Mr. Talmadge is the only man in the race worthy of being governor of Georgia."[61]

Candidates in Georgia's 1946 elections campaigned on platforms that addressed a variety of issues, from road improvements and industrial development to teacher pay raises and veterans services.[62] Conservative and reactionary veterans who publicly articulated a position during these campaigns more often than not neglected to mention these issues. Rather, the key question to them was whether the state and region's political traditions would withstand the racial implications of the war. Christopher De Mendoza, a war veteran, wrote to congressional candidate Prince Preston in order "to open an outlet in my chest to let out what is in it." Noting that Preston's opponent, incumbent Hugh Peterson, had done little for veterans over the years, De Mendoza pointed out that Peterson had, to his credit, fought consistently against the "F.E.P.C. and social equality." And that, De Mendoza informed Preston, "is exactly what I want you to do." After all, he continued, Georgia "was the best state in the union [until] the influence coming down here from the North" turned it into a haven for "Negroes lovers." Thus, he continued, "today we are not living in a democratic country but under a dictatorship like Germany, Russia, Italy, and Japan." In fact, "we are slaves under the dictatorship of a bunch of fools in the Congress and 'Negroes lovers' in the Supreme Court."[63]

In Coffee County, a group of veterans ran campaign ads in the local newspapers with a picture of Eugene Talmadge beside a large headline that read "Georgia Can Restore the Democratic White Primary and Retain the County-Unit System." Declaring that, if Talmadge was elected, recent court rulings would not defeat the white primary in Georgia, the veterans advocated writing the county-unit system "in to the state constitution." In case these arguments were not compelling enough, they spelled out the consequences of a Talmadge defeat: "Hear [sic] is what will happen if our Democratic white primary is not restored and preserved," one ad read: "The Negroes will vote in a block [sic]" and dictate to white citizens who should be elected. "Proof of this was shown in the recent election of the Fifth Congressional District where the vote of one Negro ward carried the election. . . . The same thing can happen all over Georgia," they warned, "if Negroes are allowed to vote in the Democratic White Primary and if the county Unit System is abolished." Remember, veterans ominously added, "if Georgia, now feeling progressive tremblors that could shake the entire South, elects Talmadge Governor again, not even a Supreme Court ruling will prevent a return to 'White Supremacy' as only Talmadge can support it." To "Preserve our Southern Traditions and Heritage," citizens should "Vote for Talmadge and a White Primary!"[64] Thus, predicted Don Prince of Atlanta, "Eugene Talmadge will be elected governor of Georgia because the veterans who hail from this state will vote almost in a bloc for the man who has kept faith with them . . . a person must be very naïve to believe that the white primary is not the main and vital issue in this present campaign."[65]

Openly adopting the rhetoric, ideology, and extralegal tactics of the recently defeated enemy discredited the extreme reactionism of the Georgia Klan and the Columbians. City, state, and county authorities essentially broke up both organizations through infiltration and prosecution.[66] The more mainstream variant of southern conservatism, however, fared much better. White veterans helped elect Eugene Talmadge as governor in 1946, supported Herman Talmadge's claim to that office in 1947 and 1948 (following Eugene Talmadge's death in 1946), and voted in the state legislature to enact the white primary bill thereafter.[67]

In fact, the momentum for democratic and racial change seemed to have waned nationally and regionally by 1947, as the developing cold war with its virulently anti-Communist tinge undercut the legitimacy of progressive social reform.[68] In the South, both black and white veterans made the political equality of blacks an important issue in the battle to redirect the region's future. Their conservative counterparts circumscribed what they could achieve and contributed to the reactionary climate that hindered all political challengers in the South, progressive or moderate. Even white veterans who pursued very moderate agendas found it prudent to reaffirm their commitment to racial stability.

Indeed, many returning white veterans found neither racial discrimination nor social change nearly as disturbing as the slow economic growth and venal officials that hampered many southern communities. Military service had a direct influence on their political attitudes because it had exposed them to a more modernized world. The paved highways, efficient sanitation systems, advanced educational facilities, and public health services encountered in the course of their wartime journeys often revealed glaring deficiencies at home.[69] During the war, shortages and hidebound officials had perpetuated and exacerbated shoddy infrastructure and meager services in many southern communities. Postwar complacency promised to continue that pattern, even as the demand for services and diversified development increased. For many southern white veterans, the war exerted a dual influence—exposing them to a level of development unattained at home *and* convincing them that corruption, inefficiency, electoral fraud, and machine politics impeded their postwar opportunity for prosperity.

Moreover, much like their progressive counterparts—black and white—these veterans brought home a sense of civic entitlement that chafed under the thumb of local and state political incumbency. Their energetic efforts to oust entrenched Bourbon leaders, to campaign for development and growth, and to eradicate bureaucratic inefficiency and governmental corruption, however, developed more from a burning desire for economic modernization than from a progressive mandate derived from the war.

This ambition had important political repercussions. Armed with a new and critical perspective on home, Georgia's white veterans returned to mount insurgent revolts against old-guard leadership and political machines sustained by electoral fraud, corrupt patronage, and civic apathy, none of which conformed to the principles of honest and democratic government that many believed they had fought to defend.[70] In 1946 alone, white veterans mounted a strong challenge to Eugene Talmadge's reactionary bid for governor, toppled the Cracker regime in Augusta, and overturned the political machine led by John

Bouhan in Savannah.[71] The political shock waves that these insurgencies generated reverberated throughout Georgia's cities, towns, and rural communities, drawing an unprecedented number of citizens into state and local politics. The diversity and demands of a new, more engaged constituency—a political by-product of the war—compounded the political turmoil of the postwar era and heightened pressure on the state's traditional leadership either to change or to relinquish power to a new generation.[72]

For many of Georgia's white soldiers and sailors, World War II was a disconcerting experience—and not simply because of the hard lessons of combat. "You were exposed to the world," recalled Griffin Bell, a former U.S attorney general and veteran of World War II, and furthermore, "you had different ideas than the parochial world you had lived in before you went into the military." J. H. Bottoms, a boatswain's mate in the navy, agreed: "I was born and reared in Georgia and never realized what a place it really was until I got out of it."[73]

Discovering what kind of place Georgia "really was" came, in part, from encountering a level of development and modernization not found at home. Having entered the military at a time when Georgia was still struggling to overcome the burden of the Great Depression, veterans were frequently amazed at the development, prosperity, and sophistication of other states and nations. Private James Moffett marveled at the cultural sophistication in Tokyo after attending a concert by the Nippon Philharmonic Orchestra, and he wondered why Atlanta came up short in comparison: "It's generally believed in various sections of the country . . . that the South is backward in every respect," he noted. After all, "less than a year after V-J day," the Japanese "have mustered an orchestra capable of giving a concert comparable to many heard in the United States." Yet Atlanta "can't compare insofar as culture . . . is concerned, with a city that has been the objective of bombing and foreign occupation." John J. Flynt, a veteran and candidate for the state legislature, remarked during his 1946 political campaign that "in comparison with some of the places [I have] seen . . . there [is] much to be done back home . . . in health, education, housing and roads."[74]

What seemed to impress Georgia's white veterans even more than what they saw, however, was what they heard. Homesick for the cotton fields, provincial towns, and scruffy cities of the Empire State of the South, Georgia's servicemen and -women encountered far less sympathy than recrimination and ridicule from non-southerners (and even foreigners), who rarely let pass an opportunity to belittle their state. Discovering that their own home defined "bad government" and "backwardness" in the minds of other Americans was a humbling experience that few veterans forgot.

Eugene Talmadge's tenure as governor in the 1930s and early 1940s was indelibly linked in the minds of many of the state's servicemen and -women with the embarrassment of hailing from a state so poorly regarded by the rest of the nation and world.[75] Georgia's GIs entered the armed forces with Talmadge's reputation already well established. However, his reckless attack on the University of Georgia's board of regents in 1941 became a new source of embarrassment, and Georgia's soldiers cringed at the remarks and ridicule it earned. "At least forty of my company are Northerners" who watched Talmadge's feud with the board of regents unfold "with great interest," wrote one soldier to a friend in Atlanta: "What could I say about my home state after such a farce was enacted?" "Small wonder," he lamented, "that Northerners have such views about the South." Filipinos in Manila put Georgia sergeant Norman Tant on the spot by questioning him about the racial implications of Talmadge's behavior. "I was ashamed and I could give no adequate explanation," he later recalled. To Tant, as well as many other GIs, Talmadge's actions "stank 10,800 miles from Georgia."[76]

Not surprisingly, many of Georgia's white veterans found Talmadge's reactionary bid for governor in 1946 an unpleasant reminder of the many unflattering remarks they had just endured. "I had an opportunity to see Georgia from the outside," complained Thomas Y. Lovett of Athens: "I had the humiliation of being constantly reminded that my state was one of the most backward in the nation, and we Georgians were often called electors of dictators and demagogues for governors." J. C. Huddleston had the same opinion: "You would be surprised at the things that have been said by people from other states about the kind of rule the state of Georgia [has had]." In fact, "what they know and say about Talmadge would fill several volumes. . . . [M]ost of them classify him as alongside of Hitler."[77] "Hitler, Mussolini, and Tojo [are] gone," noted veteran E. G. Wilkes of Atlanta, and soon, he predicted, "Eugene Talmadge is joining them. Never has a man done more to retard the progress and growth of a state." In fact, Wilkes noted, "men from all sections of the nation during my six-year cruise in the Navy couldn't understand why the people of Georgia would elect a man like Talmadge." As far away as Japan, embarrassed GIs were "sick and tired," explained Captain Frank Morrison, "of being ragged and ribbed about [the] loud-mouthed, demagogic and dishonest government we have in Georgia."[78]

Non-southerners not only took shots at Georgia's colorful political heritage but also pointed out the economic and social problems that plagued the state. Recalling that no one had "greater regard for Georgia" when he entered the service, Lewis Adams Jr. of Carrollton was soon "shocked and awakened" by "the many unfavorable but true things" his shipmates knew about his home state. Adams grew too embarrassed to claim his place of birth because he tired of hearing "how low Georgia stood in comparison with other states in education, how high it stood in illiteracy, physical unfitness, syphilis, murder, etc."[79] A Georgia soldier stationed in Orlando, Florida, remarked to a reporter that a soldier away from home liked nothing better "than being able to brag to his buddies about conditions at home." Still, "he likes to do it honestly," and nothing, he ruefully admitted, was "so irritating as having to 'take it' when somebody launches an attack on his state which he knows is justified."[80]

For many of Georgia's GIs, a welcome reprieve from such insults came with Talmadge's defeat and Ellis Arnall's election as a moderately progressive governor in 1942. The image of poverty, backwardness, and reactionary, corrupt politics that dogged them in the early years of the war began to fade as the new governor demonstrated a more modern, businesslike, and democratic approach to state government. Georgia became the embodiment of urbane and progressive government rather than its antithesis, and the state's servicemen and -women appreciated the difference.[81]

Bill Boring, a reporter for the *Atlanta Constitution* who had served in North Africa during the war, first heard of Arnall while he was in Egypt, where the accolades for the new governor surprised and pleased him. Accustomed to hearing, "From Georgia, huh? It's a great state but how does a man like that Talmadge get elected Governor?" Boring "got a big lift in Cairo" when someone spoke well of Arnall, "particularly since all my life I have been accustomed to listening to indignities heaped upon my governor." Similarly, a "Cracker in service" noted that Arnall "really made a name for Georgia, and brought her forward from the lowest depths of corrupt government to a democracy admired by 47 states."[82] Lieutenant P. D. Cunningham agreed. While stationed in Walla Walla, Washington, he welcomed Arnall's election as a chance for the "boys away from home [to] stop apologizing for Ol' Gene's antics."[83]

The setbacks and hardships that many veterans encountered when they returned home transformed war-induced revelations into active opposition to the Bourbon status quo. Proud, ambitious soldiers who had basked in the praise showered on Arnall's administration came home to find the reactionary, undemocratic, archaic, and venal habits that had prompted negative comment outside the South still alive and well even after four years of war.

Georgia's white veterans consistently articulated a conviction that they *had* fought for principles, values, and rights irreconcilable with the continued rule of undemocratic and corrupt government at home. Survival may have been the driving force for most soldiers during the war, but defending democracy and "good government" against dictatorship and "bad government" became the meaning that many white veterans drew from their participation after they returned. This "recovered" sense of mission defined the war as a fight against government removed from popular influence and unrestrained by concerns of political honesty, racial harmony, and community betterment. The lessons of the recent war, veterans explained, demanded vigilance against the same thing at home. Sergeant Harry Baxter of Ashburn, Georgia, noted that veterans who "have made sacrifices in the name of democracy to overthrow dictators and tyrants in Europe and Asia" will not "return to power in their home state men who have shown beyond a doubt that they have all the characteristics and instincts of would be dictators." This mandate for vigilance against homegrown dictators was enmeshed with a conviction that service in the war earned one a right to economic prosperity.[84]

Veterans returned to their home and family "to try to fulfill the way of life which they dreamed of and planned for during the war years," stated James W. Green of Atlanta, and they "want to be assured of a way of life which will warrant their having fought the most costly war in history." Thus, reminded Green, "let us not forget the purpose behind these four years of sacrifice and death." C. W. Carver of College Park in Atlanta spent three and a half years in the Pacific theater "fighting for a better place to live," while H. P. Dasher and his "buddies" passed the war "in their foxholes, dodging bullets, [and] dreaming of home and what they could come back to."[85]

However, wartime dreams of postwar abundance and prosperity faded amid job shortages and housing scarcities as the country lurched through reconversion. The war had fueled Georgia's economic growth, but not sufficiently to guarantee a better standard of living right away to all returning veterans.[86] The complaints made to Georgia's newspapers revealed smoldering frustration with postwar conditions, particularly regarding employment and housing. "We expected to find things a little tough," remarked "Ex-Sarge" in Atlanta, "but little did we dream how things could have gotten in such a rotten state of affairs." Noting that her husband had served in the army for five years, including almost two years overseas, Mrs. W. R. Lewis expressed "thorough disgust" at the treatment meted out to returning veterans. Laid off only two months after his discharge, her husband searched fruitlessly for comparable work. "At 36 he's told he's too old to work," Mrs. Lewis complained, although, she pointedly noted, "he wasn't too old for the Army." And, she claimed, even firms participating in the GI Bill's on-the-job training program preferred veterans with relevant experience. "Human memory is short-lived," Mrs. Lewis bitterly concluded; World War II veterans were "being given the 'run-around' just as veterans were after the last war."[87] Other veterans blamed job shortages on labor disputes that brought important sectors of the economy to a standstill shortly after V-J Day. "GIs returning to 'civilization' are having difficulty in finding 'on-the-job' training in this strike-ridden land," proclaimed a "$20 GI" to the *Atlanta Journal.* Seeking to find jobs for themselves and other returning servicemen, veterans from Valdosta petitioned the federal government to hire them to operate plants closed by strikes "if the strikers refuse to resume work."[88]

For many of Georgia's white veterans, housing shortages, inflated prices, and menial jobs called into question the whole purpose behind the war. They wondered why the oft-heralded economic impact of war mobilization had fallen so short of their dreams of abundance and prosperity. The ridicule that Georgia's soldiers had endured during the war illuminated the state's political and economic shortcomings, but postwar conditions demonstrated in very personal terms the cost of maintaining a long tradition of civic apathy and political corruption. War mobilization put local institutions and leadership to the test by straining not only resources and services but also popular faith in the fitness of incumbents to rule. Traditional excuses for spending as little as possible to maintain streets, schools, and sewage systems, to regulate the proliferation of vice and crime, to build public housing, and to develop plans to recruit industry fell flat in the wake of the development and spending that came with the war.

Thus a newly critical perspective born in the war gained credence under the pressure of home-front conditions. Veterans believed that complacency caused communities to languish while opportunities to capitalize on wartime growth passed by. Meanwhile, local administrations, machines, and factions throughout Georgia routinely stuffed ballot boxes and defrauded voters of the democracy and clean government that many believed they had fought to defend. Veterans grew disgusted with parochial and conservative leaders who seemed ill-suited to govern; as a result, in 1946 white veterans across the state invaded the public arena in order to claim their rights to "good government," honest elections, and economic opportunity.

In Georgia, veterans flocked to support the "good government" campaign of James V. ("Jimmy") Carmichael against gubernatorial candidates Eugene Talmadge and Eurith D. Rivers, two former governors whose past administrations evoked memories of bayonet rule, national ridicule, and indictments for scandal and fraud. White veterans organized Carmichael-for-Governor Clubs in counties and towns throughout the state (as well as in Tokyo, Japan), appeared with Carmichael regularly on the stump, and made numerous speeches on his behalf at rallies and over the radio.[89]

Veterans liked Jimmy Carmichael because his platform, which advocated fiscal conservation, industrial development, agricultural diversification, improved education, and a positive national image, reflected their own vision of what constituted "good government." Veterans in the Student-League-for-Good-Government proclaimed that Talmadge's formal administration amounted to "Six years of . . . Virtual Dictatorship" and "Four Years of Rivers Was Greed, Graft, and Shame" and that it was "small wonder that daily more and more thinking Georgians are turning to efficient, clean-cut Jimmy Carmichael." In fact, World War II veteran C. W. Carver noted that "the State of Georgia will always be in a rut and looked down upon by the other 47 states as long as we allow reckless politicians to have the run of the state. I spent three and one-half years in the Pacific fighting for a better place to live," he added, and "in order to have that place we must have good government." Thus, "here's one vote for Carmichael."[90]

John Sammons Bell, a veteran of the Pacific War, campaigned actively for Carmichael, and Bell's powerful, well-crafted appeal linked participation in the war with opposition to Talmadge. He had entered the army in 1941, received the Purple Heart and the Bronze Star for his participation in the Pacific theater, and joined the Carmichael campaign when he returned home. "In the South Pacific, four of us were sitting on the Russell Islands," announced Bell in a WSB radio broadcast shortly before the election. "The fighting in Guadalcanal was over [and] we were making preparations" for the next invasion. With his three friends, Bell declared, he discussed returning home, and "each and every one of those four soldiers said when we get back home, we are going to do our best to make America a better America." Only Bell survived the war, however, and upon his return he proclaimed, "I feel it a bounded duty to carry on their fight for good government." Veterans

Struggle to Define the Political Legacy of World War II   263

supported Carmichael and opposed Talmadge, Bell trumpeted, because "we are determined to continue in peace to fight for the things we fought for in war." Thus "we shall keep the faith of our battle dead" by voting for Carmichael.[91]

Veterans' programs for modernization and political change revealed their faith in good government and economic development as panaceas for the state's persistent problems. To black and progressive white veterans, *progress* meant reforming the region's worst racial habits. To pro-modernization veterans it meant modernizing the economy, making the administration of government efficient and fiscally responsible, cleaning up ramshackle towns and overcrowded cities, and repairing and expanding old infrastructures. All of this, as if by magic, would attract new industries, boost agriculture, elevate the incomes of all southerners, and thereby resolve the region's racial, social, and economic ills.

Veterans in the B-29ers-for-Carmichael Club spelled out a platform that Carmichael and his veterans supporters articulated throughout the state.[92] Carmichael pledged to keep Georgia out of debt, never to increase taxes unless the increase was for education and was approved by the voters, to improve veterans' services as well as general health and pension programs, and to accomplish all of this "within the Georgia income." Home rule promised local control over local matters, and improved rural roads and agricultural markets helped farmers. Guided by the maxim that "the very foundation of good government is economy," Carmichael promised to run the state "like you run your business" because good government was crucial to "create an atmosphere that will attract industry."[93]

Veterans in other cities and towns throughout Georgia followed suit, pledging to bring prosperity, national respect, and honest politics to their communities.[94] The state's strongest urban machines, in Augusta and Savannah in particular, faced strong challenges from veterans who were disgusted with electoral fraud, economic stagnation, corruption, arbitrary tax assessments, and rule by decree. White veterans led anti-machine coalitions of civic reformers and businessmen against the incumbents sustained by the Cracker Party in Augusta and the Bouhan machine in Savannah. Similar efforts took place in Gainesville, McRae, Americus, and many other Georgia communities in the state's first postwar elections of 1946.[95]

Veterans' calls for modernization proved to be popular, attracting unprecedented numbers to the polls and pushing registration and voting to record levels in Americus, Columbus, Brunswick, Gainesville,

Augusta, Savannah, and statewide. More citizens than ever before, black and white, turned out to state their concerns for the future and to express a new political voice that grew, in large part, from the war's impact. "Now that I'm home again and settled," explained Columbus veteran Walter Player as he registered to vote, "I think it's important to participate in elections, exercising a vote in our democratic form of government."[96] In communities in which citizens directly experienced machine rule and economic stagnation—and because local elections were not affected by the county-unit system—the postwar campaign for modernization often unseated the forces of southern political and economic tradition, at least temporarily. The Citizens Progressive League defeated the Bouhan machine in Savannah, and the Independents broke the hegemony of the Cracker Party in Augusta.[97] Statewide, however, the county-unit system combined with the threat of black voting to defeat Carmichael.[98]

The fight for modernization and good government in Georgia sounded remarkably progressive and farsighted. Ultimately, however, it expressed a conservative vision that failed to fulfill the imperative democratic reform induced by the war. Many white veterans believed that entrenched and corrupt machines were dictatorial—not because they denied civic and economic rights to black southerners and workers, but because their corruption, intimidation, and reaction infringed on the rights and ambitions of *white* southerners. Ballot-box stuffing and political intimidation violated every citizen's constitutional right to an equal voice in public affairs, but, even more insidiously—according to many white veterans—such practices perpetuated a corrupt and backward image that discouraged industrial recruitment. For the majority of white veterans, the key postwar issue was modernization, particularly the creation of more democratic and honest administrations that created jobs to raise the standard of living to a level that most veterans felt they deserved. The majority of politically active white veterans in Georgia articulated a vision of progress that reflected an unwavering popular faith in the restorative powers of economic development and governmental efficiency.

The racially tense atmosphere of 1946, however, precluded the separation of issues of race from those of modernization. Veterans challenging the political status quo confronted a race-baiting response designed to command the support of white citizens by arousing their racial fears. From Talmadge in the gubernatorial race to Roy V. Harris of the Crackers in Augusta to opponents of the Citizens Progressive League in Savannah, race became the rhetorical ploy that old-guard defenders enlisted to offset the moral advantage veterans enjoyed in challenging their control.[99]

Deflecting these attacks required, at best, mastering a delicate balancing act, since most white veterans' campaigns directly benefited from the recent expansion of the black electorate. Thus these veterans made a fateful choice by adopting a Janus-faced approach to change which rejected anything that impeded modernization while affirming whatever promised to sustain racial stability.

James Carmichael's struggle to respond to Talmadge's race-baiting attack suggests how difficult this balancing act could be. Talmadge tried to paint Carmichael as the newest vanguard of a liberal Yankee plot to integrate the South, as indicated by his pledge to obey federal law by allowing blacks to vote in Georgia's Democratic primary.[100] The Carmichael campaign tried to negate this attack by combining an assault on the resurgent Ku Klux Klan and Talmadge's racial extremism with a strong defense of Georgia's county-unit system.[101] More explicitly, pro-Carmichael veterans regularly took to the stump to proclaim their candidate's southern loyalties and the immutability of Jim Crow. Lon Sullivan, a veteran of both world wars, dismissed the importance of the race issue by reminding Georgians that "no Negroes go to white schools in Georgia, and they never will. We have no Negro sheriffs, policemen, or congressmen," he added, "and we never will." Veteran George Doss Jr., an avid Carmichael supporter and chairman of the Student League for Good Government, agreed. Talmadge had been predicting for twenty years that blacks would "take over" Georgia, Doss argued, yet that had not happened. Rather than offer a positive program, Talmadge "screams 'Nigger, Nigger, Nigger'" to cloak the real issue: good government versus his own past gubernatorial record. In fact, Doss explained, "we all know that letting the Negro vote in your primary will not bring the results that he claims." "You know Georgians well enough to know that whites and Negroes are never going to mix in schools, restaurants, picture shows or other public places and institutions," Doss assured white voters, and "in every county in Georgia there are far more whites than Negroes registered." Thus "there is no county where the Negro can possibly gain control." As for Carmichael, proclaimed the B-29ers-for-Carmichael Club, "he adheres to Southern racial traditions."[102] Though Carmichael later regretted his defense of the county-unit system, the veterans who supported him apparently did not question the irony in defining good government as a vehicle for modernization rather than as a guarantor of real political democracy, even as the county-unit system defeated their own candidate.[103]

Other campaigns proclaimed the southern loyalties of white veterans even more explicitly. In Augusta, Independents successfully campaigned against the long-incumbent Cracker Party by promising to end local bossism and establish a modern efficient administration and by declaring their commitment to white supremacy. "We independent candidates bow to no one in their love for and loyalty to the traditions of the South," trumpeted the Independents, and "you know that we are against FEPC. You know we are Southerners through and through."[104]

The war fostered among most politically active white veterans a desire for economic development, prosperity, modernization, and clean, efficient government. These were goals important enough to moderate the racial attitudes of some veterans, as in the case of Savannah's Citizens Progressive League, and to compel others to neglect the needs and demands of black southerners in favor of maintaining white support, as in the case of veterans who supported Carmichael and opposed the Crackers in Augusta.[105]

More important than *who* won these battles, however, was what remained once the political dust of the postwar 1940s had settled. Despite the dynamic growth sparked by the war, despite the moderation of racial attitudes that sometimes came with serving alongside black soldiers, despite a keen desire to improve Georgia's image in order to attract industry, and despite a fairly broad sense of civic entitlement and obligation, the persistent strength of southern racial tradition still limited political change. Indeed, the struggle between change and tradition that defined southern veteran activism continued to animate southern political discourse and events in the following decades. The progressive racial reform that black and white veterans pursued bore fruit in the civil rights movement of the 1950s and 1960s. Reactionary veterans continued to lead the region in the "massive resistance" to integration that followed the *Brown* decision in 1954. Both the progressive impulse to southern reform and the extreme reactions against it, however, lost out to the ascendance of the chamber of commerce policies that white veterans helped to legitimize. Indeed, the ethos of conservative growth popularized by veterans in their campaigns for political and economic change became the guiding philosophy behind the policies and expansionism of the Sun Belt era. The industry and development that transformed the southern landscape in the decades following World War II helped to produce a region that expanded faster and grew more rapidly than the rest of the country, but the region also remained, in many ways, poor and racially divided.

The embodiment of Georgia's contradictory political legacy was

Herman Talmadge, a Pacific War veteran who followed in his father's footsteps with his assumption of the governorship in 1947 (extralegally) and 1948. He crafted a strong statewide political machine sustained by a program that offered unprecedented expenditures for education, public services, and industrial recruitment and a stalwart defense of Jim Crow. Talmadge pushed through a 3 percent sales tax to fund the Minimum Foundation Program, which effectively created the first real public education system in the state. Moreover, over the course of his administrations he introduced a tax-reform program conducive to attracting industry and built ten thousand miles of new roads. Talmadge also tried to reestablish the white primary as his first act as governor in 1947, and he continued to rant against blacks, integration, the NAACP, the federal courts, and communism, earning a reputation as one of the region's foremost defenders of white supremacy. Subsequent Georgia governors Marvin Griffin and Ernest Vandiver followed suit. All were veterans of World War II.[106]

Veteran activism defined the political legacy of World War II as an engine of significant economic and political change that traveled, by and large, along a quintessentially southern track. Although it produced a program for change that was more moderate than the reactionary provincialism of prior days, it offered little social economic uplift to needy black and white southerners. The veterans who won the fight against fascism overseas ensured that the South's approach to change remained enmeshed in the contradictions and ironies of its past.

Epilogue: Ugly Roots
Race, Emotion, and the Rise of the Modern Republican Party in Alabama and the South

Glenn Feldman

FOR ALMOST A century after the Civil War, the Republican Party existed only on the periphery of southern society and its polity. The vast majority of white southerners viewed Republicans with the most intense dislike and suspicion—a revulsion so deep and so abiding that it is impossible to state it too strongly. Southerners considered white Republicans an especially abhorrent lot, ranking them just above the freed blacks they occasionally tolerated as political partners. Some even regarded white Republicans, both the native scalawag sort and the northern carpetbag variety, as the actual inferiors—socially, politically, *and morally*—of the South's large black population. As William Faulkner would write decades later, the South's past never died; in fact, it wasn't even the past.[1] Nowhere was this observation more telling than in the region's persistent bedevilment by the memory of war and Reconstruction—a twin recollection of the most intimate violation—both attributable, ultimately, to the despised Republican Party.

All of this eventually changed, of course. Today when we speak of the "Solid South," we no longer speak of the Solid *Democratic* South. Today, and for the last couple of decades, the "Solid South" means the Solid *Republican* South—at least in terms of presidential elections and, increasingly, in down-ticket races as well. The South is the place where we are able to see most clearly the GOP's rise from its leprous origins, through respectability and competitiveness, to ascendance and, finally, to ever-growing dominance. Yet the trauma of civil war and Republican reconstruction cannot be overstated. It left the South with a seething hatred and fear of everything Republican, black, federal, and liberal—a burning memory that, it is not too much to write, was consuming and all-pervading in politics and society. For the next seven decades, the "Solid South" was almost completely and exclusively Democratic in its politics and in its political and associated moral culture. Anything even remotely connected with the Republican Party was anathema in the South, indelibly associated with the traumatic, caricatured, and largely inaccurate collective memory of corrupt and incompetent "black rule," backed by the bristling bayonets of an invading army of northern, federal aggression.[2] From Redemption onward, Republican candidates, including national presidential candidates, received only a handful of votes in the southern states. That is, until, the election of 1928.

From 1865 to 1928 this was the Democratic Party, the "Solid Democratic South," sometimes referred to by its proper name in places like Alabama: the "Conservative and Democratic Party." During these years there were several sporadic, and not inconsequential, challenges to the Solid South—Republicans, independents of various stripes, and finally the Populists of the 1890s.[3] But in the latter part of that decade, southern whites of all kinds—Bourbon Democrats and Independents—agreed on the overriding goal of white supremacy, Jim Crow, and a whites-only politics.[4] In Alabama, whites of various political persuasions —separated mainly by economic issues—temporarily subsumed them to disfranchise blacks in the state's new 1901 constitution, and they made certain that blacks stayed excluded by legislating an all-white Democratic primary into effect the next year and purging the Republican Party of black participation. Contrary to much of the traditional writing on this subject, many plain whites actually supported the disfranchisement of blacks. Hill-country representatives such as J. Thomas "Cotton Tom" Heflin of Chambers County favored suffrage restriction because, as he put it, "I believe as truly as I believe that I am standing here, that God almighty intended the negro to be the servant of the white man." Thomas L. Bulger, a representative of the hill-country whites of Tallapoosa County, admitted that "What we would like to do in this county, more than any other two things, is to disfranchise the darkeys and educate the white children." "The plain English of it," according to William H. Denson, a leading representative of Alabama's plain hill-country whites in Etowah County, "is to eliminate the negro from the ballot box. . . . The rejection of the unfit is going on." "And in that step," he vowed, "I give my heart and my hand and trust to the God that made us to preserve the supremacy of the white race."[5]

In Alabama, whites of various strains on economic issues were of virtually one mind on race. The major sticking point in disfranchisement was whether whites of plain origins would also be caught up in the net of black disfranchisement. In the closing moments of the nineteenth century and the opening ones of the twentieth, many whites of all stations joined together to doom black voters in Alabama until the 1960s. It was the most notable occurrence yet of using race as a glue to bond whites of differing economic and cultural outlooks into common cause, and as such it constituted the first germ of the modern Republican Party—at least in Alabama.

The 1928 presidential election foreshadowed future political developments by making crystal clear the power of the race issue in southern politics.[6] A large number of white southern Democrats, furious over the choice of New York governor Al Smith to bear the national party standard, bolted the party of their fathers and committed the serious heresy of lending their support to a Republican, Herbert Hoover. In the 1928 South, though, these rebels could not yet afford to call themselves "Republicans" without consigning themselves to the furthest outreaches of society—and truth be told they were more anti-Democrats than actual Republicans as the GOP was constituted in the 1920s. So they took the euphemism "Hoovercrats." Yet their support of the Republican candidate marked the closest presidential election up until that time in the South. A "wet," Irish-Catholic product of Tammany Hall and, most importantly, a relative liberal on the race question, Alfred Emmanuel Smith was the physical embodiment of everything the white South found repugnant. In this election, the Outer South states of Tennessee, Texas, North Carolina, Virginia, and Florida registered a distinct crack in the Solid South by casting a majority of their votes for the Republican.[7] Still, just over half of Alabama's white Democrats held their noses and voted for Smith because they believed the Democratic Party in the South, regardless of one particular candidate, to be the most important guardian of white supremacy and the racial status quo ever conceived.

Alcohol, Catholicism, urbanization, and ethnic purity were all major issues in the 1928 election. But in Alabama and the Deep South, race eclipsed every other issue as both sides attempted to out-race-bait the other in what amounted to an extremely bitter "political" civil war. In Alabama a strong coalition of Klan-Republican-Prohibitionist bolters opposed Smith's candidacy by employing the most ruthless methods, circulating broadsheets to every corner of the state charging the Democrat with having to pander to "Harlem negroes" to be elected. Various titles were used, none of them subtle: "Al Smith, the Negro Bootlicker," "Al Smith, the Negro Lover," "Nigger, Nigger, Nigger," "Smith's Negro

Babies," "Tammany and the Negro," and "More Nigger." Klan rallies designed for the whole family lynched Al Smith dummies—replete with hanging, throat-slashing, and spurting fake blood—and promised to lynch the New Yorker, come November, "with good Christian votes." Loyalist Democrats fought back by invoking the emotional specter of Reconstruction drummed into every southern schoolboy and -girl by the age of ten. The caricature, which relied on the canted texts of the "Dunning School" of Reconstruction historiography, was replete with corruption, "ignorant" black rule, Yankee and federal oppression, and dire threats to white womanhood. "We have a white man's government in Alabama, and we are going to keep it unless federal bayonets again tear our heritage from us," Congressman George Huddleston, an economic progressive, broadcast in opposing Herbert Hoover. Future Alabama governor Frank M. Dixon warned that the Republican's election would reconstitute the Reconstruction era's "Negro rule" and again bring "down the heels of the ex-slaves on the throats of Southern men and women." Another future governor, Benjamin Meek Miller, bragged that "no nigger" had helped to nominate Al Smith at the Democratic National Convention but rather "900 Anglo Saxons." Former governor Bill Brandon raised himself from his sickbed long enough to warn of "negro domination . . . the perils of Republican misrule . . . [and] the slimy trail of the carpetbagger" should the GOP candidate prevail in Alabama. An Alabama woman, distraught at having to practice integration at Herbert Hoover's Commerce Department in Washington, said, "Think of [it,] a Secretary of Commerce having to stoop to niggers . . . [and] nigger politicians . . . to win. I wonder how Mr. Hoover would like to have the women of his family use the same toilet that colored people use." The woman confided that she and other southern white women in Washington had a pet name for the black employees at the Commerce Department: "Hoover's Chocolates . . . [and] we all wish we could make him eat them." Perhaps the most dramatic moment came when Alabama's oligarchs imported the notorious Theodore "the Man" Bilbo from Mississippi to plead their cause before a record Birmingham crowd. "The Republican Party of the North is the negro Party of the South," Bilbo told the Alabama audience as a contingent of Confederate veterans dramatically ringed the stage. "It is [the] Republican 'nigger' organization of Alabama. . . . And [i]f you . . . desert to the Negro Republican Party you will live to regret it. . . . [T]here will be blood spilled—the blood of your children, some of them yet unborn."[8]

As the standard-bearer for the Democratic Party, Smith eventually carried Alabama—but only by the slimmest of margins. In fact, quite a few veteran observers of Alabama politics were convinced that vote fraud on a large scale in the Black Belt—a place renowned for voting irregularities—was the only reason Smith even carried the state.

To a remarkable degree, the 1928 election represented a fierce family split among white southerners over the best way to preserve white supremacy. Although both sides agreed on the ultimate aim of preserving white supremacy in the South, they disagreed bitterly over how to achieve that result. The bolters chose the Republican Party but, out of deference to (and wise recognition of) the region's Reconstruction memory, called themselves Hoovercrats. Alabama's Loyalists, despite their serious misgivings, decided to remain inside the Democratic tent. During the years leading up to and including the campaign, the state's Hoovercrats and nascent Republicans operated in close physical and spiritual proximity to the state's powerful Ku Klux Klan, as well as the forces most clearly identified with Prohibition, religious fundamentalism, traditional family values, nativism, xenophobia, religious, ethnic, and racial intolerance, and conventional white, Anglo-Saxon, Protestant notions of morality—enforced at the end of a whip or a gun, if necessary. In essence, for Alabama, the 1920s KKK provided a second major germ of modern Republicanism. It is likely that it did so in much of the greater South as well. By contrast, the Loyalists were more cosmopolitan, mostly business conservatives, concerned with preserving their favorable political and economic position, and not as likely to get worked up over issues like alcohol, Catholics, Jews, immigrants, or conventional forms of morality. Yet both factions were ultraconservative on the race issue. While the Loyalists were determined opponents of the Klan, they fought the order as a *political* adversary and as an unsubtle police force against racial change—one that threatened to dry up northern capital investment and bring down an unwanted federal invasion and real racial change on the heads of racially conservative white southerners.[9] The Loyalists shared an interest—indeed an obsession—with their fledgling Republican or Hoovercrat challengers in maintaining white supremacy. The raucous 1928 episode made clear that if the two sides could ever be glued together using race or some equally emotional adhesive, the product of such a union would be invincible in the Deep South. As shocking and, perhaps, overheated as it might initially seem, there is no way around the conclusion that a critically important part of the Republican appeal in the modern South may accurately be termed "neo-Kluxism."

"Neo-Kluxism" denotes a focus redux on racial, cultural, ethnic, moral, religious, and even gender-relations homogeneity that bears striking parallels with the Ku Klux Klan of the 1920s and 1940s. That is, the "second KKK" and its 1940s incarnation posed as the self-conscious preservers of home and hearth in the South, a concept constituted by the interaction of several fundamental building blocks of conservative (read: predominant) southern culture: white supremacy, Anglo-Saxon, evangelical Protestantism, "dry," patriarchal, traditional family values, religious, ethnic, moral, and social conservatism, ethnic purity, and nativism, patriotism, and "100 percent Americanism." The 1940s version did a very similar thing, with the exception of being poorer and more working class in membership than middle class, and having that fact reflected in its deemphasis on mainline Protestantism for more fringe, Pentecostal, charismatic, Church of God, and Holiness church support. The main adversaries of the KKK in Alabama and the South from 1915 through the 1960s were the "best people," persons variously referred to as the "Bourbons," "Redeemers," "bosses," "planter-industrialist clique," the "Big Mule/Black Belt coalition," and so forth. In 1928 they made up the ranks of Loyalist Democracy, but in 1948 they made up the Dixiecrats in alliance with the KKK. Their concerns were primarily white supremacy, economic conservatism, low taxes, fiscal retrenchment, malapportionment, "laissez-faire" defined as government support for business in the form of corporate welfare, subsidies, low-interest loans, low corporate and property taxation, weak or nonexistent unionism, inadequate spending on social services, and the preservation of a strict hierarchical and socially, economically, and politically stratified society—in short, "Bourbon values" or, as historian Numan V. Bartley has termed it, "neo-Bourbonism."[10] In Alabama, the marriage of neo-Kluxism and neo-Bourbonism—with a courtship that began around 1936 and continued through the 1940s, 1950s, and 1960s—eventually produced the offspring of the modern GOP. Most critically, the shared primary value of white supremacy—and anti-federalism both racial and economic—provided the essential glue for the union. It acted to bind the rigid ethnic, religious, moral, and social conservatism of neo-Kluxism with the intense economic conservatism of neo-Bourbonism in the modern South.

The realization among neo-Bourbons and neo-Kluxers that they had to bury their factional class squabbles and wed in order to preserve white supremacy and laissez-faire became clearer as they perceived that the national Democratic Party could no longer be their home. Both elements had to find a new home, something different from the national Democratic Party, because it became clearer day by day through the 1940s and beyond that they could no longer call themselves "Democrats" and still adhere to white supremacy and anti-federalism—which was *the* priority value for both. In response, they pooled their resources, first to bolt and then to build a new party—a new, viable southern GOP—in order to protect white supremacy and home rule, since it was clear that the national Democratic Party was no longer going to do so. Republican ascendance in Alabama was based on protecting white, Anglo-Saxon, native-born, male-dominated, evangelical Protestant, family values, and "patriotic" society—or strict, and even exclusionary, ethnic, religious, and social conservatism. But the ascendant GOP also stood for the Bourbon economic values of old. The critical glue—the secret of the marriage—that kept the two groups welded together was composed of race and the "Reconstruction Syndrome." It was a preoccupation and fixation with preserving white supremacy and an allegiance to the hallowed anti-federal values of the syndrome—anti-liberal, anti-outsider/foreigner, and anti-Yankee. The union was possible because both the neo-Kluxist and the neo-Bourbon strains put race and the maintenance of white supremacy at the very pinnacle of their values and priorities—and because race and the manipulation of racial fears free of federal meddling was the Bourbons' most reliable weapon to keep plain whites and blacks divided in order to preserve a privileged class status. The result for the modern GOP in Alabama was an absolutely unbeatable—even unassailable—combination of values, mores, and issues which are even today virtually irresistible to the majority of southern whites. These are values that are held very dear, which many white southerners perceive as having "made this country great," and which many accurately charge the national Democratic Party with having moved away from since the 1940s.

In recent decades, race (in the form of civil rights, voting rights, "law and order," busing, affirmative action, and welfare) has been increasingly supplemented by a myriad of other factors that constitute a "politics of emotion": religion, morality, family values, abortion, homosexuality, school prayer, display of the Ten Commandments, the Confederate battle flag, and gun control. As white supremacy alone once did for Bourbon Democracy, these issues, together with a more muted race issue, work to keep lower- and working-class Republicans—most captivated by the social, ethnic, religious, and moral proscriptions of neo-Kluxism—contentedly and often unwittingly supporting the neo-Bourbon program of economic conservatism. Perhaps most maddening to many liberals, mass emotional support was often purchased with the cheap coin of nothing more than neo-Bourbon lip service or symbolic displays for the most divisive issues of social conservatism.

During the Great Depression, events moved southern Democrats ever further away from the national party. In 1936 a watershed of sorts was reached when, for the first time, African Americans voted for the party of Roosevelt in greater numbers than the party of Lincoln. Liberal New Deal policies that appealed to blacks, Jews, Catholics, immigrants, labor unionists, and the working poor increasingly alienated the white, Anglo-Saxon, Protestant, rural, Democratic South. For a time, the extraordinary exigencies associated with the unprecedented economic crisis of the Great Depression muted southern white discontent with the increasing liberalism of the national Democratic Party. Alabama's—and the South's—allegiance and receptivity to economic liberalism was predominantly exceptional and expedient, an extraordinary temporary measure to gain relief, income, and survival during an emergency that was by its very nature abnormal, ephemeral, exceptional, and fleeting. It did not contradict the region's essential conservatism in a lasting or fundamental way. More, though, the increasingly obvious racial liberalism of First Lady Eleanor Roosevelt and the New Dealers surrounding her worked as a powerful corrosive against the southern New Deal coalition of farmers, unionists, the poor, and rural whites, like those of North Alabama, grateful for TVA electricity.

In 1938, simmering tensions boiled over as southern congressmen released a ten-point "Conservative Manifesto" detailing their unhappiness with Franklin Roosevelt's New Deal—despite the South's receipt of considerable federal monies from New Deal programs. One frustrated white southerner accurately, if crudely, summed up increasing discontent with the national Democratic Party under FDR: "You ask any nigger in the street who's the greatest man in the world. Nine out of ten will tell you Franklin Roosevelt. That's why I think he's so dangerous."[11]

The exigencies of World War II only exacerbated southern racial tensions, with women and blacks taking the places of white males in the workplace and with southern customs finding themselves under increasing challenge by an influx of non-southerners into Dixie. Franklin Roosevelt's institution of a Fair Employment Practices Committee (FEPC) and Harry Truman's Executive Order 1088, desegregating the armed forces, shook southern racial conventions to the core. While white southerners damned the new Democratic racial liberalism and clung steadfastly to Jim Crow, actual racial integration was practiced long before *Brown* in southern workplaces and even in the "cradle of the Confederacy," at federal installations such as Montgomery's Maxwell Air Force Base. Enforcement of FEPC nondiscrimination directives resulted in a race riot in Mobile's shipyards and serious unrest in other places across Alabama. Crisis was reached in 1948 after President Truman released a four-point civil rights package: proposals for federal legislation outlawing lynching, segregation, and the poll tax and for making the FEPC permanent. Long-suffering southern Democrats again bolted the party of their fathers, meeting first in Jackson, Mississippi, and then Birmingham, Alabama, to found a new political party: the States' Rights Democrats, or "Dixiecrats." Although the Dixiecrat revolt eventually "failed" in the sense that Harry Truman won the 1948 election, and the revolt did not spread significantly beyond the former Confederate states, the disaffected southerners did carry Alabama, Mississippi, Louisiana, and South Carolina—with their all-important electoral votes—and polled over a million votes in the popular election. More importantly, the Dixiecrat revolt crystallized and *politicized* southern Democratic disenchantment with the national party—principally over the intertwined issues of race and federal power—and, in effect, baptized the Republican Party into viability in southern environs. For years now, assorted Republicans have denied the Dixiecrat tie with their modern party as something that smacks of ugly racial animus, but in the frank words of a Democrat-turned-Republican who ought to know (former GOP congressman and senatorial and gubernatorial candidate James E. Martin of Alabama), "The nucleus of the Republican Party was in '48."[12]

The union that had only been hinted at in the bolt of 1928 actually occurred in 1948 as Alabama's Big Mule/Black Belt alliance of wealthy planters and industrialists merged with the KKK in the Dixiecrat movement. Disenchantment had grown steadily during the New Deal years, especially after the historic 1936 departure of blacks from the party of Lincoln. Wartime racial liberalism under the Truman administration had only made things worse, according to most of the white South. At Birmingham's Municipal Auditorium in July 1948, all of the laissez-faire, anti-federal, economic conservatism of the planter-industrialist clique was present along with the religious and moral narrowness of the KKK. Racial conservatism and opposition to civil rights served as the irresistible glue that bound them together. In the late 1940s a KKK that again terrorized Alabamians for infringements of traditional moral conformity locked arms with a Dixiecrat ally. But the Dixiecrats also featured the Bourbon variety of strident economic conservatism. Even the split between the Dixiecrats and their Loyalist adversaries was, again, more an argument over means than ends. Both groups rejected Truman's civil rights initiatives, and both disparaged the growing leftward drift on race manifested by the national Democratic Party and the administrations of Franklin Roosevelt and Harry Truman. The Dixiecrats advocated resistance to civil rights by bolting the Democratic Party; the Loyalists urged opposition by fighting civil rights within the party, where they could rely on patronage, deal making, and congressional seniority. The Dixiecrat episode amounted to the third germ of the modern Republican Party in the South.

Loyalist Alabama Democrats made clear that they would fight Truman's civil rights package within the regular Democratic Party—through the seniority and committee system in the House and Senate, and by filibuster if necessary—a tack that had served them well repeatedly in thwarting prior attempts at federal anti-lynching statutes. The Loyalists routinely emphasized that they "agree[d] in principle" with the States' Righters but parted ways on the question of methods. Some, such as former state attorney general A. A. Carmichael, explained his loyalism by stating that the Dixiecrat revolt would only let the "carpetbagger, nigger-loving Republicans" benefit—underscoring that in 1948 Alabama Democratic loyalism was a far cry from racial liberalism. Loyalist forces included the chastened Tom Heflin and racial "liberals" such as George Wallace of Barbour County. Even in 1948, calling Wallace a liberal on racial matters was dubious at best. The "Little Judge" had remained behind in Philadelphia after the infamous Alabama and Mississippi delegate walkout at the Democratic National Convention. That and other early acts earned the young Wallace a reputation for liberalism more deserved on the economic front than the racial. It is not as clearly recalled that Wallace stayed behind in order to place Senator Richard B. Russell's name into nomination for president. He nominated the Georgian (with apologies to William Jennings Bryan) by vowing that Russell was the man to see that "the South shall not be crucified on the cross of civil rights."[13]

Dixiecrats in Alabama were capable of being just as blunt. Attorney and prominent politico Horace C. Wilkinson swore that he would "rather die fighting for states' rights than live on Truman boulevard in a Nigger heaven." While former governor Frank M. Dixon and perennial state Democratic chair Gessner T. McCorvey usually managed a more restrained posture in public, preferring to speak of states' rights as a high constitutional and philosophical issue, in private they let their hair down. "It may be that the time has come for us to see established in the South a great big mongrel brotherhood of mixed races," Dixon told a local judge, "but I don't think so." "As a cosmopolitan and a church man," he confided to another close friend, "I can justify, in theory, racial amalgamation. [But] as a Southern man with the normal human dislike of foreigners . . . I doubt my ability to put Christian charity into practice. . . . The progeny of a cornfield ape blackened with the successive suns of Africa and Alabama, mated with a swamp gorilla from the Louisiana rice fields [is supposed to have] promise as great as the sons of the great American families. . . . But I prefer to keep my faith." For his part, McCorvey could barely conceal his delight when he got hold of a "corking good glossy picture" of a black St. Louis attorney at the Democratic National Convention in Philadelphia. Letting Dixon in on his plan to surreptitiously distribute the photo throughout the state in order to boost the Alabama Dixiecrat cause, McCorvey gushed: "I don't think I ever saw a human being whose picture more closely resembled a gorilla."[14]

In the states' rights stronghold of Alabama, intraparty strife preoccupied Democrats in the critical years after the Dixiecrat revolt, as the state's Republican Party fought to emerge as a viable player for the first time.[15] In 1954 and 1958 the Alabama GOP took a long stride toward that goal when disaffected Dixiecrat leader and newspaper publisher Thomas Abernethy joined the Republicans and ran two very successful campaigns for governor, principally by exploiting the race issue. Not one to sugarcoat political issues, Abernethy asked Alabamians point-blank "whether the NAACP or the people are to run Alabama."[16] Perennial gubernatorial candidate and arch-racist Rear Admiral John G. Crommelin allied with the Republican Party, and States' Rights leader Ludie Abernethy (the wife of Thomas Abernethy) became a major player and national committeewoman in the suddenly vital GOP.[17] In Alabama, leading conservative Democrats left the party of their fathers in growing numbers. Horace Hall's *Dothan Eagle*, a conservative Democratic newspaper since its founding, was so incensed over the national Democratic Party's pursuit of civil rights legislation that it converted to Republicanism. In 1952 the *Montgomery Advertiser*, known as the venerable "old Grandma" in Alabama, announced with much fanfare that its 1948 bolt to the States' Rights cause had not been sufficient. It endorsed a Republican for the first time since it began publishing newspapers, back in 1826. A slew of Dixiecrat notables, representing thousands of other whites in the state, turned to the Republican Party—at least in national elections.[18] Sidney Smyer, Frank P. Samford, John Temple Graves II, Wallace Malone, Laurie Battle, Ed O'Neal, H. M. Abercrombie, Sam M. Johnston, Asa Young, Joseph G. Burns, Ross Diamond Jr., Donald Comer, Winton Blount, Hubert Baughn, and W. H. Albritton all entered the Republican column—and took with them thousands.[19] The Albrittons, an influential family of Covington County attorneys, were actually so prominent in party politics that they furnished state electors for the Dixiecrats in 1948 and for the Republican ticket in 1956. Race and local control of race relations remained the prime mover. "We have all been disturbed about our school situation," patriarch W. H. Albritton confided to Frank Dixon, "the great threat of 'Federal Aid' which would result in the totalitarian State domination of the mind of America. We have been seeking some way to finance private schools or segregated school systems and leave education in the hands of the people of the various States free from Federal control." "It is simply insane," Albritton felt, "to seek 'Federal Aid' with the ensuing 'Federal control.' The remedy . . . the way to stop 'Federal control,' is to retain and channel [tax] funds into our local school systems and private institutions rather than send it to Washington."[20]

But perhaps the most important Dixiecrat move to the Republican column was that of Gessner McCorvey. For McCorvey, the conversion was especially painful because it ran diametrically opposite to his well-cultivated persona as the actual embodiment of Democratic protection of white supremacy. The powerful Mobile attorney served four separate terms as chairman of the state Democratic Executive Committee and in 1948 personally oversaw the capture of the party's machinery for the States' Rights ticket. During the midst of the Dixiecrat campaign, an angry McCorvey had ordered one newspaper editor to "Please get it out of your head that I am a Republican or a Republican sympathizer. I was just brought up to believe that voting a Republican ticket was something that was not done by Southern white men." Yet by 1952, McCorvey had defected to the Republican Party. A few major States' Righters—Horace Wilkinson, Bruce Henderson, and Bull Connor in Alabama and Lester Maddox in Georgia—stayed in the Democratic Party, but most of these holdouts increasingly drifted toward third-party "Independent" Democracy. Former Alabama governor Frank Dixon remained tight-lipped about his personal voting record after 1948. Still, Dixon's personal correspondence reveals that he helped organize speakers for the White Citizens' Council while he flirted with Republicanism and recommended the organization of local Republican committees in Alabama, and he allowed that "a good many" Alabama Dixiecrats "of my political belief" were leaving the Democratic Party for the ranks of the GOP. Louisiana boss Leander Perez, a States' Rights ally who operated closely with Alabama's leading Dixiecrats, also switched to the Republican Party and was, characteristically, more direct in public about his rationale and revulsion for the racial situation.

"Do you know what the Negro is?" Perez asked a journalist. "Animals right out of the jungle. Passion. Welfare. Easy life. That's the Negro. And if you don't know that, you're naïve." He traced the civil rights movement back to Franklin Roosevelt and the Democratic Party and "all those Jews who were supposed to have been cremated at Buchenwald and Dachau but weren't, and Roosevelt allowed two million of them illegal entry into our country."[21]

After 1952, the Republican Party increasingly began to appear as the logical home for whites in the Deep South, regardless of their class or social rank. The party was formed largely on the basis of being "the" preserver of white supremacy, combined with a large dose of anti-federal government sentiment. The combination appealed powerfully to former Dixiecrats (both the old KKK type and the wealthier planter-industrialist type), segregationist Loyalist Democrats, new suburban white voters, and economic and social conservatives of all kinds. Modern Republican strength is sometimes laid to the cohesiveness and growth of the GOP-dominated "suburbs." It should be recalled here that in the South, as elsewhere, the "suburbs" often means lily-white affluence galvanized by white flight after the *Brown* decision. The "suburbs" also means upper-class in-migrants to the South who often brought with them an affinity for business and a profound distaste for federal intervention in economic matters, unless it came in the form of government subsidies or tax exemptions. This selective laissez-faire of the new migrants jelled nicely with the traditional, more principally race-centered anti-federalism of their new southern home.

Here, at last, was a party that could accommodate all kinds of white southerners under the single umbrella of white supremacy and antipathy to the federal government. While the national Democratic Party has often been thought of as an umbrella party of divergent interests held under one tent, actually the modern Republican Party in places like Alabama was, in many ways, the umbrella party of whites. In the GOP, whites of varying social rank took cover under the canopy of white supremacy and segregation during the most violent civil rights storms of the 1940s, 1950s, and 1960s. When they emerged from the thunder and lightning, they came out Republicans.

In 1957, the nascent GOP received a serious but temporary setback across the South from President Dwight Eisenhower's enforcement of the U.S. Supreme Court's racial integration order at Little Rock. Far from indicating that a "New South" was emerging, southern distress over Little Rock, and its brief disgust with national Republicanism, demonstrated very clearly that the white South had not moved ... the national parties had. In a rather fundamental way, the white South had not changed since 1860—despite the hullabaloo made over a "New South" by boosters, Yankee investors, and, in fact, historians. While some took the visual appearance of a white southern partisan movement—from Democrat to Republican—to be a political sea change, such a "move" was really just a trick played on the eyes of wistful observers. In actuality, the major *parties* moved on race. *Politically and ideologically,* white southerners remained standing very still.[22]

Growing receptivity among southern whites for the GOP, after Harry Truman's assaults, was almost killed in its infancy at Little Rock. To Republicans, the confrontation in Arkansas demonstrated just how ephemeral white southern allegiance could be if a political party failed to protect the tabernacle of white supremacy or states' rights—a lesson not lost on those most influential in Republican Party councils. Even if national GOP officials were wont to forget that race had "brung them to the dance" in the South, former Dixiecrats like Ludie Abernethy were not bashful about reminding their new party brethren of this cold reality. Mrs. Abernethy denounced Ike's use of federal troops, whom she compared to "Hitler's Gestapo," and warned that "millions of persons" in the South, distressed over Democratic liberalism, had turned to the Republicans for racial conservatism, and wanted and fully expected "restoration of a government that would be constitutional as well as clean."[23] Still, despite Little Rock, these years mostly saw mounting white disaffection with the national Democratic Party's increasingly clear racial liberalism.

Even when the disillusionment of Republicans over Little Rock led to an exit from the GOP, the absence was often temporary. Racially conservative white southerners could flirt with third-party movements, but ultimately they had nowhere else to go besides the Republican Party. The odyssey of W. T. Witt of Birmingham was exemplary. "When the Democrat[ic] Party, beginning with Roosevelt, began to lean toward the Communists," Witt explained, "I left it" for the Republican Party. A local GOP activist, Witt accepted election shortly after Little Rock to the presidency of the Jefferson County Republican Club, the most populous county in the state. He "thanked the members for having elected me . . . and then stated to them that I was not only resigning . . . the club but also was renouncing the Republican Party." "When the 'pottage eaters' sold Mr. Eisenhower a 'mess' and he sent soldiers to Little Rock to place bayonets in white girls' backs to force them to carry out a Russian-type decree sponsored by the NAACP, he cleaned the slate of all the gains the Republican Party has made since the Civil War,"

Witt declared. "Now a more suitable name . . . would be the 'Stupid Party.' Can't you envision Khrushchev & Co. holding up their vodka before gulping it down and praising the President's . . . 'civil rights'?" Despite the obvious sincerity and emotion in his conversion statement, within a short time Witt returned to the Republican fold.[24]

The 1960s phase of the civil rights movement led, not coincidentally, to the clear coming-of-age of the Republican Party in the South as white southern Democrats tried desperately—and in many cases vainly—to disassociate themselves from the national Democratic Party and its civil rights program.[25] In 1962, high-profile Republican convert James E. Martin ran a breathlessly close race against longtime incumbent Democratic senator Lister Hill. A North Alabama oil man, Martin eagerly cashed in on southern white resentment against John and Robert Kennedy's support of the Freedom Riders and other civil rights initiatives— most notably the revisited Reconstruction nightmare of using federal marshals in Montgomery and federal troops to integrate the University of Mississippi—sins of such proportion that the Kennedys have still not been forgiven in the South. After JFK's assassination, southern white hostility shifted to Bobby Kennedy, Lyndon Johnson, and Hubert Humphrey, who had made himself unforgettable in the South by delivering a strong call for civil rights legislation at the critical 1948 Democratic National Convention.[26] In Alabama, GOP chief John Grenier, who would soon serve as national director of the Republican Party, effectively capitalized on white racial insecurities to build momentum for his party and for Barry Goldwater. Later, Grenier admitted that "we were aware not only of the liberal attitudes on race that Lyndon Johnson . . . promoted . . . were foreign to Southerners, but his liberal economic scheme of giving away everything to appease the small black minority was ridiculous in the minds of most Southerners."[27] Running as an extreme right-wing Republican presidential candidate, Goldwater swept the Deep South in 1964 as Jim Martin and other Republican segregationists rode his coattails to victory in Alabama's congressional and state elections. Some Republicans were hoping the race issue would actually carry him further. One California Goldwater leader was so confident that he crudely prophesied, "the nigger issue will put him in the White House." In the South, perhaps nothing summed up the Goldwater campaign so much as his famous admission that the Republican Party was "not going to get the Negro vote as a bloc in 1964 or 1968, so we ought to go hunting where the ducks are."[28]

It is significant not only that Goldwater swept the Deep South but also that that is about all he swept. In addition to his home state of

Arizona, Goldwater prevailed in only five other states: Alabama, Mississippi, Georgia, Louisiana, and South Carolina—with the exception of Georgia the same states won by Dixiecrat presidential candidate Strom Thurmond in 1948. In Alabama, Goldwater won sixty-three of sixty-seven counties. In the only four all-black precincts in the state he garnered less than 2 percent of the vote. His coattails swept in five Republicans out of Alabama's seven allotted U.S. congressmen: Jim Martin (who would go on to make dramatically close race-based runs for governor and U.S. senator), William Dickinson, John Buchanan, Glenn Andrews, and Jack Edwards.[29]

Once it became clear that the racial liberalism of FDR and Harry Truman would be continued by the national Democratic Party, huge numbers of conservative southern whites reconciled themselves to leaving the party for good. No longer could the fight against the national Democratic Party's racial liberalism be contained within the party tent—or even by mounting an independent movement as in 1928 and 1948. As he signed the 1964 Civil Rights Bill into law, Lyndon Johnson—a son of the Texas soil intimately aware of the power of race in southern politics—clearly understood this. No sooner had he signed the act than he slumped forward, took his head in his hands, and told his press secretary: "I've just given the South to the Republicans for a generation."[30]

While it is true that a slightly higher percentage of Republicans than Democrats in the House and Senate actually voted for the Civil Rights Act, the law was indelibly and accurately associated in the public mind with John Kennedy, Lyndon Johnson, Hubert Humphrey, and even Harry Truman—Democrats all.[31] The reason, it seems almost unnecessary to explain, why the total Democratic percentage of support for the bill was lower than the Republican percentage is that the South—as it had for decades where anti-lynching and civil rights measures were concerned—voted as a bloc against the bill.[32] Conservative southern Democrats in both houses—then in the throes of conversion to the modern GOP *precisely because* of Democratic advocacy for civil rights—voted as a unit against the measure. Far from indicating some kind of modern Democratic hostility to the cause of civil rights, congressional Democratic opposition to the bill was yet another in a long line of conservative southern Democratic rearguard actions against civil rights, racial equality, federal anti-lynching laws, and the like—in effect, against racial modernity. In a very real way, it was the last hurrah for the conservative Democratic South on a congressional level, a conservative bloc that would eventually be replaced by the conservative Republican

South. By the same token, it was the last hurrah for the old-guard, racially liberal northern wing of the Republican Party—the Dirksens, the Romneys, the Rockefellers—who were about to see themselves thrust into political exile within their own party by a conservative purge of the GOP at the 1964 national convention in Miami. Recent attempts by right-wing radio and television pundits to cast this congressional opposition to the 1964 Civil Rights Act as evidence of some kind of latent Democratic hostility to racial equality stems from either the most staggering ignorance of history or the most cynical manipulation of context to distort the reality of present-day politics.[33] Either way, it is historically irresponsible and a disservice to legitimate historical inquiry.

A fairer present-day recognition from the Right of the lead role the Democratic Party took during the civil rights movement, and even a kind of covetousness of the present-day Democratic stranglehold on black votes, usually emanates from the northern wing of latter-day Republicanism or from a young GOP generation in the South. Neither group, generally, has a particularly solid grasp on the political/economic nature of the GOP's historical ascendance in the South: how Republican economic conservatism replaced Bourbon Democratic economic conservatism in the South only because the GOP was able to get on the "right side" of race and thereby win the votes of masses of plain southern whites who otherwise would have had little incentive to vote the GOP label. Thus in 2003 a senior editorial page writer at the *Wall Street Journal* could fervently recommend that George W. Bush "lead his Party on race" and actually provide an outline of how to do so. "For starters," Republicans "should work to retire the Southern strategy. Don't make excuses for it. Don't euphemize it. Say it was wrong and now it's over. End the pit stops at Bob Jones University, the strained defenses of the Confederate flag, the coded references to states' rights." In giving credit to the Democratic Party for their "stalwart behavior during the civil rights movement," the same writer laments that the Democrats have become the "default Party for minorities" and urges Bush the Younger to exploit the considerable "racial capital" he allegedly gained with blacks for his "forthright" handling of the Trent Lott imbroglio to make inroads on the dismal 8 percent of the black vote that Bush gained in the 2000 presidential election—"to make his Party more amenable to minorities and especially blacks."[34]

During the Second Reconstruction, Democratic identification with civil rights and voting rights made it clear that the party could no longer be the home for whites in Alabama. As the First Reconstruction created the Solid Democratic South, the Second Reconstruction has virtually created a Solid Republican South. In retrospect, George Wallace's brand of independent politics was only a pit stop for thousands of white Alabama Democrats who were then on their way to a more permanent home in the Republican Party. To be sure, the trajectory of many States' Righters to the GOP was fraught with fits and starts, and sometimes detours. Many former Dixiecrats split their tickets—voting Republican in national elections, but continuing to vote as, and think of themselves as, Democrats in local and state elections—at least for a time. "I am a life-long Democrat," explained one, "who takes pride in having never voted for a Democratic President." Many of these same individuals—disgusted with the national Democratic Party's racial and economic liberalism—its "drift toward socialism"—participated in George Wallace's independent movement as a rest stop on the way to a more permanent home in the GOP. "People will ease their way into the Republican Party by way of the American Independents," a confident John Mitchell put it in 1970. "We'll get two-thirds to three-fourths of the Wallace vote in nineteen seventy-two." Mitchell, who served as Richard Nixon's attorney general, knew a thing or two firsthand about the South, being married to outspoken Alabama native Martha Mitchell. A close student of the States' Rights movement in Alabama concurred that the Dixiecrats were "a halfway house along the road to Republicanism."[35]

As Dan T. Carter realized in his magisterial work on George Wallace, the Alabama governor was immensely important to the emergence of the modern GOP in the South, and across the nation.[36] Yet Wallace was not an originator or a pioneer. Instead he was the ultimate practitioner, the embodiment and articulator of the racial and anti-federal politics and intolerant rhetoric originated by many others before him—notably the Dixiecrats of the 1940s. As such, Wallacism was the fourth germ of modern southern Republicanism.

Made respectable and competitive by its effective use of the race issue, the Alabama GOP spent the remainder of the 1960s trying to find a way not to be "out-niggered" by Alabama's most formidable politician, perennial governor, and third-party candidate for president.[37] Wallace's masterful use of the race issue to own the governor's mansion and use it as a springboard for presidential runs in 1964, 1968, 1972, and 1976 amounted to a major challenge to the Republican Party's ability to compete for the hearts and minds of conservative white Alabamians perpetually transfixed by the race issue.

There is little question that Wallace himself, one of the most astute students of southern politics around, fully realized the debt Republicans eventually owed him for their strength in his native region. "It sounds like to me, when I hear all this talk," he said years later, "that the Republicans have stolen a lot of their thoughts and their words and their principles from George Wallace. You know, I should have copyrighted all of my speeches. If I had, the Republicans in Alabama, throughout the South, and all over the nation would be paying me hundreds of thousands of dollars. They owe everything they have to my kind of Democratic thinking." Master conservative Republican strategist Kevin Phillips cheerfully corroborated Wallace's claim, seeing it as a good thing for the modern Republican Party—in both a regional and a national sense. After noting that four of the five 1968 Wallace states had gone Goldwater Republican in 1964, Phillips explained that Richard Nixon's candidacy confirmed that "the GOP [w]as the ascending Party of the local white majority" and that Wallace's American Independent Party was merely "a way station" for "some longtime Republicans, but the great majority were conservative Democrats who have been moving—and should continue to move—towards the GOP." Wallace, the GOP's leading political strategist chortled, had "principally won those in motion between a Democratic past and a Republican future."[38] Those most in the know about how things worked politically in the South agreed. Howard "Bo" Callaway, a Democratic Georgia governor-turned-Republican who served as Richard Nixon's southern director during the 1968 presidential campaign, concurred: "The ideas expressed by George Wallace are the ideas a great many Republicans espouse."[39]

In Alabama, Hubert Baughn was the perfect exemplar—the physical embodiment and manifestation—of the thesis that the modern Republican Party owes the largest part of its dominance in the South to the successful appropriation of the race issue and white supremacy away from the old conservative Democratic Party that owned the "Solid South." Baughn served as the publisher and editor of *Alabama Magazine: News Digest of the Deep South* and, later, *South: The News Magazine of Dixie*, from the magazine's inception in 1936 until his retirement in the 1970s. Both versions of the magazine were arguably the most passionate, outspoken, and consistently accurate indices of conservative white sentiment in Alabama and the South. Both were bankrolled by Alabama's Big Mule/Black Belt coalition—the planter-industrialist alliance that dominated state politics from Redemption in 1874 to the mid-1960s.[40] More importantly, the Big Mule/Black Belt coalition was solidly Democratic from 1874 on. They represented the Loyalist side of the equation during the heated 1928 Hoovercrat "bolt." During the 1930s, though, increasing unhappiness with Franklin Roosevelt's New Deal, relative racial liberalism, and other, less important matters led to rumblings among the privileged. During the World War II crisis, the coalition grew increasingly disillusioned with Roosevelt's FEPC and later with Harry Truman's desegregation orders. The break came in 1948 as the planter-industrialist coalition (and its mouthpiece *Alabama*) occupied the vanguard in the Dixiecrat exodus from the national Democratic Party. Baughn patched up old feuds with plain-white tribunes like Horace Wilkinson as the Birmingham political boss abandoned class pursuits to help planter-industrialist stalwarts Gessner McCorvey and Frank Dixon lead Alabama's States' Rights insurgency—making the "Heart of Dixie" one of the best-organized and -financed of the Dixiecrat states. Baughn's and *Alabama*'s editorial and content policies reflected these changes at every point, as the most conservative southern Democrats were pushed into the arms of alternative political parties by the national Democratic Party's increasingly obvious racial liberalism. In Alabama, with Harry Truman kept off the ballot by Dixiecrat machinations at the state level, Strom Thurmond polled 80 percent in 1948. But by 1950 the state's Democratic Loyalists had recaptured control of the party machinery, effectively snuffing out the possibility of another intraparty revolt in 1952.

During the early 1950s, Alabama's planters and industrialists furnished the most prominent members of a rapidly expanding Republican Party. The emerging GOP, so long the unwanted stepchild of southern politics, accommodated the disillusionment over race of the expatriate white conservatives leaving Alabama's Democratic Party by eagerly catering to their white supremacist beliefs. It was at this critical point that the modern Republican Party chose its course. Once the national Democratic Party decided to support the cause of civil rights for African Americans, the Republican Party could have followed suit. The route was still a possibility. While history often seems inevitable in retrospect, at the time decisions occur and courses are followed, they are chosen, not preordained.

The GOP could have followed the Democratic lead in sponsoring a Second Reconstruction. After all, the Republican Party did have a proud civil rights heritage. Abraham Lincoln had been a Republican. The party's northern old guard had among it the most liberal politicians on race to be found anywhere in the country. But instead the Republican brass in Alabama welcomed Thomas Abernethy with open arms. In fact, they threw open the party with undisguised jubilation that Abernethy's decision to run for governor on a Republican ticket would finally transform Alabama's GOP into a "real" party—a force to be reckoned with. This is significant because Abernethy was not just any Democrat or even any *Dixiecrat*. He was firmly embedded in the minds of black Alabamians as one of the causes—correctly or not—for Klan-related bombing violence on Birmingham's "Dynamite Hill." Just one day before a bomb exploded at a black physician's house in the contested Smithfield district, Abernethy had unleashed a particularly blistering tirade against civil rights, broadcast across Alabama by statewide radio hookup. Alabama's Republicans followed up on the Abernethy conversion coup by having the national GOP chairman visit Birmingham and issue a formal invitation to Dixiecrats to join the GOP because we "both stand in opposition to the Socialist Democratic Party of the Truman Administration." In 1956, state Republican chairman Claude Vardaman was even more direct. "You can go home and tell your people," he told disgruntled Democrats, "that if they are interested in preserving segregation in Alabama, then their man is Dwight D. Eisenhower."[41]

During the 1960s, George Wallace realized that the success of his fledgling Independent movement depended on the perception that there was no discernible difference between the two major parties. To this end, he repeated his mantra that there "wasn't a dime's worth of difference" between the two parties.[42] Would that it were so. As it was, the modern Republican Party in Alabama chose the racist path of white supremacy. At the very same time that the national Democratic Party estranged white Alabama Democrats over civil rights and the role of the federal government, the Republican Party made a choice. It endorsed racism, advertised its commitment to white supremacy, and did its best to attract disaffected Democrats by billing itself as the party opposed to civil rights. In Alabama, Republicans built their party by endorsing civil rights resistance, exploiting racial tensions, and doing all they could to fill the yawning void left by the old conservative Democratic Party. The GOP did everything it could to convince Alabama voters that it—not the new national Democratic Party—was the real guardian of white supremacy and segregation.

To be sure, there was significant variation on the race question among the Democrats who converted to the GOP. Not all, by a long shot, were race-baiters the stripe of Thomas Abernethy or Jim Martin. Many were segregationists of a more moderate variety. There is also no question that the Alabama Democratic Party during this time continued to harbor some states' rights enthusiasts that were every bit the peers of Democrat expatriates on the race issue. Even more, old-guard northern Republicans like Nelson Rockefeller, George Romney, Everett

Dirksen, Jacob Javits, and the Ripon Society represented much more liberal thinking on the race issue. Still, what *was* centrally important is that the liberal wing of the Republican Party lost its power struggle with the conservatives, punctuated by the 1964 nomination of Barry Goldwater (orchestrated in large part by Alabama GOP chieftain John Grenier). Even more important is that in Alabama the Republican Party made the choice to use the race issue to build a viable, and eventually dominant, modern party at the very time the Democratic Party was losing ground in the South due to its identification with the national Democratic Party's racial liberalism. The Republican racial offensive also made it increasingly difficult for "Alabama Democrats"—who claimed they were conservative on race—to keep themselves divorced in the popular mind from the racially liberal national Democratic Party. Many—Armistead Selden, Laurie Battle, Don Collins, and a host of others—constantly on the defensive over race, and realizing the futility of their cause, eventually crossed over to become Republicans.[43]

Tragically, it was this choice—the same essential choice that George Wallace made in 1958 to "out-nigger" the competition—that the Alabama GOP made on which to build their modern party.[44] Wallace's choice was made to his permanent ignominy. The unfortunate Republican choice, while made to the party's electoral advantage in places like Alabama, was also made to its everlasting discredit.

As the invigorated state Republican Party broadcast its determination to be Alabama's guardian of the temple of white supremacy—and as the state Democratic Party fought a losing battle against being associated with the racially liberal policies of Harry Truman, Hubert Humphrey, Adlai Stevenson, Estes Kefauver, and other national Democrats—Alabama's Big Mules and Black Belt planters increasingly populated the ranks of the new GOP. Hubert Baughn and *Alabama Magazine* accurately reflected this watershed—first as "Solid South" Democrats, then Dixiecrats, then Eisenhower Democrats who voted Republican in national elections, and increasingly as "independent" Democrats of the George Wallace stripe, and, finally, as Republicans (and proud of it!) who made up the ranks of the new Republican Party so accurately and prophetically described by Kevin Phillips. Baughn's editorials—as acidic and, at times, openly racist as they could be—were not important in and of themselves.[45] They were not even that significant as indices of Baughn's thought. The editorials were important because they represented, for three and a half decades, the deepest hopes, fears, plans, and beliefs of the powerful industrial, banking, insurance, and utility interests that paid the freight.[46] This new majority, of which Baughn and his magazine were a stalwart part, was the new Solid *Republican* South upon whose back the national Republican majority eventually emerged during the 1980s.

Disaffected Democrats responded in droves by turning to a Republican Party that courted them principally on the basis of white supremacy. Race was more often than not the primary consideration in their conversion. "When you vote for President Johnson," explained one, "you will vote to mix the races" and for the "Communist rights program.... The President's acts are making the Democratic Party the negro Party." Lyndon Johnson "understand us" southerners so well, another wrote bitterly, that "he helped ... railroad the satanic 'civil rights act of 1964' through. Such thinking is exactly why the Democratic Party is controlled by socialists now." A rural preacher who vehemently opposed civil rights reacted angrily to public charges of being a "turn-coat Democrat" for supporting Republican candidates. "It is rather ridiculous," he spat, "to accuse anyone of trying to tear down that [the Democratic Party] which has already been torn down by a crowd of wild-eyed, fuzzy-minded politicians who are trying to brainwash the American public."[47]

While some have written that the South changed *politically,* no such fundamental change occurred. A new party label was adopted for many, but essential conservative ideology on race and the federal government stayed the same for the white South. In fact, many white southerners defended their defection from the Democratic Party—then and today—as, in reality, no defection at all. A common proverb, with more than a seedling of truth, sprang up throughout the region: "I didn't leave the Democratic Party. The Democratic Party left me." Few articulated the defensive creed as well as Don Collins, an Alabama state legislator who formally, dramatically, and publicly switched parties in 1966. "I campaigned as a conservative or Southern Democrat . . . an old-fashioned Democrat," Collins informed a standing-room-only meeting of both houses of the state legislature as he issued a formal statement of principles of conversion. "My thinking was accepted, and my thinking has not changed. I have not changed. While I have not changed, and while the people of Alabama have not changed, the political philosophy of the national Democratic Party has changed and has left me an orphan." The following month Collins confidently predicted that the "semantical, or name-only, conversion of our friends who think and act Republican, yet from habit, call themselves Democrats" would be easy. "We will not have to ask them to turn away from established habits, actions, and customs," he explained. "We only have to convert our friends in name only from . . . Democrat to Republican. Most Southerners are *already* Republican—but they don't know it."[48]

During the late 1960s and early 1970s, Richard Nixon's masterful use of a "Southern Strategy," designed to appeal subtly to southern white insecurities on race without appearing too bluntly racist, led to the Republican consolidation of the South that Ronald Reagan and George Bush the Elder enjoyed, as predicted by Kevin Phillips. A national Republican ascendance built upon a solid Republican South disenchanted with the national Democratic Party's racial liberalism was precisely laid out and predicted by the legendary GOP strategist in *The Emerging Republican Majority,* which became, in effect, the bible of the "Southern Strategy." Phillips based his calculations and projections, as hauntingly accurate as a Nostradamus quatrain was supposed to be, on large-scale demographic shifts that favored the conservative Sunbelt of the West and South as opposed to shrinking liberal population centers in the old industrial Northeast. "Substantial Negro support is not necessary to national Republican victory," Phillips concluded bluntly. "The GOP can build a winning coalition without Negro votes." In a particularly Machiavellian passage, Phillips recommended that, although Republicans did not need black votes, the GOP should actually work to maintain black voting rights in the South because of the salutary effect it would have in pushing angry white southerners further into the arms of the GOP. "Far from contrary to GOP interests," Phillips explained, continued black voting "is essential if Southern conservatives are to be pressured into switching to the Republican Party—for Negroes are beginning to seize control of the national Democratic Party." In a less guarded moment, Phillips distilled his strategy down to a simple, if disturbing, formula: "Who hates whom: 'That is the secret.'" "The trick," as one close student of the strategy has written, "was to use the emotional issues of culture and race to achieve what . . . John Mitchell had"—more euphemistically—"called a 'positive polarization' of American politics."[49]

Phillips's analysis found itself echoed in several other best-selling political treatises of the time that forecast the demise of the Democratic Party, principally Kirkpatrick Sale's *The Power Shift* and Richard M. Scammon and Ben J. Wattenberg's *The Real Majority.* While still in galley form, the latter became must reading in the Nixon White House and apparently played a role in his administration's conceptualization of the "Silent Majority." First recommended to Nixon by a young speechwriter named Patrick J. Buchanan, *The Real Majority* echoed right-wing criticism of the Democratic Party, but from the perspective of two

Democratic journalists. They, like the party's conservative critics, reasoned that the Democrats had erred fatally in allowing themselves to be sucked into becoming not only the party of blacks, due to its championship of civil rights, but also the party of a whole host of other un-American undesirables: women libbers pushing for abortion rights and the Equal Rights Amendment, homosexuals, Latino and other new and poverty-stricken immigrants, the urban poor, welfare dependents, war-protesting students in the streets, and Americans opposed to compulsory school prayer. They dubbed the subject "The Social Issue" and reasoned that Democrats were on the losing end of it.[50]

In 1988, George H. W. Bush's advisers, Lee Atwater and Roger Ailes, would cynically employ the infamous Willie Horton issue to sink Democratic candidate Michael Dukakis and provide the quintessential Republican demonstration of race to carry Dixie and use the South as the most reliable bedrock of national GOP strength.[51] But actually, John Mitchell, Richard Nixon, Pat Buchanan, Kevin Phillips, and Lee Atwater finished what had been started much earlier by the South Carolina tandem of Strom Thurmond and Harry Dent: building Republican dominance in the South on the foundation of white supremacy and racism, and using that solid southern bedrock of GOP dominance as the launching point for the emergence of a national Republican majority. The idea that Barry Goldwater had started the "Southern Strategy" was so much "bullshit," according to Richard Nixon. Nixon saw Eisenhower, whom he had served as vice-president in 1952 and 1956, as the real pioneer of the "Southern Strategy" and believed that Goldwater had actually blundered in 1964 by being too transparent on race. By appealing to the "foam-at-the-mouth segregationists," Nixon reasoned, Goldwater had "won the wrong [southern] states"—Alabama, Mississippi, Louisiana, South Carolina, and Georgia—and in the process alienated much of the rest of the country. Nixon and his advisers were after a much more subtle racial appeal. They "scrupulously avoided explicit references to race" in developing a "racial policy conservative enough to entice the South from Wallace, but not so radical as to repel the . . . 'swing states' of California, Ohio, Illinois, Pennsylvania, and New Jersey." Harry Dent advised Nixon to "follow [Kevin] Phillips' plan" but to "disavow it publicly." Nixon ordered chief aide-de-camp H. R. Haldeman to "use Phillips . . . study his strategy . . . go for Poles, Italians, Irish . . . learn to understand the Silent Majority . . . don't go for Jews & Blacks."[52] Since that time, Ronald Reagan, George Bush, Newt Gingrich, and Bush the Younger have to a great extent been the beneficiaries of a strategy that has appealed well to white voters, favorable population shifts, and a consequent Republican majority ascendance.

Much of Reagan's appeal in the South was, without question, racial. Reagan won his southern spurs in 1964 as one of Goldwater's most ardent supporters, making him a political darling in Dixie. In his 1976 run for the Republican presidential nomination, Reagan cultivated white racial resentments by railing against "welfare queens" and assuring voters that they were justifiably outraged when "some strapping young buck" ahead of them in the grocery store paid for his T-bone steaks with food stamps. In 1980, Reagan's handlers chose Neshoba County, Mississippi—site of the infamous slaying of civil rights workers Goodman, Chaney, and Schwerner—to kick off his presidential campaign by making the call for "states' rights" in a section where it was pregnant with meaning. Strom Thurmond lined up behind the Californian, and Klan groups throughout the South rushed to endorse him. As he listened to notorious racist J. B. Stoner rail outside of Atlanta, one white voter summed up southern support for Reagan based on race. "I'm not a member of the Klan . . . [or] that National States' Rights Party," he said, "but some of the things that Mr. Stoner says I know are right." "I don't consider myself a racist," the voter explained. "I'm for black people having their rights . . . but I'm also for white people having a few rights too. . . . For one, [Stoner] says the black people are getting more rights than the white people . . . and that's right; they get more welfare, food stamps, and the law's on their side. . . . [Y]ou see 'em riding down the road in a Cadillac full of children and you know they're going to pick up their welfare check, and you know it isn't right. It just isn't right." "The Democratic government of Lyndon Johnson and Jimmy Carter turned everything over to the blacks," he said, "they spend my tax money for welfare and food stamps. . . . Well, I'm sick of all that. Back in the sixties and early seventies I voted for George Wallace for President whenever I had the chance. . . . I'll vote for Ronald Reagan for President because I think he wants to . . . give some of the government back to the white people. I guess it's just about that simple."[53] In 1980 Reagan won every state in the South except for Jimmy Carter's home state. In 1984 he won them all—even Georgia.[54]

Recent Republican success in the South has been based largely on the party's being seen as the protectors of "angry white men," the white, Anglo-Saxon, Protestant majority, patriotism, and religion.[55] The most important element in this unbeatable combination in the South was the Republican capture of the mantle of white supremacy from the Democratic Party during the Second Reconstruction. Along with this mantle came the related scepter of opposition to the federal government and its nefarious intervention. This fit perfectly into the traditional Republican stance on economic issues. The GOP in the South was able to use its opposition to federal intrusion on race matters as a foundation to include opposition to federal intrusion on a host of other fronts: prayer in public schools, taxes, business regulation, workplace safety laws, environmental regulation, mandated equal rights for women, and what they referred to as the "creeping socialism" of Medicare, Medicaid, and welfare.[56] Race issues, of course, remained centrally important, and were expressed in opposition to crime, busing, affirmative action, welfare, and other issues amenable to coded reference. But race was used as the glue to stick on other issues that had anti–federal government potential—more class-oriented and traditional economically conservative issues: Republican opposition to taxes, environmental protections, worker safety, labor unions, mandated gender equity, and the programs of the New Frontier and Great Society "Welfare State."

While the modern GOP agenda has been cast (and often received) as, on its surface, having very little to do with race, in actuality its major issues were grounded very firmly on the issue.[57] Recent practitioners of the "Southern Strategy" have heeded well the words of the strategy's original architects: to make "obvious but not too blunt appeals to race" that would be clear to white southerners but not crude enough to alienate the rest of the country—and, of course, to deny that such a strategy even existed if charged with it. Historian Dewey W. Grantham described Nixon's approach as "a wide-ranging campaign to exploit the racial fears and prejudices of white Americans, particularly in the South . . . despite . . . lip service . . . paid to racial justice." For example, Nixon "made effective use of the highly emotional issue of busing"; he "tried hard to appeal to white segregationist sentiment in the Southern states." "It was a cynical strategy," journalists Reg Murphy and Hal Gulliver agreed, "this catering in subtle ways to the segregationist leanings of Southern voters—yet pretending with high rhetoric that the real aim was simply to treat the South fairly, to let it become part of the nation again."[58]

Messages on taxes, guns, religion, patriotism, conventional gender roles, abortion, "family values," and "big government spending" are all undergirded by the race issue to make them particularly attractive in the South.[59] For example, opposition to taxes was not simply opposition on a philosophical level. The tax issue was tied to the issue of "federal programs," which to many white southerners meant taxpayer-supported federal programs to benefit "lazy" black Americans. Gun control and crime were also skillfully tied to racial conservatism. Guns became synonymous with personal protection against a grasping federal government that could and would ram unwelcome legislation down the throats of the people, as well as personal protection against criminals, associated so closely and for so long in the white mind with African Americans. Abortion and morality have also long had a racial lining to them in the popular consciousness.[60]

In Alabama, Republicans at all levels fought hard to overcome the Reconstruction stigma attached to their party label and to sell the modern GOP as the new party of white supremacy. Jim Martin railed about federal invasions and states' rights at every opportunity. Bill Dickinson filled the pages of the *Congressional Record* with attempts to discredit black voting rights by charging that interracial sex had occurred between the Montgomery-to-Selma marchers and thus invalidated their whole cause. In the late 1960s, Dickinson proposed a constitutional amendment to subject federal judges to a six-year review so as to exercise "some control" of the judiciary and defended Vice-President Spiro Agnew as misunderstood due to biased attacks from a "liberal media."[61] John Buchanan, a Baptist minister and U.S. congressman eventually unseated for being too moderate, damned the civil rights work of Martin Luther King Jr. and federal government interference in southern race relations "presided over by a vast, all-powerful bureaucracy in Washington."[62] Hubert Baughn's editorials in *Alabama* (and later *South*) not so subtly tied the civil rights cause to the concept of a primitive race of subhumans undeserving of basic civil or political rights. The editorials, and indeed even what passed for "news" text, routinely condemned the "savagery" of the civil rights movement, its "drumbeaters" and "gun-wielding savages" working for "uncivilized rights."[63] Assorted Republicans, disgusted with the Democratic Party's racial liberalism, branded civil rights protests as "unChristian," "treason," "Congo-like outbreaks," and "Demon-strations" that ran counter to the laws of God and man. One relatively new Republican, a Baptist preacher, energetically deplored the "civil rights hypocrites . . . hell raisers [and] Black savage revolutionaries" who had crammed such "bitter medicine . . . down the throats of decent law-respecting people in the South."[64]

Virtually any fruit of the civil rights movement received like treatment from the new Republican activists—damned as both heresy and treason in an approach that increasingly blurred the lines between church and state. To those most disgusted with the national Democrats' racial liberalism, the Civil Rights Act of 1964 was "satanic." Voting rights was a "blunder" that allowed "illiterates to vote by a mere 'touch of the pen.'" School integration was the "ultimate folly" that led to the closing of perfectly good schools simply "in order to satisfy the idiotic, egotistical and unreasonable whims of starry-eyed 'pseudo-intellectuals.'"[65] Guidelines on nondiscrimination in education from the Department of Health, Education, and Welfare were the orders of a federal "gestapo" that had the "odor of the carpetbagger" all over them.[66] The Equal Employment Opportunity Commission (EEOC) was a "big stick that the federal government place[d] at the hands of zealots. . . . [A]nytime a civil rights group or a Washington commission dedicated to the Negro's uplift by law or bayonet seeks a scapegoat—the South gets it. . . . [E]very time a Negro is turned down for a job . . . [the EEOC] drag[s] in the race question." The Great Society programs of Lyndon Johnson were a "Satanic Tyranny insidiously creeping over our nation and our family." "The only way to get out," a disgusted southerner advised, is to "get back to God."[67] "You cannot pour a half gallon into a half-pint," another Republican complained about the civil rights laws. "Neither can we create responsible citizens out of a rabble of savages barely removed from the jungle."[68] Liberal U.S. Supreme Court decisions were to blame, concluded another angry Republican, the kind that "have convinced an immature negro race, church and labor officials that they and their children are immune to local . . . laws."[69] GOP congressman John Buchanan provided representative Republican resentment against the Civil Rights Act of 1966 as the "latest . . . pet legislation of the Liberal Establishment . . . in fact more uncivil than civil." "Every section of this nation cries in dismay that this freedom-strangling legislation is not conducive to civic harmony and welfare," Buchanan complained. "Its compulsive nature would further regiment our nation. . . . The House was stampeded into consideration of [it] . . . under threats of ethnic revolution." What we really need, the Republican congressman preached, "is legislation to deal firmly with the agitators, demonstrators, commentators and mobsters who create strife and arouse racial hatred."[70] Conservative Democrats like Armistead Selden tried desperately to hang on by deploring the Civil Rights Act of 1966 as "the latest in . . . a long line of federal force bills [and] . . . civil agitation." Like many others, Selden eventually gave up and joined the GOP.[71]

Martin Luther King served as a lightning rod for modern Republican outrage over civil rights, often buttressed with righteous religious indignation. Just several decades later, in a new Republican South, "compassionate conservatism" would dictate ritualistic and public homage to the memory and dream of "Dr. King"—especially once a year, in January, on Martin Luther King Day. But such was hardly the case during the growing pains of the modern GOP. Disaffected Democrats, in transition to the Republican standard over race, denounced King in the most bitter terms that melded the political and the religious as "Mahatma Martin" and a "false prophet . . . in league with the devil."[72] Recent converts to the Republican Party damned King as "Martin Lucifer King" and mourned his "un-American phony civil rights and anti-Vietnam jackassery" as they deplored liberalism as one big conglomeration of racial anarchy and un-American, communistic war protest.[73] The pages of *South* cursed King as "Martin Luther King Cong . . . that preacher-agitator [from] . . . Atlanta . . . a ruthless agitator . . . a menace to law and order . . . [and] an avaricious . . . advocate of ill will." His followers were "outright Communists, bleeding hearts and political opportunists."[74] Baptist congressman John Buchanan blamed the rise of crime in America on "men like Dr. Martin Luther King and his insidious doctrine."[75] In 1966, upon seeing that Alabama voters had to pick between segregationist Democrat Lurleen (Mrs. George) Wallace and segregationist Republican Jim Martin—and that Georgians were also to choose between two segregationists, Democrat Lester Maddox and Republican Bo Callaway—Hubert Baughn rejoiced: "it would appear that Mahatma King and his disciples are all registered up with no place to go."[76]

At the end of the turbulent 1960s the *Alabama Independent,* mouthpiece of the Independent way station for transient Democrats on their way to the GOP, explained clearly how, in the South, race was the engine that drove the modern Republican Party:

> The Republican Party was just another dirty word since the days of Reconstruction . . . [until] the Communist traitors stealthily took over grandpa's old Democratic Party. When we finally awoke . . . we got mad, real mad . . . we even voted Republican. . . . [T]he younger generation . . . even join[ed] the Republican Party . . . [Republicans] went into office on this new wave of rebellion against the old "Liberal Establishment," which in the South, had taken the form of the old Democratic Party . . . [while] the country [had gone to] . . . the "One Worlders," Fabian Socialists and Communists into whose slimy hands it had fallen. . . . "One Worlders" . . . beg[an] their campaign of hate promoted by the mass news media against the White Christians in the South . . . the "Bible Belt" . . . conjur[ing] up an image of the typical White Southerner;

"nigger hating" ... "rednecks" "bigots." ... Their weapon? Naturally, the "Civil Rights" Movement ... Nazi-type legislation ... the festering sore of rebellion against all decency known as the "Civil Rights Movement" ... the race-baiting "Civil Rights Movement" ... the Communist-inspired "Civil Rights Movement!"[77]

Central to this politics and to the success of the GOP in the South was the Republican capture of the race issue away from the Democratic Party.[78] As long as George Wallace existed as a viable factor, GOP co-option of the race issue could never be complete—neither could their eclipse of the Democratic Party. Once Wallace was gone from the national scene (ca. 1972) and the liberalism of the national Democratic Party allowed the southern GOP to capture the race issue, the GOP was in the driver's seat in the South, at least in national elections. Once the national Democratic Party became identified with racial liberalism—first with Roosevelt and Truman, but decisively with the Kennedy brothers, Lyndon Johnson, and Hubert Humphrey—the Democratic Party in the South was put on the defensive and had to fight an increasingly rearguard action, especially when the leading Democrat and leading politician in the state, George Wallace, was clearly anything but in concert with the national Democratic Party, especially on the race issue.

And make no mistake, in Alabama the racial foundation has been in place for the Republican Party for some time now. In recent years the racial-political divide has become so stark that it is virtually accepted as common knowledge for many in the state. In much of the popular consciousness, the party split is first and foremost a racial split: the Democratic Party is the "party of blacks" and the Republican Party is the "party of whites."[79] On a street corner in Mobile, a white native—startled to learn that the white woman with whom she is conversing is a Democrat—blurts out: "My, I've never met a white person who voted for a Democrat!" At a tennis club in the hills of North Alabama, a local Republican activist is shocked to learn that a club member is also a Democrat. "You're a Democrat?" he asks her. "Be serious now. You're white, you can't be a Democrat." Across the state, candidates for political office bruise their heads against what can only be called a "color ceiling." White Democrats find the going especially rough. "I can't tell you how many [white] people came up to me during the campaign," a recent candidate for state office recounted, "and said, 'But you're white. How can you be a Democrat?' And I said, 'But I am!'" Other white Democratic candidates confirm the experience.[80]

From the Republican perspective, this polarization is not only real but a good thing. It is true that the state is not completely dominated by the GOP quite yet and that the racial split is not total. Patronage, family tradition, local dynamics, a few stubborn white liberals, and even the persistence of such a thing as a conservative "Alabama Democrat"—if the image is effectively conveyed—still exist and still preserve some Democratic allegiance and split tickets, especially at the county courthouse and state legislature. If a single, winning issue is ridden hard enough, combined with a mass black turnout—as in the 1998 "education lottery" gubernatorial race—Democratic victory on the state level is still possible. But this is a shrinking phenomenon.

In sum, the racial split has served the Alabama GOP well. State Republican Party chairman Marty Connors recently reported that Republicans own nearly three-quarters (and growing) of all political posts in the state, and, he gleefully predicted, soon "the Democrats" will have nothing to fight over except "the money of the plaintiff attorneys, [the] affection of labor leaders (not rank and file), Joe Reed and his ADC [the black Alabama Democratic Conference] . . . minority [voters] . . . and a handful of aging college professors." After explaining that the Republican primary was growing and growing, and the Democratic primary was becoming smaller and *blacker,* Connors unwittingly revealed much about his ideal definition of "Alabama" by gloating, "So, the democrat primary is looking less and less like Alabama . . . and ours is looking more and more."[81]

With the foundation of the race issue firmly in place, southern Republicans have been able to draw upon the powerful tradition in the South of evangelical religion, fundamentalist values, traditional family values, "100 percent Americanism" conformity, and super-patriotism to round out their newly ascendant "politics of emotion." To a large extent, Republican success in the South has been predicated on the party's ability to articulate these issues in such a simplistic way as to blur shades of gray and subsume any semblance of complexity.[82] As the national Democratic Party supported the civil rights movement, the modern GOP increasingly profited in the South. And while the *ideology* of the old "Reconstruction Syndrome"—with its prohibitions against racial equality, liberalism, Yankee activism, and a grasping federal government—remained compelling in the 1960s (perhaps more so than ever), the *language* of the syndrome grew increasingly inappropriate to a Republican-dominated South. Because the Reconstruction Syndrome had arisen in response to Abraham Lincoln and, later, Radical Republican sponsorship of abolition, black suffrage, and the First Reconstruction, the language of the syndrome was filled with unflattering references to rascally "carpetbaggers" and scoundrelly "scalawags"—Republicans all—as the chief villains in the South's ongoing morality play. Growing Republican success in the 1960s South, however, rendered this language ill-suited, although the hallowed ideas it represented had never been more powerful. The answer was the morphing of the Reconstruction Syndrome into a politics of emotion. Same ideas, different lexicon—with a Republican twist of religion and morality thrown into the mix.[83]

The result has been a maximum resonance with southern sensibilities on what may be called the "Holy Trinity" of southern politics: God, country, and race. It is a simple language, devoid of complexity, that all white southerners, regardless of class, education, or knowledge of specific issues, can parrot—indeed, had been accustomed to speaking for so long, only with a conservative Democratic accent. In the southern GOP's new emotional language, the modern Democratic Party came to be understood as the party of undesirables: "niggers, queers, and atheists."[84] Gone was any distinction between protesting an unjust war in Vietnam and being unpatriotic—even treasonous. Erased was any difference between tolerating alternative lifestyles, believing that gay Americans should have civil liberties, and desiring the eradication of the traditional family and wanting to see everyone in America become a homosexual. Lost was any realization that those who stand against compulsory prayer in schools do not, by definition, hate God and want to erode the Judeo-Christian ethic and end Western civilization itself. Some of them might happen to be religious (Christians, in fact), value religious freedom and pluralism, and believe that a separation of church and state is worth preserving. Obliterated was any distinction between those who believe in a woman's right to choose and the advocation of abortion as a common contraceptive. Glossed over was any cognizance that advocates of background checks and bans on assault weapons may not be at all interested in the complete abolition of firearms from the country. Buried were any differences between those who favored spending on Social Security, Medicare, and other social programs and Socialists—or worse yet, Communists—unpatriotic, subversive traitors all, bent on the overthrow of the Republic.[85] The politics of guilt by association and the slippery slope have seldom enjoyed more potency than in the modern Republican South since 1948.

And more, it is important to realize that little of this has been by accident. Republican-style racial politics have taken powerful hold in Dixie, but not without considerable effort. In 1964, Alabama Republican chieftain John Grenier apparently sent an army of operatives throughout the small towns of the South—to cafeterias, barbershops, laundromats, hair salons, and the like—to talk up how voting for a Democrat would mean the racial apocalypse, and how voting for Republicans like Barry Goldwater was the South's only salvation. The Republican moles studiously avoided making public appearances or giving newspaper interviews, instead sowing rumors that the Democratic fair-employment law would mean laying off white millworkers and that the public accommodations measure would mean small-town shops and businesses overrun with black customers. The efforts continued even after George Wallace dropped out of the race, resulting in small towns throughout the South being in a very "ugly mood" when representatives of the Johnson-Humphrey ticket arrived to campaign.[86]

Weighing the career of H. Lee Atwater, the modern GOP's ultimate strategist and campaign activist, makes this point very clear. Some have credited, or debited as the case may be, Atwater for being the creator of negative campaigning in American politics. But, like George Wallace, Atwater was not an originator or a pioneer, only the most influential and seminal of American political strategists in the modern era. A South Carolina native, Atwater was a neo-Confederate student of Sun Tzu, Niccolo Machiavelli, and several Confederate generals who learned his racial politics at the knee of fellow South Carolinians Strom Thurmond and Harry Dent, and who ended leaving his legacy to protégés who today number among the GOP's top strategists: Mary Matalin, Tucker Eskew, and Karl Rove. Manic, obsessive, and a remarkably charismatic individual, Atwater had a passion for junk food, distance running, Tabasco sauce, and playing the guitar. He poured his considerable talent and energy into manipulating perceptions over reality, emotion over thought, and preying on the most divisive and intense passions he could arouse in the electorate—and was unapologetic about doing so. "Republicans in the South could not win elections by talking about issues," he forthrightly acknowledged. "You had to make the case that the other candidate was a bad guy." And nobody did this better than Atwater. Doing field research on what he affectionately called "swing voters," Atwater concentrated on feelings and negative images, as he frequented bars, Waffle Houses, and massage parlors to find out what the masses wanted to hear and to make politics "more consumer driven, in touch with the customer/voter." For Atwater and the new Republican politics, it was all about perception over reality, and using mass media to manipulate those perceptions. "It's not what happens to us that matters," Atwater concluded according to his empathetic biographer, "it's how we *interpret* what happens to us. The interpretation establishes an attitude, which can then be catered to emotionally. Therefore, the political goal was to get in front of the interpretation—mental crowd control: *When we want your opinion, we'll give it to you!*" Perception, Atwater believed, was far stronger than reality. A master at using impressionistic images and symbols, he was steadfast in his belief that once a perception was established, it "can't be busted up even with opinion changes on specific issues that my opponent might accomplish."[87]

Central in all of this was a fairly low estimation of the political instincts and acumen of the average voter, Atwater's critical "swing voters." According to Atwater's biographer, the "average voter could absorb only a limited amount of information about his candidate, Lee thought, and should never be bewildered with specifics. The average voter was kind of slow, actually—would perceive facts as ideas.... So you could throw fact after fact at a voter ... who might never be able to connect the dots." "The National Enquirer readership is the exact voter I'm talking about," Atwater quipped. "I've learned a lot about politics simply by going to wrestling matches." As Atwater saw his job in 1988, he had to push George H. W. Bush's candidacy by "tap[ping] voters' emotions instead of their brains" by finding the one "specific example, the outrageous abuse, the easy-to-digest tale that made listeners *feel*—usually repulsion—rather than *think*." Enter Willie Horton. Later, on his cancer deathbed at the age of forty, Atwater apologized for the infamous ad (Harry Dent would insist that he had *repented* rather than apologized)—and, to a degree, turned his back on the whole way of doing politics that he had lifted to an art form as chairman of the national Republican Party. "I do think that we can end strident personality campaigning," he wrote to one of the earliest southern Democratic victims of his style, "and that we can change the nature of American politics and make it geometrically more positive than it has been the last few years simply by cutting a lot of the bullshit, getting sincere, honest solutions to critical problems, and not insulting the American electorate." Unfortunately, it appears that Atwater's ultimate legacy was the opposite of this late wish. One of his earlier prognostications was far more accurate: that the GOP would consolidate its power in the South as "the first step in the process of building a national Republican majority ... by the year 2000."[88]

With the base of racism taken from Dixie's old conservative Democrats and planted firmly in the soil of a new Republican South, the southern GOP has been able to make itself invincible by fusing together different strains of traditional southern culture and values: white supremacy, anti-federalism, xenophobia, anti-liberalism, laissez-faire economics, religious fundamentalism, traditional gender roles, super-patriotism, isolationism and jingoism, traditional moral conformity, and so forth. The party's strategists have been able to fuse these elements onto the central adhesive of race. This, of course, was a central part of the 1920s Klan program, so popular in the South, the Midwest, and the West, and so fundamental to the 1928 Hoovercrat bolt on behalf of the GOP. In modern terms, the southern GOP has translated it into issues such as opposition to anything or anyone that challenged or differed from traditional American and family values, and has done so in a way that frequently strains the limits of logical connection.[89] Calls for respect for people being called African Americans, Native Americans, Asian Americans, and the like were not seen as a celebration of diverse heritage and cultural pluralism but rather as a threat to the dominant white, Anglo-Saxon, Protestant culture, as politically correct hyphenated Americanism run amok. The proposed Equal Rights Amendment, women's rights, feminism, and gender equity was not seen as an equity and justice issue but as a threat to traditional gender roles and family values based, in part, on the Bible. Global peacekeeping missions and the United Nations were targeted, as in the 1920s heyday of the KKK, as evidence of an international "one-world" conspiracy and a threat to American sovereignty and ethnic purity. Much of the recent anti-French and anti-UN feeling over the 2003 Iraq War would have warmed the hearts of Barry Goldwater's John Birch supporters, once derided along with their candidate as "extremist." Insistence on conformity with traditional moral values, the pro-life position, and general Bible thumping and flag waving became synonymous with the preservation of traditional American values and an increasing impatience with any form of religious, ethnic, or cultural pluralism. While values such as these may not play well back in Peoria, they play every evening to sold-out crowds in Dixie. Kevin Phillips had put it this way back in 1968: "[John] Wayne may sound bad to people in New York, but he sounds great to the schmucks we're trying to reach through John Wayne. The people down there along the Yahoo Belt."[90] The resemblances between the program of "100 percent Americanism" of the 1920s KKK (including its infatuation with white supremacy and moral conformity) and the "neo-Kluxism" of the modern GOP are more than merely striking—they are family cousins. And it was no accident that in 1928 the Klan-backed Hoovercrat movement nearly took Alabama for the Republican Party, and might have were it not for widespread fraud and irregularities in the Black Belt.

As the internet and cable television have revolutionized media, it has grown even easier to cater to the desire for simplicity in our lives—even in our politics. The proliferation of cable channels, AM stations, and internet websites has, paradoxically, contributed to a growing political isolation wherein citizens are capable of becoming media consumers who pick and choose a menu of ideas—seemingly legitimate because of their existence as "published" media—that serve instead to reinforce existing prejudices and partial understandings while insulating the consumer from annoying information that might contradict deeply held prior views. Along with the proliferation has come a steady drumbeat from the political Right about the unreliability and "liberal" bias of mainstream media. Faced by this relentless assault, venues of traditional media have shown signs of succumbing to the "Limbaugh Effect." Horrified at the thought of being criticized as "the liberal media," these outlets have gone out of their way to make time and space for the most extreme faces associated with what was previously considered the Far Right.[91] The entry of the Religious Right into politics further dichotomized modern political discourse, granting it almost the tenor of a millennial struggle between good and evil, righteousness and wickedness, with clear lines drawn between virtue and wickedness. In such a worldview, almost no tactic was placed off limits in the waging and winning of a political holy war.

The price of simplicity, though, is considerable. As our culture has grown more complex and fast-paced, people have less and less time, money, interest, energy, educational expertise, or even inclination to study political issues on their own. In such a culture, many people want their politics simple—"fast-food politics" to go. They just do not have the time for, or interest in, complexity and nuance. In the South, the modern Republican Party has mastered the art of giving the people what they want, simple issues with clear-cut heroes and villains: people who love life versus baby-killers; believers versus the godless; patriots versus traitors and evildoers; responsible taxpayers versus lazy parasites and "welfare queens."[92]

Today, many Republicans, in the South and elsewhere, would bristle with indignation at the suggestion that the modern emergence of their party, particularly in the South, has been based largely on racial and other forms of intolerance. Many would not consider themselves racists in a personal sense—and many certainly are not. Still, the lines of continuity that stretch from the disfranchisement movement and the second KKK to the modern GOP are clear—at least in Alabama. And the line from the GOP co-option of the race issue away from the Democratic Party is also clear. Without the race issue, the GOP was not a serious factor in southern politics. With it—fortified by other emotional and moral issues—the party is dominant.

On August 1, 2000, Condoleezza Rice ascended the dais at the Republican National Convention in Philadelphia. A forty-two-year-old African American woman and the former provost of Stanford University, Rice appeared as a well-known authority on foreign-policy issues and a rumored cabinet member should Republican candidate George W. Bush win the presidency. More importantly, she was present at the convention to speak as a young, intelligent, articulate black woman—a native of Birmingham, Alabama, no less—whose presence and Republican convictions were on display to persuade African American voters to leave the Democratic Party to which they had been overwhelmingly faithful since 1936. Rice's appearance at the Republican convention—along with those of General Colin Powell, George P. Bush (the Hispanic son of Florida governor Jeb Bush), and Chaka Khan and other minority singers and entertainers—was a thinly veiled attempt to convince minorities to vote Republican, to accept the warmer, fuzzier, inclusive Republican rhetoric of "compassionate conservatism," "Leave No Child Behind," and "uniter not divider" put forth by George W. Bush and his handlers.[93] Rice explained her allegiance to the GOP in terms of her Alabama roots. Her father, she told the convention—and, by extension, the country—had been denied the right to vote in 1952 Alabama by Democrats. Ever since, Rice said, she had looked to the Republican Party for inclusion.[94] Her message was clear: millions of African Americans should now look to the GOP for meaningful political participation as well.

Rice's exposition, while partially accurate in a technical sense, could not have amounted to a more perverse distortion of reality. Southern white Democrats, like the very registrars who had disfranchised her father and other blacks in 1952 Alabama, also left the Democratic Party—first in trickles in 1948, then in droves during the 1950s and 1960s—to form the heart, soul, and much of the sinew and flesh of the new Republican majority in the former Confederate states. Moreover, the new Solid *Republican* South—in which a Democrat (unless he was named George Wallace) found it increasingly difficult to win election, also made up the strongest part of the emerging Republican majority across America outlined so prophetically by conservative politico Kevin Phillips.

In fact, the Republican Party in places like Rice's home state of Alabama had been politically anemic from Reconstruction until 1952, identified in the popular consciousness as the "party of Lincoln" that had enabled—with the assistance of federal bayonets—incompetent blacks and corrupt carpetbaggers and scalawags to put the prostrate South through nine circles of hell. Not until the "bolt" of 1928 and, to a far greater extent, the "Dixiecrat" revolt of 1948 did the Republican Party learn how to play the politics of race. As the national Democratic Party became increasingly identified with the racial liberalism and civil rights initiatives of John and Robert Kennedy, Lyndon Johnson, and Hubert Humphrey, the southern GOP capitalized on white backlash. Once it claimed the mantle of the "party of white supremacy," the Republican Party was on its way to dominance in the South. One by one, high-profile conservative southern Democrats repudiated their party and embraced the GOP—conversions that represented thousands of rank-and-file Democrats moving to the Republican Party: Strom Thurmond and Albert Watson in South Carolina, Tom Abernethy, Jim Martin, and Jabo Waggoner in Alabama, Jesse Helms in North Carolina, Trent Lott in Mississippi, Leander Perez and David Duke in Louisiana, Phil Gram in Texas, Bo Callaway in Georgia, and many others. By the 1990s, even George Wallace considered himself a Republican.[95] Harry Dent and Richard Nixon's subtly racist "Southern Strategy" and Lee Atwater's cynical use of race on behalf of Ronald Reagan and George Bush were wildly successful in Dixie. Republican presidential candidates, for example, have grown stronger and stronger in Condi Rice's Alabama ever since 1952—the year Democratic registrars did not allow her father to vote.[96] In recent elections, Republicans have failed miserably with black voters in Dixie yet won an overwhelming percentage of the white vote. In 1984 only 12 percent of white Alabamians voted for Democratic presidential candidate Walter Mondale, while 88 percent went for Ronald Reagan. Black percentages in Alabama were exactly the opposite. In 1988, George Bush got 70 percent of Alabama's white vote; Democrat Michael Dukakis received 78 percent of the state's black vote. In 1992 and 1996, respectively, Bill Clinton received 85 and 92 percent of the state's black vote. Alabama's racial divide in electoral politics has only sharpened in recent years. In the 2000 election, Al Gore won a virtually impossible 98 percent of Alabama's black vote, while George W. Bush won almost 80 percent of the state's white vote.[97] The strongest Gore county in the United States was located in Alabama's Black Belt.[98]

At a national level, Republican opposition to integration, busing, affirmative action, crime, welfare, slave reparations, bans on racial profiling, and, in some instances, even an apology for slavery, and many other issues—as well as the prominence of famously intolerant Republicans the stripe of Jerry Falwell, Pat Robertson, Pat Buchanan, Strom Thurmond, Jesse Helms, Bob Barr, Newt Gingrich, David Duke, John Ashcroft, Dick Armey, and Tom DeLay, not to mention Rush Limbaugh and an army of national and local imitators—have kept Republicans and their defense of white supremacy foremost in the minds of both white southerners and black voters. The Trent Lott fiasco was merely the loudest and most recent to do so—and the one with the most serious potential repercussions for costing the GOP any shot at the exponentially growing Latino minority vote.[99] In the past eleven presidential elections, over four decades' worth, Alabama has gone for the regular Democratic presidential candidate only one time. That was in 1976 (and it was reasonably close) when a neighboring Georgia boy headed the Democratic ticket.[100]

There is much to suggest that modern Republican dominance of the South—and, by extension, the nation—has been built on the back of white supremacy, racism, and emotional intolerance. In fact, modern Republican dominance in Alabama—and by inference the South, and by further inference the nation—appears to have been built upon a firm but very ugly foundation, the ultimate kind of white flight in reaction to the civil rights movement. In Alabama there are spiritual and direct links to the disfranchisement constitution of 1901, the Ku Klux Klan of the 1920s, the Dixiecrats of 1948, and the Wallacism of the 1960s. Disfranchisement, the KKK, Dixiecrats, and George Wallace—as unfortunate as it is, these are among the most elemental building blocks of the modern Republican Party in the South—in some respects, they are more important than any others. The maintenance of white supremacy has been the ultimate determinant of the character of the "Solid South" politically. Stated another way: whichever party managed to capture the race issue—to defend white supremacy ("out-nigger" the other party, in Wallace's crude phrasing)—would control the South. Ultimately, it is within this important context that the civil rights struggles which roiled in the 1940s and 1950s South should be understood.

Southern politics is not now—nor has it ever been, predominantly—about politics. It's about culture. This is the great irony of southern politics (and increasingly about American politics as well): that most people in the South are fueled by *cultural* dictates, not *political* ones.

This thesis has found expression in various ways over the decades: the power of the "Reconstruction Syndrome," the salience of a "politics of emotion," the resonance of "God and country" issues, the portability of the "New Racism," the continued strength of a race-based and morality-based political and social conformity, the relevance of a "fast-food politics," and the perpetual power of perception over reality. At root, despite their differences in emphasis and in time period, all of these things are about culture: what is the predominant culture in the South, and what is presented by its elite as the dominant culture. Race has long served as the vital core for this cultural orthodoxy, but the outer layers are cultural in their essence as well—prevailing regional orthodoxies on class, gender and sex, religion, war, patriotism, jingoism, morality, nativism and xenophobia, taxes, and the federal government.

In such a polity, cultural IQ matters much more than knowledge about actual policies or matters of governance. For the bulk of the citizenry, knowledge of what constitutes the "southern way of life" is enough to know how to stand on civil rights. Cognizance of what comprises regional mores on religion, not constitutional requisites, is sufficient for voters to form a position on school prayer or display of the Ten Commandments—and to demand elected officials to do the same.[101] For the Lee Atwaters of the world it is enough to know how people *perceive* candidates and character rather than any correlation with actual reality or the electorate's knowledge of a real issue. In the white, male, rural, working-class culture of the new important voting cadre of "NASCAR Dads," it is enough to perceive that voting for Democrats is "for wooses" and that the Democrats are somehow "out of control."[102] No actual knowledge about a specific policy, or how what was once Goldwater-era extremism has been converted into present-day mainstream conservatism, need be necessary.[103]

At root this state of affairs reveals an ugly but important truth about much of our democracy in the twentieth and twenty-first centuries. It makes plain that once the two major political parties stopped being Tweedledum and Tweedledee on race, once one of the major parties actually tried to make the country live up to part of its founding creed of "equal rights for all," it doomed itself to electoral defeat and, according to some, increasing irrelevance. The ascendance of "The Social Issue," as Scammon and Wattenberg dubbed it, did not bespeak the essential wisdom of the electorate. On the contrary, it revealed a fundamental and difficult truth about much of white America—perhaps a majority. Both white ethnic northerners and white southerners were a lot more comfortable with a racially, ethnically, and sexually exclusive polity, society, and economy—even those whites who do not partake in a significant way in the economic rewards associated with this status quo—than in striving toward a genuinely inclusive America. This truth reveals that "the people"—far from comprising a wise and moderating influence in politics—have too often been, especially once mass media and modern religion caught up to the elite rhetoric, ever susceptible to a demagogy that preys on their most primal and irrational fears, jealousies, prejudices, and emotions. As a country and as a people, we have not been the better for it.

Notes

FOREWORD

1. W. E. B. Du Bois, "The Heart of the South," *Crisis,* May 1917, 18.
2. See, e.g., John Dittmer, *Black Georgia in the Progressive Era, 1900–1920* (Urbana: University of Illinois Press, 1980); Robin D. G. Kelley, *Hammer and Hoe: Alabama Communists during the Great Depression* (Chapel Hill: University of North Carolina Press, 1990); Tera Hunter, *To 'Joy My Freedom: Southern Black Women's Lives and Labors after the Civil War* (Cambridge: Harvard University Press, 1997); Leon F. Litwack, *Trouble in Mind: Black Southerners in the Age of Jim Crow* (New York: Knopf, 1998); William Chafe, Raymond Gavins, and Robert Korstad, eds., *Remembering Jim Crow: African Americans Tell about Life in the Segregated South* (New York: New Press, 2001).

PROLOGUE

1. Charles W. Eagles, "New Histories of the Civil Rights Era," *Journal of Southern History* 66 (November 2000): 815–49; Charles M. Payne, "The Social Construction of History," in *I've Got the Light of Freedom: The Organizing Tradition and the Mississippi Freedom Struggle* (Berkeley: University of California Press, 1995), 413–41; Steven F. Lawson, "Freedom Then, Freedom Now: The Historiography of the Civil Rights Movement," *American Historical Review* 96 (April 1991): 456–71; Adam Fairclough, "Historians and the Civil Rights Movement," *Journal of American Studies* 24 (December 1990): 387–98; George Rehin, "Of Marshalls, Myrdals, and Kings: Some Recent Books about the Second Reconstruction," *Journal of American Studies* 22 (April 1988): 87–103; and Dan T. Carter, "From Segregation to Integration," in *Interpreting Southern History: Historiographical Essays in Honor of Sanford W. Higginbotham,* ed. John B. Boles and Evelyn Thomas Nolen (Baton Rouge: Louisiana State University Press, 1987), 408–33.

The civil rights movement as a "black freedom struggle" is most closely associated with the work of Clayborne Carson. See Carson, "Civil Rights Reform and the Black Freedom Struggle," in *The Civil Rights Movement in America*, ed. Charles W. Eagles (Jackson: University Press of Mississippi, 1986), esp. 23, 27; and Carson, *In Struggle: SNCC and the Black Awakening of the 1960s* (Cambridge: Harvard University Press, 1981). "Black initiative" in the movement is also discussed in Armstead L. Robinson and Patricia Sullivan's "Introduction: Reassessing the History of the Civil Rights Movement," in *New Directions in Civil Rights Studies*, ed. Armstead L. Robinson and Patricia Sullivan (Charlottesville: University Press of Virginia, 1991), 1–7, esp. 6. A recent work that effectively studies the national and local movements is Glenn T. Eskew, *But for Birmingham: The Local and National Movements in the Civil Rights Struggle* (Chapel Hill: University of North Carolina Press, 1997). Two that address the tie between economic issues and civil rights are Diane McWhorter, *Carry Me Home: Birmingham, Alabama; The Climactic Battle of the Civil Rights Revolution* (New York: Simon and Schuster, 2001); and Susan Youngblood Ashmore, "Carry It On: The Civil Rights Movement and the War on Poverty in Alabama, 1964–1969" (Ph.D. diss., Auburn University, 1999). Recent studies also examine the role of music in the movement: see Brian Ward, *Just My Soul Responding: Rhythm and Blues, Black Consciousness, and Race Relations* (Berkeley: University of California Press, 1998), and Timothy B. Tyson, *Radio Free Dixie: Robert F. Williams and the Roots of Black Power* (Chapel Hill: University of North Carolina Press, 1999). Several focus on the critical intersection between religion and civil rights: see Mark Newman, *Getting Right with God: Southern Baptists and Desegregation, 1945–1995* (Tuscaloosa: University of Alabama Press, 2001); Charles Marsh, *God's Long Summer: Stories of Faith and Civil Rights* (Princeton: Princeton University Press, 1997); and Andrew Michael Manis, *A Fire You Can't Put Out: The Civil Rights Life of Birmingham's Fred Shuttlesworth* (Tuscaloosa: University of Alabama Press, 1999). David L. Chappell's intriguing work has addressed religion as well as the role of native-born southerners in the movement, persons he calls *Inside Agitators: White Southerners in the Civil Rights Movement* (Baltimore: Johns Hopkins University Press, 1996); see also his "A Stone of Hope: Prophetic Religion, Liberalism, and the Death of Jim Crow," *Journal of the Historical Society* 3 (March 2003): 129–62, and "Religious Ideas of the Segregationists," *Journal of American Studies* 32 (1998): 45–72. Steven F. Lawson and Charles Payne's *Debating the Civil Rights Movement, 1945–1968* (Lanham, Md.: Rowman and Littlefield, 2000) is an introduction to the movement framed around questions of the importance of governmental involvement versus grassroots activism. A magisterial study by J. Mills Thornton III explores the intersection between municipal politics and the movement: *Dividing Lines: Municipal Politics and the Struggle for Civil Rights in Montgomery, Birmingham, and Selma* (Tuscaloosa: University of Alabama Press, 2002). Among the leading works on Martin Luther King Jr. and his role in the movement are David J. Garrow, *Bearing the Cross: Martin Luther King, Jr., and the Southern Christian Leadership Conference* (New York: Morrow, 1986); Taylor Branch, *Parting the Waters: America in the King Years, 1954–63* (New York: Simon and Schuster, 1988); and Adam Fairclough, *To Redeem the Soul of America: The Southern Christian Leadership Conference and Martin Luther King, Jr.* (Athens: University of Georgia Press, 1987).

2. August Meier paid a good deal of attention to the "antecedents" of the modern civil rights struggle in his "Epilogue: Toward a Synthesis of Civil Rights History," 211–24, as do Robinson and Sullivan themselves in their "Introduction," 6, both in Robinson and Sullivan, *New Directions in Civil Rights Studies*. Vincent Harding's and Martha Norman's chapters in the same book suggest a long-term view of the struggle, with the classic 1954–65 decade understood as a highlight. Dan T. Carter, Steven F. Lawson, and Charles W. Eagles, in their later historiographical essays, all recommend that work be done on the pre-1954 phases. See also Manning Marable, *Race, Reform, and Rebellion: The Second Reconstruction in Black America, 1945–1982* (Jackson: University Press of Mississippi, 1984).

3. Examples include John Dittmer, *Local People: The Struggle for Civil Rights in Mississippi* (Urbana: University of Illinois Press, 1994); John Egerton, *Speak Now against the Day: The Generation before the Civil Rights Movement in the South* (New York: Knopf, 1994); Adam Fairclough, *Race and Democracy: The Civil Rights Struggle in Louisiana, 1915–1972* (Athens: University of Georgia Press, 1995); Patricia Sullivan, *Days of Hope: Race and Democracy in the New Deal Era* (Chapel Hill: University of North Carolina Press, 1996); and Stephen G. N. Tuck, *Beyond Atlanta: The Struggle for Racial Equality in Georgia, 1940–1980* (Athens: University of Georgia Press, 2001).

4. I discussed this idea of the "two sides of the civil rights coin" earlier in several places. See Glenn Feldman, "The Ku Klux Klan in Alabama, 1915–1954" (Ph.D. diss., first draft, Auburn University, 1996), 682, 741; Feldman, "Review of Kimberley L. Phillips, *AlabamaNorth: African-American Migrants, Community, and Working-Class Activism in Cleveland, 1915–1945*," *Labor History* 41 (August 2000): 366–67; and Feldman, "Introduction: The Pursuit of Southern History," in *Reading Southern History: Essays on Interpreters and Interpretations*, ed. Glenn Feldman (Tuscaloosa: University of Alabama Press, 2001), 9. Other scholars have, of course, more generally emphasized the importance of looking at southern white racial attitudes and behavior to better understand the civil rights movement. See, e.g., Lawson, "Freedom Then, Freedom Now," 466; Eagles, "New Histories," 842–43; and J. Mills Thornton III, "Challenge and Response in the Montgomery Bus Boycott of 1955–1956," *Alabama Review* 33 (July 1980): 163–235 (reprinted in *The Walking City: The Montgomery Bus Boycott, 1955–1956*, ed. David J. Garrow [Brooklyn: Carlson, 1989], 323–79). August Meier, in an effort to undermine the classic 1954–65 periodization of the drive for civil rights, paradoxically and unwittingly contributed to periodization of the movement by freezing white backlash in the 1950s. He implied that notable "Southern white backlash" to the movement only "came after the cresting of the postwar threats to freedom of speech epitomized by McCarthyism" ("Epilogue," 216).

5. This complaint is being increasingly heard in various forms. Paul M. Gaston's new afterword to his republished classic, *The New South Creed: A Study in Southern Myth-making* (1970; reprint, Montgomery: NewSouth Books, 2002), laments how easily the conservative South refigured its New South Creed to accommodate the results of the civil rights movement. Diane McWhorter, Pulitzer Prize–winning author of *Carry Me Home*, ends her lectures around the country

by concluding that "in a sense, the segregationists won," as evidenced by the dominance of a modern Republican South. Diane McWhorter to author, e-mail, November 11, 2002.

6. I discussed the "Reconstruction Syndrome" in *Reading Southern History*, 5–6, and in *Politics, Society, and the Klan in Alabama, 1915–1949* (Tuscaloosa: University of Alabama Press, 1999), 75, 187, 327. Rev. J. M. Glenn of Union Springs, Alabama, a Methodist preacher for sixty-nine years, supplied a representative example of "Reconstruction Syndrome" thought and language in a 1957 diatribe against civil rights: "The negro agitator [Martin Luther] King and his wife," "so-called 'Democrats' of the Northern socialist kind" who made "Moscow rejoice," and "various agitators . . . brought ill will and division" by their civil rights activities, "where before there was [only] peace and good will between the races." Instead of King and other "Negro preachers [who] are the leaders in the work of agitation," Rev. Glenn expressed his preference for Booker T. Washington, George Washington Carver, Robert R. Moton, and other "worthy leaders . . . [who] taught real racial pride" and did not incite "one-tenth of the people in this nation (colored)" to try to "dominate a nation of 160 million." Glenn traced his present disgust with the national Democratic Party and civil rights "agitators" to Reconstruction. "Though then a child," the minister wrote, "I have very vivid recollections of Reconstruction Days. We had hoped such days were in the past, but dirty and unprincipled politicians are again at work . . . call[ing] for federal bayonets to enforce racial mixing on trains, buses, in schools, housing, etc." J. M. Glenn to editor, *South: The News Magazine of Dixie*, January 21, 1957, 4. For an example of economically conservative and white supremacist beliefs fused together and understood as American ideas "upon which this nation was built," see John C. Sheffield, "The Second Secession," February 1937, box 2, folder 5, Frank M. Dixon Personal Papers, Alabama Department of Archives and History, Montgomery.

7. Feldman, *Reading Southern History*, 6, 364.

8. The subtlety of modern racial appeals is a major theme in Earl Black and Merle Black, *The Rise of Southern Republicans* (Cambridge: Belknap Press, Harvard, 2002). It is also addressed in Thomas Byrne Esdall and Mary D. Esdall, *Chain Reaction: The Impact of Race, Rights, and Taxes on American Politics* (1991; New York: Norton, 1992), 19, 27, 28.

9. On the embarrassment to the GOP of the Trent Lott controversy, see, e.g., Jim VandeHei, "Lott Says Bush Aides Undermine Bid to Stay," *Washington Post*, December 19, 2002; Pay Murphy, "Cynical Politics, Not Virtue, Ousted Lott," *Idaho Mountain Express*, December 24–30, 2002; and Thomas Sowell, "Lott Is Too Much" and "Lott, Race, and Hypocrisy: Part I," both in www.jewishworldreview.com and www.NewsAndOpinion.com, December 13 and 17, 2002. The "New Racism" so permeates some sections of the South that even first- and second-graders in some southern Catholic parochial schools knew nothing about the 2000 presidential election except that "Al Gore is a baby killer, Al Gore is a baby killer." Notes from conversation with PW, the mother of an elementary school student and active member of the parish Our Lady of Sorrows Catholic Church, Birmingham, Alabama, January 24, 2003.

10. This point obviously relates to the recent outpouring of literature on

"whiteness." A discussion of this literature is beyond the scope of this study. Readers should see recent overviews of the subject, e.g., Peter Kolchin, "Whiteness Studies: The New History of Race in America," *Journal of American History* 89 (June 2002): 54–73.

11. The starting point for understanding this period is still several classic works: C. Vann Woodward, *Origins of the New South, 1877–1913* (Baton Rouge: Louisiana State University Press, 1951); George Brown Tindall, *The Emergence of the New South, 1913–1945* (Baton Rouge: Louisiana State University Press, 1967); and Paul M. Gaston, *The New South Creed: A Study in Southern Myth-making* (New York: Knopf, 1970). See also Edward L. Ayers, *The Promise of the New South: Life after Reconstruction* (Chapel Hill: University of North Carolina Press, 1992). In the postbellum South, white supremacy, segregation, caste, and the rest of it in its particulars (lynching, peonage, sharecropping, tenancy, convict-lease, disfranchisement, the KKK, and vigilante terror) contained both racial and economic elements because these enforcement mechanisms were an essential part of the apparatus and machinery of a mutually supporting, self-reinforcing, symbiotic relationship and system between race and class. Jim Crow and racism kept black economic prospects at a depressed level. They limited the educational opportunities, and thus economic opportunities, for blacks and preserved white economic superiority, which, in turn, was used by many whites precisely as a rationale to justify the maintenance of white supremacy and the further suppression of black fortunes in a vicious cycle of race and class. As a result, white supremacy brought tangible, material benefits to whites—in addition to the psychological and emotional benefits of feeling membership in a superior status and culture. Whites of all kinds benefited and thus had a rational stake and claim in the preservation of white supremacy, Jim Crow, and disfranchisement.

12. See, e.g., Daniel Letwin, *The Challenge of Interracial Unionism: Alabama, 1878–1921* (Chapel Hill: University of North Carolina Press, 1998); Brian Kelly, *Race, Class, and Power in the Alabama Coalfields, 1908–21* (Urbana: University of Illinois Press, 2001).

13. Recent work on lynching includes W. Fitzhugh Brundage, *Lynching in the New South: Georgia and Virginia, 1880–1930* (Urbana: University of Illinois Press, 1993); Stewart E. Tolnay and E. M. Beck, *A Festival of Violence: An Analysis of the Lynching of African Americans in the South, 1882–1930* (Urbana: University of Illinois Press, 1995); and James H. Madison, *A Lynching in the Heartland: Race and Memory in America* (New York: Palgrave, 2001).

14. Sheldon Hackney, *Populism to Progressivism in Alabama* (Princeton: Princeton University Press, 1969); William Warren Rogers Sr., *The One-Gallused Rebellion: Agrarianism in Alabama, 1865–1896* (Baton Rouge: Louisiana State University Press, 1970); Lawrence Goodwyn, *The Populist Moment: A Short History of the Agrarian Revolt in America* (New York: Oxford University Press, 1978).

15. An example of this type of member of the black middle class was Rev. P. Colfax Rameau, Ph.D., "race leader" and grand president of the Southern Federation of Afro-American Industrial Brotherhood. Rameau, whose organization was heavily subsidized by Birmingham's industrial interests, preached, literally, against organized labor. The United Mine Workers (UMW), for Rameau, was a "bolshevist labor organization that is seeking to drive my people out of the

mines and the state" even though it was one of the very few organizations in the South even attempting some form of biracial cooperation. During a 1920–21 coal strike, he lobbied against this "band of bolshevist labor barons" trying to "plunder and devastate" Alabama's rich mineral deposits. "God's only Son came and taught to 'Render unto Caesar that which is Caesar's,'" the minister preached, but the UMW says "if I can't rule, I will devastate murder and ruin." Rev. P. Colfax Rameau, Ph.D., to Governor Thomas E. Kilby, October 14, 1920, file: Coal Strike Sept.–Nov. 1920, drawer 2, Alabama's Governors Papers, Thomas E. Kilby, Alabama Department of Archives and History, Montgomery.

16. There were also psychological and emotional bases of racism, of course. Some illustrate the ties between race and class: a type of class-based racism. Many elite whites took comfort in what can only be called a social Darwinist conception of class-based racism. That is, they chose to believe that they, as white elites, were wealthier and more privileged because of their native and inherited superior intelligence, hard work, thrift, industry, innovation, the capacity to "lift themselves up by their bootstraps," and the entrepreneurial spirit—not because they had inherited wealth, education, or start-up capital from parents or grandparents. Thus they were the "deserving rich," and poor whites and blacks were, conversely, the "deserving poor," who were poor because they were less intelligent and did not adhere to the time-honored traits of hard work, industry, thrift, innovation, and entrepreneurialism. A challenge to this worldview also posed a challenge to the legitimacy of their place at the apex of such a society—and to the ultimate Grand Designer of nature itself. Many poor and working-class whites also adhered to a version of class-based racism that helped them reconcile and make sense of the uncomfortable fact that they were the economic peers of blacks, competitors for the same jobs. Their racism helped them live with, and accept the facts of, their troubled economic existence by rationalizing that—no matter how hard their row was to hoe—at least they were better than *somebody.* They might have to work alongside blacks, but they did not have to eat with or socialize with blacks or have them in their homes and churches because, after all, they were socially superior. And this superiority was immutable.

17. Michael J. Klarman, "*Brown,* Racial Change, and the Civil Rights Movement," *Virginia Law Review* 80 (February 1994): 7–150; and Klarman, "How *Brown* Changed Race Relations: The Backlash Thesis," *Journal of American History* 81 (June 1994): 81–118. The remainder of volume 80 of the *Virginia Law Review* was devoted to essays evaluating the Klarman thesis by David J. Garrow, Gerald N. Rosenberg, and Mark Tushnet.

18. Robert Korstad and Nelson Lichtenstein, "Opportunities Found and Lost: Labor, Radicals, and the Early Civil Rights Movement," *Journal of American History* 75 (April 1988): 786–811, quotes on 799 and 800. See also Michael Honey, *Southern Labor and Black Civil Rights: Organizing Memphis Workers* (Urbana: University of Illinois Press, 1993).

19. Comment at "Politics 2001 Workshop," Alabama AFL-CIO State Convention, Mobile, Alabama, October 30, 2001 (first quote); author's conversation with ELB, a longtime liaison between education and organized labor, Birmingham, Alabama, June 11, 2003 (second quote); the third example is from labor

education class with three United Paperworkers International Union (UPIU) locals in Columbia, South Carolina, March 17, 1998. Alan Draper argues compellingly that labor leaders recognized and fought for the opportunity present in the early civil rights movement but were confronted by a recalcitrant rank and file; see his *Conflict of Interests: Organized Labor and the Civil Rights Movement in the South, 1954–1968* (Ithaca: ILR Press, Cornell University, 1994).

20. See Mary L. Dudziak, "Desegregation as a Cold War Imperative," *Stanford Law Review* 40 (November 1988): 61–120; Dudziak, *Cold War Civil Rights* (Princeton: Princeton University Press, 2000); and Thomas Borstelmann, *The Cold War and the Color Line: American Race Relations in the Global Arena* (Cambridge: Harvard University Press, 2001).

21. Meier, "Epilogue," 223; Lawson, "Freedom Then, Freedom Now," 456; Julian Bond, "The Politics of Civil Rights History," in Robinson and Sullivan, *New Directions in Civil Rights Studies,* 13–14. Kris Shepard reviewed recent works that addressed the connection between race and growing conservative strength in "Conservatism and Its Cousins in Twentieth-Century America," *Historical Journal* 41 (September 1998): 901–8.

22. Esdall and Esdall, *Chain Reaction,* 14–15 (first quote), 49 and 284 (second quote). On the clear association of the Democratic Party with the civil rights movement and the Second Reconstruction, see ibid., 5, 7–9, 10, 12, 20, 32–37, esp. 35, and 215. Richard M. Scammon and Ben J. Wattenberg, *The Real Majority* (1970; New York: Primus, 1992). See also Numan V. Bartley, *The New South, 1945–1980* (Baton Rouge: Louisiana State University Press, 1995), 397–431, 456–70.

23. Esdall and Esdall, *Chain Reaction,* 19, 25, and 30 ("legitimate"), 28 and 29 ("majoritarian values"). Democrats have let themselves be "corrupt[ed]" into speaking for only a black and radical minority of the country, and "pressed an agenda [that] . . . provoked often divisive reactions," while conservatives are only reacting to being "under pressure" to take advantage of racial divisions that present themselves (26, 30). A recent study that actually blames the U.S. Supreme Court for destroying American cities, driving a wedge between a Democratic liberal elite and a former-Democratic white working class, and contributing to the Republican organization of whites across class lines, is Peter H. Irons, *Jim Crow's Children: The Broken Promises of the* Brown *Decision* (New York: Viking, 2002). See review by Anders Walker on h-south-net.msu.edu (December 2003).

CHAPTER 1

1. Box 51, Bayard Rustin Files, Fellowship of Reconciliation Papers [hereafter cited as FOR Papers], Swarthmore College Peace Collection, Swarthmore College, Swarthmore, Pennsylvania. The lyrics for "You Don't Have to Ride Jim Crow" were co-written by Bayard Rustin, Johnny Carr, Donald Coan, Doreen Curtis, and A. C. Thompson at the FOR/CORE-sponsored Interracial Workshop in Washington, D.C., on July 7, 1947. The music was an adaptation of the traditional Negro spiritual "There's No Hidin' Place Down Here."

2. *Baltimore Afro-American,* January 26, 1946; *People's Voice* (New York), June 15, 1946, Box II-B 190, Papers of the NAACP, Library of Congress, Washing-

ton, D.C., contains numerous documents related to Irene Morgan and the 1946 U.S. Supreme Court decision in *Morgan v. Virginia*. See especially "Opinion by Justice Herbert B. Gregory," typescript, June 6, 1945; "Argument in Irene Morgan Case," undated typescript; "Irene Morgan, Appellant vs. Commonwealth of Virginia . . . Brief of Appellee," undated typescript; and "Virginia Goes A'Courtin'," *Headlines and Pictures*, May 1946, 15. On the racial situation in Baltimore during the 1940s, see the Papers of the Baltimore Branch of the NAACP, box C77, Papers of the NAACP; and the extensive coverage in the *Baltimore Afro-American*. For brief accounts of the Morgan incident, see Catherine A. Barnes, *Journey from Jim Crow: The Desegregation of Southern Transit* (New York: Columbia University Press, 1983), 45; Richard Kluger, *Simple Justice* (New York: Random House, 1975), 237–38; and Jack Greenberg, *Race Relations and American Law* (New York: Columbia University Press, 1959), 118–19.

3. *Baltimore Afro-American*, January 26, 1946.

4. Ibid.; *People's Voice*, June 15, 1946 (quote). According to Morgan's brother-in-law, James Finney, Morgan's mother, Ethel Amos, was a key supporter of her daughter's fight for justice. "Irene's mother deserves a lot of credit for this," Finney told Virginia Gardner of the *People's Voice*; "her mother got to work and raised the money to make bond for Irene when she decided to appeal her conviction in the lower court." Gardner added that "at the time the elderly woman took up the cudgel in her daughter's case, Irene had no attorney, no advisers."

5. "Opinion by Justice Herbert B. Gregory," and "Irene Morgan, Appellant vs. Commonwealth of Virginia—Brief of Appellee," box II-B 190, Papers of the NAACP. In Virginia the official name of the state supreme court is the Supreme Court of Appeals of Virginia.

6. Barnes, *Journey from Jim Crow*, 3–4, 10, 14, 18, 44–47; Spottswood Robinson, "Memorandum Covering Transportation Cases," ca. January 1945, box II-B 190, Papers of the NAACP; Ray Stannard Baker, *Following the Color Line: American Negro Citizenship in the Progressive Era* (New York: Harper and Row, 1964), 31; Gunnar Myrdal, *An American Dilemma: The Negro Problem and American Democracy* (New York: Harper and Brothers, 1944), 635.

7. Barnes, *Journey from Jim Crow*, 2–19, quote on 16; *Plessy v. Ferguson*, 163 U.S. 537 (1896); *Chiles v. Chesapeake and Ohio Railway Company*, 218 U.S. 71 (1910); *McCabe v. Atchison, Topeka and Santa Fe Railway Company*, 235 U.S. 151 (1914). For an excellent summary of the *Plessy* decision, see Kluger, *Simple Justice*, 73–83.

8. Barnes, *Journey from Jim Crow*, 1–2, 5–7, 14–44; Kluger, *Simple Justice*, 73, 77, 105–226, 238; "Argument in Irene Morgan Case," Papers of the NAACP; *Hall v. DeCuir*, 95 U.S. 485 (1878); *Mitchell v. United States*, 313 U.S. 80 (1941).

9. Spottswood W. Robinson III to Thurgood Marshall, January 11, 1945, and Marshall to Robinson, January 15, 1945, folder 1, box II-B 190, Papers of the NAACP; Robinson, "Memorandum Covering Transportation Cases"; Barnes, *Journey from Jim Crow*, 44–45; Mark V. Tushnet, *Making Civil Rights Law: Thurgood Marshall and the Supreme Court, 1936–1961* (New York: Oxford University Press, 1994), 72–73; Carl T. Rowan, *Dream Makers, Dream Breakers: The World of Justice Thurgood Marshall* (Boston: Little, Brown, 1993), 106; Juan Williams, *Thurgood Marshall: American Revolutionary* (New York: Random House, 1998), 145.

10. *Irene Morgan v. Commonwealth of Virginia,* 184 Va. 24, in *Virginia Reports,* 184 (Richmond, 1946), 39.

11. "Argument in Irene Morgan Case"; "Irene Morgan, Appellant, vs. Commonwealth of Virginia—Brief for Appellee"; Richard E. Westbrooks to Thurgood Marshall, June 15, 1945; memorandum to Mr. Wilkins from Thurgood Marshall, November 28, 1945; Clifford Forster (ACLU) to Marian Perry, January 10, 1946; "Memorandum for Bulletin on Irene Morgan Case"; Earl B. Dickerson (National Bar Association) to Thurgood Marshall, February 5, 1946; "Virginia 'Jim-Crow' Law Argued before Supreme Court: Decision Pending," *NAACP Bulletin,* March 28, 1946, all in box II-B 190, Papers of the NAACP. See also Barnes, *Journey from Jim Crow,* 45–46; Tushnet, *Making Civil Rights Law,* 73–75; Kluger, *Simple Justice,* quote on 238; Williams, *Thurgood Marshall,* 145–46; and Rowan, *Dream Makers, Dream Breakers,* 106.

12. *Smith v. Allwright,* 321 U.S. 649 (1944); Kluger, *Simple Justice,* 234–38, quote on 237; Tushnet, *Making Civil Rights Law,* 74–75, 99–115. On the Columbia, Tennessee, crisis, see Gail O'Brien, *The Color of the Law: Race, Violence, and Justice in the Post-World War II South* (Chapel Hill: University of North Carolina Press, 1999). On the significance of Jackie Robinson in the immediate postwar era, see Jules Tygiel, *Baseball's Great Experiment: Jackie Robinson and His Legacy* (New York: Oxford University Press, 1983); Arnold Rampersad, *Jackie Robinson: A Biography* (New York: Knopf, 1997); and Randy Roberts and James Olson, *Winning Is the Only Thing: Sports in America since 1945* (Baltimore: The Johns Hopkins University Press, 1989), 25–45. For a perceptive analysis of the political context of the racial crosscurrents of the mid-1940s, see Patricia Sullivan, *Days of Hope: Race and Democracy in the New Deal Era* (Chapel Hill: University of North Carolina Press, 1996), 133–275; and Sullivan, "Southern Reformers, the New Deal, and the Movement's Foundation," in *New Directions in Civil Rights Studies,* ed. Armstead L. Robinson and Patricia Sullivan (Charlottesville: University Press of Virginia, 1991), 81–104. See also John Egerton, *Speak Now against the Day: The Generation before the Civil Rights Movement* (New York: Knopf, 1994), 330–532.

13. *Morgan v. Virginia,* 328 U.S. 373 (1946); Kluger, *Simple Justice,* 236–38; "Question Ducked," *Time,* June 10, 1946. Barnes, *Journey from Jim Crow,* 47, notes that "Chief Justice Harlan Fiske Stone had been prepared to dissent in *Morgan.* Because he died on April 22, 1946, before the decision was handed down, his views were not made public, but in conference, the Chief Justice had maintained that racial seating on buses was a predominantly local matter which the states could regulate."

14. Folder 1, box II-B 190, Papers of the NAACP, contains numerous clippings, press releases, and congratulatory telegrams related to the *Morgan* decision. See also the clippings in the Tuskegee Institute Race Relations Clippings File (microfilm), reel 96, Tuskegee University Archives, Tuskegee, Alabama; and the *Baltimore Afro-American,* June 8–July 27, 1946.

15. "National Leaders Hail Supreme Court Decision on Jim Crow Buses," press release, typescript, June 10, 1946, and telegram, Adam Clayton Powell to Walter White, June 6, 1946, both in folder 1, box II-B 190, Papers of the NAACP; *Baltimore Afro-American,* June 15, 1946 (McGehee quote). A June 10, 1946, editorial in the *Washington Post* noted that Representative Powell "had introduced

a bill to abolish Jim Crow practices in interstate transportation a year and a half ago."

16. Telegram, Walter White to a long list of political and civil rights leaders, June 5, 1946, folder 1, box II-B 190, Papers of the NAACP; *Chicago Defender*, June 15, 1946 (Winborne, Coleman, Sparks, and Bailey quotes); *Baton Rouge State-Times*, June 4, 1946; *Baltimore Afro-American*, June 15, 1946 (Talmadge quote); Barnes, *Journey from Jim Crow*, 50–51. On Talmadge's racial demagoguery, see William Anderson, *The Wild Man from Sugar Creek: The Political Career of Eugene Talmadge* (Baton Rouge: Louisiana State University Press, 1975).

17. *Chicago Defender*, June 15, 1946; *Baltimore Afro-American*, June 15–July 27, 1946; Barnes, *Journey from Jim Crow*, 52–53, 62–65.

18. Tushnet, *Making Civil Rights Law*, 75–76; Barnes, *Journey from Jim Crow*, 62–65; Robert L. Carter to Daniel E. Byrd, June 12, 1946, folder 1, box II-B 190, Papers of the NAACP, expresses Carter's early suspicion that "the bus companies' rules and regulations requiring segregation, apart from state statutes, are not affected by the Morgan case. Where such rules are inaugurated, as we expect them to be, we will have to go to court in an attempt to have them set aside as being unreasonable and invalid."

19. *Baltimore Afro-American*, June 15, 1946 (quote); "Virginia Goes A'Courtin'," 15, claimed that Morgan was having "domestic problems" during the spring of 1946: "In April she left her service job and her husband who works as a maintenance man in one of Manhattan's less swanky apartment houses." *People's Voice*, June 15, 1946. At the time of the decision, she was employed "as a practical nurse for the children of Mr. and Mrs. Harold Wolff, writers, 70 Haven Ave." On Marshall's unshakable commitment to the NAACP's legal and constitutional civil rights strategy during the 1940s, see Tushnet, *Making Civil Rights Law*, 67–136; Williams, *Thurgood Marshall*, 145–66; and Kluger, *Simple Justice*, 213–314.

20. Williams, *Thurgood Marshall*, 167–69; Kluger, *Simple Justice*, 190–91; Roy Wilkins, with Tom Matthews, *Standing Fast: The Autobiography of Roy Wilkins* (New York: Penguin, 1984), 190, 205–6, 210–11. On the NAACP youth councils and other sources of direct-action advocacy within the NAACP, see Joanne Grant, *Ella Baker: Freedom Bound* (New York: Wiley, 1998), 50–51, 93; and Adam Fairclough, *Race and Democracy: The Civil Rights Struggle in Louisiana, 1915–1972* (Athens: University of Georgia Press, 1995), xi–xx, 110–11, 272–83, 296, 407–8. On the NAACP and anti-communism, see Wilson Record, *Race and Radicalism: The NAACP and the Communist Party in Conflict* (Ithaca: Cornell University Press, 1964).

21. Although there is no comprehensive study of radical civil rights activism during the 1930s and 1940s, a number of monographs discuss the activities of individual activists and specific organizations. See especially August Meier and Elliott Rudwick, *CORE: A Study in the Civil Rights Movement* (Urbana: University of Illinois Press, 1975), 3–40; Jervis Anderson, *Bayard Rustin: Troubles I've Seen* (New York: HarperCollins, 1997), 3–149; Daniel Levine, *Bayard Rustin and the Civil Rights Movement* (New Brunswick: Rutgers University Press, 2000); Jervis Anderson, *A. Philip Randolph: A Biographical Portrait* (New York: Harcourt Brace Jovanovich, 1973); Paula E. Pfeffer, *A. Philip Randolph: Pioneer of the Civil Rights Movement* (Baton Rouge: Louisiana State University Press, 1990); Jo Ann O.

Robinson, *Abraham Went Out: A Biography of A. J. Muste* (Philadelphia: Temple University Press, 1981), 109–37; Dan T. Carter, *Scottsboro: A Tragedy of the American South* (Baton Rouge: Louisiana State University Press, 1969); John A. Salmond, *A Southern Rebel: The Life and Times of Aubrey Willis Williams, 1890–1965* (Chapel Hill: University of North Carolina Press, 1983); Frank T. Adams, *James A. Dombrowski: An American Heretic, 1897–1983* (Knoxville: University of Tennessee Press, 1992); Robert F. Martin, *Howard Kester and the Struggle for Social Justice in the South, 1904–1977* (Charlottesville: University Press of Virginia, 1991); Michael K. Honey, *Southern Labor and Black Civil Rights: Organizing Memphis Workers* (Urbana: University of Illinois Press, 1993); Anthony P. Dunbar, *Against the Grain: Southern Radicals and Prophets, 1929–1959* (Charlottesville: University Press of Virginia, 1981); John M. Glen, *Highlander: No Ordinary School, 1932–1962* (Lexington: University Press of Kentucky, 1988); Thomas A. Kreuger, *And Promises to Keep: The Southern Conference on Human Welfare, 1938–1948* (Nashville: Vanderbilt University Press, 1967); H. L. Mitchell, *Mean Things Happening in This Land* (Montclair, N.J.: Allanheld, Osmun, 1979); Nell Irvin Painter, *The Narrative of Hosea Hudson: His Life as a Negro Communist in the South* (Cambridge: Harvard University Press, 1979); Robin D. G. Kelley, *Hammer and Hoe: Alabama Communists during the Great Depression* (Chapel Hill: University of North Carolina Press, 1990); Mark Naison, *Communists in Harlem during the Depression* (Urbana: University of Illinois Press, 1981); Anne C. Loveland, *Lillian Smith: A Southerner Confronting the South* (Baton Rouge: Louisiana State University Press, 1986); Sullivan, *Days of Hope;* and Egerton, *Speak Now.*

22. Robinson, *Abraham Went Out,* 3–118; Meier and Rudwick, *CORE,* 4–34; Anderson, *Bayard Rustin,* 61–77, 81–110; James Farmer, *Lay Bare the Heart: An Autobiography of the Civil Rights Movement* (New York: New American Library, 1985), 70–161. See also Nat Hentoff, *Peace Agitator: The Story of A. J. Muste* (New York: Macmillan, 1963); and Lawrence S. Wittner, *Rebels against the War: The American Peace Movement, 1941–1960* (New York: Columbia University Press, 1969), 1–181.

23. Anderson, *Bayard Rustin,* 114–24, 183–96, 224–35; Bayard Rustin, *Down the Line: The Collected Writings of Bayard Rustin* (Chicago: Quadrangle Books, 1971), ix–61; Raymond Arsenault, "Bayard Rustin and the 'Miracle in Montgomery,'" in *A History of the African American People,* ed. James O. Horton and Lois E. Horton (Detroit: Wayne State University Press, 1997), 156–57; James Peck, *Freedom Ride* (New York: Simon and Schuster, 1962); Farmer, *Lay Bare the Heart,* 2–32, 101–16, 165–66, 195–221; Meier and Rudwick, *CORE,* 4–19, 131–417.

24. Anderson, *Bayard Rustin,* 6–95; Levine, *Rustin and the Civil Rights Movement,* 7–29; Charles Moritz, ed., *Current Biography Yearbook, 1967* (New York: H. W. Wilson, 1967), 360; Taylor Branch, *Parting the Waters: America in the King Years, 1954–1963* (New York: Simon and Schuster, 1988), 168–71; Adam Fairclough, *To Redeem the Soul of America: The Southern Christian Leadership Conference and Martin Luther King, Jr.* (Athens: University of Georgia Press, 1987), 23–24; Robinson, *Abraham Went Out,* 111; Anderson, *A. Philip Randolph,* 249–74, 275 (first quote), 280–81, 378–80; Pfeffer, *A. Philip Randolph,* 51–90; Milton Viorst, *Fire in the Streets: America in the 1960s* (New York: Simon and Schuster, 1979), 200–208; Bayard Rustin, "The Negro and Non-Violence," *Fellowship* 8 (Oc-

tober 1942): 166–67 (second quote); Rustin, *Down the Line*, ix–xv, 11. On Carl Rachlin, see Anderson, *Bayard Rustin*, 41–44, 157, 271; Meier and Rudwick, *CORE*, 143, 151, 168, 173, 180, 226, 271, 277, 283, 412; and *New York Times*, January 4, 2000 (obituary).

25. Rustin, *Down the Line*, 6–7; Levine, *Rustin and the Civil Rights Movement*, 32–33. On Mayor Ben West, see David Halberstam, *The Children* (New York: Random House, 1998), 111–14, 127, 179, 198, 200, 210–13, 230–34, 719; and "Ain't Scared of Your Jails," episode 3 of the documentary film series *Eyes on the Prize: America's Civil Rights Years* (Boston: Blackside, 1986).

26. Anderson, *Bayard Rustin*, 96–110, quote on 111; Levine, *Rustin and the Civil Rights Movement*, 27–28, 34–51; Moritz, *Current Biography Yearbook, 1967*, 360–61; Rustin, *Down the Line*, ix–x, 5–52; Branch, *Parting the Waters*, 171–72; Fairclough, *To Redeem the Soul of America*, 24; Robinson, *Abraham Went Out*, 111–17; Viorst, *Fire in the Streets*, 208–10; Pfeffer, *A. Philip Randolph*, 62, 142, 150–68; Meier and Rudwick, *CORE*, 12–20, 34–50, 57, 64.

27. *New York Times*, July 13, 1993 (obituary); James Peck, *Underdogs vs. Upperdogs* (Canterbury, N.J.: n.p., 1969); Peck, *Freedom Ride*, 15–38, quotes on 39; Meier and Rudwick, *CORE*, 35; James Peck, interview by James Mosby Jr., February 19, 1970, Ralph Bunche Oral History Collection, Moorland-Spingarn Research Center, Howard University, Washington, D.C. [hereafter cited as RBOHC]; Nancy L. Roberts, *American Peace Writers, Editors, and Periodicals: A Dictionary* (Westport, Conn.: Greenwood Press, 1991), 221–22.

28. Farmer, *Lay Bare the Heart*, 33–65.

29. Ibid., 117–28, quote on 129. In a 1970 interview, Jim Peck stated: "I feel that Mr. Farmer's only asset was that he was an effective public speaker.... Therefore we needed somebody like Marvin Rich to really do the brain work, strategy, and basic work required in running a national organization." Peck interview. Following Farmer's death in 1999, an *Associated Press* wire service story emphasized the strange power of his voice: "Diabetes stilled the legs that had walked treacherous miles on the roads of the hostile South during the Freedom Rides of the 1960s. But, oh, that voice! Right up to his final days, nothing had muted the mighty, flowing baritone that helped mold and inspire the civil rights movement for one generation, then brought it back to life for college students of a later time." *St. Petersburg (Fla.) Times*, July 11, 1999. See also Farmer's interview in "Ain't Scared of Your Jails," episode 3 of the documentary film series *Eyes on the Prize*.

30. Farmer, *Lay Bare the Heart*, 129–33; Sullivan, *Days of Hope*, 150; John B. Kirby, "Race, Class, and Politics: Ralph Bunche and Black Protest," in *Ralph Bunche: The Man and His Times*, ed. Benjamin Rivlin (New York: Holmes and Meier, 1990), 36–39; see also Pfeffer, *A. Philip Randolph*; Anderson, *Bayard Rustin*, 58.

31. Farmer, *Lay Bare the Heart*, 135 (first quote), 71 (second quote), 133–46; James Farmer, interviewed by John Britton, September 28, 1968, RBOHC. On Howard Thurman, see Walter E. Fluker and Catherine Tumber, eds., *A Strange Freedom: The Best of Howard Thurman on Religious Experience and Public Life* (Boston: Beacon Press, 1998); Walter E. Fluker, *They Looked for a City: A Comparative Analysis of the Ideal Community in the Thought of Howard Thurman and Martin Luther King, Jr.* (Lanham, Md.: University Press of America, 1989); Luther E.

Smith, *Howard Thurman: The Mystic as Prophet* (Richmond: Friends United Press, 1992); and Alton B. Pollard II, *Mysticism and Social Change: The Social Witness of Howard Thurman* (New York: Peter Lang, 1992).

32. Meier and Rudwick, *CORE*, 4–17, quote on 18; Farmer, *Lay Bare the Heart*, 67–116; Anderson, *Bayard Rustin*, 93; George Houser, interview, RBOHC; Farmer interview.

33. Farmer, *Lay Bare the Heart*, 115–16, 149–61, quote on 116; Meier and Rudwick, *CORE*, 19–25, 42–44; Robinson, *Abraham Went Out*, 111–17; Houser interview; Anderson, *Bayard Rustin*, 93–95.

34. Farmer, *Lay Bare the Heart*, 165–66.

35. Houser interview; George M. Houser, "A Personal Retrospective on the 1947 Journey of Reconciliation," paper given at Bluffton College, September 1992, typescript, box 1, Congress of Racial Equality Collection [hereafter cited as CORE Collection], Swarthmore College Peace Collection, Swarthmore College, Swarthmore, Pennsylvania; George M. Houser, "'Thy Brother's Blood': Reminiscences of World War II," *Christian Century*, August 16, 1995, 774; Meier and Rudwick, *CORE*, 5–6, 16–21, 29, 34.

36. Houser, "A Personal Retrospective," 3–4.

37. On Wilson Head's freedom ride, see John A. Salmond, *"My Mind Set on Freedom": A History of the Civil Rights Movement, 1954–1968* (Chicago: Ivan R. Dee, 1997), 3–4, 87, 149; Houser interview; Houser, "A Personal Retrospective," 2–6; Anderson, *Bayard Rustin*, 114–16; Meier and Rudwick, *CORE*, 20, 34; Peck, *Freedom Ride*, 14–15; Rustin, *Down the Line*, 13; Robinson, *Abraham Went Out*, 113–14.

38. Houser, "A Personal Retrospective," 5–6 (quotes); George M. Houser and Bayard Rustin, "Memorandum Number 2: Bus and Train Travel in the South," box 20, FOR Papers; Peck, *Freedom Ride*, 16; Meier and Rudwick, *CORE*, 34; Grant, *Ella Baker*, 91–92.

39. Robert L. Carter to Daniel E. Byrd, June 12, 1946, George Houser to Marian Perry, October 9, 1946, W. A. C. Hughes to Thurgood Marshall, July 8, 1946, Robert L. Carter, Memos to Walter White, July 26, September 26, 1946, all in box II-B 190, Papers of the NAACP; *Baltimore Afro-American*, June 26, July 6 and 27, November 2, 1946; *Los Angeles Tribune*, September 21, 1946; *Kansas City Plaindealer*, September 20, 1946; *Chicago Defender*, August 17, November 30, 1946; *Oklahoma City Black Dispatch*, December 9, 1946; *Memphis World*, November 15, 1946; *Atlanta Daily World*, November 27, 1946; Houser, "A Personal Retrospective," 6–8; Barnes, *Journey from Jim Crow*, 52–53, 62–63; Tushnet, *Making Civil Rights Law*, 74–76; Peck, *Freedom Ride*, 17; Meier and Rudwick, *CORE*, 34–35; Anderson, *Bayard Rustin*, 114–15. On the Fellowship of Southern Churchmen, see Robert F. Martin, "Critique of Southern Society and Vision of a New Order: The Fellowship of Southern Churchmen, 1934–1957," *Church History* 52 (March 1983): 66–80; and Martin, *Kester and the Struggle for Social Justice*.

40. Thurgood Marshall to Dear Sir [members of NAACP Legal Committee], November 6, 1946, box II-B 190, Papers of the NAACP; *New York Times*, November 23, 1946 (quote); Anderson, *Bayard Rustin*, 114–15.

41. Bayard Rustin, "Our Guest Column: Beyond the Courts," *Louisiana Weekly*, January 4, 1947; Anderson, *Bayard Rustin*, 115–16.

42. On Truman and the President's Committee on Civil Rights, see John

Hope Franklin, "A Half-Century of Presidential Race Initiatives: Some Reflections," *Journal of Supreme Court History* 24 (1999): 227–30; William C. Berman, *The Politics of Civil Rights in the Truman Administration* (Columbus: Ohio State University Press, 1970); and Donald R. McCoy and Richard T. Ruetten, *Quest and Response: Minority Rights and the Truman Administration* (Lawrence: University Press of Kansas, 1973). See also President's Committee on Civil Rights, *To Secure These Rights: The Report of the President's Committee on Civil Rights* (Washington, D.C.: Government Printing Office, 1947).

43. Peck, *Freedom Ride*, 17; Houser, "A Personal Retrospective," 6–7 (quote). Rustin and Houser traveled together to Washington, D.C.; Richmond and Petersburg, Virginia; and Chapel Hill, Greensboro, Winston-Salem, and Asheville, North Carolina. Houser traveled alone to Nashville and Knoxville, Tennessee, and Louisville, Kentucky. Rustin and Houser, "Memorandum Number 2"; Houser interview. During the scouting trip, Rustin and Houser met Floyd McKissick, a young black attorney practicing in Durham, North Carolina, who would later serve as CORE's national chairman (1963–66) and national director (1966–68). On McKissick see Meier and Rudwick, *CORE*, 293–94, 381, 396, 402–24.

44. Houser, "A Personal Retrospective," 7–8; Rustin and Houser, "Memorandum Number 2."

45. Rustin, *Down the Line*, 13–14; Houser, "A Personal Retrospective," 7–8; Meier and Rudwick, *CORE*, 35; Anderson, *Bayard Rustin*, 116.

46. Peck, *Freedom Ride*, 15–16 (quotes); Houser, "A Personal Retrospective," 8; Anderson, *Bayard Rustin*, 116; Meier and Rudwick, *CORE*, 35–36.

47. Bayard Rustin and George Houser, "You Don't Have to Ride Jim Crow" (Washington, D.C.: Interracial Workshop, 1947). Copies of this pamphlet can be found in reel 25, CORE Papers, microfilm edition (Washington, D.C.: University Publications of America), and in the "George Houser Scrapbook—Journey of Reconciliation 1947," box 2, CORE Collection.

48. Peck, *Freedom Ride*, 16.

49. Ibid., 18 (quote); "Log—Journey of Reconciliation," April 9–23, 1947, typescript, box 51, Bayard Rustin Files. Wally Nelson maintained the log. Houser, "A Personal Retrospective."

50. "Log—Journey of Reconciliation," 1–2; Rustin and Houser, "You Don't Have to Ride Jim Crow," 1 (quote); Rustin, *Down the Line*, 14; Houser, "A Personal Retrospective," 9–10; Peck, *Freedom Ride*, 18; Anderson, *Bayard Rustin*, 117; Conrad Lynn, *There Is a Fountain* (Westport, Conn.: Lawrence Hill, 1979), 109 (quote).

51. "Log—Journey of Reconciliation," 2; Rustin and Houser, "You Don't Have to Ride Jim Crow," 1; Houser, "A Personal Retrospective," 10 (quote); Rustin, *Down the Line*, 14–15, 16 (quote).

52. Rustin, *Down the Line*, 15 (first and second quotes); "Log—Journey of Reconciliation," 2–4; Houser, "A Personal Retrospective," 10–11; Anderson, *Bayard Rustin*, 117; Lynn, *There Is a Fountain*, 109–10, 111 (third quote).

53. Rustin, *Down the Line*, 16–17 (quotes); "Log—Journey of Reconciliation," 5–6; Peck, *Freedom Ride*, 18–20; Houser, "A Personal Retrospective," 11–12.

54. "Log—Journey of Reconciliation," 6–7; Houser, "A Personal Retrospective," 12–14; Houser interview; Peck, *Freedom Ride*, 20–21; Anderson, *Bayard Rustin*, 118; Egerton, *Speak Now*, 422–23, 556–59. The "George Houser Scrapbook—

Journey of Reconciliation 1947" contains numerous clippings on the Chapel Hill incident. See especially *Greensboro Daily News,* April 15, 17, and 18, 1947; *Pittsburgh Courier,* April 19, 1947; and *Carolina Times,* April 26, 1947. On Frank Porter Graham, see Warren Ashby, *Frank Porter Graham: A Southern Liberal* (Winston-Salem, N.C.: John F. Blair, 1980).

55. Houser, "A Personal Retrospective," 12 (quote); Peck, *Freedom Ride,* 20–21; *Pittsburgh Courier,* April 19, 1947.

56. "Log—Journey of Reconciliation," 6 (quotes), 7; Houser interview; Peck, *Freedom Ride,* 21–22; Rustin, *Down the Line,* 17; Anderson, *Bayard Rustin,* 118; *New York Times,* April 14, 1947.

57. Rustin, *Down the Line,* 17 (first quote); Peck, *Freedom Ride,* 21 (second and third quotes); Houser interview; "Log—Journey of Reconciliation," 7; *Pittsburgh Courier,* April 19, 1947. The North Carolina A&T professor was Eugene Stanley.

58. Peck, *Freedom Ride,* 22 (quotes), 23; "Log—Journey of Reconciliation," 7; Rustin, *Down the Line,* 17; *Pittsburgh Courier,* April 19, 1947. Anderson, *Bayard Rustin,* 119, offers a detailed but largely inaccurate account of the pursuit.

59. Peck, *Freedom Ride,* 23; *New York Times,* April 14, 1947; *Greensboro Daily News,* April 17, 1947 (first quote); *Chicago Defender,* May 3, 1947 (second quote).

60. *Greensboro Daily News,* April 18, 1947 (quotes); *Carolina Times,* April 26, 1947. Houser, "A Personal Retrospective," 13–14, notes: "I always had a guilt feeling about this incident because we left Charles Jones to face the wrath of the taxi drivers and others of their ilk in Chapel Hill. He was already a marked man in the community because he was always on the cutting edge of racial and social issues (such as union organization) which divided the community." Conservative editors and reporters in North Carolina often printed diatribes against Jones. See, e.g., the editorial in the *Charlotte Textile Times,* April 15, 1947 (typescript copy in "George Houser Scrapbook—Journey of Reconciliation 1947"), which declared: "The town of Chapel Hill, N.C., has for several years been affiliated with a 'crank' a Presbyterian preacher named Charles M. Jones, who was brought there from Tennessee. He is the type of minister who, like the Holy Rollers and the sect which handles live snakes, interprets the Bible to suit his own warped ideas and he seems to be hipped upon the subject of social equality with Negroes. When, during the war, a Negro band was sent to Chapel Hill to furnish music for Navy preflight trainees, Mr. Jones saw a great opportunity. He began to invite Negroes to his church for ice cream socials and encouraged white girls to attend and have dates with Negro men. Encouraged by the success of that effort, Mr. Jones invited students and professors from a Negro college at Durham, N.C., to a breakfast at his church. Four students and a professor accepted and each was seated at breakfast beside a white girl. . . . There are always a few crack-pot students in a university or college, but it is unusual for them to have the encouragement and support which they receive at Chapel Hill." In 1953, conservative critics of Jones's civil rights activism prompted a Presbytery inquiry that led to his resignation from the Presbyterian ministry. See Ashby, *Frank Porter Graham,* 305–9; "Deplore Secrecy in the Jones Case," *Christian Century,* March 4, 1953, 245; "Presbyterian U.S. Commission Fires Chapel Hill Pastor," *Christian Century,* March 18, 1953, 319–20; and "Pastor vs. Presbytery," *Time,* February 23, 1953, 53.

61. Peck, *Freedom Ride,* 23.

62. Rustin, *Down the Line*, 18 (first and second quotes); "Log—Journey of Reconciliation," 8; Houser, "A Personal Retrospective," 14, 15 (third quotes).

63. Peck, *Freedom Ride*, 24–26 (quotes); Rustin, *Down the Line*, 18; Houser, "A Personal Retrospective," 16; *Asheville Citizen*, April 19, 1947; *Pittsburgh Courier*, April 26, 1947; *Baltimore Afro-American*, April 26, 1947; James Peck, "Not So Deep Are the Roots," *Crisis*, September 1947, 274. On Felmet, see the Joe Felmet Papers, Southern Historical Collection, University of North Carolina, Chapel Hill; for the FBI files on Felmet see the Journey of Reconciliation folder, box 20, FOR Papers.

64. Peck, *Freedom Ride*, 26 (quotes); Rustin, *Down the Line*, 18; Curtiss Todd to Thurgood Marshall, April 19, 1947, Robert L. Carter to Curtiss Todd, April 23, 1947, box II-B 184, Papers of the NAACP.

65. Homer A. Jack, "Journey of Reconciliation," *Common Ground*, Autumn 1947, 22, 23 (quote); Houser, "A Personal Retrospective," 14–15; Houser interview.

66. Jack, "Journey of Reconciliation," 23–24 (quotes); Rustin, *Down the Line*, 19; Houser, "A Personal Retrospective," 15–16.

67. Rustin, *Down the Line*, 19; Houser, "A Personal Retrospective," 15–16.

68. Jack, "Journey of Reconciliation," 24; Rustin, *Down the Line*, 19–21; Houser, "A Personal Retrospective," 16–17; Houser interview; Peck, "Not So Deep Are the Roots," 273, 274 (quote); *Lynchburg News*, April 23–24, 28, 1947; *Lynchburg Advance*, April 29, 1947. "Log—Journey of Reconciliation," 9–11, provides a detailed summary of Houser and Nelson's bus and train trip from Lynchburg, Virginia, to Washington, D.C.

69. Peck, *Freedom Ride*, 27 (quote); "Log—Journey of Reconciliation," 11; Rustin, *Down the Line*, 14. For a sampling of the press reaction to the Journey of Reconciliation, see "George Houser Scrapbook—Journey of Reconciliation 1947." On the public reaction to and press coverage of Jackie Robinson's first months as a major league ballplayer, see Tygiel, *Baseball's Great Experiment*, 174–200.

70. *Baltimore Afro-American*, April 26, 1947.

71. Rustin, *Down the Line*, 22–25; Jack, "Journey of Reconciliation," 26.

72. Rustin, *Down the Line*, 21–22; Peck, "Not So Deep Are the Roots," 282; Jack, "Journey of Reconciliation," 24; Houser, "A Personal Retrospective," 17; *Pittsburgh Courier*, May 3, 1947; *Knoxville News-Sentinel*, May 21, 1947; *Lynchburg Advance*, April 29, 1947; Workers Defense League, "Bus Companies Urged To Obey Supreme Court Ruling Outlawing Jimcrow," press release, typescript, May 6, 1947, and "Group Finds Bus Companies Evading Supreme Court's Anti–Jim Crow Ruling," FOR press release, typescript, April 28, 1947, both in box 51, Bayard Rustin Files.

73. Peck, "Not So Deep Are the Roots," 274 (first quote); *New York Times*, May 22, 1947; *Long Island Daily Press*, May 21, 1947; Anderson, *Bayard Rustin*, 122 (second quote); "Chapel Hill Judge Sentences Rustin and Roodenko," *Fellowship*, July 1947; C. Jerry Gates to Roy Wilkins, May 27, 1947, and to Thurgood Marshall, May 27, 1947, box II-B 184, Papers of the NAACP; *Call*, July 2, 1947 (third quote).

74. *Durham Morning Herald*, March 18, 1948; *Chicago Defender*, March 27, 1948; *Pittsburgh Courier*, March 27, 1948; *Asheville Times*, December 14, 1948; *State of North Carolina v. Johnson et al.* (1949), Orange County, North Caro-

lina, NC 723; "Carolina Journey Members Lose North Carolina Appeal," *Fellowship*, February 1949, reel 3, Bayard Rustin Papers, microfilm edition (Washington, D.C.: University Publications of America); Bayard Rustin to C. Jerry Gates, May 13, June 5, 1947, reel 44, CORE Papers; C. Jerry Gates to Roy Wilkinson, May 27, 1947, C. Jerry Gates to Robert L. Carter, June 16, 1947, Robert L. Carter to C. Jerry Gates, July 25, 1947, Robert L. Carter to George Houser, February 8, 1949, "Journey of Reconciliation, 1949, Chapel Hill Case" folder, reel 44, CORE Papers; Anderson, *Bayard Rustin*, 122, 123 (quote). The Virginia Supreme Court of Appeals later overturned Lee's conviction. See *Norvell Lee v. Commonwealth of Virginia* (1949), Record no. 3558; and Martin A. Martin to George Houser, October 12, 1949, reel 44, CORE Papers.

75. C. E. Boulware to George Houser, January 18, 1949, Robert L. Carter to George Houser, February 8, 1949, Minutes of FOR/CORE Legal Committee Meeting, February 11, 1949, George Houser to Nelle Norton, February 12, 1949, Conrad Lynn to Andrew Johnson, February 14, 1949, Andrew Johnson to George Houser, March 12, 1949 (first quote), FOR press release, typescript, March 20, 1949, all in "Journey of Reconciliation, 1949, Chapel Hill Case" folder, reel 44, CORE Papers; George Houser to Dear Fellows, November 13, 1948, and George Houser to Bayard Rustin, November 20, 1948, reel 3, Bayard Rustin Papers; Anderson, *Bayard Rustin*, 123, 130–34; "Negro Acclaimed at Home and Abroad Sentenced to North Carolina Road Gang," FOR/CORE press release, typescript, March 9, 1949, box 51, Bayard Rustin Files (second quote).

76. Rustin, *Down the Line*, 26–49, quote on 29; Anderson, *Bayard Rustin*, 135–36; Levine, *Rustin and the Civil Rights Movement*, 61–65. See also the correspondence and clippings (including the *New York Post* series) in reel 3 of the Bayard Rustin Papers (microfilm); and the reports and correspondence in the Roxboro Prison Report folders, box 51, Bayard Rustin Files.

77. Houser, "A Personal Retrospective," 17–21; Peck, *Freedom Ride*, 27; Bayard Rustin, "From Freedom Ride to Ballot Box: The Changing Strategies of Black Struggle," typescript of lecture delivered as part of the William Radner Lecture Series, Columbia University, October 9–11, 1973, 31, reel 18, Bayard Rustin Papers; Anderson, *Bayard Rustin*, 123; Meier and Rudwick, *CORE*, 38–39; Barnes, *Journey from Jim Crow*, 60–65; Levine, *Rustin and the Civil Rights Movement*, 64–67.

CHAPTER 2

1. For more on Howard's role at the 1954 conference called by Governor Hugh White, see John Dittmer, *Local People: The Struggle for Civil Rights in Mississippi* (Urbana: University of Illinois Press, 1994), 38–40.

2. *Chicago Tribune*, August 10, 1957; Oakwood Junior College, Student's Application Blank, June 30, 1924, T. R. M. Howard Papers, Eva B. Dykes Library, Oakwood College, Huntsville, Alabama; Mary Howard vs. Arthur Howard, Judgement, April 4, 1911, Petition in Equity, Calloway County, Circuit Court, Kentucky Department for Libraries and Archives, Public Records Division, Frankfort, Kentucky; Marriage Bonds, 1913–14, Calloway County, Calloway County Court House, Murray, Kentucky.

3. Hodding Carter, "He's Doing Something about the Race Problem," *Saturday Evening Post,* February 23, 1946, 64. The first known appearance of Howard's new middle name was in T. R. M. Howard, "The Hour Has Come," *Oakwood Junior College Bulletin* 15 (March 1928), Betterment Society Number, 30.

4. Howard to Joseph A. Tucker, July 26, 1926, March 26, 1928, Howard Papers; Harold D. Singleton, telephone interview, December 5, 2002; Charles Edward Dudley Sr., "Moments in Black History: Theodore R. M. Howard, M.D., of Murray, Ky.," *North American Regional Voice,* December 1989, 18.

5. Anti-Saloon League of America, *Proceedings,* January 15–19, 1930, 18.

6. Howard to Leo F. Thiel, September 27, 1929, and Howard to Tucker, March 14, 1931, Howard Papers; *California Eagle,* September 8, 1933.

7. *California Eagle,* July 7, 1933; Edward M. Boyd, telephone interview, July 21, 2000. For more on Bass, see Charlotta A. Bass, *Forty Years: Memoirs from the Pages of a Newspaper* (Los Angeles: Charlotta A. Bass, 1960); and Rodger Streitmatter, *Raising Her Voice: African-American Women Journalists Who Changed History* (Lexington: University Press of Kentucky, 1994), 95–106.

8. *California Eagle,* July 14, 1933, May 4, 1934; Boyd interview.

9. *California Eagle,* July 7, August 4, 1933.

10. Ibid., August 18, September 1, 1933, February 3, 1934.

11. Ibid., August 18, 25, 1933.

12. Ibid., August 4, 1933, June 22, 1934.

13. Ibid., April 13, 1934.

14. Ibid., May 4, 11, 25, June 8, 1934.

15. "Baccalaureate and Commencement," *Medical Evangelist,* June 20, 1935, 1–3; *California Eagle,* June 21, 1935.

16. Singleton interview; Annabelle Simons, telephone interview, April 20, 2000; Charles E. Dudley Jr., telephone interview, April 20, 2000; Dudley, "Moments in Black History," 18; Rayfield Lewis, "Complete Health Center," *Message Magazine,* Ingathering Issue, February 12, 1938, 12; *Nashville Globe,* May 24, 1940.

17. David T. Beito, *From Mutual Aid to the Welfare State: Fraternal Societies and Social Services, 1890–1967* (Chapel Hill: University of North Carolina Press, 2000), 182.

18. Ibid.

19. For more on the history of Mound Bayou, see Janet Sharp Hermann, *The Pursuit of a Dream* (New York: Vintage Books, 1981).

20. Beito, *From Mutual Aid to the Welfare State,* 185.

21. Ibid., 185–86.

22. Ibid., 189; Myrlie Evers, *For Us, the Living* (New York: Doubleday, 1967), 89–90; Dittmer, *Local People,* 32–33.

23. Howard to Claude A. Barnett, April 29, 1946, in August Meier and Elliott Rudwick, eds., *The Claude A. Barnett Papers, Associated Negro Press, 1918–1967* (Frederick, Md.: University Publications of America, 1986), Series I, Race Relations, Black Towns, reel 4.

24. Will Whittington to Howard, September 27, 1945, Correspondence, box 188, folder 2, William L. Dawson Papers, Moorland-Spingarn Collection, Howard University, Washington, D.C.

25. John E. Rankin to Walter Sillers Jr., June 7, 1945, box 50, folder 18, Walter Sillers Jr. Papers, Charles W. Capps Jr. Archives and Museum, Delta State University, Cleveland, Mississippi; Sillers to Rankin, June 8, 1945, box 50, folder 18, Sillers Papers; *Jackson Advocate,* March 23, 1946; Theodore G. Bilbo to Howard, June 7, 1945, folder 2, box 1129, Theodore G. Bilbo Papers, McCain Library and Archives, University of Southern Mississippi, Hattiesburg.

26. Whittington to Howard, September 27, 1945, box 188, folder 2, Dawson Papers; Sillers to Rankin, June 18, 1945, box 50, folder 18, Sillers Papers; *Jackson Advocate,* March 23, 1946; Kenneth V. Vickers, "John Rankin: Democrat and Demagogue" (M.A. thesis, 1993, Mississippi State University), 25–30, 42, 86, 104.

27. Will Whittington to Howard, September 27, 1945, and Jesse O. Redmon Jr. to William L. Dawson, October 12, 1945, box 188, folder 2, Dawson Papers; *Jackson Advocate,* April 12, 1947.

28. Benjamin A. Green to Dawson, March 25, 1946, and Howard to Dawson, March 20, 1946, box 188, folder 2, Dawson Papers.

29. Barnett to Howard, April 20, 1946, and Howard to Barnett, April 29, 1946, in Meier and Rudwick, *Barnett Papers,* Series I, Race Relations, Black Towns, reel 4.

30. *Jackson Advocate,* March 22, 1947, January 29, 1949.

31. Beito, *From Mutual Aid to the Welfare State,* 188; *Jackson Advocate,* November 15, 1947.

32. Beito, *From Mutual Aid to the Welfare State,* 188; *Memphis World,* September 2, 1949.

33. Charles M. Payne, *I've Got the Light of Freedom: The Organizing Tradition and the Mississippi Freedom Struggle* (Berkeley: University of California Press, 1995), 17; James C. Cobb, *The Most Southern Place on Earth: The Mississippi Delta and the Roots of Regional Identity* (New York: Oxford University Press, 1992), 204–5; David L. Cohn, *Where I Was Born and Raised* (Boston: Houghton Mifflin, 1948), 324–25.

34. Payne, *I've Got the Light of Freedom,* 13–17.

35. Adam Nossiter, *Of Long Memory: Mississippi and the Murder of Medgar Evers* (Reading, Mass.: Addison-Wesley, 1994), 40; Earl M. Lewis, "Negro Voter in Mississippi," *Journal of Negro Education* 26 (Summer 1957): 334–35; Dittmer, *Local People,* 28; Payne, *I've Got the Light of Freedom,* 24–25; Mississippi Regional Council of Negro Leadership, *Prospectus of the First Annual Meeting of the Mississippi Regional Council of Negro Leadership* (Mound Bayou, Miss.: n.p, 1952), 11, copy in the author's possession.

36. Aaron Henry with Constance Curry, *Aaron Henry: The Fire Ever Burning* (Jackson: University Press of Mississippi, 2000), 80; *Memphis World,* November 23, 1951; (Memphis) *Tri-State Defender,* December 1, 1951.

37. *Tri-State Defender,* December 1, 1951.

38. *Mississippi Enterprise* (Jackson), November 24, 1951; Mississippi Regional Council of Negro Leadership, *Prospectus,* 7.

39. *Tri-State Defender,* December 15, 1951; *Memphis Commercial Appeal,* December 19, 1951.

40. *Mississippi Enterprise,* November 24, 1951; Maury S. Knowlton to Howard, December 17, 1951, box 30, folder 1, Sillers Papers; *Tri-State Defender,* Decem-

ber 1 and 19, 1951; Howard et al. to "Dear Leader," December 12, 1951, box 30, folder 1, Sillers Papers.

41. Statement of Delta Council with Reference to the Proposed Negro Organization, Cleveland, Mississippi, December 28, 1951, Sillers Papers; *Clarksdale Press Register,* January 3, 1952; Henry, *Aaron Henry,* 79–80.

42. Mississippi Regional Council of Negro Leadership, *Prospectus,* 16, 17; Henry, *Aaron Henry,* 80; *Clarksdale Press Register,* October 14, 1953.

43. Mississippi Regional Council of Negro Leadership, *Prospectus,* 13–14.

44. Ibid.

45. Ibid., 15; *Jackson Advocate,* February 7, 1953.

46. *Jackson Advocate,* February 7, 1953.

47. Mississippi Regional Council of Negro Leadership, *Prospectus,* 12. For more on this argumentative approach, see Mary L. Dudziak, *Cold War Civil Rights: Race and Image of American Democracy* (Princeton: Princeton University Press, 2000).

48. *Tri-State Defender,* December 1, 1951; Mississippi Regional Council of Negro Leadership, *Prospectus,* 14.

49. Mississippi Regional Council of Negro Leadership, *Prospectus,* 15.

50. *Mississippi Enterprise,* November 24, 1951; *Jet,* December 6, 1951, 9.

51. *Tri-State Defender,* November 17, 1951; Jerry Thornbery, "Amzie Moore and His Civil Rights Allies," paper presented at the annual meeting of the Southern Historical Association, November 12, 1993, copy in the author's possession. Aaron Henry had first heard of Howard after reading a 1946 article in the *Saturday Evening Post* by Hodding Carter: "When we did meet, I told Dr. Howard how much I admired him, that we were fortunate to have a man like him in our community, and that I would like to help promote his ideas. A close friendship developed from our meeting." Henry, *Aaron Henry,* 79.

52. *Jackson Advocate,* May 17, 1951; Mississippi, Insurance Department, *Biennial Report,* March 1, 1951, to February 29, 1952, 154, 245; Mississippi, Insurance Department, *Annual Report,* March 1, 1952–February 28, 1954, 168; Mississippi Regional Council of Negro Leadership, *Prospectus,* 4–6; Howard to Barnett, April 26, 1954, Meier and Rudwick, *Barnett Papers,* Series I, Race Relations, Black Towns, reel 4; Maurice L. Sisson to Board Member, February 12, 1952, Correspondence, 1955–56, box 1, folder 2, Amzie Moore Papers, Wisconsin Historical Society, Archives, Madison; Thornbery, "Amzie Moore and His Civil Rights Allies," 4; Henry, *Aaron Henry,* 79; Nossiter, *Of Long Memory,* 38.

53. Mississippi Regional Council of Negro Leadership, *Prospectus,* 16; Henry, *Aaron Henry,* 80–82; Payne, *I've Got the Light of Freedom,* 59.

54. Mississippi Regional Council of Negro Leadership, *Prospectus,* 4–6; *Jackson Advocate,* June 5, 1948; George A. Sewell and Margaret L. Dwight, *Mississippi Black History Makers* (Jackson: University Press of Mississippi, 1984), 245; Beito, *From Mutual Aid to the Welfare State,* 181–82.

55. Mississippi Regional Council of Negro Leadership, *Prospectus,* 4–6; Dudley interview.

56. Julius E. Thompson, *Percy Greene and the Jackson Advocate: The Life and Times of a Radical Conservative Black Newspaperman, 1897–1977* (Jefferson, N.C.: McFarland, 1994), 82; *Jackson Advocate,* February 1, 1947, July 1, 22, 1950.

57. Payne, *I've Got the Light of Freedom*, 191–92.

58. Charles Evers, telephone interview, September 9, 1999. John Dittmer finds that the occupations of NAACP leaders in Jackson, Mississippi, during the 1940s and early 1950s facilitated a similar level of independence from white control (*Local People*, 30).

59. Dittmer, *Local People*, 33; E. M. Lewis, "Negro Voter in Mississippi," 348; *Tri-State Defender*, October 9, 1954.

60. Henry, *Aaron Henry*, 80.

61. Dittmer, *Local People*, 26, 28; Payne, *I've Got the Light of Freedom*, 57; *Jackson Advocate*, August 16, 1952; E. M. Lewis, "Negro Voter in Mississippi," 348; *Clarksdale Press Register*, January 7, 1955.

62. Mississippi Regional Council of Negro Leadership, *Prospectus*, 4–6; Henry, *Aaron Henry*, 73; Dittmer, *Local People*, 26, 29–32, 39–42, 48, 53; Thornbery, "Amzie Moore and His Civil Rights Allies," 6.

63. Thompson, *Percy Greene and the Jackson Advocate*, 32–59; Dittmer, *Local People*, 28; *Chicago Defender*, January 4, 1947; *Memphis World*, March 15, 1949; Henry, *Aaron Henry*, 83; Mississippi Regional Council of Negro Leadership, *Prospectus*, 15.

64. *Jackson Advocate*, February 8, 1947, May 19, 1952, January 24, 1953.

65. Myrlie Evers, *For Us, the Living*, 72–77; Henry, *Aaron Henry*, 80.

66. Myrlie Evers, *For Us, the Living*, 87–88; Henry, *Aaron Henry*, 80–81; Evers interview; Mississippi Regional Council of Negro Leadership, *Prospectus*, 13; Homer Wheaton, telephone interview, June 14, 2000; Maurice L. Sisson, telephone interview, October 22, 1999; Charles Tisdale, telephone interview, January 2, 2001.

67. *Jackson Advocate*, October 4, 1952; *Chicago Defender*, October 11, 1952; Release, Brutality by Highway Patrolmen of Negroes in Mississippi to Cease, ca. October 1952, file on Mississippi Pressures, Howard, T. R. M., box 422, Group 2, NAACP Papers, Library of Congress, Washington, D.C.

68. Payne, *I've Got the Light of Freedom*, 59; *Tri-State Defender*, August 2, 1952; Dittmer, *Local People*, 28, 70; Henry, *Aaron Henry*, 81.

69. *Clarksdale Press Register*, April 8, 1952; *Jackson Advocate*, May 3, 1952; *Tri-State Defender*, May 10, 1952. Dawson had campaigned extensively in the South for the Truman campaign in 1948. William J. Grimshaw, *Bitter Fruit: Black Politics and the Chicago Machine, 1931–1991* (Chicago: University of Chicago Press, 1992), 81.

70. *Memphis World*, May 6, 1952; *Tri-State Defender*, May 10, 1952.

71. *Tri-State Defender*, May 17, 1952; *Memphis World*, May 6, 1952.

72. Myrlie Evers, *For Us, the Living*, 88; Kay Mills, *This Little Light of Mine: The Life of Fannie Lou Hamer* (New York: Dutton, 1993), 40–41; Payne, *I've Got the Light of Freedom*, 154; Evers interview.

73. *Jackson Advocate*, August 16, 1952; *Tri-State Defender*, August 2, 1952; *Memphis World*, October 7, 1952.

74. *Jackson Advocate*, May 9, 1958; Archibald Carey to T. R. M. and Helen Howard, May 4, 1953, box 15, folder 103, Archibald Carey Papers, Chicago Historical Society.

75. Sisson, Tisdale, and Wheaton interviews.

76. Ibid.

77. Dittmer, *Local People*, 32–33; Gloster Current to Walter White, September 30, 1952, memorandum, and Ruby Hurley to Walter White, memorandum, October 8, 1952, both in Group II, box 381, NAACP Papers; "The Accomplishments and Objectives of the Regional Council of Negro Leadership," NAACP, file on Mississippi Pressures, Group II, box 422, NAACP Papers; Mississippi Regional Council of Negro Leadership, *Prospectus*, 6; Payne, *I've Got the Light of Freedom*, 41–42, 61.

78. Dittmer, *Local People*, 32–34; Payne, *I've Got the Light of Freedom*, 61.

79. Dittmer, *Local People*, 36; *Clarksdale Press Register*, November 21, 1952; *Tri-State Defender*, February 21, 1952; *Jackson Advocate*, February 7, 1953.

80. *Jackson Advocate*, February 7, 1953; *Clarksdale Press Register*, October 14, 1953.

81. *Clarksdale Press Register*, November 12 and 21, 1953; *Jackson Clarion-Ledger*, December 25, 1953.

82. Nossiter, *Of Long Memory*, 41.

83. *Clarksdale Press Register*, November 3, 1953; Dittmer, *Local People*, 43. The state NAACP recruited people representing a wide spectrum of opinion as "special consultants" to the conference, including Howard, Ruby Hurley, Fred Miller, Percy Greene, and W. A. Bender. Eighth Annual Conference of Mississippi Branches, November 6–8, 1955, Mississippi, Branch File, Group C98, NAACP Papers.

84. *Memphis World*, November 20, 1953; *Delta Democrat Times* (Greenville, Miss.), November 16, 1953.

85. *Delta Democrat Times*, November 16, 1953; *Clarksdale Press Register*, November 6, 1953; *Tri-State Defender*, December 27, 1952; *Jackson Clarion-Ledger*, November 7, 1953; *Jackson Advocate*, October 17, 1953, May 15, 1954.

86. Henry, *Aaron Henry*, 83; *Jackson Advocate*, May 15, 1954.

87. Payne, *I've Got the Light of Freedom*, 50, 56; Myrlie Evers, *For Us, the Living*, 98, 102; *Clarksdale Press Register*, January 22, 1954; Officers of the Mississippi State Conference of NAACP Branches, January 1, 1954," NAACP 1940–1955, Branch File, Geographical File, Mississippi State Conference of Branches, 1954–55, Group II, C98, NAACP Papers.

88. *Tri-State Defender*, May 8 and 15, 1954; *Mississippi Enterprise*, April 17, 1954; *Jackson Advocate*, April 27, 1954.

89. *Memphis World*, May 11, 1954; *Tri-State Defender*, May 15, 1954, May 22, 1955; Benjamin Hooks, telephone interview, June 15, 2000.

90. For more on Howard in subsequent years, see David T. Beito and Linda Royster Beito, "*The Most Hated, and the Best Loved, Man in Mississippi*": *The Life of Dr. T. R. M. Howard* (forthcoming); Beito and Beito, "T. R. M. Howard, M.D.: A Mississippi Doctor in Chicago Civil Rights," *A.M.E. Church Review* 117 (July–September 2001): 58–59.

CHAPTER 3

1. George Holmes, review of *Uncle Tom's Cabin*, from *Southern Literary Messenger* 8 (October 1852), reprinted in *Uncle Tom's Cabin Norton Critical Edition*, ed. Elizabeth Ammons (New York: Norton, 1994), 468–69, 475, 477.

2. The outer limit for white southern liberals, more accurately "moderates," was segregation, which few of their number opposed in the 1940s. Though they wished to see amelioration of the harsh and demeaning features of the system by bringing improvements in black employment and housing and by guaranteeing the ballot and fair, dispassionate dispensation of justice, liberals tended to agree with *Atlanta Constitution* editor Ralph McGill, who in 1943 wrote approvingly that segregation would "be retained for a long time."

For overviews of the ideology of twentieth-century southern liberalism, see Morton Sosna, *In Search of the Silent South: Southern Liberals and the Race Issue* (New York: Columbia University Press, 1977); John Egerton, *Speak Now against the Day: The Generation before the Civil Rights Movement in the South* (Chapel Hill: University of North Carolina Press, 1994); Patricia Sullivan, *Days of Hope: Race and Democracy in the New Deal Era* (Chapel Hill: University of North Carolina Press, 1996). McGill's quote is from Egerton, *Speak Now*, 307.

3. Harvard Sitkoff, "Racial Militancy and Interracial Violence in the Second World War," *Journal of American History* 58 (December 1971): 671; Gunnar Myrdal, *An American Dilemma* (New York: Harper and Row, 1944), 997; Egerton, *Speak Now*, 276; Pete Daniel, "Going among Strangers: Southern Reactions to World War II," *Journal of American History* 77 (December 1990): 893.

4. Doris Kearns Goodwin, *No Ordinary Time: Franklin and Eleanor Roosevelt/The Home Front in World War II* (New York: Simon and Schuster, 1994), 629; Blanche Wiesen Cook, *Eleanor Roosevelt*, vol. 1, *1884–1933* (New York: Viking, 1992), 407.

5. Hollinger Barnard, ed., *Outside the Magic Circle: The Autobiography of Virginia Foster Durr* (Tuscaloosa: University of Alabama Press, 1984), 49; ER quoted in Allida Black, *Casting Her Own Shadow: Eleanor Roosevelt and the Shaping of Postwar Liberalism* (New York: Columbia University Press, 1996), 20; James Coker to Mrs. Roosevelt, November 12, 1937, and Friendship Methodist Episcopal Church Bible class, Wilkesboro, North Carolina, to Mrs. Roosevelt, December 26, 1937, both in Official File 93, box 7, FDR Papers, FDR Library, Hyde Park, New York.

6. Black, *Casting Her Own Shadow*, 20; Eleanor Roosevelt, "Should Wives Work?" *Good Housekeeping*, December 1937, 211.

7. Harold Ickes, *The Secret Diary of Harold L. Ickes: The First Thousand Days, 1933–1936* (New York: Simon and Schuster, 1953), 284–85. ER biographer Blanche W. Cook notes that Ickes disliked ER, perhaps because she reminded him of his wife, "a forceful, independent woman of wealth" with whom he endured "a difficult marriage." Blanche Wiesen Cook, *Eleanor Roosevelt*, vol. 2, *1933–1938* (New York: Viking, 1999), 67.

8. George Wolfskill and John A. Hudson, *All But the People: Franklin D. Roosevelt and His Critics, 1933–1939* (London: Macmillan, 1969), 43. Republicans attempted to make an issue of the First Lady's public role in the 1936 contest, stressing that Landon's wife would be no part of campaign trips and had never held a press conference. Joseph Lash, *Eleanor and Franklin* (New York: Norton, 1971), 447.

9. Ruth Stevens, *"Hi-Ya Neighbor"* (n.p.: Tupper and Love, 1947), 57.

10. Wolfskill and Hudson, *All But the People*, 87.

11. Ralph Bunche, *The Political Status of the Negro in the Age of FDR*, ed.

Dewey W. Grantham (Chicago: University of Chicago Press, 1973), 33; Wolfskill and Hudson, *All But the People,* 91; Cook, *Eleanor Roosevelt, 1933–1938,* 345; Mrs. J. E. Andrews to President Franklin D. Roosevelt, April 7, 1935, in Official File 93, FDR Papers. The newsletter was called the *Georgia Woman's World;* it was distributed to every delegate at the 1936 anti-FDR rally hosted in Macon, Georgia, by Eugene Talmadge and funded by the Liberty League.

12. Allida Black, "Championing a Champion: Eleanor Roosevelt and the Marian Anderson Freedom Concert," *Presidential Studies Quarterly* 21 (Fall 1990): 725–26.

13. "67% Approve First Lady's D.A.R. Stand," *Washington Post,* March 19, 1939.

14. Mrs. A. W. Taylor to Franklin D. Roosevelt, n.d., filed May 29, 1944, Official File 93, FDR Papers. In 1945 when the Daughters of the American Revolution (DAR) again refused the hall to singer Hazel Scott, wife of Adam Clayton Powell, First Lady Bess Truman ignored Congressman Powell's demand that she resign her DAR membership and pointedly accepted DAR hospitality at a tea. In most of the nation the episode spawned unfavorable comparisons between the two First Ladies, but in the South it sparked more applications for DAR membership. Maurine Beasley, "Bess (Elizabeth Virginia Wallace) Truman," in *American First Ladies,* ed. Lewis G. Gould (New York: Garland, 1996), 457; Mrs. S. L. Hollingsworth to Senator Theodore Bilbo, n.d. [January 1946], box 1010, Theodore G. Bilbo Papers, University of Southern Mississippi, Hattiesburg.

15. Martha Swain, *Pat Harrison: The New Deal Years* (Jackson: University Press of Mississippi, 1978), 209.

16. Howard Odum, *Race and Rumors of Race* (Chapel Hill: University of North Carolina, 1943), 171; Gail W. O'Brien, *The Color of the Law: Race, Violence, and Justice in the Post–World War II South* (Chapel Hill: University of North Carolina, 1999), 89–108.

17. John Morton Blum, *V Was for Victory: Politics and American Culture during World War II* (New York: Harcourt, Brace, Jovanovich, 1976), 193; Marion M. Crisp, Blaine, AR to ER, March 26, 1944, in ER Papers, 190.1, FDR Library; Raper interview with Will Ratliff, April 4, 1943, Arthur Raper Papers, Southern Historical Collection, University of North Carolina, Chapel Hill. I am indebted to my colleague Gail O'Brien for this last citation.

18. Odum, *Race and Rumors of Race,* 56–66, 92, 105–6, 110–11; Thomas Sancton, "Trouble in Dixie," *New Republic,* January 4, 1943, 11–14; Sancton, "Race Fear Sweeps the South," *New Republic,* January 18, 1943, 81–83.

19. Odum, *Race and Rumors of Race,* 73–80, 81–89; Sancton, "Race Fear Sweeps the South," 83.

20. Bryant Simon, "Fearing Eleanor: Whiteness and Wartime Rumors in the American South, 1940–1945," paper presented at Cambridge University, April 1999, p. 2.

21. Frank Daniels to Jonathan Daniels, August 5 and 25, 1942, in Jonathan W. Daniels Papers, Southern Historical Collection, University of North Carolina, Chapel Hill.

22. Sancton, "Race Fear Sweeps the South," 83.

23. ER quoted in Odum, *Race and Rumors of Race*, 83; FBI report quoted in Robert A. Hill, *The FBI's RACON: Racial Conditions in the United States during World War II* (Boston: Northeastern University Press, 1995), 255.

24. Quoted in Pamela Tyler, *Silk Stockings and Ballot Boxes: Women and Politics in New Orleans, 1920–1963* (Athens: University of Georgia Press, 1996), 101.

25. Mrs. J. H. Gibbs, Palmetto, Georgia, to ER, November 16, 1942, quoted in Simon, "Fearing Eleanor," 3–4; Mrs. J. T. Stephens, Selma, Alabama, to FDR, October 20, 1944, Official File 93, box 6, FDR Papers.

26. Anonymous letter, Washington, D.C., to ER, July 3, 1942, http://foia.fbi.gov Eleanor Roosevelt part 12D no. 62-28371-190.

27. Sancton, "Race Fear Sweeps the South," 83.

28. Jessie Daniel Ames, interview by Jacquelyn Dowd Hall, p. 35 of transcript G-3, Southern Oral History Project, University of North Carolina, Chapel Hill.

29. Lash, *Eleanor and Franklin*, 672; FBI report from Baltimore, March 17, 1943, http://foia.fbi.gov Eleanor Roosevelt, identification number illegible; Malvina Thompson to Steve Early, July 30, 1943, PPF 2, container 2, FDR Papers.

30. Valerie Nicholson, "No 'Nice' Home Would Receive Her," *Southern Pines (N.C.) Pilot*, November 15, 1962, in North Carolina Collection, University of North Carolina, Chapel Hill; Frank Daniels to Jonathan Daniels, August 25, 1942, Daniels Papers.

31. "Ed" to Steve Early, March 30, 1943, PPF 2, container 2, FDR Papers.

32. Quoted in Thomas Sancton, "The Race Riots," *New Republic*, July 5, 1943, 630.

33. "Texan" to J. Edgar Hoover, September 8, 1943, http://foia.fbi.gov Eleanor Roosevelt Part 1, no. 62-62735-9.

34. *Congressional Record*, 78th Cong., 2nd sess. (1944), vol. 90, part 6, June 20, 1944, 6253; Mrs. Floyd Jones, "wife of Warrant Officer, U.S.N.," to Bilbo, March 25, 1944, Bilbo Papers.

35. "Mixing of Races at CIO Canteen Draws New Fire," unidentified clipping (March 2, 1944) in Official File 93, FDR Papers; Mrs. L. M. Standifer, Chattanooga, Tennessee, to ER, n.d., Mrs. M. M. McConnell, Gallatin, Tennessee, to ER, March 10, 1944, "An Outraged Woman," Lakeland, Florida, to ER, February 28, 1944, and Bertie Mae Loner to ER, March 1, 1944, all in box 2962, ER Papers.

36. Mary Malone and eleven others, Lynchburg, Virginia, to FDR, February 22, 1944, [name illegible], Arlington, Virginia, to FDR, February 7, 1942, and Mr. And Mrs. George B. Rogers, Atlanta, to FDR, December 23, 1943, all in PPF 2, FDR Papers.

37. Howard C. Smith to Senator Lister Hill, January 4, 1943, quoted in Virginia Van der Veer Hamilton, *Lister Hill: Statesman from the South* (Chapel Hill: University of North Carolina Press, 1987), 115; Mrs. J. T. Stephens, Selma, Alabama, to FDR, October 20, 1944, and E. P. Crow, Atlanta, to FDR, February 18, 1944, both in Official File 93, FDR Papers; Brown Hayes, Corinth, Mississippi, to FDR, August 21, 1944, PPF 2, container 2, FDR Papers.

38. Eleanor Roosevelt, "Freedom: Promise or Fact," in Allida Black, ed., *What I Hope to Leave Behind: The Essential Essays of Eleanor Roosevelt* (Brooklyn: Carlson, 1995), 165; *Raleigh News and Observer*, February 1, 1950; ER, "Race, Religion,

and Prejudice," *New Republic*, May 11, 1942, 630; ER to L. W. Bates, February 23, 1942, 190.1, ER Papers.

39. ER, "Race, Religion, and Prejudice," 630; ER, essay written for the Joint Commission on Social Reconstruction, October 1945, in Black, *What I Hope to Leave Behind*, 168; ER, "The Negro and Social Change," ibid., 146.

40. ER, "Some of My Best Friends Are Negro," in Black, *What I Hope to Leave Behind*, 171–76.

41. Gunnar Myrdal, *An American Dilemma*, vol. 1, *The Negro in a White Nation* (New York: McGraw-Hill, 1964), 60–61.

42. Lillian Smith, *Killers of the Dream* (New York: Norton, 1949), 19–20.

43. ER, "Some of My Best Friends Are Negro," 176. Emphasis mine.

44. Quoted in Black, *Casting Her Own Shadow*, 87. Interviews that my students have conducted with their southern grandparents, born in the 1930s and earlier, reveal that belief in ER's racially mixed blood was not uncommon. This belief persisted until her death. "The mixed breed is treacherous, clever, and shrewd," wrote a southern correspondent to the FBI in 1961. "She wishes all mankind to become mongrels because she is one." March 8, 1961, http://foia.fbi.gov Eleanor Roosevelt Part 02 illegible identification number.

45. Hamilton, *Lister Hill*, 115; George B. Tindall, *The Emergence of the New South, 1913–1945* (Baton Rouge: Louisiana State University Press, 1967), 716–17.

46. Bryant Simon, "Race Reactions: African American Organizing, Liberalism, and White Working-Class Politics in Postwar South Carolina," in *Jumpin' Jim Crow: Southern Politics from Civil War to Civil Rights*, ed. Jane Dailey, Glenda Elizabeth Gilmore, and Bryant Simon (Princeton: Princeton University Press, 2000), 254; Bunche, *Political Status of the Negro*, xix.

47. Tindall, *Emergence of the New South*, 556 (first quote); William Anderson, *The Wild Man from Sugar Creek: The Political Career of Eugene Talmadge* (Baton Rouge: Louisiana State University Press, 1975), 210, 225 (second, fourth, and fifth quotes); Bilbo quote from Thurston E. Doler, "Theodore Bilbo's Rhetoric of Racial Relations" (Ph.D. diss., University of Oregon, 1968), 211.

48. Mrs. J. T. Stephens, Selma, Alabama, to FDR, October 20, 1944 (first and third quotes), and Chester B. Collins, Fort Worth, to FDR, May 26, 1944 (second quote), both in Official File 93, box 6, FDR Papers; Loretta Carlisle to ER, April 18, 1944, box 2962, ER Papers (fourth quote).

49. Ethridge quoted in Tindall, *Emergence of the New South*, 714; John Temple Graves, "The Southern Negro and the War Crisis," *Virginia Quarterly Review* 18 (Autumn 1942): 500–517; Virginius Dabney, "Nearer and Nearer the Precipice," *Atlantic Monthly*, January 1943, 94–100; David Cohn, "How the South Feels," *Atlantic Monthly*, January 1944, 47–51.

50. *Chicago Defender*, May 30, 1942, in PPF 2, container 2, FDR Papers.

51. Rayford Logan, ed., *What the Negro Wants* (Chapel Hill: University of North Carolina Press, 1944), 136 (Randolph), 205 (Wilkerson), 28 (Logan), 115 (Wilkins), 319 (Brown). W. T. Couch, the University of North Carolina Press editor, had solicited the essays from black opinion makers, selecting liberal, moderate, and conservative individuals. When even the most conservative essayist in the group wrote flatly that "all Negroes must condemn any form of

segregation based on race, creed, or color anywhere in our nation," a shocked Couch, generally considered a "liberal," penned an awkward introduction to the book in which he defended segregation as right for the foreseeable future.

52. FBI report from E. P. Guinane, Birmingham, Alabama, to J. Edgar Hoover, October 7, 1942, http://foia.fbi.gov Eleanor Roosevelt no. 100-2218; Graves quoted in Hamilton, *Lister Hill*, 115; Mrs. Paul T. Norris, Quinton, Alabama, to ER, April 4, 1944, Fred D. Oakley to ER, March 5, 1944, and Willie King Jones, Austin, Texas, to ER, April 8, 1944, all in box 2962, ER Papers.

53. Interviews with confidential sources; James T. Wooten, *Dasher: The Roots and the Rising of Jimmy Carter* (New York: Summit Books, 1978), 96.

54. Frank Daniels to Jonathan Daniels, August 25, 1942, Daniels Papers.

55. Archie Bunker, in *All in the Family*, 25th-anniversary show, quoted in Simon, "Fearing Eleanor," 21.

56. Along these lines, the author's grandmother, born in 1899 in rural south Georgia, maintained stoutly her entire life that Eleanor Roosevelt was "no lady."

57. ER to Evans C. Johnson, September 18, 1942, Collection no. 3064, Southern Historical Collection, University of North Carolina at Chapel Hill; unknown writer to J. Edgar Hoover, October 12, 1943, in FBI website, http://foia.fbi.gov Eleanor Roosevelt, Part 12c, no. 100-0-19681.

58. Cohn, "How the South Feels," 49.

CHAPTER 4

1. Quoted in Dorothy Tilly, "Christian Social Relations in the Southeastern Jurisdiction," *Methodist Woman*, n.d., n.p., copy in Dorothy Rogers Tilly Papers, Robert H. Woodruff Library, Emory University, Atlanta, Georgia.

2. John Patrick McDowell, *The Social Gospel in the South: The Woman's Home Mission Movement in the Methodist Episcopal Church, South, 1889–1939* (Baton Rouge: Louisiana State University Press, 1982).

3. Information on Tilly's early life is found in the biographical sketch introducing the Tilly Papers; Arnold Shankman, "Dorothy Tilly and the Fellowship of the Concerned," in *From the Old South to the New: Essays on The Transitional South*, ed. Walter J. Fraser Jr. and Winfred B. Moore (Westport, Conn.: Greenwood Press, 1981), 241 [hereafter cited as "Tilly and the FOC"]; Shankman, "Dorothy Rogers Tilly," in *Encyclopedia of Religion in the South*, ed. Samuel S. Hill Jr. (Macon: Mercer University Press, 1984), 782; *Macon Telegraph*, June 3, 1962; *Wesleyan Christian Advocate*, March 18, 1965.

4. Dorothy Tilly, "The Fellowship of the Concerned," *The Woman's Press*, February 5, 1950, 8 [hereafter cited as "The FOC"]; Shankman, "Dorothy Rogers Tilly," 782.

5. Apropos of Tilly and her FOC colleagues was the designation "city mothers," first suggested by Jessie Ash Arndt, "Women's Crusade Spurs Fairer Treatment of Negroes in Southern U.S.," *Christian Science Monitor*, January 9, 1953, n.p., copy in Tilly Papers.

6. See Joel Williamson, *The Crucible of Race: Black-White Relations in the American South Since Emancipation* (New York: Oxford University Press, 1984).

For a fuller discussion of Methodist racial views in this period, see Robert Watson Sledge, "A History of the Methodist Episcopal Church, South, 1914–1939" (Ph.D. diss., University of Texas, May 1972), 197–200.

7. Elmer T. Clark, *The Negro and His Religion* (Nashville: Cokesbury Press, 1924), 48.

8. *Alabama Christian Advocate*, July 15, 1926, 2.

9. Sledge, "History of the Methodist Episcopal Church"; Ann Wells Ellis, "The Commission on Interracial Cooperation, 1919–1944: Its Activities and Results" (Ph.D. diss., Georgia State University, 1975), preface. On the relation of the 1906 Georgia governor's race to the Atlanta riot, see C. Vann Woodward, *Tom Watson: Agrarian Rebel* (1938; reprint, Savannah: Beehive Press, 1973), 327–28; Mark Bauerlein, *Negrophobia: A Race Riot in Atlanta, 1906* (San Francisco: Encounter Books, 2001).

10. Helena Huntington Smith, "Mrs. Tilly's Crusade," *Collier's*, December 30, 1950, 66; Shankman, "Tilly and the FOC," 242–43; Ellis, "Commission on Interracial Cooperation," 178–89. For a fuller examination of the Association of Southern Women for the Prevention of Lynching, see Jacqueline Dowd Hall, *Revolt against Chivalry: Jessie Daniel Ames and the Women's Campaign against Lynching* (New York: Columbia University Press, 1979).

11. Alice G. Knotts, "Bound by the Spirit, Found on the Journey: The Methodist Women's Campaign for Southern Civil Rights, 1940–1968" (Ph.D. diss., Iliff School of Theology and the University of Denver, 1989), 29–39.

12. Robert Moats Miller, "Methodism and American Society, 1900–1939," in *The History of American Methodism*, vol. 3, ed. Emory Stevens Bucke (Nashville: Abingdon Press, 1964), 355.

13. Specific efforts to influence the South away from segregation remained a minority approach within the Methodist Episcopal Church. Such periodic efforts are highlighted in ibid., 367–68, citing the *Evanston News-Index*, April 4, 1919, 1, and the *Journal of the General Conference of the Methodist Episcopal Church*, 1924, 295.

14. Frederick A. Norwood, *The Story of American Methodism: A History of the United Methodists and Their Relations* (Nashville: Abingdon Press, 1974), 407–9.

15. W. Edward Orser, "Racial Attitudes in Wartime: The Protestant Churches during the Second World War," *Church History* 41 (March 1972): 337–53.

16. "Southern Methodist Women Ask Searching Question," *Christian Century*, April 21, 1937, 509.

17. Orser, "Racial Attitudes in Wartime," 345.

18. *Pittsburgh Courier*, December 21, 1940, quoted in Richard M. Dalfiume, "The 'Forgotten Years' of the Negro Revolution," *Journal of American History* 55 (June 1968): 91–94.

19. Orser, "Racial Attitudes in Wartime," 351–52, citing *Zion's Herald*, July 8, 1942, 656.

20. "Address of the Council of Bishops," *Daily Christian Advocate*, April 27, 1944, 27, 28; Frank L. Robertson, "'White Supremacy'—'Master Race,'" *Wesleyan Christian Advocate*, February 14, 1947, 6.

21. *Wesleyan Christian Advocate*, October 28, 1948, 6.

22. Ibid., August 19, 1948, 6–7.

23. Quoted in the *Report of Interracial Leadership Conference,* Wesley Memorial Church, Atlanta, Georgia, January 28–29, 1957, 40–41.

24. Message on Race Relationships, Board of Social and Economic Relations of the Methodist Church, January 14, 1955, cited in *Report of Interracial Leadership Conference,* 1, 41.

25. Statement on Supreme Court ruling, June 13, 1954, and Janice Treadway to Bishop Arthur J. Moore, June 14, 1954, box 20, Arthur J. Moore Papers, Robert H. Woodruff Library, Emory University, Atlanta, Georgia.

26. Episcopal Address to the 1956 General Conference and "The Methodist Church and Race," both quoted in *Report of Interracial Leadership Conference,* 43–47.

27. *Wesleyan Christian Advocate,* September 1, 1955, 8. See also the 1956 Episcopal Address of the Methodist College of Bishops, Southeastern Jurisdiction, ibid., July 26, 1956, 2–3, 11. The bishops' frank admission that many Methodists were not yet ready to follow Christian discipleship on the matter of ending segregation was at least an improvement over one Mississippi Presbyterian church, which in 1964 even more candidly confessed, "we know that this is not what Jesus Christ would do," before it proceeded to exclude African Americans from its worship. See Joel L. Alvis Jr., *Religion and Race: Southern Presbyterians, 1946–1983* (Tuscaloosa: University of Alabama Press, 1994), 97–98.

28. Copy of resolution in box 20, Moore Papers.

29. Copy of telegram, W. B. Rouse to Chairman, Methodist Bishops, December 7, 1954, box 20, Moore Papers.

30. Stanley Frazer, "The Methodist Church and Segregation," *Wesleyan Christian Advocate,* August 19, 1954, 3.

31. Meeting of the Association of Methodist Ministers and Laymen, December 14, 1954, see "Preservation of Central Jurisdiction to Be Discussed," *Wesleyan Christian Advocate,* December 2, 1954, 7; G. Stanley Frazer to Bishop Arthur J. Moore, January 24, 1955, box 20, Moore Papers.

32. Donald E. Collins, *When the Church Bell Rang Racist: The Methodist Church and the Civil Rights Movement in Alabama* (Macon, Ga.: Mercer University Press, 1998), 19–20.

33. Resolution of the Lindale Methodist Church, February 4, 1952, and Josie Lee Herrin to Arthur J. Moore, May 30, 1952, both in box 20, Moore Papers.

34. Ellen D. Bunn to the Board of Missions of the Methodist Church, April 1, 1954, box 20, Moore Papers.

35. Report of Workshop no. 3, *Report of Interracial Leadership Conference,* 95.

36. Mrs. E. C. Dowdell to Bishop James O. Andrew, 1861, cited by Knotts, "Bound by the Spirit," 6.

37. Knotts, "Bound by the Spirit," 40–45, citing *Thirteenth Annual Report of the Woman's Missionary Council,* 1923, 136; McDowell, *The Social Gospel in the South,* 109–11.

38. Knotts, "Bound by the Spirit," 142, 172; Thelma Stevens, "Advance in Human Rights," and "Advance—In Training, in Cooperation, and in Human Relations," *Methodist Woman,* September 1949, 19–20; *Journal of the Women's Division of the Board of Global Ministries,* Annual Report, January 17, 1953, 38. This latter source refers to the minutes of the Woman's Division of Christian Service

of the Board of Missions of the Methodist Church. Each year's minutes bound together in one volume includes both the Annual Report and the Journal of the Executive Committee. Citations come from the quarterly "Report and Recommendations of the Department of Christian Social Relations and Local Church Activities to the Woman's Division of Christian Service of the Board of Missions of The Methodist Church." Since after 1968 all such volumes of the successor organization were entitled *Journal of the Women's Division of the Board of Global Ministries,* these annual volumes issued between 1940 and 1968 are also designated as *Journal* hereafter.

39. *Journal,* Annual Report of the Woman's Division, 1943–1944, 189.

40. "Christian Social Relations and Local Church Activities: A Program of Action for 1945," *Methodist Woman,* January 1945, 16.

41. Knotts, "Bound by the Spirit," 137–38, citing *Journal,* Sixth Annual Meeting, November 27–December 3, 1945, 14; Knotts, "Bound by the Spirit," 141; *Journal of the General Conference of the Methodist Church,* 1948, 1093, 1096, 1099.

42. Knotts, "Bound by the Spirit," 184, 187, citing Thelma Stevens and Margaret R. Bender, "Information and Action," *Methodist Woman,* January 1954, 25.

43. *Journal,* Annual Report, January 16, 1954, 54; "Affirmations of the Assembly," *Methodist Woman,* July–August 1954, 43.

44. Knotts, "Bound by the Spirit," 190–91, citing *Journal,* Executive Committee Meeting, September 1954, 76–77; *Journal,* Executive Committee Meeting, September 1955, 29.

45. Marianne D. Fink, "The Methodist Church and Segregation: An Open Letter to the Wesleyan Christian Advocate," *Wesleyan Christian Advocate,* September 9, 1954, 11. Along with running Fink's rejoinder to Frazer, editor F. M. Gaines issued the cautious disclaimer that articles did not represent the views of the *Advocate* or the Methodist Church, adding: "The two articles published represent the two schools of thought on segregation. A continued discussion of the subject would probably result in more heat than light. So please let the *Advocate* sing the Amen and dismiss the subject."

46. *Eleventh Annual Report of the Woman's Missionary Society of the North Georgia Conference* (Gainesville, Ga.: n.p., 1921), 29; Dorothy Tilly, "Leadership School," *Wesleyan Christian Advocate,* May 14, 1937; Ruth H. Collins, "We Are the Inheritors," *Response* 3 (July–August 1971): 31.

47. *Eleventh Annual Report of the Woman's Missionary Society of the North Georgia Conference,* 29; Knotts, "Bound by the Spirit," 164–65, citing Thelma Stevens, *Legacy for the Future: The History of Christian Social Relations in the Women's Division of Christian Service, 1940–1968* (Cincinnati: Women's Division, Board of Global Ministries, United Methodist Church, 1978), 48; Arndt, "Women's Crusade"; Smith, "Mrs. Tilly's Crusade," 66; R. H. Collins, "We Are the Inheritors," 31.

48. Tilly, "Leadership School."

49. Shankman, "Tilly and the FOC," 242–43; Ellis, "Commission on Interracial Cooperation," 178–89; memorandum on meeting of Tilly and Ellis Arnall, October 27, 1942, box 35, CIC Papers, Atlanta University; Smith, "Mrs. Tilly's Crusade," 67.

50. See John E. Talmadge, *Rebecca Latimer Felton: Nine Stormy Decades* (Athens: University of Georgia Press, 1960), 36–45. On Felton's Holiness activities, see Briane Turley, *A Wheel within a Wheel: Southern Methodism and the Georgia Holiness Association* (Macon, Ga.: Mercer University Press, 1999), 139, 172–73, 176–77.

51. *Atlanta Journal,* October 24, 1904; Rebecca Felton to *Atlanta Journal,* November 15, 1898.

52. *Wesleyan Christian Advocate,* September 27, 1940, 1, 13.

53. Knotts, "Bound by the Spirit," 158, citing unpublished material submitted to the *North Georgia Review* and a letter from Ames to Lillian Smith, December 30, 1941, Jesse Daniel Ames Papers, Southern Historical Collection, University of North Carolina Library, Chapel Hill.

54. Arndt, "Women's Crusade."

55. R. H. Collins, "We Are the Inheritors," 31; Shankman, "Tilly and the FOC," 243; Smith, "Mrs. Tilly's Crusade," 67; report of interview of Tilly with Governor Jim Nance McCord of Tennessee, March 6, 1946, Guy Johnson Papers, Archives of the Southern Regional Council, Robert W. Woodruff Library, Atlanta University Center, Atlanta, Georgia.

56. Ellis, "Commission on Interracial Cooperation," 86–87; Dorothy Tilly to "Dear Friend," August 19, 1942, Tilly Papers; "Interview between Ellis Arnall and Mrs. Tilly and Mrs. McDougald," August 1942, box 22 ("Politics, Ellis Arnall"), CIC Papers; Smith, "Mrs. Tilly's Crusade," 29.

57. Press release from Roosevelt's address, Lake Junaluska, North Carolina, July 25, 1944, box 2, folder 1, Tilly Papers.

58. Eleanor Roosevelt, *This I Remember* (1949; reprint, Westport, Conn.: Greenwood Press, 1975), 329–30.

59. Smith, "Mrs. Tilly's Crusade," 29, 66.

60. Shankman, "Tilly and the FOC," 243; transcripts of the President's Committee on Civil Rights, box 4, Tilly Papers.

61. President's Committee on Civil Rights, *To Secure These Rights* (New York: Simon and Schuster, 1947), 151–73. For a brief summary of the report and the southern members' dissent, see John Egerton, *Speak Now against the Day: The Generation before the Civil Rights Movement in the South* (New York: Knopf, 1994), 415–16.

62. *Journal,* Eighth Annual Meeting, Women's Division of the Board of Missions, The Methodist Church, December 2–12, 1947, 15–16; Knotts, "Bound by the Spirit," 131; Rachelle McClure to Dorothy Tilly, November 11, 1947, Tilly Papers.

63. Smith, "Mrs. Tilly's Crusade," 66; Shankman, "Tilly and the FOC," 243; *Atlanta Constitution,* January 30, 1948, 23.

64. Egerton, *Speak Now,* 482–83.

65. *Wesleyan Christian Advocate,* July 29, 1948, 11; Smith, "Mrs. Tilly's Crusade," 66.

66. *Springfield Register,* February 14, 1949, clipping in Tilly Papers.

67. *Louisville Times,* February 14, 1950.

68. Tobias to Tilly, November 5, 1948, Tilly Papers.

69. *Journal,* Executive Committee Meeting, September 9, 1952, 36.

70. Tom C. Clark to Dorothy Tilly, October 28, 1947, Tilly Papers.
71. Smith, "Mrs. Tilly's Crusade," 67.
72. Tilly, "The FOC," 8–9; Shankman, "Tilly and the FOC," 244; "Southern Church Women Draft Action Program," *New South* 4 (September 1949): 2–3; "Church and Conscience in the South," *New South* 6 (February 1951): 1–4; *The Fellowship of the Concerned* (leaflet), n.p., n.n.
73. Smith, "Mrs. Tilly's Crusade," 29.
74. Shankman, "Tilly and the FOC," 245.
75. Arndt, "Women's Crusade."
76. Tilly, "The FOC," 9; Arndt, "Women's Crusade."
77. Tilly, "The FOC," 9.
78. Smith, "Mrs. Tilly's Crusade," 29.
79. Tilly to Mr. C. A. [Esther] Meeker, June 11, 1956, Archives of the Southern Regional Council, Robert W. Woodruff Library, Atlanta University Center, Atlanta, Georgia.
80. Shankman, "Tilly and the FOC," 245.
81. Smith, "Mrs. Tilly's Crusade," 67.
82. Franklin Archer, "The New Attack," *Anderson (S.C.) Independent,* November 17, 1947.
83. Smith, "Mrs. Tilly's Crusade," 67.
84. "To the Two Southern Residents Of The Civil Rights (?) Committee," anonymous letter to Tilly and Frank Graham, mailed to Tilly on February 8, 1948, copy in Tilly Papers.
85. Knotts, "Bound by the Spirit," 174; S. High, "Methodism's Pink Fringe," *Reader's Digest,* February 1950, 134–38.
86. Shankman, "Tilly and the FOC," 246–47; Florence Robin, "Honeychile at the Barricades," *Harper's,* October 1962, 174; Tilly to Dear Friends [in Alabama], December 17, 1958, and Tilly to Bill Cleghorn, December 5, 1958, Dorothy Tilly and the Fellowship of the Concerned Papers, Archives of the Southern Regional Council, Atlanta University Center, Atlanta, Georgia.
87. Shankman, "Tilly and the FOC," 247; Tilly to Mrs. Page Wilson, April 10, 1964, Tilly and the Fellowship of the Concerned Papers; Chester Davis, "Capturing the Strategic Foothills," *Winston-Salem Journal and Sentinel,* February 22, 1953; R. H. Collins, "We Are the Inheritors," 31.
88. Shankman, "Tilly and the FOC," 244; Smith, "Mrs. Tilly's Crusade," 67.
89. Tilly, "The FOC," 9.
90. Smith, "Mrs. Tilly's Crusade," 29.
91. Tilly to Mrs. W. Murdock McLeod, August 6, 1956, Tilly and the Fellowship of the Concerned Papers.

CHAPTER 5

1. Charles S. Johnson, *Growing Up in the Black Belt: Negro Youth in the Rural South* (1941; reprint, New York: Schocken, 1967), 325–27; Charles S. Johnson, "Democracy and Social Control in Race Relations," 1942, folder 15, box 160, Charles S. Johnson Papers, Fisk University, Nashville, Tennessee.
2. Phillip J. Johnson, "The Limits of Interracial Compromise: Louisiana,

1941," *Journal of Southern History* 64 (May 2003): 346; Greta De Jong, *A Different Day: African-American Struggles for Justice in Rural Louisiana, 1900–1970* (Chapel Hill: University of North Carolina Press, 2002). The term "parish" in Louisiana is synonymous with the term "county" in other states.

3. Richard H. King, *Civil Rights and the Idea of Freedom* (New York: Oxford University Press, 1992), 4.

4. The classic argument for the emergence in the 1940s of a labor-based, Left-leaning civil rights movement, to be subsequently destroyed by anti-Communist repression, is Robert Korstad and Nelson Lichtenstein, "Opportunities Found and Lost: Labor, Radicals, and the Early Civil Rights Movement," *Journal of Southern History* 75 (December 1988): 786–811.

5. For the attack on the NAACP after *Brown*, see Numan V. Bartley, *The Rise of Massive Resistance: Race and Politics in the South during the 1950s* (Baton Rouge: Louisiana State University Press, 1969), 213–22; Aldon D. Morris, *The Origins of the Civil Rights Movement: Black Communities Organizing for Change* (New York: Free Press, 1984), 26–39; Mark V. Tushnet, *Making Civil Rights Law: Thurgood Marshall and the Supreme Court, 1936–1961* (New York: Oxford University Press, 1994), 287–300; Adam Fairclough, *Race and Democracy: The Civil Rights Struggle in Louisiana, 1915–1972* (Athens: University of Georgia Press, 1995), 194–211.

6. Fairclough, *Race and Democracy*, 23–25, 29–31, 108–9, 113–19, 154–55, 165–66, 179.

7. John Beecher to Lawrence W. Cramer, "Field Report on New Orleans, Louisiana," March 7, 1942, and "Supplement to New Orleans Report," March 16, 1942, both in Office Files of John Beecher, Headquarters Files, reel 78, Fair Employment Practices Committee (microfilm), Alderman Library, University of Virginia.

8. John A. Davis to Malcolm Ross, February 29, 1944, Headquarters Files, reel 75, Tension File, Fair Employment Practices Committee.

9. Adam Fairclough, "Racial Repression in World War Two: The New Iberia Incident," *Louisiana History* 32 (Spring 1991): 183–207.

10. Merl E. Reed, "The FEPC, the Black Worker, and the Southern Shipyards," *South Atlantic Quarterly* 74 (Autumn 1975): 446–87.

11. Anthony J. Badger, "Huey Long and the New Deal," in *Nothing to Fear: New Perspectives on America in the Thirties*, ed. Stephen W. Baskerville and Ralph Willett (Manchester: Manchester University Press, 1985), 73–74; Alan Brinkley, *Voices of Protest: Huey Long, Father Coughlin, and the Great Depression* (New York: Vintage, 1983), 32; William Ivy Hair, *The Kingfish and His Realm: The Life and Times of Huey P. Long* (Baton Rouge: Louisiana State University Press, 1991), 99, 151, 170–71, 274–75, 303.

12. Korstad and Lichtenstein, "Opportunities Found and Lost," 786; Alan H. Draper, *Conflict of Interest: Organized Labor and the Civil Rights Movement in the South, 1954–1968* (Ithaca: Cornell University Press, 1994), 11–13. See also Bruce Nelson, *Divided We Stand: American Workers and the Struggle for Racial Equality* (Princeton: Princeton University Press, 2001).

13. Richard Dalfiume, "The 'Forgotten Years' of the Negro Revolution," *Journal of American History* 55 (June 1968): 90–106.

14. Harvard Sitkoff, "Racial Militancy and Interracial Violence in the Second

World War," *Journal of American History* 58 (December 1971): 661–81; Harvard Sitkoff, "African American Militancy in the World War II South," in *Remaking Dixie: The Impact of World War II on the American South*, ed. Neil R. McMillen (Jackson: University Press of Mississippi, 1997), 70–95.

15. Fairclough, *Race and Democracy*, 54–72; Thurgood Marshall to A. P. Tureaud, July 6, 1942, folder 23, box 49, Alexander Pierre Tureaud Papers, Amistad Research Center, Tulane University, New Orleans.

16. Fairclough, *Race and Democracy*, 78.

17. Ibid., 65–68, 71, 99–102.

18. Ernest J. Middleton, *History of the Louisiana Education Association* (Washington, D.C.: National Education Association, 1984), 85, quote on 149. The Louisiana Colored Teachers Association changed its name to the Louisiana Education Association in 1947.

19. Fairclough, *Race and Democracy*, 102–5, 133–34.

20. Matthew Polk, interview by Kate Ellis, July 22, 1994, New Iberia, Louisiana, Behind the Veil Oral History Project, Special Collections, Perkins Library, Duke University; J. H. Scott, interview by Joseph L. Logsdon, 1966, p. 44, Earl K. Long Library, University of New Orleans; Joseph L. Logsdon, "Oral History of A. P. Tureaud, Sr.," transcript of tape 10, private collection of Joseph L. Logsdon; Huey Long quote from proverb among black Louisianans, possibly apocryphal (author's conversations).

21. P. J. Johnson, "Limits of Interracial Compromise," 130–31.

22. "Morris Henry Carroll," http://monroefreepress.com/history/blkhis11.htm. It is worth noting that Carroll also developed business interests that made him a wealthy man.

23. *Monroe (La.) Morning World*, May 2, 1956; *Monroe News-Star*, May 4, 1956; Special Agent in Charge, New Orleans, to Director, "Mae Lucky et al.," June 15, 1956, FBI file 56-1553-27, pp. 40–43, 126–28, in author's possession (acquired by Freedom of Information Act).

24. Fairclough, *Race and Democracy*, 179–86; Glen S. Jeansonne, *Leander Perez: Boss of the Delta* (Baton Rouge: Louisiana State University Press, 1977), 244–49.

25. John H. Fenton and Kenneth R. Vines, "Negro Registration in Louisiana," *American Political Science Review* 51 (September 1957): 704–13; Frederick D. Wright, "The History of Black Political Participation to 1865," in *Blacks and Southern Politics*, ed. Lawrence W. Morland, Robert P. Steed, and Tod A. Baker (New York: Praeger, 1987), 22 (quote).

26. *Louisiana Weekly*, June 5, 24, 1950, November 3, 1951.

27. Fairclough, *Race and Democracy*, 129–31; Mary Alice Fontenot and Vincent Riehl, *The Cat and St. Landry: A Biography of Sheriff D. J. "Cat" Doucet of St. Landry Parish, Louisiana* (Baton Rouge: Claitor's Publishing Division, 1972), 87, 100; Melissa Fay Greene, *Praying for Sheetrock: A Work of Nonfiction* (New York: Fawcett Columbine, 1991).

28. "[Deleted]-Subjects; Alvin Hamilton Jones et al.-Victims," FBI file 44-3207-10, July 7, 1950; FBI reports, June 16, 1950, file 44-3207-6, July 7, 1950, file 44-3207-10, and September 18, 1950, file 44-3207-12, Brotherton Library, University of Leeds, England.

29. Fairclough, *Race and Democracy*, 184–85.

30. J. Mills Thornton III argues that the rise of black voting after 1944 helped to precipitate the breakdown of established political machines and fostered the emergence of divisions among white politicians. This in turn, he argues, persuaded blacks that they possessed the political influence to effect social change; moreover, if the white power structure appeared sufficiently vulnerable, this political self-confidence prompted blacks to employ nonviolent direct action in an effort to achieve their goals. See Thornton, *Dividing Lines: Municipal Politics and the Struggle for Civil Rights in Montgomery, Birmingham, and Selma* (Tuscaloosa: University of Alabama Press, 2002).

31. Christopher Waldrep, "War of Words: The Controversy over the Definition of Lynching, 1899–1940," *Journal of Southern History* 66, no. 1 (2000): 94; Margery Dallet, "The Case of Clinton Clark," August 17, 1940, folder 19, box 3, Harold N. Lee Papers, Tulane University; *Louisiana Weekly*, August 24, 1940.

32. Juan Williams, *Thurgood Marshall: American Revolutionary* (New York: Times Books, 1998), 142; August Meier and Elliott Rudwick, "The Origins of Nonviolent Direct Action in Afro-American Protest: A Note on Historical Discontinuities," in *Along the Color Line: Explorations in the Black Experience* (Urbana: University of Illinois Press, 1976), 362–63; *Louisiana Weekly*, November 29, 1947; Consumers' League—NAACP leaflet, December 1947, folder 67, NAACP Papers (New Orleans Branch), Earl K. Long Library, University of New Orleans; *Byrd v. City of New Orleans*, February 2, 1948, folder 18, box 5, Daniel E. Byrd Papers, Amistad Research Center, Tulane University; Oakley Johnson to Aubrey Grossman, September 10, 1950, Oakley Johnson Papers, Schomburg Library, New York City.

33. N. C. Newbold, "Lumberton Negro School Strike," October 21, 1946, folder 16, General Correspondence, Division of Negro Education, Department of Public Instruction, North Carolina State Archives, Raleigh; *Charlotte Observer*, October 11, 1946; *Raleigh News and Observer*, October 9, 1946; Taylor Branch, *Parting the Waters: America in the King Years, 1954–63* (New York: Simon and Schuster, 1988), 19–21; *Louisiana Weekly*, September 15, 1951; Daniel E. Byrd to Thurgood Marshall, March 5, 1953, folder 1, box 1, and Byrd, "Activity Report," March 1953, folder 1, box 4, both in Byrd Papers.

34. Morris, *Origins of the Civil Rights Movement*, 17–25; Emmett Harold Buell, "The Politics of Frustration: An Analysis of Negro Political Leadership in East Baton Rouge Parish, 1953–1966" (M.A. thesis, Louisiana State University, 1967), 116–27.

35. *Louisiana Weekly*, June 25, 1949.

36. *New York Times*, June 16, 21, 1953; *Baton Rouge Morning Advocate*, June 16–22, 1953; *Louisiana Weekly*, July 4, 1953.

37. Meier and Rudwick, "Origins of Nonviolent Direct Action," 365–66; Plaintiff's Petition, *Jemison v. City of Baton Rouge*, folder 4, box 31, Tureaud Papers.

38. Fairclough, *Race and Democracy*, 148–51.

39. Samuel Lubell, *The Future of American Politics* (New York: Harper and Brothers, 1951), 118–20; *Labat v. Bennett*, 365 F.2d 698 (1966); Frank T. Read and Lucy S. McGough, *Let Them Be Judged: The Judicial Integration of the Deep South* (Metuchen, N.J.: Scarecrow Press, 1978), 336–44.

40. A. P. Tureaud to E. A. Johnson, July 15, 1950, folder 8, box 10, Tureaud Papers; Daniel E. Byrd to Thurgood Marshall, September 12, 1951, folder 1, box 1, Byrd Papers.

41. Louise Metoyer Bouisse, interview by Kate Ellis, June 20, 1994, Behind the Veil Oral History Project; J. B. Henderson, interview by Michelle Wallace, July 20, 1994, tape 1, ibid.; Edran Auguster, interview by Michelle Wallace, June 19, 1994, tape 1, ibid.

42. Bruce Nelson, *Workers on the Waterfront: Seamen, Longshoremen, and Unionism in the 1930s* (Urbana: University of Illinois Press, 1988), 81–82; Nelson, *Divided We Stand;* A. L. Glenn Sr., *History of the National Alliance of Postal Employees, 1913–1955* (Washington, D.C.: National Alliance of Postal Employees, n.d.); Cornelius Hendricks, "The National Alliance of Postal and Federal Employees," *Crisis,* April 1977, 148–49.

43. Constance Baker Motley, interview by Jack Bass, June 21, 1979, pp. 71–72, Jack Bass Collection, Law Library, Tulane University; Constance Baker Motley, *Equal Justice under Law: An Autobiography* (New York: Farrar, Straus and Giroux, 1998), 107.

44. Daniel E. Byrd to Thurgood Marshall, April 9, 1953, folder 3, box 1, Byrd Papers; E. A. Johnson, "Report on Atlanta Meeting," in minutes of Executive Board and Regional Board, folder 15, box 12, Tureaud Papers; "Suggested Program for Southern Branches, 1954–1955," folder 7, box 4, Byrd Papers; Joseph T. Taylor, "Desegregation in Louisiana: One Year Later," *Journal of Negro Education* 24 (Summer 1955): 264–67; *Louisiana Weekly,* June 5, 1954; *New Orleans Times-Picayune,* May 18, 1954 (quoted), in Taylor, "Desegregation in Louisiana," 267.

CHAPTER 6

1. James and Esther Cooper Jackson interview, tape recording, January 5, 2001, Brooklyn, New York.

2. Formed in 1938 by southern New Dealers and other liberals in the wake of the Roosevelt administration's "Report on the Economic Condition of the South," SCHW organized state committees and a regional staff to work toward liberalizing and modernizing the South along the lines outlined in the report. SCHW's support for federal intervention to end racial discrimination certainly contributed to its collapse after only ten years, but the organization's internal divisions, including a split among its supporters into "center" and "popular front" factions, also became crucial elements in its early death. Active participation of several important SCHW board members in Henry Wallace's 1948 presidential campaign increased southern segregationists' accusations that SCHW was controlled by Communists and stopped vital foundation grants and union donations.

3. David Caute, *The Great Fear: The Anti-Communist Purge under Truman and Eisenhower* (New York: Secker and Warbug, 1978), 178–79, quote on 178.

4. William Patterson, ed., *We Cry Genocide: The Historic Petition to the United Nations for Relief from a Crime of the United States Government against the Negro People* (New York: Civil Rights Congress, 1951), 178.

5. Ralph Powe, longtime CRC legal director, does not fit this description. A

Tuskegee and Howard Law School graduate, Powe was the son of black sharecroppers from Cheraw, South Carolina. Another exception is the English writer Jessica Mitford, who for many years served as a CRC leader in the San Francisco area.

6. Gerald Horne, *Communist Front? The Civil Rights Congress, 1946–1956* (Rutherford, N.J.: Fairleigh Dickinson University Press, 1988), 32–35.

7. The Smith Act of 1940, the first peacetime sedition act since 1798, made it a crime to join, endorse, organize, publish, or use the mails to distribute material supporting "any society, group or assembly of persons who teach, advocate or encourage . . . overthrow of the government of the United States." It provided for ten-year sentences and fines up to $10,000 for those so convicted. Earlier espionage acts condemned verbal attacks on the American form of government, but the Smith Act bans only advocacy of acts of violence or force to overthrow the government. *Digest of the Public Record of Communism in the United States* (1955; reprint, New York: Arno Press, 1977), 188–205.

8. Horne, *Communist Front*, quotes on 16 and 22; "Press Release From: Civil Rights Congress," November 11, 1950, and September 6, 1951, reel 7, box 7, part 1, Civil Rights Congress Papers, Schomburg Center for Research in Black Culture, New York Public Library [hereafter cited as CRC Papers]; W. L. Patterson to J. M. Coe, August 2, 1951, box 37, folder 35, John Moreno Coe Papers, Special Collections Department, Robert H. Woodruff Library, Emory University, Atlanta, Georgia.

9. Numan V. Bartley, *The New South, 1945–1980* (Baton Rouge: Louisiana State University Press, 1995), 71.

10. "For Immediate Release—Report on the first Texas CRC Conference," July 9, 1946, 3, reel 31, box 86, part 2, CRC Papers; Jackson interview.

11. Chester M. Morgan, *Redneck Liberal: Theodore G. Bilbo and the New Deal* (Baton Rouge: Louisiana State University Press, 1985), 250–51.

12. Ibid.; Robin D. G. Kelley, *Hammer and Hoe: Alabama Communists during the Great Depression* (Chapel Hill: University of North Carolina Press, 1990), 221.

13. Patricia Sullivan, *Days of Hope: Race and Democracy in the New Deal Era* (Chapel Hill: University of North Carolina Press, 1996), 194.

14. Laurent Franz to Milt (Milton Kaufmann), September 23, 1946, reel 5, Oakley Johnson Papers, Schomburg Center for Research in Black Culture, New York Public Library.

15. The committee included such notables as Adam Clayton Powell, Oscar Hammerstein II, Gene Kelly, Leonard Bernstein, Fannie Hurst, Alaine Locke, David O. Selznick, and Albert Einstein and was chaired by Quentin Reynolds and Vincent Sheehan. See Horne, *Communist Front*, 56.

16. Sullivan, *Days of Hope*, 56, 22, quote on 22; Jackson interview; Denton L. Watson, *Lion in the Lobby: Clarence Mitchell, Jr.'s Struggle for Passage of Civil Rights Laws* (Lanham, Md.: Rowman and Littlefield, 2002), 189.

17. Sullivan, *Days of Hope*, quote on 218; *Smith v. Allwright*, 321 U.S. 649 (1944); A. Wigfall Green, *The Man: Bilbo* (Baton Rouge: Louisiana State University Press, 1963), 206–19; Jackson interview.

18. Charles G. Hamilton to Director, CRC, December 19, 1947, reel 28, box 83, CRC Papers; Griffin Fariello, *Red Scare: Memories of the American Inquisition:*

An Oral History (New York: Norton, 1995), 470–71; Caute, *The Great Fear*, 90; Report no. 1115, 80th Cong., 1st sess., House of Representatives, "Report on Civil Rights Congress as a Communist Front Organization," November 17, 1947; John Egerton, *Speak Now against the Day: The Generation before the Civil Rights Movement in the South* (Chapel Hill: University of North Carolina Press, 1994), 221.

19. The SCHW became the subject of a scathing HUAC report published in June 1947. Although the committee refused to give SCHW board members a chance to speak at its hearings, their investigators concluded that SCHW's supposed interest in southern social and economic problems "deviously camouflaged" a "Communist-front organization."

20. Jackson interview; Kelley, *Hammer and Hoe*, 224–28.

21. Horne, *Communist Front*, 45.

22. Ibid, 182–206; Laurent Franz to Milt (Milton Kaufmann), September 23, 1946, reel 5, Johnson Papers; see also the series of letters between William Patterson and Larkin Marshall, 1949–1951, reel 24, box 80, part 2, CRC Papers.

23. Sylvia H. Thompson interview, tape recording, January 6, 2001, New York. As to the incongruity of an organization supposedly allied with "godless Communism" calling on God in its meetings, Thompson says that was just the way things were done in the South in 1946.

24. Ibid.; Don E. Carleton, *Red Scare! Right Wing Hysteria, Fifties Fanaticism, and Their Legacy in Texas* (Austin: Texas Monthly Press, 1985), 44; *Sweatt v. Painter*, 339 U.S. 629 (1950).

25. "For Immediate Release"; J. T. Kelly to Milton Kauffman, August 12, 1946, reel 31, box 86, part 2, CRC Papers; Bartley, *The New South*, 76. The "Georgia murders" involved a lynching near Monroe in Walton County, where two black women and two black men, one a recent veteran in uniform, were killed by a mob of white men. These brutal lynchings represented only the tip of an iceberg of southern mob violence in the year after the war; lynch mobs murdered veterans and other blacks who took part in civil rights activities from northern Louisiana to eastern North Carolina. The new militant attitudes of returning black servicemen, and especially the voting drives of the NAACP and other civil rights organizations, caused an "anti-black rampage" across the South in 1945 and 1946.

26. The petition, concerned primarily with international control of atomic weapons, was originally adopted by a World Peace Congress at Stockholm in March 1950. HUAC denounced it as a defense of Communist aggression in Korea and named the Peace Information Center and its successor, the American Peace Crusade, as the petition's American sponsors. House Report 378, "Report on the Communist 'Peace' Offensive: A Campaign to Disarm and Defeat the United States," 82nd Cong., 1st sess., April 25, 1951.

27. "For Immediate Release"; Carleton, *Red Scare*, 56–63, quotes on 57, 59, and 61; Horne, *Communist Front*, 138–39, 314–15, quotes on 314–15.

28. Oakley C. Johnson, "The New Orleans Story," reel 1, Johnson Papers; see especially 207–9.

29. Ibid.

30. Ibid., 207–8, and see also multiple examples of Johnson's LCRC corre-

spondence on reel 4; Thompson interview; Horne, *Communist Front,* 197–202, quote on 202; Oakley C. Johnson to Aubrey Grossman, April 8, 1951, reel 26, box 81, part 2, CRC Papers; Sarah H. Brown, *Standing against Dragons: Three Southern Lawyers in an Era of Fear* (Baton Rouge: Louisiana State University Press, 1998), 108–10.

31. Adam Fairclough, *Race and Democracy: The Civil Rights Struggle in Louisiana, 1915–1972* (Athens: University of Georgia Press, 1995), 143; Johnson, "The New Orleans Story," reel 1, 212–19; Johnson to William Patterson, May 2, 1951, reel 4, Johnson Papers.

32. Benjamin E. Smith, "Before a Committee of the Board of Administrators of Tulane University, February–April, 1953, In the Matter of Dr. Robert Hodes and Tulane University: Brief for Dr. Hodes," 33–34, 36, box 92, National Lawyers Guild Papers, Martin Luther King Center for Non-Violent Social Change, Atlanta, Georgia; *Ward v. United States,* 344 U.S. 924 (1953); see also Ellen Schrecker, *No Ivory Tower: McCarthyism and the Universities* (New York: Oxford University Press, 1986), 141–44; and Brown, *Standing against Dragons,* 105–13. It is interesting to note that Hodes's and Roosevelt Ward's lawyers (Smith and Coe) were officers of both SCEF and the National Lawyers Guild (another popular front association with roots in the 1930s).

33. Horne, *Communist Front,* 202; Fairclough, *Race and Democracy,* 143.

34. Raymond A. Mohl, "'South of the South?': Jews, Blacks, and the Civil Rights Movement in Miami, 1945–1960," *Journal of American Ethnic History* 18, no. 2 (1999): 5–13, quote on 5.

35. Milton Wolff to William L. Patterson, February 9, 1949, reel 24, box 80, part 2, CRC Papers; Mohl, "South of the South," 5–13, quote on 5.

36. *State of Florida ex. rel Benemovsky v. Sullivan, Sheriff,* 37 So. 2nd 798, 907 (1948); Sylvia Thompson, telephone interview by author, tape recording, December 18, 1991, New York.

37. Brown, *Standing against Dragons,* 69–71; *Benemovsky v. Sullivan.*

38. Bella Fisher to Len (Goldsmith), December 16, 1948, and Goldsmith to Fisher, December 20, 1948, reel 24, box 80, part 2, CRC Papers.

39. Matilda (Bobby) Graff to Leon Josephson, March 24, 1949, and William Patterson to Graff, March 28, 1949, ibid.; Mohl, "South of the South," 14.

40. Statement released to the *Miami Daily News* by the Executive Board of the Greater Miami Chapter of the Civil Rights Congress, March 26, 1949, "Miami's Own Whirligig," n.d. (1949), and Bobby Graff to William Patterson, May 4, 1950, all in reel 24, box 80, part 2, CRC Papers. See also Brown, *Standing against Dragons,* 132; and Mohl, "South of the South," 14.

41. Horne, *Communist Front,* 203–12; For publicity pieces and correspondence regarding the Ingram case, see reel 7, box 7, part 1, CRC Papers, and reel 5, Johnson Papers. For the CRC and the NAACP, see William Lawrence to Marve Bovington, May 28, 1948, "Pat" to Joseph Cadden, April 5, 1948, Walter White to the Civil Rights Congress, April 22, 1948, and William Patterson to Mr. R. Hanson, November 18, 1949, reel 5, Johnson Papers. The release of the Ingrams, like the commutation of the death sentence in the Gilbert case, was a rare occurrence: almost all of the CRC's southern cases ended with the death or continued incarceration of their clients.

42. Eric Rise, *The Martinsville Seven: Race, Rape, and Capital Punishment* (Charlottesville: University Press of Virginia, 1995), 153, 99–116, quotes on 116 and 153.

43. Horne, *Communist Front*, 78–93, quote on 80; "For General Release Monday, January 31, 1949, From: Kevin Mullen, Civil Rights Congress," box 12, reel 12, part 1, CRC Papers.

44. Horne, *Communist Front*, 78–97, quote on 79; *McGee v. Jones*, box 36, folder 24, Coe Papers; "For General Release Monday, January 31, 1949, From: Kevin Mullen, Civil Rights Congress," box 12, reel 12, part 1, CRC Papers.

45. *McGee v. State*, 47 So. 2d 155, 339 U.S. 958 (1950); J. M. Coe to Bella Abzug, May 9, 1951, 44, box 36, folder 24, Coe Papers.

46. Communists were given forty-eight hours to leave town or suffer both a $100 fine and 180 days in jail. *Digest of the Public Record of Communism*, 458–61; Caute, *The Great Fear*, 568–69; *Trainor v. Cannon*, box 35, folder 27, and *Hall v. City of Birmingham*, box 35, folder 26, Coe Papers; *Florida Times-Union*, October 10, 1950, 17.

47. Editorials, *Birmingham News*, October 5, 16, 1950, box 35, folder 26, Coe Papers. Active in the Methodist Church as a young man, Sam Hall had joined the staff of the *Anniston Star* in the 1930s. Discouraged over the Depression and opposed to racial segregation, he joined the Communist Party a few years later. After he served in the navy during the war, the party trained him as an organizer and sent him to North Carolina, where he met and married another Communist worker fresh from organizing the CRC in Houston, Sylvia Bernard. The party assigned the newlyweds to Birmingham just after James and Esther Cooper Jackson left, though several of the Jackson's friends remained to welcome them.

48. Thompson interviews, 1991, 2001. Sylvia Bernard Hall remarried and is today known as Sylvia Bernard Thompson.

49. Thompson interviews, 1991, 2001; J. M. Coe to Mynelle Cook, March 20, 1954, box 3, folder 22, Coe Papers. Hall was probably the party's district organizer in New Orleans when he met Coe. See "Scope of Soviet Activity in the United States," part 12, Senate Committee on the Judiciary, Subcommittee to Investigate the Administration of the Internal Security Act and other Internal Security Laws, Hearings April 5–6, 1956 (New Orleans), 84th Cong., 2nd sess., 710.

50. Patterson, *We Cry Genocide*, 171, 31, 5.

51. Ibid., 5.

52. Maurice Jackson, "Patterson, William L.," in *Encyclopedia of the American Left*, ed. Mari Jo Buhle, Paul Buhle, and Dan Georgakas (Urbana: University of Illinois Press, 1992), 565; Horne, *Communist Front*, 172–74; "The Emmett Till Murder and Its Racist Roots" and "The Murder of Emmett Louis Till and the Verdict of Acquittal," reel 12, box 12, part 1, CRC Papers.

53. Harvey Klehr, John Earl Haynes, and Fridrikh Igorevich Firsov, *The Secret World of American Communism (Annals of Communism)* (New Haven: Yale University Press, 1995), 13–14; Charles H. Martin, "Communism," in *The Encyclopedia of Southern Culture*, ed. Charles Reagan Wilson and William Ferris (Chapel Hill: University of North Carolina Press, 1989), 1393.

54. Jackson interview; for Jack O'Dell see Fariello, *Red Scare*, 413–18, 500–506; Esther Cooper Jackson, ed., *Freedomways Reader: Prophets in Their Own Country* (Boulder, Colo.: Westview Press, 2000), xviii.

55. Charles Eagles, *Jonathan Daniels: the Evolution of a Southern Liberal* (Knoxville: University of Tennessee Press, 1982), 127; for a rebuttal to Eagles's argument see Horne, *Communist Front*, 24.

56. Horne, *Communist Front*, 172–74, quote on 172; Aubrey William note on CRC pamphlet called "Mississippi, USA: An Innocent Negro Faces Death," reel 5, Johnson Papers; J. A. Dombrowski to Benjamin Mays, March 5, 1954, box 16, folder 9, James A. Dombrowski Papers, State Historical Society of Wisconsin, Madison.

57. Fairclough, *Race and Democracy*, 137.

CHAPTER 7

1. *Ebony*, November 1985, 60–76.

2. E. D. Nixon to John H. Johnson, November 13, 1985, E. D. Nixon Collection, Alabama State University Special Collections, Montgomery. There is no scholarly biography of E. D. Nixon. Lewis V. Baldwin and Aprille V. Woodson's *Freedom Is Never Free: A Biographical Portrait of Edgar Daniel Nixon, Sr.* (Atlanta: United Parcel Service Foundation, 1992) is an uneven and frequently inaccurate short profile. On Nixon's (controversial) role in the Montgomery Bus Boycott, see John White, "Nixon *Was* the One: Edgar Daniel Nixon, the MIA, and the Montgomery Bus Boycott," in *The Making of Martin Luther King and the Civil Rights Movement*, ed. Brian Ward and Anthony J. Badger (New York: New York University Press, 1996), 45–63.

3. Robin D. G. Kelley, "'We Are Not What We Seem': Rethinking Black Working-Class Opposition in the Jim Crow South," *Journal of American History* 80 (June 1993): 79, 102.

4. Jack Santino, *Miles of Smiles, Years of Struggle: Stories of Black Pullman Porters* (Urbana: University of Illinois Press, 1989), 52.

5. Bernard Mergen, "The Pullman Porter: From 'George' to Brotherhood," *South Atlantic Quarterly* 73 (1974): 224–25. Mergen adds that the Pullman porter "had a special status in the black community because he knew what was happening all over the country" (228).

6. Eliot Wigginton, *Refuse to Stand Silently By: An Oral History of Grass Roots Social Activism in America, 1921–1964* (New York: Doubleday, 1992), 22.

7. Earl and Miriam Selby, *Odyssey: Journey through Black America* (New York: Putnam, 1971), 48–49.

8. These early biographical details have been taken from several autobiographical fragments in the E. D. Nixon Collection. See also "When Montgomery Was Not Like St. Louis" in Wigginton, *Refuse to Stand Silently By*, 22–24; and Steven M. Millner, "The Montgomery Bus Boycott: A Case Study in the Emergence and Career of a Social Movement," in *The Walking City: The Montgomery Bus Boycott, 1955–1956*, ed. David J. Garrow (Brooklyn: Carlson, 1989), 416–17.

9. Studs Terkel, *Hard Times: An Oral History of the Great Depression* (New York: Pantheon Books, 1970), 144.

10. Wigginton, *Refuse to Stand Silently By,* 23–24. In a short autobiographical sketch, Nixon relates that before he began work as a Pullman porter "I had begin [sic] to feel that the law in the South was right, since I had not been anywhere except Birmingham, Selma, Mobile and Montgomery. But after several trips east, west and north, I soon learned that the laws in the South was legally right according to the interpretation, but was morally wrong. I had felt that being the last one hired and the first one fired was the law of the land. Likewise, I thought that living in back-yards was the best that the average Negro could do." Nixon Collection.

11. Wigginton, *Refuse to Stand Silently By,* 23.

12. Terkel, *Hard Times,* 119.

13. Santino, *Miles of Smiles,* 55.

14. E. D. Nixon to Paula F. Pfeffer, December 1, 1972, in possession of the author.

15. *Black Worker,* November 15, 1929, 3. In a June 3, 1927, memorandum, Randolph observed that white Americans "cannot imagine that Negroes have grown up from little children. They can't believe that we are able to handle our own affairs, that we are moving into the period of self-reliance, nor can white people believe that there are any Negroes who are not subject to corruption with money; hence the Brotherhood is a marvel to them. Thus we are making history for our race." Mergen, "The Pullman Porter," 229. Subsequent commentators agree that the BSCP was as much a racial as a labor movement: "To the Negro community the porter's Brotherhood was a racial rather than a purely occupational movement, and the differences of opinion which it aroused were mainly differences over racial tactics. Race militancy versus salvation through white philanthropy, and the union of white and black labor against white capital versus a rapprochement between white capital and black labor against the white worker were policies dividing the Brotherhood's supporters from its opponents. It was well-nigh impossible for a Negro leader to remain neutral toward the union, and the position which he took toward it became a fundamental test." Sterling D. Spero and Abram Harris, *The Black Worker: The Negro and the Labor Movement* (1933; New York: Atheneum, 1982), 436. The origins and subsequent history of the BSCP are covered by William H. Harris, *Keeping the Faith: A. Philip Randolph, Milton P. Webster, and the Brotherhood of Sleeping Car Porters, 1925–37* (Urbana: University of Illinois Press, 1977). See also Brailsford R. Brazeal, *The Brotherhood of Sleeping Car Porters: Its Origin and Development* (New York: Harper and Brothers, 1946). A. Philip Randolph's life and times have been most recently examined by Paula F. Pfeffer, *A. Philip Randolph: Pioneer of the Civil Rights Movement* (Baton Rouge: Louisiana State University Press, 1990); but see also Jervis Anderson, *A Philip Randolph: A Biographical Portrait* (New York: Harcourt, Brace Jovanovich, 1973). Briefer but judicious estimates of Randolph are found in William H. Harris, "A. Philip Randolph as a Charismatic Leader, 1925–1941," *Journal of Negro History* 64 (1979): 301–15; and Benjamin Quarles, "A. Philip Randolph: Labor Leader at Large," in his *Black Mosaic: Essays in Afro-American History and Historiography* (Amherst: University of Massachusetts Press, 1988), 151–77.

16. Santino, *Miles of Smiles,* 38–39.

17. "E. D. Nixon: Porter on God's Freedom Train," undated manuscript in possession of the author.

18. Wigginton, *Refuse to Stand Silently By*, 27–28.

19. Ibid.

20. Terkel, *Hard Times*, 120–21.

21. Hollinger F. Barnard, ed., *Outside the Magic Circle: The Autobiography of Virginia Foster Durr* (Tuscaloosa: University of Alabama Press, 1990), 252–53. Durr also recalled that under Jim Crow she could not call their mutual acquaintance, Rosa Parks, by her first name: "I couldn't call her Rosa until she could call me Virginia. Now she finally does, and that took twenty-odd years. I had to call them Mrs. or Mr. until they could call me by my first name" (253).

22. Terkel, *Hard Times*, 121.

23. Norman Lumpkin, interview, Statewide Oral History Project, Alabama Center for Higher Education, Tuskegee Institute, 1963, vol. 3, p. 1.

24. Nixon Collection.

25. E. D. Nixon to J. B. Hill, February 7, 1944, ibid.

26. E. D. Nixon to J. B. Hill, April 25, 1944, ibid.

27. "Significant Reminiscences of Alabama History in the Making: Autobiography of E. D. Nixon," undated manuscript, ibid.

28. S. S. Seay Sr., *I Was There by the Grace of God* (Montgomery: S. S. Seay Educational Foundation, 1990), 170.

29. Ralph J. Bunche, *The Political Status of the Negro in the Age of FDR* (Chicago: University of Chicago Press, 1973), 285–87, 401.

30. Selby and Selby, *Odyssey*, 50 (quote). An indefatigable letter writer (and typist) but acutely conscious of his grammatical failings, Nixon remembered that he "generally gave someone my theory of what I wanted in a letter and some principal or somebody would put it into a decent letter. I think it was Mrs. Rosa Parks who was later in the NAACP with me, helped me write that letter to Mrs. Roosevelt. I wanted [her] to know what we was up against, and I told her that I'd appreciate it if she'd direct my letter to the proper authority." Ibid. Loula Dunn to George Syme Jr., February 25, 1942, Mildred Patterson, Director USO Travellers Aid Service, March 19, 1943, and George Syme to E. D. Nixon, March 30, 1942, all in Nixon Collection.

31. William C. Powell, "An Open Letter to the Colored Citizens of Montgomery," April 25, 1942, Nixon Collection. In an unpublished autobiographical fragment, Nixon relates bitterly: "When we got this USO club put together, I was told to start with I'd have to have a committee to handle it, funds and everything. We got a group together and one of the professors over at Alabama State nominated me for chairman. You know what happened to the nomination? Died on the floor for lack of a second. A sister nominated her brother and another sister seconded the motion and it was carried. He had nothing in the world to do with bringing the USO club to town." Manuscript of interview with E. D. Nixon, n.d., in possession of author.

32. Pfeffer, *A. Philip Randolph*, 173.

33. On the Freedom Train and its reception in the South see James Gregory Bradsher, "Taking America's Heritage to the People: The Freedom Train Story," *Prologue* 17, no. 4 (1985): 229–45; Stuart J. Little, "The Freedom Train: Citizen-

ship and Postwar Political Culture, 1946–1949," *American Studies* 34 (Spring 1993): 35–67; and John White, "Civil Rights in Conflict: The 'Birmingham Plan' and the Freedom Train, 1947," *Alabama Review* 52 (April 1999): 121–41.

34. *Alabama Tribune,* December 12, 1947.

35. E. D. Nixon to Walter White, November 13, 1947, American Heritage Foundation Freedom Train Folder: Papers of the NAACP, part 15: Segregation and Discrimination: Complaints and Responses, 1940–1955, series B: Administrative Files, box A-359, Library of Congress, Washington, D.C. (Bethesda, Md.: University Publications of America, 1993), microfilm, reel 6 [hereafter cited as AHFFT Folder].

36. E. D. Nixon to American Heritage Foundation, December 1, 1947, AHFFT Folder. He also sent a copy of this letter to Walter White with the comment: "We are putting forth every effort to have the Freedom Train by-pass Montgomery, we have already been ignored by the local committee." Nixon to Walter White, ibid. According to an article in the *Alabama Tribune,* Nixon had also contacted Edward Shugrue, president of the American Heritage Foundation, who "promised that we would get results or the train wouldn't stop in Montgomery." C. C. Beverly, "Strange as It Seems," *Alabama Tribune,* January 10, 1948.

37. Rosa Parks to Gloster B. Current, December 19, 1947, AHFFT Folder.

38. "Priceless Documents Draw 10,000 to Freedom Train," *Montgomery Advertiser,* December 28, 1947, 1.

39. "Two Races Mingle Amicably on Freedom Train in Mobile," undated and unnamed newspaper clipping, AHFFT Folder.

40. (Montgomery) *Alabama Journal,* November 22, 1954, front page.

41. *Montgomery Advertiser/Alabama Journal,* October 2, 1955, 2B.

42. "According to Their Rules," *Alabama Tribune,* October 14, 1955.

43. Edward R. Crowther, "Alabama's Fight to Maintain Segregated Schools," *Alabama Review* 42 (July 1990): 215.

44. NAACP Minutes: Montgomery Branch, 1954–56, Schomburg Center for the Study of Black Culture, New York Public Library.

45. Dorothy A. Autrey, "The National Association for the Advancement of Colored People in Alabama, 1913–1952" (Ph.D. diss., University of Notre Dame, 1985), 96, 102.

46. Nixon to Walter White, December 14, 1944, AHFFT Folder.

47. Donald Jones to Ella Baker, September 14, 1945, ibid.

48. Nixon Collection.

49. Nixon to W. G. Porter, November 13, 1945, AHFFT Folder.

50. In a 1968 interview, Nixon provided more detail on the Amanda Baker episode and his meeting with Governor Sparks. A student at the State Teacher's college, Baker had been raped, drenched with acid, and then murdered. Nixon told Sparks that if he would offer a reward for "the arrest and conviction of the guilty Party who committed the crime against Amanda Baker . . . the Negro citizens would like that reward deposited in the Alabama National Bank." Nixon agreed to match the $250 offered by Sparks, and "the next morning we walked down to the bank and deposited that $250.00, in the name of the Amanda Baker Fund, and it stayed there four years; and, of course, nobody never was caught." E. D. Nixon, interview by Stanley Smith, transcript, 8–9, Montgomery, February

1968, Moorland-Spingarn Research Center, Civil Rights Documentation Project, Howard University, Washington, D.C.

51. Selby and Selby, *Odyssey*, 51–52. On the Southern Conference for Human Welfare and its offshoot, the Southern Conference Education Fund, see Linda Reed, *Simple Decency and Common Sense: The Southern Conference Movement, 1938–1963* (Bloomington: Indiana University Press, 1991); and Patricia Sullivan, *Days of Hope: Race and Democracy in the New Deal Era* (Chapel Hill: University of North Carolina Press, 1996).

52. "Let the Record Show," undated pamphlet, Nixon Collection.

53. Roberta Hughes Wright, *The Birth of the Montgomery Bus Boycott* (Southfield, Mich.: Charro Book Co., 1991), 34.

54. David J. Garrow, ed., *The Montgomery Bus Boycott and the Women Who Started It: The Memoir of Jo Ann Gibson Robinson* (Knoxville: University of Tennessee Press, 1987), 28.

55. Fred D. Gray, *Bus Ride to Justice* (Montgomery: Black Belt Press, 1994), 28.

56. Ralph D. Abernathy, "The Natural History of a Social Movement: The Montgomery Improvement Association," in Garrow, *The Walking City*, 111, 143.

57. Martin Luther King Jr., *Stride toward Freedom: The Montgomery Story* (New York: Harper and Row, 1958), 39.

58. Rosa Parks with Jim Haskins, *Rosa Parks: My Story* (New York: Dial Books, 1992), 72–73.

59. Baldwin and Woodson, *Freedom Is Never Free*, 51.

60. Western Union telegrams, n.d., Nixon Collection.

61. Joseph F. Wilson, *Tearing Down the Color Bar: A Documentary History of the Brotherhood of Sleeping Car Porters* (New York: Columbia University Press, 1989), 246.

62. Ibid., 258.

63. Howell Raines, *My Soul Is Rested: Movement Days in the Deep South Remembered* (New York: Putnam, 1977), 37.

64. Roy Wilkins with Tom Mathews, *Standing Fast: The Autobiography of Roy Wilkins* (New York: Viking Press, 1982), 236–37.

65. *Black Worker*, December 1955, 1.

66. Ibid., April 1956, 1, 3.

67. Taylor Branch, *Parting the Waters: America in the King Years, 1954–63* (New York: Simon and Schuster, 1988), 186.

68. Wilkins, *Standing Fast*, 228.

69. Ibid., 225–28.

70. Baldwin and Woodson, *Freedom Is Never Free*, xi.

71. Nixon to Martin Luther King Jr., June 3, 1957, Martin Luther King Papers, Special Collections, Mugar University Library, Boston University. Although Nixon's relations with King steadily worsened during and after the bus boycott, Nixon did commend King for electing not to pay a fine following his arrest in Montgomery in September 1958: "when you choosed [sic] to serve time rather than to pay a fine was the most courageous stand made in that direction since Bayard Rustin served time [in 1947] in [North] Carolina. And because of your courage in face of known danger I want to commend you for your stand for people of color all over the world, and especial [sic] the people in Montgomery.

Your action took the fear out of the Negroes and made the white man see himself as he is." Nixon to King, September 9, 1958, in Clayborne Carson et al., eds., *The Papers of Martin Luther King, Jr.,* vol. 4, *Symbol of the Movement: January 1957–December 1958* (Berkeley: University of California Press, 2000), 492.

72. "E. D. Nixon Retires," *Black Worker,* October 1964, 7.

73. Daniel Guerin, *Negroes on the March: A Frenchman's Report on the American Negro Struggle* (London: Grange, 1956), 179. See also Robert Korstad and Nelson Lichtenstein, "Opportunities Found and Lost: Labor, Radicals, and the Early Civil Rights Movement," *Journal of American History* 75 (December 1988): 786–811. They comment that during the early 1940s it had become "commonplace for sympathetic observers [like Guerin] to assert the centrality of mass unionization in the civil rights struggle" (787).

CHAPTER 8

1. John A. Salmond, *A Southern Rebel: The Life and Times of Aubrey Willis Williams, 1890–1965* (Chapel Hill: University of North Carolina Press, 1983), 181. Portions of this essay were previously published in another form in the April 1992 *North Carolina Historical Review,* and the editor acknowledges with thanks the North Carolina Office of Archives and History's permission to use this material.

2. John Egerton, *Speak Now against the Day: The Generation before the Civil Rights Movement in the South* (New York: Knopf, 1994), 259, 341–59; John A. Salmond, *The Conscience of a Lawyer: Clifford J. Durr and American Civil Liberties, 1899–1975* (Tuscaloosa: University of Alabama Press, 1990), 92–94.

3. For the SCHW, see Linda Reed, *Simple Decency and Common Sense: The Southern Conference Movement, 1938–1963* (Bloomington: Indiana University Press, 1991); Thomas Krueger, *And Promises to Keep: The Southern Conference for Human Welfare, 1938–1948* (Nashville: Vanderbilt University Press, 1967); Patricia Sullivan, *Days of Hope: Race and Democracy in the New Deal Era* (Chapel Hill: University of North Carolina Press, 1996).

4. Sullivan, *Days of Hope,* 202–4; John A. Salmond, *Miss Lucy of the CIO: The Life and Times of Lucy Randolph Mason* (Athens: University of Georgia Press, 1988), 120–21, 140–42; Margaret Fisher to members of Executive Board, Committee for Georgia, December 31, 1945, box 12, Glenn Waddington Rainey Papers, Robert H. Woodruff Library, Emory University, Atlanta, Georgia.

5. Sullivan, *Days of Hope,* 204, 214–16.

6. Ibid., 206–7; Mary Price to James Dombrowski, January 10, 1946, and Price to Mary McLeod Bethune, February 9, 1946, collection 19, box 3, Southern Conference for Human Welfare Papers, Robert W. Woodruff Library, Atlanta University Center, Atlanta, Georgia [hereafter cited as SCHW Papers]; Minutes of Board Meeting, Committee for North Carolina, March 26, 1946, collection 19, box 5, SCHW Papers. For a good recent account of Mary Price and her work, see Sayoko Uesugi, "Gender, Race, and the Cold War: Mary Price and the Progressive Party in North Carolina, 1945–1948," *North Carolina Historical Review* 77 (July 2000): 269–311.

7. Sullivan, *Days of Hope,* 206; Foreman to Mary Price, September 30, 1945,

Dombrowski to Price, April 6, 1946, Price to Dombrowski, February 22, 1946, and Price to Gertrude Weil, October 22, 1946, all in collection 19, box 3, SCHW Papers.

8. Branson Price to Susan Reed, September 24, 1946, collection 19, box 3, SCHW Papers; Sullivan, *Days of Hope*, 207.

9. Sarah Cunningham, "Woman beyond Her Times," *The Churchwoman: An Interdenominational Magazine* 32 (December 1966): 5–13; Helena Huntington Smith, "Mrs. Tilly's Crusade," *Colliers*, December 1950, 29, 66–67. Both are offprints in box 2, Dorothy Rogers Tilly Papers, Special Collections, Robert H. Woodruff Library, Emory University, Atlanta, Georgia.

10. Smith, "Mrs. Tilly's Crusade"; see also Florence B. Robin, "Honeychile at the Barricades," *Harpers' Magazine*, October 1962, 173–77, box 2, Tilly Papers; "Workbook of the Fellowship of the Concerned," October 23, 1968, box 4, Tilly Papers.

11. Smith, "Mrs. Tilly's Crusade," 66–67.

12. Ibid.; see also Report of Mrs. Tilly on Fellowship of the Concerned Activities, First Quarter, 1956, box 1, Tilly Papers; Jessie Ash Arndt, "Women's Crusade Spurs Fairer Treatment of Negroes in the United States," *Christian Science Monitor*, January 9, 1953, clipping in box 2, Tilly Papers.

13. Robert F. Martin, "Critique of Southern Society and Vision of a New Order: The Fellowship of Southern Churchmen, 1934–1957," *Church History* 52 (March 1983): 66–67.

14. Anthony P. Dunbar, *Against the Grain: Southern Radicals and Prophets, 1929–1959* (Charlottesville: University Press of Virginia, 1981), 59–75; Robert F. Martin, *Howard Kester and the Struggle for Social Justice in the South, 1904–77* (Charlottesville, University Press of Virginia, 1991); Thomas B. Cowan, "History of the Fellowship of Southern Churchmen," typescript, n.d., Walter Sikes to FSC members, October 1, 1943, and Howard Kester to FSC members and friends, November 21, 1944, all in Fellowship of Southern Churchmen Papers, Southern Historical Collection, Wilson Library, University of North Carolina at Chapel Hill [hereafter cited as FSC Papers].

15. Kester to FSC members and friends, November 21, 1944, Morton to Kester, March 30, 1974, and to Anthony Dunbar, January 3, 1978, all in FSC Papers; Nelle Morton, interview by Dallas Blanchard, June 25, 1983, Southern Oral History Collection, Southern Historical Collection, Wilson Library, University of North Carolina at Chapel Hill [hereafter cited as SOHC]; Dunbar, *Against the Grain*, 229.

16. Kester to FSC members and friends, November 21, 1944, Morton to Kester, March 30, 1974, and to Anthony Dunbar, January 3, 1978, all in FSC Papers; Morton interview; Dunbar, *Against the Grain*, 229. Herrin, Ashby, and Williams were all graduate students at the time, while Lowenstein was an undergraduate. Ashby later taught philosophy at the Women's College of the University at Greensboro. Herrin, then a Southern Baptist chaplain at the University at Chapel Hill, was later tried for heresy and recalled that his work for the FSC precipitated the incident. J. C. Herrin, interview by Dallas Blanchard, January 18, 1985, SOHC; Morton to David Burgess, April 30, 1945, FSC Papers.

17. Morton to William Jernagin, January 31, 1947, Don West, "The Case for

Work Camps," typescript, n.d., and "Have You Heard about This Work Camp?" FSC flyer, n.d., all in FSC Papers.

18. Eugene Smathers to Nelle Morton, February 21, 1945, and FSC newsletter, August 1945, ibid.

19. Smathers to Morton, July 17, 1946, Elizabeth Taylor to Jean ——, July 26, 1946, and Morton to David Burgess, December 20, 1946, ibid.

20. FSC application blank, May 1946, Morton to Henry Linter, May 7, 31, 1946, Gustav Lohse to Morton, May 1946, and Elizabeth Taylor to Morton, May 3, 1946, ibid.

21. Morton to David Jones, July 23, 1946, Cornelia Lively to Charles Frantz, September 6, 1946, William Klein to Morton, September 2, 1946, and Morton to Tony Dunbar, January 3, 1978, ibid.; Hibbard Thatcher, interview by Dallas Blanchard, August 3, 1985, SOHC.

22. FSC newsletter, February 1947, FSC Papers.

23. Nelle Morton, *The Journey Is Home* (Boston: Beacon Press, 1985), 188; Morton to Garland Anderson, May 2, 1947, and Jack Anderson to Morton, July 14, 15, 16, 19, 1947, all in FSC Papers.

24. Morton, *The Journey Is Home*, 189; Jack Anderson to Morton, July 30, 1947, FSC Papers; *Raleigh News and Observer*, August 19, 1947.

25. Cowan, "History of the Fellowship of Southern Churchmen"; *Raleigh News and Observer*, August 19, 1947; *Greensboro Daily News*, August 21, 1947.

26. David Burgess to Morton, January 10, 1948, Burgess to Morton, Richard Comfort, and Kester, May 17, 1948, Morton to Kester, Comfort, Burgess, and David McVoy, May 19, 1948, Morton to Ann Stephens, June 12, 1948, Morton to Charles Malone, June 23, 1948, Ann Stephens to work campers, August 16, 1948, and FSC newsletter, September 1948, all in FSC Papers.

27. Morton to Henry Hill, May 18, 1948, ibid.

28. Morton to Mr. and Mrs. Greg Ritchie, June 11, 1948, and "Brief Account of July 16, 1948 of Friday night Recreation," ibid.

29. *Atlanta Journal*, July 17, 1948; Rosalie Oakes to Cornelia Lively, September 28, 1948, Lively to campers, October 4, 1948, Greg and Pegi Ritchie to Lively, August 13, 17, 1948, Scotty Cowan to Morton, September 3, 1948, and Morton to Hester, March 30, 1948, all in FSC Papers.

30. Morton to Rev. R. W. Underwood, January 7, 1947, FSC newsletter, February 1947, Shelby Rooks to Morton, February 6, 1947, and clipping from *Columbus (Ga.) Tribune*, ibid.

31. Morton, *The Journey Is Home*, 247; Morton to Rustin and Houser, October 14, 1946, FSC Papers.

32. Morton, *The Journey Is Home*, 247; Cornelia Lively to Maynard Catchings, April 30, 1947, and Houser to Morton, May 14, 1947, both in FSC Papers.

33. Conrad Lynn to Morton, February 23, 1949, and Houser to C. E. Boulware, March 9, 1949, both in FSC Papers. The fourth rider decided not to risk imprisonment and disappeared; *Morgan v. Virginia*, 328 U.S. 373 (1946).

34. Rustin to Morton, March 14, 21, 1949, Rustin to Boulware, March 16, 1949, and Morton to Howard Kester, March 30, 1974, ibid.

35. Minutes of Executive Committee meeting, September 3, 1951, and Kes-

ter to Jones, November 11, 1951, ibid; James McBride Dabbs to FSC Members, March 21, 1963, James McBride Dabbs Papers, Southern Historical Collection, Wilson Library, University of North Carolina at Chapel Hill; Morton interview; Martin, *Howard Kester*, 144–45.

36. Sullivan, *Days of Hope*, 235; Egerton, *Speak Now*, 528–29; Price to Dombrowski, October 28, 1946, collection 19, box 3, SCHW Papers.

37. Salmond, *Miss Lucy of the CIO*, 164–66; Sullivan, *Days of Hope*, 274; Minutes of the CNC Executive Board, October 21, 1947, February 8, 1948, box 12, Rainey Papers; Price to Rev. William Poteat, January 9, 1948, collection 19, box 5, SCHW Papers; Minutes of the Executive Board, Committee for Georgia, February 15, April 12 and 26, July 26, 1947, box 12, Rainey Papers.

38. Thatcher interview.

CHAPTER 9

1. A new state constitution, drafted and ratified under the direction of Governor Ellis Arnall's wartime administration, abolished the poll tax for all of Georgia's citizens. On this and other electoral law changes that occurred under Arnall's administration during the war see Numan V. Bartley, *The Creation of Modern Georgia*, 2nd ed. (Athens: University of Georgia Press, 1990), 194–95. This essay originally appeared as "Winning the Peace: Georgia Veterans and the Struggle to Define the Political Legacy of World War II," *Journal of Southern History* 66, no. 3 (2000): 563–604. The editor is grateful to the *Journal of Southern History* for permission to reprint it here.

2. For general discussions of the impact of the war on African Americans and the struggle for black civil rights see Mary Penick Motley, ed., *The Invisible Soldier: The Experience of the Black Soldier, World War II* (Detroit: Wayne State University Press, 1967); Phillip McGuire, *Taps for a Jim Crow Army: Letters from Black Soldiers in World War Two* (Santa Barbara, Calif.: ABC-CLIO, 1982); Richard M. Dalfiume, *Desegregation of the U.S. Armed Forces: Fighting on Two Fronts, 1939–1953* (Columbia: University of Missouri Press, 1969); Harvard Sitkoff, *The Struggle for Black Equality, 1954–1980* (New York: Hill and Wang, 1981); and Neil A. Wynn, *The Afro-American and the Second World War* (New York: Holmes and Meier, 1975).

3. The Supreme Court decision abolishing the southern white primary rendered in *Smith v. Allwright* in 1944 was applied to Georgia through the Primus King case decided in early 1946. On the King case see Bartley, *Creation of Modern Georgia*, 201.

4. Law finally came to believe that his not receiving an overseas assignment was "a blessing in disguise," since many of the men with whom he had trained did not return. W. W. Law interview, November 15 and 16, 1990, Transcript Series E, Georgia Government Documentation Project, Special Collections and Archives, William Russell Pullen Library, Georgia State University, Atlanta [hereafter cited as GGDP].

5. Samuel A. Stouffer et al., *Studies in Social Psychology in World War II*, vol. 1, *The American Soldier: Adjustment during Army Life* (Princeton, N.J.: Sun-

flower University Press, 1949), 513–14 (first quote) and 515 (second and third quotes); Joyce Thomas, "The 'Double V' Was for Victory: Black Soldiers, the Black Protest, and World War II" (Ph.D. diss., Ohio State University, 1993), 171.

6. Robert J. Norrell, *Reaping the Whirlwind: The Civil Rights Movement in Tuskegee* (New York: Knopf, 1985), 60–61.

7. Horace Bohannon found that most black ex-servicemen in Georgia had definite, if modest, postwar goals. What they most wanted, he recalled, was "a decent job. They wanted to work. They wanted to make it." After all, Bohannon noted, "they had lived, they'd seen other circumstances, and they'd seen other peoples. And by now they knew that all every man wants is a job, and security for his family and so forth." Horace Bohannon interview, June 16, 1989, manuscript no. 2854, audiotapes, Hargrett Library, University of Georgia, Athens.

8. Horace Bohannon to George Mitchell, Ft. Valley, Georgia, January 11, 1945, document series VII: 3, microfilm, reel 188, frame 257, Southern Regional Council Archives, Special Collections, Robert W. Woodruff Library, Atlanta University Center.

9. "Statements by Teachers, Principals, and Administrators," Atlanta University Seminar, Summer 1946, document series VII: 35, microfilm, reel 189, frames 1289–94, Southern Regional Council Archives.

10. Figures, as well as a detailed examination of the experience of black veterans in the South and their access to the GI Bill, may be found in David Onkst, "'First a Negro . . . Incidentally a Veteran': Black World War Two Veterans and the G.I. Bill of Rights in the Deep South, 1944–48," 18 and 29–30, manuscript in possession of the author.

11. "Statements by Teachers, Principals, and Administrators."

12. Southern black veterans often established their own organizations rather than joining segregated chapters of the American Legion or the Veterans of Foreign Wars. Information on such veteran organizations in Alabama, Mississippi, and Tennessee may be found in *Birmingham World,* March 8, 1946; *Atlanta Daily World,* October 1, 1946, 6; *Jackson (Miss.) Advocate,* September 7, 1946; and *Memphis World,* August 23, 1946.

13. Bohannon interview.

14. "Fourteen Points of Action of GVL, Inc.," December 1945, document series VII: 4, microfilm, reel 190, frame 931, Southern Regional Council Archives; Bohannon interview. Veteran services organizations such as the American Legion (which required segregated chapters), as well as government offices, usually had white counselors who often did not prioritize serving black veterans. According to Bohannon, black veterans often felt more comfortable with, and received better service from, black counselors when trying to navigate through the inevitable bureaucratic red tape involved in applying for federal or state benefits.

15. Bohannon interview (first and third quotes); "Fourteen Points of Action of GVL, Inc." (second quote). See also Paul Douglas Bolster, "Civil Rights Movements in Twentieth-Century Georgia" (Ph.D. diss., University of Georgia, 1972), 106.

16. Doyle Combs interview, October 13, 1989, audiotape, Transcript Series E, GGDP.

17. "Fourteen Points of Action, GVL., Inc."

18. *Savannah Herald,* April 24, 1946, 6 (first quote), and June 5, 1946, 7 (second quote). Supporting the CPL gave black citizens of Savannah an opportunity to gain political influence by helping overthrow an entrenched political machine that had provided few services for blacks since its inception in the 1930s. See editorial in the *Savannah Tribune,* December 12, 1946, 4 and 8.

19. *Savannah Morning News,* May 1, 1946, 12; and *Savannah Evening Press,* July 5, 1946, 18 (quotes). For more details on the Savannah voter-registration campaign see *Savannah Herald,* May 1, 1946, 2 and 9; R. W. Gadsen interview, July 10, 1947, for "Who Runs Georgia?" unpublished manuscript, Transcript Series B, GGDP; Bolster, "Civil Rights Movements," 119; and Alexander Heard interview, July 17, 1991, accession no. A-344, transcript, Southern Oral History Program, Southern Historical Collection, Louis Round Wilson Library, University of North Carolina, Chapel Hill [hereafter cited as SOHP].

20. *Savannah Morning News,* May 13, 1946, 10, July 2, 1946, 16, and July 18, 1946, 14; *Savannah Herald,* July 25, 1946, 8; Bolster, "Civil Rights Movements," 123.

21. The ACRC was a new umbrella organization that encompassed several black civil rights groups in Atlanta and Fulton County. On the ACRC voter-registration campaign see David Andrew Harmon, "Beneath the Image: The Civil Rights Movement and Race Relations in Atlanta" (Ph.D. diss., Emory University, Atlanta, 1991), 33–56; Bolster, "Civil Rights Movements," 116 ff.; and Jacob Henderson interview, July 24, 1992, videotape, and Jacob Henderson interview, June 1989, Transcript Series E, both in GGDP. Campaign material from the ACRC drive can also be found in the Clarence Bacote Collection (currently being processed) and in the Atlanta Urban League Papers, box 7, document series 2, manuscript no. 597, Grace Towns Hamilton Papers, both in Special Collections Department, Robert W. Woodruff Library, Atlanta History Center. See also *Birmingham World,* March 19, April 30, and May 7, 1946.

22. Veterans' Division memo, March 28, 1946, 7, folder 1, box 7, document series 2, manuscript no. 597, Hamilton Papers (first quote); *Birmingham World,* March 19, 1946.

23. Harmon, "Beneath the Image," 47, 72; Bolster, "Civil Rights Movements," 117, 122.

24. On similar activities throughout Georgia, see *Birmingham World,* January 15, 1946, 5, and April 19, 1946, 4; *Atlanta Journal,* May 23, 1946, 1, and June 14, 1946, 1; *Atlanta Daily World,* March 28, 1946, 2; *Augusta Chronicle,* February 10, 1946, 1; *Brunswick News,* November 1, 1945, 8, and March 21, 1946, 8; and *Columbus Enquirer,* June 2, 1946, 10-C, and September 27, 1946, 7-A.

25. Donald L. Grant, *The Way It Was in the South: The Black Experience in Georgia* (New York: Birch Lane Press, 1993), 363–65, 368–70. In Mississippi, e.g., black veterans' efforts to oust Senator Theodore G. Bilbo failed to rid the state of its most notorious reactionary. Nonetheless, veterans' courage in testifying against "the Man" in a later congressional investigation of electoral chicanery encouraged others to take action. By 1950 some twenty thousand black Mississippians were registered to vote, far short of their overall percentage in the population but a significant start, nonetheless, in a state known for its rabid racism. See Kenneth H. Williams, "Mississippi Civil Rights, 1945–1954" (Ph.D. diss.,

Mississippi State University, 1985), 89–99, 108; and Steven F. Lawson, *Black Ballots: Voting Rights in the South, 1944–1969* (New York: Columbia University Press, 1976), 128.

26. World War II veteran Hodding Carter, editor of the Greenville, Mississippi, *Delta Democrat Times,* believed that his observation of the British attitude toward Egyptian colonials and natives while serving as Middle East editor for *Yank* magazine awakened him to the destructiveness of discrimination, prodding him toward a moderate racial liberalism in his editorials after the war. Congressman Frank E. Smith of Mississippi learned through his experiences with integration at Fort Sill, Oklahoma, that "compelling authority" could cause widespread acceptance of racial change, and he ultimately became somewhat of a racial moderate in Congress, at least by Mississippi standards. See Ann Waldron, *Hodding Carter: The Reconstruction of a Racist* (Chapel Hill: Algonquin Books, 1993), 128–29; Frank E. Smith, *Congressman from Mississippi* (New York: Pantheon Books, 1964), 59, 66–67, 71–72; and James C. Cobb, *The Most Southern Place on Earth: The Mississippi Delta and the Roots of Regional Identity* (New York: Oxford University Press, 1992), 210–11.

27. *Atlanta Constitution,* July 17, 1946, clipping (first quote), Scrapbook no. 7 entitled "1946 Gubernatorial Campaign," James V. Carmichael Papers, Special Collections Department, Robert H. Woodruff Library, Emory University; Morton Sosna, "More Important Than the Civil War: The Impact of World War II on the South," in *Perspectives on the American South: An Annual Review of Society, Politics, and Culture,* ed. James C. Cobb and Charles R. Wilson, vol. 4 (New York: Gordon and Breach, 1987), 154–55 (second quote).

28. Harold Fleming interview, January 24, 1990, accession no. A-363, transcript, SOHP.

29. Ibid. (all quotes); *Washington Post,* September 6, 1992.

30. After the war, Mackay became an avid defender of the democratic political rights of all Georgians and developed a reputation as a maverick southern liberal in the state and national legislatures. James Mackay interviews, March 28, 1986, and March 31, 1987, Transcript Series B, GGDP.

31. *Atlanta Constitution,* February 16, 1947, 10-A, February 9, 1947, 4-A. See also Joseph Rabun interview for "Who Runs Georgia?," unpublished manuscript, Transcript Series B, GGDP.

32. White veterans with burgeoning, but as yet untapped, progressive inclinations returned to a state beset by both the forces of change and a reactionary resistance to reform. The growing presence of the Congress of Industrial Organization, the reformist efforts of the Southern Regional Council and the Southern Conference for Human Welfare, and the political activism of black veterans, the NAACP, and other organizations generated a resurgent Ku Klux Klan, reactionary campaigns for public office, and a wave of racial violence and anti-unionism. See Numan V. Bartley, *The New South, 1945–1980* (Baton Rouge: Louisiana State University Press, 1995), for the conservative trends of the postwar years in the South.

33. Fleming interview; *Washington Post,* September 6, 1992. The race-baiting that occurred following the war, as Georgia conservatives worked to reinstate a white primary, moved Joseph Rabun to mount a protest that ultimately cost

him his pulpit. Rabun convinced the Georgia Baptist Convention to condemn Eugene Talmadge's white supremacy campaign in the fall of 1946, and he testified in early 1947 before a state legislative committee against a bill to reinstate the white primary. Rabun had lived "by those beliefs" ever since his conversion, he told an Atlanta reporter, but now "he had faced 100 days of battle-fire for them; he had known four years of war. Thus," he declared, "it was little enough that as a private citizen I should exercise my right as such in a democracy, to speak in behalf of them." *Atlanta Constitution,* February 16, 1947, 10-A. Rabun's comments inspired much controversy among his congregants, particularly since the church was the home of the Talmadge family. After resisting calls to resign, Rabun eventually stepped down from that pulpit later in 1947. Rabun interview, p. 2; *Atlanta Constitution,* February 9, 1947, 4. Also see John Egerton, *Speak Now against the Day: The Generation before the Civil Rights Movement in the South* (New York: Knopf, 1994), 423-24.

34. The AVC condemned racial segregation and discrimination and worked to advance progressive causes and candidates. See *Atlanta Daily World,* November 14, 1946, 3: *Birmingham World,* May 10, 1946, 7; Egerton, *Speak Now,* 340, 382, 468; and AVC pamphlet, Robert Thompson Biographical File, Special Collections, Robert W. Woodruff Library, Atlanta University Center.

35. *Bellringer,* October 20, 1947, 1, box 13 (first quote), Glenn Rainey Collection, Special Collections Department, Robert H. Woodruff Library, Emory University; AVC pamphlet, Robert Thompson Biographical File (second quote). For more on the AVC in Georgia, see *Atlanta Constitution,* July 10, 1946, 4, and July 23, 1946, 3; "Southern Activity," American Veterans Committee bulletin, March 1948, folder entitled "American Veterans Committee, 1944-45," box 5, Gilbert Harrison Papers, Library of Congress, Washington, D.C.; Marcus Gunter to George Mitchell, December 15, 1946, document series VII: 6, microfilm, reel 188, frames 456-523, Southern Regional Council Archives; Robert Thompson interviews, June 5, 1989, audiotape and transcript, Transcript Series E and G, GGDP; and Annie McPheeters interview, June 8, 1992, Transcript Series J, GGDP.

36. Lorraine Nelson Spritzer, *The Belle of Ashby Street: Helen Douglas Mankin and Georgia Politics* (Athens: University of Georgia Press, 1982), 98.

37. *Atlanta Constitution,* July 9, 1946, E-1 (first and second quotes). George Stoney became acquainted with the community of Atlanta liberals as a researcher for Gunnar Myrdal's *An American Dilemma: The Negro Problem and Modern Democracy* (New York: Harper and Brothers, 1944). "Josephine Wilkins and Maggie Fisher [of the Southern Conference for Human Welfare's Georgia Committee] suggested that I work for Helen Douglas Mankin," he recalled. George Stoney interview, June 13, 1991, transcript no. A-346, SOHP. Many of Mankin's positions paralleled those taken by the national AVC. See, e.g., *Atlanta Daily World,* October 8, 1946, 3.

38. Convinced that "sinister forces might be back of all this" (meaning the county-unit system's nullification of Mankin's and Carmichael's popular majorities), a coterie of Atlanta liberals affiliated with the Southern Conference for Human Welfare, the Southern Regional Council, and the Urban League obtained a Rosenwald Fund grant to ferret out the "hidden influences" that ostensibly ran the state. Progressive white veterans Calvin Kytle and James Mackay

carried out the research to discover "Who Runs Georgia?" After interviewing numerous politicians, editors, writers, and community leaders, Mackay and Kytle concluded that a cabal of large economic interests, particularly the Georgia Power Company and the railroads, essentially controlled politics throughout the state. Mackay and Kytle compiled their interviews and conclusions into a manuscript that remained unpublished until recently by the University of Georgia Press. According to Kytle, however, at the time it became "the most famous unpublished report of Georgia politics because the Talmadge people stole it" and enlisted it in the next campaign. See Calvin and Elizabeth Kytle interview, January 1, 1991, interview no. A-365, transcript, SOHP; and Mackay interview.

39. Plaintiffs for the two lawsuits were Mrs. Robert Thurman of the League of Women Voters; Cullen Gosnell, chairman of the political science department at Emory University; and Earl P. Cooke, a law student at Georgia Tech and veteran of World War II. These units were styled *Thurman and Gosnell v. J. Lon Duckworth* and *Cooke v. Fortson*. See *Atlanta Journal,* August 2, 1946, 1.

40. Ibid.

41. "A group of veterans is out today to raise $40,000 in a month's time to wage political battle against minority rule," announced one Savannah newspaper as veterans in the GVMR set up a central office in Atlanta from which to coordinate their fund-raising efforts. See *Savannah Morning News,* September 22, 1946, 27.

42. GVMR members included Alexander Heard, a navy veteran from Savannah who headed the committee in the First Congressional District; George Doss Jr. of the Student League for Good Government at the University of Georgia; James M. Crawford, veteran of seventeen months as an enlisted man in the infantry and in the Army's Tenth Armored Division; Elizabeth Penn Hammond, veteran of forty months as an enlisted woman and officer in the Women Accepted for Voluntary Emergency Service; and Richard T. Brooke, veteran of seventeen months as an enlisted man in the navy. See "Personal Histories," Georgia Veterans for Majority Rule, August 1946, document series VII: 43, microfilm, reel 190, frames 730 and 733, Southern Regional Council Archives.

43. Georgia Veterans for Majority Rule, October 1946, document series V-1, entitled the Lucy Randolph Mason Papers in *Operation Dixie: The CIO Organizing Committee Papers, 1946–1953,* Special Collections, Perkins Library, Duke University (first and second quotes) [hereafter cited as Mason Papers]; Georgia Veterans for Majority Rule, n.d., document series Pt. 4, microfilm reel 7, frames 729–31, NAACP Papers, John C. Hodges Library, University of Tennessee, Knoxville (third and fourth quotes).

44. Lucy Randolph Mason remarked on the "pall of fear" hanging over Georgia after Eugene Talmadge's reelection as governor, making organizing for any progressive cause difficult. See Lucy Randolph Mason to Barry Bingham, September 8, 1946, frame 343, and Lucy Randolph Mason to Eleanor Roosevelt, September 8, 1946, frame 344, both in document series V-1, reel 63, Mason Papers; and V. O. Key Jr., *Southern Politics in State and Nation* (New York: Knopf, 1949), 121. For more on this veteran organization, including the obstacles it faced, see Jennifer E. Brooks, "From Hitler and Tojo to Talmadge and Jim Crow: World War Two Veterans and the Remaking of Southern Political Tradition"

(Ph.D. diss., University of Tennessee, Knoxville, 1997), chap. 5; Mackay interview; *Savannah Morning News,* August 11, 1946, B-2; "Personal Histories," Georgia Veterans for Majority Rule, reel 190, frames 731–33; Georgia Veterans for Majority Rule, October 1946, document series V-1, reel 63, frame 413, Mason Papers; and Georgia Veterans for Majority Rule, n.d., document series Pt. 4, reel 7, frames 729–31, NAACP Papers.

45. *Atlanta Constitution,* February 5, 1947, 1, 4. On testimony at the committee hearing see Egerton, *Speak Now,* 389.

46. "While it is important to not be too optimistic," stated a reporter for the *Atlanta Constitution* on June 24, 1945, "many practical Atlantans feel sure this area will meet the shock of transition from war to peace with less pain than many other areas." Specifically, "there will be some sort of job . . . available to everyone wanting to work." On predictions of full employment see ibid., April 22, 1945, E-1, June 24, 1945, 1, August 19, 1945, 2-B, August 21, 1945, 1, August 22, 1945, 1, August 24, 1945, 1, August 26, 1945, 9-A, and August 27, 1945, 1; and *Savannah Evening Press,* April 27, 1946, 14.

47. On unemployment at the end of the war see *Savannah Morning News,* January 24, 1946, 14 (quote), and April 5, 1946, 14; *Atlanta Constitution,* September 6, 1945, 8; and *Atlanta Journal,* January 13, 1946, 9-D. According to the Georgia Department of Labor in February 1946, employment in the state dropped "from a peak" of "502,500 in the third quarter to 1943" to 435,000 soon after V-J Day. "The drop was attributed to cutbacks in shipyards and war plants," reported the *Atlanta Journal,* as well as in "textile plants engaged in war production." See *Atlanta Journal,* February 5, 1946, 6. The Douglas (Ga.) *Coffee County Progress* reported on May 16, 1946, that in Douglas, the county seat, "the volume of unemployed ex-servicemen . . . is still unusually high."

48. In the Midwest, returning veterans hoping to become independent farm operators found that high prices made it difficult to purchase good land, even with the help of GI Bill credit benefits. See *New York Times,* April 28, 1946, IV-8.

49. For a discussion of the chaotic social and economic aftermath of the war of the South and the United States generally see Bartley, *Creation of Modern Georgia,* 179, 197–98, 199–203; George Brown Tindall, *The Emergence of the New South, 1913–1945* (Baton Rouge: Louisiana State University Press, 1967), 687–73; Bartley, *New South,* 1–73; and Richard Polenberg, *War and Society: The United States, 1941–1945* (Philadelphia: Lippincott, 1972), 99–153.

50. Lucy Randolph Mason to John Roy Carlson, April 15, 1946, document series V-1, reel 63, frame 269, Mason Papers.

51. Report on Atlanta Klavern no. 1, September 23, 1946, folder 3, box 1, microfilm, reel 1, Stetson Kennedy Papers, Special Collections and Archives, William Russell Pullen Library, Georgia State University, Atlanta.

52. The following sources from reel 1, Kennedy Papers, describe the Klan's "strong-arm" inner circle: Klavalier Klub Meeting, May 1, 1946, folder 3, box 1; "Information Relative to the Klavalier Klub," folder 4, box 1; and Report on the Atlanta Ku Klux Klan, May 6, 1946, folder 3, box 1.

53. See the following in reel 1, Kennedy Papers: Klan report, Atlanta, May 6, 1946, folder 3, box 1; report on Klavalier Klub meeting, May 1, 1946, folder 3, box 1; Klavalier Klub Activities, 1948, folder 4, box 1; report on meeting of At-

lanta Klavern no. 1, April 29, 1946, folder 3, box 1; "Info Relative to Klavalier Klub," 1948, folder 4, box 1; Meeting of Klavalier Klub, May 15, 1946, folder 3, box 1; Report by John Brown, Atlanta Klavern no. 1 meeting, April 829, 1946, folder 3, box 1; "Info Relative to Klavalier Klub," 1948, folder 4, box 1; Meeting of Klavalier Klub, May 15, 1946, folder 3, box 1; and Report by John Brown, Atlanta Klavern no. 297 meeting, April 18, 1946, folder 3, box 1. Also see *Atlanta Journal,* September 16, 1948, 5.

54. Brief discussions of the Columbians may be found in Brooks, "From Hitler and Tojo to Talmadge and Jim Crow," chaps. 1 and 4; J. Wayne Dudley, "'Hate Organizations' of the 1940s: The Columbians, Inc.," *Phylon,* September 3, 1981, 262–74; and Spritzer, *Belle of Ashby Street,* 117. Also see *Atlanta Daily World,* November 1, 1946, 1, October 31, 1946, 1 and 8, November 1, 1946, 9, November 3, 1946, 3, December 10, 1946, 1, and December 11, 1946, 4. Informants infiltrating this organization reported regularly on its activities to Ralph McGill, editor of the *Atlanta Constitution.* See, e.g., Grey to AF, October 1, 1946, and Ned to AF, November 8, 1946, folder 1, box 51, Series V: Subject Files, Ralph McGill Papers, Special Collections Department, Robert H. Woodruff Library, Emory University. Stetson Kennedy played a key role in this infiltration, and his papers include a variety of firsthand information on the Columbians. See folder entitled "Columbians," reel 1, Kennedy Papers.

55. AF to Ned, September 3, 1946, folder 1, box 51, Series V: Subject Files, McGill Papers (first quote); *The Bellringer,* September 7, 1946, 2, microfilm, reel 190, Southern Regional Council Archives (last quote).

56. See Dudley, "'Hate Organizations' of the 1940s," 296; *Atlanta Daily World,* November 5, 1946, 1 and 6; "Atlanta Version of Mein Kampf," folder 6, box 1, reel 1, and Ned to AF, November 3, 1946, folder entitled "Columbians," reel 1, both in Kennedy Papers. Although a few veterans joined the Columbians, it is possible to assign too much significance to their association with the group. The group had trouble sustaining its membership, not only because of competitive, obviously twisted egos among the leadership but also because few southerners, veteran or civilian, could stomach an organization that closely parroted the antics and philosophy of the Nazis. Nonetheless, the presence of some veterans illustrated the extent to which they would go to defend southern racial tradition.

57. Herman Talmadge, speech delivered for Eugene Talmadge, May 4, 1946, transcript and audiotape, accession no. Draft APR. 19923, GGDP.

58. Guy Alford to Prince Preston, July 31, 1946, folder entitled "Emmanuel," box 33, Prince Preston Papers, Richard B. Russell Library, University of Georgia, Athens.

59. *Atlanta Journal,* May 9, 1946, 14.

60. Ibid., August 20, 1946, 14.

61. Ibid., June 7, 1946, 18.

62. See, e.g., *Atlanta Constitution,* July 19, 1946, 1 and 13, and July 24, 1946, 8; *Atlanta Journal,* July 14, 1946, 10-A; *Savannah Evening Press,* May 27, 1946, 2; *Augusta Chronicle,* March 13, 1946, 1 and 2; and La Fayette (Ga.) *Walker County Messenger,* August 2, 1946, 1.

63. While "in the First World War we used to sing 'The Yanks Are Coming,'"

De Mendoza added, "now we are going to sing 'The Negroes are coming.'" Christopher De Mendoza to Prince Preston, July 12, 1946, folder entitled "Liberty," box 33, Preston Papers.

64. *Coffee County Progress,* June 20, 1946 (first quote), July 4, 1946, 10.

65. *Atlanta Journal,* July 1, 1946, 10.

66. See ibid., December 10, 1946, 1, December 11, 1946, 4, and January 5, 1947, B-1.

67. State representative Garland T. Byrd, a combat veteran elected in 1946 from Taylor County, proclaimed on January 2, 1947, that a "Herman Talmadge Victory Is a Victory for Veterans!" in the *Atlanta Statesman,* a pro-Talmadge political rag published in Hapeville, Georgia, and associated with Roy V. Harris, the Augusta Cracker politico. More than three hundred World War II veterans in Floyd County reportedly drafted a petition sympathetic to Herman Talmadge and critical of press coverage of the two-governors controversy. "We the undersigned, being veterans of World War II, who fought for fairness and justice in Georgia . . . are absolutely and completely for Herman Talmadge and pledge to him (a fellow veteran) our full support in his legal and moral right to the Governorship of the State of Georgia." See ibid., January 13, 1947. For the controversy, see Bartley, *Creation of Modern Georgia,* 204. State representative Culver Kidd, a war veteran from Baldwin County elected in 1946, recalled supporting Herman Talmadge during the gubernatorial controversy, which earned him an appointment as chairman of the Institutions and Property Committee. John J. Flynt, yet another veteran elected to the state legislature in 1946, recalled taking a "bad beating" in the press and from his hometown constituency in Spalding County for supporting Talmadge and his white primary bill. Culver Kidd interview, October 3, 1988, Transcript Series B, and John J. Flynt interview, July 13, 1947, for "Who Runs Georgia?," unpublished manuscript, Transcript Series B, both in GGDP.

68. See Bartley, *New South,* 38–73, for an incisive discussion of "The Rise and Fall of Postwar Liberalism."

69. Having "been around the country and in a few other cities," for example, "Just Another GI" found that when looking at New Orleans, "I have not got too much to brag about." If New Orleans is the "Pride of the South," he added, "there should be more beautiful places to visit and . . . they should be kept clean. . . . Several soldier friends of mine visited New Orleans before they were in the army and some don't ever want to go back." *New Orleans Times Picayune,* January 26, 1946.

70. The same phenomenon marked postwar politics in virtually every southern state. Submitting to a "dictatorial" ring that thrived on ballot stuffing, nepotism, and profiteering at the public expense seemed unconscionable to veterans in Yell County, Arkansas, e.g., who promised in 1946 to wage the "damnedest campaign you ever saw" against local bossism. "We were told we were fighting for democracy," these former soldiers explained, but "democracy [does not] exist in Yell County, so we're still fighting for it." *Atlanta Constitution,* August 1, 1946, 10-A. The Battle of Athens stands as the most widely known postwar veterans' revolt. In Athens, Tennessee, disgust with the practices of a corrupt county ring compelled veterans not only to run their own candidates for office

but also to wage a heated gun battle to prevent the election from being stolen. A sensationalized image of gun-wielding, crusading hillbilly veterans shooting it out with brutish, corrupt courthouse thugs blazed across national headlines in the summer of 1946. "If democracy is good enough for Germany and the Japs," declared one Athens combat veteran, "it's good enough for McMinn County!" See C. Stephen Bynum, *The Battle of Athens* (Chattanooga, Tenn.: Paidia Productions, 1987), 3–4 (quote), 7–8, 119; *Newsweek,* August 12, 1946, 30–32, September 9, 1946, 38, and January 27, 1947; *Commonweal,* August 12, 1946, 419–20; Theodore H. White, "The Battle of Athens, Tennessee," *Harper's Monthly,* January 1947, 54–61; and Lones Seiber, "The Battle of Athens," *American Heritage* 35 (February–March 1985): 72–79.

71. The Cracker Party of Augusta was a long-incumbent Democratic Party organization in Richmond County headed by Roy V. Harris, reactionary former speaker of the Georgia House. For more on the Cracker Party and the veteran-led Independent revolt against it in 1946 see James C. Cobb, "Colonel Effingham Crushes the Crackers: Political Reform in Postwar Augusta," *South Atlantic Quarterly* 77 (Autumn 1979): 507–19.

72. Voter turnout for the 1946 gubernatorial election was more than twice that for the 1942 election, in which Ellis Arnall had defeated Talmadge. See William Anderson, *The Wild Man from Sugar Creek: The Political Career of Eugene Talmadge* (Baton Rouge: Louisiana State University Press, 1975), 210–11; Joseph L. Bernd, *Grass Roots Politics in Georgia: The County Unit System and the Importance of the Individual Voting Community in B-factional Election, 1942–1954* (Atlanta: Emory University Research Committee, 1960), 66–71; and Harold Paulk Henderson, *The Politics of Change in Georgia: A Political Biography of Ellis Arnall* (Athens: University of Georgia Press, 1991), 50, 145, 166–68.

73. Griffin Bell interview, September 19, 1990, Transcript Series B, GGDP (first quote); *Atlanta Journal,* April 29, 1946, 10 (second quote). Many observers at the time noticed, and were pleased by, the broadened perspective of the state's returning white solders. "Georgians . . . returning from lands all over the earth are bringing in new visions and ideas," reported the *Gainesville Eagle,* and having "seen and experienced many new things . . . they can do much to broaden the horizons of Georgia today." The *Augusta Chronicle* agreed, remarking that "most, if not all of these young men are quite different in their outlook and actions, from the timid, apathetic, secure in the rut, average run of the time [sic] citizen." *Gainesville Eagle,* May 9, 1946; *Augusta Chronicle,* March 9, 1946, 4.

74. *Atlanta Constitution,* August 7, 1946, E-1 (Moffett quote), and July 21, 1946, 14-a (Flynt quote). Veterans in other southern states remarked on and acted from similar experiences. Arkansas veteran Orval E. Faubus, who rose to political prominence in Governor Sidney S. McMath's administration and later became one of the South's leading architects of massive resistance, was influenced by the modern world he had observed in Germany during and after the war. Having used the enemy's good roads, Faubus recalled thinking that "Germany was a poor country and I wondered what they would think if they knew that when I, a representative of a wealthy country, went back I would have to get a mule to get home." Diane D. Blair, *Arkansas Politics and Government: Do the People Rule?* (Lincoln: University of Nebraska Press, 1988), 17. In Polk County,

Tennessee, heartened by the success of their comrades in nearby Athens, veterans formed a Good Government League in 1946 to oust the Crump-allied Burch Biggs machine, declaring to Congressman Estes Kefauver that "Machine Rule has brought decay and stagnation to Progress in Polk County, and citizens have at last rebelled." R. E. Barclay to U.S. Representative Estes Kefauver, telegram, October 1946, folder entitled "Qualifying Petitions, 1944–6," box entitled "1946 Political Files," Estes Kefauver Collection, Special Collections, Hoskins Library, University of Tennessee–Knoxville.

75. Few would dispute that during his term as agricultural commissioner and as governor in the 1930s and early 1940s Talmadge had provided plenty of ammunition to fuel Yankee ridicule. Not every politician was in a position to make political capital out of an investigation into his misuse of funds, but Talmadge was. In one of his most infamous feats as agriculture commissioner, Talmadge used state money to purchase from local farmers eighty-two carloads of Georgia hogs, which were shipped to Chicago for sale, all without any legal appropriation of funds for that purpose. Ardently opposed to the New Deal, Talmadge responded to the hog farmers' dilemma during the Great Depression with an illegal appropriation of state funds to buy and market Georgia hogs. In the ensuing controversy, prompted, in part, by the state's loss of approximately $13,000 on the deal, Talmadge publicly declared that "If I stole, it was for farmers," which delighted his wool-hat followers but embarrassed uptown Georgians. During Talmadge's time as governor, his antics reached new heights of absurdity, reactionism, and downright meanness. He pastured a cow on the statehouse lawn, kept the state government in a state of martial law for months in order to consolidate his control of state agencies, and declared those who served in the Civilian Conservation Corps to be "bums and loafers." In 1934 he remarked that "the next President . . . should be able to walk a two-by-four," a comment that splashed across national headlines. That same year, Talmadge called out the state national guard in a brutal suppression of Georgia workers in the Great Textile Strike of 1934, during which thousands were incarcerated in barbed-wire prison camps and one worker was beaten to death in front of his family. The following year, Talmadge provoked an impasse with the Georgia General Assembly by vetoing old-age pensions, seven constitutional amendments, and hundreds of local measures. Later in 1935, the legislature adjourned without appropriating money to operate the state government in 1936. In the ensuing imbroglio, Talmadge defied state law and political convention by having the state adjutant general physically remove the state treasurer from office and then try to open the state vault with blowtorches. Such antics—and there were plenty of others—not only gained widespread local coverage but also directed national attention to Georgia's "banana republic" politics. Talmadge publicly bragged about having read *Mein Kampf* seven times just as war broke out in Europe, and more and more observers drew a connection between his style of rule and the dictatorships overseas. In the wake of the 1936 conflict with the legislature, newspapers in Georgia remarked that Talmadge "is getting to be worse than Hitler or Mussolini" and that he was a "paper-mache dictator" who administered "lynch law" in Georgia. Nor did Talmadge try to deflect his critics, declaring that "I'm what you call a minor dictator. But did you ever see anybody

that was much good who didn't have a little dictator in him?" Quotes in Anderson, *Wild Man from Sugar Creek,* 57–58, 59, 60, 73, 194.

76. "Arnold" to James Setze Jr., July 15, 1941, folder 1, box 1 entitled "Letters to James Setze Jr., 1940–August 1941" (first quote), World War II Miscellany Papers, Special Collection Department, Robert H. Woodruff Library, Emory University [hereafter cited as Setze Letters]; *Atlanta Constitution,* May 15, 1946, clipping, Scrapbook no. 6, Carmichael Papers (Tant quote). "Frank" wrote to James Setze about reading of "the Georgia students and Governor Talmadge in Life and Time. That sure is a mess." "Larry" wrote to Setze from Missouri: "It sure is a disgrace that Talmadge's meddling caused such a loss of prestige to the University of Georgia." "Frank" to James Setze Jr., n.d., folder 2, box 1, and "Larry" to James Setze Jr., January 11, 1942, folder 3, box 1, both in Setze Letters.

77. *Atlanta Journal,* July 26, 1846, 18 (first quote), and May 28, 1946, 10 (second quote).

78. *Atlanta Constitution,* July 16, 1946, E-1 (first quote); and clipping, ca. 1946, Scrapbook no. 6, 1946 Gubernatorial Campaign, Carmichael Papers (second quote).

79. *Atlanta Journal,* May 22, 1946, clipping, Scrapbook no. 6, Carmichael Papers.

80. "Georgia soldier," Orlando, Florida, August 15, 1944, clipping, folder entitled "Servicemen's reactions to Georgia," box 16, Lamar Q. Ball Collection, Georgia Department of Archives and History, Atlanta.

81. Arnall's accomplishments included a new state constitution, a constitutional board of regents, a state board of education, a law providing absentee ballots to out-of-state and overseas soldiers, lowering the age of voter eligibility to eighteen, abolishing the poll tax for all citizens, significantly increasing expenditures for education, creating a teacher-retirement plan, and liquidating the long-standing state debt without raising taxes. See Bartley, *Creation of Modern Georgia,* 194.

82. *Atlanta Constitution,* July 3, 1946, 1 (first quote); *Atlanta Journal,* May 10, 1946, 18 (second quote).

83. Cunningham to James Setze Jr., September 29, 1942, folder 6, box 1, Setze Letters.

84. Sergeant Harry Baxter, July 2, 1946, WSB Radio broadcast, transcript, accession no. Draft APR.1993.18, GGDP.

85. *Atlanta Journal,* October 28, 1946, 10 (first quote), May 15, 1946, 12 (second quote); and *Atlanta Constitution,* August 23, 1946, E-1 (third quote).

86. War mobilization fostered significant economic growth in Georgia and the South, boosting the region's overall industrial capacity by almost 40 percent. Along with new aircraft, munitions, rubber, and chemical industries came the expansion of traditional industries such as textiles, lumber, and mining. This growth, combined with increasing agriculture prices, generated more income, which encouraged the development of a nascent consumer market in the South. In Georgia, wartime development boosted per capita incomes from 57 percent of the national average in 1940 to 73 percent in 1960. The arrival of more than sixteen hundred new manufacturing establishments between 1930 and 1947 and the emergence of a burgeoning consumer market spurred diversification and

expansion of jobs in both the white- and blue-collar sectors of the economy. The prosperity induced by World War II seemed an abrupt change after years of unrelenting depression, a change that promised to eradicate the South's image as a "benighted" region burdened by its past and saddled with an unwelcome, though deserved, reputation as the nation's "number one economic problem." While pump-priming federal spending did much to boost southern economic growth, it failed to "neutralize the South's economic heritage." Much of this development was uneven, favoring the Gulf Southwest within the South and larger cities within Georgia. In addition, with much of this development centered on war production, reconversion shut down plants that were important sources of wartime employment. For example, Huntsville, Alabama; Columbia, Tennessee; and Brunswick, Savannah, and Marietta, Georgia, all suffered immediately after the war from the closure of war industries, which contributed to local racial tension and political instability. See Tindall, *Emergence of the New South*, 694, 700–701; and Bartley, *Creation of Modern Georgia*, 186–87, 181–83.

87. *Atlanta Journal*, February 19, 1946, 10 (first quote), July 23, 1946, 10 (second quote).

88. Ibid., March 13, 1946, 10 (first quote); *Atlanta Constitution*, February 10, 1946, A-15 (second quote).

89. For examples of veterans' support of Carmichael's gubernatorial campaign see clippings from *Atlanta Constitution*, April 28, 1946, and from *Atlanta Journal*, April 30, 1946, in Scrapbook no. 6, Carmichael Papers; *Atlanta Journal*, May 5, 1946, 16-A, May 12, 1946, 18-A, May 14, 1946, 6, and June 13, 1946, 6; and *Waycross (Ga.) Journal Herald*, May 16, 1946, 1.

90. Student-League-for-Good-Government, advertisement, folder 5 entitled "Georgia Politics," reel 2, Kennedy Papers (first quote); and *Atlanta Journal*, May 22, 1946, clipping, Scrapbook no. 6, Carmichael Papers (second quote).

91. John Sammons Bell, Fulton County-for-Carmichael-Club, WSB Radio broadcast, July 11, 1946, accession no. Draft APR.1993.22.uc-m84-20/56b, GGDP.

92. The B-29ers-for-Carmichael Club also included former employees of the Bell Bomber plant in Marietta, Georgia, managed by Carmichael. See B-29ers-for-Carmichael Club, WSB Radio broadcast, July 5, 1946, transcript, accession no. Draft APR.1993.20.uc-M84-20/49thb and 461, GGDP.

93. B-29ers-for-Carmichael Club; James V. Carmichael, WSB Radio broadcast, June 15, 1946, transcript, accession no. Draft APR.1993.c-M84-20/29a and 29b, GGDP. See also *Atlanta Journal*, May 26, 1946, 6-A.

94. Smaller communities in Georgia that experienced veteran insurgencies (or in which veterans were particularly active) included Telfair County, Douglasville, La Fayette, Rabun County, Emmanuel County, Milledgeville, Athens, Clarkesville, Valdosta, Waycross, Albany, Talbotten, Cartersville, and La Grange.

95. Similar campaigns occurred across the South. Former serviceman Sidney McMath rode a wave of veteran support to become governor of Arkansas in 1948. In 1946 veterans helped former serviceman deLesseps S. Morrison oust the Long machine in New Orleans and seize the mayoralty, and white former soldiers in Alabama facilitated the formation of a long-lasting political machine by electing populist-progressive and veteran James E. Folsom to the governorship. See Jim Lester, *A Man for Arkansas: Sid McMath and the Southern Reform Tradition*

(Little Rock, Ark.: James W. Bell Publishers, 1976); Edward F. Haas, *DeLesseps S. Morrison and the Image of Reform: New Orleans Politics, 1946–1951* (Baton Rouge: Louisiana State University Press, 1974).

96. *Columbus Enquirer,* May 26, 1946, 10-D, June 2, 1946, 10-C.

97. See note 71 above for information on the Independents, a veteran-led insurgency against the Cracker Party in Augusta.

98. Carmichael received a solid plurality of votes, around 700,000, but the majority of county-unit votes went to Talmadge. See Bartley, *Creation of Modern Georgia,* 203–4.

99. In announcing his campaign for governor in 1946, Talmadge minced few words in appealing to his constituency's southern and racial nationalism. Declaring that the white primary issue was the most important question facing the region and the state of Georgia, Talmadge announced that "alien and Communistic influences from the East are agitating social equality in our state." In fact, he alleged, "they desire Negroes to participate in our white primary in order to destroy the traditions and heritages of our Southland." Thus, "if elected Governor," Talmadge promised, "I shall see that the traditions which were fought for by our grandparents are maintained and preserved . . . unfettered and unhampered by radical Communistic and alien influence." Talmadge capitalized also on national controversies and implied that the outcome of the gubernatorial race would affect issues that actually could be settled on by Congress. In a speech at Summerville, e.g., Talmadge attacked "socialized medicine" and the FEPC, pretending to explain how these questions threatened white supremacy in Georgia. "If they get across the FEPC and the socialized medicine, too," he alleged, "if you apply for a doctor, they might send you to a Negro doctor right here in this county." See *Montgomery Advertiser,* April 7, 1946, 25; and Eugene Talmadge, n.d., WSB Radio broadcast, transcript, accession no. Draft APR.1993.uc-M84-20/113a, 106, GGDP. Probably the only Georgia politician who could approach Talmadge in racial hyperbole and demagoguery for political effect was Roy V. Harris of the Cracker Party in Augusta. As an incumbent state legislator whose reelection was opposed by the Independents, Harris led the Crackers in attacking their opponents as carpetbaggers intent on eliminating the white primary in Georgia. Dubbing the white primary as the vehicle used by "the old Confederate veterans to wrest control of this state from the hands of the carpet-baggers, scalawags, and Negroes," a political ad for the Cracker legislative candidates proclaimed the importance of maintaining a racially exclusive primary. The "colored people" who "vote as a block [*sic*]" and "take orders from Washington and New York" aim to defeat southern congressmen, pass a permanent FEPC bill, and end segregation in all public facilities as well as promote intermarriage "of the races." The result, the Crackers warned, would be "the end of Augusta's development and growth" because "we will either have race riots or the white people will leave the community." Having declared white supremacy to be the overarching issue, the Crackers then tried to put the Independents on the spot by challenging them to take a position on the white primary. "This is the most important election in Georgia since we got rid of the scalawags, carpetbaggers, and Negro government," trumpeted Harris, yet "I have been asking this question [about the white primary] for two weeks

but I have received no answer." *Augusta Chronicle,* April 13, 1946, 8, April 12, 1946, 1 and 9.

100. Rather than attacking Carmichael directly, Talmadge often focused his most vitriolic efforts on his old rival Ellis Arnall, who had endorsed his opponent. For example, his race-baiting attacks on Arnall for refusing to defend the white primary labeled Arnall as the leader of a Yankee-liberal-black plot to overturn Georgia's racial traditions, a conspiracy that Carmichael's election as governor would only further. "Ellis 'Benedict' Arnall opened the breach in the dike that has protected Southern manhood, Southern womanhood, and Southern childhood for three quarters of a century," Talmadge accused, and Arnall had gone "further than any white man in America to promote [racial equality] in Georgia." Quoted in Henderson, *Politics of Change,* 166. On Talmadge's racial antics during the gubernatorial campaign of 1946 see Anderson, *Wild Man from Sugar Creek,* 229–31; and Bartley, *Creation of Modern Georgia,* 201–3.

101. Throughout the campaign, Carmichael sought to make the Klan the only racial issue, linking both Talmadge, endorsed by the Georgia Klan, and Rivers, a former member, to the reconstituted KKK. At Vienna, Georgia, Carmichael flayed his opponents for granting the Klan significant influence during their gubernatorial administrations. "Georgia cannot have prosperity if the governor uses tax money to endow the imperial wizard of Ku Klux Klan," he proclaimed in one speech for a rural audience. "There are crows that wear costumes of red suspenders [i.e., Talmadge], and there are crows that wear black bow ties as their insignia [i.e., Rivers] . . . when these two flocks of crows get together after dark . . . they cannot be told apart because they all wear white nightshirts. . . . And instead of going Caw, Caw, Caw as they do in the daytime, they go: Klux, Klux, Klux." *Jackson (Miss.) Advocate,* May 25, 1946, 1; *Birmingham World,* May 24, 1946, 1; James Carmichael speech, WSB Radio broadcast June 1, 1946, transcript, accession no. Draft APR.1993.4, GGDP. Carmichael often emphasized the need to obey the law and respect the courts as a way to deflect his opponents' attack on the white primary issue. "The welfare of any community . . . depends upon the maintenance of the law and order, or respect for the courts, of reasonableness in dealing with one another," Carmichael stated, and Talmadge's and Harris's antics aimed "to disturb the good relations that exist in Georgia between the races," inviting a "disregard for law and . . . an invitation to lawless chaos." Thus, he continued, "my platform means that the county unit system will be preserved as part of our law and that control of Georgia politics will remain with the people of our state and will not pass to Roy Harris and his stooges." Preserving the county-unit system and all other laws regulating primary elections, Carmichael promised, "means that the statutes against fraud, against ballot box stuffing, against fake registration lists, against the voting of dead folks on election day, will not be repealed in the interest of any political gain." James V. Carmichael, June 15, 1946, WSB Radio broadcast, transcript, accession no. Draft APR.1993.10.uc, GGDP (Carmichael quote).

102. Lon Sullivan speech, WSB Radio broadcast, July 13, 1947, accession no. Draft APR.1993.14.uc-M-84-20/32b and 59a, GGDP (first quote); George Doss Jr., WSB Radio broadcast B-49ers, also hurried to affirm Carmichael's southern "le-

gitimacy" by proclaiming "here's Jimmy's stand" on race relations; "He adheres to Southern racial tradition. [He] was born in, reared in, lives in, and expects to die in Cobb County, Georgia." B-29ers-for-Carmichael Club, WSB Radio broadcast, July 5, 1946, transcript, accession no. Draft APR.1993.20.uc-M84-20/49b and 46a, GGDP (third quote).

103. In an interview shortly after the election, Carmichael confided that his capitulation on the county-unit system—he personally regarded it as evil and undemocratic—rendered him unsuitable to be governor. See James V. Carmichael interview, July 23, 1947, for "Who Runs Georgia," unpublished manuscript, Transcript Series B, GGDP.

104. *Augusta Chronicle,* April 13, 1946, 1–2, April 14, 1946, 7.

105. In Savannah, where black veterans helped an upstart reformist coalition of white veterans defeat the corrupt John Bouhan machine, the CPL fulfilled African American demands to improve services to black neighborhoods, appoint a Negro Advisory Committee, and hire black police officers. Racial conservation in the CPL, however moderate compared to other administrations in the South, nonetheless soon caused a rupture in the relationship between CPL mayor John Kennedy and the new Negro Advisory Committee. Black war veteran W. W. Law, a supporter of the CPL and member of the committee, resigned when Mayor Kennedy refused to allow integrated lines for viewing the traveling Freedom Train exhibit. See W. W. Law interview; *Savannah Evening Press,* May 27, 1947, 2; *Savannah Tribune,* November 28, 1946, 1 and 8, February 6, 1947, 1 and 7; *Savannah Morning News,* October 27, 1946, 4; and *Savannah Herald,* February 6, 1947, 1 and 8.

106. See Harold P. Henderson and Gary L. Roberts, eds., *Georgia Governors in an Age of Change: From Ellis Arnall to George Busby* (Athens: University of Georgia Press, 1988); and Bartley, *Creation of Modern Georgia.*

EPILOGUE

1. See, e.g., the (Birmingham) *Alabama Independent,* July 10, 1969, 7. Of course, pockets of Republican strength existed in the South—most notably in the mountain Republican strongholds that overlapped with pro-Union sentiment during the Civil War: east Tennessee, western North Carolina, northwest Georgia, north Alabama, and northeast Mississippi. See Alexander P. Lamis, *The Two-Party South* (New York: Oxford University Press, 1984). The famous quote is from Faulkner's *Requiem for a Nun.*

2. For discussions of this prevailing view of Reconstruction, see Paul M. Gaston, *The New South Creed: A Study in Southern Mythmaking* (New York: Knopf, 1970), 130–31; Gaines M. Foster, *Ghosts of the Confederacy: Defeat, the Lost Cause, and the Emergence of the New South, 1865–1913* (New York: Oxford University Press, 1987); and virtually anything by Fred Arthur Bailey, such as "Free Speech and the 'Lost Cause' in the Old Dominion," *Virginia Magazine of History and Biography* 103 (April 1995): 237–66. For the enduring importance of the Civil War in southern history, see, e.g., Susan-Mary Grant and Peter J. Parish, eds., *Legacy of Disunion: The Enduring Significance of the American Civil War* (Baton Rouge: Louisiana State University Press, 2003); David R. Goldfield, *Still Fighting*

the Civil War: The American South and the Civil War (Baton Rouge: Louisiana State University Press, 2002); and David W. Blight, *Race and Reunion: The Civil War in American Memory* (Cambridge: Belknap Press, Harvard, 2001).

3. Due to time and space constraints, I am glossing over some very important history here, which has been documented and its significance explained in a number of works, not the least of which are C. Vann Woodward, *Origins of the New South, 1877–1913* (Baton Rouge: Louisiana State University Press, 1951); and Edward L. Ayers, *The Promise of the New South: Life after Reconstruction* (New York: Oxford University Press, 1992). Other works should be consulted. On Alabama, alone, see Michael W. Fitzgerald, *The Union League Movement in the Deep South: Politics and Agricultural Change during Reconstruction* (Baton Rouge: Louisiana State University Press, 1989); Sheldon Hackney, *Populism to Progressivism in Alabama* (Princeton: Princeton University Press, 1969); William Warren Rogers Sr., *The One-Gallused Rebellion: Agrarianism in Alabama, 1865–1896* (Baton Rouge: Louisiana State University Press, 1970); Samuel L. Webb, *Two-Party Politics in the One-Party South: Alabama's Hill Country, 1874–1920* (Tuscaloosa: University of Alabama Press, 1997); Daniel Letwin, *The Challenge of Interracial Unionism: Alabama Coal Miners, 1878–1921* (Chapel Hill: University of North Carolina Press, 1998); and Brian Kelly, *Race, Class, and Power in the Alabama Coalfields, 1908–21* (Urbana: University of Illinois Press, 2001). Southwide, see Michael Hyman, *The Anti-Redeemers: Hill Country Political Dissenters in the Lower South from Redemption to Populism* (Baton Rouge: Louisiana State University Press, 1990); and, more recently, Michael Perman, *Struggle for Mastery: Disfranchisement in the South, 1888–1908* (Chapel Hill: University of North Carolina Press, 2001). See also the excellent recent state studies: Jane Elizabeth Dailey, *Before Jim Crow: The Politics of Race in Postemancipation Virginia* (Chapel Hill: University of North Carolina Press, 2000); and Stephen Kantrowitz, *Ben Tillman and the Reconstruction of White Supremacy* (Chapel Hill: University of North Carolina Press, 2000). The literature on the Populist movement is vast. At the very least, the following should be consulted: Lawrence Goodwyn, *The Populist Moment: A Short History of the Agrarian Revolt in America* (New York: Oxford University Press, 1978); Bruce M. Palmer, *"Man Over Money": The Southern Populist Critique of American Capitalism* (Chapel Hill: University of North Carolina Press, 1980); and Barton C. Shaw, *The Wool-Hat Boys: Georgia's Populist Party* (Baton Rouge: Louisiana State University Press, 1984).

4. This, above all, is the lesson that may be taken from Malcolm Cook McMillan's classic *Constitutional Development in Alabama, 1798–1901: A Study in Politics, Sectionalism, and the Negro* (Chapel Hill: University of North Carolina Press, 1955). On the more general subject of disfranchisement, see also J. Morgan Kousser, *The Shaping of Southern Politics: Suffrage Restriction and the Establishment of the One-Party South, 1880–1910* (New Haven: Yale University Press, 1974); and Perman, *Struggle for Mastery*.

5. McMillan, *Constitutional Development in Alabama*; Allen W. Jones, "Political Reforms of the Progressive Era," *Alabama Review* 21 (July 1968): 173–94; *Official Proceedings of the Constitutional Convention of the State of Alabama, May 21st 1901 to Sept. 3, 1901* (Wetumpka, Ala.: Wetumpka Printing Co., 1940), 3:2841 (Heflin quote) and 3:3377 (Bulger quote); *Minutes of the Democratic State*

Convention, March 29, 1899, 23, 25–27 (Denson quote). Alabama's privileged Redeemers made no secret of the fact that they also meant to disfranchise blacks in the 1901 Alabama Constitution. John B. Knox, Anniston industrialist and former chair of the state Democratic Executive Committee, explained that "There is a difference . . . between the uneducated white man and the ignorant Negro. There is in the white man an inherited capacity for government, which is totally wanting in the Negro. . . . The Negro . . . is descended from a race lowest in intelligence and moral perceptions of all the races of men." *Official Proceedings, 1901,* 1:12. Future U.S. senator Captain Frank S. White agreed that "We have disfranchised the African in the past by doubtful methods, but in the future we will disfranchise [him] by law. The cancer that has been eating upon the body politic . . . must be taken away." *Minutes of the Democratic State Convention,* April 25, 1900, 5, Alabama Department of Archives and History, Montgomery [hereafter cited as ADAH].

6. The years between 1901 and 1928, while eventful and interesting in their own right, are beyond the scope of this part of the essay. The focus of this portion is to look at highlights of white voter cooperation in Alabama and the South across class and party lines—two of the most notable of which occurred in 1901 and 1928.

7. V. O. Key Jr., *Southern Politics in State and Nation* (1949; reprint, Knoxville: University of Tennessee Press, 1984), 317.

8. Glenn Feldman, *Politics, Society, and the Klan in Alabama, 1915–1949* (Tuscaloosa: University of Alabama Press, 1999), 185 (broadsheet quotes); Huddleston to Hammill, October 4, 1928 (quote), box 210, folder: Birmingham City Commission, Alabama Governors Papers, Benjamin Meek Miller, ADAH; Anonymous to Coleman A. Blease, c. 1928 (Commerce Department quote), box 5, folder 14, William Brockman Bankhead Papers, ADAH. Other quotes in *Birmingham News,* November 4–6, 1928, and Hugh D. Reagen, "Race as a Factor in the Presidential Election of 1928 in Alabama," *Alabama Review* 30 (Fall 1993): 6–7, 12–17. *Birmingham News,* November 5–6, 1928 (Bilbo quote). For the anti-Smith Klan rally, see *New York Times,* July 8, 1928, 2. The Alabama KKK fought Smith's election by impugning his moral character as a "negro lover" for associating too closely with African Americans: "Although Al Smith's skin may be white, his heart is as black as that of any African that roams the jungles. . . . Smith was raised with the negroes. He lived with the negroes. He moves and associates with the negroes now. He eats with the negroes. Therefore we cannot say that he is the equal of the negro because the negro is better than he is. Any white man that makes the negro his equal is not as good as the negro." *Alabama Ku Klux Klan Newsletter,* September 1928, Oliver Day Street Papers, ADAH.

9. Feldman, *Politics, Society, and the Klan,* chaps. 9 and 10; Glenn Feldman, *From Demagogue to Dixiecrat: Horace Wilkinson and the Politics of Race* (Lanham, Md.: University Press of America, 1995), 87–98. For example, Rev. Bob Jones Sr., a Baptist minister, spoke throughout Alabama on behalf of Klan-backed political candidates and to Klan dens during the 1920s. His speeches were often laced with nativism, jingoism, and anti-Catholicism. After the rise of the Religious Right in the 1980s, the university he founded in Tennessee and then South Carolina—Bob Jones University—became a pilgrimage site for aspiring Republi-

can presidential candidates. During the 2000 presidential campaign, the background of the university's founder, along with the more recent racial and sexual-orientation policies of the school, became a national issue. See Feldman, *Politics, Society, and the Klan,* 38, 40, 65–66, 131, 170, 175, 182; *Mobile Register,* February 25, 2000; *Washington Post,* February 18, 2000; *Huntsville (Ala.) Times,* February 16, 2000; Rives Moore, The Interfaith Alliance, "News Release," February 18, 2000; Libby Quaid, "Democrats Swipe at Ashcroft over Bob Jones Visit," *Associated Press,* February 22, 2000; Robert A. George, "Bush's Missed Opportunity," *Salon.com,* February 22, 2000; John Leo, "The Company He Keeps," *U.S. News and World Report,* March 6, 2000; Janelle Carter, "Democrats in Congress Seek Condemnation of Bob Jones U.," *Associated Press,* February 29, 2000; Reg Henry, "Watch Out for a School Named Bob," *Pittsburgh Post-Gazette,* March 14, 2000; Jay Reeves, "Book Links Founder of Bob Jones U. with Alabama Klan," *Associated Press,* March 18, 2000; Libby Quaid, "Democrats Seizing on Bob Jones Issue," *Associated Press,* April 14, 2000; and Juliet Eilperin and Hanna Rosin, "Bob Jones: A Magnet School for Controversy," *Washington Post,* February 25, 2000. The differences between "pragmatic" and "principled" opposition are outlined in Feldman, *Politics, Society, and the Klan,* 8–9, 226–27, 326–27.

10. I use the term "neo-Bourbon" here in essentially the same sense that Numan V. Bartley described in *The Rise of Massive Resistance: Race and Politics in the South during the 1950s* (Baton Rouge: Louisiana State University Press, 1969), 17–20.

11. Anthony J. Badger, *The New Deal: The Depression Years, 1933–40* (New York: Farrar, Straus and Giroux, 1989), 271 (quote). Growing southern white disenchantment with FDR and the national Democratic Party's racial liberalism oozed out in many forms—some of it official, like the "Conservative Manifesto," others more extreme. "[A] darkey drives the Donkey now," lamented Ku Klux Klansmen when the 1936 campaign revealed the defection of black voters from the Republican to the Democratic Party. "The Negro Goes Democratic," *Kourier Magazine* 12 (August 1936): 20. KKK political cartoons featured Franklin and Eleanor Roosevelt singing: "You kiss the niggers and I'll kiss the Jews. And we'll stay in the White House as long as we choose." Wyn Craig Wade, *The Fiery Cross: The Ku Klux Klan in America* (New York: Simon and Schuster, 1987), 259, 275.

12. *Birmingham News,* July 12, 1998, 1A.

13. Harry Mell Ayers to Lister Hill, August 10, 1948 (first quote), box 367, folder 32, J. Lister Hill Papers, Special Collections Department, University of Alabama, Tuscaloosa; *Birmingham News,* September 2, 1948 (Carmichael); *Birmingham News,* July 15, 1948 (Wallace).

14. *Birmingham News,* March 22, 1948 (Wilkinson); William D. Barnard, "Race, Class, and Party: Frank M. Dixon and the Dixiecrat Revolt of 1948 in Alabama," in *The Public Life of Frank M. Dixon: Sketches and Speeches* (Montgomery: ADAH Historical Series no. 18, 1979), 78–79 (first Dixon quote); Dixon to Hall Jr., November 1944 (second Dixon quote), in Grover C. Hall Jr. Papers, ADAH; McCorvey to Dixon, August 21, 1948, Alabama Governors Papers, Frank M. Dixon, ADAH [hereafter cited as Dixon Papers].

15. As Kari Frederickson and others have made clear, the movement of Dixiecrats to the Republican Party was not immediate or wholesale. See Frederickson,

The Dixiecrat Revolt and the End of the Solid South, 1932–1968 (Chapel Hill: University of North Carolina Press, 2001), 228–38. Also see Paul Maxwell Smith, "Loyalists and States' Righters in the Democratic Party of Alabama, 1949–1954" (unpublished M.A. thesis, Auburn University, 1966), 94; and George Brown Tindall, *The Disruption of the Solid South* (Athens: University of Georgia Press, 1972), 3–5, 51–72.

16. Miscellaneous clippings, box 12, folder 12, "Republicans," Series IV, Charles E. Dobbins Papers, Auburn University Archives, Auburn, Alabama; *Montgomery Advertiser*, December 4, 1952; *Birmingham Post-Herald*, May 26, 1956. *Talladega Daily Home*, November 2, 1954 (Abernethy quote), in James Lamar Sledge III, "The Alabama Republican Party, 1865–1978" (Ph.D. diss., Auburn University, 1998), 160.

17. Miscellaneous clippings, box 12, folder 12, "Republicans," Series IV, Dobbins Papers.

18. For the conversion of the *Dothan Eagle*, see *Birmingham News*, July 15, 1948; for that of the *Montgomery Advertiser*, see Feldman, *From Demagogue to Dixiecrat*, 168. Dixiecrats moved to the GOP, conceding that they had "never voted the Republican ticket" before but were now because "there is only one way out for the South . . . to present demands to these left-wingers who are running the national Democratic Party and unless those demands are met to tell them goodbye. I am sick and tired of the South being kicked around." Bradley to Shepperd, December 12, 1957, box 2, folder 24, Dixon Papers.

19. Citations for moves of prominent Alabama Dixiecrats to the GOP: Graves discussed in *Alabama: The News Magazine of Dixie*, March 25, 1949, 8–11; Battle in *Alabama*, December 24, 1948, 6–7; Smyer in *Birmingham Post-Herald*, February 23, 1966; McCorvey, Comer, Malone, and Blount mentioned in Frederickson, *Dixiecrat Revolt*, 228; Abernethy, Comer, O'Neal, Malone, Abercrombie, Johnston, Young, McCorvey, Burns, Diamond, Battle, and "many other States' Rights officeholders and officials," including two state Democratic Executive Committee members from the First District and a whole raft of Montgomery Dixiecrats who called themselves "Jeffersonian Democrats," then "Eisenhower Democrats," before moving officially into the GOP, are mentioned in Smith, "Loyalists and States' Righters," 91–92, 93 (quote), 97–101, 103–4, 106.

20. W. H. Albritton to Dixon, March 6, 1959, box 2, folder 17, Dixon Papers. See also *Birmingham Post-Herald*, May 26, 1956.

21. McCorvey to editor, *Roanoke Leader*, October 9, 1948, Alabama Governors Papers, James E. Folsom, ADAH. On McCorvey's defection to the GOP see Dixon to E. H. Ramsey, December 9, 1954, box 3, folder 25, Dixon Papers. On Dixon, see Dixon to E. H. Ramsey, December 9, 1954 (quote), box 3, folder 25, ibid. See also Dixon to E. H. Ramsey, August 7, 1952, box 3, folder 25, and August 19, 1963, box 3, folder 17, and Dixon to Governor Marvin Griffin, September 17, 1957, box 3, folder 8, all in ibid. Wilkinson and Henderson mentioned in Smith, "Loyalists and States' Righters," 91. *Baton Rouge State-Times*, April 3, 1965 (first Perez quote); *Kansas City Star*, January 26, 1964 (second Perez quote). Both quotes in Glen Jeansonne, *Leander Perez: Boss of the Delta* (Baton Rouge: Louisiana State University Press, 1977), xv, see also 193–94, 331–34. Perez also served for a time as George Wallace's point man in Louisiana. See *South*, January 1968, 18.

22. I discussed this point previously: "White Southerners as a whole have yet to change. There is not yet a 'New South' in this respect. What changed were the names of the national parties that were willing to cater to Southern views on race and white supremacy—from the Democrats, to the Dixiecrats and States' Rights Democrats, to the Republican Party in more recent years. In the checkered evolution of the national parties on the race issue, the only truly consistent posture has been that adopted by the Southern white conservative voter. In short, the parties changed their positions; the white South has not. . . . The key point is that it has been the parties that changed over the years, not Southern voters. White Southerners can still be won over by conservative patriotic posturing and appeals (albeit more subtle than before) to the seemingly primordial fear of the African American." *From Demagogue to Dixiecrat,* 194 and 195.

23. *Birmingham News,* September 14, 1958.

24. W. T. Witt to editor, *South,* January 13, 1958, 4 (quote); W. T. Witt to editor, *South,* September 28, 1964, 4.

25. Although Democratic officeholders such as John Kennedy have been criticized regularly for being timid, late, and not completely on board the modern civil rights movement, the risks they took and the prices they paid for supporting the movement—however late and incomplete—were real. For criticism of presidential timidity and federal hesitancy and reluctance, see Armstead L. Robinson and Patricia Sullivan, "Introduction: Reassessing the History of the Civil Rights Movement," 3–4; Julian Bond, "The Politics of Civil Rights History," 8–9; and August Meier, "Epilogue: Toward a Synthesis of Civil Rights History," 217, all three in *New Directions in Civil Rights Studies,* ed. Robinson and Sullivan (Charlottesville: University Press of Virginia, 1991); Steven F. Lawson, "Freedom Then, Freedom Now: The Historiography of the Civil Rights Movement," *American Historical Review* 96 (April 1991): 470; and Steven F. Lawson and Charles Payne, *Debating the Civil Rights Movement, 1945–1968* (Lanham, Md.: Rowman and Littlefield, 2000). For the clear identification of the Democratic Party with the Second Reconstruction and civil rights, see Thomas Byrne Esdall and Mary D. Esdall, *Chain Reaction: The Impact of Race, Rights, and Taxes on American Politics* (1991; New York: Norton, 1992), 5, 7–9, 10, 12, 20, 32–37, esp. 35, and 215.

26. Conversations with JW, Tupelo, Mississippi, September 12, 2003 (on Kennedy liberalism). As mayor of Minneapolis, Humphrey had indelibly identified himself with the cause of civil rights by delivering a fiery oration on behalf of the Truman program at the 1948 Democratic National Convention in Philadelphia: "I ask the Democratic Party to march down the high road of progressive democracy. I ask this Convention to say in unmistakable terms that we proudly hail and will courageously support our President and leader, Harry Truman, in his great fight for civil rights." And later, at a critical point in the adoption of a civil rights plank: "There will be no hedging, and there will be no watering down. . . . There are those who say to you—we are rushing this issue of civil rights. I say we are a hundred and seventy-two years late. The time has arrived for the Democratic Party to get out of the shadow of states' rights and walk forthrightly into the bright sunshine of human rights." Frederickson, *Dixiecrat Revolt,* 118–19, 129.

27. *Nation*, February 1965, in Wayne Greenhaw, *Elephants in the Cottonfields: Ronald Reagan and the New Republican South* (New York: Macmillan, 1982), 57. Grenier obviously meant only white southerners when referring to "Southerners."

28. Rick Perlstein, *Before the Storm: Barry Goldwater and the Unmaking of the American Consensus* (New York: Hill and Wang, 2001), 374 (Goldwater supporter). The famous "duck" quote can be found in many places, e.g., Fred J. Cook, *Barry Goldwater: Extremist of the Right* (New York: Grove Press, 1964), 155–56.

29. Jack Bass and Walter DeVries agreed that the 1964 election clearly demonstrated that "In Alabama, Republican development was tied to the politics of race." *The Transformation of Southern Politics: Social Change and Political Consequence since 1945* (New York: Basic Books, 1976), 78. Election results reported in Sledge, "The Alabama Republican Party," 221–22.

30. Jake Tapper, "Democratic Bigots," *Salon.com*, July 17, 2000; Paul Begala, "Banana Republicans," *MSNBC.com/news*, November 13, 2000, 4.

31. See note 25 above.

32. Numan V. Bartley, *The New South, 1945–1980* (Baton Rouge: Louisiana State University Press, 1995), 339.

33. On the significance of the conservative purge of the northern liberal wing of the GOP at the 1964 Republican National Convention in Miami, see Jonathan Soffer's review of Rick Perlstein's *Before the Storm* on H-NET (July 2001). Representative right-wing media venues where the Democratic record on civil rights is distorted are myriad. See Sean Hannity, *Let Freedom Ring: Winning the War of Liberty over Liberalism* (New York: Regan Books, 2002); Rush Limbaugh, "Strom Thurmond and Dixiecrats Were Democrats," December 13, 2002, "Bill Clinton's Racist Roots," November 8, 2001, and "Republicans Passed the Civil Rights Act," August 17, 2000, all on www.rushlimbaugh.com; Thomas Sowell, "Lott, Race, and Hypocrisy: Parts I and II," www.jewishworldreview.com and www.NewsAndOpinion.com, December 17 and 18, 2002; Betty Boatman, "The Trent Lotts of the Left," *San Francisco Bay Area Independent Media Center*, www.indymedia.org, January 6, 2003, "Robert Byrd—The Democrats' Lott," www.NewsMax.com, December 29, 2002, and "White House Wannabe Edwards Has Ex-Klansman for Mentor," www.NewsMax.com, January 2, 2003.

34. Jason L. Riley, "President Bush Needs to Lead His Party on Race," *Wall Street Journal*, January 16, 2003, A12.

35. *South*, April 1966, 38 (first quote); Dan T. Carter, *From George Wallace to Newt Gingrich: Race in the Conservative Counterrevolution, 1963–1994* (Baton Rouge: Louisiana State University Press, 1996), 44 (Mitchell quote); Smith, "Loyalists and States' Righters," v (third quote).

36. Dan T. Carter, *The Politics of Rage: George Wallace, the Origins of the New Conservatism, and the Transformation of American Politics* (New York: Simon and Schuster, 1995); and Carter, *From George Wallace to Newt Gingrich*.

37. The original source for Wallace's infamous promise is Marshal Frady, *Wallace*, 2nd ed. (New York: New American Library, 1976), 127. Through a succession of interviews with Wallace confidantes, Dan Carter has since substantiated that Wallace did, indeed, make the remark. See *The Politics of Rage*, 96.

38. "You can sure tell they've listened to me, can't you?" said Wallace about southern Republicans in an August 1981 interview. Interview cited in Greenhaw, *Elephants in the Cottonfields,* 97 (all Wallace quotes). Kevin P. Phillips, *The Emerging Republican Majority* (New York: Anchor Books, 1970), 462–63.

39. Reg Murphy and Hal Gulliver, *The Southern Strategy* (New York: Scribner, 1971), 1.

40. *Alabama: The News Magazine of the South* and *South: The News Magazine of Dixie,* 1936–1973.

41. Emory O. Jackson to Thurgood Marshall, April 13, 1950, and Arthur D. Shores to Thurgood Marshall, April 12, 1951, both in part 5, reels 19 and 20, Papers of the NAACP, Library of Congress, Washington, D.C.; *Birmingham Post-Herald,* February 11, 1952 (national chair's quote); *Birmingham News,* October 10, 1956 (Vardaman). See also Sledge, "The Alabama Republican Party," 148, 164.

42. The Wallace quote can be found in many places; see, e.g., Greenhaw, *Elephants in the Cottonfields,* 78.

43. Don Collins's 1966 conversion was especially poignant. See ibid., 89–97, where Collins is quoted at length.

44. Recent GOP claims of inclusiveness and receptivity to minorities would be amusing, based on the party's pedigree of exclusion in the South, were the results of this exclusion not so tragic. For such claims see Dave Boyer and Andrew Cain, "Democrats Are Edgy as Bush Woos Blacks: Seek to Blunt His Message to NAACP," *Washington Times,* July 12, 2000; and Tapper, "Democratic Bigots."

45. See note 63 below and its subject matter in the text.

46. Week after week, *Alabama*'s and *South*'s corporate contributors were the state's leading banks, corporations, insurance companies, and utilities, among them Alabama Power Company, Vulcan Life, Blount Brothers Construction, City Federal Savings and Loan, U.S. Pipe and Foundry, First National Banks across the state, Founders Life Insurance, Protective Life, Harbert Construction, Molton, Allen and White Real Estate, Hayes International, Blue Cross and Blue Shield of Alabama (medical insurance), Southern United Life, American Materials and Supply, Federated Investments, Great Southern Investment, The Life Insurance Company of America, and Alexander City Manufacturing. See, e.g., *South,* January 1966 and February 1966; the lead editorial in the latter issue bordered on prescribing a eugenics program to deal with America's race problem and the "welfare state."

47. E. E. Williams to editor, *South,* September 28, 1964, 4 (first quote); Walter Masterson to editor, *South,* October 12, 1964, 4 (second quote); Fred Peters to editor, *South,* September 28, 1964, 4 (third quote). Many others extremely distraught over racial liberalism turned to the Republican Party. See, e.g., Frank Morrissey to editor, *South,* August 3–17, 1964, 4; and John Troutman to editor, *South,* September 28, 1964, 4. On Peters's religious background, see Fred Peters to editor, *South,* May 25, 1964, 4, and September 14, 1964, 4.

48. Proverb quoted in Tim Baer oral interview by Melody P. Izard, December 27, 2001, 2–3, Birmingham, Alabama, interview in possession of the author. Baer is currently the state director of the Alabama GOP. Still, even Don Collins

could become confused by the trajectory of the parties and come to state occasionally, albeit inaccurately, that the South—as represented by southern white voters—was changing. "I do believe that Alabama and the South are changing," Collins predicted, "and that we will see a new day for Republicanism and that day is *now.*" Greenhaw, *Elephants in the Cottonfields,* 92 (first Collins quote), 95 (second Collins quote), 94 (third Collins quote).

49. Phillips, *The Emerging Republican Majority,* 461–74. George Brown Tindall dismissed Phillips's book as one of a recent spate of "wonders . . . major creations [that] have rolled off the psephological assembly lines . . . a nine-days' wonder . . . emerged from a shallow perspective . . . that perfectly illustrated the hazards of prophecy." *Disruption of the Solid South,* 3 and 5. Phillips's quote about the GOP not needing "Negro votes," 468, and about GOP support for black voting rights, 464. Phillips on his formula and Carter's analysis in *From George Wallace to Newt Gingrich,* 43. Reg Murphy and Hal Gulliver also prematurely wrote off the power of the plan in *The Southern Strategy,* 269–73, and even erringly prophesied that "a future Southern Strategy would demand their [black voters'] inclusion," 225.

50. Kirkpatrick Sale, *Power Shift: The Rise of the Southern Rim and Its Challenge to the Eastern Establishment* (New York: Random House, 1975); Richard M. Scammon and Ben J. Wattenberg, *The Real Majority* (1970; New York: Primus, 1992); Esdall and Esdall, *Chain Reaction,* echoes this interpretation.

51. Lee Atwater gave a deathbed confession expressing remorse for using the race issue so blatantly to sink Dukakis's candidacy. Atwater confessed that his, GOP ad man Roger Ailes's (the later head of Fox News' "fair and balanced"), and Jim Baker III's use of the Willie Horton ad was an effort to "strip the bark off the little bastard." According to Atwater, they wanted to make "Willie Horton . . . his [Dukakis's] running mate." Quoted in John Brady, *Bad Boy: The Life and Politics of Lee Atwater* (Reading, Mass.: Addison-Wesley, 1997), 182 and 316.

52. Transcript of Richard Nixon interview by Herbert Parmet, November 16, 1988 (first quote), in possession of Dan T. Carter, quoted in Carter, *From George Wallace to Newt Gingrich,* 27; Harry Dent to Richard Nixon, October 13, 1969 (second quote), box 2, Harry Dent Files, Richard Nixon Presidential Materials, National Archives [hereafter cited as NA], College Park, Maryland; H. R. Haldeman Notes, January 8, 1970 (third quote), box 41, H. R. Haldeman Papers, Nixon Presidential Materials, NA. Dent, Haldeman, and other quotes in D. T. Carter, *From George Wallace to Newt Gingrich,* 28, 44.

53. On the racial aspects of Reagan's support, see D. T. Carter, *From George Wallace to Newt Gingrich,* 55–59, 64 (Reagan quote); and Greenhaw, *Elephants in the Cotton Fields,* 11–14, 180–87, 252; Begala, "Banana Republicans" (states' rights quote); *Miami Herald,* October 1980, quoted in Greenhaw, *Elephants in the Cotton Fields,* 187 (voter's quote); see also 182–83, 233. See also chap. 9 of Esdall and Esdall, *Chain Reaction,* 172–97.

54. Election results in William J. Cooper Jr. and Thomas E. Terrill, *The American South: A History* (New York: McGraw-Hill, 1991), 2:52.

55. GOP appeals to angry white males in South have been so successful largely because these voters saw the gains of blacks, women, and other minorities in "zero-sum terms," i.e., that a gain for blacks, women, and other minori-

ties could only come at their own expense. They didn't see the 1960s as "opening up" society in a positive way, as the government helping to facilitate opportunity and access for minorities. They saw the 1960s as fostering a "liberal culture" of entitlement and dependency for minorities which cost them, because they understood improvements for minorities occurring only at their expense—not a "rising tide lifts all boats" but as "a rising tide for them means we're sinking," e.g., affirmative action, the eradication of discrimination in workplace hiring and promotion. General zero-sum theory as economic thought about behavior is laid out in Lester C. Thurow, *The Zero-Sum Society: Distribution and the Possibilities for Economic Change* (New York: Basic Books, 1980). Esdall and Esdall recognized the zero-sum character of the issue in *Chain Reaction*, 9.

56. Bill Leavell, "Crying Towel," *South*, March 1966, 20 (quote). References to the Democratic Party's program as being "socialistic or even Communistic" became common during the 1960s. Republican congressman William L. Dickinson criticized one Great Society program as "all-out welfare statism.... There can be nothing more socialistic or even Communistic.... This country, built upon individual enterprise, cannot survive by glorifying the incompetents, the ignorant and the shiftless." *South*, March 1966, 3. For similar denouncements see *South*, November 1966, 3; and Frank Morrissey to editor, *South*, May 1966, 4.

57. On this important point, see Esdall and Esdall, *Chain Reaction*, 19, 27, 28.

58. Cooper and Terrill, *The American South*, 2:750 (first quote); Dewey W. Grantham, *The Life and Death of the Solid South: A Political History* (Lexington: University Press of Kentucky, 1988), 178–79; Murphy and Gulliver, *The Southern Strategy*, 3.

59. Michael Hill, arch-conservative president of the neo-Confederate "League of the South," celebrated the red-blue divergence in the "fly-over states" of the 2000 presidential election and contrasted Bush and Gore voters on a host of issues—prominent among them "programs for minority [read: black] 'victim' groups." Hill pegged the "Bush constituency" as being "mainly made up of white European stock that favors gun ownership, Christian morality, less government, fewer programs for minority 'victim' groups, and a strict interpretation of the Constitution" versus a Gore constituency that favors "gun control, big government, more programs, high taxes, the normalization of deviant behavior, a secular notion of human rights, and a very loose construction of [the] ... Constitution." Dr. J. Michael Hill, "Election 2000: Time for a Divorce between Madonna and Merle," www.dixienet.org, January 24, 2001.

60. Race is fundamentally tied to the major tenets of the modern Republican agenda—even when it seems to be completely unrelated—and is therefore so salient and powerful, especially in the South. After all, race has long resonated with the majority of white southerners. These basic connections were formed in the fiery cauldron of southern politics from the late 1940s through the 1960s. The modern GOP agenda is made up of seven major planks: (1) opposition to taxes, (2) pro-religion (especially evangelical religion and "traditional family values"), (3) pro-guns, (4) anti-Communism, (5) super-patriotism, (6) opposition to the federal government, and (7) opposition to women's rights and gay rights.

(1) Taxes: much of the opposition to increased taxes rests upon (a) an unhappiness with being taxed by the federal government to redistribute income to "unworthy, inferior human beings," i.e., "no-good, lazy," stereotypical blacks, "welfare queens," chronically dependent on the state and liberal, big-government programs of the Democratic New Deal, Fair Deal, New Frontier, and Great Society, etc.; and (b) taxation for these government programs, which disproportionately benefit undeserving and lazy blacks, is tied to and painfully reminiscent of an overreaching federal government that invaded the South twice, the second time to compel compliance with civil rights laws and desegregation in an intransigent South clinging to "massive resistance" and its notions of states' rights. (For good examples of this type of anti-tax sentiment, see *South,* February 1965, 26, March 1965, 9, and January 1965, 30).

(2) Pro-religion, "traditional family values," the "moral character" issue, and the rise of the Christian Right: (a) Martin Luther King Jr., although a member of the cloth, was seen by many civil right opponents as the personification of evil, a perversion of religion, as "Martin Lucifer King"—a notion tied, of course, to the conviction that God had ordained segregation and opposed civil rights, and hence the "movement" itself was tied to godlessness and was an abomination; (b) the civil rights movement was a Communist plot in which Jews were using blacks as their stooges to overthrow the United States; (c) the Supreme Court's 1962 school prayer decision was seen as just one more way in which the federal government, as with civil rights, was forcibly imposing alien ideas and a foreign will on a recalcitrant South. As with the civil rights movement and desegregation, only immorality and moral decay would follow; (d) the civil rights movement was rife with immorality between the races, miscegenation, and black promiscuity and profligacy, e.g., on the march from Selma to Montgomery. (For good examples of these beliefs, see Dennis J. Davis to editor, *South,* February 1965, 4, and *South,* August 1965, 4 [Martin "Lucifer" King quote], and Feldman, *Politics, Society, and the Klan* and *From Demagogue to Dixiecrat.*)

(3) Crime: "law and order" was a major issue during the 1960s and was related to attempts to limit and license gun ownership in order to deal with (a) black criminals who were supposed to be congenitally immoral and predisposed to crime ("scientific racism"), as a race, as well as with an (b) overreaching, tyrannical central government that was dominated by a Democratic Party catering to northern liberals and the black vote and imposing its will on race and civil rights on a resistant South as it had during the First Reconstruction. (For good examples, see the Thurman Sensing column in *South,* March 1965, 27, and *South,* May 13, 1963, 3, on the NRA.)

(4) Communism and patriotism: (a) this was a well-established, old theme from the KKK days of conspiracy theories of Communist Jews using black stooges to take over the South and America; (b) there were a few members of the civil rights movement, as with unions, who had flirted with communism or did have actual Communist ties; (c) the federal government, now in the hands of the liberal, northern-dominated national Democratic Party, was "on the Socialistic road" (*South,* January 1965, 3, and February 1966, 4) and "drifting toward Socialism" through its expansion of taxation and government social programs, most of which benefited undeserving and inferior blacks. And, after all, govern-

ment programs sponsored by the Democratic Party equaled socialism, and socialism equaled communism, in essence. By a kind of "transitive law of politics," the Democratic Party was tantamount to communism and, thus, treason. The 1998 impeachment charges against President Clinton, with frequent mention of treason charges, were not original, but rather reminiscent of this 1960s theme earlier targeted at Supreme Court justices William O'Douglas (Democrat) and Earl Warren (liberal Republican) by the John Birch Society. (Good examples: *South*, March 1965, 3, H. W. Stokes to editor, *South*, March 1965, 4, *South*, editorial, January 1965, 3, Cress Joiner to editor, *South*, February 1965, 4, Chet Schwarzkopf to editor, *South*, October 1965, 4.)

(5) Super-patriotism: (a) this point was closely linked to the point about communism, the federal government, and the Democratic Party, in some way, suspected of being in league with forces that wanted to overthrow America—Socialists and Communists; (b) the civil rights movement was fundamentally un-American and unpatriotic, riddled with Communists who wanted to make trouble for the United States during a time of war, also supported by the Democrats; (c) protest against the Vietnam War (also identified with Democrats such as Robert Kennedy and Hubert Humphrey) and Eugene McCarthy was thought of as a form of disloyalty, unpatriotic, even treasonous behavior—criticizing government policy during wartime. Moreover, in parts of the public mind the civil rights movement, with its protests on behalf of blacks, was indelibly linked with the war protests through street protests, student demonstrations in Mississippi "Freedom Summer," and anti-Vietnam protests; (d) liberalism itself, with its emphasis on solving problems instead of celebrating the country's virtues, was often thought of as essentially unpatriotic and disloyal.

(6) Federal government: (a) thought of as out of control, socialistic, an unconstitutional tool of white liberals and black civil rights activists, a gravy train for unworthy blacks, tyrannical in stomping on states' rights to compel the white South to do things on race it did not want to do, taking taxes to support programs for undeserving blacks; and (b) is tied to gun control because of the need to have arms in the hands of ordinary citizens to oppose a Leviathan-like federal government. (Frank Morrissey to editor, *South*, January 1965, 4, Hal Steadman to editor, *South*, January 1965, 4, welfare specifically mentioned in *South*, February 1965, 30.)

(7) Women's rights and gay rights: (a) are immoral because God put males in charge of the household, and both usurp the institution of marriage on which society was based; (b) are tied to civil rights because the women's liberation movement got a huge boost in Title VII of the Civil Rights Act of 1964; (c) like the civil rights movement, they are immoral because they are tied to abortion rights and sexual deviance. Democrats favor expanded women's rights and advocate civil liberties for homosexuals, and abortion had long been tied in the popular mind with unwed black teens.

These seven central issues of modern southern Republicanism—not only predicated on race but also tied to the original "Reconstruction Syndrome" and the Second Reconstruction to result in a "politics of emotion" of modern southern Republicanism—have helped mightily in leading to modern GOP control over the South.

61. William L. Dickinson to editor, *South,* March 1967, 4 (quote), and November 1969, 4.

62. John H. Buchanan Jr. to editor, *South,* January 1966, 21.

63. *South,* August 1969, 22 (first quote), March 1965, 3 (second quote), August 31, 1964, 3 (third quote), 15 (fourth quote).

64. Doris J. Davis to editor, *South,* February 1965, 4 (first and second quotes); Rev. Fred A. Peters to editor, *South,* September 1966, 4 (third quote); Frank Morrissey to editor, *South,* September 14, 1964, 4 (fourth quote); Peters to editor, *South,* September 1969, 4 (fifth quote).

65. Walter Masterson to editor, *South,* October 12, 1964, 4 (first quote); G. V. Timmons to editor, *South,* September 1969, 4 (second and fourth quotes); *South,* January 1969, 3 (third quote).

66. *South,* April 1966, 3 (first quote), 34 (second quote).

67. *South,* May 1967, 3 (first quote); Norman L. Hall to editor, *South,* October 1967, 4 (second quote).

68. Chet Schwarzkopf to editor, *South,* October 1965, 4. Schwarzkopf's turn to Republicanism was succinctly expressed by his reasoning that "for over a generation America has been weakened by an era of dough-headed lunacy, nurtured by irresponsible liberals, shrilling do-gooders, Communist-line troublemakers, beatniks, college revolutionaries, limp-rag demonstrators and other[s] . . . who have appeared sadly in need of a good old-fashioned flogging. . . . Dewey-eyed liberalism appears to have failed. . . . The hour is upon us to advance into an era of common sense."

69. C. C. McLean, M.D., to editor, *South,* March 1966, 4.

70. John H. Buchanan Jr. to editor, *South,* August 1966, 4.

71. Armistead Selden to editor, *South,* August 1966, 4. Selden also damned the federal government's "so-called" education "guidelines" and called for less "federal control over local schools." Selden to editor, *South,* June 1967, 4.

72. Gordon Ellis to editor, *South,* February 1966, 4 (first quote). The "Mahatma" comparison was also a favorite of Hubert Baughn's; see "Major Squirm," *South,* October 1966, 22. C. M. Cason Sr. to editor, *South,* August 1965, 4 (second quote). In 2003, e.g., President George W. Bush paid ritualistic homage to King, calling him a "great American" and praising the "the power of his words, [and] the clarity of his vision," while declaring that "there's more to do." "Bush: More to Do to Attain King's Dream," *Associated Press,* January 20, 2003. Yet within the same fortnight, Bush masterfully combined the yin and the yang of "compassionate conservatism" by overseeing a behind-the-scenes removal of Trent Lott as Senate Majority Leader, while publicly proclaiming neutrality, in order to stop the bleeding in Republican ranks over Lott's racially insensitive remarks and to appease a right wing long disenchanted with Lott's feeble leadership on conservative issues. During the same week as his King remarks, Bush publicly denied that Lott's comments had hurt the GOP, refused to apologize for them (either himself or as the head of the Republican Party), renominated Charles Pickering, a controversial Lott protégé who had failed to win confirmation to the Fifth Circuit U.S. Court of Appeals from a Democratic-controlled Senate in 2002 because of disturbing racial parts of his judicial record, and, in a historic move, directly interposed his administration against affirmative-action "quotas" in a

Michigan case before the U.S. Supreme Court. See Jim VandeHei, "Lott Says Bush Aides Undermine Bid to Stay," *Washington Post,* December 19, 2002; Gail Russell Chaddock, "GOP Right Long Frustrated with Lott," *Christian Science Monitor,* December 19, 2002; "Bush: Iraq Attack Would 'Cripple' Economy" (for denial of any damage to GOP from Lott remarks), *Associated Press,* January 1, 2003; Mike Allen, "Bush Plans No Apology over Lott Remarks," *Washington Post,* January 12, 2003; "The Revenge of Trent Lott" (on Pickering), *New York Times,* January 9, 2003; Cynthia Tucker, "Bush Wants to Elevate Judge with Suspect Past" and "Bush's Attack on 'Quotas' Conveniently Ignores the Facts," both in *Atlanta Journal-Constitution,* January 11 and 23, 2003, respectively; Neil A. Lewis, "President Faults Race Preferences as Admission Tool," *New York Times,* January 16, 2003; and Nicholas D. Kristof, "A Boy and His Benefits," *New York Times,* January 24, 2003. On the conservative appropriation of King as a symbol of respectability and even alleged racial conservatism, see Paul M. Gaston, "Missing Martin," *Facing South: A Progressive Southern News Report,* August 28, 2003 (Atlanta: Institute for Southern Studies and *Southern Exposure* magazine), www.southernstudies.org.

73. Fred Morrissey to editor, *South,* December 1966, 4 (first quote); Fred Peters to editor, *South,* May 1967, 4 (second quote).

74. *South,* December 1966, 13 (first quote), March 1968, 22 (second quote), March 1965, 3 (third quote).

75. John H. Buchanan Jr. to editor, *South,* September 1966, 4.

76. *South,* October 1966, 22.

77. *Alabama Independent,* July 10, 1969, 7.

78. During the 1960s the South underwent almost a kind of collective obsessive-compulsive disorder in its polity and society—principally over the race issue. The experience allowed all seven of the issues discussed in note 60 to become very real to white southerners, through the power of perception, and to eventually provide for the ascendance of the southern GOP in the South in the place of the once all-powerful conservative Democratic Party. See note 85. An obsessive-compulsive disorder is precisely that: obsessive. It begins with a single thought that has some splinter of rationality, but through a never-ending process of obsessive worry, anxiety, and preoccupation it blows up into irrational thoughts and conclusions. The thoughts that make it up are invasive—they pop up all the time and in all areas of one's life. And, perhaps most importantly, they hang their hat on one nail, which is real, although usually very isolated and insignificant in reality. Yet, through continuous obsession over that issue and tying everything to it, the thought is extrapolated to the nth degree. The result is an irrational conclusion that bears very little relation to the original premise or rational thought. Such conclusions were extremely detrimental to the health of the Democratic Party, especially in the South. All white southerners needed was one example—no matter how isolated or unrepresentative—of a bad or outdated tax, or of tax revenue being "wasted," to conclude, after enough obsessing, that federal taxes were a form of tyranny, that Democrats favored such tyrannical rule by an overreaching central power, and that such taxation was a usurpation of the U.S. Constitution. Objections to mandatory school prayer led, through enough obsessing, to the conclusion that Democrats and liberals were

godless—the kiss of death in the religious South. Defense of due process and other constitutional protections against search and seizure, after enough fixating, became the conclusion that Democrats "coddled" crime and favored criminals over law enforcement. Legislation mandating background checks and waiting periods for the purchase of firearms, through enough worrying, became translated into the conclusion that Democrats favored the confiscation of all firearms in America in order to facilitate a "federal gestapo" that could break down doors at will. Any previous flirtation with the Communist Party by a current liberal became, through the obsession process, the same as Democrats being unpatriotic, suspect, treasonous, and disloyal. Protest of Vietnam or any unjust or controversial war became the same as treason and infidelity on the part of all liberals. Advocacy of rights for women and tolerance of homosexuals and other minorities, through enough anxiety, resulted in a conclusion that Democrats actually favored the eradication of the institution of the family and the decline of Western civilization itself. For examples of the label "Reconstruction II" being pinned on the modern civil rights movement, see *South,* May 1965, 5; Frank Morrissey to editor, *South,* September 1965, 29; *South,* May 1965, 5–6. For the "ungodly encroachment" of the federal government, a favorite of the Dixiecrats, see Feldman, *From Demagogue to Dixiecrat,* 136. And for "all-powerful central government" see *South* editorial, January 1965, 3.

79. Racial identification with the parties is a point also made in Esdall and Esdall, *Chain Reaction,* 259–60 and 270–71.

80. The Mobile Democrat was originally a Pennsylvania native. JLK to author (e-mail), January 11, 2002 (Mobile quote); author to ELB (e-mail), January 11, 2002 (North Alabama quote), confirmed in conversation, January 11, 2002; Carol Ann Vaughn to author (e-mails), January 8 and 17, 2002; anonymous to author (e-mail), January 13, 2002 (third quote).

81. Marty Connors, "The Sea Change of Alabama Primary Politics," *AlaGOP.org,* November 2, 2001 (first quote); Marty Connors, interview by Melody P. Izard, Birmingham, Alabama, December 18, 2001, 4 (second quote).

82. On black/white media depictions and sound bites with no sensitivity to complexity, see Sheldon Hackney, *The Politics of Presidential Appointment: A Memoir of the Culture War* (Montgomery: NewSouth Books, 2002). In fact, among some right-wing radio types, the alleged liberal inability to reduce complex issues down to simple black-and-white, often misleading and moralistic terms is actually lampooned as a "weakness" that should ensure conservative dominance in talk radio for some time to come. See Leonard J. Pitts Jr., "Just What We Need: More On-Air Yahoos," *Miami Herald,* February 24, 2003, 1B.

83. On the "New Racism," see note 9 of the Prologue to this volume.

84. "Why don't you leave the niggers behind and come join us?" was the invitation proffered to two white Democratic political scientists in the mid-1980s by a friendly South Carolina Republican. Earl Black and Merle Black, *Politics and Society in the South* (Cambridge: Harvard University Press, 1987), 313. Modern Republican appeals in the South have more often been couched in terms that have been described as a "more genteel type of racism" (ibid., 288). Donald S. Strong outlined this kind of subtle Republican racism in "Further Reflections on Southern Politics," *Journal of Politics* 33 (May 1971): 254. Reg Mur-

phy and Hal Gulliver described the Republican approach as "a sort of reasonable button-down-collar country club" racism and a "button-down-collar downtown segregationist" view in *The Southern Strategy*, 48 and 25.

85. Arch-conservative Michael Hill praised the Bush "majority of common folks who still revere 'God, Guts, and Guns.'" He also described this common majority of "white European stock" as favoring "Christian morality" and "fewer programs for minority 'victim' rights" while contrasting them with an Al "Gore constituency [of] . . . elites and their various minority clients" that favored "more programs, high taxes, [and] the normalization of deviant behavior" [read: homosexuality]. Hill, "Election 2000." One depressed union leader distilled general labor frustrations by describing his fruitless efforts to convince rank-and-file Alabama workers to vote Democratic as running into a concrete wall of Republican allegiance, due to what he termed "The Three G's: God, Guns, and Gays." Comment at "Politics 2001 Workshop," Alabama AFL-CIO State Convention, Mobile, Alabama, October 30, 2001. On people being opposed to public school prayer because "they hate God so much," from conversations with JW, Tupelo, Mississippi, September 13, 2003.

86. On Grenier, see Ralph McGill to Lyndon Johnson, September 30, 1964 (quote), and Johnson to McGill, October 5, 1964, both in White House Correspondence Files, box 84, folder PL 2, Lyndon Johnson Presidential Library and Museum, Austin, Texas.

87. Brady, *Bad Boy*, 70 (Atwater quote), 147 (second quote, Atwater), 147–48 (third quote, Brady), and 148 (fourth quote, Atwater). See also, e.g., xvi, 153, and 158 for places to tap into voters' minds, xvii and 38–39 for ties to Mary Matalin and Karl Rove, and 69 for affection for the Confederacy.

88. Brady, *Bad Boy*, 148 (first, second, and fourth quotes), xvi (on Dent), 153 (second part of third quote, Atwater) 298 (fifth quote, Atwater) and xi (sixth quote, Atwater). Esdall and Esdall, *Chain Reaction*, 145 (first part of third quote, Atwater); see also 144 and 220–23.

89. See note 78. With all of these examples, perception outweighs reality—so much so that it may be said, in the end, that perception *is* reality—or might as well be. Because the vast majority of native white southerners view the liberal questioning of Vietnam as "unpatriotic," then liberals *are* unpatriotic in the minds of these southerners—and no amount of logic, reasoning, or rational disputation is likely to change that perception. In this kind of unassailable, impregnable strength, then, perception actually becomes reality—because in real-life politics that is how these liberals are approached, as unpatriotic. It is similar with immorality. Many native white southerners view liberals as immoral and godless because of the school prayer controversy or tolerance of the gay lifestyle and advocacy of civil rights and medical insurance for homosexuals, so much so that this perception—that citizens who oppose compulsory prayer in schools, or the posting of the Ten Commandments in public places, or prayer before a high-school football game, must therefore hate God and not be religious—is so strong that it determines how the vast majority of native white southerners view and actually treat liberals. It is their reality, and no amount of rational disputation, or explanation about the constitutional separation of church and state, or trying to point out the difference between "toleration" of gays as human beings

with basic human and civil rights is categorically different from wanting all households to be gay, or an opposition to the family as a basic and important institution in society, makes the least bit of difference, because the efficacy of emotion is so overwhelming. This is so because of the emotional southern personality. The South and the "politics of emotion" are a perfect fit. Once the GOP adopted the emotional strategy, it quickly became apparent that the match between the South and the GOP was made in heaven. The southern penchant for emotionalism exacerbates southern patriotism, conservatism, religiosity, etc. This is really not new. Southern politics have longed turned on the emotional issue of race, and once upon a time, when the conservative Democratic Party specialized in defending white supremacy, the quintessential emotional issue, the Democratic Party owned the South. When the Republican Party was able to take the race issue away from the Democratic Party, because of the national Democratic Party—and add other emotional issues to their arsenal—they also took the South. As long as the Republican Party maintains its grip on race and "God and country" issues, it will most likely own the South. With the South as a bedrock, national Republican strategists built a national Republican majority. Without race, there would be no Republican Party in the South. There never was before. And without the "Solid Republican South," there would be no Republican majority in America. George W. Bush, Florida or no, would probably not be in the White House. For many liberal Democrats, the ultimate frustration is that noble virtues such as morality, patriotism, religion, and so forth have been appropriated and employed in an emotional way to lend unquestioning support (seen as God-ordained, moral, and patriotic) for a raft of conservative Republican economic and social policies that have little to do with these original virtues. Esdall and Esdall, *Chain Reaction,* 71 and 215, realize that perceptions play a role in politics, but they describe the process as one of inevitable blurring of distinctions rather than the fruit of the purposeful manipulation of emotions and images.

90. On second thought, Peoria might not be such a good example. As was made evident by the ubiquitous red-and-blue electoral college maps shown on every television station during the 2000 Bush-Gore electoral dispute, the Republicans swept the "fly-over country" of the South, West, and Midwest, while Democratic strength was constricted to the industrial Northeast and several large population centers along the Atlantic and Pacific Coasts. Phillips quoted in Joe McGinnis, *The Selling of the President, 1968* (New York: Trident Press, 1969), 125.

91. For example, Ann Coulter received a full page in *Time* magazine to push her best-selling book, *Treason: Liberal Treachery from the Cold War to the War on Terrorism* (New York: Crown Forum, 2003), a book dedicated to the rehabilitation of Joseph McCarthy and to the thesis that Democrats are, and always have been, dangerous traitors to the country. See "Ten Questions for Ann Coulter," *Time,* July 14, 2003, 8. According to Coulter, the "myth of 'McCarthyism' is the greatest Orwellian fraud of our times. Liberals are fanatical liars, then as now. . . . [McCarthyism] is sheer liberal hobgoblinism. Liberals weren't hiding under the bed during the McCarthy era. They were systematically undermining the nation's ability to defend itself. . . . Liberals denounced McCarthy because

they were afraid of getting caught, so they fought like animals to hide their own collaboration with a regime as evil as the Nazis." Ann Coulter, "I Dare Call it Treason," June 26, 2003; see also "We Don't Care, Liberals," June 5, 2003, both syndicated columns on *Townhall.com*. For a more rational and coherent view that takes stock of Coulter's many factual errors and distortions from a nonpartisan perspective, see Brendan Nyhan, "Screed: With Treason, Ann Coulter Once Again Defines a New Low in America's Political Debate," *Spinsanity.org*, June 30, 2003. For a sample of the drumbeat about alleged liberal bias in the mainstream media, see Patrick J. Buchanan, "Is Liberal Media Bias a Myth?" *Townhall.com*, June 16, 2003. Right-wing radio talk-show host Michael Savage was given a weekend cable television show on MSNBC in March 2003. Four months later he was fired for telling an unidentified caller on the air that he was a "sodomite" who "should only get AIDS and die, you pig. How's that? Why don't you see if you can sue me, you pig? You got nothing better [to do] than to put me down, you piece of garbage? You have got nothing to do today, go eat a sausage and choke on it." Savage then asked for a different caller who "didn't have a nice night in the bathhouse who's angry at me today." David Bauder, "MSNBC Fires Savage for Anti-Gay Remarks," *Associated Press, Miami Herald*, July 7, 2003. On a somewhat milder level, former Florida congressman Joe Scarbrough has a show on MSNBC, and Laura Ingraham has moved seamlessly between MSNBC and Fox News.

92. On GOP media and technology proficiency, see Esdall and Esdall, *Chain Reaction*, 10–11. For examples of this kind of dichotomy, see notes 59 and 85. The upshot of the modern GOP use of a "politics of emotion" in the South has been very similar to how the old Bourbon Democrats once used the "Reconstruction Syndrome." The result, to a large extent, has been that, because of these emotional issues, unsuspecting common white folk have voted with the GOP with little or no clue as to—or inclination to learn—the underlying Republican economic agenda that has unstintingly favored the country's most privileged individuals and corporations. See also note 82.

93. On the orchestrated effort to include minorities at the GOP convention, see *Los Angeles Times*, July 30, 2000. This was not the first time the GOP used black entertainers at its national convention to portray an image of inclusiveness. In 1984, Lee Atwater approved the idea of having Ray Charles and his black female backup singers perform at that summer's convention to send "the proper message: No racists here, thank you." Brady, *Bad Boy*, 183. Actually, "compassionate conservatism" was introduced, explained, and first discussed as a strategic concept by one of the fathers of the "Southern Strategy," Harry S. Dent of South Carolina. See Harry S. Dent, *The Prodigal South Returns to Power* (New York: Wiley, 1978), 299.

94. For Rice's speech, see *New York Times*, August 2, 2000. On George W. Bush's speech to the NAACP—the first by a Republican since his father's in 1988—see Boyer and Cain, "Democrats Are Edgy." Rice's speech at the Republican National Convention seems to have been part of a coordinated strategy to woo black voters to the GOP by "reminding . . . [them] that there have been plenty of friendly Republicans since [Abraham] Lincoln," such as Dwight Eisenhower and Everett Dirksen of Illinois, "as well as Democrats like" Lester Mad-

dox and George Wallace. In the three weeks leading up to the convention, George W. Bush and Republican National Committee (RNC) chairman Jim Nicholson made the pitch to the NAACP's national convention, with Nicholson actually arguing that "it's the Democrats—not Republicans—who should be reluctant to come before this . . . organization." Black Oklahoma representative J. C. Watts and former RNC chair Haley Barbour made the same argument on CNN's *Crossfire,* and another black Republican, Cherylyn Harley, deputy RNC press secretary and author of Nicholson's NAACP speech, repeatedly argued the same line. "It's absurd for a Republican to claim that the modern Republican Party of the year 2000 has done more for blacks than Democrats. That's outrageous," historian Douglas Brinkley correctly responded. "That's playing historical games." Congressman Watts's father, a lifelong black southerner, furnished his own plain-folk response to his son: "A black man voting for a Republican is like a chicken voting for Colonel Sanders." Jake Tapper, "Democratic Bigots" (above quotes). See also John H. McWhorter, "Uncivil Rights Activists," *Wall Street Journal,* December 11, 2001.

95. *Birmingham News,* July 12, 1998, 1A. Wallace had actually sent a personal envoy, segregationist Republican congressman Jim Martin of Alabama, to approach Barry Goldwater about Wallace running as the vice-presidential candidate on the 1964 Republican ticket. "It must be apparent to a one-eyed nigguh who can't see good outa his other eye," Wallace had said, "that me and Goldwater would be a winning ticket. We'd have the South locked up, then him and me could concentrate on the industrial states of the North and win." Wallace quoted in D. T. Carter, *The Politics of Rage,* 220.

96. Actually, voter registration in Alabama is not conducted through political parties, so the Democratic Party per se did not turn Rice's father away from the polls. But, by all chances, the actual voting registrars who did were, in 1952, conservative Democrats.

97. I would like to thank Professor Patrick J. Cotter of the Department of Political Science, University of Alabama, Tuscaloosa, and Southern Opinion Research for making these figures available to me.

98. In a September 2003 state referendum, Alabama's Republican governor Bob Riley went off the reservation to propose a record $1.2 billion tax hike that would have more fairly distributed the tax burden in a state routinely recognized as having the most malformed tax system in America. Moreover, Riley campaigned vigorously for the plan as a religious and moral duty to "the least of those among us." The package would have targeted Alabama's woefully undertaxed corporations, utilities, and large landholding farm and timber interests while lessening the burden on lower- and working-class families; it resulted in a campaign against the plan that had a definite racial subtext. Alabama's Republican Party—from its state chairman to its state and county executive committees—repudiated Riley and his plan, even importing former House power Dick Armey of Texas to stump against it. Conservative radio talk-show host Russ Fine even recommended that Riley be expelled from the Republican Party. In the end, Alabama's electorate crushed the plan in a 68 percent–32 percent vote that had clear racial meaning. Riley's plan prevailed in only thirteen of Alabama's sixty-seven counties, all of them in the heavily African American

Black Belt. Whites, especially the blue-collar and middle-class variety, voted heavily against the plan, with the rural, white North Alabama counties that had supplied Riley with the strongest support in his 2002 Republican gubernatorial race going most heavily against the tax plan. *Birmingham News,* September 10, 2003.

99. Trent Lott served an apprenticeship under "fanatical segregationist Democrat" William Colmer, a Mississippi congressman, joined the Sons of Confederate Veterans, and actively worked to keep James Meredith from racially integrating the University of Mississippi. In a 1984 interview with neo-Confederate *Southern Partisan* magazine, Lott bragged that "the spirit of Jeff Davis lives in the 1984 Republican platform" and condemned the fact that Martin Luther King Jr.'s birthday had been set aside as a national holiday. Meanwhile, Bill Clinton was pegged by modern racial conservatives as a president for blacks, a traitorous "Oreo turned inside out." Black novelist Toni Morrison evaluated Clinton's racial sensitivity as a positive. He was, she declared, "America's first black liberal President." Joe Conason, "Why Lott and Barr Hate Clinton," *Salon.com,* December 22, 1998 (above quotes). Elsewhere, Morrison deemed Clinton "our first black President. Blacker than any actual black person who could ever be elected in our children's lifetime." Ellis Cose, "Getting Ready for the Fire This Time," *Newsweek,* January 22, 2001, 29 (Morrison quote). See also Alicia Montgomery, "Ashcroft Whistles Dixie," *Salon.com,* January 3, 2001. For references on the Trent Lott controversy, see note 72 above.

100. In 1976, Jimmy Carter won in Alabama over Republican Gerald Ford by 56 percent to 43 percent. John L. Moore, ed., *Congressional Quarterly's Guide to U.S. Elections,* 3rd ed. (Washington, D.C.: Congressional Quarterly Inc., 1994), 464.

101. Over 75 percent of Alabamians supported state supreme court chief justice Roy Moore's recent display of a 5,300-pound granite statue in the Rotunda of the state judicial building. Bill Rankin, "Alabama's Pryor Breaks Faith with Stand on Commandments," *Atlanta Journal-Constitution,* August 31, 2003. See also Kyle Whitmire, "Rock of Rages Revisited," *Birmingham Weekly,* August 21–28, 2003, 4; and "Alabama Baptists Endorse Commandments But Not Roy Moore," www.newsmax.com, November 21, 2003. For sentiment expecting elected officials to follow popular opinions on the matter, regardless of superior federal court orders or constitutional mandates, see Lionel Ledbetter, Adamsville, to editor, *Birmingham News,* December 9, 2003, 8A, and also Mary Orndorff, "Aderholt Renews Push for Commandments Bill," *Birmingham News,* September 5, 2003, 1C, 2C.

102. Quotations from a Democratic aide to North Carolina senator John Edwards and Virginia governor Mark Warner in Mara Liason, "Democrats Seek to Fire Up 'NASCAR Dad' Vote," on "Morning Edition," *NPR.org,* September 19, 2003 (first quote); Scott Shepard, "GOP Owns the Votes of 'NASCAR Dads,'" *Atlanta Journal-Constitution,* August 31, 2003 (Dennis Hurley).

103. For an example of how the bar of mainstream conservatism has moved far to the right over the past few decades, see Nixon conservatism described as "liberal" by today's standards in Matthew Miller, "Something to Talk About," *New York Times,* September 4, 2003.

Contributors

Raymond Arsenault is the author of *The Wild Ass of the Ozarks: Jeff Davis and the Social Bases of Southern Politics* (1988), *Crucible of Liberty: Two Hundred Years of the Bill of Rights* (1991), and *St. Petersburg and the Florida Dream, 1888–1950* (1996). Professor Arsenault is also an editor of the Florida History and Culture series, published by the University Press of Florida, and is a professor of history at the University of South Florida. He is currently at work on a history of the Freedom Riders. Arsenault received his Ph.D. in history from Brandeis University in 1981.

David T. Beito is professor of history at The University of Alabama. He is the author of *From Mutual Aid to the Welfare State: Fraternal Societies and Social Services, 1890–1967* (2000) and *Taxpayers in Revolt: Tax Resistance during the Great Depression* (1989). He received his doctorate in history from the University of Wisconsin in 1986.

Linda Royster Beito is chair of the Department of Social Sciences at Stillman College and is the author of *Leadership Effectiveness in Community Policing* (1999). She is currently at work, with David T. Beito, on a biography of T. R. M. Howard. Dr. Beito earned her Ph.D. in political science at The University of Alabama in 1996.

Jennifer E. Brooks is assistant professor of commons and history at Tusculum College. Her dissertation, "From Hitler and Tojo to Talmadge and Jim Crow: World War Two Veterans and the Remaking of Southern Political Tradition," is under advance contract. Dr. Brooks's work has also appeared in the *Journal of Southern History*. She completed her doctoral degree in history at the University of Tennessee in 1997.

Sarah Hart Brown is the author of *Standing against Dragons: Three Southern Lawyers in the Era of Fear, 1945–1965* (1998). Professor Brown's work has also appeared in the *Georgia Historical Quarterly* and the *Florida Historical Quarterly*. She earned her Ph.D. in history from Georgia State University in 1996 and is currently an associate professor of history at Florida Atlantic University.

Adam Fairclough is the author of *Teaching Equality: Black Schools in the Age of Jim Crow* (2001), *Better Day Coming: Blacks and Equality, 1890–2000* (2001), *Race and Democracy: The Civil Rights Struggle in Louisiana, 1915–1972* (1995), *Martin Luther King, Jr.* (1990), and *"To Redeem the Soul of America": The Southern Christian Leadership Conference and Martin Luther King, Jr.* (1987). He took his Ph.D. in history from Keele University in 1977 and taught at the Universities of Ulster, Liverpool, Leeds, and Saint David's University College. Professor Fairclough has served as the chair of the American History Department at the University of East Anglia since 1997.

Glenn Feldman is associate professor at the Center for Labor Education and Research in the School of Business at the University of Alabama at Birmingham. He is the author of *Politics, Society, and the Klan in Alabama, 1915–1949* (1999), *From Demagogue to Dixiecrat: Horace Wilkinson and the Politics of Race* (1995), and *The Disfranchisement Myth: Poor Whites and Suffrage Restriction in Alabama* (2004). Professor Feldman edited *Reading Southern History: Essays on Interpreters and Interpretations* (2001) and is the coeditor, with Kari Frederickson, of the Modern South series at The University of Alabama Press. He holds a Ph.D. in history from Auburn University (1996).

Andrew M. Manis is the author of *A Fire You Can't Put Out: The Civil Rights Life of Birmingham's Reverend Fred Shuttlesworth* (1999), which won the 2000 Lillian Smith Book Award, and *Southern Civil Religions in Conflict: Black and White Baptists and Civil Rights, 1947–1957* (1987). Manis is also the coeditor (with Marjorie L. White) of *Birmingham's Revolutionary: Fred Shuttlesworth and the Alabama Christian Movement* *for Human Rights* (2000). Dr. Manis completed his doctorate in religious history at the Southern Baptist Theological Seminary in 1984 and is lecturer in American history at Macon State College.

John A. Salmond is professor emeritus of American history at La Trobe University in Bundoora, Victoria, Australia, the author of twelve books and many articles, and the editor of several books. Among Salmond's books are *"My Mind Set on Freedom": A History of the Civil Rights Movement, 1954–1968* (1997), *Gastonia, 1929: The Story of the Loray Mill Strike* (1995), *The Conscience of a Lawyer: Clifford Durr and American Civil Liberties, 1899–1975* (1990), *Miss Lucy of the CIO: The Life and Times of Lucy Randolph Mason, 1882–1959* (1988, a recipient of the Gustavus Myers Center for Civil Liberties Award), *A Southern Rebel: The Life and Times of Aubrey Willis Williams* (1983), and *The Civilian Conservation Corps: A New Deal Case Study* (1967). Professor Salmond took his doctoral degree in history at Duke University in 1964.

Patricia Sullivan is associate professor of history at the University of South Carolina. She is the author of *Days of Hope: Race and Democracy in the New Deal Era* (1996), and coeditor (with Waldo E. Martin Jr.) of *Civil Rights: An Encyclopedia* (2000) and (with the late Armistead L. Robinson) of *New Directions in Civil Rights Study* (1990). She is currently working on a history of the NAACP and is also editing a collection of Virginia Durr's letters. Sullivan received her Ph.D. in history from Emory University in 1983.

Pamela Tyler is the author of *Silk Stockings and Ballot Boxes: Women and Politics in New Orleans, 1920–1963* (1996). Dr. Tyler's work has also appeared in the *Gulf Coast Historical Review* and *Southern Studies*. She received her doctorate in history at Tulane University in 1989 and is presently an associate professor of history at North Carolina State University.

John White is reader emeritus in American studies at the University of Hull, England. His books include *Slavery in the American South* (1970), *Reconstruction after the American Civil War* (1977), *Black Leadership in America, 1895–1968* (1985), and *Billie Holiday: Her Life and Times* (1987); he also coedited (with Brian Holden Reid) *American Studies: Essays in Honour of Marcus Cunliffe* (1990). Professor White completed his doctoral degree in history at the University of Hull in 1975.

Index

Abercrombie, H. M., 278
Aberdeen, MS, 177
Abernathy, Ralph, 12, 214–15, 219
Abernethy, Ludie: and disgust with Little Rock, 281; conversion to Republican party, 278
Abernethy, Thomas: and Dixiecrats, 278; conversion to Republican party, 278, 288; importance of conversion, 287–88
Abolition, 299
Abortion, 4–5, 14, 274, 300, 304, 314n. 9; relationship to race issue, 294–95
Abzug, Bella, 11; and Willie McGee execution, 190–91
Accomodationism. *See* racial accommodation
Adams, Louis, 50
Adams, P. M., 252
Affirmative action, 294, 307, 382n. 55, 386n. 72
Africa, 33–34
African Methodist Episcopal Church (AME), 35, 106
Agnew, Spiro: attacks on "liberal media," 295
Agriculture, 77, 102

Ailes, Roger: and Fox News channel, 382n. 51; and Willie Horton ad, 382n. 51; as Bush I adviser, 292
Alabama, 7, 11, 12, 14, 30, 35; as Goldwater state, 292; backlash against civil rights and rise of Republican party, 268–309; Communist party in, 186; criticism of Eleanor Roosevelt, 104, 108, 110, 112–13; disfranchisement in, 375n. 5; Dumas bill passes in, 125; mountain Republicanism in, 374n. 1; racial divide in presidential elections, 306; racial inferiority of blacks, 112; SCHW in, 223–24; strength of Dixiecrats in, 287; 2003 tax reform referendum, 392n. 98; voting returns in presidential elections, 306; won by the Dixiecrats and Goldwater, 283
Alabama Christian Advocate: favors segregation, 118–19
Alabama Coalition Against Hunger, 219
Alabama Democratic Conference, 299
"Alabama Democrats," 210–11, 289, 299
Alabama Republican party, 381n. 48; disowns sponsor of tax reform plan, 392n. 98

Index

Alabama Independent, 297
Alabama Magazine, 286–87, 289–90; list of corporate contributors, 381n. 46
Alabama Republican Party: chooses white supremacy, 287–89
Albritton, W. H.: as Dixiecrat, 278–79; conversion to Republican party, 278–79; favors segregated schools, 279; on danger of federal aid to schools, 279
Alcohol. *See* Anti-Saloon League; prohibition; Roosevelt, Eleanor, and controversy over women and alcohol
Alexander, Will, 119. *See also* Committee on Interracial Cooperation
All Citizens Registration Committee, 243–44, 361n. 21
American Civil Liberties Union (ACLU), 33, 40, 177
American Council of Race Relations, 241
American Dilemma, An, 25, 98, 121
American Federation of Labor (AFL), 13, 149
American Federation of Teachers, 153
American Friends Service Committee, 36
American Heritage Foundation, 209. *See also* "Freedom Train"
American Independent Party, 286, 297. *See also* Wallace, George C.
American Veterans Committee, 248–49, 363n. 34
Americanism. *See* patriotism
Ames, Jesse Daniel: and domestic work, 105; and lynching, 105, 131
Amos, Ethel, 318n. 4
Anderson, Jervis, 39
Anderson, Marian, 101
Andrews, Glenn: rides Goldwater's coattails, 283
Anglo-Saxons, 3, 273–74, 293, 303, 383n. 59, 389n. 85
"Angry white males," 293–94, 382n. 55
Anniston, AL, 375n. 5
Anniston Star, 350n. 47

Anti-Defamation League, 139
Anti-intellectualism, 296, 386n. 68
Anti-Redeemers. *See* independents; Populists
Anti-Saloon League, 69
Anti-Semtism. *See* Jews, and anti-Semitism
Arizona: won by Goldwater, 283
Arkansas, 102, 281. *See also* Little Rock
Armey, Dick, 307; stumps against Alabama tax reform bill, 392n. 98
Arnall, Ellis, 223, 259–60; abolishes poll tax, 359n. 1; accomplishments of, 370n. 81; attacks on by Eugene Talmadge, 373n. 100; pressured by Methodist women, 132–33; stumbles on race, 111, 132
Arsenault, Raymond, 9, 10, 12–13, 15
Ashby, Warren, 228, 357n. 16. *See also* Graham, Frank Porter (biography of)
Ashcroft, John, 9–10, 307
Asheville, NC, 50, 59–60, 216
Ashland, OH, 38
Ashmore, Susan Youngblood, 311n. 1
Asia, 33
Association of Colored Women, 119
Association of Methodist Ministers and Laymen, 125
Association of Southern Women for the Prevention of Lynching, 119
Associated Negro Press of Chicago, 74
Athens, TN (battle of), 367n. 70
Atlanta, 45, 100, 138, 141, 225–26, 297; and Dorothy Tilly, 116–17, 135; and failed project, 232–33; Columbians and Klan, 252–53
Atlanta Constitution, 142, 247, 333n. 2
Atlanta Journal, 131
Atwater, H. Lee, 308; and blacks at 1984 convention, 391n. 93; and "southern strategy," 292, 301–2, 306; and Willie Horton ad, 292, 302; deathbed confession of, 382n. 51; manipulation of emotions and perceptions, 301–2, 308; mentorship by Strom Thurmond and Harry Dent, 301; protégés, 301

Auburn, NY, 36
Augusta, GA, 130
Austin, TX, 41, 181
Avant, Edward, 65
Azbell, Joe, 215

Baer, Tim, 381n. 48
Backlash. *See* civil rights, backlash against; "two sides of the civil rights coin;" violence; "white backlash" thesis
Bailey, Thomas, 30
Baker, Amanda (murder of), 213, 354n. 50
Baker, Ella, 12, 46, 212
Baker, Ray Stannard, 25
Baker, James A. "Jim" III, 382n. 51
Baldwin, Roger, 33, 40. *See also* American Civil Liberties Union
Baltimore, 21, 23–24, 31
Baltimore Afro-American, 29, 52, 63, 67
Bankhead, Tallulah: and civil rights rally in New York, 217
Banks, Dennis, 50, 60, 63
Baptists, 93, 200, 295, 297, 357n. 16, 376n. 9; in Georgia, 362n. 33; in Louisiana, 156; southern wing, 123
Barbour, Haley, 391n. 94
Barnes, Catherine, 25
Barnett, Claude, 74
Barr, Bob, 307
Bartley, Numan V., 273, 377n. 10; on "liberal" becoming a negative word, 174
Bass, Charlotta A., 70
Bass, Jack, 380n. 29
Bates, Daisey, 198
Baton Rouge: bus boycott in, 163–65
Battle, Clinton, 85
Battle, Laurie C.: conversion to Republican party, 278, 289
Baughn, Hubert: as Dixiecrat, 278; as "Eisenhower Democrat," 289; as Republican, 289; conversion to Republican party, 278; rapprochement with old class foes, 287; support for George Wallace, 289;

support for segregationists, 297; tie between modern GOP and racism, 286–87, 289–90, 295
Beaumont, TX: riot, 148
Beito, David, 7, 9, 12
Beito, Linda Royster, 7, 9, 12
Belgium, 223
Bell, Griffin, 257
Bell, John Sammons, 262–63
Beloit, Harvey, 157
Bender, W. A., 85, 332n. 83
Benemovsky, Leah, 11, 186–87
Benemovsky v. Sullivan, 191
Bernard, Sylvia, 11, 180–81, 183, 186, 191–92, 350n. 47; on religion and communism, 348n. 23, 350n. 48
Bernstein, Arnold, 157
Bernstein, Leonard, 347n. 15
Berrigan brothers (the), 18
Bethune, Mary McLeod, 11, 47, 224; friendship with Eleanor Roosevelt, 109
Bethune Cookman Institute, 41
Bible, 14, 42, 303; classes on and alcohol, 99
Biblical Seminary (of New York), 228
Big Lick, TN, 228–30
Big Mule/Black Belt coalition, 273, 286–87; corporate contributors to Alabama Magazine, 381n. 46; support for Dixiecrats, 289; support for George Wallace, 289; support for Republicans, 289
Big Mules, 7
Bilbo, Theodore G., "the Man," 75, 111, 148; criticism of Eleanor Roosevelt, 107; "Oust Bilbo" campaign against, 174–78, 361n. 25; poetic indictment of, 170, 172, 193; role in "bolt of 1928," 271
Birdsong, T. B., 87
Birmingham, 10, 176; and "Dynamite Hill," 288; as home of Condoleezza Rice, 305; persecution of communists in, 191–92; police squad, 191; racial tensions in, site of 1948 Dixiecrat convention, 276; 113; site of

1938 SCHW meeting, 97, 100–1; visit of national GOP chairman, 288
Birmingham, Dave, 211
Birmingham Post-Herald, 29
Bi-vocational (ministers), 83–84
Black-and-Tan Republicans, 87, 131
Black Belt, 7; of Alabama, 231, 272, 304, 306; of North Carolina, 230. *See also* Big Mule/Black Belt coalition
Black Boy, 54
Black Mountain, NC, 227
Black Power, 220. *See also* Garvey, Marcus; X Malcolm
Blacks: as inherently inferior, 122, 375n. 5; as lazy, 293, 294, 304, 383n. 60; as savages, 295–96
Bladsacker, Alvin, 182
Block, Emmanuel, 176
Blount, Winton: conversion to Republican party, 278
Bob Jones University: and "southern strategy," 284, 376n. 9
Bogdanow, Morris, 181–82
Bohannon, Horace, 240–42, 360nn. 7, 14
Bolivar County, MS, 80
"Bolt of 1928," 269–72, 303–4, 376n. 8. *See also* "neo-Kluxism"
Bond, Julian 18, 195
Borah, Wayne G., 153
Boston, 39
Boston University, 41
Bouhan, John (machine), 243–44, 256–57, 263–66, 374n. 105. *See also* Savannah
Bouisse, Louise Metoyer, 167
Bourbons, 4–5, 259–60, 269, 273, 391n. 92
Bourgeoisie. *See* middle class
Bowling Green, 62
Boycotts. *See* Baton Rouge, bus boycott in; economic boycott; service station boycott; Mongtomery Bus Boycott; New Orleans, department store boycott in
Boyd, Edward M., 70
Boyd, Helen N., 70, 72. *See also* Howard, T. R. M.

Boyd, John Dewey, 93
Brandon, William W., "Plain Bill," 271
"Bread-and-butter unionism," 14
Brinkley, Douglas: on blacks and GOP, 391n. 94
Broadway, 34
Bromley, Ernest, 50
Brooks, Roy Cyril (case of), 182–83
Brooks, Jennifer E., 8, 13, 14, 16
Brooklyn Dodgers, 27
Brotherhood Mobilization, 43
Brotherhood of Sleeping Car Porters (BSCP), 13, 199–205, 216, 219, 352n. 15. *See also* Nixon, E. D.; Randolph, A. Philip
Browder v. Gayle, 218
Brown, Charlotte Hawkins, 235
Brown, Lee, 185
Brown, Louis, 183
Brown, Sarah Hart, 9–16
Brown, Sterling, 113
Brown vs. Board of Education, 1, 6, 9–11, 16, 29, 280; and conservatism, 266–67; referred to, 95
Brown v. Board of Education II, 169
Bryan, William Jennings, 277
Buchanan, John: criticizes civil rights, 295; criticizes Martin Luther King, 295, 297; rides Goldwater's coattails, 283
Buchanan, Patrick J., 291, 307; and "southern strategy," 292
Buchenwald, 280
Buckeye Cove, NC, 232
Bulger, Thomas L., 269
"Bull Connor" ordinance, 191
Bunche, Ralph, 42, 100, 196
Bunker, Archie, 114
Bureaucracy. *See* federal government, resentment of bureaucracy and regulation
Burnham, Louis, 175
Burns, Joseph G., 278
Burton, E. P., 82, 87
Burton, Harold, 28
Bush, George H. W.: and 1988 election, 306; and Willie Horton ad, 292, 302, 382n. 51; profits from

"southern strategy," 291, 292–93, 306. *See also* Matalin, Mary
Bush, George P., 305
Bush, George W., 9–10, 305, 386n. 72; and removal of Trent Lott, 386n. 72; and 2000 election, 306, 390n. 90; profits from "southern strategy," 292–93; ritualistic praise for Martin Luther King, 386n. 72; speech to NAACP, 391n. 94; supported by neo-Confederates, 383n. 59, 389n. 85; urged to take lead on race relations, 284; use of "politics of emotion," 389n. 89. *See also* "compassionate conservatism;" red-blue divide; Rove, Karl
Bush, Jeb, 305
Business (black). *See* Howard, T. R. M.
Bussing, 168, 294, 307
Byrd, Daniel, 153, 163, 167–68

Cable television, 304
Cahoon, Ray, 231
Cajun country, 159–60
California, 10, 45, 282, 292–93
California Eagle, 70–71
California Economic, Commercial, and Political League, 70–72, 77–78, 89
Callaway, Austin (lynching of), 131
Callaway, Howard "Bo": conversion to GOP, 306; on connection between George Wallace and modern Republicans, 286
Calvinism, 127
Canterbury (Dean of), 186
Carey, Archibald, 89
Carleton, Don E., 181–82
Carmichael, A. A.: and 1948 Democratic loyalism, 277
Carmichael, James V., 244, 262–63, 265, 372n. 99, 373n. 100; attacks on Eugene Talmadge and Roy V. Harris, 373n. 101; judges own capitulation on race issue, 374n. 103. *See also* Arnall, Ellis; Harris, Roy V.; Talmadge, Eugene
Carr, Mrs. Johnnie, 12, 214
Carroll, Henry, 157–58

Carson, Clayborne, 311n. 1
Carter, Dan T.: on George Wallace remark, 380n. 37; on pre-1954 period, 313n. 2; on significance of George Wallace, 285
Carter, Hodding, 330n. 51, 362n. 26
Carter, Jimmy, 114; and 1976 election, 307, 393n. 100; disliked for racial liberalism, 293
Carter, Lillian, 114
Carter, Robert L., 31, 320n. 18
Carver, George Washington, 314n. 6
Case Bill, 248
Caste system. *See* racial caste system
Cathey, Sam, 60
Catholics, 17; and abortion, 314n. 9; and "bolt of 1928," 270, 272; anti-Catholicism, 376n. 9; in Louisiana, 144, 151–52, 159, 169; quit over segregation, 167; vacillation on segregation, 169
Chaka Khan, 305
Chapel Hill, NC, 230; and Journey of Reconciliation, 46, 55–59; liberal makeup of, 55–56, 224, 228, 233–34, 357n. 16. *See also* Graham, Frank Porter; Jones, Charles M.
Chapital, Arthur J., 167
Chappell, David L., 311n. 1
Chapple, Levye, 82, 89
Character (moral, as an issue), 4, 5
Charles, Ray: plays at 1984 Republican convention, 391n. 93
Cheney State Teachers College, 36
Chicago, 8, 10, 33, 43, 45, 50, 60–61, 181; and black congressman, 75, 88; and black newspaper, 112–13; and Methodist conference, 124; and Pullman porters, 201
Chicago Christian Advocate, 121
Chicago Defender: lauds Eleanor Roosevelt, 112–13
Chicago Committee of Racial Equality, 43
Chicago Council against Racial and Religious Discrimination, 50
Chiles v. Chesapeake and Ohio Railway, 25–26, 47

China, 45
Christ, Jesus, 80, 130; teachings of and civil rights, 133–34
Christian(s), 18, 33, 80; ideals of, 117, 136, 227, 339n. 27
Christian Century, 38
Christian Socialism, 227
Church of God, 273
Cincinnati, 44, 50
City College of New York, 36
City Park, (New Orleans): desegregation of, 147
Civil rights: as communistic, 170–97, 297–98; backlash against, 2, 8–10, 295, 313n. 4; backlash against and rise of modern Republican Party, 268–309; bureaucratic approach to, 13–16; continuity with pre-*Brown* period, 2–3, 6, 8, 161–62, 313n. 2; discontinuity with pre-*Brown* period, 161–62; groups in the South, 222–37; historiography of, 1–2, 311n. 1; legal-administrative approach to, 13–16; networks among activists, 11–12; related to later conservative politics, 17–18, 313n. 5; religion and, 15, 16–17, 315n. 15; traditional periodization of movement, 1–2, 8, 313n. 2. *See also* "lost opportunities" thesis; NAACP; Republican party; "white backlash" thesis
Civil Rights Act of 1964: Democratic and Republican support for, 283–84; meaning of, 283; right-wing distortion of, 283–84, 380n. 33
Civil Rights Act of 1966: opposition to, 296
Civil Rights Congress (CRC), xiii, 9–12, 170–97; and religion, 348n. 23; assessment of, 196–97; cooperation and competition with the NAACP, 172, 180; in Alabama, 179; in Asheville, 179; in Houston, 179, 180–82; in Jackson, 179; in Louisiana, 149; in Memphis, 179; in Macon, 179–80; in Miami, 179; in Mississippi, 179; in New Orleans, 179, 182–85; in Texas, 174
Civil War, 3, 268–69, 281, 374n. 1
Clancy, Frank "King," 161
Clark, Elmer T., 118
Clark, Tom C., 137
Clarksdale, MS, 85
Class, 4, 6–8, 220–21, 308, 315n. 11; business and race tensions, 113; class-based liberalism, 18–19; consciousness, 14; rapprochement within Dixiecrats, 287; suppression of class differences, 376n. 6; suppression of class differences in modern GOP, 280, 299–300, 307–9, 376n. 6, 391n. 92. *See also* conservatism, economic conservatism; labor; middle class; NAACP, divisions and activities in; New Deal Coalition; plain whites; "politics of emotion;" race, class, and gender (relationship between); *We Cry Genocide*; working class
"Class-based racism," 316n. 16
Cleghorn, Bill: sends photographers to Fellowship of the Concerned meeting, 142
Cleveland, 44, 46
Cleveland, MS, 74, 82
Clinton, Bill, 11; and 1992 election, 306; and 1996 election, 306; described as "first black president," 393n. 99; impeachment of, 383n. 60
Clinton, Hillary: compared to Eleanor Roosevelt, 11
Coahoma County Citizens Association, 92
Cobb, W. Montague, 75
Coe, John Moreno, 11; and Civil Rights Congress, 174, 184, 186, 189–92, 350n. 49
Coffin, William Sloane, 18
Cohn, David L., 112
Cold War, xiii, 8, 9–10, 17, 160, 235–36, 255–56. *See also* McCarthyism
Coleman, Clayton, 30
College of Medical Evangelists, 69–70

Collins, Don: conversion to Republican party, 289, 381n. 48; importance of conversion, 290–91
Colmer, William, 393n. 99
"Color ceiling," 298
Colorado, 45
Columbia, SC, 14
Columbia, TN, 27; riot, 132
Columbia University, 34
Columbians (the), 251–53, 366n. 56
Colvin, Claudette, 215
Combs, Doyle, 242
Comer, Donald: conversion to Republican party, 278
Committee of Racial Equality, 37, 43. *See also* Congress of Racial Equality
Committee on Interracial Cooperation, 119, 131; argues that women oppose lynching, 132
Common Ground, 64
Communism (and communists), 9–10, 11, 13, 15, 34, 223, 298, 300, 315n. 15; alleged gulf with liberals, 15; and anti-communism, 170–97; and religion, 348n. 23; and the Civil Rights Congress, 170–97; in Alabama, 186, 191–92, 194, 350n. 47; in Florida, 191; in Louisiana, 149–50; relationship with civil rights, 10, 33, 36–37, 42, 101–2, 125, 141, 195–96, 298, 372n. 99, 383n. 60. *See also* Civil Rights Congress; cold war; Jews; "lost opportunities" thesis; McCarthyism; socialism
"Communist Eleven." *See* Foley Square Smith Act
Communist party, xii, xiii, 37
"Compassionate conservatism," 5, 296, 305; term introduced by Harry Dent, 391n. 93
Confederate flag, 4, 274
Confederate generals, 301
Congregationalism, 34
Congress (U.S.), xiii, 31, 41. *See also* House of Representatives; Senate
Congressional Record, 295

Congress of Industrial Organizations (CIO), 13, 55, 57; and CIO Political Action Committee, 176; and civil rights, 101–2, 149–50, 176, 223, 251, 362n. 32; financing the SCHW, 236
Congress of Racial Equality (CORE), 9, 12, 15, 162; and the Journey of Reconciliation, 21–67, 233
Connor, Theophilus Eugene "Bull": and communists, 191–92; and Dixiecrats, 279
Connors, Marty, 299; referred to, 392n. 98
Conservatism, 2, 4–5, 16, 18, 266–67, 313n. 5; economic, 273, 276–77, 280, 284, 294, 303; extreme right as becoming "mainstream," 304, 308, 393n. 103; social, 273, 276–77, 280, 284. *See also* Bourbons; Conservative Democratic party; culture; "fast-food politics;" liberalism; "neo-Bourbonism;" "neo-Kluxism;" "politics of emotion;" "Reconstruction Syndrome;" Republican party; "the new racism;" white supremacy, relationship to conservatism
Conservative and Democratic party, 269, 389n. 89. *See also* Big Mule/Black Belt coalition; Bourbons
"Conservative Manifesto," 275, 377n. 11
Constitution (U.S.), 26, 387n. 78; embraced by conservatives, 383n. 59; requirements of, 308
Convict-lease system, 7
Cook, Blanche Wiesen, 333n. 7
Coon, John, 157
Cotter, Patrick J., 392n. 97
Cotton, 77
Couch, Bill, 252
Couch, W. T., 336n. 51
Coulter, Ann: and rehabilitation of Joseph McCarthy, 390n. 91; in *Time* magazine, 390n. 91
County-unit system: in Georgia, 248–51, 253–55, 265, 363n. 38
Courts, Gus, 85
Covington County, 279

Cracker party, (Augusta), 256–57, 263–66, 367n. 67, 368n. 71
Creoles, 151–52
Crime, 294, 307, 387n. 78; black-on-black, 80
Crommelin, John G., 278
Crump, "Boss" Ed: referred to, 145, 368n. 74
Cuban-American, 229
Cultural IQ, 308
Culture: and conservatism, 272–74, 382n. 55; culture as the basis of southern politics, 307–9; homogeneity of, 272–73; pluralism of, 303; southern, 273–74. See also "neo-Kluxism;" "politics of emotion;" "Reconstruction Syndrome;" red-blue divide
Culture thesis, 307–9. See also class, suppression of class differences, and within GOP; labor, divisions between leadership and rank-and-file; plain whites; "politics of emotion;" religion, divisions between leadership and flocks
Cumberland County, TN, 232
Cumberland plateau (Tennessee), 228–29
Current, Gloster, 90, 209

Dabney, Virginius, 112
Dachau, 280
Dailey, Jane, 16
Dailey Worker, 181
Dalfiume, Richard, 150
Dallas, 181
Danbury, CT, 40
Daniel, Pete, 98
Daniels, Frank, 103, 114
Daniels, Jonathan, 12, 103, 222
Daughters of Eleanor, 103
Daughters of the American Revolution: bar Hazel Scott from singing in hall, 334n. 14; bar Marian Anderson from singing in hall, 101; Eleanor Roosevelt resigns from, 101
Davis, Abraham Lincoln, 156
Davis, Angela, 194

Davis, Jefferson, 73, 393n. 99
Dawson, William L., 75; campaigns for Harry Truman, 331n. 69; relationship to T. R. M. Howard, 89; visit to Mississippi, 88
Dean, S. P., 230–31
Decatur, AL, 203
De Jong, Greta, 146
De Mendoza, Daniel, 254–55
Declaration of Independence, 136
Deep South, 5, 10, 15, 185; and Journey of Reconciliation, 29, 42, 46
DeLay, Tom, 307
Delta Council (of Mississippi), 78–79
Delta Council of Negro Leadership, 78–79
Democratic party, xii, 5, 14, 18–20, 28–29; alleged failures of, 291–92, 307–9; and Dixiecrat revolt, 276–80, 283, 287; and 1964 Civil Rights Act, 283–84; and Mississippi Freedom Democrats, 89; appeal to blacks during New Deal, 275, 377n. 11; as communistic, 297, 300, 383n. 60, 386n. 68; as party of blacks, 298–99; as party of "undesirables," 292, 300; as socialistic, 297, 300; class differences in, 280; decline of in South, 268–309, 377n. 11; fissures along racial fault line, 18–20, 273, 291–92, 293, 317n. 23; identification with modern civil rights movement, 281, 283–85, 287–88, 293, 317n. 22, 379n. 26; loss of race issue to GOP, 304–5, 389n. 89; loyalists and race, 277; persistence of some small strength, 299; retention of white supremacists in, 288; strengthened in South by Civil War and Reconstruction, 268–69. See also liberalism, alleged failures of; New Deal Coalition; obsessive-compulsive (nature of 1960s); Solid Democratic South; "Solid South"
Demographic shifts, 291
Denson, William H., 269
Dent, Harry S: and "southern strategy," 292, 306; introduces term "compas-

sionate conservatism," 391n. 93; mentorship of Lee Atwater, 301; on Lee Atwater and Willie Horton ad, 302
Depression. *See* Great Depression
Detroit, 13, 178, 181, 188
DeVries, Walter, 380n. 29
Dewey, Thomas E., 386n. 68
Dexter Avenue Baptist Church, 216
Diamond, Ross, Jr., 278
Dickinson, William L.: criticizes Democratic party as communistic, 383n. 56; criticizes Great Society as communistic, 383n. 56; denounces Montogmery-to-Selma march, 295; rides Goldwater's coattails, 283
Dillard College, 182, 184
Dirksen, Everett, 284, 288–89
Disfranchisement, 269–70, 305; as first germ of modern GOP, 269–70, 307; in Alabama, 375n. 5
District of Columbia, 24
District of Columbia Court of Appeals, 47
Dittmer, John, 331n. 58
Dixie, 18, 30, 102
Dixie Sereneders, 71
Dixiecrats, 273, 276–78, 287; as third germ of modern GOP, 276–77, 285, 306, 307; conversions to Republican party, 278–80, 377n. 15, 378n. 18; grievances and founding of, 276; in Georgia, 137; in Mississippi, 74
Dixon, Frank M., 271; Dixiecrats and, 277–78; flirtation with Republicanism, 279; racism of, 277–78; rapprochement with old class foes, 287; ties to White Citizens' Councils, 279
Dombrowski, James A., 17, 236; founded Fellowship of Southern Churchmen, 227
Domingeaux, Jimmie, 150
Doss, George, Jr., 265
Dothan Eagle: conversion to Republican party, 278
Double V campaign, 24, 121, 175

Doucet, D. J. "The Cat," 160
Douglass, Frederick, 127
Draper, Alan, 149, 316n. 19
Drew, R. L., 76, 82, 85, 87, 92
Du Bois, W. E. B., xi, 78
Dukakis, Michael, 292, 382n. 51; and 1988 election, 306
Duke, David, 306, 307
Duke University, 224
Dumas Bill, 125
Dunn, Loula, 207–8
Dunning School (of Reconstruction), 271
Durham, 55, 65, 324n. 43, 325n. 60; race conference at, 113
Durr, Clifford A., 222
Durr, Virginia, 11, 12, 16, 235; and E. D. Nixon, 204; on women and alcohol, 98–99; racial etiquette and, 353n. 21
Dutch Reformed, 17, 34

Eagles, Charles W., 313nn. 2, 4, 351n. 55
Earle, Willie (lynching of), 138, 139, 225–26
Early, Steve, 106
East Texas, 41, 42
Eastland, James, 177, 193–94, 196
Ebony, 198
Economic boycott (against Klan), 132
Economic growth, 370n. 86. *See also* class
Edsall, Mary, 18
Edsall, Thomas Byrne, 18
Education, 7, 8; attempted integration in Montgomery, 211; in Louisiana, 147, 162–63, 166–69; integration, 211, 279, 296, 386n. 71; integration in Mississippi, 90–94; lottery, 299; spending equalization as improvement, 91–92; trade or vocational, 7. *See also* Louisiana Education Association; "white backlash" thesis
Edwards, Jack: rides Goldwater's coattails, 283
Einstein, Albert, 347n. 15
Eisenhower, Dwight D., 188; and Little Rock, 280–82; as candidate for white supremacy, 288

Eleanor Roosevelt Vocational School for Colored Youth, 100
El Paso, 181
Eleanor Clubs, 102–5
Elks clubs, 83
Ellender, Allan J., 159
Ellington, Duke, 72
Emerging Republican Majority, The, 291
Emotion in politics. *See* "politics of emotion"
Employment discrimination. *See* affirmative action; Equal Employment Opportunity Commission; Fair Employment Practices Committee
Energy Peace Campaign, 36, 37
Entrepreneurialism. *See* Howard, T. R. M.
Environment: regulation of, 294
Episcopals, 39
Equal Employment Opportunity Commission (EEOC), 296, 382n. 55
Equal protection clause (of the Fourteenth Amendment), 249
Equal Rights Amendment, 292, 294, 303. *See also* gender
Eskew, Glenn T., 311n. 1
Eskew, Tucker: as protégé of Lee Atwater, 301
Ethnicity, 2, 270, 291–92, 296, 308; pluralism of, 303
Ethridge, Mark, 112
Eugenics, 381n. 46
Europe, 40
Evangelicals, 18, 299, 383n. 60
Evers, Charles, 11, 84, 89
Evers, Medgar, 8, 11, 16, 86, 92; applies to 'Ole Miss, 93–94; contemplates violent resistance, 91
Evers, Myrlie, 11, 86–89
Executive Order 8802, 148
Executive Order 1088, 275

Fairclough, Adam, 7–15; on anti-radicalism, 196–97; on Dillard University case, 184
Fair Deal, 383n. 60
Fair Employment Practices Committee (FEPC), 13, 37, 121, 148, 266, 275, 287, 372n. 99; creation of, 97; permanent FEPC as part of Truman's package, 276; Theodore Bilbo's opposition to, 175. *See also* Truman, Harry S, civil rights package of
Falwell, Jerry, 18, 307
Family values. *See* morality; "politics of emotion;" Republican party, and traditional family values
Farm Security Administration, 130
Farmer, James, 12, 15, 17, 34–35, 40–42, 44; estimations of, 322n. 29; place in history, 198
Farmer, James Leonard, Sr., 41
Farmer, Pearl Houston, 41
Farmers: and black labor, 102; as part of New Deal coalition, 275; bi-vocational, 83–84
Fascism, 10, 17. *See also* cold war; Columbians; Hitler, Adolf; Ku Klux Klan; McCarthyism; Nazis
"Fast-food politics," 304, 308, 389nn. 85, 89; alleged liberal weakness at simplifying issues, 388n. 82
Faubus, Orval E., 368n. 74
Faulkner, William, 268
Federal Bureau of Investigation, 107, 336n. 44; and the Civil Rights Congress, 171; in Louisiana, 160; investigates Eleanor Clubs, 104; report on Birmingham, 113
Federal government: antipathy to, 59, 97, 274, 276, 280, 288, 294, 303, 308, 383n. 59; involvement in civil rights, 10; lynching investigation, 147; relationship to race issue, 160, 294, 383n. 60; resentment of bureaucracy and regulation, 294–95; resentment of judiciary, 295–96, 383n. 60. *See also* Dixiecrats; "politics of emotion;" "Reconstruction Syndrome;" Wallace, George C.
Feduccia, F. D., 88
Feldman, Glenn, 313n. 4, 314n. 6
Fellowship, 38

Fellowship House, 43, 51
Fellowship of Christian Athletes, 18
Fellowship of Concerned Women, 8
Fellowship of Reconciliation (FOR), 9, 12; and the Journey of Reconciliation, 33–34, 37–39, 43–46, 48, 50–51, 66
Fellowship of Southern Churchmen (FSC), 8, 11, 17, 227–35; and Journey of Reconciliation, 47, 55, 233–35
Fellowship of the Concerned (FOC), 17, 117, 138–43
Felmet, Joseph, 50, 56–57, 60, 67
Felton, Rebecca Lattimer, 131–32
Felton, William H., 131
Feminism. *See* abortion; Equal Rights Amendment; gender
Field Foundation, 173
Fifth Amendment, 183–84
Fine, Russ, 392n. 98
Fink, Marianne D.: rebuts argument for segregation, 340n. 45
Finney, James, 318n. 4
First Amendment, 183–84
Fisher, Margaret, 11, 223, 235–36
Fisk University, 145
Fleming, Harold, 245–46, 247–48
Flora McDonald College, 227
Florida, 11, 30, 41, 305; criticism of Eleanor Roosevelt, 106
Flynt, John J., 367n. 67
Foley Square Smith Act (trials), 171, 186
Folsom, James E. "Big Jim," 210, 224, 371n. 95
Fontenot, J. Y., 159
Fontenot, L. Austin, 160
Food, Tobacco, and Agricultural Workers, 149
Food stamps, 293
Ford, Gerald R., 393n. 100
Foreman, Clark, 12, 223, 236
Fosdick, Harry Emerson, 33
Fourteenth Amendment, 31, 153, 249
FOX News channel, 382n. 51, 390n. 91
France: antipathy toward, 303
Franklin, John Hope, 225

Franklin, Mitchell, 183
Frantz, Laurent, 176–77, 179–80, 190
Frazer, Stanley: argument in favor of segregation, 124–25, 340n. 45; argument rebutted, 129–30, 340n. 45
Fredericksburg, VA, 47
Frederickson, Kari: on movement of Dixiecrats to GOP, 377n. 15
Free blacks: in New Orleans, 151–52
"Freedom marchers," 95
"Freedom rides," xii, 9, 10, 15, 17, 63; and Journey of Reconciliation, 33–36, 39, 44, 53
"Freedom Train," 209–10
Freedomways, 194
Freedomways Reader, 195
Fundamentalism, 299, 303

Gallup, George: polling on Eleanor Roosevelt, 101
Gannon Theological Seminary, 142, 232–33
Gardner, Virginia, 318n. 4
Garth, Nat, 230
Garvey, Marcus, 70, 202
Gaston, Paul M., 313n. 5; on ritual homage for Martin Luther King, 386n. 72
Gates, C. Jerry, 55, 65
Gay rights, 4, 14, 19, 274, 300; anti-gay remarks, 390n. 91; identification with Democratic party, 292, 383nn. 59–60, 389n. 89
Geater, James, 208
Gender, 4, 11, 14, 19, 303, 308; and Eleanor clubs, 102–5; and masculinity, 308, 383n. 59, 389n. 85; and "neo-Kluxism," 272–73, 274; and women's liberation movement, 292, 294, 300, 382n. 55; involvement of women in civil rights, 11, 235; mixed blood, 336n. 44; racial double-standard of sexual assaults, 80; relationship to race issues, 80, 294–95, 303, 383n. 60; southern anxiety over interracial sex, 109–11; women's propensity for civil rights,

126–43. *See also* abortion; Equal Rights Amendment; Roosevelt, Eleanor, on gender roles, racial and sexual rumors about; Roosevelt, Franklin, criticized Eleanor's independence

Georgia, 8, 11, 12, 17, 30, 226, 232–33, 293, 297, 306; and Dorothy Tilly's civil rights activities, 116–43, 226; and Eleanor Roosevelt, 104, 337n. 56; and SCHW in, 236; as Goldwater state, 283, 292; Columbians in, 251–53; Jimmy Carter from, 307; KKK in, 251–53; mountain Republicanism in, 374n. 1; poll tax abolished in, 359n. 1; violence in, 348n. 25; war veterans and racial responses, 238–67. *See also* county-unit system

Georgia Veterans for Majority Rule, 249–50

Georgia Veterans League, 241–42

Georgia Woman's World, 333n. 11

Georgia Workers Education Service, 232

Germany, 37

Gestapo, 281, 296; "federal gestapo," 387n. 78

Gettysburg Address, 136

GeWinner, Hoke, 252

Ghandi, Devadas, 66

Ghandi, Mohandas, 33, 36–37, 49; and non-violent social protest, 34, 38–39, 42–43, 47; mentioned, 297

GI Bill, 178

Gilbert, Leon (case of), 173, 349n. 41

Gingrich, Newt, 19, 307; profits from "southern strategy," 292–93

Glenn, J. M., 314n. 6

Global government, 303. *See also* "one worlders;" United Nations

Gloucester County, VA, 21

Glustrom, Johnny, 248

"God and country issues": mentioned, 4, 308, 389n. 89

Goff, Irving, 186

Goldsmith, Len, 187

Goldwater, Barry, 19; and purge of liberal wing of GOP, 289, 380n. 33; and "southern strategy," 292; appeal in South, 282–83; approached by George Wallace for 1964 running mate, 392n. 95; "extremism" converted into mainstream conservatism, 304, 308, 393n. 103; racist appeal of 1964 campaign, 282–83, 292, 300–1; supported by Ronald Reagan, 293

"Good government" movement (and modernization), 260–67

Goodman, Chaney, and Schwerner (murders of), 293

GOP. *See* Republican party

Gore, Al, 314n. 9; and 2000 election, 306, 390n. 90; opposed by neo-Confederates, 383n. 59, 389n. 85. *See also* red-blue divide

Gosnell, Cullen, 364n. 39

Graff, Bobbi, 185, 188

Graff, Emmanuel, 185

Graham, Frank Porter, 12, 224, 233; and Journey of Reconciliation, 55, 58; and President's Committee on Civil Rights, 134–135

Gramm, Phil, 306

Grantham, Dewey W.: on "southern strategy," 294

Graves, John Temple II, 112; as Dixiecrat, 278; conversion to Republican party, 278; on race tensions in Birmingham, 113

Graves, Lam, 52

Gray, Fred D., 12, 214

Great Depression, xi, xiii, 2, 8, 150; and Journey of Reconciliation, 33, 36, 39

Great Society, 294, 296, 383n. 60

Green, Benjamin A., 74, 75

Green, Sam, 139

Greenbackers, 7

Greene, Melissa Fay, 160

Greene, Percy, 85–86, 88, 332n. 83; break with T. R. M. Howard, 93

Greensboro: and Journey of Reconciliation, 56, 59; sit ins at, xii, 50, 198

Greensboro Daily News, 231
Greenville, SC, 99, 138, 225–26
Gregory, Herbert, 26
Grenier, John, 380n. 27; and Alabama Republican party, 282; and Goldwater campaign, 282, 289, 300–1; on Lyndon Johnson and race, 282; role in purge of liberal wing of GOP, 289; use of race issue, 300–1
Gretna, LA, 182–83
Greyhound Bus Company, 21–22, 45, 52–55
Griffin, Marvin, 267
Grossman, Aubrey, 183
Groveland, FL: rape case in, 187
Guerin, Daniel: and "lost opportunities" thesis, 356n. 73; estimation of interracial unionism, 220–21
"Guilt by association," 125, 300
Gulliver, Hal, 294; on Kevin Phillips, 382n. 49
Gun control, 4, 14, 274, 300, 383n. 59, 389n. 85; relationship to race issue, 294, 383n. 60.

Haldeman, H. R., 292
Haley, Alexander, 218
Hall, Gus, 188
Hall, Horace: conversion to Republican party, 278
Hall, Sam, 11, 183, 186, 191–92, 350n. 49; biographical sketch of, 350n. 47
Hall, Sylvia Bernard. *See* Bernard, Sylvia
Hall v. DeCuir, 25–26
Hamer, Fannie Lou, 11, 89
Hamilton, Charles F., 177–78
Hammerstein, Oscar II, 347n. 15
Hammond, LA, 147
Hampton Institute, 100, 106
Hampton Roads, VA, 21
Hannity, Sean: on distortion of civil rights voting, 380n. 33
Harding, Vincent, 313n. 2
Harlan, John: dissent in *Plessy v. Ferguson,* 134
Harlem, 29, 36

Harris, Roy V., 264–65, 367n. 67, 368n. 71; attacks on, 373n. 101; racism of, 372n. 99
Harrison, Pat, 101
Hartman, L. O., 121
Hartsfield, William B., 141, 244
Harvard University, 39
Haskin, Estelle, 119
Hastie, William, 12, 25, 27
Hastings Law School, 173
Hate, 136, 291
Hayes, R. W., 250
Hayes Store, VA, 21–22
Haygood Memorial Methodist Church, 117
Haynes, J. K., 155
Health. *See* medicine
Health, Education, and Welfare (Department of), 296
Heard, Alexander, 364n. 42
Heflin, J. Thomas, 148, 269; and 1948 Democratic loyalism, 277
Height, Dorothy, 198
Helms, Jesse, 306–7
Henderson, Bruce, 279
Henry, Aaron, 82, 85, 87, 330n. 51
Herrin, J. C., 228; tried for heresy, 357n. 16
Highlander Folk School, 205
High Point, NC, 44
Hill, J. B., 206
Hill, J. Michael: support for George W. Bush, 383n. 59, 389n. 85. *See also* League of the South
Hill, Leslie Pinckney, 36
Hill, Lister, 113, 282
Hill, Oliver, 26, 168
Hillsboro, NC, 67
Hispanics, 292, 305, 307
Hitler, Adolf, 121, 170, 175, 193; Eisenhower compared to, 281. *See also* Nazis
Hodes, Jane, 183
Hodes, Robert, 183, 194; dismissal from Tulane University, 184, 349n. 32
Holiness movement, 273

Holliday, Billie, 162
Holly Springs, MS, 41
"Holy Trinity" (of southern politics), 300
Homosexuality. See gay rights
Honey, Michael, 13. See also "lost opportunities" thesis
Hoover, Herbert, 270–72
Hoover, J. Edgar, 106–7, 115, 181; investigates Eleanor Clubs, 104
Hoovercrats, 270–72. See also "bolt of 1928"
Hopkins, Archie 35
Horne, Gerald, 176–77, 183, 351n. 55
Horton, Myles, 12, 16, 205
Horton, Willie (advertisement), 292, 302, 382n. 51
House of Representatives (U.S.), 75, 131, 178
Houser, George, 12, 17; and Journey of Reconciliation, 34, 39, 43–46, 48–52, 54, 56–57, 64, 66, 233–35; travels of, 324n. 43
House Un-American Activities Committee (HUAC), 178; denounces SCHW, 348n. 19
Houston, 179; branch of the Civil Rights Congress, 179, 180–82
Houston, Charles, 49, 150–51
Howard, T. R. M., 68–95, 332n. 83; alleged conservatism of, 80; bipartisanship of, 89; criticized by NAACP, 90–91; flees Mississippi, 94–95; joins NAACP, 93–94; parents of, 68; referred to, xii, 7–12, 16; rejects separate-but-equal doctrine, 91–95; upbringing of, 68–69
Howard University, 26, 42, 75, 100, 346n. 5
Howell, Clark, 119
Huddleston, George, 271
Humes, H. H., 83, 93
Humphrey, Hubert H.: and 1964 campaign, 301; and protest of Vietnam, 383n. 60; disliked for racial liberalism, 282–83, 289, 298, 301, 306, 379n. 26; speech at 1948 Democratic convention, 379n. 26
Hungary, 194
Hunter, Charles (case of), 187
Hurley, Ruby M., 90, 332n. 83
Hurst, Fannie, 347n. 15
Hyde Park, NY, 133

Ickes, Harold, 29; on Eleanor Roosevelt, 99, 333n. 7; racial liberalism of, 148, 175
Illinois, 25, 292
Immigrants, 270, 272, 292
Independents, 269. See also American Independent party
India, 33
Individualism, 4
Ingraham, Laura, 390n. 91
Ingram, Rosa Lee (case of), 188–89, 349n. 41
Institutionalized racism, 6
International Labor Defense, 170–71, 179
International Longshoremen's and Wharehousemen's Union, 168, 183, 185
International Longshoremen's Association, 168
International Order of Knights and Daughters of Tabor, 72–77, 95
Internet, 304
Interstate Commerce Commission, 30
Iraq: 2003 war in, 303. See also France; United Nations
Irish, 270, 292
Italians, 292
Ivy League, 39

Jack, Homer, 50, 61–62, 64
Jackson Advocate, (Mississippi), 85–86, 93
Jackson, Esther Cooper, xii, 11, 175, 178, 188, 194, 350n. 47
Jackson, James, 11, 177, 183, 350n. 47
Jackson, Mahalia, 88
Jackson, MS, 276, 331n. 58
Jackson, Robert, 28, 193

Jacksonville, FL, 191
Japanese-Americans, 70, 229
Javits, Jacob, 288–89
Jeanmard, Jules, 159
Jefferson County Republican Club, 281
Jefferson, George, 76
Jefferson School of Social Science, 180
Jet, 82, 198
Jews, 39, 272, 292; and anti-Semitism, 100, 185, 280; connection in public mind with communism, 11, 180, 383n. 60; ideals of, 117; involvement in civil rights, 11, 185, 280
Jim Crow. *See* segregation
John Birch Society, 303; advocates impeachments, 383n. 60
Johns, Barbara, 163
Johnson, Andrew, 50, 55, 66
Johnson, Carrie Parks, 119, 127
Johnson, John H., 198–99
Johnson, Lyndon B.: and Great Society, 294, 296; and implications of 1964 Civil Rights Act, 283, 290; and 1964 campaign, 301; disliked for racial liberalism, 282–83, 290, 293, 296, 298, 301, 306
Johnson, Mary Lea, 183
Johnson, Mordecai, 42
Johnson, Oakley, 163, 182–85, 192–94
Johnson, Phillip J., 145–46
Johnston, Sam M., 278
Jones, Alvin H., 159, 160, 184
Jones, Bob, 376n. 9. *See also* Bob Jones University
Jones, Charles M.: activities of, 228, 325n. 60; and Journey of Reconciliation, 55–58, 228, 234, 325n. 60
Jones, Donald, 212, 213
Jones, John C. (lynching of), 147
Jones, Walter B.: issues injunction outlawing NAACP in Alabama, 218
Journey of Reconciliation, 21–67, 233–35; referred to, 9
Judaism. *See* Jews
Judeo-Christian ethic, 300

Judiciary. *See* federal government, resentment of judiciary
Justice Department (U.S.), 9, 30, 160, 169

Kefauver, Estes, 289
Kelley, Robin D. G., 175
Kennedy, Edward M. "Teddy,": as inheritor of southern hostility toward Kennedys, 282
Kennedy, John F., 194; and "freedom rides," 282; criticized for being late and timid on civil rights, 379n. 25; disliked for racial liberalism, 283, 298, 306
Kennedy, Robert F., 228; and "freedom rides," 282; and protest of Vietnam, 383n. 60; disliked for racial liberalism, 282, 298, 306
Kennedy, Stetson, 193; infiltrates Georgia Klan, 252
Kentucky, 9, 10, 28, 49, 59, 137, 226
Kenya, 91
Kester, Howard Anderson "Buck," 15, 17, 227, 235
Killers of the Dream, 126
King, Martin Luther, Jr., 12, 34–35, 137, 194, 198–99, 226, 235; and E. D. Nixon, 355n. 71; and Montgomery Improvement Association, 83, 214–17; criticized for protesting Vietnam, 297; disparaged, 296–97, 314n. 6, 383n. 60; honored in recent years, 296–97, 386n. 72; national holiday for resented by some, 218–19, 393n. 99
King, Primus (case of), 359n. 3
King, Richard H., 146
Klarman, Michael J., 9–10, 19. *See also* "white backlash" thesis
Knights of Labor, 7
Knights of Peter Claver, 155
Knotts, Alice G., 127
Knowlton, Maury S., 79
Knox, John B., 375n. 5
Knoxville, 61–62

Kolchin, Peter, 314n. 10
Korean War, 182, 348n. 26
Korstad, Robert, 13, 149. *See also* "lost opportunities" thesis
Krushchev, Nikita, 194, 282
Ku Klux Klan, 8, 30, 54, 122, 191, 265, 303–4, 307; and "bolt of 1928," 270–72, 376nn. 8, 9; and draft board, 184; disgust with Democratic racial liberalism, 377n. 11; in Georgia, 251–53, 362n. 32; in Miami, 185; in Montgomery, 204; Klavalier squads, 252–53; opposition to, 119–20, 139, 157; "second Klan," 273; support for Ronald Reagan, 293; threats against Dorothy Tilly, 141, 226–27; ties to Theodore Bilbo, 176. *See also* Columbians; "neo-Kluxism"
Kytle, Calvin, 248–49, 363n. 38

Labor, 6–8; alliance with "The Group" faction of NAACP in New Orleans, 152–53; anti-union strategies, 7, 315n. 15, 362n. 32; backlash against civil rights, 13; division between leadership and rank-and-file, 13–14, 299, 316n. 19, 389n. 85; division between national, state, and local branches of, 13–14; divisions between white and black members of, 13–14, 168; divisions within unions, 13–14; interracial unionism, 220–21; mixed record of, 12–13; work for civil rights, 13, 183; worker safety laws, 294. *See also* AFL; AFL-CIO; class; Guerin, Daniel; Knights of Labor; "lost opportunities" thesis; Nixon, E. D.; race, class, and gender (relationship between); Randolph, A. Philip; UMW
Labor unions. *See* labor
Lafayette, LA, 147
La Grange, GA, 131
La Grange Ministerial Association, 131
Laissez-faire. *See* conservatism, economic; taxes, antipathy to

Lake Charles, LA, 147
Lake Junaluska, NC, 123, 133
Landon, Alf, 333n. 8
Language (of Reconstruction), 299–300
Laurel, MS, 190
Law, W. W., 239–40, 359n. 4, 374n. 105
Lawson, James, 18
Lawson, Steven F., 18, 311n. 1, 313nn. 2, 4
League of the South, 383n. 59, 389n. 85
Leave No Child Behind (act), 305
Lebeau, LA, 159
Ledbetter, Huddie "Ledbelly," 36
Lee, Davis: boycotted in Montgomery, 210
Lee, George W., 85
Lee, Norvell, 66
Lehman, Herbert, 29
Leigh Avenue Baptist Church, 53
Lest, Muriel, 36
Lewisburg, PA, 39
"Liberal media." *See* Agnew, Spiro; "Limbaugh effect;" Limbaugh, Rush; media, as the "liberal media"
Liberalism, 2; alleged failures of, 13–16, 18–20, 307–9; alleged gulf with radicals, 15–16; alleged weakness at oversimplifying issues, 388n. 82; becoming a bad word, 174, 296; decline of New Deal coalition, 18–20, 268–309, 317n. 23, 382n. 55; frustration with emotional appeals, 274; rareness of southern racial liberalism, 10. *See also* conservatism; Democratic party; "lost opportunities" thesis; media, as the "liberal media;" "popular front;" "Reconstruction Syndrome;" "Southern liberals;" white supremacy, relationship to conservatism
Liberty League, 333n. 11
Lichtenstein, Nelson, 13, 149. *See also* "lost opportunities" thesis
"Limbaugh effect," 304. *See* media, as the "liberal media"
Limbaugh, Rush, 19, 304, 307; and distortion of civil rights voting,

380n. 33. *See also* media, as the "liberal media"
Lincoln, Abraham, 136, 299; party of, 287
Little Rock, AR (crisis): relationship to rise of Republican party, 280–82
Local control. *See* states' rights
Local schools. *See* education, integration in
Locke, Alain, 347n. 15
Logan, Rayford, 113
Loma Linda University. *See* College of Medical Evangelists
Long, Earl, 157–58, 169; and Long machine, 371n. 95
Long, Huey P.: factions in Louisiana, 157; relative moderation of, 148–49, 156–57
Long, Russell B., 156
Longshoremen, 168
Los Angeles, 10, 70–71, 201
"Lost opportunities" thesis, 13–15, 316n. 19, 343n. 4, 356n. 73; in Louisiana, 149–50
Lott, Trent, 5, 306; interviews with neo-Confederates, 393n. 99; laments holiday for M. L. King, 393n. 99; scandal, 284, 307, 314n. 9, 386n. 72; segregationist background of, 393n. 99
Lottery: as election issue, 299
Louisiana, 25, 46, 278, 306; and George Wallace, 378n. 21; and Leander Perez, 378n. 21; as Goldwater state, 292; black education in, 147, 162–63, 166–69; black voting in, 147, 155–56; civil rights in, 7, 9–11, 16–17, 144–69; lynching in, 147, 162; race and labor in, 149–50; segregation in, 147; won by the Dixiecrats and Goldwater, 283
Louisiana Education Association, 154–55
Louisiana Farmers Union, 149
Louisiana Public Service Commission, 30
Louisiana Weekly, 48

Louisville, 37, 62, 124, 226
Louisville and Nashville Railroad, 206
Lowenstein, Allard, 228, 357n. 16
Lubell, Samuel, 165–66
Lucy, Arthurine, 1
Lumberton, NC, 163
Lynching, 1, 77, 97; and Methodists, 131–32; anti-lynching bill as part of Truman's package, 276, 283; differing definitions of, 162; emotional nature of, 69; in Louisiana, 147, 162; postwar, 348n. 25. *See also* sexual assaults; Truman, Harry S, civil rights package of; violence
Lynn, Conrad, 50, 53–54, 59

Macchiavelli, Niccolo, 291, 301
Mackay, James, 246–47, 249, 362n. 30, 363n. 38
Macon, 179; anti-FDR conference, 333n. 11
Maddox, Lester, 279, 297
Magnolia Mutual Life Insurance Company, 74, 86, 95
Malcolm X, 70
Mallory, Arenia, 83
Malone, Wallace D.: conversion to Republican party, 278
Mandell, Arthur, 181
Manhattan, 39
Manis, Andrew M., 10, 11, 17
Mankin, Helen Douglas, 223, 244, 248–49, 253–54
Marine Cooks and Stewards, 149
Marshall, Larkin, 180
Marshall, Thurgood, 11–12, 89; and bus boycott, 218; and Civil Rights Congress, 181; and Journey of Reconciliation, 25–28, 30, 32, 47–49; and legal strategy of NAACP, 150–51, 166–67; and Medgar Evers' application to 'Ole Miss, 93–94; emphasis on school desegregation, 168; work with A. P. Tureaud, 154–55
Marshall, TX, 41
Marshall Foundation, 173
Martin, James E.: approaches Gold-

water on behalf of George Wallace, 392n. 95; conversion to Republican party, 288, 306; on ties between Dixiecrats and Republicans, 276; race for governor, 297; race for Senate, 282; rides Goldwater's coattails, 282–83; uses racial appeals, 295
Martin, Martin A., 26
"Martinsville Seven": trial of in Virginia, 189
Maryland, 23–24
Masculinity, 308. *See also* gender
Mason-Dixon Line, 44
Mason, Lucy Randolph, 12, 223, 235–36, 364n. 44
Mason, Will, 68–69
Masons, 72
"Massive resistance," 16, 169, 383n. 60
Matalin, Mary: as protégé of Lee Atwater, 301
Matthews, Robert L., 212
Matthews v. Southern Railway, 47
Mau-Mau rebellion, 91, 210
Maynor, Dorothy, 55, 233
Mays, Benjamin E., 196
McCabe v. Atchison, Topeka, and Santa Fe Railroad, 25
McCall, Willis, 187
McCallister, Frank, 232
McCarthy, Eugene, 383n. 60
McCarthy, Joseph, 142, 390n. 91
McCarthyism, 9–10, 13, 16–17, 125, 162; and backlash, 147, 235–37, 313n. 4; and the Civil Rights Congress, 170–97; attempt at rehabilitation of, 390n. 91; black sympathy for, 81. *See also* "lost opportunities" thesis
McCorvey, Gessner T.: conversion to Republican party, 279; Dixiecrats and, 277; racism of, 277–78; rapprochement with old class foes, 287
McDowell, John Patrick, 116, 127
McGee, Willie (execution of), 182, 189 91, 196
McGill, Ralph, 247, 333n. 2

McGirt, William, 58
McKaine, Osceola, 12, 223–24
McKelphin, Joseph: lawsuit of, 153–54
McKissick, Floyd, 324n. 43
McMath, Sidney, 368n. 74, 371n. 95
McWhorter, Diane, 311n. 1, 313n. 5
Means, Theodore, 183
Media: and politics, 19, 391n. 92; as the "liberal media," 295, 304, 390n. 91; combined effect with "religious right" to make conservatism more extreme, 304, 308, 393n. 103; 309; revolution in and reinforcement of prejudices, 304. *See also* "religious right"
Medicare, 300
Medicine: and T. R. M. Howard, 68–95
Meeropol, Abe: writes "Strange Fruit," 162
Meier, August, 17, 162, 313nn. 2, 4
Memphis: Crump machine politics in, 145
Memphis Commercial Appeal, 78
Memphis Tri-State Defender, 78, 88
Memphis Women's Interracial Conference, 119
Meredith, James, 393n. 99
Mergen, Bernard, 200
Methodist Episcopal Church, South, 118, 338n.13
Methodist Woman, 140–41
Methodists, 11, 17, 314n. 6; and civil rights, 116–43; and Journey of Reconciliation, 41, 43, 45, 50; and lynching, 131–32; and segregation, 338n. 13, 339n. 27; and southern race relations, 118–27; educational work of, 128–31; opinion before *Brown* decision, 118–23; opinion after *Brown* decision, 123–27; politics and civil rights and, 132–34; reaction to *Brown* decision, 129–30; reunification of branches, 118, 120; women and civil rights, 126–43. *See also* Calvinism; Wesleyan-Armenianism

Miami, 10, 179, 201; and 1968 Republican convention, 284, 380n. 33; Civil Rights Congress in, 185–88
Miami Daily News, 188
Miami University, 41
Michigan, 386n. 72
Middle-class: blacks, 7–8, 11, 12; whites, 18, 227. *See also* Howard, T. R. M.; NAACP; Nixon, E. D.
Middlesex County, VA, 23, 24
Midwest, 29, 43, 365n. 48
Miller, Alexander, 139
Miller, Benjamin Meek, 271
Miller, Fred, 332n. 83
Mississippi, 10–12, 29–30, 293, 306; and T. R. M. Howard, 68–95; as Goldwater state, 292; criticism of Eleanor Roosevelt, 108, 113; mountain Republicanism in, 374n. 1; on by the Dixiecrats and Goldwater, 283; planters in, 102; Presbyterians in, 339n. 27; voting in, 81–82, 87–88, 361n. 25. *See also* Mississippi Delta; "Oust Bilbo" campaign
Mississippi Delta, xi, 7, 8, 12, 15, 84, 231; and T. R. M. Howard, 68–95. *See also* Delta Council; Mound Bayou
Mississippi Freedom Democrats, 89, 195
Mississippi "Freedom Summer," 383n. 60
Mississippi Junior College, 83
Mississippi Negro Democrats, 86
Mississippi State Democratic Association, 86, 88
Missouri, 10–12
Mitchell, Arthur, 25
Mitchell, J. Douglas, 24
Mitchell, John: and "southern strategy," 285, 291–92
Mitchell, Martha, 285
Mitchell v. Arkansas, 25
Mitford, Jessica, 346n. 5
Mobile, AL, 279, 298; riot in shipyards, 148, 276
Moderates. *See* "southern liberals"

Mohl, Raymond A.: on Miami, 185
Mondale, Walter P.: and 1984 election, 306
Monroe, LA, 157–58
Montgomery, AL, 10, 12, 15, 23; and black USO, 207–8; attempted school integration, 211; attitudes toward black voting, 206–7; civil rights in, 198–221; home of Stanley Frazer, 124; integration at Maxwell Air Force Base, 275; marshal law declared in, 282; meeting of FOC photographed, 142; voter registration in, 206–7, 208–9
Montgomery Advertiser: conversion to Republican party, 278
Montgomery Bus Boycott, 1, 16, 34, 214–19, 220; referred to, 95, 162
Montgomery Improvement Association, 83, 214–19
Montgomery Negro and Civil Improvement League, 206
Montgomery Voters League, 208–9
Montgomery Welfare League, 205
Moore, Amzie, 16, 82, 85, 87, 91–92
Moore, Arthur J., 125
Moore, Roy: and Ten Commandments controversy, 393n. 101
Morality (and values), 4, 5, 14, 19, 299, 308, 383n. 59, 389nn. 85, 89; and "bolt of 1928," 270–73; relationship of "family values" to race issue, 294–95, 303, 383n. 60. *See also* "neo-Kluxism;" "the new racism"
Morgan, Chester M., 175
Morgan, Irene, 15, 21–24, 26, 30–31, 67
Morgan v. Commonwealth of Virginia, 26, 28–32, 45–47, 53–54, 59–60, 64, 234, 317n. 2
Mormon, Natalie, 46
Morris, Chester, 65
Morrison, deLesseps S. "Chep," 156, 161, 371n. 95
Morrison, Toni: dubs Bill Clinton "first black president," 393n. 99
Morton, Nelle, 11, 17, 227–35

Motley, Constance Baker, 168
Moton, Robert R., 314n. 6
Mound Bayou, MS, 73–95
MSNBC, 390n. 91
Murphy, Reg, 294; on Kevin Phillips, 382n. 49
Murray, KY, 68
Murray, Paula, 12, 46
Muste, A. J., 12, 34, 37, 44–46, 48
Myrdal, Gunnar, 25, 98, 121; on types of race customs, 109–10

NAACP Legal Defense Fund, 166
NASCAR dads, 308
Nashville, 37–38, 72
Nashville Christian Advocate, 120
National Association for the Advancement of Colored People (NAACP), xi, xii, 10, 72, 97, 176, 199, 251, 278; and definition of lynching, 162; and Journey of Reconciliation, 22, 24–26, 28–32, 47–50, 52, 66; and Little Rock, 281; competition and cooperation with the Civil Rights Congress, 172, 180, 196; class tensions within, 12, 15–16; divisions and activities in Louisiana, 146, 166–69; divisions and activities in Mississippi, 77, 85, 90–91, 93–94, 332n. 83; divisions and activities in Montgomery, 208–9, 211–15, 217–18; hostility to T. R. M. Howard, 90–91; Howard joins, 93–94; in Georgia, 362n. 32; legal activism of, 12, 13, 166–69; relationship with other civil rights groups, 12, 172; speech of George W. Bush to, 391n. 94; struggle in New Orleans, 151–54; struggles within, 15–16, 151–54. *See also* Hastie, William; Houston, Charles; NAACP Legal Defense Fund; Marshall, Thurgood
National Committee for Rural Schools, 216
National Conference of Methodist Youth

National Federation for Constitutional Liberties, 171
National Lawyers Guild, 180, 349n. 32
National Maritime Union, 40, 194
National Negro Congress, 42, 171
National States' Rights party, 293
Nativism. *See* immigrants; xenophobia
Nazis(m), 104, 121–22, 193, 298, 366n. 56, 390n. 91
Neal, Benjamin F., 122
Nearing, Scott, 33
Negro Digest, 109
Nelson, Andrew, 183
Nelson, Bruce, 168
Nelson, Wallace, 50, 53–54, 59, 63
"Neo-Bourbonism," 273–74, 280, 377n. 10; merger with "neo-Kluxism," 273
Neo-Confederates: support for George W. Bush, 383n. 59, 389n. 85; ties to Trent Lott, 393n. 99
"Neo-Kluxism," 272–74, 280; as second germ of modern GOP, 272, 293, 303–4, 307; defined, 272–73; merge with "neo-Bourbonism," 273
Neshoba County, MS, 293
"New abolitionists," 101–2
New Deal, xi, xii, xiii, 1, 8, 12, 18, 383n. 60; and "new abolitionists," 101–2; Theodore Bilbo's support for, 175
New Deal Coalition, 275; breakup of, 18–20, 108, 275–77, 287, 291–92, 317n. 23. *See also* Democratic party
New Frontier, 294, 383n. 60
New Iberia, LA, 167–68
New Jersey, 292
New Orleans, 12, 15, 46, 47, 179; bussing in, 165; department store boycott in, 162–63; status in 1940, 144; struggle within NAACP, 151–54
New Orleans States, 184
New Orleans Times-Picayune, 184
"New Racism." *See* "The New Racism"
New Republic, 105
New South, 2–3, 7
New Testament, 42

New York, 31, 33–34, 36–37, 39, 43–47, 49–50, 54; and southern race customs, 109; Lower East Side of, 185; meetings in, 216; school in, 180
New York Council for a Permanent FEPC, 50
New York Post, 67
New York Times, 29, 48
Newport News, 106
Newsom, Adam, 82
Nicholson, Jim: on Republicans and NAACP, 391n. 94
Niebuhr, Reinhold, 33
Nixon, E. D., 9–13, 16, 353nn. 30, 31; and Brotherhood of Sleeping Car Porters, 199–200, 216, 352nn. 10, 15; and M. L. King, 355n. 71; and Montgomery Bus Boycott, 214–19; and NAACP, 208–9, 211–15, 354n. 36; and Virginia Durr, 204; bitterness of, 198, 218–20; disparages SCHW, 213; finally gets his due, 220–21; life and civil rights activities of, 198–221; poverty of upbringing, 200–201; runs for office, 210; resignation from MIA, 218–19; speaks in New York, 216–17; threats by Klan, 204; writings on, 351n. 2
Nixon, Richard M.: and "southern strategy," 285–86, 291–92, 294, 306; as "moderate" by recent standards, 393n. 103; influenced by A. Philip Randolph, 201–2; keeping Pat Nixon at home, 114; on the need for a subtle racial appeal, 292; rejects Goldwater as innovator, 292; sees Eisenhower as originator of "southern strategy," 292
Noe, James A., 157–58
Norfolk, 21–22
Norman, Martha, 313n. 2
North, xi, 10, 14, 29, 35, 233–34. *See also* Yankees
North Alabama, 298, 392n. 98
North Carolina, 9, 11, 12, 14, 226, 306; and Journey of Reconciliation, 30, 44, 49, 50–51, 54, 59; mountain Republicanism in, 374n. 1; religion in, 99; SCHW, 224–25, 236; sentiment favoring segregation, 124. *See also* Chapel Hill
North Carolina A & T, 50, 57, 198, 325n. 57
North Carolina Christian Advocate, 120
North Carolina Supreme Court, 65–66
Northeast, 29
Northeast Methodist Episcopal Church, 118
Northerners: involvement in civil rights, 10; racism of, 14. *See also* federal government; "outside agitators"
Nossiter, Adam, 92
Nostradamus, 291
Nuremburg Trials, 28

O'Brien, Gail, 334n. 17
O'Dell, Jack, 183, 194
O'Douglas, William: threatened impeachment of, 383n. 60
O'Neal, Ed, 278
Oakes, Rosalie, 232
Oakwood College, 68–69
Obsessive-compulsive (nature of 1960s politics), 387n. 78
Odum, Howard W., 101
Ohio, 28, 35, 42, 292
Okinawa, 245–46
Old Dominion. *See* Virginia
Old Guard. *See* Republican party, purge of liberal wing
Old South, 2, 3
'Ole Miss. *See* University of Mississippi
"One-hundred percent Americanism." *See* patriotism
"One Worlders," 297, 303. *See also* global government; United Nations
Orange County, NC, 67
Organized labor. *See* labor
Orser, W. Edward, 120
"Other-worldliness," 81
Our Lady of Sorrows Catholic Church, 314n. 9

420 Index

"Oust Bilbo" campaign, 174–78, 195. See also Bilbo, Theodore G.
"Outside agitators" 10, 97, 139, 23–34. See also xenophobia
Outer South. See Upper South
Oxford, OH, 41, 54

Paris, 40
Parks, Rosa, 12, 23, 35, 198–99, 226, 353n. 21; and E. D. Nixon, 209, 215–217
Paternalism, 7
Patriotism, 4, 9, 14, 308, 389n. 89; relationship to white supremacy and conservatism, 126, 273, 293–94, 300, 303–4, 314n. 6, 383n. 60. See also "politics of emotion;" "Reconstruction Syndrome"
Patronage, 299
Patterson, F. D., 76
Patterson, John M., 218
Patterson, William: and Civil Rights Congress, 173, 174, 179, 181, 183, 187, 192; and Ingram case, 188; and We Cry Genocide, 192–94; snubbed by liberals, 196. See also Civil Rights Congress
Paul (Saint), 130
Payne, Charles, 311n. 1
Peck, James "Jim," 11, 12, 15, 17; and Journey of Reconciliation, 34, 39–40, 50–52, 54–57, 60, 63; on James Farmer, 322n. 29
Peck, Samuel, 39
Pelican State. See Louisiana
Pennsylvania, 35, 292
Pentecostals, 273
People's Defense League, 153
Peoria, IL, 303, 390n. 90
Perceptions (versus reality), 301–2, 308, 389nn. 85, 89. See also "politics of emotion"
Perez, Leander, 169; and Dixiecrats, 279; anti-Semitism of, 280; as George Wallace leader in Louisiana, 378n. 21; control of Plaquemines Parish, 159; conversion to Republican party, 279–80, 306; racism of, 149, 279–80
Peter (Saint), 130
Petersburg, VA, 53–54
Philadelphia: and 1948 Democratic convention, 277
Philippines, The, 45
Phillips, Kevin R.: evaluated by George Brown Tindall, and Reg Murphy and Hal Gulliver, 382n. 49; on connection between George Wallace and modern Republicans, 286, 289; on John Wayne, 303; on manipulating plain-white emotions, 303–4; on "southern strategy," 291, 292–93, 303–4; predicts Republican majority, 291–93, 305–6
Phipp, T. J., 65
Phoebus, VA, 230–31
Pickering, Charles, 386n. 72
Piedmont, 44
Pinkard, Otis, 240
Pittsburgh Courier, 52; referred to, 112
Plain whites: and disfranchisement, 269–70; and culture thesis, 307–9; and Klan, 252–53; economic competition with blacks, 111, 165, 252–53, 316n. 16; manipulation of emotions, 4, 301–2, 303–5, 391n. 92; vote against tax reform, 392n. 98; working-class racism, 165, 225–26. See also Atwater, H. Lee; class; culture thesis; labor, division between leadership and rank-and-file; "politics of emotion;" religion, division between leadership and flocks; "southern strategy"
Planters. See agriculture; black belt; Bourbons; farmers
Plessy v. Ferguson, 25–26, 28, 166; and age of segregation, 145
Pluralism. See culture, pluralism of; ethnicity, pluralism of; religion, pluralism of
Poland, 230; and Poles, 292
Political correctness, 5
Politics. See civil rights, related to later

politics; conservatism; culture thesis; Democratic party; Dixiecrats; liberalism; "politics of emotion;" Republican party; South, ostensible political transformation
"Politics of emotion," 5–8, 14, 19, 274, 291, 294–95, 308–9, 383n. 60; and modern Republican party, 299–305, 391n. 92; defined, 4–5; mentioned, 389n. 89; "Reconstruction Syndrome" morphs into, 300; versus "politics of reason," 315n. 11. *See also* conservatism; "fast-food politics;" "Reconstruction Syndrome;" "the new racism"
"Politics of reason," 5, 315n. 11
Polk, Matthew, 157
Poll tax, 97, 111; abolished in Georgia, 359n. 1. *See also* Soldier Vote Bill; Truman, Harry S, civil rights package of; voter rights; voting
Poor whites. *See* plain whites
"Popular front" 170–97, 349n. 32. *See also* communism; liberalism
Population. *See* demographic shifts
Populists, 7, 269
Porter, William, 211
Potomac Railroad, 47
Poverty. *See* class; farmers; plain whites; urban poor
Powe, Ralph, 346n. 5
Powell, Adam Clayton, Jr., 29, 89, 319n. 15, 334n. 14, 347n. 15; at civil rights rally, 217
Powell, Colin, 305
Power Shift, The, 291
Prayer in schools, 4, 274, 292, 294, 300, 308; in Sixties, 387n. 78; opposed because people "hate God," 389nn. 85, 89
Praying for Sheetrock, 160
"Pre-civil rights movement," 146–47
Presbyterians, 55–56, 228, 325n. 60; and segregation, 339n. 27
President's Committee on Civil Rights, 49, 117, 134–37
Price, Mary, xii, 11, 224–25, 235–36

Primitive Baptists, 200
Prince Hall Masons, 155
Professors, 299
Progressive Democratic Association (Alabama), 210
Progressive Era, 118
Progressive Party, 186
Progressive Voters League, 85
Prohibition, 69, 272
Protestants, 3, 293, 303
Pullman (railroad cars and porters), 200–5. *See also* Brotherhood of Sleeping Car Porters
Psychology. *See* "politics of emotion;" white supremacy, emotional and psychological aspects of

Quakers, 17, 33, 35–36, 38

Rabun, Joseph, 247, 362n. 33
Race. *See* race, class, and gender; "the new racism;" white supremacy
Race and Industrial department, 39, 45–46
Race, class, and gender (relationship between), 4–8, 315n. 11
Race Relations Sunday, 128
Racial accommodation, 92–93, 314n. 6, 315n. 15
Racial caste system: as a misnomer, 145
Racial profiling, 307
Racial quotas. *See* affirmative action
Racism. *See* "politics of emotion;" "the new racism;" white supremacy
Radical Republicans, 299–300
Radicals. *See* communism
Radio. *See* talk radio
Rainach, William N., 169
Raleigh, NC, 54
Raleigh News and Observer, 103
Rameau, P. Colfax, Rev., Ph.D., 315n. 15
Ramey, Ben, 180–81
Ramspeck, Robert, 223
Randle, Worth, 50
Randolph, A. Philip, 12, 13–17, 198, 352n. 15; and Journey of Reconciliation, 37, 42, 47; and "March on

Washington," 148–50; calls for nonviolent direct action, 162; effect on E. D. Nixon, 201–5, 216–17, 352n. 15; evaluation of by Eleanor Roosevelt, 109; writings, 113

Rankin, John E., 177–78, 185; and black veterans hospital, 74–75

Rape. *See* sexual assaults

Raper, Arthur, 102

Reader's Digest, 142

Reagan, Ronald, 18; and 1984 election, 306; campaigns for Goldwater, 293; Klan support for, 293; opens 1980 campaign in Neshoba County, Mississippi, 293; profits from "southern strategy," 291–93, 306; racial appeal of, 293; supported by Strom Thurmond, 293

Real Majority, The 291–92

Reconstruction, xi, 3–5, 372n. 99; and unpopularity of Republican party in the South, 268–69, 285; historiography of, 271; memories of and civil rights, 101–2, 282, 383n. 60, 372n. 99

"Reconstruction complex," 250

"Reconstruction Syndrome," 268–69, 274, 308, 314n. 6, 383n. 60; defined, 3–4; morphing into "politics of emotion," 300; overcome by Republican party, 299–300, 391n. 92

Red-Blue divide: in 2000 election, 383n. 59, 389n. 85, 390n. 90. *See also* culture

Redeemers. *See* Bourbons

Redemption, 269

"Red scare." *See* cold war; McCarthyism

Reed, Joe, 299

Reed, Stanley, 28, 31

Regional Council of Negro Leadership, xii, 78–95

Regulation, 294. *See also* federal government, antipathy to

Reinhardt Junior College, 116

Religion, 4, 19, 308, 387n. 78; and communism, 348n. 23; and fundamentalism, 272; and Hoovercrats, 271; and political conservatism, 14, 271, 290, 293, 304, 315n. 15, 316n. 16; and traditional family values, 272; division between leadership and flocks, 16–17; pluralism of, 303; relationship to racism, 269, 277–78, 290, 294–96, 383n. 60; religious groups, 8; Republican blurring of line between church and state, 295–96; use of for civil rights, 15–17; use of in disfranchisement, 269. *See also* Baptists; Catholics; Church of God; Congregationalism; Dutch Reformed; Episcopals; fundamentalism; "God and country" issues; Holiness movement; Jews; media, combined effect with "religious right;" Methodists; Pentecostals; Presbyterians; Protestants; Quakers; "religious right;" Seventh Day Adventists; social gospel; Ten Commandments; "the new racism;" Unitarians

"Religious right," 18–19; combined effect with media revolution to make conservatism more extreme, 304, 308–9, 393n. 103; entry into politics, 304. *See also* media, as the "liberal media"

Reparations, 307

"Report on the Economic Conditions of the South," 346n. 2

Representation: views of, 393n. 101

Republican convention of 2000, 305

Republican party, xiii, 5, 12, 17–19, 25, 28; alliance with Klan and prohibitionists, 270–72; and "fast-food politics," 304; and "Limbaugh effect," 304; and Little Rock crisis, 280–82; and 1964 Civil Rights Act, 283–84, 290, 295–98, 306; and "politics of emotion," 299–305; and purge of liberal wing, 283–84, 288–89, 380n. 33; and "southern strategy," 291–95; and "the new racism," 5, 308, 314n. 9; appropriation of George Wallace's politics, 285–86,

381n. 38; as party of Lincoln, 287, 306; as party of whites, 298–99; attempt to pose as inclusive, 284, 391nn. 93, 94; blurring line between church and state, 295–96; black, 89; black-and-tans, 87; blurring shades of grey, 299–300, 304, 388n. 82, 389nn. 85, 89; chooses to abandon racial moderation, 287–89, 381n. 44; competition with George Wallace for white vote, 19, 285–86, 289, 292, 307, 381n. 44; denial of racism, 304–5; disfranchisement as first germ of modern GOP, 269–70; during Reconstruction, 268–69, 271; link to Conservative Democratic party, 4–5, 391n. 92; link to Dixiecrats, 276–80, 285, 377n. 15, 378n. 18; makeup of 1920s judiciary and chilly atmosphere for civil rights, 12; media proficiency of, 391n. 92; merger between "neo-Bourbonism" and "neo-Kluxism," 273–74, 280, 287; "neo-Kluxism" as second germ of modern GOP, 272–73, 293, 303–4, 307; overcoming relationship to Reconstruction, 295, 297–98, 299–300, 393n. 99; pro-business orientation of, 391n. 92; relationship to race and Reconstruction, 4–5, 17–18, 271, 279, 295, 299–300, 317n. 23; southern distaste for after Civil War, 268–69; strength in mountain regions, 374n. 1; suburbs and, 280; target Eleanor Roosevelt, 333n. 8; use of emotional issues, 5, 293, 300–6, 314n. 9, 389n. 89; use of racial backlash for party's rise, 17–19, 268–309, 313n. 5, 314n. 9, 317n. 23, 380n. 29, 388n. 84. *See also* Atwater, H. Lee; "bolt of 1928;" "compassionate conservatism;" conservatism; Dent, Harry; "fast-food politics;" federal government, antipathy to; "Limbaugh effect;" media, as the "liberal media;" Phillips, Kevin; "politics of emotion;" "religious right;" Rove, Karl; Solid Republican South; "southern strategy;" "the new racism;" Thurmond, J. Strom

Reynolds, Quentin, 347n. 15

Rice, Condoleezza: claim about Democratic voting registrars, 392n. 96; speech at 2000 Republican national convention, 305–6, 391n. 94

Rich, Marvin, 322n. 29

Richmond, 24, 42, 47, 53–54

Right-to-Work Committee, 187

Right-to-work laws, 14

Riley, Bob: enmity of fellow state Republicans, 392n. 98; religious tenor of tax referendum pitch, 392n. 98; tax reform plan, 392n. 98

Ripon Society, 288–89

Rise, Eric, 189

Rivers, Henry C., 245

Roberts, Oral, 18

Robertson, Pat, 18, 307

Robeson, Paul, 186, 193

Robinson, Armstead L., 311n. 1

Robinson, Jackie, 27, 80

Robinson, Jo Ann Gibson, 12, 214–15, 226

Robinson, Spottswood, 12, 26–27, 49

Rockefeller, Nelson, 284, 288–89

Romney, George, 284, 288–89

Roodenko, Igal, 11, 50, 54, 56–57, 65

Roosevelt, Eleanor, 10–12, 16, 96–115, 121, 217, 275; and anxieties of white South, 109–15; and conspiracy theories about, 102–5; and controversy over women and alcohol, 98–99; and enmity of white southerners, 96–115, 141, 175; and ties to Jews, 377n. 11; as not ladylike, 337n. 56; challenges segregated seating at SCHW, 100–1; compared to Harriet Beecher Stowe, 96, 115; disliked by "southern liberals," 112; friendship with Dorothy Tilly, 117, 133–34; friendship with E. D. Nixon, 208; friendship with Mary Price, 224; Hillary Clinton compared to, 11;

on Christ's teachings and civil rights, 133–34; on gender roles, 98–99, 107–8; opposed by Republicans, 333n. 8; opposes Civil Rights Congress, 196; personality of, 98; racial and sexual rumors about, 103–6; sexual anxieties about, 107–8, 110–11; suspicion that she is of mixed blood, 336n. 44. *See also* Eleanor clubs; Ickes, Harold

Roosevelt, Franklin D., 12–13, 37, 121; and judiciary, 25–26; and New Deal, 275; and ties to Jews, 280, 377n. 11; anti-FDR rally in Macon, 333n. 11; criticized about Eleanor's independence, 99, 103, 108, 114; on South as nation's "number-one economic problem," 98; presidency of, 96–97; racial and sexual rumors about, 103–6; reluctance on race, 148; unpopularity because of racial liberalism, 275, 280, 283, 287, 298. *See also* Roosevelt, Eleanor

Roosevelt, Theodore: lunch with Booker T. Washington, 131

Roxboro, NC, 67

Rove, Karl: as protégé of Lee Atwater, 301

Royal House of Eleanor, 103

Rudwick, Elliott, 162

Rush, Lever (execution of), 74

Russia. *See* Soviet Union

Rust College, 41

Rustin, Bayard, 12, 15, 17, 355n. 71; and Journey of Reconciliation, 34–39, 40, 43–45, 48–59, 64, 233–35; on America's democratic pretensions, 66; serves time in North Carolina, 65–67; trip to India, 66–67; travels of, 324n. 43

Rustin, Florence, 35

Rustin, Janifer, 35

Rustin, Julia, 35

Sacco and Vanzetti (case of), 173

Safety and health. *See* labor, worker safety laws

St. Augustine's College, 54

St. James Methodist Church, 124

St. Louis, 10, 72, 201–2, 278

St. Lucia, 173

Saints Junior College, 83

Sale, Kirkpatrick, 291

Salmond, John A., 8–15, 17

Salisbury, NC, 106

Saluda, Virginia, 22, 24, 26

Samford, Frank P.: conversion to Republican party, 278

Sampson, Edith, 109

Samuel Houston College, 41

San Antonio, 181

Sancton, Thomas, 105

Savage, Michael: anti-gay remarks, 390n. 91

Savannah, 251, 256–57, 361n. 18, 374n. 105

Scales, Junius, 236

Scammon, Richard M., 291, 308

Scarborough, Joe, 390n. 91

School prayer. *See* prayer in schools

"Scientific racism," 383n. 60

Scott, Hazel, 334n. 14

Scott, J. H., 157

"Scottsboro Boys" (rape cases), 170, 173

Seals, Hilton, 57

Second Reconstruction, 3, 5, 17–18; identification with Democratic party, 285, 294, 296, 317n. 22; "Reconstruction II" as term, 387n. 78

Segregation, xi, xii, xiii, 6, 8, 168, 269; age of from *Plessy* to *Brown*, 145; and Journey of Reconciliation, 23–25, 27, 29–33, 39, 41–42, 44–45, 47, 49, 50, 52–53; anti-segregation bill as part of Truman's package, 276; as issue for modern GOP, 287–88; demoralizing effects of, 69; extreme examples of, 60; in Armed Forces, 245–46, 275; separate-but-equal doctrine, 91–92. *See also* education, integration in; Truman, Harry S, civil rights package of

Selden, Armistead, 289; conversion to

Republican party, 296; criticizes federal control over schools, 386n. 71
Selznick, David O., 347n. 15
Senate (U.S.): southern filibusters, 97, 111
Service-station boycott (Mississippi), 86–87
Seventh Day Adventists, 22, 68–72, 83
Sexual assaults: of white men on black women, 80
Sexuality. *See* gender
Shaw, William M., 158
Sheehan, Vincent, 347n. 15
Shepard, Kris, 317n. 21
Shiloh Baptist Church, 59
Shreveport, LA, 147; and first NAACP branch in Deep South, 146
Shridharani, Krishnaial, 38
"Silent majority," 291
Sillers, Walter J., Jr., 91; and black veterans hospital, 74–75; and Dixiecrats, 74; background of, 74; meets with black delegation, 92
Simmons, Roscoe Conklin, 174
Simon, Bryant: on Eleanor clubs, 103
Simplicity. *See* "fast-food politics"
Sinclair, Upton, 71
Sisson, Maurie L., 89–90
Sisters of Eleanor, 103
Sitkoff, Harvard, 150
Slavery: apology for, 307
"Slippery slope," 300
Smathers, Eugene, 228–29
Smith Act, 347n. 7. *See also* Foley Square
Smith, Al, 270–72, 376n. 8. *See also* "bolt of 1928"
Smith, B. F., 79
Smith, Ellison D. "Cotton Ed," 111
Smith, Frank E., 362n. 26
Smith, Gerald L. K.: racial extremism of, 149
Smith, Hoke, 119
Smith, Lillian, 126, 132, 235
Smith, Perry M., 72, 74; feud with T. R. M. Howard, 76, 83
Smithfield, AL, 288

Smith v. Allwright, 27–29, 98, 111, 121; and Georgia, 359n. 3; and Louisiana, 156; and Montgomery, 208–9
Smyer, Sidney: conversion to Republican party, 278
Social Darwinism: and racism, 316n. 16
Social Gospel, 43, 116, 119, 127, 143
Socialists, 33, 37, 42, 71, 300; and civil rights, 101–2, 125; as epithet to denote racial liberalism, 141, 288, 290, 383n. 60; Christian socialism, 227; "drift toward socialism," 285, 294; Fabian socialists, 297. *See also* communism
Social Security, 300
Soldier Vote Bill, 97, 111
Solid Democratic South, 5, 268
Solid Republican South, 5, 268, 290, 299, 305–7, 389n. 89
"Solid South," 268, 307
Sons of Confederate Veterans, 393n. 99
South (magazine), 286–87, 289–90, 297
South, xi, xii, xiii, 3–6, 9, 11, 14–18; culture as basis for its politics, 307–9; defensiveness of, 98; enmity of whites toward Eleanor Roosevelt, 96–115; ostensible political transformation of, 281–82, 290–91, 379n. 22, 381n. 48; reasons for racial anxiety, 109–15
South Carolina, 12, 14, 226, 306, 376n. 9; as Goldwater state, 292; as home of Strom Thurmond, Harry Dent, and Lee Atwater, 292, 301; Republicans and race, 388n. 84; won by the Dixiecrats and Goldwater, 283
Southern Christian Leadership Conference, 194, 219
Southern Conference Educational Fund, 125, 178, 196, 349n. 32
Southern Conference for Human Welfare, 11, 97, 149, 170–71, 172–73, 178, 223–25, 251; aid Georgia veterans on voting, 249, 362n. 32; denounced as a "Communist-front organization," 348n. 19; Eleanor

Roosevelt challenges segregation at, 100; history of, 346n. 2; in Alabama, 223–24; in Georgia, 236; in North Carolina, 224–25; spurned by E. D. Nixon, 213
Southern Federation of Afro-American Industrial Brotherhood, 315n. 15
"Southern liberals": and race, 112, 333n. 2; held fast on segregation, 333n. 2. *See also* Cohn, David L.; Couch, W. T.; Dabney, Virginius; Ethridge, Mark; Graves, John Temple II; McGill, Ralph
Southern Negro Youth Congress, 42, 149, 155–56, 170–71, 172–73, 177–78; as the "first SNCC," 195
Southern Patriot, 178
Southern Regional Council, 119, 130, 132, 135, 247, 362n. 32; and the Fellowship of the Concerned, 139
"Southern strategy," 5, 284, 291–95, 306, 391n. 93; disingenuousness of denials, 292, 294. *See also* Atwater, H. Lee; Dent, Harry; Phillips, Kevin
Southern University, 167
"Southern way of life," 125, 308
Southern Workers Defense League, 50, 60
Sovereignty. *See* global government; states' rights; United Nations
Soviet Union, 37, 81, 126, 195–96
Sparks, Chauncey, 30, 213, 354n. 50
Spike, Robert, 18
Stalin, Joseph, 194
Stanley, Eugene (Louisiana attorney general), 162
Stanley, Eugene, 50, 325n. 57
Staples, Abram, 27
Statesman, The 135
States' rights, 4, 383n. 60
States' Rights Democratic party. *See* Dixiecrats
Statesville, NC, 59
Stevenson, Adlai, 289
Stewart, John, 117
Stewart, Ollie, 52, 63
Stone, Harlan Fiske, 28, 319n. 13

Stoner, J. B., 293
Stoney, George, 248, 363n. 37
Stowe, Harriet Beecher, 96, 115
"Strange Fruit," 162
Stringer, Emmett, 85, 89; as head of Mississippi NAACP, 92, 93
Student Non-Violent Coordinating Committee (SNCC), 38, 195
Suburbanization (and rise of GOP), 280
Suffrage, 299. *See also* disfranchisement
Sullivan, Patricia, 223–24, 311n. 1
Super-patriotism, 4
Supreme Court (U.S.), xi, 15; and all-white primary, 98, 111, 121; and county-unit system, 249–50; and interstate travel, 25, 27–29, 31, 47–48, 51
Swannanoa, NC, 232–33, 235
Sweatt, Herman, 181
Sweatt v. Painter, 166
Swing voters, 301–2
Sylvester, Ray, 58

Taborians. *See* International Order of Knights and Daughters of Tabor
Take Your Choice, 175
"Talented tenth," 8, 78
Talk radio, 304
Tallahatchie County, MS, 90–91
Talmadge, Eugene, 30, 111, 148, 251, 253–55, 362n. 33; and anti-FDR rally, 333n. 11; attacks on, 373n. 101; attacks on Ellis Arnall, 373n. 100; career of, 369n. 75; global infamy, 258–59; in race against Ellis Arnall, 132–33; racism of, 369n. 75, 372n. 99; reelection of, 364n. 44; veto overridden, 130
Talmadge, Herman E., 135, 188, 244, 253, 255, 362n. 33, 367n. 67; conservatism on race, 266–67; contradictory legacy of, 266–67
Tammany Hall, 270
Taxes, 18, 20; Alabama tax reform referendum, 392n. 98; antipathy to, 3, 273, 280, 293–94, 304, 308, 383n. 59, 389n. 85; in Sixties,

387n. 78; relationship to racial resentments, 293–95, 383n. 60, 392n. 98. *See also* "Reconstruction Syndrome"
Taylor, Bayard, 35
Taylor, Herman, 65
Ten Commandments, 4, 274, 308, 389n. 89; controversy over in Alabama, 393n. 101
Tennessee, 9, 10, 12, 49, 59, 176, 226–27, 376n. 9; and Highlander Folk School, 205; mountain Republicanism in, 374n. 1; race tensions in, 111
Tennessee Valley Authority (TVA), 275
Terkel, Studs, 203–4
Texas, 11, 27, 41, 283, 306, 392n. 98; and black education, 145; criticism of Eleanor Roosevelt, 112
"The Group." *See* New Orleans, struggle within NAACP
"The New Racism," 5, 308, 314n. 9
"The Social Issue," 292, 308
The Three "G's," 389n. 85
The Voice of the South, 158
Thomas, Norman, 33
Thompson, Malvina, 106
Thompson, Melvin E., 244
Thompson, Sylvia Bernard Hall. *See* Bernard, Sylvia
Thornton, J. Mills III, 311n. 1, 313n. 4, 345n. 30
Thurman, Howard, 33, 42–43, 47
Thurman, Robert Mrs., 364n. 39
Thurmond, Strom J., 307; and "southern strategy," 292; campaigns for Ronald Reagan, 293; conversion to GOP, 306; level of victory in Alabama, 287; mentorship of Lee Atwater, 301; states won in common with Goldwater, 283. *See also* Dixiecrats; Lott, Trent
Tidewater, 21, 23
Till, Emmett (lynching of), 1, 94, 193
Tilly, Dorothy Rogers, 11, 16–17, 225–27, 235, 237; and President's Committee on Civil Rights, 134–37, 225; civil rights activities of, 116–43; 225–27; founds Fellowship of the Concerned, 138–43; friendship with Eleanor Roosevelt, 117, 133–34; work with Methodist women, 126–43
Tilly, Milton Eben, 116–17, 119, 134, 141
Time, 28
Tindall, George Brown: on Kevin Phillips, 382n. 49
Tisdale, Charles, 90
Title VII (of the Civil Rights Act of 1964), 383n. 60
Tobias, Channing, 137
Todd, Curtiss, 65
Tojo, 170, 175, 193
Tolson, Melvin, 41
To Secure These Rights, 134–37, 192. *See also* Presidents Committee on Civil Rights
Trailways Bus Company, 52, 54–55
Transport Workers Union, 149
"Trenton Six" (New Jersey), 192
Trial lawyers, 299
Trotskyism, 34
Truman, Bess, 334n. 14
Truman, Harry S, 29, 49, 188; and black veterans hospital, 76; civil rights package of, 276, 379n. 26; committee on civil rights, 117, 134–47; denounced as socialist, 288; disliked for racial liberalism, 141, 283, 287–89, 298; integration of Armed Forces, 275, 287; veto of Case Bill, 248. *See also* President's Committee on Civil Rights; *To Secure These Rights*
Tucker, Rosina, 200
Tulane University, 183–84, 349n. 32
Tureaud, A. P., 11, 151, 153–55, 157; education lawsuit of, 166–69; work with Thurgood Marshall, 154–55
Turner, John B., 241
Tushnet, Mark V., 31
Tuskegee, 76, 105
Tuskegee Institute, 76, 346n. 5; and definition of lynching, 162

"Twenty-Two Days on a Chain Gang," 67
"Two sides of the civil rights coin," 313n. 4
Tyler, Pamela, 10
Tyrell County, NC, 230–31
Tyson, Timothy B., 311n. 1
Tzu, Sun, 301

"Uncle Toms," 54, 71, 93
Union College, 69
Union Theological Seminary, 45
Unions. *See* labor
Unitarians, 50, 64
United Mine Workers of America, 315n. 15
United Nations, 192–93, 229–30; antipathy toward, 303
United Nations Relief and Rehabilitation Agency, 229–30
United Negro and Allied Veterans, 180
United Order of Friendship of America, 76–77, 82, 85. *See also* Regional Council of Negro Leadership
United Services Organization (USO), 12; in Montgomery, 207–8, 353n. 31
University of Alabama, 1
University of California, 173
University of Chicago, 43
University of Cincinnati, 66
University of Georgia, 116, 258
University of Mississippi: integration of, 393n. 99; Medgar Evers' application to, 93–94; riots, 282
University of North Carolina at Chapel Hill, 55, 134, 224
University of North Carolina at Greensboro, 224
University of North Carolina Press, 113, 336n. 51
University of Texas, 42, 166, 180–81
University of Virginia, 8
Upholsterers International Union of North America, 44
Upper South, 9, 10, 31, 46, 49, 270
Urban League, 90, 100
Urban poor, 292

Vandiver, Ernest, 267
Vardaman, Claude O., 288
Veterans, 8; and racial responses to World War II, 238–67; as candidates, 371n. 95; black, 239–41; in Georgia, 238–67; insurgencies of, 371n. 94
Veterans Administration: hospital, 74–76
Veterans Services Project, 240
Vietnam War, 389n. 89; protest against, 292, 296–97, 300, 383n. 60
Violence, 2, 7–8; as backlash against civil rights, 113, 313n. 4, 348n. 25. *See also* civil rights, backlash against; Columbians; Ku Klux Klan; lynching
Violent resistance: contemplated by Medgar Evers, 91
Virginia, 9, 100, 173; and black education, 145; and Journey of Reconciliation, 22–29, 44, 49, 53, 59, 65. *See also* "Martinsville Seven"
Virginia Supreme Court, 24, 26
Virginia Tidewater, 21, 23
Virginia Union College, 53
Voter Education Project, 195
Voter registration: drive in Mississippi, 87–88; in Georgia, 242–44; in Montgomery, 206–7, 208–9; in North Carolina, 224
Voting rights, 109, 171; in Louisiana, 147, 155–56; in Mississippi, 81–82, 87–88, 361n. 25. *See also* county-unit system; disfranchisement

Waco, 181
Waffle House, 301
Waggoner, James T. "Jabo," 306
Walker, Martin, 58
Wallace, George C., 14, 19, 305; and Dan T. Carter on, 285; and Leander Perez in Louisiana, 378n. 21; and 1948 Democratic loyalism, 277; appeal to white working class, 13–14; attempts to run as GOP vice-presidential candidate, 392n. 95;

choice to "out-nigger" the competition, 289, 307, 380n. 37; claims not "a dime's worth of difference" between major parties, 288; competition with Republicans for white vote, 19, 285, 292, 298, 301; considers self a Republican, 306; drops out of 1964 campaign, 301; Lee Atwater compared with, 301; on Republican debt to him, 285–86, 381n. 38; puts Richard Russell's name into nomination for president, 277; racist appeal of, 285–86, 289, 293; "reformed" version of, 220; sends envoy to approach Barry Goldwater, 392n. 95; supported by E. D. Nixon, 220; voters support Ronald Reagan as his successor, 293; Wallacism as fourth germ of modern GOP, 285–86, 289, 293, 307, 381nn. 38, 44
Wallace, Henry A., 175, 178, 186, 236
Wallace, Lurleen (Mrs. George C.), 297
Wallingford, CT, 39
Wall Street Journal, 284
War, 308. *See also* Iraq; Vietnam
Ward, Brian, 311n. 1
Ward, Roosevelt (case of), 184, 186, 349n. 32
Warm Springs, GA, 100
Warren, Earl, 29; threatened impeachment of, 383n. 60
War Resisters League, 40
War veterans. *See* veterans
War Without Violence, 38
Washington, D.C., 27, 37, 43, 45–46, 50–53, 62–63; and segregation at, 101; controversy at CIO-sponsored canteen, 107–8; enmity toward, 59. *See also* District of Columbia
Washington, Booker T., 314n. 6; influence on T. R. M. Howard, 69, 70, 78, 84; lunch at White House, 131
Watkins, William T., 124
Watson, David, 243
Watson, Albert, 306
Wattenberg, Ben J., 291, 308
Watts, J. C., 391n. 94

Wayne, John, 303
We Challenged Jim Crow, 64
We Cry Genocide, 172, 192–94, 196
Welfare, 280, 292–94, 307; "welfare queens," 293, 304, 383n. 60; "welfare state," 294, 381n. 46, 383n. 56
Wesleyan-Armenianism, 127
Wesleyan Christian Advocate (Macon), 120; arguments for and against segregation, 129–30, 340n. 45
Wesleyan College, 116
Wesley Memorial Methodist Church, 138
West, 29
West, Ben, 38
West Chester High School, 35
West Chester, PA, 35–36
What the Negro Wants, 113
Wheaton, Homer, 90
"White backlash" thesis (of Michael J. Klarman), 8–10, 19, 316n. 17
White Citizens' Councils, 158, 169, 279
White, Edward, 25
White, Frank S., 375n. 5
White, Hugh, 91
White, J. H., 83
White, John, 9, 10, 12–13, 17, 36
White, Lulu, xii, 180–81
White, Walter, 10, 12, 30–31, 49; and E. D. Nixon, 209, 212, 354n. 36; and Regional Council of Negro Leadership, 90; friendship with Eleanor Roosevelt, 100, 109; opposes *We Cry Genocide*, 196
"Whiteness" studies, 314n. 10
White supremacy, 4; and enmity toward Eleanor Roosevelt, 96–115; as an issue in 1928 election, 270–72; emotional and psychological aspects of, 5–8, 316n. 16; rational aspects of, 6–8, 315n. 11; relationship to conservatism, 276–77, 287–88, 314n. 6, 316n. 16, 317n. 21; subtlety of racial appeals, 314n. 8
Whitfield, Henry, 65
"Who Runs Georgia?" 363n. 38
Wilberforce University, 35; quartet of, 35

Wiley College, 41
Wilkerson, Doxey, 113
Wilkins, Roy, 12, 66, 113, 198, 218
Wilkinson, Horace C.: Dixiecrats and, 277, 279; racism of, 277; rapprochement with old class foes, 287
Williams, Aubrey W., 10, 222–23, 225, 236; opposes Civil Rights Congress, 196
Williams, Aubrey W., Jr., 228, 357n. 16
Williams, G. William: cancels appearance in Alabama, 210–11
Williams, W. C. (lynching of), 147
Williamson, Joel R., 118
Wilson, Roy S., 166
Winborne, Stanley, 30
Winston-Salem, NC, 13, 59, 60
Witt, W. T.: and Republican party, 281–82; disgust with Little Rock, 281–82
Wolff, Milton, 179–80, 185–86
Women. *See* gender
Women's Missionary Council, 119
Women's National Association for the Preservation of the White Race, 100
Women's Political Council, 215
Women's Society for Christian Service, 117
Work, Monroe, 162
Workers Defense League News Bulletin, 40
Working class, 12, 16, 18; alienation by racial liberalism, 274, 317n. 23; racism of, 165. *See also* class; labor; "lost opportunities" thesis; middle-class blacks; NAACP; New Deal Coalition; plain whites; Wallace, George C.
Works Progress Administration, 130, 148, 205
World Communion Sunday, 128
World War I, xi
World War II, xii–xiii, 1, 8, 16, 24, 33–34, 45; and attitudes of blacks, 77, 101; and economic growth, 370n. 86; conspiracy theories during, 102–5; increasing racial tensions, 97–98, 102–5, 110–11, 113, 120–21, 348n. 25
Worthy, William, 50, 61
Wright, Ernest, 153
Wright, J. Skelly, 169
Wright, Nathan, 50, 61–62
Wright, Richard, 54

Xenophobia, 3, 272, 303, 308; liberals as "outsiders," 141–42. *See also* immigrants; "outside agitators;" "Reconstruction Syndrome"

Yankees, 3, 67. *See also* northerners
Yazoo City, MS, 83
Young, Asa, 278
Young Communist League (YCL), 36–37
Young Women's Christian Association: in Atlanta, 232

Zero-sum theory, 382n. 55
Zimmerlee, John, 252
Zion's Herald, 121